WITHDRAWN

Poetry for Students

Poetry for Students

Presenting Analysis, Context, and Criticism on Commonly Studied Poetry

Volume 13

Elizabeth Thomason, Editor

Foreword by David Kelly

GALE GROUP
THOMSON LEARNING

Detroit • New York • San Diego • San Francisco
Boston • New Haven, Conn. • Waterville, Maine
London • Munich

Poetry for Students

Staff

Editor: Elizabeth Thomason.

Contributing Editors: Reginald Carlton, Anne Marie Hacht, Michael L. LaBlanc, Ira Mark Milne, Jennifer Smith, Carol Ullmann.

Managing Editor, Content: Dwayne D. Hayes.

Managing Editor, Product: David Galens.

Publisher, Literature Product: Mark Scott.

Literature Content Capture: Joyce Nakamura, *Managing Editor*. Arlene Johnson, *Editor*.

Research: Victoria B. Cariappa, *Research Manager*. Cheryl Warnock, *Research Specialist*. Sarah Genik, Ron Morelli, Tamara Nott, Tracie A. Richardson, *Research Associates*. Nicodemus Ford, *Research Assistant*.

Permissions: Maria Franklin, *Permissions Manager*. Shalice Shah-Caldwell, *Permissions Associate*.

Manufacturing: Mary Beth Trimper, *Manager, Composition and Electronic Prepress*. Evi Seoud, *Assistant Manager, Composition Purchasing and Electronic Prepress*. Stacy Melson, *Buyer*.

Imaging and Multimedia Content Team: Barbara Yarrow, *Manager*. Randy Bassett, *Imaging Supervisor*. Robert Duncan, Dan Newell, *Imaging Specialists*. Pamela A. Reed, *Imaging Coordinator*. Leitha Etheridge-Sims, Mary Grimes, David G. Oblender, *Image Catalogers*. Robyn V. Young, *Project Manager*. Dean Dauphinais, *Senior Image Editor*. Kelly A. Quin, *Image Editor*.

Product Design Team: Kenn Zorn, *Product Design Manager*. Pamela A. E. Galbreath, *Senior Art Director*. Michael Logusz, *Graphic Artist*.

Copyright Notice

Since this page cannot legibly accommodate all copyright notices, the acknowledgments constitute an extension of the copyright notice.

While every effort has been made to secure permission to reprint material and to ensure the reliability of the information presented in this publication, Gale Research neither guarantees the accuracy of the data contained herein nor assumes any responsibility for errors, omissions, or discrepancies. Gale accepts no payment for listing; and inclusion in the publication of any organization, agency, institution, publication, service, or individual does not imply endorsement of the editors or publisher. Errors brought to the attention of the publisher and verified to the satisfaction of the publisher will be corrected in future editions.

This publication is a creative work fully protected by all applicable copyright laws, as well as by misappropriation, trade secret, unfair competition, and other applicable laws. The authors and editors of this work have added value to the underlying factual material herein through one or more of the following: unique and original selection, coordination, expression, arrangement, and classification of the information. All rights to this publication will be vigorously defended.

Copyright © 2001
The Gale Group
27500 Drake Rd.
Farmington Hills, MI 48331-3535

All rights reserved including the right of reproduction in whole or in part in any form.

ISBN 0-7876-4691-1
ISSN 1094-7019
Printed in the United States of America.

10 9 8 7 6 5 4 3 2 1

National Advisory Board

Jennifer Hood: Young Adult/Reference Librarian, Cumberland Public Library, Cumberland, Rhode Island. Certified teacher, Rhode Island. Member of the New England Library Association, Rhode Island Library Association, and the Rhode Island Educational Media Association.

Christopher Maloney: Head Reference Librarian, Ocean City Free Public Library, Ocean City, New Jersey. Member of the American Library Association and the New Jersey Library Association. Board member of the South Jersey Library Cooperative.

Kathleen Preston: Head of Reference, New City Library, New City, New York. Member of the American Library Association. Received B.A. and M.L.S. from University of Albany.

Patricia Sarles: Library Media Specialist, Canarsie High School, Brooklyn, New York. Expert Guide in Biography/Memoir for the website *About.com* (http://biography.about.com). Author of short stories and book reviews. Received B.A., M.A. (anthropology), and M.L.S. from Rutgers University.

Heidi Stohs: Instructor in Language Arts, grades 10-12, Solomon High School, Solomon, Kansas. Received B.S. from Kansas State University; M.A. from Fort Hays State University.

Barbara Wencl: Library Media Specialist, Como Park Senior High School, St. Paul, Minnesota. Teacher of secondary social studies and history, St. Paul, Minnesota. Received B.S. and M.Ed. from University of Minnesota; received media certification from University of Wisconsin. Educator and media specialist with over 30 years experience.

Table of Contents

Guest Foreword
 "Just a Few Lines on a Page"
 by David J. Kelly x

Introduction xii

Literary Chronology xv

Acknowledgments .xvii

Contributors xix

An African Elegy (by Robert Duncan) 1
 Author Biography 2
 Poem Text 3
 Poem Summary 4
 Themes 6
 Style 7
 Historical Context 7
 Critical Overview 8
 Criticism 9

Birches (by Robert Frost) 13
 Author Biography 14
 Poem Text 14
 Poem Summary 15
 Themes 17
 Style 18
 Historical Context 18
 Critical Overview 19
 Criticism 20

Table of Contents

Blood Oranges (by Lisel Mueller) 33
   Author Biography 34
   Poem Text 34
   Poem Summary 34
   Themes 37
   Style 38
   Historical Context 39
   Critical Overview 40
   Criticism 41

Cavalry Crossing a Ford
(by Walt Whitman) 49
   Author Biography 50
   Poem Text 50
   Poem Summary 50
   Themes 52
   Style 53
   Historical Context 54
   Critical Overview 56
   Criticism 56

The Conquerors (by Phyllis McGinley) 65
   Author Biography 66
   Poem Text 67
   Poem Summary 67
   Themes 69
   Style 70
   Historical Context 71
   Critical Overview 73
   Criticism 74

Darwin in 1881
(by Gjertrud Schnackenberg) 82
   Author Biography 83
   Poem Text 83
   Poem Summary 84
   Themes 87
   Style 88
   Historical Context 89
   Critical Overview 90
   Criticism 91

Daylights (by Rosanna Warren) 100
   Author Biography 101
   Poem Text 101
   Poem Summary 102
   Themes 103
   Style 103
   Historical Context 104
   Critical Overview 105
   Criticism 105

For the White poets who would be Indian
(by Wendy Rose) 111
   Author Biography 112
   Poem Text 112
   Poem Summary 112
   Themes 114
   Style 116
   Historical Context 116
   Critical Overview 118
   Criticism 118

I felt a Funeral, in my Brain
(by Emily Dickinson) 135
   Author Biography 136
   Poem Text 137
   Poem Summary 137
   Themes 138
   Style 139
   Historical Context 140
   Critical Overview 141
   Criticism 142

i was sitting in mcsorley's
(by e. e. cummings) 150
   Author Biography 151
   Poem Text 151
   Poem Summary 152
   Themes 153
   Style 154
   Historical Context 155
   Critical Overview 156
   Criticism 156

The Idea of Order at Key West
(by Wallace Stevens) 162
   Author Biography 163
   Poem Text 164
   Poem Summary 164
   Themes 167
   Style 168
   Historical Context 169
   Critical Overview 170
   Criticism 171

Leda and the Swan
(by William Butler Yeats) 180
   Author Biography 181
   Poem Text 181
   Poem Summary 182
   Themes 183
   Style 185
   Historical Context 186
   Critical Overview 188
   Criticism 189

The Song of the Smoke
(by W. E. B. Du Bois) 194
    Author Biography 195
    Poem Text 196
    Poem Summary 197
    Themes 200
    Style 201
    Historical Context 202
    Critical Overview 204
    Criticism 205

To His Excellency General Washington
(by Phillis Wheatley) 211
    Author Biography 212
    Poem Text 212
    Poem Summary 213
    Themes 214
    Style 215
    Historical Context 216
    Critical Overview 217
    Criticism 218

To the Virgins, to Make Much of Time
(by Robert Herrick) 225
    Author Biography 226
    Poem Text 226
    Poem Summary 226
    Themes 227
    Style 228
    Historical Context 228
    Critical Overview 230
    Criticism 230

We Live by What We See at Night
(by Martín Espada) 239
    Author Biography 239
    Poem Text 240
    Poem Summary 240
    Themes 241
    Style 243
    Historical Context 243
    Critical Overview 244
    Criticism 245

Glossary 251

Cumulative Author/Title Index 271

Cumulative Nationality/Ethnicity Index 277

Subject/Theme Index 281

Cumulative Index of First Lines 287

Cumulative Index of Last Lines 293

Just a Few Lines on a Page

I have often thought that poets have the easiest job in the world. A poem, after all, is just a few lines on a page, usually not even extending margin to margin—how long would that take to write, about five minutes? Maybe ten at the most, if you wanted it to rhyme or have a repeating meter. Why, I could start in the morning and produce a book of poetry by dinnertime. But we all know that it isn't that easy. Anyone can come up with enough words, but the poet's job is about writing the *right* ones. The right words will change lives, making people see the world somewhat differently than they saw it just a few minutes earlier. The right words can make a reader who relies on the dictionary for meanings take a greater responsibility for his or her own personal understanding. A poem that is put on the page correctly can bear any amount of analysis, probing, defining, explaining, and interrogating, and something about it will still feel new the next time you read it.

It would be fine with me if I could talk about poetry without using the word "magical," because that word is overused these days to imply "a really good time," often with a certain sweetness about it, and a lot of poetry is neither of these. But if you stop and think about magic—whether it brings to mind sorcery, witchcraft, or bunnies pulled from top hats—it always seems to involve stretching reality to produce a result greater than the sum of its parts and pulling unexpected results out of thin air. This book provides ample cases where a few simple words conjure up whole worlds. We do not actually travel to different times and different cultures, but the poems get into our minds, they find what little we know about the places they are talking about, and then they make that little bit blossom into a bouquet of someone else's life. Poets make us think we are following simple, specific events, but then they leave ideas in our heads that cannot be found on the printed page. Abracadabra.

Sometimes when you finish a poem it doesn't feel as if it has left any supernatural effect on you, like it did not have any more to say beyond the actual words that it used. This happens to everybody, but most often to inexperienced readers: regardless of what is often said about young people's infinite capacity to be amazed, you have to understand what usually does happen, and what could have happened instead, if you are going to be moved by what someone has accomplished. In those cases in which you finish a poem with a "So what?" attitude, the information provided in *Poetry for Students* comes in handy. Readers can feel assured that the poems included here actually are potent magic, not just because a few (or a hundred or ten thousand) professors of literature say they are: they're significant because they can withstand close inspection and still amaze the very same people who have just finished taking them apart and seeing how they work. Turn them inside out, and they will still be able to come alive, again and again. *Poetry for Students* gives readers of any age good practice in feeling the ways poems relate to both the reality of the time and place the poet lived in and the reality of our emotions. Practice is just another word for being a student. The information given here helps you understand the way to read poetry; what to look for, what to expect.

With all of this in mind, I really don't think I would actually like to have a poet's job at all. There are too many skills involved, including precision, honesty, taste, courage, linguistics, passion, compassion, and the ability to keep all sorts of people entertained at once. And that is just what they do with one hand, while the other hand pulls some sort of trick that most of us will never fully understand. I can't even pack all that I need for a weekend into one suitcase, so what would be my chances of stuffing so much life into a few lines? With all that *Poetry for Students* tells us about each poem, I am impressed that any poet can finish three or four poems a year. Read the inside stories of these poems, and you won't be able to approach any poem in the same way you did before.

David J. Kelly
College of Lake County

Introduction

Purpose of the Book

The purpose of *Poetry for Students* (*PfS*) is to provide readers with a guide to understanding, enjoying, and studying poems by giving them easy access to information about the work. Part of Gale's "For Students" Literature line, *PfS* is specifically designed to meet the curricular needs of high school and undergraduate college students and their teachers, as well as the interests of general readers and researchers considering specific poems. While each volume contains entries on "classic" poems frequently studied in classrooms, there are also entries containing hard-to-find information on contemporary poems, including works by multicultural, international, and women poets.

The information covered in each entry includes an introduction to the poem and the poem's author; the actual poem text; a poem summary, to help readers unravel and understand the meaning of the poem; analysis of important themes in the poem; and an explanation of important literary techniques and movements as they are demonstrated in the poem.

In addition to this material, which helps the readers analyze the poem itself, students are also provided with important information on the literary and historical background informing each work. This includes a historical context essay, a box comparing the time or place the poem was written to modern Western culture, a critical overview essay, and excerpts from critical essays on the poem. A unique feature of *PfS* is a specially commissioned critical essay on each poem, targeted toward the student reader.

To further aid the student in studying and enjoying each poem, information on media adaptations is provided (if available), as well as reading suggestions for works of fiction and nonfiction on similar themes and topics. Classroom aids include ideas for research papers and lists of critical sources that provide additional material on the poem.

Selection Criteria

The titles for each volume of *PfS* were selected by surveying numerous sources on teaching literature and analyzing course curricula for various school districts. Some of the sources surveyed included: literature anthologies; *Reading Lists for College-Bound Students: The Books Most Recommended by America's Top Colleges*; textbooks on teaching the poem; a College Board survey of poems commonly studied in high schools; and a National Council of Teachers of English (NCTE) survey of poems commonly studied in high schools.

Input was also solicited from our advisory board, as well as educators from various areas. From these discussions, it was determined that each volume should have a mix of "classic" poems (those works commonly taught in literature classes) and contemporary poems for which information is often hard to find. Because of the interest in expanding the canon of literature, an emphasis was also placed on including works by international, multicultural, and women poets. Our advisory board members—educational professionals—helped pare down the list for each volume. If a work was not selected for the present volume, it was often noted as a possibility for a future volume. As always, the editor welcomes suggestions for titles to be included in future volumes.

How Each Entry Is Organized

Each entry, or chapter, in *PfS* focuses on one poem. Each entry heading lists the full name of the poem, the author's name, and the date of the poem's publication. The following elements are contained in each entry:

Introduction: a brief overview of the poem which provides information about its first appearance, its literary standing, any controversies surrounding the work, and major conflicts or themes within the work.

Author Biography: this section includes basic facts about the poet's life, and focuses on events and times in the author's life that inspired the poem in question.

Poem Text: when permission has been granted, the poem is reprinted, allowing for quick reference when reading the explication of the following section.

Poem Summary: a description of the major events in the poem, with interpretation of how these events help articulate the poem's themes. Summaries are broken down with subheads that indicate the lines being discussed.

Themes: a thorough overview of how the major topics, themes, and issues are addressed within the poem. Each theme discussed appears in a separate subhead and is easily accessed through the boldface entries in the Subject/Theme Index.

Style: this section addresses important style elements of the poem, such as form, meter, and rhyme scheme; important literary devices used, such as imagery, foreshadowing, and symbolism; and, if applicable, genres to which the work might have belonged, such as Gothicism or Romanticism. Literary terms are explained within the entry, but can also be found in the Glossary.

Historical Context: this section outlines the social, political, and cultural climate *in which the author lived and the poem was created*. This section may include descriptions of related historical events, pertinent aspects of daily life in the culture, and the artistic and literary sensibilities of the time in which the work was written. If the poem is a historical work, information regarding the time in which the poem is set is also included. Each section is broken down with helpful subheads.

Critical Overview: this section provides background on the critical reputation of the poem, including bannings or any other public controversies surrounding the work. For older works, this section includes a history of how the poem was first received and how perceptions of it may have changed over the years; for more recent poems, direct quotes from early reviews may also be included.

Criticism: an essay commissioned by *PfS* which specifically deals with the poem and is written specifically for the student audience, as well as excerpts from previously published criticism on the work (if available).

Sources: an alphabetical list of critical material used in compiling the entry, with full bibliographical information.

Further Reading: an alphabetical list of other critical sources which may prove useful for the student. It includes full bibliographical information and a brief annotation.

In addition, each entry contains the following highlighted sections, set apart from the main text as sidebars:

Media Adaptations: if available, a list of audio recordings as well as any film or television adaptations of the poem, including source information.

Topics for Further Study: a list of potential study questions or research topics dealing with the poem. This section includes questions related to other disciplines the student may be studying, such as American history, world history, science, math, government, business, geography, economics, psychology, etc.

Compare and Contrast: an "at-a-glance" comparison of the cultural and historical differences between the author's time and culture and late twentieth century or early twenty-first century Western culture. This box includes pertinent parallels between the major scientific, political, and cultural movements of the time or place the poem was written, the time or place the poem

Introduction

was set (if a historical work), and modern Western culture. Works written after the mid-1970s may not have this box.

What Do I Read Next?: a list of works that might complement the featured poem or serve as a contrast to it. This includes works by the same author and others, works of fiction and nonfiction, and works from various genres, cultures, and eras.

Other Features

PfS includes "Just a Few Lines on a Page," a foreword by David J. Kelly, a professor of English, College of Lake County, Illinois. This essay provides a straightforward, unpretentious explanation of why poetry should be marveled at and how *Poetry for Students* can help teachers show students how to enrich their own reading experiences.

A Cumulative Author/Title Index lists the authors and titles covered in each volume of the *PfS* series.

A Cumulative Nationality/Ethnicity Index breaks down the authors and titles covered in each volume of the *PfS* series by nationality and ethnicity.

A Subject/Theme Index, specific to each volume, provides easy reference for users who may be studying a particular subject or theme rather than a single work. Significant subjects from events to broad themes are included, and the entries pointing to the specific theme discussions in each entry are indicated in **boldface**.

A Cumulative Index of First Lines (beginning in Vol. 10) provides easy reference for users who may be familiar with the first line of a poem but may not remember the actual title.

A Cumulative Index of Last Lines (beginning in Vol. 10) provides easy reference for users who may be familiar with the last line of a poem but may not remember the actual title.

Each entry may include illustrations, including a photo of the author and other graphics related to the poem.

Citing Poetry for Students

When writing papers, students who quote directly from any volume of *Poetry for Students* may use the following general forms. These examples are based on MLA style; teachers may request that students adhere to a different style, so the following examples may be adapted as needed.

When citing text from *PfS* that is not attributed to a particular author (i.e., the Themes, Style, Historical Context sections, etc.), the following format should be used in the bibliography section:

Angle of Geese. *Poetry for Students*. Eds. Marie Napierkowski and Mary Ruby. Vol. 2. Detroit: Gale, 1997. 5–7.

When quoting the specially commissioned essay from *PfS* (usually the first piece under the "Criticism" subhead), the following format should be used:

Velie, Alan. Essay on "Angle of Geese."*Poetry for Students*. Eds. Marie Napierkowski and Mary Ruby. Vol. 2. Detroit: Gale, 1997. 8–9.

When quoting a journal or newspaper essay that is reprinted in a volume of *PfS*, the following form may be used:

Luscher, Robert M. "An Emersonian Context of Dickinson's 'The Soul Selects Her Own Society.'" *ESQ: A Journal of American Renaissance* Vol. 30, No. 2 (Second Quarter, 1984), 111–16; excerpted and reprinted in *Poetry for Students*, Vol. 1, eds. Marie Napierkowski and Mary Ruby (Detroit: Gale, 1997), pp. 266–69.

When quoting material reprinted from a book that appears in a volume of *PfS*, the following form may be used:

Mootry, Maria K. "'Tell It Slant': Disguise and Discovery as Revisionist Poetic Discourse in 'The Bean Eaters,'" in *A Life Distilled: Gwendolyn Brroks, Her Poetry and Fiction*. Edited by Maria K. Mootry and Gary Smith. University of Illinois Press, 1987. 177–80, 191; excerpted and reprinted in *Poetry for Students*, Vol. 2, eds. Marie Napierkowski and Mary Ruby (Detroit: Gale, 1997), pp. 22–24.

We Welcome Your Suggestions

The editor of *Poetry for Students* welcomes your comments and ideas. Readers who wish to suggest poems to appear in future volumes, or who have other suggestions, are cordially invited to contact the editor. You may contact the editor via E-mail at: ForStudentsEditors@galegroup.com. Or write to the editor at:

Editor, *Poetry for Students*
The Gale Group
27500 Drake Rd.
Farmington Hills, MI 48331–3535

Literary Chronology

1591: Robert Herrick is born in London.

1648: Robert Herrick's "To the Virgins, to Make Much of Time" is published.

1674: Robert Herrick dies in Devonshire, England.

1754: Phillis Wheatley is born in West Africa (present-day Senegal).

1776: Phillis Wheatley's "To His Excellency General Washington" is published.

1784: Phillis Wheatley dies on December 5.

1819: Walt Whitman is born on May 31 on Long Island, New York.

1830: Emily Dickinson is born on December 10, in Amherst, Massachusetts.

1865: Walt Whitman's "Cavalry Crossing a Ford" is published.

1865: William Butler Yeats is born on June 13 in the Dublin suburb of Sandymount.

1868: W. E. B. Du Bois is born on February 23 in the western Massachusetts town of Great Barrington.

1874: Robert Frost is born on March 26 in San Francisco, California.

1879: Wallace Stevens is born on October 2 in Reading, Pennsylvania.

1886: Emily Dickinson dies on May 15 in Amherst, Massachusetts, after an unspecified illness contracted in 1884.

1892: Walt Whitman dies on March 26 in Camden, New Jersey.

1894: E. E. Cummings is born in Cambridge, Massachusetts.

1896: Emily Dickinson's "I Felt a Funeral, in my Brain" is published.

1905: Phyllis McGinley is born on March 21.

1907: W. E. B. Du Bois's "The Song of the Smoke" is published.

1916: Robert Frost's "Birches" is published.

1919: Robert Duncan is born on January 7 in Oakland, California.

1923: William Butler Yeats wins the Nobel Prize in literature.

1924: Lisel Mueller is born on February 8 in Hamburg, Germany.

1925: E. E. Cummings's "i was sitting in mcsorley's" is published.

1928: William Butler Yeats's "Leda and the Swan" is published.

1934: Wallace Stevens's "The Idea of Order at Key West" is published.

1939: William Butler Yeats dies on January 28 in Roquebrune, France.

1948: Wendy Rose is born on May 7 in Oakland, California.

1949: Wallace Stevens wins the Bollingen Prize in Poetry from Yale University.

Literary Chronology

1950: Wallace Stevens wins the National Book Award for poetry for *The Auroras of Autumn*.

1953: Rosanna Warren is born on July 27 in Fairfield, Connecticut.

1953: Gjertrud Schnackenberg is born on August 27 in Tacoma, Washington.

1954: Wallace Stevens wins the National Book Award and the Pulitzer Prize for *Collected Poems*.

1955: E. E. Cummings wins the National Book Award special citation for *Poems, 1923–1954*.

1955: Wallace Stevens dies of cancer on August 2 in Hartford, Connecticut.

1957: Martin Espada is born in Brooklyn, New York.

1958: E. E. Cummings wins the Bollingen Prize in Poetry from Yale University.

1959: Robert Duncan's "An African Elegy" is published.

1960: Phyllis McGinley's "The Conquerors" is published.

1961: Phyllis McGinley wins the Pulitzer Prize for poetry for the collection *Times Three*, in which "The Conquerors" appeared.

1962: E. E. Cummings dies of natural causes.

1963: W. E. B. Du Bois dies on August 27 in Accra, Ghana.

1963: Robert Frost dies on January 29 in Boston, Massachusetts.

1978: Phyllis McGinley dies on February 22.

1980: Wendy Rose's "For the White poets who would be Indian" is published.

1982: Gjertrud Schnackenberg's "Darwin in 1881" is published.

1984: Rosanna Warren's "Daylights" is published.

1986: Lisel Mueller's "Blood Oranges" is published.

1987: Martin Espada's "We Live by What We See at Night" is published.

1988: Robert Duncan dies of a heart attack on February 3 in San Francisco, California.

Acknowledgments

The editors wish to thank the copyright holders of the excerpted criticism included in this volume and the permissions managers of many book and magazine publishing companies for assisting us in securing reproduction rights. We are also grateful to the staffs of the Detroit Public Library, the Library of Congress, the University of Detroit Mercy Library, Wayne State University Purdy/Kresge Library Complex, and the University of Michigan Libraries for making their resources available to us. Following is a list of the copyright holders who have granted us permission to reproduce material in this volume of *Poetry for Students* (*PfS*). Every effort has been made to trace copyright, but if omissions have been made, please let us know.

COPYRIGHTED MATERIALS IN *PfS*, VOLUME 13, WERE REPRODUCED FROM THE FOLLOWING PERIODICALS:

The Antioch Review, v. 41, Spring, 1983. Copyright © 1983 by the Antioch Review Inc. Reproduced by permission of the Editors.—*Freedomways*, v.5, 1965. Copyright © 1965 by Freedomways Associates, Inc. Reproduced by permission.—*The Kenyon Review*, v. vi, Winter, 1984 for "Separateness and Solitude in Frost" by Patricia Wallace. Copyright © 1984 by Kenyon College. All rights reserved. Reproduced by permission of the author.—*Sewanee Review*, v. 84, Summer, 1976. Copyright © 1976 by The University of the South. Reproduced with permission of the editor.

COPYRIGHTED MATERIALS IN *PfS*, VOLUME 13, WERE REPRODUCED FROM THE FOLLOWING BOOKS:

Bruchac, Joseph. From *Survival This Way: Interviews with American Indian Poets*. University of Arizona Press, 1987. Copyright © 1987 The Arizona Board of Regents. All rights reserved. Reproduced by permission of the author.—Bunge, Nancy L. From *Finding the Words: Conversation with Writers Who Teach*. Swallow Press, 1985. Copyright © 1985 by Nancy L. Bunge. All rights reserved. Reproduced by permission of the author.—Duncan, Robert. From *The Norton Anthology of Modern Poetry*, second edition. Edited by Richard Ellmann and Robert O'Clair. W.W. Norton & Company. Copyright © 1988, 1973 by W.W. Norton & Company, Inc. All rights reserved. Reproduced by permission of the Estate of Robert Duncan.—Espada, Martin. From *Trumpets From the Island of Their Eviction*. © 1994 by Bilingual Press/ Editorial Bilingüe, Arizona State University, Tempe, AZ. All rights reserved. Reproduced by permission.—Frost, Robert. From *The Poetry of Robert Frost*. Edited by Edward Connery Lathem. Henry Holt and Company, 1969. Copyright © 1969 by Holt, Rinehart and Winston, Inc. Reproduced by permission.—Herrick, Robert. From *English Poetry*. Chadwyck-Healey Ltd, 1992–1995. Copyright © 1992–1995 Chadwyck-Healey Ltd. Reproduced by permission.—Kemp, John C. From ***Robert Frost and New England***. Princeton University Press, 1979. Copyright © 1979 by Princeton University Press. All rights reserved. Reproduced by permission.—Mueller, Lisel. From *Second Language*. Louisiana State University Press, 1986. Copyright © 1986 by Lisel Mueller. All rights reserved. Reproduced by permission.—Richmond, M.A. From *Bid the Vassal Soar*. Howard University Press, 1974. Copyright © 1974 by Merle A. Richmond. All rights reserved. Reproduced by permission.—Rollins, Roger B. From *Robert Herrick*. G.K. Hall, 1999.—Rose, Wendy. From *The Remembered Earth*. Edited by Geary Hobson. Red Earth Press, 1979. Copyright © 1979 by Red Earth Press. Reproduced by permission of the author.—Schnackenberg, Gjertrud. From *Portraits and Elegies*. Farrar, Straus and Giroux. Copyright © 1982, 1986 by Gjertrud Schnackenberg. Reproduced by permission of Farrar, Straus and Giroux, LLC.—Stevens, Wallace. From *The Collected Poems of Wallace Stevens*. Faber and Faber Ltd., 1955. Reproduced by permission.—Warren, Rosanna. From *Each Leaf Shines Separate*. W.W. Norton & Company, 1984. Copyright © 1984 by Rosanna Warren. Reproduced by permission.—Wheatley, Phillis. From *The Poems of Phillis Wheatley*. Revised and enlarged edition, edited with an introduction by Julian D. Mason, Jr. Copyright © 1989 by the University of North Carolina Press. Used by permission of the publisher.—Whitman, Walt. From *Walt Whitman: Poetry and Prose*. The Library of America, 1982. Copyright © 1982 by Literary Classics of the United States, Inc., New York, N.Y. All rights reserved. Reproduced by permission.—Yeats, W. B. From *Variorum Edition of the Poems of W.B. Yeats*. Edited by Peter Allt and Russell K. Alspach. Macmillan Publishing Company. Copyright 1903, 1906, 1907, 1912, 1918, 1919, 1924, 1928, 1931, 1933, 1934, 1935, 1940, 1944, 1945, 1946, 1950, 1956, 1957, by Macmillan Publishing Company. Copyright 1940 by George Yeats. Renewed 1986 by Catherine C. Alspach. Reproduced by permission.

PHOTOGRAPHS AND ILLUSTRATIONS APPEARING IN *PfS*, VOLUME 13, WERE RECEIVED FROM THE FOLLOWING SOURCES:

Cummings, E.E. (lounging on a bed, holding a cigarette), 1938, photograph. AP/Wide World Photos. Reproduced by permission.—Dickinson, Emily, photograph of a painting. The Library of Congress.—DuBois, W.E.B. (three-quarter view from his right, young), photograph. The Library of Congress.—Duncan, Robert, photograph by Nata Piaskowski. Courtesy of New Directions. Reproduced by permission.—Espada, Martin, photograph. Reproduced by permission.—Four busts of prehistoric man's evolution, photograph. Corbis-Bettmann. Reproduced by permission.—Frost, Robert (wearing dark suit, lighter colored tie a bit rumpled), photograph. The Library of Congress.—Herrick, Robert, photograph by Schiavonetti. Archive Photos, Inc. Reproduced by permission.—McGinley, Phyllis, Connecticut, 1964, photograph. AP/Wide World Photos. Reproduced by permission.—Mueller, Lisel, Illinois, 1997, photograph. AP/Wide World Photos. Reproduced by permission.—Stevens, Wallace (wearing light striped suit), photograph. The Library of Congress.—Union cavalry column lined along river, Rappahannock River, Virginia, 1862, photograph. National Archives and Records Administration.—Warren, Rosanna, photograph by Mark Richards. Reproduced by permission.—Wheatley, Phillis, in white empire style dress and pearls, lithograph by Lemercier, Benard and Co. New York Public Library. Reproduced by permission.—Whitman, Walt (butterfly on right hand), photograph. The Library of Congress.—Yeats, William Butler, late 1800's, photograph. Library of Congress.

Contributors

Bryan Aubrey: Aubrey holds a Ph.D. in English Literature from the University of Durham, England. He has worked as editor for Lynn C. Franklin Associates and as a freelance writer and editor. Original essay on *Darwin in 1881*.

Greg Barnhisel: Barnhisel holds a Ph.D. in American literature from the University of Texas at Austin. He has taught English as assistant professor at Southwestern University in Georgetown, Texas. He has published articles on Ezra Pound, and has worked as a freelance writer and editor. Original essay on *The Idea of Order at Key West*.

Jonathan N. Barron: Barron is an associate professor of English at the University of Southern Mississippi. He has co-edited *Jewish American Poetry* (from the University Press of New England), and *Roads Not Taken: Rereading Robert Frost* (forthcoming from the University of Missouri Press), as well as a forthcoming collection of essays on the poetic movement, New Formalism. In 2001, he has become the editor-in-chief of *The Robert Frost Review*. Original essay on *Birches*.

Adrian Blevins: Blevins, a poet and essayist who has taught at Hollins University, Sweet Briar College, and in the Virginia Community College System, is the author of *The Man Who Went Out for Cigarettes*, a chapbook of poems, and has published poems, stories, and essays in many magazines, journals, and anthologies. Original essay on *Cavalry Crossing a Ford*.

Sheldon Goldfarb: Goldfarb has a Ph.D. in English and has published two books on the Victorian author William Makepeace Thackeray. Original essay on *I felt a Funeral, in my Brain*.

Joyce Hart: Hart is a freelance writer, copyeditor, and former editor of a literary magazine. Entry on *The Conquerors*. Original essays on *The Conquerors*, *Daylights*, and *For the White poets who would be Indian*.

Pamela Steed Hill: Hill has had poems published in over 100 journals and has been nominated for a Pushcart Prize three times. Her first collection, *In Praise of Motels*, was published in 1999 by Blair Mountain Press. She is an associate editor for University Communications at Ohio State University. Entries on *Darwin in 1881*, *For the White poets who would be Indian*, and *We Live by What We See at Night*. Original essays on *Darwin in 1881*, *For the White poets who would be Indian*, and *We Live by What We See at Night*.

David J. Kelly: Kelley is a professor of English, College of Lake County, Illinois. He is also a fiction writer and playwright. Entries on *Blood Oranges*, *Cavalry Crossing a Ford*, *The Song of the Smoke*, and *To His Excellency General Washington*. Original essays on *Blood Oranges*, *Cavalry Crossing a Ford*, *The Song of the Smoke*, and *To His Excellency General Washington*.

Judi Ketteler: Ketteler has taught literature and English composition and is currently a freelance writer based in Cincinnati, Ohio. Original essays on *For the White poets who would be Indian* and *To the Virgins, to Make Much of Time*.

Uma Kukathas: Kukathas is a freelance editor and writer. Entry on *Leda and the Swan*. Original essay on *Leda and the Swan*.

Daniel Moran: Moran is a secondary-school teacher of English and American literature. He has contributed several entries and essays to the Gale series *Drama for Students*. Entries on *I felt a Funeral, in my Brain* and *To the Virgins, to Make Much of Time*. Original essays on *I felt a Funeral, in my Brain* and *To the Virgins, to Make Much of Time*.

Wendy Perkins: Perkins has a Ph.D. in English from the University of Delaware, is an assistant professor of English at Prince George's Community College, Maryland, and has published widely in the field of twentieth-century American and British literature. Original essays on *Birches*, *The Idea of Order at Key West*, *Leda and the Swan*, and *To the Virgins, to Make Much of Time*.

Doreen Piano: Piano is a Ph.D. candidate in English at Bowling Green State University. Original essay on *We Live by What We See at Night*.

Paul Pineiro: Pineiro is a published poet and the supervisor of English at Montgomery High School in New Jersey. Original essay on *I felt a Funeral, in my Brain*.

Dean Rader: Rader is an assistant professor of English at Texas Lutheran Univerity in Seguin, Texas. He has published widely in the field of twentieth-century American poetry and on Wallace Stevens in particular. Entry on *The Idea of Order at Key West*. Original essay on *The Idea of Order at Key West*.

Chris Semansky: Semansky holds a Ph.D. in English from Stony Brook University and teaches writing and literature at Portland Community College in Portland, Oregon. His collection of poems *Death, But at a Good Price* received the Nicholas Roerich Poetry Prize for 1991 and was published by Story Line Press and the Nicholas Roerich Museum. Semansky's most recent collection, *Blindsided*, has been published by 26 Books of Portland, Oregon. Entries on *An African Elegy*, *Daylights*, and *i was sitting in mcsorley's*. Original essays on *An African Elegy*, *Daylights*, and *i was sitting in mcsorley's*.

Erica Smith: Smith is a writer and editor. Entry on *Birches*. Original essays on *Birches*, *Cavalry Crossing a Ford*, *i was sitting in mcsorley's*, and *The Song of the Smoke*.

Erika Taibl: Taibl has a master's degree in English writing and writes for a variety of educational publishers. Original essay on *Darwin in 1881*.

An African Elegy

Robert Duncan

1959

"An African Elegy" is one of the most controversial poems that Duncan ever wrote. Editor John Crowe Ransom accepted the poem for publication in *The Kenyon Review* in 1942 calling it "very brilliant." However, after Duncan published his essay "The Homosexual in Society" in Dwight MacDonald's radical monthly *Politics,* "outing" himself and arguing (in part) that gay culture needed to see itself as more fully a part of mainstream society, Ransom changed his mind and decided not to publish the poem. Ransom wrote: "We are not in the market for literature of this type." By *literature of this type,* Ransom meant poetry that, in his view, was an "obvious homosexual advertisement." The curious thing about Ransom's rejection of the poem is that he did not read any homosexual content in it when he accepted it, but only after reading Duncan's essay. Ransom, though he praised the essay, disagreed with it and considered homosexuality an "abnormality." In response to Ransom's new reading of "An African Elegy," Duncan wrote, "The theme of the poem is not homosexuality; nor does the darkness stand for homosexuality. The dark continent in the poem is not what one hides, but what is hidden from one. . . . It would be rather astounding in an overt homosexual that what was held back, imprisoned in the unconscious, was the homosexual desire." Duncan wanted Ransom to publish their correspondence about the poem in *The Kenyon Review,* but Ransom refused. The poem was eventually published in 1959.

The poem itself is difficult. Written in eight free-verse stanzas, it is full of symbols and allusions to both Africa and Western literature. The central symbolic metaphor is how the dark jungles of Africa are like the dark and unknown places of the human mind and heart. Duncan loads the poem with African animal imagery and references to famous women (both real women and literary characters), such as Virginia Woolf, Ophelia, and Desdemona, who either committed suicide or were murdered. Death, personified as a "dog-headed man," appears everywhere in the poem, eliciting varying responses from the speaker.

Duncan said that the poem was, in part, inspired by Spanish poet Frederico Garcia Lorca's poem "El Rey de Harlem" (The King of Harlem). Lorca was a heavily persecuted gay writer whom Duncan admired. Even practiced readers of modern poetry, however, would be hard-pressed to find any evidence of a homosexual theme or imagery in the poem.

Robert Duncan

Author Biography

Robert Duncan is one of the twentieth century's most enigmatic and romantic poets. His dedication to poetry as an act of magic and self-creation has enlarged the scope of what is possible for other poets to do. Born to Edward Howard and Marguerite Wesley Duncan on January 7, 1919, in Oakland, California, Duncan was given up for adoption shortly after birth and raised as Robert Edward Symmes. He resumed using his original surname in 1942. At three years old, Duncan suffered an eye injury in a fall, making him cross-eyed. Duncan has written about his altered way of physically perceiving the world in his poems, and critics have made connections between his writing and his injury, especially in regards to the blurring of identities and distinctions in his poetry. Duncan's adopted parents were "orthodox theosophists," and his upbringing was steeped in hermetic lore and the occult. Theosophy, a nineteenth-century spiritual movement founded on the ideas of Madam Helena Petrovna Blavatsky, incorporated principles from both Eastern and Western religions and held reincarnation as one of its central doctrines. Theosophists saw correspondences in language and nature and believed that the physical world itself was a system of symbols pointing to a deeper reality. Duncan's parents read fairy tales and myths to him and provided him with a storehouse of poetic material, which he would draw from throughout his life.

At the University of California at Berkeley, Duncan began publishing his poems in the school's literary journal, *The Occident*, and meeting regularly with a circle of literary friends which included Pauline Kael, Virginia Admiral, and Lili Fabilli. After two years at Berkeley, Duncan moved to New York City, where he became involved with a group of writers gathered around Anaïs Nin that included Henry Miller, Lawrence Durrell, and Nicolas Calas. This was a rich time in Duncan's life during which he developed friendships with poets Russel Sanders and Jack Johnson and a number of abstract expressionist painters who were to influence his own thinking about the possibilities for poetry. In 1942, Duncan met Kenneth Rexroth, one of the central figures in mid-twentieth-century American poetry and a shaper of the San Francisco Renaissance in which Duncan was a major player. Duncan, who saw himself as a spiritual quester and wanderer, married Marjorie McKee in 1943, but the couple divorced shortly after when McKee had an abortion. In 1944, Duncan wrote and published the groundbreaking essay, "The Homosexual in Society," in which he both "outed" himself as a gay man *and* criticized the homosexual culture's attitude of superiority. In 1951, Duncan began what was to be a lifelong partnership with artist Jess Collins.

In the mid 1940s, Duncan returned to San Francisco and became a vital part of the burgeoning literary scene there, later known as the San Francisco Renaissance. Writers involved in this renaissance included Philip Whalen, Jack Spicer, Philip Lamantia, and Robin Blaser, among others. Never a follower of any one literary school or trend, Duncan was active in a number of groups, including the Maidens, a San Francisco circle of writers who gathered for readings and discussions, and the Black Mountain group, which included Robert Creeley, Charles Olson, Larry Eigner, and John Cage. Duncan taught at the experimental Black Mountain College for a few terms in 1956 with some of the latter poets and, after Olson died, became the leading spokesman for open form, or Projectivist, poetry. Duncan published his poetry with a number of presses, many of them small. His best-known books include *The Opening of the Field* (1960), *Roots and Branches* (1964), and *Bending the Bow* (1968).

Never one to promote his own writing or to participate in the kind of reputation mongering in which so many writers engage, Duncan has nevertheless gained a steady, if modest, stream of new readers through the years. His poetry, learned and sometimes obscure, is at once intensely personal and passionately public. He strove to give meaning to his own life by seeing it as a part of all life. Poetry, for Duncan, did more than merely reflect society; it helped determine what it would be.

Robert Duncan died of a heart attack on February 3, 1988, in San Francisco, California.

Poem Text

In the groves of Africa from their natural wonder
the wildebeest, zebra, the okapi, the elephant,
have entered the marvelous. No greater marvelous
know I than the mind's
natural jungle. The wives of the Congo   5
distil their red and the husbands
hunt lion with spear and paint Death-spore
on their shields, wear his teeth, claws and hair
on ordinary occasions. There the Swahili
open his doors, let loose thru the trees   10
the tides of Death's sound and distil
from their leaves the terrible red. He
is the consort of dreams I have seen, heard
in the orchestral dark
like the barking of dogs.   15

Death is the dog-headed man zebra striped
and surrounded by silence who walks like a lion,
who is black. It was his voice crying come back,
that Virginia Woolf head, turnd
her fine skull, hounded and haunted, stopt,   20
pointed into the scent where
I see her in willows, in fog, at the river of sound
in the trees. I see her prepare there
to enter Death's mountains
like a white Afghan hound pass into the forest, 25
closed after, let loose in the leaves
with more grace than a hound and more wonder
    there
even with flowers wound in her hair, allowing
    herself
like Ophelia a last
pastoral gesture of love toward the world.   30
And I see
all our tortures absolved in the fog,
dispersed in Death's forests, forgotten. I see
all this gentleness like a hound in the water
float upward and outward beyond my dark hand.   35

I am waiting this winter for the more complete
    black-out,
for the negro armies in the eucalyptus, for the cities
laid open and the cold in the love-light, for hounds
women and birds to go back to their forests and
    leave us
our solitude.   40

Negroes, negroes, all those princes,
holding cups of rhinoceros bone, make
magic with my blood. Where beautiful Marijuana
towers taller than the eucalyptus, turns
within the lips of night and falls,   45
falls downward, where as giant Kings we gathered
and devour her burning hands and feet, O
    Moonbar
thee and Clarinet! those talismans
that quickened in their sheltering leaves like
    thieves,
those Negroes, all those princes   50
holding to their mouths like Death
the cups of rhino bone,
were there to burn my hands and feet,
divine the limit of the bone and with their magic
tie and twist me like a rope. I know   55
no other continent of Africa more dark than this
dark continent of my breast.

And when we are deserted there,
when the rustling electric has passt thru the air,
once more we begin in the blind and blood throat 60
the African catches; and Desdemona, Desdemona
like a demon wails within our bodies, warns
against this towering Moor of self and then
laments her passing from him.

And I cry, Hear!   65
Hear in the coild and secretive ear
the drums that I hear beat. The Negroes, all those
    princes
holding cups of bone and horn, are there in halls
of blood that I call forests, in the dark
and shining caverns where   70
beats heart and pulses brain, in
jungles of my body, there

Othello moves, striped black and white,
the dog-faced fear. Moves I, I, I,
whom I have seen as black as Orpheus, 75
pursued deliriously his sound and drownd
in hunger's tone, the deepest wilderness.

Then it was I, Death singing,
who bewildered the forest. I thot him
my lover like a hound of great purity 80
disturbing the shadow and flesh of the jungle.
This was the beginning of the ending year.
From all of the empty the tortured appear,
and the bird-faced children crawl out of their
    fathers
and into that never filld pocket, 85
the no longer asking but silent, seeing nowhere
the final sleep.

The halls of Africa we seek in dreams
as barriers of dream against the deep, and seas
disturbd turn back upon their tides 90
into the rooms deserted at the roots of love.
There is no end. And how sad then
is even the Congo. How the tired sirens
come up from the water, not to be toucht
but to lie on the rocks of the thunder. 95
How sad then is even the marvelous!

Poem Summary

Stanza 1

Elegies are poems written to lament someone's death. In "An African Elegy" death isn't literal but figurative. The speaker is lamenting the death of a part of himself. The opening stanza creates a symbolic landscape full of exotic African creatures such as wildebeests, zebras, elephants, and okapi, a giraffe-like animal found in the Congo. Swahili are part of the Bantu peoples of eastern and central Africa. Duncan makes an explicit connection between the "marvelous" jungle in which the animals live and the "mind's / natural jungle." "Marvelous" primarily has a positive meaning here, but it picks up less benign associations as the poem develops. The preparation and hunting rituals engaged in by the Congolese men and women create a strange and ominous atmosphere in which death is omnipresent.

Stanza 2

Developing the image of death with which he ends the first stanza, Duncan personifies death here as "the dog-headed man zebra striped / and surrounded by silence who walks like a lion, / who is black." This image might also be a literal description of one of the hunters. Duncan uses dog imagery throughout the poem, often to suggest contradictory ideas. Like dogs, death variously appears as a loyal companion, a guide, and a frightening presence. The speaker associates this image of death with British writer Virginia Woolf, who drowned herself in the River Ouse. Death calls Woolf back to the river to drown herself. Woolf suffered from depression and battled emotional demons throughout her life. The images the speaker uses to describe Woolf's journey toward death are dream-like, spectral, and enigmatic. The speaker empathizes with Woolf's emotional torment. Toward the end of the stanza, he compares her to Ophelia, a character from Shakespeare's play *Hamlet,* who, emotionally unbalanced, commits suicide by drowning. These two figures become symbolic representations for all of humanity, whose "tortures" the speaker sees "absolved in the fog, / dispersed in Death's forests, forgotten." Here death is seen as a rescuer, a primal and natural part of the world into which all must eventually journey. Note that Woolf is a variant of wolf, an animal closely associated with the dog.

Stanza 3

In the previous stanzas, the speaker describes what he sees and hears. In this stanza, he announces his desire: "I am waiting this winter for the more complete black-out." This image and the ones that follow are symbolic, that is images that arise from the speaker's subconscious. Symbolic imagery does not have a one-to-one correlation to things or ideas outside of itself; rather symbols open up a realm of association, which can either be private (known only to the poet) or public (familiar to the common reader). "Negro armies in the eucalyptus" is an obscure image but one which suggests the idea of waiting. Who, though, is the "us" to whom the speaker refers? If the poem is read as a statement on homosexuality, as at least one reader has interpreted it, it might refer to the gay community itself, which has been persecuted and ostracized. Another possibility for the "us" is all the people who have suffered like the speaker himself, people of similar sensibilities, for example, Virginia Woolf. The third possibility is that the "us" is universal as in all humanity. Again the image of dogs, figured as "hounds," appears. This stanza suggests a contradiction in the speaker's desire. He wants "hounds / women and birds to go back to their forests and leave us / our solitude." Yet those very images, associated with death, are the ones that can "absolve tortures."

Stanza 4

This stanza describes a ritual in which Negro princes drink the blood of the speaker from cups made of rhinoceros bone and then, using magic, "tie and twist [him] like a rope." This stanza echoes lines from Spanish poet Frederico Garcia Lorca's poem "El Rey de Harlem." Duncan himself has noted that this scene describes a sado-masochistic ritual in which the speaker casts himself in the role of victim. The speaker describes himself and others as "Kings" ("as giant Kings we gathered / and devour her burning hands and feet") possibly transformed through the smoking of marijuana, a plant with psychoactive chemicals. He then invokes the names of both "moonbar" and "clarinet" as talismans, that is, objects that hold magical powers. Duncan was well versed in the occult and the practice of magic and alchemy, and he frequently uses images from those fields in his poetry. Moonbar is a pearly white, opaque gemstone, usually pale blue with green and gold mottling, and considered a magic stone. Duncan repeats the image of burning hands and feet later in the stanza, foreshadowing his reference to Orpheus, son of Apollo and the muse Calliope, who was dismembered by the Maenads, a group of women who worshipped Dionysius. The last three lines highlight the symbolic nature of the ritual itself. The speaker is saying that what goes on inside of him, the "dark continent of my breast," is as strange and tormenting as the scene just described.

Stanza 5

This stanza refers to the process of dying and death. "The rustling electric" is life itself, the energy that constitutes the animate world. Desdemona is the wife of Othello, a black African (Moor) in Shakespeare's *Othello*. Her figure holds some significance for the speaker, as she too is a victim. She is murdered by her husband in a jealous rage when he suspects her of having an affair with his best friend. That she "wails within our bodies" further underscores the idea of victimization implicit throughout the poem. However, that she both "warns / against this towering Moor of self" and "laments her passing from him" seems to imply that she, and, by implication, the speaker, and possibly all of humanity are never simply victims but somehow always complicitous in whatever happens to them. Human beings are always both victims and victimizers. "Catches" is a word that Duncan has used in other poems. It has multiple meanings. On the one hand, it can mean the thing that is caught, as in a net of "catches"; on the other hand, it can mean being caught (i.e., what "catches" one).

Stanza 6

In this stanza the speaker's sense of self dissipates into others. The images of the negroes and

Media Adaptations

- Modern American Poetry sponsors a Robert Duncan web site at http://www.english.uiuc.edu/maps/poets/a_f/duncan/duncan.htm (last accessed April 2001).

- Kent State University lists a bibliography of Duncan's work in its special collection at http://www.library.kent.edu/speccoll/literature/poetry/duncan.html (last accessed April 2001).

- The Theosophical University Press has a glossary of theosophical terms available online at http://www.theosociety.org/pasadena/etgloss/mi-mo.htm (last accessed April 2001).

- The American Academy of Poets offers a 1969 audiocassette of Duncan reading from *The Opening of the Field, Roots and Branches,* and *Bending the Bow*.

the rhinoceros-bone cups again appear. Duncan makes the symbolism more explicit in this stanza, as he compares the "halls / of blood that I call forests" to "the dark / and shining caverns where / beats heart and pulses brain, / in jungles of my body." The figure of Othello, here "striped black and white" represents the complexity of the speaker's desire. Othello was largely a good man who gave in to his jealousy and rage. The repetition of the pronoun "I" highlights the ecstatic pitch of the speaker's emotion. Disembodied, he witnesses himself "as black as Orpheus," possibly a reference to *Orphé noire*, a French film which retells the story of Orpheus. The speaker's identification with Orpheus makes sense when the reader understands that Orpheus was the son of Calliope, one of the nine muses, and was revered for his music and verse. It is said that Orpheus had the ability to tame wild animals with his music.

Stanza 7

In this stanza, the speaker makes peace with Death. The image of the hound appears again, this time signifying an emotional release of sorts for the speaker. The souls of the dead now appear out of "all of the empty," a kind of limbo. Other images in this stanza symbolize the relentlessness of desire "that never filld pocket," and the incessant nature of being, "seeing nowhere / the final sleep," the inability to die.

Stanza 8

This stanza universalizes the speaker's vision. "The halls of Africa," for Duncan, symbolically representative of the zone of "the marvelous," is a place both desired and feared. These final images speak to the impossibility of love, as "seas / disturbd turn back upon their tides / into the rooms deserted at the roots of love." The first sentence of the fifth line makes literal what was figurative in the image of the "bird-faced children crawl[ing] out of their fathers" in the preceding stanza; "There is no end." The final image of the "tired sirens / com[ing] up from the water not to be touchd" both describes and emphasizes the complex nature of human desire.

Themes

Death

"An African Elegy" presents death as a subconscious force that is not fully present to the speaker except in symbolic terms. Duncan charts his relation to death through introspection, likening his own mind to Africa's jungles. His descriptions of those jungles are replete with images of suffering and death: "Death is the dog-headed man zebra striped /and surrounded by silence who walks like a lion, / who is black." For Duncan, Death is both an ominous seducer, who beckons Virginia Woolf to "come back" to the river to complete her suicide, and a welcome presence, who can rescue people from torment: in death "all our tortures [are] absolved in the fog, / dispersed in Death's forests, forgotten." The death drive, popularized in the philosophical idea of *Thanatos,* is alternately welcomed and rebuffed in Duncan's poem. As an elegy, this poem mourns not physical death, per se, but the fact that death must be a necessary part of the exotic and the beautiful, the zone of the "marvelous."

Race and Racism

Any poem titled "An African Elegy" and written by a white American will necessarily touch on the idea of race. Duncan's poem, written in 1942, though using Africa and the Congo in symbolic terms, nonetheless presents Africans in stereotypical ways. His representations of Africa as a dark

Topics for Further Study

- After researching the basic beliefs of Theosophy, give a report to your class outlining them. Are there connections you can draw between any of these beliefs and Duncan's poem?

- Keep a dream diary for one month, writing down as much and as many of your dreams as you can remember. Then catalog all of the images and stories. Do certain images or stories reccur? What do these images and stories tell you about that month in your life?

- Write a poem or story about the creation of the universe using symbols that are personally meaningful to you. Do not worry if these symbols will be accessible to others. Then write a short essay describing why you chose those particular symbols.

- Research the use of magic by the Swahili. Do you see any similarities with the rituals Duncan describes in his poem?

and unknowable place and of Africans as an inscrutable and exotic people who engage in barbaric rituals play on popular misconceptions of the continent and its people. Further, Duncan's depiction of African princes as those responsible for drinking his blood and torturing him in (what Duncan has described) a sado-masochistic ritual reinforce stereotypes of African men as sexually aggressive and dominant. These images, presented as symbolic renderings of the speaker's subconscious desires, serve as a historical index of American attitudes toward Africans in the early 1940s.

Nature

"An African Elegy" makes a comparison between the natural world and human nature, suggesting that the latter, at its root, is a variation of the former. Duncan makes the comparison explicit in the first, fourth, and final stanzas. For example, in the fourth stanza, he states, "I know / no other continent of Africa more dark than this / dark continent of my breast." Human beings have long debated their own nature, asking what accounts more for who we are, society or natural laws. This question is sometimes framed in terms of a debate between nature and nurture. Some philosophical and religious traditions, especially those associated with Western Judeo-Christianity, see the desires of the human body as a result of sin and humanity's separation from God. Others see the body's desires as natural, and religious and social prescriptions for behavior as unnatural. By using the natural world as the primary vehicle for describing human nature, and by making that natural world essentially mysterious and unknowable, Duncan suggests that true human nature is ultimately concealed from humans. All that human beings have access to is myth and imagery to explain themselves to themselves.

Style

Symbol

"An African Elegy" uses symbolic imagery to carry the emotional weight of the poem. Some of Duncan's primary symbols include the Congo, Africa and African nature, African Negroes, blood, and dogs. These images represent a complex of ideas including the unconscious elements of human desire, the ubiquity and reality of death, and the tenuousness of human identity and of life. In the West, Africa has often been used by writers as a symbol of human beings' baser instincts and desires. Joseph Conrad's novel *Heart of Darkness*, which presents the Congo as a place of violence, ignorance, and barbarity, is one such example. Many of Duncan's images, however, are obscure and sometimes inaccessible to beginning readers of poetry. He attempts to use them as pointers to a deeper, more complex reality than that which human beings experience. That reality can only be expressed in images.

Diction/Tone

Although the poem is called an elegy, its tone shifts between celebration and lament, sometimes approaching a kind of self-destructive ecstasy. The first stanza prepares the reader for this vacillation as it begins with the statement, "No greater marvelous / know I than the mind's / natural jungle," and then shifts to a description of the ominous nature of Death's sounds. Duncan's archaic spelling, sometimes using *t* instead of *-ed* endings for the past tense (e.g., "stopt" instead of "stopped"), his inversion of subjects and verbs, and his exotic word choice give his poem a formal and often magical tone.

Historical Context

In the early 1940s when Duncan wrote "An African Elegy," a group of poets and critics, who came to be known as the New Critics, helped to determine what kind of poetry would be published and read in the coming decades. Writers associated with this trend in criticism include Allen Tate, R. P. Blackmur, Cleanth Brooks, William K. Wimsatt, and John Crowe Ransom, who edited the *The Kenyon Review* and whose book *The New Criticism* (1941) gave the group its name. The members of the New Critics, who were mostly southerners and politically conservative, held formalist views of literature and argued that poems and stories be considered for their inherent value. This meant that literary works should be regarded as self-contained objects, separate from the traditions, histories, and authors that helped to produce them. Though they never established a doctrine as such, New Critics introduced critical principles and terms into the study of literature that remain today. It is ironic that Ransom rejected "An African Elegy" *after* reading Duncan's essay on homosexuals in society, for it shows that Ransom did not practice what he preached. By 1959, when Duncan finally published the poem, New Criticism had become entrenched in English departments throughout the United States and helped form the theoretical background against which millions of students would come to learn literature.

At about the same time, in Asheville, North Carolina, a progressive school in the arts was developing. Black Mountain College, founded in 1933, was an experiment in community education and appealed to many musicians, dancers, and writers who considered themselves part of the artistic avant-garde. Duncan taught there in 1956, as did other poets and writers associated with Duncan such as Charles Olson, Robert Creely, Paul Blackburn, and Denise Levertov. Olson's theory of poetry, as outlined in his essay "Projective Verse" (1950), became a doctrine of sorts for Black Mountain poets. He was also the leader of the college and the poets. These writers all shared a desire to explore the creative process and to integrate the arts. They saw poems as fields of meaning into which anything and everything was permitted and readers as active participants in meaning-making. Olson saw poetry beginning with the human body. He believed that the way a poem appears on the page should be related to how the poet experienced it and how the reader will experience it. Creely applied Olson's theories to his own poetry, writing a process-oriented poetry

Compare & Contrast

- **1958:** Patrice Lumumba founds the Movement National Congolais (MNC), which becomes the most dominant political party of the Democratic Republic of Congo.

  1960–1965: Political turmoil engulfs The Democratic Republic of Congo. Lumumba is assassinated by forces loyal to Colonel Mobutu Sese Seko, who eventually takes over the government in 1965.

  1971: Seko renames the country the Republic of Zaire and asks Zairean citizens to change their names to African names.

  1997: Seko is overthrown by Laurent Kabila and Rwandan-backed rebels, who "re-rename" the country the Democratic Republic of Congo.

  2000: Political unrest continues in the Democratic Republic of Congo.

- **1956:** Allen Ginsberg's poem "Howl" is published and embraced by the counterculture. In the poem, Ginsberg calls for America to wake up from its middle-class, sterile slumber that crushes the human soul and to end the "human war" on its own people.

  1997: Ginsberg dies at 70. The Beat culture, for which Ginsberg was a central figure, is a historical curiosity and has been reduced to slogans and symbols used in advertising campaigns.

---

which drew attention to the writer's thinking as he went along. Levertov, on the other hand, focused on the perceiving rather than the thinking mind as it detailed the surfaces of ordinary objects to evoke their presence and underlying meanings. Duncan, while influenced by Olson's thinking, attempted to create a poetry that was closer to religion or religious vision. His use of Greek myth and classical literature gave his writing an erudite, almost ethereal feel at times. Projectivist verse was regularly published by journals including *The Black Mountain Review* and *Origin.* Painters, photographers, musicians, and dancers such as Merce Cunningham, Robert Rauschenberg, John Cage, and Jess Collins (Duncan's life-partner) also taught or gave presentations at Black Mountain.

Although there are references to Africa and the Congo throughout Duncan's poem, they are symbolic rather than historical references. When Duncan wrote this poem, the United States had just become involved in World War II. Duncan himself spent time in the army but was granted a psychiatric discharge in 1941. Thanks to the war, the country was finally coming out of the Great Depression, as more than fifteen million Americans worked for the armed forces. African Americans, however, didn't benefit from the job boom. One group, the Brotherhood of Sleeping Car Porters, marched on Washington, D.C., calling for an end to discrimination. Shortly after this protest, President Franklin Delano Roosevelt issued Executive Order 8802 creating the Fair Employment Practices Commission to investigate complaints and make discrimination in war industries illegal.

Critical Overview

Although associated with the Projectivist school of Black Mountain poetry, Duncan is known as a romantic poet and a mystic whose verse often baffles readers. For example, John Crowe Ransom, after accepting "Sections Towards an African Elegy" (the original title of "An African Elegy") in 1943, returned it to Duncan the next year writing: "It seems to me to have obvious homosexual advertisement, and for that reason not to be eligible for publication." Ransom had re-read Duncan's poem after reading Duncan's essay "The Homosexual in Society" and saw things in it he hadn't before. "Is it not possible," he wrote Duncan, "that you have made the sexual inferences inescapable, and the poem unavailable?" Duncan biographer Ekbert Faas writes that even though Duncan acknowledged to Ransom that the sexual inferences in the poem were "inescapable," Faas himself does not find them as such. Faas sees Ransom's refusal to publish "An African Elegy" as the "sudden end to what easily might have turned into a successful literary career sanctioned by the new Critical establishment."

Mark Andrew Johnson praises Duncan's "powerful imagery" and "roiling vowels" in the poem and notes that the use of Shakespearean characters anticipates Duncan's "The Venice Poem." In his introduction to his volume *The Years as Catches,* Duncan writes that "An African Elegy," along with a few other of his early poems, displayed "exaggerated pretensions" and "falseness." That Duncan chose to publish the poem again anyway demonstrates his willingness to accommodate even the "falseness" of his past writing, for it too forms part of his ongoing work.

Criticism

Chris Semansky

Semansky publishes widely in the field of twentieth-century culture and poetry. In the following essay, he discusses the difficulty of reading "An African Elegy" and suggests a strategy.

It's a fact; some poems are more difficult to read than others. Some are straightforward, using images from the contemporary world and requiring little if any knowledge of other poetry, history, myth, or philosophy from their readers. Others require all of this background knowledge and more. Poems such as T. S. Eliot's "The Waste Land," for example, considered a modern masterpiece by many critics, contain a veritable encyclopedia of allusions to Western myth and intellectual history. In addition, its form, a collection of fragmented speeches and imagery, makes reading it a challenge. Robert Duncan's poem "An African Elegy," though much briefer and nowhere near as dense with allusions and history as "The Waste Land," is also a difficult poem to read. Its difficulty in part stems from its fragmented structure and its refusal to make the terms of its symbolism accessible in any conventional way. Even seasoned literary critics have had difficulty with Duncan's poems, including "An African Elegy." Writing of Duncan's "drifting conglomerations [of symbols and allusions]," poet and critic James Dickey writes that Duncan "never courted a readership but rather a special kind of reader, who grants the poet a wide

> *"Don't cogitate. Let the images resonate, reverberate, becoming what they will."*

latitude in developing his art, even in its most extreme moments.... The number of such readers is necessarily limited, but fierce in devotion." One strategy for reading Duncan's poems is to first understand his own approach toward poetry and composition and then to adjust your expectations and reading practices accordingly.

The first thing to understand about Duncan is his concept of the poem as a compositional field. *Field* in this case is a metaphor for space. Duncan conceives of poems as spaces in which all materials are welcome. Readers, therefore, should not read the poem as a story or a piece of writing with any one message or theme. Rather, they should read with an eye and an ear to the repetition of particular images, sounds, phrases, symbols, or structures, all of which Duncan uses—much as a painter uses color, line, or shape—to suggest ideas or emotions. Duncan, an ardent admirer of modern collage, saw his own verse as a kind of grand collage in which his given material was words. In this light, the individual images that Duncan uses as pieces of his collage might not make sense if readers strive to interpret them in a traditional fashion, pinning them down to specific definitions. However, by taking in the images and their multiple meanings and letting them build up, readers will find that the accumulated images will yield an emotional effect, even if readers are unable to articulate that effect in any coherent or conventional way.

To better comprehend Duncan's images it's necessary to know that Duncan is using them as symbols. Symbols don't have a one-to-one relationship to the outside world but rather weave a web of associations to various ideas and themes. Symbols open up the possibility for meaning rather than limiting meaning to one idea or thing. In his *Dictionary of Symbols,* scholar J. E. Cirlot writes:

> This language of images and emotions is based ... upon a precise and crystallized means of expression, revealing transcendent truths, external to Man (cosmic order) as well as within him (thought, the moral order of things, psychic evolution, the destiny of the

What Do I Read Next?

- Robert Bertholf edited a collection of thirty-five letters between Duncan and the poet H. D. in 1991, titled *A Great Admiration: H. D. / Robert Duncan Correspondence 1950–1961*. Duncan and H. D. admired each other's poetry intensely.

- Ekbert Faas' biography of Duncan, *Young Robert Duncan: Portrait of the Poet As Homosexual in Society*, provides a detailed biography of the poet through 1950.

- Black Sparrow Press published Robert J. Bertholf's *Robert Duncan: A Descriptive Bibliography* in 1986. The book is difficult to obtain but contains an exhaustive and useful collection of secondary sources on Duncan.

- Critics generally agree that Duncan's 1960 collection *The Opening of the Field* begins the poet's mature phase of work. This collection contains what is perhaps Duncan's best-known poem, "Often I Am Permitted to Return to a Meadow."

- Ian Reid and Robert Bertholf edited a collection of essays and tributes to Duncan in 1979. *Robert Duncan: Scales of the Marvelous* contains essays by Denise Levertov, Michael Davidson, Thom Gunn, and Don Byrd.

- Duncan was a fierce and outspoken opponent to the war in Vietnam. James Mersmann's 1974 *Out of the Vietnam Vortex: A Study of Poets and Poetry* examines Duncan's poetry and life in light of the poet's commitment to the idea of community.

- Sherman Paul's *The Lost America of Love: Rereading Robert Creely, Edward Dorn, and Robert Duncan*, published in 1981, is a diary of sorts detailing Paul's close reading of these important poets' work.

- Cary Nelson's *Our Last First Poets: Vision and History in Contemporary American Poetry* (1981) examines the relationship between history and poetics in a few of Duncan's poems. Nelson is a leading Marxist literary critic.

---

soul); furthermore, it possesses a quality which . . . increases its dynamism and gives it a truly dramatic character. This quality, the essence of the symbol, is its ability to express simultaneously the various aspects (thesis and antithesis) of the idea it represents.

Symbols are both particular and general, then. They are a prism of an idea or theme, irreducible. Africa, as the figurative space for Duncan's idea of the "marvelous" is, in effect, a symbolic topography of images, all of which contribute to this idea. The first stanza contains many of the symbolic images that will be repeated throughout the poem.

> In the groves of Africa from their natural wonder
> the wildebeest, zebra, the okapi, the elephant,
> have entered the marvelous. No greater marvelous
> know I than the mind's
> natural jungle. The wives of the Congo
> distil their red and the husbands
> hunt lion with spear and paint Death-spore
> on their shields, wear his teeth, claws and hair
> on ordinary occasions. There the Swahili
> open his doors, let loose through the trees
> the tides of Death's sound and distil
> from their leaves the terrible red. He
> is the consort of dreams I have seen, heard
> in the orchestral dark
> like the barking of dogs.

The animal imagery here creates a strange and exotic landscape. Most American-born readers have probably never encountered any of these creatures except in a zoo or on television. Their appearance, then, indicates otherness and difference, a way of being unfamiliar to most readers. The speaker compares his own mind to this sense of strangeness. It too is other or strange to him, and this is exhilarating and frightening at the same time. The ritual of hunting preparation by Congolese men and women also contributes to this sense of the exotic; it underscores the presence and importance of death in their lives. Like the speaker later in the poem, the Congolese men inhabit the identity of another, "wear[ing] . . . [the lion's] teeth, claws and hair / on ordinary occasions." The idea of ordinariness resonates in the last animal image in the stanza, the barking of dogs. Dogs are domestic animals; they are also scavengers and hunters and known as being loyal. Associating dogs with death highlights the ordinariness of death in the lives of the other. The "terrible red" is another symbol of death's many forms.

Duncan repeats the images introduced in the first stanza throughout the poem, letting them accrue meaning and power in much the same way a moonbar or magic stone (an image Duncan uses later) accrues power for its holder. The "barking of dogs" in the first stanza becomes "Death . . . the dog-headed man" in the second stanza. Hounds appear over and over again: white Afghan hounds, hounds in water, hounds of "great purity / disturbing the shadow and flesh of the jungle." By repeating this image but altering it slightly and using it in a different context each time, Duncan imbues the image of the dog/hound with symbolic resonance. The dog is at once death itself, death's companion, and a bewildering presence that requires a reassessment of its significance each time it appears.

The image of the "Negro" is also central to the poem. Duncan presents the image of Swahili men, Negro armies, Negro princes, Negro Kings, and Othello almost always as hunters or aggressors who act on him or others, often in a violent manner, making magic with his blood, twisting him like a rope. As symbolic images that inhabit the zone of the marvelous, these figures simultaneously inspire fear and awe. They function in the poem as markers of the speaker's desire, as parts of himself just beginning to make themselves known to him through these images. In a letter to John Crowe Ransom, the editor of the magazine that initially accepted the poem for publication, Duncan attempts to explain the poem's theme:

> The theme of the unknown is seen variously; as the figure of Death, the unknown self . . . or as the darkness of repressed desires, the unknown content of the mind as it goes on. Negroes, Africa and the black of love are all symbols of subconscious forces. . . . The rising figures from the subconscious discovered in the poem then were Death, my lost self, and the lost love-object . . . projected in the mind as the images of the women distilling their red (the object feared and hated) and the image of Virginia Woolf (the object loved and desired).

This explanation is Duncan attempting to understand the poem *after* it was written. Duncan is not interested in intentionality in his poems. When he composes, images often appear. He doesn't sit down and think about how he will use the image of the dog or the image of the African princes to mean something specific. For Duncan, the writing of poetry is itself a means of self-exploration, a therapy of sorts suited to figuring out his identity and desires, to probe the unknown self, as he has written, to "exercise my faculties at large." His poems are often an expression of something he does not understand about himself or about the world as much as they are about what he does understand. In "Pages from a Notebook," Duncan writes the following about his relationship to the composing process:

> In one way or another to live in the swarm of human speech. This is not to seek perfection but to draw honey or poetry out of all things. After Freud, we are aware that unwittingly we achieve our form. It is, whatever our mastery, the inevitable use we make of the speech that betrays to ourselves and to our hunters (our readers) the spore of what we are becoming. I study what I write as I study out any mystery. A poem, mine or another's, is an occult document, a body awaiting vivisection, analysis, x-rays.

It is interesting that the words "spore" and "hunter" appear in this journal entry, as they also appear in "An African Elegy." As with "hunters," readers can infer that both of these words function symbolically in Duncan's universe. Hunting is an act of looking and thinking, of being prepared for what might appear. This description also fits Duncan's work as a poet. Hunting is also a form of wanting or desiring an object. The object of desire in Duncan's poem, though, is never made explicit. All the reader knows is that some *thing* is desired, and whatever it is, is never achieved. This idea is expressed in the poem's final stanza when, for the first time, what the speaker is lamenting in this elegy becomes clear.

> The halls of Africa we seek in dreams
> as barriers of dream against the deep, and seas
> disturbd turn back upon their tides
> into the rooms deserted at the roots of love.
> There is no end. And how sad then
> is even the Congo. How the tired sirens
> come up from the water, not to be toucht
> but to lie on the rocks of the thunder.
> How sad then is even the marvelous!

Duncan laments that the idea of the exotic and the unknown—"The halls of Africa"—that human beings fantasize and dream about are neither truly exotic nor unknown because we already have ideas of them as such. The true unknown, Duncan suggests, is "the deep," the part of the human soul that can never be described in symbolic imagery or metaphor, the part that transcends language itself. That human beings desire and go on desiring when there is no hope to fulfill that desire is the sad thing. The final image of the sirens, those beautiful mythological sea-nymphs whose ravishing songs caused men to drown themselves, underlines this, while also echoing the manner in which Ophelia and Virginia Woolf died.

When reading Duncan, try not to think about or to figure out what his images mean. Rather, try to inhabit the "marvelous" itself. Don't cogitate. Let the images resonate, reverberate, becoming what they will. Receptive readers, even beginning readers of Duncan's poems, will discover that their own minds can accommodate the exotic and strange as well. They'll discover that the marvelous is the poem itself in the act of becoming, and that as readers they participate in that act.

Source: Chris Semansky, Critical Essay on "An African Elegy," in *Poetry for Students,* The Gale Group, 2001.

Sources

Bertholf, Robert J., ed., *A Great Admiration: H. D. / Robert Duncan Correspondence 1950–1961,* Lapis Press, 1991.

Bertholf, Robert J., and Ian W. Reid, eds., *Robert Duncan: Scales of the Marvelous,* New Directions, 1979.

Cirlot, J. E., *A Dictionary of Symbols,* Philosophical Library, 1971.

Dickey, James, *Babel to Byzantium: Poets and Poetry Now,* Straus & Giroux, 1968, pp. 173–77.

Duncan, Robert, "Pages from a Notebook," in *The New American Poetry,* edited by Donald M. Allen, Grove Press, 1960, pp. 400–07.

———, *Selected Poems,* edited by Robert J. Berthoff, New Directions, 1993.

———, *The Years as Catches: First Poems, 1939–1946,* Oyez, 1966.

Ellingham, Lewis, *Poet Be Like God: Jack Spicer and the San Francisco Renaissance,* University Press of New England, 1988.

Faas, Ekbert, *Towards a New American Poetics: Essays and Interviews: Charles Olson, Robert Duncan, Gary Snyder, Robert Creeley, Robert Bly, Allen Ginsberg,* Black Sparrow Press, 1978.

———, *Young Robert Duncan: Portrait of the Poet As Homosexual in Society,* Black Sparrow Press, 1983.

Foster, Edward Halsey, *Understanding the Black Mountain Poets,* University of South Carolina Press, 1984.

Johnson, Mark Andrew, *Robert Duncan,* Twayne Publishers, 1988.

Letters from Duncan to John Crowe Ransom, Washington Universities Libraries, St. Louis, Missouri.

Ray, Kevin, "Obvious Advertisement: Robert Duncan and the *Kenyon Review,*" *Fiction International,* 1992, pp. 287–91.

For Further Study

Allen, Donald, ed., *The New American Poetry,* Grove Press, 1960.

> This groundbreaking anthology collects poems from many of the most influential poets writing in America since World War II, including Duncan and many of the Black Mountain poets.

Duberman, Martin, *Black Mountain: An Exploration in Community,* Anchor Books, 1973.

> Duberman provides an insider's look at the experimental college where Duncan taught briefly in the mid-1950s. This is an invaluable study of one of the most celebrated intentional communities of its time, its birth, growth, and death.

Duncan, Robert, *Selected Poems,* edited by Robert J. Berthoff, New Directions, 1993.

> Including eleven additional poems, this second edition of Duncan's *Selected Poems* is a good place to start for students who want to read more of Duncan's work.

Harris, Mary Emma, *The Arts at Black Mountain College,* MIT Press, 1987.

> Harris examines the innovative ways the arts were taught at Black Mountain College and the ideals that many of the artists shared.

Birches

Robert Frost
1916

"Birches" is one of Robert Frost's most popular and beloved poems. Yet, like so much of his work, there is far more happening within the poem than first appears.

"Birches" was first published in the *Atlantic Monthly* in August of 1915; it was first collected in Frost's third book, *Mountain Interval,* in 1916. "Birches," with its formal perfection, its opposition of the internal and external worlds, and its sometimes dry wit, is one of the best examples of everything that was good and strong in Frost's poetry.

The main image of the poem is of a series of birch trees that have been bowed down so that they no longer stand up straight but rather are arched over. While the poet quickly establishes that he knows the real reason that this has happened—ice storms have weighed down the branches of the birch trees, causing them to bend over—he prefers instead to imagine that something else entirely has happened: a young boy has climbed to the top of the trees and pulled them down, riding the trees as they droop down and then spring back up over and over again until they become arched over. This tension between what has actually happened and what the poet would like to have happened, between the real world and the world of the imagination, runs throughout Frost's poetry and gives the poem philosophical dimension and meaning far greater than that of a simple meditation on birch trees.

Robert Frost

Author Biography

Robert Frost is universally identified with New England, his home for many years and the setting for much of his poetry. However, he was born in San Francisco, California, on March 26, 1874, and did not move to New England until after the death of his father in 1885 when his mother resettled the family to Lawrence, Massachusetts. There, Frost attended Lawrence High School where he was the co-valedictorian with his eventual wife, Elinor.

Frost was admitted to Harvard but did not have the money to go to school there. He briefly went to Dartmouth College in New Hampshire and worked at a variety of teaching and other jobs. He married Elinor in 1895 and began attending Harvard as a special student, but he left in 1899 to take up farming to support his family.

Frost published a few poems in 1894, and between 1899 and 1912, he wrote articles and poems and worked as a teacher in New Hampshire. In 1912, he moved his family to England in order to concentrate on his writing. While in England, he published his first book of poems, *A Boy's Will*, in 1913 and was enthusiastically reviewed by the American modernist poet Ezra Pound (1885–1978), who soon made his acquaintance. In 1914, *North of Boston*, his second book, was published; in 1915, when Frost returned to the United States, *North of Boston* was published there and became a major success, bringing him immediate fame.

From then on, Frost settled into a career of writing and teaching, holding jobs at several major universities. He rapidly became known as one of the most important American poets of the twentieth century. He won the Pulitzer Prize for poetry four times. In 1961, he was invited to read one of his poems at President John F. Kennedy's inauguration.

Frost's personal life, in contrast to his professional success, was often painful and bitter. Only four of his six children survived to adulthood; one of his daughters died after giving birth, another was institutionalized for mental illness, and his son committed suicide. His marriage was often stormy, and Frost has been accused of being cruel and domineering to his family. He strongly disliked left-wing politics and programs, such as the New Deal, which earned him the distrust of many literary critics. He was disappointed that he never received the Nobel Prize for literature.

Robert Frost died at the age of eighty-eight on January 29, 1963, in Boston, Massachusetts.

Poem Text

<pre>
When I see birches bend to left and right
Across the lines of straighter darker trees,
I like to think some boy's been swinging them.
But swinging doesn't bend them down to stay
As ice storms do. Often you must have seen them   5
Loaded with ice a sunny winter morning
After a rain. They click upon themselves
As the breeze rises, and turn many-colored
As the stir cracks and crazes their enamel.
Soon the sun's warmth makes them shed crystal   10
    shells
Shattering and avalanching on the snow crust—
Such heaps of broken glass to sweep away
You'd think the inner dome of heaven had fallen.
They are dragged to the withered bracken by the
    load,
And they seem not to break; though once they are   15
    bowed
So low for long, they never right themselves:
You may see their trunks arching in the woods
Years afterwards, trailing their leaves on the
    ground
Like girls on hands and knees that throw their hair
Before them over their heads to dry in the sun.   20
But I was going to say when Truth broke in
With all her matter of fact about the ice storm,
I should prefer to have some boy bend them
</pre>

As he went out and in to fetch the cows—
Some boy too far from town to learn baseball,
Whose only play was what he found himself,
Summer or winter, and could play alone.
One by one he subdued his father's trees
By riding them down over and over again
Until he took the stiffness out of them,
And not one but hung limp, not one was left
For him to conquer. He learned all there was
To learn about not launching out too soon
And so not carrying the tree away
Clear to the ground. He always kept his poise
To the top branches, climbing carefully
With the same pains you use to fill a cup
Up to the brim, and even above the brim.
Then he flung outward, feet first, with a swish,
Kicking his way down through the air to the ground.
So was I once myself a swinger of birches.
And so I dream of going back to be.
It's when I'm weary of considerations,
And life is too much like a pathless wood
Where your face burns and tickles with the cobwebs
Broken across it, and one eye is weeping
From a twig's having lashed across it open.
I'd like to get away from earth awhile
And then come back to it and begin over.
May no fate willfully misunderstand me
And half grant what I wish and snatch me away
Not to return. Earth's the right place for love:
I don't know where it's likely to go better.
I'd like to go by climbing a birch tree,
And climb black branches up a snow-white trunk
Toward heaven, till the tree could bear no more,
But dipped its top and set me down again.
That would be good both going and coming back.
One could do worse that be a swinger of birches.

Poem Summary

"Birches" is a poem of fifty-nine lines without any stanza breaks. However, the poem does contain several sections that move from naturalistic description to a fanciful explanation of why the birches are bowed, and it concludes with philosophical exploration of a person's existence in the world.

Lines 1–4

Frost opens the poem with an image of the birches bent "left and right / across the lines of straighter darker trees" (lines 1–2) and quickly puts forth one explanation for how they got that way: a boy had been swinging on them. Right away, however, he admits this is false, saying in line 4, "But swinging doesn't bend them down to stay." However, the image of the playful boy is a powerful one for Frost, and he will soon return to it.

Lines 5–11

The first break in the poem occurs in line 5 when Frost admits that it is ice storms, not boys, who bend down the birch trees. The next few lines are a beautiful description of birch trees, their branches frozen and encrusted with ice in the morning after an ice storm. However, their beauty is only short-lived; soon, in line 9, the sun "cracks and crazes their enamel"—the ice, which breaks and falls into the snow. This is the first hint of destruction in the poem (other than the birches themselves).

Lines 12–20

Frost makes another break in line 13 when he raises the symbolic level of the poem with the sentence "You'd think the inner dome of heaven had fallen." This line not only anticipates the last lines of the poem, but it also signals the beginning of a retreat from reality. The language of the poem becomes more "poetical"; for the first time, Frost uses a simile, comparing the bowed birch trees to girls on all fours, their hair hanging down in front of them. More than just destruction, the imagery now turns to symbols of conquest: the birches are bowed so that they can never right themselves; the image of the girl is also the image of a captive kneeling before her captor. This becomes an important theme in later parts of the poem.

Lines 21–27

The second really significant break (the first was in line 5) occurs now. Frost dismisses the ice storm as a cause of the birches' condition in favor of his original explanation that a boy had bent them—despite the fact that he knows that a boy didn't do it:

> But I was going to say when Truth broke in
> With all her matter of fact about the ice storm,
> I should prefer to have some boy bend them

The word *prefer* is very important here. Frost rejects the narrow limitations of the outside world in favor of his own poetic vision. However, this world must necessarily have its own limits, for it inhabits only his own mind. Likewise, the boy is separated from other people and plays alone.

Lines 28–35

In these lines, Frost returns to the theme of conquest. The boy "subdues" his father's trees, riding them until he takes the "stiffness" out of them, leaving him, in lines 31–32, absolutely victorious over the trees: "not one was left / For him to conquer." The boy's conquest of the trees mirrors the

Media Adaptations

- A videocassette, *New England in Autumn* (1998), distributed by Monterey Home Video, includes footage of Robert Frost's homes in New England and readings of his works.

- Another video, *Robert Frost* (1988), includes interviews with Seamus Heaney and other poets and a dramatic reading by Joan Allen of one of Frost's poems.

- Henry Holt & Co. has produced an interactive computer resource on CD, *Robert Frost: Poems, Life, Legacy* (1998). It includes an interactive documentary, 1,500 pages of critical and biographical literature, and 69 poems read by Frost himself.

---

victory of Frost's poetic imagination over the real world, for now his vision has completely supplanted the ice storm as the cause of the trees' condition.

Lines 36–40

These lines contain a description of the boy's technique for climbing and bending the trees. He must take painstaking care to reach the top of each tree, which Frost describes in line 38 as similar to the care that one must take to fill a cup "Up to the brim, and even above the brim." This is an important line. Frost is here describing a method of reaching beyond the limits of things (filling a cup beyond the brim) to a realm beyond the real. This is not just the internal world of his imagination but something even greater—a theme he will begin to develop more fully in the concluding sections of the poem. Also, the care taken by the boy is similar to the careful construction involved in writing a poem, making the boy's actions in climbing the trees a parallel for Frost's act of creating the poem.

Lines 41–47

Frost begins this section (lines 41–42) with a note of nostalgia: "So was I once myself a swinger of birches. / And so I dream of going back to be."

This longing for the simpler days of childhood stands in sharp contrast with the pain of the adult world, which is described as a "pathless wood." But this section also further develops the theme of the imagined world versus the real world: the boy's birch climbing has been wholly imaginary, a peaceful, playful time when one person can alone remake the world as he imagines it; in contrast, the real world lashes out at the narrator, and it is clear that he will achieve no victory over it.

Lines 48–53

Frost now, in line 48, develops his idea of escaping into an imaginary world: "I'd like to get away from earth awhile." However, he also makes it clear in lines 52–53 that he does not want to permanently escape the real world and that such a fate is not even desirable: "Earth's the right place for love: / I don't know where it's likely to go better." It is almost as if the limits of the real world must exist in order for the imaginative world to exist. This is similar to the theme of Frost's contemporary, the American poet Wallace Stevens (1879–1955), in his poem "Sunday Morning," in which he calls death "the mother of beauty." The real world makes possible the fantasies of the poetic imagination and makes them more poignant because they cannot be reality.

Lines 54–59

In the concluding section of the poem, Frost ties these ideas together with the image of the birch trees. The act of his poetic imagination—reaching beyond the limits of reality—is now likened to climbing the birch tree. The motion of the tree, which allows a person to climb to its top only to bend down and drop him back on the ground, is in fact the way Frost wants his imagination to work: to allow him only to approach "heaven" and then to bring him back to the real world. This also ties in with the image of filling a cup beyond its brim (line 38): it is possible to exceed the limits of the real world but only a little bit, or else there is disaster. The poem's concluding line, which at first seems to be a bit of folksy wisdom—"One could do worse than be a swinger of birches"—contains darker possibilities: one could certainly do worse by not making the attempt, that is, by not using one's imagination, or one might actually escape—the birch might not swing, but instead it might allow the climber to leave the world of limitations entirely behind. The limits of the real world may be painful, but they define one as a person (or as a poet); if it is a solitary existence, it is still existence.

Without limits, there can be no love (see line 52) or, for that matter, any other human emotion. Frost thus brings the poem back to the duality he expressed in the first lines of the poem. The real world provides the limits that make his poetry possible.

Themes

The Imagination vs. the Real World

One important theme of "Birches" is how Frost uses his poetic imagination to transcend the limits of the real world. He rejects the true reason the birches have been bent over in favor of his own fanciful explanation. On some level, he is claiming that this act of the imagination embodies a larger "truth" and is a worthy task, one that must be made with great care and diligence.

On the other hand, Frost makes it clear that one must remain within the natural world itself and that complete escape into the world of the imagination is impossible and not even desirable. It is this tension within the poem that makes each world both appealing and painful—the real world might be a place of pain, but it is also the place for love; the imaginary world is innocent, but it is also solitary and, by extension, loveless.

The Need for Limits

In "Birches" and many other Frost poems, the limits imposed by the real world are seen not only as a consequence of being in the world but as a necessary condition for existing as a person. The borders of the world define a person and place him or her in the real world, just as the birch trees are bent back toward the earth by the ice storm. In much of Frost's work, the idea that one could remove all the barriers between oneself and the world is at best undesirable and at worst terrifying. Thus, in "Birches," Frost pleads that "no fate willfully misunderstand me / And half grant what I wish and snatch me away." The removal of limits would leave one's personality groundless, with no way to define itself. Thus, wherever one looks in "Birches," one will find people or forces imposing limits: both the boy and the ice storm bend the birches, gravity pulls the narrator back down to earth as he climbs "toward heaven," surface tension holds water just past the brim of a cup.

This theme runs throughout Frost's work and can be found in many other of his poems, for example, "Mending Wall," "For Once, Then, Something," and "Desert Places," one of the most terrifying poems he ever wrote.

Topics for Further Study

- Frost remarks that "Earth's the place for love" and does not want to be separated from it. Do you agree? What do you think this means about Frost's attitude about the afterlife?

- Frost's poems are intimately connected with the natural environment and climate of New England; for example, the ice storms that bend down the birches. What is unique about the climate or area in which you live? Search for poems in which your area or climate has been celebrated.

- Write a poem about your own childhood or on how you remember your childhood. Do you think you were more innocent then than now? If so, or if not, explain whether or not that childhood innocence is something to be desired.

Conquest

Related to both the above themes is the idea of conquest, which occurs often in the first two-thirds of the poem. The ice storm conquers the trees, bending them down almost in supplication; the boy also bends the trees down in Frost's imagination. This expands the idea of the need for limits that push the boundaries of those that naturally occur. Thus, the poetic imagination becomes, in a sense, an act of conquest, allowing the poet to vanquish the natural world with his own mind. It is both the ultimate limit and the ultimate expression of his individuality—he stands alone in a world of his own making.

Some critics have also seen the images of conquest in terms of psychoanalytic theory. James Ellis, for example, notes that the boy "subdues" his father's trees, implying a kind of Oedipal conflict where the boy must symbolically kill his father in order to become his own person. In this reading, climbing the trees has overtly sexual meanings, and the trees themselves are phallic objects.

Pastoralism and Nature Poems

A pastoral is a kind of poem that is about rural life. It generally presents the natural world as unspoiled and idyllic as compared to the corrup-

Compare & Contrast

- **1915:** War rages across northern France; T. S. Eliot publishes "The Love Song of J. Alfred Prufrock" in *Poetry;* "Birches" appears in the *Atlantic Monthly.* Frost is forced to return to America by the war, while Eliot moves to London.

    1948: Eliot receives the Nobel Prize for literature. By this time, Frost had won the Pulitzer Prize for poetry an unprecedented four times (1924, 1931, 1937, 1943)—yet, much to his dismay, he is never considered for the Nobel Prize. This is perhaps due to his deep association with New England and the apparent concern of his poetry only with its landscape, as opposed to Eliot's more cosmopolitan life and his concern with the universal issues of life and religion.

    1961: Frost is selected to read his poem "The Gift Outright" at President John F. Kennedy's inauguration. Frost at this point has held the position of official U.S. Poet Laureate, from 1958 to 1959.

    1992: Derek Walcott, the Caribbean poet, wins the Nobel Prize for literature.

tion and troubles of city life. In some respects, "Birches," as well as many other Frost poems, can be considered a pastoral in that it has a rural setting and represents the boy's solitary life as something to be desired. However, this picture is complicated by the fact that Frost admits freely that it does not actually exist; thus, his preferring it to reality is somewhat ironic because he knows it is false.

Style

Frost, unlike his great contemporaries such as T. S. Eliot, Ezra Pound, Wallace Stevens, and William Carlos Williams, never stopped using traditional forms in his poems. He continued using strict meter and rhyme forms throughout his career, famously remarking that free verse—poetry written without strict meter or rhyme—was like "playing tennis without a net."

"Birches" is written in blank verse. Blank verse is a kind of unrhymed, metered poetry that is very common in English. It consists of five "feet" (syllable groups) of two syllables each, in which the first syllable of each foot is unstressed and the second stressed: dah-DUH. This stress pattern is called iambic pentameter: an iamb is the two-syllable foot just described, and pentameter simply means that there are five feet in each line.

Blank verse has a long and glorious history in English poetry. It is the verse pattern of Shakespeare and Marlowe's plays, for example, and such other poems as Wordsworth's "The Prelude" and Keats' "The Eve of St. Agnes." As with all more formal verse patterns, it had fallen into disuse in the twentieth century but was still sometimes used, for example, Wallace Stevens' "Sunday Morning." Frost's stubborn use of traditional poetic forms not only reflected his personality but ties in with the theme of limits remarked upon above.

Historical Context

It is perhaps ironic that "Birches," set in a peaceful, almost idyllic New England landscape, first appeared during one of the most destructive wars in history. "Birches" was first published in 1915, when World War I was raging on the European continent. "Birches" shows little sign of the larger conflict that was engulfing the world; it is in no sense a war poem, and it displays no obvious political content. However, it is notable that there are many violent acts either shown or implied in the poem and that the language of conquest is conspicuous in the middle section of the poem.

Although Frost first reached prominence around the end of World War I, he had little in common with other poets, such as T. S. Eliot and Ezra Pound, who also became famous at that point. For one thing, he was over ten years older than either poet; for another, he lacked the rebel sensibility that led the younger poets to reject traditional forms in favor of a new poetics that are today called modern. Pound and Eliot were influenced by poets such as Baudelaire, author of "Flowers of Evil," and by his successors, French symbolist poets such as Paul Verlaine, Arthur Rimbaud, and Stephane Mallarme. Their poems not only made use of a rich vocabulary of symbolic expression (often drawn from religious or mythological sources) but also turned away from traditional verse forms, which they found too rigid and artificial to express their ideas and feelings. Pound and Eliot (in his early period) worked within a style known as imagism, a successor to the symbolist movement, which strove to find concrete, arresting images that contained powerful symbolic associations and to create a vivid picture in the reader's mind.

Frost, however, looked back to an earlier tradition. He remained within the bounds of regular verse forms, and his primary influences were poets from the late-nineteenth and early-twentieth centuries, such as the English novelist and poet Thomas Hardy (1840–1928) and the American poet Edward Arlington Robinson (1869–1935). Typically for Frost, however, he cited earlier poets as his influences: the American essayist and poet Ralph Waldo Emerson (1803–1882) and, even further back, the Roman poets Horace and Virgil.

Frost's language, though, reflected the changes sweeping through the world of poetry. He rejected the stilted, artificial poetry of many nineteenth-century poets (including Robinson) in favor of a language, despite its use of such words as "e'en" and "twere," that sounds like the speech of ordinary people. His descriptions of the natural world are both arresting images and complex symbols that carry the weight of his moral convictions. So, although most of his poems do not reflect the political and historical realities of the time they were written (only late in his life, when Frost had become somewhat of a political figure himself as perhaps America's most well-known and beloved poet, does his poetry begin to reflect these things) and despite their backwards-looking forms, they remain very much, poems of their time.

Critical Overview

"Birches" has been viewed as an important expression of Frost's philosophical outlook as well as a transitional poem that signaled a significant change in his literary development. Critic Jeffrey Hart, writing in *Sewanee Review,* terms "Birches" a "Frostian manifesto" due to the poem's skeptical tone regarding spiritual matters. Hart draws attention to the first part of the poem, where Frost presents the fantastic idea that the trees were bent by a boy, then discredits this thought with a more rational explanation regarding ice storms. In this manner, according to Hart, Frost casts doubt on the irrational aspects of the spiritual realm and upholds the value of earthly reality. "Birches," the critic writes, "asserts the claims of Frost's skepticism and sense of human limits against the desire for transcendence and the sense of mysterious possibility." A similar conclusion is reached by Floyd C. Watkins in an essay published in *South Atlantic Quarterly*. Watkins explains that Frost "contemplates a moment when the soul may be completely absorbed into a union with the divine. But he is earthbound, limited, afraid. No sooner does he wish to get away from earth than he thinks of 'fate'— rather than God. And what might be a mystical experience turns into fear of death, a fear that he would be snatched away 'not to return.'"

John C. Kemp, in his book *Robert Frost and New England,* notes that "Birches" was written at a time when Frost's work took a new direction. In 1913, the poet was completing work on *North of Boston,* a collection that is considered one of his finest. "Birches" was also composed in 1913 but was withheld from *North of Boston*. Kemp believes that Frost made this decision because he "evidently knew that he had done something different in ['Birches'], something not quite appropriate to the tone and dramatic impetus of the other poems" that were published in the volume. In specifying what that difference is, Kemp argues that the poems in *North of Boston* often reflect the observations of "perplexed and uncertain" outsiders as they observe rural New England life. "Birches" on the other hand, expresses the "confident, affirmative, and dominating" voice of the "Yankee farmer." The farmer is a self-assured native who delivers pronouncements and wisdom based on his experiences in the countryside. Frost's later poetry continued and intensified this attitude, according to Kemp, making "Birches" a precursor of Frost's subsequent work. The critic also contends that this change in direction ultimately harmed Frost's poetry. "By adopting the stance of the Yankee farmer," Kemp writes, "Frost committed himself to conventional poses and slighted his original, imaginative impulses."

Criticism

Erica Smith

Smith is a writer and editor. In this essay, she argues that, while "Birches," like so many of Robert Frost's poems, is a delicate balancing act of memory and imagination, reality and fantasy, and heaven and earth, the poet's intent is not to judge these things but to find his own way among them.

Many people read Frost's poetry, especially better-known poems such as "The Road Not Taken" or "Stopping by Woods on a Snowy Evening," and come away with a sense of Frost as a rustic, good-natured painter of nature scenes. While Frost was indeed a great poet of the natural world, his vision was far more complex and nuanced than most readers realize at first. One of his great concerns was how a person can define himself or herself in the world—that is, what does it mean to be conscious and what is the relation between the external, observed world and the interior world of the mind and imagination? And his view of nature never forgets the vision of Emerson, the great romantic philosopher and poet who nevertheless held that all life comes from the death of other things.

Themes of estrangement and alienation abound in the poetry of Robert Frost. Yet his attitude towards estrangement is complex. On the one hand, being separated from people and things is lonely, dangerous, and maddening; but at the same time, giving in, tearing down barriers, and allowing oneself to merge with the outside world means losing definition, selfhood, one's sense of identity. Neither alternative is totally satisfactory, and both provide a constant tension that runs through the very heart of much of his greatest work.

For example, consider the trees at the beginning of "Birches." They are separated from the "straighter, darker trees" behind them, alone and beaten down. Yet at the same time, the fact that they have been bowed means that they have been part of the larger world and have been buffeted by its forces. They are both alienated and a part of the world. They may stand in defeat, but they still stand. In that respect, they exist as emblems of the darker part of Frost's vision.

That Frost considers some alienation not only a consequence of being alive, but perhaps its defining characteristic, can be seen in his attitude toward barriers and limits. "Birches" treats two such kinds of limits: the natural limits that are created and enforced by the outer world and the inner, self-defined limits created by the mind and the imagination. In the end, both are necessary, in a sense, but Frost definitely seems to have a preference for one over the other.

Natural limits occur throughout the poem, but they are most directly treated from lines 5 through 20 and from lines 45 through 52. Frost's view of these limits is complex, neither condemning them fully nor embracing them.

Consider the description of the ice-laden trees in the beginning of the poem (lines 6–11). First, it should be noted, we are inclined to view the ice storm negatively because Frost has used it to refute his hoped-for explanation in line 3 of why the trees have become bowed: "I like to think some boy's been swinging them." Yet the storm, which has encrusted the branches with crystalline ice, makes them far more beautiful than they were before. They delight both eye and ear as they "click upon themselves" (line 7) and the sun "cracks and crazes their enamel" (line 9)—a line which conjures up an image of a vase whose enamel has been specially heated so that it cracks into a multicolored pattern of cracks (and which perhaps echoes, unconsciously, the image of the urn in John Keats' poem "Ode on a Grecian Urn.") The storm, despite impinging upon the trees, has given them the ability to become more lovely.

Yet another natural limit intrudes upon this scene: the sun, which causes the ice to melt and slide off the trees' branches and lie scattered around them. Frost thinks of heaven when he looks at this shattered ice, and from this point forward, imagination begins to intrude upon the natural world: the poem's first simile soon follows, and in a short while we have entered his fantasy, where it is a boy, not an ice storm, that has brought down the trees.

This fantasy lasts from lines 23 through 40, and Frost says that this is the one he "prefers." Yet, this fantasy, while it allows escape from the limits imposed by the outside world, is in its own way just as limited. The boy, while freed from the constraints of time and able to play in any season, is totally alone and isolated. And his freedom from the constraints of the natural world means that he is just as alienated from it as he is from other people.

Also, his world still limits what he can do. Climbing the trees requires painstaking care—as much care as trying to fill a cup beyond its brim. And he can only subdue things, not connect to them; when he is done with the birches, they are limp and unable to stand alone any longer. The imaginary world has affected them just as badly as the natural world and its ice storms.

The image of conquest, however, is an important one. Both the natural world of the ice storm and the imaginary world of the boy affect the birches in the same way, and the imagery is the same for both: that of violence, of bending another person to your will. The birches, after the ice storm is finished with them, are reduced to an attitude of supplication, like girls on their hands and knees. That they will never stand up straight again makes the victory of the ice storm complete; it has forever changed what they were, imposed its limits permanently on them.

The boy also takes all the "stiffness" out of his father's trees and does so until "not one was left / For him to conquer" (lines 31–32). On the face of things, his victory is as complete as the ice storm's. But it is undermined by our knowledge that this is a fantasy, that Frost himself has told us that it is ice storms, not boys, that affect birch trees so. However, the image of the trees as girls is an example of a simile; in other words, to see the totality of the ice storm's victory in the poem, we must use the tools of the imagination. Each side in this debate is limiting—and reinforcing—the other.

Following the fantasy of the boy among the trees, Frost returns to the natural world but depicts it in a very imaginative way. He describes a "pathless wood" in which the narrator wonders alone and afraid, burdened down with the hard choices of being an adult, his face burning and tickling "with the cobwebs / Broken across it, and one eye is weeping / From a twig's having lashed across it open" (lines 45–48).

Now the natural world is attacking the poet himself, rather than just the object of his consideration. It is imposing its limits upon him and inflicting pain as it does so. Yet this whole passage is itself a simile. Once again, in order to understand how the natural world limits us, we must turn to the imagination.

In the same way, the narrator's imaginative escape at the end of the poem relies on a specific image, that of climbing up the birch tree. The urge to move upwards, out of the naked reality of the world and into the timeless world of the mind—of heaven—is defeated once again by the outside world, which drags the tree down and places the narrator back in it. And this is what he wants: not the absolute conquest of the imagination displacing the real world, nor the awful destruction of him-

> *One of his great concerns was how a person can define himself or herself in the world—that is, what does it mean to be conscious and what is the relation between the external, observed world and the interior world of the mind and imagination?"*

self—in a very real way, a death—that would result from his surrender to the outside world. Instead, he must exist along the arch of the birch tree, the curved path between two opposite poles, a narrow way to exist but the only way to exist and be his own person—and poet. Return now to the image of the ice-bound birches: the natural world has affected them and made them more than they were; so too does it affect the poet and make it possible—necessary—for him to use his imagination and create a poem. Thus Frost "likes to think" that it is boys who bow down birch trees.

There are glimpses of the terror Frost puts into other poems, such as "Design" or "Desert Places," in "Birches"—the passage about the woods is certainly frightening when one considers that Frost is using it as a metaphor for everyday life—but it never reaches the depths that those poems approach. Rather, it maps out the way we all are: we desire escape, freedom from death and time, but we cannot stand the alienation that such escape entails; we need the limits of being in the world. Thus, dark and pathless as the woods are, they remain "the best place for love." We need the world as much as our imagination and so must all go on being "swingers of birches."

Source: Erica Smith, Critical Essay on "Birches," in *Poetry for Students,* The Gale Group, 2001.

Jonathan N. Barron

Barron is associate professor of English at the University of Southern Mississippi. He has co-

What Do I Read Next?

- *The Poetry of Robert Frost* (1969) includes all of the poems mentioned in this article and remains the standard source for Frost's work.

- The American poet Galway Kinnell also features New England as the setting for many of his poems. His *Selected Poems* (1982) includes "For Robert Frost," an account not only of his visit with Frost but an assessment of his life and career as a poet.

- *Homage to Robert Frost* (1996) includes essays about Frost and his poems by (among others) Nobel Prize winners Joseph Brodsky, Seamus Heaney, and Derek Walcott.

- Peter Davison's *The Fading Smile: Poets in Boston, 1955–1960* (1994) examines Robert Frost, Robert Lowell, and Sylvia Plath, among others, who were some of the best poets working in the United States at the time.

---

edited Jewish American Poetry *(from the University Press of New England) and* Roads Not Taken: Rereading Robert Frost *(forthcoming from the University of Missouri Press), as well as a forthcoming collection of essays on the poetic movement, New Formalism. Beginning in 2001, he will be the editor in chief of* The Robert Frost Review. *In the following essay, he shows how "Birches" is really a profound meditation on the meaning of and need for poetic metaphors in everyday life.*

Of all the poets in his generation, Robert Frost is the most surprisingly subtle. Compared to such American poets as Ezra Pound, T. S. Eliot, Marianne Moore, and Wallace Stevens, Frost's poetry seems to be accessible, straightforward, free of learned allusions and difficult language. The subtlety, however, reveals itself whenever readers begin to closely read a Frost poem. The careful attention close reading requires demonstrates just how complex, even tricky, Frost's poetry can be. A look at "Birches," for example, will show that, while it is a simple tale of a boyhood experience, it is also a profound meditation on the meaning of, and the need for, poetic metaphors. While a number of scholars have examined Frost's theory of metaphor, even those who have turned their attention to "Birches" do not go into the detail that a close reading requires. Of the recent critics who do, two are exemplary: Judith Oster's *Towards Robert Frost: The Reader and the Poet* and George Bagby's *Frost and the Book of Nature*.

Yet for all their insight into the meaning of metaphor in this poem, neither Bagby nor Oster accounts for the metaphorical richness of "Birches." When one does, one finds that, from the very first lines, metaphor is a central issue in this poem. The poem begins with a simple declaration. The poet tells his readers that, when he sees "birches bend to left and right," he likes to imagine what caused them to be so bent. He says, "I like to think some boy's been swinging them." Given this relatively flat declaration, the first three lines of the poem seem as straightforward as any three lines of poetry can be. But notice that Frost's explanation for the bent trees is actually just a wish, an imagined possibility, not a fact. He says, "I like to think." And, after he admits his own fantasy, he corrects that imaginative, poetic idea with a naturalistic fact: "But swinging doesn't bend them down to stay / As ice storms do." That natural fact, at war with his poetic imagination, ought to put an end to his delightful image of a boy's exuberant play among the trees. Notice, though, that this naturalistic fact does not put an end to Frost's imaginative desire to create metaphors.

What poets call a caesura, a pause, occurs in line 5 with the period in the middle of the line. This caesura is immensely important because it stops the intrusion of the natural fact midway through the line. Frost, in effect, will not let natural science have the last word. Instead, after stating the natural fact of the ice storm, he appeals directly to his readers: "you must have seen them." It is as if Frost were asking his readers to confirm his own sense that bent trees are a strange and even exciting phenomenon—so strange that they are worthy of metaphors. Describing the trees after the ice storm, Frost's language is both exact and vivid. Then, in line 9, he begins to get carried away: his language becomes poetic, which is to say that it becomes metaphorical. Describing the effect of wind and light on the ice in the trees, he says that the "stir" of the wind "cracks and crazes their [the trees'] enamel." Well, the birches do not really have enamel on them; that is a metaphor for the ice. And what does "crazes" mean? In a 1918 talk, "The Unmade Word," to high school students about this very poem, he asked the students about his use of the word "crazes." One of the students took notes on the talk and later described it. Frost asked, "Where do you think I got that word 'crazes'? [no answer] Mr. Frost went to the blackboard, and drew a pattern of crackly china." The word, as this anecdote reveals, is a metaphor to explain the image of the trees. And this is not the only metaphor. It is just the beginning of a series of metaphors. In the next four lines (which comprise a complete sentence), one finds even more. It is as if, having created one metaphor, he finds he cannot stop himself from creating even more. He goes so far as to say that "You'd think the inner dome of heaven had fallen." Again, in his talk to the high school students mentioned above, Frost said, "I wonder if you think I fetched that word dome too far?" After asking that question, he added, "but I like it."

These are not the only metaphors in this part of the poem. After comparing the trees to china or pottery, and then to heaven, Frost next makes the most alluring and surprising metaphor of them all: he compares the trees to "girls on hands and knees that throw their hair / Before them over their heads to dry in the sun." Here, he introduces a sensual image and prepares the way for a serious theme about love that will emerge only at the end of the poem. But at this point, in the first twenty lines, it is enough to notice that Frost has devoted more than half of his lines (twelve) to metaphors about the ice on the trees. Without using *like* or *as*, the first part of Frost's poem is little more than a comparison of ice-storm-bent trees to various other things and people. Then, in line 21, Frost returns to his beginning: he returns to line 4. In line 21, he basically apologizes to the reader for ever even mentioning the fact of the ice storm:

> But I was going to say when Truth broke in
> With all her matter of fact about the ice storm,
> I should prefer to have some boy bend them

These seemingly simple statements are in fact amazingly complicated. For "Truth," the mundane natural fact of the ice storm, was, in the previous twenty lines, already undercut by the poetic imagination of Frost's many metaphors. And the imagined ideal of a boy is, in the lines that follow, presented not as something startling and imaginative, but as a fact. In other words, "Truth" with a capital "T" may well be the fact that an ice storm bent the trees—but, in this poem, it is depicted as a fantasy of heavenly domes, young girls, and pottery. The imagination, by contrast, which would rather have a boy bend those trees, is described in non-

> "... Frost wants his readers to focus only on his idea of life's meaning. So far, in this poem, Frost has said that life is a difficult journey filled with pain. He has shown through his own example how that pain can be tempered, even eradicated, through the salvific power of the poetic imagination."

metaphorical, realistic imagery. Indeed, from line 21 to line 40, Frost offers a set of brilliant, exciting, and powerfully vivid images of a boy swinging the trees down to their present bent shape. Even though this is supposed to be his imagination at work, the language is almost entirely descriptive, offering almost no metaphors.

In line 41, Frost then explains why his fantasy seemed to be so real. He admits, "So was I once myself a swinger of birches. / And so I dream of going back to be." These lines are the very meat and substance of the poem. They explain why Frost is so committed both to metaphor and to his own image of a boy rather than to an ice storm as the explanation for these trees' shape. When he says that he "dreams of going back" to being a "swinger of birches," he is using that image as a metaphor for a state of being, for a time of life, for the condition of youth. He says as much in the next lines, which are powerful precisely for their honesty. And, in them, one learns why metaphors are necessary. They demonstrate to readers that metaphors are psychological tools by which one copes with everyday life:

> It's when I'm weary of considerations,
> And life is too much like a pathless wood
> Where your face burns and tickles with the cobwebs
> Broken across it, and one eye is weeping
> From a twig's having lashed across it open.

Look at the imagery here. Comparing life's journey to a wood without paths, to a place where there are no roads, no directions, Frost explains that it will be inevitable that in such a situation one will become injured. One's face, even one's eyes, will be damaged. There will be pain. Frost explains his sense of getting older, of travelling on life's journey through this metaphor of the woods. And by comparing life to a wood and adulthood to a journey through it, he tells his readers that young people are far happier than adults since they do not have to go anywhere. They get to swing and play. In fact, *they* damage the trees. In other words, the trees have to submit to the boy; they have to bend to *his* will. Older people, says Frost, are not so fortunate; they have to submit to nature. They walk with "one eye weeping."

Given this realization that youth is a far more pleasant experience than maturity, a realization stated entirely in metaphorical terms, Frost admits that, though he is an adult, he would much rather be a swinger of birches; he would rather, as he says in line 48, "get away from earth awhile / And then come back to it and begin over." Immediately, however, Frost realizes that these lines have another implication. They can be interpreted as meaning that he *really* wants to get away from earth; they can be interpreted to mean that, in other words, he wants to die, that he wants to leave the world altogether. Not intending to imply that at all, he adds ironically and even humorously, "May no fate willfully misunderstand me / And half grant what I wish and snatch me away."

By insisting that this is not a poem about the afterlife, that it is not a meditation on death or a contemplation of suicide, Frost wants his readers to focus only on his idea of life's meaning. So far, in this poem, Frost has said that life is a difficult journey filled with pain. He has shown through his own example how that pain can be tempered, even eradicated, through the salvific power of the poetic imagination. The poetic imagination allows one to make metaphors, and the metaphors offer comfort when nothing else will. The poem, then, is a profound meditation on the meaning of aging, of maturity, and above all on the necessity of making metaphors.

What happens next, however, is especially mysterious, and only a close reading reveals just how strange it is. After Frost insists that he is not in any way asking for death or putting all his faith and hope into an imagined afterlife, he writes, "Earth's the right place for love." What makes this mysterious is that love has not been an issue anywhere in the previous 51 lines. Why does he make it an issue here? What, as the rock star Tina Turner would say, has love got to do with it? The concluding seven lines offer a tentative and profound answer. In them, Frost not only defends the need for his own metaphor of a boy, rather than an ice storm, being the cause of the trees' shape, but he also defends his refusal to adopt the conventional Christian attitude that life on Earth is but a prelude to the afterlife. As one Catholic scholar of Frost, Edward Ingebretson, put it, these lines show that for Frost "Love is the soul's essential gravity." Also, when Frost in these concluding lines, turns to love, he says that life on Earth must be about the experience of human love. For Frost, the purpose of life, as of love, is poetic. As he says, "I don't know where it's likely to go better." Together, these two lines—"Earth's the right place for love: / I don't know where it's likely to go better"—constitute Robert Frost's creed. And, as the Frost scholar James M. Cox put it, they are also "Frost's greatest lines—lines which reveal the grace and loss and gain of all Frost's life and language." These lines, it must be said, are not the boy's words. They are Frost the poet's words. The boy, a swinger of trees, has not yet come to this realization, but Frost implies that he will. Still, the boy has not yet come to any of that, and his life without considerations, without the need to forge paths, without pain, enables him to be the master, not the mastered. Such a situation certainly holds its attractions. A man of this world, Frost readily admits his own need for the boy's youthful experience of mastery, irresponsibility, and play. At the same time, he wishes for the adult world despite the pains that come with it. Frost concludes, "That would be good both going and coming back." By this, Frost means that if he could have his way, he would have both attitudes at once. A mature man, he would, at the same time, like to be a boy.

In the final line, when Frost says, "One could do worse than be a swinger of birches," one might well ask, what could be worse? The answer is that to be only such a swinger is to forsake love altogether. While one might want to forsake the "pathless wood" of life to be such a swinger, Frost implies that, in the end, one will have a lonely, hollow existence based on power and will. The playfulness of youth comes with its own price. Nonetheless, Frost will not give up on that dream, that metaphor, either. For if he were to forsake his imagined world of a boy swinging on trees, he would be left only with a mechanistic, nonpoetic, scientific view—truth. To insist on the need for his own metaphor of the boy is to insist, as well, on the importance of love, the least practical and sensible of emotions.

Source: Jonathan N. Barron, Critical Essay on "Birches," in *Poetry for Students,* The Gale Group, 2001.

Wendy Perkins

Perkins has published widely in the field of twentieth-century American and British literature. In the following essay, she examines how Frost uses images of nature in his poem to reflect its themes.

Robert Frost's "Birches" presents vivid, personal descriptions of nature as he describes a boy playfully swinging on birches. As he often does in his poetry, Frost here presents an ambiguous view of the natural world and uses that as a starting point for a questioning of larger issues. As he describes a hypothetical boy climbing high up birches and then riding them down to the ground, Frost raises questions about the nature of human existence.

The poem opens with the speaker seeing "birches bend to left and right" and imagining that a young boy has been swinging on them during play. Immediately, though, he undercuts his imaginative, pleasing image with the harsher truth of nature. He acknowledges that only ice storms could have bent the trees in such a way. Frost continues this juxtaposition of pleasant and harsh images when he contrasts the sun's warmth with the shattered ice.

The damage done by the ice causes them to "never right themselves." The speaker notes that "Truth broke in" to his pleasant vision of a boy at play. Nature can be beautiful and offer an opportunity for contemplation and escape from the pressures of life, but it also can be cruel and destructive. This duality in nature is echoed in his 1923 poem "Stopping by Woods on a Snowy Evening." In this poem, while the speaker stops to watch "woods fill up with snow," he notes the "lovely, dark and deep" setting as well as the fact that stopping there too long would result in death.

The ambiguity Frost finds in nature becomes a metaphor for the ambiguity he finds in human experience. This larger theme is first glimpsed through the boy's playing on the trees. Here, again, Frost juxtaposes positive and negative images. What at first seems like innocent play gains a darker note when the speaker describes the ultimate damage done by the boy:

> One by one he subdued his father's trees
> By riding them down over and over again
> Until he took the stiffness out of them,
> And not one but hung limp, not one was left
> For him to conquer.

Frost may be suggesting that the boy's need to subdue and conquer the trees points to the destructive side of human nature. The boy's motive

> *The ambiguity Frost finds in nature becomes a metaphor for the ambiguity he finds in human experience. This larger theme is first glimpsed through the boy's playing on the trees."*

could also stem from his feelings of isolation since he was "too far from town to learn baseball" and so was forced always to "play alone."

The speaker contrasts the more negative images of the boy's experience with the birches with his own fond memories of playing on the trees although both turn to this activity as a form of escape. The speaker longs again to be "a swinger of birches."

Frost uses harsh images of nature to suggest the speaker's world-weariness:

> And life is too much like a pathless wood. . . .
> I'd like to get away from earth awhile
> And then come back to it and begin over.

He wants to swing on the trees, not to conquer them as the boy does, but to have an opportunity to reach up toward heaven.

As the speaker describes his dream of going back to the birches, Frost introduces another topic in the poem and, as he has done with the others, presents it ambiguously. The speaker's desire to escape the earth's demands and climb toward heaven suggests he is looking for a spiritual salvation. Instead of escaping the problems of life through trying to control nature, the speaker's goal is to reach up to a higher level. Yet, when the speaker concludes that he wants to come back to earth "and begin over," Frost questions the reality of spiritual salvation:

> May no fate willfully misunderstand me
> And half grant what I wish and snatch me away
> Not to return. Earth's the right place for love:
> I don't know where it's likely to go better.

So, while the trials of life prompt him to search for a higher power that can lead him to paradise, he ultimately is more comfortable with the "Truth" of his earthly existence. Yet he would like to experience both worlds, climbing "Toward heaven, till the tree could bear no more," then dipping him down back to earth.

A further comparison of "Birches" to "Stopping by Woods on a Snowy Evening" might suggest another motive for the speaker's climbing of the birches. Critics have suggested that the speaker in "Stopping by Woods" may have a death wish. As he stops to watch the "lovely, dark and deep" woods fill up with snow, he is pulled into the tranquil scene with its "easy wind and downy flake" and could be contemplating suicide. His horse, however, recognizes the danger in staying too long on "the darkest evening of the year" next to the frozen lake and so pulls the speaker away from the brink of death. And so he decides that while the scene could offer him ultimate peace, he will remain.

The speakers in both poems feel a need "to get away from earth awhile" but also to "come back to it and begin over." Perhaps both also consider death as a movement "toward heaven" and peace. Frost's ambiguous spiritual images raise questions about the speaker's motives and about the nature of human experience but provide no concrete answers.

Two critics offer similar conclusions about "Birches." Jeffrey Hart, in his article "Frost and Eliot," published in the *Sewanee Review,* finds a skepticism about spirituality in "Birches." He argues that since the beginning of the poem, Frost has questioned reality, starting with the reason for the bent birches. Thus, he continues, Frost carries that same sense of doubt to the notion that one can attain a heavenly paradise. "Birches," he concludes, "asserts the claims of Frost's skepticism and sense of human limits against the desire for transcendence and the sense of mysterious possibility." This thesis is echoed by Floyd C. Watkins in "Going and Coming Back: Robert Frost's Religious Poetry." Watkins asserts that Frost

> contemplates a moment when the soul may be completely absorbed into a union with the divine. But he is earthbound, limited, afraid. No sooner does he wish to get away from earth than he thinks of "fate"—rather than God. And what might be a mystical experience turns into fear of death, a fear that he would be snatched away "not to return."

In another poem, "Design" (first published in 1912 as "In White" and then heavily revised and retitled in 1936), Frost also questions spirituality as he focuses on a common scene in nature. As the speaker observes a spider trap a moth on a flower, he questions not only the cruelty he finds in nature but the very existence of God:

> What brought the kindred spider to that height,
> Then steered the white moth thither in the night?
> What but design of darkness to appall?—
> If design govern in a thing so small.

In his study of modern poetry, critic David Perkins comments on Frost's style:

> the wisdom of [Frost's] poetry lies not so much in what he says as in the way he says it. The form is the major content. He keeps his balance, not coming down on one side or the other of arguments that cannot be settled. He moves forward, and momentary clarifications of an attitude or point of view rise to the surface, shimmer, and are submerged in the ongoing flow. He gives order and unity not to existence, but to an episode, a figure, and the figure has some "ulteriority" about it, a meaning beyond what is said.

In "Birches," as in many of his poems, Frost turns to the world of nature to find "an episode" that has this sense of "ulteriority" about it. In his description of a young boy, and later an older man, experiencing the pleasure of swinging on birches during a New England summer, Frost creates a perfect metaphor to express his insightful commentary on the ambiguity and complexity of the human experience.

Source: Wendy Perkins, Critical Essay on "Birches," in *Poetry for Students,* The Gale Group, 2001.

Patricia Wallace

In the following essay excerpt, Wallace explores the theme of solitude in "Birches," calling it "characteristic Frost."

Frost offers us poems written in the spirit of solitude, with all of her delights. Solitude is separateness seen upside down, or from the other side, where what are sometimes felt as limits are not barriers at all. Therefore the popularity of "Birches" isn't at all incidental to Frost's central concerns. "Birches" truly is representative Frost, but in it privacy is choice, and the sweetness of the poem is genuine, the sweetness of solitude. Because Frost's intelligence is always part of feeling in his best poems, "Birches" fills us with the recognizable delight of a world inhabited only by the self, a world made by the self, at the same time that it recognizes the limits and temptations of that satisfaction. "Birches" makes a grove of privacy, creates the place where the poet imagines the poem's central figure:

> Some boy too far from town to learn baseball
> Whose only play was what he found himself,
> Summer or winter, and could play alone.

We never feel the boy's loneliness as deprivation, but as pleasure. The imagined grove of trees becomes the scene, in the poet's mind, for a boy's playing out of his impulses, subduing and bending the world to his own shape as only solitude permits us. In this privacy there is the wide space of freedom. "Birches" is characteristic Frost because in it he confirms his own connection both to a landscape of solitude and to a solitary figure. And what we love about the poem, no matter how long we have read or studied Frost, is what first drew us to it and draws us back again: the image of the trees, at one with our memory and longing for the child's world which is the self, where everything bends to the self, and our whole being seems to spill out of us, and yet is contained, like a cup filled "even above the brim."

We like the swish upward and back as well, the swings built into the rhythms of the poem. They are the gestures of expansiveness and contraction which we know and remember in ourselves, and they are part of the poet's playfulness which includes us, unlike his teasing which excludes us. This playfulness originates in the world of solitude Frost makes for himself, and we make as we listen to the poem. But "Birches" brings intelligence to this sweetness because Frost listens to himself as he creates this world, and hears how part of solitude's sweetness depends upon its limits, the responsibility of return to the world of others. Without *that* the sweetness *would* turn sugary, as Randall Jarrell thought it did, and the delight of a world where he is the sole inhabitant would become vanity, the remove from the world of others which can make one a monster. That's why Frost swings out and back again, doubles back on himself in the poem. He has to ground solitude with the acknowledgement that "Earth's the right place for love."

Source: Patricia Wallace, "Separateness and Solitude in Frost," in *Kenyon Review*, Vol. VI, No. 1, Winter 1984, pp. 5–6.

John C. Kemp

In the following essay excerpt, Kemp analyzes "Birches" in the context of Frost's poetic output of 1913, finding it to be "an initial and highly consequential experiment."

Although Frost can be said to have reached his artistic maturity in the summer of 1913 when he completed the regional poetry that made *North of Boston* a significant contribution to American literature, he soon discovered how difficult it was to

> "The more he played the true rustic, the more favorably his audiences and commentators seemed to respond."

combine his new role as Yankee poet with his ambition to be "one of the most notable craftsmen" of the age. By December of that crucial year, the struggle to select, revise, and organize his poetry into an effective structure left him "clean shucked out," and, as the conclusion to *North of Boston* indicates, somewhat distraught and discouraged.

In the ensuing years, he sought a more reassuring regional identity, a different approach to the "poetry of the farm." Instead of presenting himself as an observer, analyst, and explorer north of Boston, he often posed as a spokesman for the region and an embodiment of its virtues. Although less faithful to his personality and background, this pose was gratifying in several ways. The more he played the true rustic, the more favorably his audiences and commentators seemed to respond. It was also easier to forget or overlook fears and uncertainties about his relationship to New England than to confront them as he had in his second collection.

His decision to place "The Wood-Pile" and "Good Hours" at the end of *North of Boston* is the most obvious evidence of his unsettled frame of mind late in 1913. Although written earlier, the two pieces seemed to present a judgment on his recent work, implying that the brilliantly dramatized regional studies were a "profanation" of New England, an unworthy artistic endeavor.

The precarious state of Frost's artistic development is also suggested by another conclusion he reached while struggling with the "larger design" of *North of Boston*: his decision to exclude from the volume a poem referred to as "Swinging Birches" in his letter of 7 August to John Bartlett. Strangely, among the twelve "New England Eclogues" described to Bartlett as destined for the "next book," only "Birches" was later found unworthy to appear in the final version.

How are we to explain this change of heart? Possibly, Frost failed to reach a satisfactory revision of "Swinging Birches" until after *North of Boston* had gone to press. It seems more likely, however, that if he had the piece well enough along to mention it to Bartlett in August, he *could* have completed it, had he been committed to it, by November, when he gave the collection to his publishers. His apparent lack of early commitment is particularly significant, given his tendency in later years to single out the poem as one of his most characteristic pieces. But his decision was the right one: "Birches" is not well suited to *North of Boston*. On the contrary, it is important as a transitional piece, prefiguring much of the post-1913 poetry.

Although not comparable to the twelve overtly dramatic poems in *North of Boston,* "Birches" is broadly similar in form to the three meditative lyrics, "Mending Wall," "After Apple-Picking," and "The Wood-Pile"; thus Frost could not have omitted it on generic grounds alone. Yet he evidently knew that he had done something different in it, something not quite appropriate to the tone and dramatic impetus of the other poems. Its speaker is a much more confident, affirmative, and dominating figure in the poem than are the other speakers. They face conflicts that leave them perplexed and uncertain, whereas the swinger of birches, surmounting all doubts and difficult questions, is given to pronouncements that have an oracular finality about them, despite their casual tone: "Earth's the right place for love. . . . One could do worse than be a swinger of birches."

It is noteworthy that two scholarly detractors of "Birches," Cleanth Brooks and Radcliffe Squires, though not concerned with its relationship to *North of Boston,* have nevertheless elected to contrast it with "After Apple-Picking," one of the 1913 meditative lyrics that *does* belong in that collection. The contrast between these poems is important because Frost shifted his focus subtly when he wrote "Birches," moving away from vivid evocation of experience (as in "Mending Wall," "After Apple-Picking," "The Wood-Pile," and the other poems in *North of Boston*) and toward ardent expression of philosophy. The speaker proclaims a Yankee identity with unprecedented confidence, coming "downstage," as Brooks phrases it, "to philosophize explicitly." His tone and the stance he takes in the poem are entirely different from what we saw in *North of Boston,* where the persona tends to be unsure of himself, a bit uncomfortable, and occasionally apologetic.

The philosophy articulated in "Birches" poses no threat to popular values or beliefs, and it is so appealingly affirmative that many readers have treasured the poem as a masterpiece. Among Frost's most celebrated works, perhaps only "Stopping by Woods on a Snowy Evening" ranks ahead of it. Yet to critics like Brooks and Squires, the persona's philosophical stance in "Birches" is a serious weakness. And another perceptive commentator, Randall Jarrell, has complained that so much popularity makes it almost impossible for us to approach Frost without "the taste of 'Birches' in our mouth—a taste a little brassy, a little sugary." Associating such an undesirable flavor with the "Yankee Editorialist side of Frost," Jarrell proposes, as a major objective for his essay "To the Laodiceans," to cleanse away this all-too-persistent pungency.

It is not the purpose of the present study to arbitrate the dispute over "Birches." No easy compromises are likely, owing to sharply conflicting tastes among Frost's readers. The didactic and philosophical element that some critics have attacked strikes others as the very core of Frost's virtue. The poet's friend Sidney Cox dedicated an entire book to expounding the philosophy of the "Swinger of Birches," with exempla from the poems and from the conversation of the master. Indeed, the brassy, sugary taste that offended Randall Jarrell may appeal to many other readers precisely because of its reassuring strength in an age of anxiety and uncertainty.

Perhaps impartial observers can accept the notion that "Birches" is neither as bad as its harshest opponents suggest nor as good as its most adoring advocates claim. There must be *some* poetry in a work that remains so delightful and touching, so vivid and quotable after half a century in the spotlight. Yet, how can we consider it a true masterpiece when a significant group of intelligent, expertly qualified, independent readers—undoubtedly a minority, but still a group to be reckoned with—has raised serious and thoughtful objections to it? What needs to be recognized is that it *is* a controversial piece, and that we can find nothing quite like it in Frost's work up through the Beaconsfield period. The intense debate it has aroused should also help us to realize that the poem is an anomaly deserving close study as an initial and highly consequential experiment with a new approach to New England poetry.

Robert Langbaum's *The Poetry of Experience* provides a theoretical basis that helps to explain the difference between "Birches" and Frost's other meditative lyrics of 1913. Langbaum has demonstrated the importance of what he calls the "extraordinary perspective" as a device "to keep the poem located—to keep the dramatic situation from turning into a rhetorical device and the landscape from turning into a metaphor for an abstract idea." Extraordinary perspectives dominate "Mending Wall," first in the speaker's perception of a mysterious "something . . . that doesn't love a wall," then in his quirky glimpses of fence mending as game, ritual, even tragedy, and finally in his climactic vision of the neighbor as an "old-stone savage." In "After Apple-Picking," the pervasive "strangeness" of looking through a thin sheet of ice leads to chimerical dreams and recollections of the harvest effort. And "The Wood-Pile" presents extraordinary perspectives not only on the "slow smokeless burning of decay" and the remarkable "small bird" who seemed to take things "as personal to himself," but also on the entire setting, where "the view was all in lines" and the speaker could not say "for certain" whether he was "here / Or somewhere else."

"Birches," on the other hand, contains three fairly lengthy descriptions that do not involve unusual perspectives. In fact, the most original and distinctive vision in the poem—the passage treating the ice on the trees—is undercut both by the self-consciousness of its final line ("You'd think the inner dome of heaven had fallen") and by the two much more conventionally perceived environments that follow it: the rural boyhood of the swinger of birches and the "pathless wood," which represents life's "considerations." As a result, the poem's ardent concluding lines—its closing pronouncements on life, death, and human aspiration—do not arise from a particular experience. Instead, they are presented as doctrines that we must accept or reject on the basis of our credence in the speaker as a wise countryman whose familiarity with birch trees, ice storms, and pathless woods gives him authority as a philosopher.

Since in "Birches" the natural object—tree, ice crystal, pathless wood, etc.—functions as proof of the speaker's rusticity, Frost has no need for extraordinary perspectives, and therefore the poem does little to convince us that an "experience," to use Langbaum's wording, "is really taking place, that the object is *seen* and not merely remembered from a public or abstract view of it." This is not to deny that the poem contains some brilliant descriptive passages (especially memorable are the clicking, cracking, shattering ice crystals in lines 7–11 and the boy's painstaking climb and sudden, exhilarating descent in lines 35–40), and without doubt, the closing lines offer an engaging exegesis of swinging birches as a way of life. But though we learn a great deal about this speaker's beliefs and preferences, we find at last that he has not revealed himself as profoundly as does the speaker in "After Apple-Picking." It is remarkable that the verb "to like," which does not appear in Frost's nondramatic poetry prior to "Birches," is used three times in this poem: "I like to think"; "I'd like to get away"; and "I'd like to go." The speaker also tells us what he would "prefer," "dream of," and "wish." But while his preferences are generally appealing, and while they seem intellectually justified, they are not *poetically* justified in the sense that Langbaum suggests when he discusses the "extraordinary perspective" as a "sign that the experience is really taking place": "The experience has validity just because it is dramatized as an event which we must accept as having taken place, rather than formulated as an idea with which we must agree or disagree."

"Mending Wall," "After Apple-Picking," and "The Wood-Pile" are centered on specific events that involve the speaker in dramatic conflicts and lead him to extraordinary perspectives. The act of repairing the wall and trying to reason with the crusty farmer, the termination of the harvest and the preparation for a winter's rest, the vagrant woodland ramble and the discovery of the perplexing woodpile—all these are events that we indeed "accept as having taken place."

Unlike the meditative lyrics Frost selected for *North of Boston,* however, "Birches" does not present a central dramatized event as a stimulus for the speaker's utterance. Although the conclusion seems sincere, and although Frost created a persuasive metaphorical context for it, the final sentiments do not grow dramatically out of the experiences alluded to. Yes, the speaker has observed ice storms that bend the birches "down to stay"; he has "learned all there is / To learn" about swinging birches; and he has struggled through the "considerations" of life's "pathless wood." But the relationship of these experiences to his present utterance—the poem—is left unclear. We would be more willing to accept what Squires calls a "contradictory jumble" of images and ideas if we were convinced (as Eliot and Pound often convince us) that the diverse materials had coalesced in the speaker's mind. Frost's confession that the poem was "two fragments soldered together" is revealing; the overt, affected capriciousness of the transitions between major sections of the poem indicates that instead of striving to establish the dynamics of dramatized experience, he felt he could rely on the force of his speaker's per-

> "And this eighteenth-century skepticism, this resistance to metaphor and analogy, takes on an ultimate importance in Frost, for all philosophical theology, all affirmation of connection between time and eternity, man and God, depends on some form of analogy: it gets us from here to there and back again."

sonality and rural background. In early editions, a parenthetical question, "(Now am I free to be poetical?)," followed line 22, making the transition between the ice storm and the country youth even more arbitrary.

By comparing "Birches" with Frost's other work in 1913 we can see that even before completing *North of Boston* he had begun to explore a different way of exploiting his new sense of identity as a New Englander. The confidence he gained while fashioning his "book of people" encouraged him to don his Yankee mask more aggressively than he had in poems like "Mending Wall" and "After Apple-Picking." Less than a year after denying to Miss Ward the "virtue in Location", he produced a poem that relies on a fundamental association of his poetic self—"So was I once myself"—with the rustic lad who tended cows and lived "too far from town to learn baseball." The poem's philosophy presupposes a philosopher who was once himself just such a rustic lad—a role that Frost was more than willing to play, even though *his* boyhood had been one of basepaths rather than cowpaths, and town sandlots rather than country pastures. (His biographer attests that he knew more about stealing bases when he was fourteen than he did about milking cows at twice that age.)

It may seem arbitrary to press too hard the issue of honesty in this poem. Art, after all, relies on fantasy and deception. Yet there are different types of fantasy and many motives for deception. If we are confident that an artist has kept faith with some personal vision or inner self, we can accept falsification of many things. When Frost presents himself as a farm worker, for instance—a mower wielding his scythe or apple picker resting his weary body—the fantasy seems sincere and convincing. When we consider Frost's career and personal history, however, we may wonder about his motives in falsifying the character of his childhood. The resulting images lack originality and inspiration. Surely "Birches" contains some vivid and forceful passages, but when a line or phrase gives us too strong a sense of the poet's calculated effort to validate his speaker's rusticity, the spell of the poem, its incantatory charm and imaginative vision, is threatened. Fortunately, in "Birches" this threat is hardly noticeable, certainly not overwhelming or repellent, unless we want it to be.

"Birches," of course, is not an extreme instance of the Yankee farmer as poetic persona. But after writing for more than twenty years, Frost had never—not in his two early experiments with a regional speaker ("The Tuft of Flowers" and "Mowing") and surely not in *North of Boston*—come so close to producing advertisements for himself as a Yankee poet. Thus this poem in 1913 was a significant step toward more blatant exhibitions soon to come. He had not been in England a year when he began to speculate about how his "New England impressions" might be jeopardized by too much exposure to alien settings. Soon the planned trip to France was called off, and shortly after *North of Boston* went to press, he started to entertain a "dream" that, having gained a name for himself in London, he could "do the rest of it from a farm in New England where I could live cheap and get Yankier and Yankier."

Source: John C. Kemp, "The Poet of New England," in *Robert Frost and New England*, Princeton University Press, 1979, pp. 134–42.

Jeffrey Hart

In the following essay excerpt, Hart shows how "Birches" represents the difference between the earthbound Frost and the transcendentalism of T. S. Eliot.

In "Birches" the poet begins by recalling that he has seen birches permanently bent by the ice that collects on them in the winter, and then he toys with a pleasant fancy. When he looks at birches bent in this way, he "likes to think some boy's been swinging them." But he knows that this is not true—that the trees bent by ice all winter are permanently bent and that swinging does not do this, and he withdraws the thought almost as soon as it is offered. In this seemingly casual discourse, a serious point is being broached: truth has asserted its claims at the expense of fancy. Ice, not a boy playing. But fancy is not defeated. It comes forward again in the form of a playful simile. The trees, bent by the ice, now arch in the woods

> Like girls on hands and knees that throw their hair
> Before them over their heads to dry in the sun.

Only "like" girls. The poet returns to the ordinary world of prosy reality:

> But I was going to say when Truth broke in
> With all her matter-of-fact about the ice-storm
> I should prefer to have some boy bend them
> As he went out and in to fetch the cows

The resistance to the metaphorical mode throughout the first part of the poem is important—indeed it is the subject of the poem: the Frostian skepticism will admit no easy beauties, and this skepticism prepares us for the emblematic passage which follows. The poet himself, we hear, was a swinger of birches when a boy, and now, when "weary of considerations" and when "life is too much like a pathless wood," he dreams of going back: "I'd like to get away from earth awhile / And then come back to it and begin over."

Frost's "pathless wood" in this poem can hardly fail to remind us of Dante. Frost too has been lost in that wood. He would like to get away from earth awhile—but only for awhile. Frost will not go on with Dante to the *Paradiso* and the heavenly love of Beatrice; the movement is back to earth, a movement analogous to those lines in which Truth successfully asserted its claims against fancy:

> May no fate willfully misunderstand me
> And half grant what I wish and snatch me away
> Not to return. Earth's the right place for love:
> I don't know where it's likely to go better.
> I'd like to go by climbing a birch tree,
> And climb black branches up a snow-white trunk
> *Toward* heaven, till the tree could bear no more,
> But dipped its top and set me down again.
> That would be good both going and coming back.
> One could do worse than be a swinger of birches.

It is the point of the birches that they climb toward heaven, but also return the poet to earth, for "earth's the right place for love: / I don't know where it's likely to go better." The skepticism is pervasive, and works both ways: *he* does not know where it is "likely" to go better. Issues of epistemology and probability lurk behind the line. We are in the mental climate of eighteenth-century skepticism, and among eighteenth-century philosophical issues; we think of Locke and Berkeley, and of Hume. And this eighteenth-century skepticism, this resistance to metaphor and analogy, takes on an ultimate importance in Frost, for all philosophical theology, all affirmation of connection between time and eternity, man and God, depends on some form of analogy: it gets us from here to there and back again. Despite his pervasive skepticism, and despite the experience evoked in the lines about the pathless wood, Frost does make his affirmation. Not only that "earth's the right place for love" but that, as in the childhood joys of swinging birches, earth enables us to climb "toward" heaven. Whether we ever get closer or not, our approach is from earth. These affirmations, moreover, are all the more potent because earned amid the surrounding skepticism. The final two lines develop enormous power: good both going away *and* coming back to earth. Then in the seemingly casual throwaway: "One could do worse."

Read in this way, "Birches" asserts the claims of Frost's skepticism and sense of human limits against the desire for transcendence and the sense of mysterious possibility. His goal is to wring a great poetry out of an irreducible minimum, to triumph over the possibility of desolation which is always present, and is never finally transcended. The triumph is in its way as impressive as Eliot's.

Source: Jeffrey Hart, "Frost and Eliot," in *Sewanee Review*, Vol. 84, No. 3, Summer 1976, pp. 425–47.

Sources

Bagby, George, *Frost and the Book of Nature*, Tennessee University Press, 1993, pp. 50–52.

Cox, Robert M, "Robert Frost and the End of the New England Line," in *Frost: Centennial Essays*, edited by Jac Tharpe, Mississippi University Press, 1974

Ellis, James, "Robert Frost's Four Types of Belief in 'Birches,'" in the *Robert Frost Review*, 1993, p. 71–3.

Frost, Robert, "The Unmade Word," in *Robert Frost: Collected Poems, Prose, & Plays*, edited by Richard Poirier and Mark Richardson, Library of America, 1995, p. 697

Hart, Jeffrey, "Frost and Eliot," in *Sewanee Review*, Vol. 84, No. 3, Summer 1976, pp. 425–47.

Ingebretsen, Ed, "Earth's the Right Place: The Sentence of Love," in *Robert Frost's "Star in a Stone Boat": A Grammar of Belief*, Catholic Scholars Press, 1994.

Jarrell, Randall, *Poetry and the Age*, Alfred A. Knopf, 1953.

Kemp, John C., *Robert Frost and New England: The Poet as Regionalist,* Princeton University Press, 1979.

Lowell, Amy, *North of Boston*, in *New Republic,* Vol. 2, February 20, 1915, p. 81.

Oster, Judith, *Toward Robert Frost: The Reader and the Poet,* Georgia University Press, 1991, pp. 59–63.

Parfitt, Matthew, "Robert Frost's 'Modern Georgics,'" in the *Robert Frost Review,* 1996, p. 54–5, 67.

David Perkins, *A History of Modern Poetry: From the 1890s to the High Modernist Mode,* Harvard University Press, 1976.

Pound, Ezra, Review of *North of Boston*, in *Poetry,* Vol. 5, No. 3, December 1914, p. 127–8.

Viereck, Peter, "Parnassus Divided," in *Atlantic Monthly,* Vol. 184, October 1949, p. 67–8.

Watkins, Floyd C., "Going and Coming Back: Robert Frost's Religious Poetry," in *South Atlantic Quarterly,* Autumn 1974, pp. 445–59.

For Further Study

Bloom, Harold, ed., *Robert Frost,* Modern Critical Views series, Chelsea House Publishers, 1986.
   This book contains many essays by leading critics about the poems of Robert Frost.

Meyers, Jeffrey, *Robert Frost: A Biography,* Houghton Mifflin Co., 1997.
   This controversial biography examines the author's personal life closely, including a previously unchronicled affair with his secretary.

Parini, Jay, *Robert Frost: A Life,* Henry Holt & Co., 1999.
   Parini's biography is more sympathetic to his subject than other biographers have been without ignoring Frost's many personal faults.

Winters, Yvor, *The Function of Criticism,* Allan Swallow, 1957.
   This book by the American poet and critic includes an essay critical of Frost and his relationship with Emerson and romanticism.

Blood Oranges

Lisel Mueller

1986

"Blood Oranges" comes from *Second Language*, Lisel Mueller's fourth book of poetry. In this poem, one sees subjects that have interested Mueller throughout her career, most notably the Holocaust in Hitler's Germany and her fascination with poetry's way of capturing the physical world so concretely that reality's horrors cannot be ignored.

An interesting aspect of this poem is that it presents Nazi Germany, from which Mueller's family fled when she was young, as a sort of safe haven, a place where a child could live comfortably in ignorance of the brutality around her. The abusive political system that Mueller looks back on here is that of Spain in 1936, where, on August 19, the famed poet and playwright Federico García Lorca was executed by Fascist rebels. García Lorca was internationally famous for his sympathetic writings about the poor common people of Spain, especially the Andalusian gypsies.

"Blood Oranges" describes Mueller as a child, living in Germany and reading acceptably pleasant German poetry from long in the past, oblivious to the Spanish political situation and unaware of the sheer greatness of the poet who was being murdered at the same time. There is a painful irony in the fact that, as García Lorca was being killed, the young girl was savoring the sweetness of oranges from Spain that are called "blood oranges." Modern readers are able to add to this scene another layer, with the knowledge that the Fascist rebels in the Spanish Civil War were supported by Adolph Hitler and that Hitler would in a short time wield

Lisel Mueller

similar control over Germany, encouraging mob action against Jews and blacks, homosexuals and gypsies.

Author Biography

Lisel Mueller was born in Hamburg, Germany, on February 8, 1924, and she grew up there during the time of Adolph Hitler's rise to power. Her parents, both teachers, immigrated to the United States when Mueller was fifteen because they openly disagreed with Hitler's policies. Her father, who had already been arrested once by the Nazis for his leftist views, fled the country first and then sent for Mueller and her mother when he was established with a position at the University of Evansville, Indiana. Mueller married her husband, Paul, when they were both nineteen, and they were together for almost sixty years, until his death in January of 2001.

Mueller received her degree from the University of Evansville in 1944. After college, she did not write poetry for ten years, feeling that it was "adolescent stuff." Instead, she worked a number of jobs, including receptionist, social caseworker, library assistant, and freelance writer. She returned to poetry when she was twenty-nine as a way of coping with the strong emotions she was experiencing after her mother died. Mueller's career as a writer ascended slowly but steadily, from her first published book at the age of forty-one in 1965 to her most recent collection, which has received universal praise. While writing, she has taught at a number of institutions, including the University of Chicago, Goddard College in Vermont, and Elmhurst College. She currently lives in Lake Forest, Illinois.

Her many impressive achievements in the field of poetry are made even more impressive by the realization that she was raised speaking German and that English is her second language. In addition, many of the brilliant visual images in her recent poetry have been drawn from memory, as her eyesight has been failing due to glaucoma, which was diagnosed in 1985.

In 1997, Mueller received a Pulitzer Prize for her book *Alive Together,* which is a compilation of poems from the past thirty-five years. Previously, she was the recipient of the National Book Award in 1981 for her book *The Need to Hold Still,* the Lamont Poetry Selection in 1975 for *The Private Life,* and the 1990 Carl Sandburg Prize for *Waving From Shore.* She has also gained fame by translating poems by Marie Luise Kaschnitz and a play by Hugo von Hofmannsthal.

Poem Text

```
In 1936, a child
in Hitler's Germany,
what did I know about the war in Spain?
Andalusia was a tango
on a wind-up gramophone,                    5
Franco a hero's face in the paper.
No one told me about a poet
for whose sake I might have learned Spanish
bleeding to death on a barren hill.
All I knew of Spain                         10
were those precious imported treats
we splurged on for Christmas.
I remember pulling the sections apart,
lining them up, sucking each one
slowly, so the red sweetness                15
would last and last—
while I was reading a poem
by a long-dead German poet
in which the woods stood safe
under the moon's milky eye                  20
and the white fog in the meadows
aspired to become lighter than air.
```

Poem Summary

Lines 1–2

Assuming that the speaker of this poem is to be identified with Mueller, the child that is described here would be about twelve. It is not always the case that a poem's main character is based on the author, even when the poem speaks as "I," but in this case there is enough in common between the two (such as similar age and German background) to assume that Mueller is actually speaking about herself. These opening lines present an unsettling dramatic contrast in their use of the phrase "a child in Hitler's Germany." Childhood is often thought of as a time of innocence, and yet the world has come to see Adolph Hitler as the embodiment of evil due to the widespread slaughter of innocents that went on during the years that he ruled Germany, 1933–1945. The two phrases contained in these first two lines, separated by a comma, never actually work into a sentence in the proper grammatical way: instead of their dovetailing into the third line, it picks up a new idea, giving the impression that each phrase is an aborted start, as if the speaker is looking for a way to talk about this subject and each time changes her mind.

Line 3

It is not unusual for a child to be unaware of complex international affairs, especially when, like the Spanish Civil War, there is no clear international consensus about how to react to what is happening. The party in power at the time was the one supported by the majority of the people, but under their rule there was anarchy, and the Spanish government was barely able to function. The Falange party that challenged them was brutal and emulated Italy's Fascist dictator Benito Mussolini, but at the time Fascism was considered by some to be a reasonable response to anarchy. It is only in the years since those turbulent times that the world has come to doubt, in retrospect, whether the loss of personal freedom under the Nazis, the Fascists, or the Falange was a reasonable price to pay for civil peace. To this day, children tend to repeat the popular sentiments they hear about political issues if society has a fairly unified approach, as seen in America's united opposition to Bosnia's president Slobodan Milosevic in the 1990s. If popular opinion is divided, though, and the issue is too complex, people tend to block it out, as this poem's speaker has done.

Lines 4–6

Andolusia is the region of southern Spain where Federico García Lorca grew up and where he was killed when he returned at the age of thirty-eight. It was a poor area that was considered to have a rustic charm especially in its tradition of tango dancing, but its culture was not taken seriously until García Lorca wrote about it. The reference to a

Media Adaptations

- A tape of Lisel Mueller reading her poetry in 1979 is available from the Poetry Center collection. Contact them at http://www.sfsu.edu/~newlit/newcatalog/916.htm (last accessed April 2001) to purchase a copy.

- Another audio recording of Mueller reading was recorded by *New Letters Magazine* at the University of Missouri in 1981.

"wind-up gramophone" indicates that Mueller's childhood home did not have electricity, but it is also a sensual image, invoking the particular sound of a machine that played records at an uneven pace from start to finish. This sensation is unforgettable and is not reproduced in the modern mechanical world. The reference to Franco is, of course, ironic: he was supported by Hitler and would have been treated like a hero by the newspaper in the state that Hitler controlled, even though the world has come to see both men as cruel dictators, responsible for millions of deaths and untold human suffering.

Lines 7–9

The fact that García Lorca was not mentioned in Mueller's youth is an indication of the relationship that the arts have with politics in general. Having just mentioned the lie that did reach her in Germany, that of Franco's heroism, the poem brings out the ironic contrast of a ruthless dictator living a life of privilege and a truly heroic man dying in obscurity. There is a subtle but potent testimony to the power and clarity of García Lorca's writing in the way that line 8 speaks in the past tense, implying that the poet feels she would, even as a youth, have been moved by the work that later moved her deeply when she did find it in adulthood. Line 9 refers to him "bleeding," as a way of making the relationship between García Lorca and the blood oranges more clear.

Line 10

The wording of line 10 is similar to the wording of line 3. While the earlier line refers to the war and to political matters in general, line 10 introduces domestic matters that would have been more interesting to a young girl.

Lines 11–12

In many European countries, oranges were given as Christmas gifts. Contemporary readers might be used to having oranges available year round and might therefore fail to see the excitement of receiving them as a Christmas present but that is because modern refrigeration and transportation methods have made it possible to move fruit to climates far from where it grows. For Germany in 1936, receiving a tropical fruit like oranges in the middle of the winter was a near miraculous treat. They were, as the poem says, "precious" and something that was available only to those who "splurged" and paid a high price. The section of Spain where oranges grow is the Andalusian section to the south, where García Lorca was raised and was eventually murdered.

Lines 13–16

The details given indicate just how much the young girl savored her oranges. Her method of eating these oranges—pulling the sections apart, lining them up, and then sucking each section slowly—is a way of making the experience "last and last," as line 16 puts it, so that the pleasure she takes in it will continue. This sort of precision in eating also indicates that the speaker was a very orderly child, an impression that reinforces her willingness to accept Franco as a hero, as the German newspapers report him to be, and to avoid the moral complexity that might result from being skeptical about the official version of the truth. Line 16 ends with a dash, indicating that the poem is changing its subject, as it did between lines 2 and 3: the scene of the child sitting at a table eating an orange does not change, but the dash is necessary to make readers change their attitude so that the poetry discussed in the last lines of "Blood Oranges" is not taken with the sense of sincere delight that the orange evokes.

Lines 17–18

The "long-dead German poet" referred to here could be a generalization about poets of the romantic age, but Mueller's use of specific imagery implies that she had a specific old poem in mind. The poem that seems to match her references most closely is "Abendlied" ("Evening Song"), by Matthias Claudius (1740–1825). The first stanza of Claudius' poem contains the same imagery that Mueller uses. It translates, roughly, "The forest stands black and silent / And out of the meadow is rising / The white fog, beautifully."

The poem's emphasis that the German poet is "long dead" is used to bring out several subtle distinctions. In recent years, it has become common to draw attention to literary figures who lack relevance to contemporary life by mentioning that they are dead. The phrase "dead white men" is used negatively to dismiss writers that are traditionally studied in school but that are not really important to the lives of modern students. In this case, however, the poem intends to praise García Lorca, the Spanish poet who is dead, so it needs to specify that the German poet's work lacks vibrancy because he has been dead a long time. This could also be a way of comparing the two cultures: in Spain, the lively war was being raged between the adherents of two ideals, Fascism and Progressivism, while Germany had settled into rule by one party, with opposing views being relegated to the past, like one long dead. Hitler had only been in power a few years, but the Nazi party had so thoroughly crushed their opposition that it seemed like their opposition was long gone.

Lines 19–20

The word "safe," used in line 19, is crucial to this poem. The speaker admires García Lorca, who has been murdered brutally, and contrasts him to the safety of the kind of poetry that the oppressive German government found acceptable. In a sense, the title represents the same two extremes that the different poets represent, with "blood" standing for the danger of being a controversial poet and "oranges" representing the small, safe comforts that a twelve-year-old girl would seek. The image of the woods standing under the moon implies a sense of mystery, of hidden truths, as the trees would shield the ground from moonlight and end up entangling this safe world with a tangle of shadows that would be absent from the "barren hill" mentioned in line 9.

Lines 21–22

The fog, like the woods, gives the poem a sense of confusion, of hidden truths. The fact that the fog "aspired" to be lighter than air but was unable to be so is symbolic of the failure of the child to transcend her situation with safe German poetry. One might think that she would be able to rise above her situation by reading, but the point that the poem makes is that poetry alone does not raise the spirit above dire circumstances, such as Nazi Germany or Fascist Spain. In the end, the hollowness of traditional poetry is presented as superficial and somewhat impotent. If this were just a matter of empathizing with García Lorca's understanding of his own country, the speaker's disappointment would be sad enough, but the poem has the added, tragic dimension of having the child situated in a society that was just as dangerous and having her be oblivious to the danger.

Themes

Ignorance

In "Blood Oranges," the poem's narrator presents a time in her childhood when, living in Germany, she was unaware of events during the Spanish Civil War that led to the death of Federico García Lorca, a great poet. It describes how she sat eating an orange that had been imported from Spain, reading mediocre German poetry. She seems to regret having been ignorant. The phrase "ignorant" has come to have a negative meaning because it has been used as an insult in recent decades, but the true, basic meaning is that one is unaware. Twice, the speaker points out her childhood ignorance while using strong, defensive language. In line 3 she asks, rhetorically, "what did I know about the war in Spain?" Readers can tell from the way the question is put that she knew nothing about the war, but phrasing it this way implies that the speaker feels a need to point out her ignorance as a child and to make readers admit that her lack of knowledge was a natural thing, that there would be no reason to think that she would have any awareness of the political situation in a foreign land. The second time that her ignorance comes up, it is phrased in an even more self-conscious, defensive way. "No one told me about a poet" she says in line 7, as if to excuse her own ignorance by blaming someone else's inefficiency. In line 10, the poem calms its defensive tone a little and sets out to explain exactly what it was that the child did know to give readers a sense of how ignorant she was. Though readers probably would not blame a child for failing to keep up with international politics, the tone that this poem takes when pointing out its speaker's childhood ignorance implies that she regrets that ignorance, that she feels the need to be defensive about it because it bothers her.

Purity

As opposed to the speaker's youthful ignorance, which she regrets, this poem makes use of the purity of childhood to contrast the horrors of the totalitarian Spanish and German governments. The detail that is given about the child's process of eating the oranges, which were, for her, a rare treat, indicates that she really had no sense of the horrors that were being inflicted by either Hitler or Franco on their respective countries, that she was untouched by worldly evil. The images from the German poem that is referred to at the end of "Blood Oranges" also indicate purity, with their references to whiteness and to milk, as if this poetry had not been contaminated by reality the way that the life and work of García Lorca was. While the child's purity is touching, as indicated in the delight in sweets and in poetry that is safe, the poem seems to indicate that the German poet should have been more complex, that purity is a luxury in which a poet cannot indulge.

Sensuality

The process of eating the orange is a sensual one for the child in the poem, which is to say that

Topics for Further Study

- Research the history of the tango and why this dance and musical style is associated with Spain's Andalusia region.

- Read interviews with Germans who remained in Germany throughout the Hitler years. Describe what daily life was like. What did Hitler's supporters say in his defense?

- Francisco Franco ruled Spain for almost forty years, until 1975. Find other poems that condemn him and his reign.

- Blood oranges derive their name from the dark red color they have on the inside. Find another fruit or vegetable that is called by a compelling title, and write a poem that makes use of that name.

- Explore the tradition of giving fruit for Christmas: where the tradition came from, how long it has been around, and in what form it exists today.

- This poem points out the shallowness of reading about peace and safety while terrible things are going on in the world. Do you think that poets who write about pleasant things are being ignorant to reality? What is the responsibility of poets to keep up with world politics? What is the responsibility of readers?

it activates her senses completely. Lines 13–16 refer to the feel of pulling the sections of the fruit apart, the look of their blood red color, and, using the most infrequently described sense of all, the taste of the oranges' sweetness. By rendering this entire experience in such vibrant terms, Mueller takes the reader into the process of eating the orange. The grown person who is narrating this poem clearly knows all the details about those oranges, which is an indication of how important they were to her as a child. By rendering them in such vivid sensuality, she gives readers the opportunity to experience the thrill of them as well. To the extent that words on a page can create an experience for the senses, this poem works to trigger the reader's nerve endings.

This depth of detail is mirrored, faintly, in the descriptions from the work of the long-dead poet. Though the final lines give descriptive details, they do not register with readers as powerfully as the description of eating the orange. To some extent, this is because the German poet's intention seems to have been different from Mueller's. If the old poetry had indeed "aspired to be lighter than air," then it makes sense that, in the turbulent political times of the 1930s, it struck the child as being too superficial to care much about. Clearly, the real-world sensuality of eating the orange was a more moving experience than the poetry that she was reading at the time. The relationship between Federico García Lorca and the oranges is blood, which is powerful in look and smell and feel, indicating what is wrong with poetry that tries not to be about reality.

Revolution and Revolt

"Blood Oranges" draws a clear distinction between Spain, where the dictator's rise was resisted, and Germany, where the dictator rose to power through normal political channels and earned the opposition of his people only when it was too late. The two countries are symbolized by, respectively, a talented poet who is murdered and a little girl enjoying a Christmas treat. Although there is no indication that Mueller is suggesting that Germany should have revolted against Hitler, still the poem does clearly take a wary view toward the "safe" feeling Germans had, the one long-dead German poet in particular. Revolution is not romanticized in this poem, though, as the Fascists who murdered García Lorca were the revolutionaries and not the established party in power. The poem is about established governments and settled governments, and it does not take a position that clearly advocates either.

Style

Free Verse

"Blood Oranges" is written in free verse. There is no strict rhythmic pattern or rhyming scheme that would assert the author's control and make readers feel that the ideas presented here are organized by a controlling hand. This lack of structure fits with what the poem is saying: it is critical of poetry that is too intellectual, aspiring to be "lighter than air," and it would be hypocritical of this poem to depend too heavily on poetic technique, which would draw more attention to the poem itself than to the dire political situation it addresses. The lack of formal rules used here is appropriate for presenting a world in disorder, where a great, talented man like García Lorca can be murdered by thugs with no consequence.

Contrast

The poem is only one stanza, but it is divided by subject matter into three parts. In the first, the speaker gives a general overview about how little she knew about events in Spain when she was a child in 1936. She did not know about the murder of García Lorca, and she thought that Franco was a hero. The second section of the poem concerns an in-depth description of how important the oranges she received for Christmas were to the girl, focusing on them with a clarity that contrasts to the vagueness of her grasp of Spanish affairs. In the third section, she describes the kind of poetry that she read in those days. This section contrasts with the section before by showing how much more real the orange was to the girl than the long-dead poet's words, and it contrasts to the first section by showing how little of an impression this poet made on her, as opposed to García Lorca, for whose sake, if she had known about him, the girl might have gone to the trouble of learning a new language.

Symbol

The symbol that binds all of these sections together is the blood oranges of the title. They are a product of Spain's Andalusia region, as was García Lorca. They were a precious treat, which indicates the child's intensity in eating them, her delight in the physical world, her joyfulness in spite of being a child in Hitler's Germany. Most importantly, blood oranges are the deep red of blood, which binds her delight in them to the mention in line 9 of García Lorca bleeding to death. Because of the connection between his blood and the fruit, eating them bears a symbolic relationship to taking

Compare & Contrast

- **1936:** Political systems gain and hold on to power by exterminating great masses of people. Soviet Russia begins purges that kill eight to ten million citizens in two years. Nazi Germany kills nearly as many during the Holocaust. A million die during the Spanish Civil War.

  Today: International peace-keeping forces from the United Nations often intercede in abusive regimes.

- **1936:** Hitler's secret police force, the Gestapo, takes over the regular German police force to spy on citizens more easily.

  1986: West Germany and East Germany are still divided, with East Germany aligned with the Soviet Union.

  Today: Having been reunited in 1990 as the Soviet Union collapsed, the Federal Republic of Germany is one of the most influential European nations.

- **1936:** The Great Depression that has affected the United States through much of the 1930s is just as devastating to the rest of the world, leading people to support dictatorships as drastic measures for relief.

  1986: The United States economy is in a recession, in large part because of unbridled government spending: the national debt doubles from 1981 to 1986, from one billion to two.

  Today: Because of the economic boom from the computer revolution, the U.S. government finally has a budget surplus.

- **1936:** Fruits grown in tropical regions very rarely make it to northern markets and then only at a great price; still, their rareness makes them popular Christmas gifts.

  1986: Refrigeration and shipping methods made it possible to enjoy produce from around the world.

  Today: Increasingly, exotic fruits show up in neighborhood supermarkets all the time.

Communion, with the great poet representing Jesus for the girl who would grow up to be a poet. The deep blood color of the oranges, as well as their precious sweetness, is contrasted with the vapid, colorless whiteness that pervades during the poem's last section, making the German poetry seem powerless and anemic. The last section does have its own symbolic theme, but it is one of mystery and deceit, with trees obscuring the moon and fog obscuring the meadow, indicating the secretiveness that is necessary in countries with totalitarian governments, such as Hitler's Germany.

Historical Context

The Spanish Civil War

During the First World War (1914–1918), Spain underwent the difficult transition from a farm-based economy to an industrial one. The rise of industry brought with it a working class, centered in the cities, which struggled against the traditional monarchy. In 1922, to retain control of the country, King Alfonso XIII asked a general of the army, Miguel Primo de Rivera, to take control of the government and run it as a military dictatorship. He ruled as dictator until 1925 and then as Prime Minister until the revolution of 1931 when Alfonso left the throne and went into exile and a new government was formed by a coalition of left-wing groups. This ruling group, the Republicans, included Liberals, Socialists, and Anarchists. They ruled the country from 1931 until 1936 but not well. Poverty and violence were everywhere. In 1933, a new political party, the Falange, rose in opposition to the government. Led by Jose Antonio Primo de Rivera, the son of the former dictator, the Falange was a Fascist group that followed the policies Benito Mussolini was using to control Italy.

With the public frustrated because of the many reforms that the Republicans had instituted in their five years in office and the Falange party pressing with serious political opposition, there came a third threat: the military, led by Francisco Franco, planned a revolution that would restore King Alfonso to power.

To suppress the rebellion, the Republican government arrested and killed a leading Falangist party member in 1936, charging him with the death of a policeman. The public outrage over this act led the Nationalists, which included the army and the Falange party, to call for revolution. Further government acts of suppression ensued, followed by further acts of rebellion. By the end of the year and for the two years that followed, Spain was a chaotic and bloody mess, with the Republican and Nationalist parties struggling for control and loyalists of each side murdering the other side's supporters whenever the chance arose. Many countries kept out of it, choosing to believe that neither side had a legitimate claim to rule although Adolph Hitler in Germany supported Franco's Nationalists. The war ended in 1939 when the Nationalists took control of Madrid. Franco ruled as a dictator until his death in 1975.

Hitler's Germany

Hitler entered politics in 1919, when he joined the National Socialist German Workers Party—the Nazis. He was elected chairman, or *Führer* of the party in 1921, and proceeded to gain attention by preaching hatred against minorities, who he claimed were taking away money and resources that rightfully belonged to real Germans. His autobiography, *Mein Kampf,* was written while he was in prison in 1923 for a plot to overthrow the German government. In 1929, the same depression that occurred in America affected economies all over the globe, and the Nazi party gained public support by playing to the nation's insecurities: they claimed that the depression was the result of a conspiracy by Jewish bankers and that Germany was suffering unfairly because of the restrictions put on the country after it surrendered at the end of the First World War in 1918. Hitler's election to the chancellorship in 1933 was taken as a mandate to pursue international expansion and to persecute Jews.

By 1936, Hitler started to be more aggressive. Having banned all political parties but his own and thus having established himself as dictator, he started a course of international expansion that eventually led to World War II. Germany invaded Rhineland, a demilitarized area to the west that was rich in natural resources. That was followed by occupation of Austria in 1938 and Czechoslovakia in 1939. When Germany invaded Poland in 1939, Britain and France, which had a pact with Poland, went to war with Germany, which led to one country after another choosing sides and entering the fight.

During the period between the invasion of Rhineland and the outbreak of the war, Hitler pursued the domestic policies that have left him remembered as one of history's most evil figures. His secret police, the Gestapo, compiled files on nearly every German citizen, encouraging neighbors, coworkers, and even children to report on anyone they thought might be a threat to the government. Ghettos were established where Jews and other minorities were sent, leaving their possessions behind to be claimed by their neighbors. Later, as the war reached its peak, Hitler's ministers decided that it was not worth the government's cost to imprison these minorities, and so they were killed in mass executions, their bodies buried in huge pits that were plowed over with steam shovels. Many Germans who lived through the Nazi years have said that they were unaware of the existence of the Death Camps that only came to the attention of the world after the war was over. Some historians have been skeptical about how the German citizens could be ignorant of such large-scale slaughter, but others believe that the combination of the Nazi effort to keep the Holocaust a secret and the general public's willingness not to think about the fate of those who were "relocated" makes their claim believable.

Critical Overview

Throughout over forty years of publishing poetry, Lisel Mueller has been a poet's poet, well revered by her peers in the writing world but not well known outside of it. "Blood Oranges" is from her fourth collection, *Second Language,* which was received, like her other works, with sweeping acclaim. "Morality is a constant preoccupation in these pages," Peter Stitt wrote of *Second Language* in the *Georgia Review,* "and is one of the reasons this volume is so powerful." Stitt also pointed out Mueller's constant, skillful use of imagery, noting that "[i]t is the objects around her, the objects she welcomes into her poems, that give meaning to the world for Mueller." Joseph Parisi, in *Booklist,* called the book a good reason for her many fans to rejoice, referring to Mueller's "uncommon empathy." Parisi's overall assessment of *Second Lan-*

guage was that "Poem for poem, this is one of the strongest volumes of this or many another year."

One of the few questions about the effectiveness of Mueller's poetry came in a generally favorable review of *Second Language* from Fred Muratori, writing in the *Library Journal*. After much praise, he pointed out that "so many poems are first-person meditations (even the frequent "you" is an 'I' in disguise) that one feels one's attention repeatedly called to the poet's sensitivities rather than to the poem." This is a minor complaint and one that not even universally observed. Alice Fulton, reviewing the same book in *Poetry*, came to the opposite conclusion to Muratori's. "Like so many plain-style poems, these equate invisibility of craft with authenticity," she wrote. "The important difference here is that one does not feel manipulated by a disingenuous sincerity. There is no see-how-sensitive-I-am posing, no subtext of self-congratulation."

The praise for Mueller's poetry accelerated when she became more widely recognized. An Associated Press article printed in the *New Standard* pointed out that Lisel Mueller's life had changed at exactly 2:15 P.M. on April 8, 1997. That was when Western Union phoned her house, forwarding the telegram message that she had been awarded the Pulitzer Prize for her book *Alive Together*. The degree of fame that came along with the Pulitzer has made Mueller more famous although she is hardly a household name. The Associate Press article, by Lindsey Tanner, made note of the fact that the Pulitzer earned her more widespread recognition than winning the National Book Award sixteen years earlier for *The Need To Hold Still*, even though the NBA is "considered the pinnacle of honors in literary circles." The fact that the Pulitzer was awarded for a book of collected poems representing a lifetime of accumulated work only serves to highlight the esteem that her peers and critics have held for Mueller all along. An example of the recognition this book earned came from John Taylor's review in *Poetry*: "She seeks to determine whether we can become aware—through poetry—of the precious gifts of the present before they are lost. Her poetry constantly turns us back to living, to the vibrant existences in our mist." These words capture the sensibility of "Blood Oranges," with its contrast between eating an orange and reading lifeless old poetry, and they apply equally well to the entire span of Mueller's long poetic career.

> *It may sound slightly irreverent to put it this way, but the whole point that Mueller is asking us to consider is whether the poetry of a man who suffered in life and was murdered can mean the same thing to an adult that a Christmas treat means to a child."*

Criticism

David Kelly

Kelly is an instructor of creative writing at College of Lake County. In the following essay, he explores how the image of the blood orange and the poet Federico García Lorca are used to mean almost the same thing and questions whether this might unintentionally diminish García Lorca's stature.

The poem "Blood Oranges," from Lisel Mueller's book *Second Language,* focuses readers' attention on the differences between innocence and ignorance, knowledge and sorrow. The poem works by creating a web out of contradictory events that all converged at one particular moment in the poet's childhood. She lived in Germany, where Adolph Hitler ruled and enjoyed popular support in the 1930s, while his reign was young and people well remembered the economic turmoil that made them turn to Hitler's extreme policies. In 1936, Hitler supported the rise of the Fascist revolution that brought Francisco Franco to power in Spain. In Spain, the poet Federico García Lorca was murdered for his democratic beliefs, while the future poet Mueller, unaware of García Lorca's persecution, enjoyed the sweetness of an orange that was imported from Spain. While eating the Spanish orange, she read insipid, "safe" German poetry, which contained empty, obscure imagery that made no comment on the sort of ruthless politics that allowed Hitler to thrive. All of these things happened

What Do I Read Next?

- Mueller won the Pulitzer Prize for her 1996 collection *Alive Together: New and Selected Poems,* which represents works selected from the previous thirty-five years.

- Mueller's work as a translator throws an interesting light on her particular interests. *The Selected Later Poems of Marie Luise Kaschnitz,* published by Princeton University Press in 1980, represents a rare opportunity to read Kaschnitz in English.

- Paulette Roeske is a friend and former student of Mueller. Roeske's newest poetry collection, *Anvil, Clock & Last,* is scheduled to be published in 2001.

- The poems that the speaker of "Blood Oranges" admired are available in both English and Spanish in *Federico García Lorca: Collected Poems,* edited by Christopher Maurer and published by Farrar, Straus and Giroux in 1991.

- Barbara Helfgott Hyett edited a book of poetry from survivors of the Holocaust in 1986, called *In Evidence: Poems of the Liberation of Nazi Concentration Camps.* It was released by University of Pittsburgh Press.

- A short book about the same subject as "Blood Oranges" is John Gorman's *The Reception of Federico García Lorca in Germany.* Published in 1973, it is now out of print but can be found in library systems.

- Poet Robert Pinsky has some of the same sensibilities as Mueller. His collection, *The Figured Wheel: New and Collected Poems, 1966–1996,* (1996) offers a good sampling of his works over several decades.

- Rita Dove was one of the judges who awarded the Pulitzer Prize to Mueller. Her *Selected Poems* was published in 1993 by Pantheon Books.

---

in 1936, and years later, when Mueller read García Lorca's poetry and the facts about his death, she realized what she had missed. She came to worship him so much that, as the poem explains, she "might have learned Spanish" for the sake of understanding his poetry.

Except for this one line explaining his importance, the poem is unclear about its speaker's relationship with García Lorca's work and what it is supposed to mean. Obviously, it is something that she admires, but what is not so obvious is whether her admiration for him is meant to be as genuine and meaningful as the experiences of her youth and whether readers should feel secure that the poet has found complete understanding now. There are many good reasons for the poem to make its readers work toward determining the significance of things that have such deep meaning for the poem's speaker that she can hardly bring herself to talk about them. Just the same, there are also good reasons for readers to want to leave a poem alone once they have settled on one clear, simple meaning. Further consideration is required.

García Lorca's life clearly altered the way that the speaker of "Blood Oranges" viewed her own life, making him a sort of hero to her. Heroism is one of the key issues that drives this poem, but its meaning is not entirely clear from the story Mueller tells. The nature of heroism changes throughout the lifetime described here, and it is not always easy for readers to keep up with the changes. There is no assurance that the heroic image that the poem grants to García Lorca, which it shows in contrast to the other elements of 1936, is meant to be true and lasting, even though that is the implication.

The false hero of this poem is, of course, Francisco Franco. The poem does not delve into Franco's tarnished place in history, other than its implication that someone who is presented as a hero by Hitler's Nazi government could obviously be nothing of the sort. The poem makes no case against Franco, but its stance against him is clearly implied by the fact that he *is* "a hero's face." The hero-figure of Mueller's childhood is nothing but a façade, an image that the child has been told to see as a hero. The decades that Spain suffered under Franco's dictatorship add to the modern reader's appreciation of childhood innocence: he was no hero. Still, historic knowledge is not necessary to appreciate the poem's basic point that children are willing to accept what heroes the world is willing to teach them to honor.

In contrast to the hollow feeling that "Blood Oranges" describes about Franco, the artificial hero, there is the very real feeling that the child had when eating the blood oranges from Spain. The child is described as doing what she could to make the most of the orange-eating experience—lining up the orange slices, sucking the juice from them slowly, trying to stay within the moment forever. All this while the poem indicates that she does not give Franco even the first moment's consideration. Childhood is often looked at as a time of naïve hero-worship, just as adulthood is often presented as a time when one loses faith in heroes, but "Blood Oranges" shows how ordinary moral dynamics were reversed in Hitler's Germany. The shallow hero figure was idealized by a corrupt society, but the very same people who were willing to call such a person a hero—in this case, represented by Mueller in her childhood—were not inclined to think twice about the true meaning of heroism.

Some poems are overly sentimental about childhood, granting to children the only real valid emotional knowledge and taking a cold look at the ways attitudes change as people mature. In fact, there have been so many poems written with this theme that readers could be forgiven for approaching any poem about childhood with the expectation that the child's point of view might be idealized and that growth might be equated with corruption. "Blood Oranges" does not glorify the innocence of children. Nor does it cast any shadow of blame on its young protagonist, as if she should have known more about poetry and world affairs at such a young age. Instead, it aims to help readers see how the human attraction to sweetness and beauty is sharpened by being deprived. There is a hint that Mueller might never have come to appreciate García Lorca's poetry if she had not been raised on mediocre stuff, just as she savors the oranges because they are an extravagance that her family splurged on only once a year.

It is interesting that no examples of García Lorca's work are presented here. He appears in the poem almost as a political figure, significant mainly for his role in the Spanish Civil War and not for the beauty of his words. Still, readers of "Blood Oranges" can hardly doubt the power of his poetry, which is eloquently indicated by the line about Mueller's willingness to learn a whole new language for his sake. The biographical facts of his life could be translated from Spanish to German easily enough, and even the poems he wrote could be read in translation, but a perfect understanding of the poet's full meaning would have required understanding his language. What she learned about his writings in later life left her wanting to know it, to feel it, more. This poem itself does not trivialize García Lorca's writing by pretending that it can capture a sense of his talent by taking any of his lines or images out of context. It is as if Mueller feels herself unworthy of having her poetry stand beside his.

If her reverence for García Lorca's work were not clear enough, the poem offers, for contrast, some images from traditional German romantic poetry. The milky-eyed moon, the woods, and the white fog struggling to rise are images that could be rendered beautifully by a poet, but they are certainly nothing that would present a threat to the Nazis' rule and would therefore have been considered "safe." These old images also are shown as failing to excite any particular sense of marvel in the child, nor in the adult she was to become. Unlike García Lorca's poetry, which was so powerful that it could not even be touched, the long-dead German poet's work is copied with ease.

The most important question raised by this poem is just how readers are to interpret the relationship between the child's excitement about eating the oranges and the adult's excitement about the poetry of Federico García Lorca. In Mueller's childhood, neither poetry nor politics excited her. Was that because of the nature of children or the particular poetry and politics that she found presented to her? It may sound slightly irreverent to put it this way, but the whole point that Mueller is asking us to consider is whether the poetry of a man who suffered in life and was murdered can mean the same thing to an adult that a Christmas treat means to a child.

The question is only disrespectful if readers consider a Christmas treat to be a trivial thing, but it clearly is important to the child in this poem—*very* important to the child. In showing the ritualized consumption of symbolic "blood," the poem even raises the act of eating oranges to the level of a sacrament, like Communion. Still, if childhood is considered a time of small concerns, of focusing on the immediate experience but missing the larger abstract importance of things, then García Lorca comes close to being represented as a toy for intellectual adults. In fact, "Blood Oranges" encourages readers to take this line of inquiry, to question its own seriousness by making its young protagonist unaware of Hitler, Franco, and the dangerous state of Europe in general in 1936. The child is not dismissed as a "mere" child in this poem, but the poem does raise the issue of how much we know about our own circumstances, about how much we ever could know, and therefore about how much anyone, even an informed adult, could be said to appreciate an heroic individual.

Clearly, this poem does not intend its readers to walk away from reading it with the idea that Federico García Lorca might, in the big picture, deserve as little regard as Hitler and Franco. It does, however, raise issues about understanding that could let readers question the poet's own level of understanding. This is intellectual honesty, the willingness to be open about how little any of us really knows. It could be that Mueller will some day look back on her feelings about García Lorca with the same fondness and pity with which she saw the child eating an orange at the time when this poem was written, but that possibility is extremely slim. The complexity of "Blood Oranges" should leave readers fairly secure that Mueller knows what is important by this time in her life.

Source: David Kelly, Critical Essay on "Blood Oranges," in *Poetry for Students,* The Gale Group, 2001.

Nancy L. Bunge

In the following interview, Bunge and Mueller discusses teaching, politics, and being bilingual and its effects on her writing.

[Nancy Bunge]: How has being bilingual influenced your consciousness of language?

[Lisel Mueller]: We learn language by imitation; even people who don't know the grammar of their own language will speak it correctly if they hear it spoken correctly. Usage is another thing we just pick up. We don't think about our native language at all. But when you switch to another language, you are conscious of *everything.* You're conscious of the grammatical constructions, you're conscious of the phrasing, you're conscious of the idioms, you're conscious of each word—what it means, how it is used in its various forms, its derivation, if there is a cognate in your own language, how it might differ—all those things become so important. And metaphor is difficult at first. Like the popular song "Under a blanket of blue": I knew from the context it couldn't be a real blanket, but I didn't know it was the sky. And I didn't know "deep purple" meant nightfall. In German, I would have understood, any American would have understood . . . except we don't really listen to the words of popular songs in our native language. We hear those words, we say those words, and we never think about what they mean or whether they make any sense. I didn't in Germany, but coming here it became extremely important to be able to understand what every word meant. It's that kind of minute attention I think you have only with a language to which you're not native. Who knows, I might not have become a poet had this not happened to me.

My poetry is largely Germanic in the sense that I usually use strong, short words and not many latinates because they sound weaker to me—conversational, essayistic. More and more latinates are coming into poetry because our whole speech is becoming more latinate. The younger people use words ending in -ion and so on much more freely than I would. Of course, that isn't unique to me. Look at Dylan Thomas or Hopkins or Roethke who almost exclusively used Germanic words, probably because they dealt with very elementary things. My poems too tend to deal with the elementary and I associate those strongly accented, strongly sounded Germanic words with elementary things. If you're going to discuss ideas, then latinates are appropriate; but I don't deal with them, at least not directly, in my poems.

A number of people have commented that a fascination with language rather than an interest in ideas is the primary impetus for writing poetry.

There are very few ideas worth talking about. Those ideas are good for all times, but unless a poet has a new way of dealing with those ideas, they become commonplace. And new insights, new connections, are inseparable from their language, which is why a paraphrase of a poem always sounds banal.

Your later poetry seems more concerned with political and moral issues than your earlier poetry, or am I imagining things?

No, I think that's true and I think the Vietnam War changed me. That's when I became angry about what was going on. Those were bad years for me, not in terms of my private life, but in terms of being involved in the shame and guilt and wrongness of this country. Like many of us at that time, I took it all very personally, and perhaps the history of Nazi Germany in the back of my mind made me feel involved with it. Also, my father was a historian much involved with contemporary history and perhaps the genes started to take.

I also thought you implied that the large ethical and political questions post-war German writers had to confront enriched their work.

World War I destroyed a lot of the assumptions, but lip service was still given to the nineteenth century virtues and values of decency and humanity and honesty. All of these assumptions were *gone* after World War II. They had all proved to be illusions. It was like starting from scratch for the writers who survived. They had a lot to catch up on. For about twenty years they had been virtually cut off from new European and American writing. There was a total physical leveling of much of Germany and thousands starved to death even after the war was over. Then there were all the revelations about the death camps and the whole *monstrous history* which had occurred as a result of the Nazis in Germany. So it was like starting from scratch both physically and spiritually. And it was important to find a new, untainted language. This is why a lot of the poetry seems very innovative as well as very stark—almost stammering to come up with something new. And the novelists had a whole new subject. The Germans have had to come to grips with their history and they get their strength from writing about it.

Your poem "The Fall of the Muse" seems critical of American poetry.

It was written against the exhibitionism I thought was going on, not just in poetry—although the confessional poets are implicated in this. It was written after the death not only of Sylvia Plath, but of Judy Garland and Marilyn Monroe and biographers on talk shows were trying to top each other with intimate details about these people's lives. I felt moral outrage about this public suffering and this *glamorizing* of suffering. The temptation is to keep upping the ante and finally all you're left with is committing suicide.

I think that some contemporary American writers romanticize neurosis and I tend to avoid teaching their work, although that may be a mistake.

For obvious historical reasons American writers tend to focus on private psychic suffering, rather than the suffering brought on by social and political injustice. That kind of suffering is no less real than the suffering of a brutalized oppressed person, but it's less shareable. We feel that someone who really has it *rough* in the world . . . we feel that kind of suffering is more justified somehow than the suffering that goes on in so much of the more privileged part of society.

I don't know which makes the better writing because some of the novels that have come out of the more realistic, proletarian writing of the thirties and so on, haven't stood up either.

There is a problem with finding subject matter in our society, partly because there is a great bias among young writers against political writing. They don't want to write about political matters at all. Robert Bly and Denise Levertov have been attacked for their engagement in these issues—the Vietnam War and nuclear disarmament and things of that sort. That seems to me a uniquely American and English tradition of disassociating writing from what goes on in the world because it's certainly not true of European writers and it's not true

> *We don't think about our native language at all. But when you switch to another language, you are conscious of everything. You're conscious of the grammatical constructions, you're conscious of the phrasing, you're conscious of the idioms, you're conscious of each word. . . ."*

of South American writers. They're all involved in the politics of their country and they write about that; in countries where they can't write about it directly, like South Africa, Eastern Block countries, and Latin American countries, they write parables. They do it in an indirect way, but it's clearly understood.

That certainly was a prejudice when I was in graduate school: bad writing is ideological and good writing is subtle and intricate. I used to think it was intellectual elitism: the best writing is the most inaccessible.

A friend once gave a poetry reading and after the reading someone came up to him and said, "I enjoyed your poetry even though I can understand it." So, yes, there has been a lot of that. Luckily, I think that is changing.

Some people have said that it's not good for literature to have so many writers sheltered by the academy.

I don't know that it makes writing any less good, but I think it probably does make it more uniform. A lot of poets of our time sound very much alike; perhaps that's come out of the fact that most of us are teachers or writing students rather than working at Sears or driving a truck, or whatever. Writers used to have to support themselves in ways that had nothing to do with writing and this may make a difference in terms of struggling by yourself.

You've written that you did exercises to teach yourself how to write poetry. Do you remember what they were?

I did things like getting books on prosody out of the library and doing some of the things that were explained in there. For example, I would read about the villanelle and I would make myself write a villanelle. It was just a matter of reading books that explained the various forms and experimenting with them; I learned how they worked and tried to do some of them myself.

Do you use anything like that with your students?

It depends on the level of the students. Recently I've been teaching in a tutorial program and dealt largely with students who are already writers, graduate students. They know what they want to do and so I don't give them exercises. I let them write and then we discuss the work at hand. I suggest poets for them to read because I can see certain directions which I would like them to go in or certain things which I feel are not good about their work and I want them to read people they can learn from.

I've done some poetry in the schools and I give exercises with kids because you can't just say, "Sit down and write a poem." You have to give them specific instructions. Younger children are wonderful at metaphor. "Something is like something else" is a very simple way of explaining metaphor. "What does this remind you of?" "What is the color pink like for you?" Blue is an interesting color because some kids come up with all sad images and others come up with wonderful exhilarating blue images. Also, with natural phenomena, they're wonderful. I remember one kid saying, "Hail is like God dropping the ice cube out of his martini."

Should I have my students read work they will understand even if it means they'll be reading Sandburg?

It depends on the student. It depends on the age and the level you're talking about. If you're teaching graduate students, no. Or if you have some ambitious young intellectual who will want to read only things that he or she can't understand . . . But high school students, yes, Give them something they can enjoy because most of them don't like poetry to begin with, or think they won't like it, so give them work that can somehow touch on their own experience, that's simple enough and yet respectable poetry. Don't give them Rod McKuen, don't give them Edgar Guest, but . . . Sandburg may not be the greatest poet we've ever had, but he was a poet. You need to start with something you don't feel bad about giving them, but which will engage their interest.

You have to grab them where they are. Then you may be able to get them to go on from there, but if you give them something that shuts them out at the beginning, you'll never get them.

I was interested by your poem about giving your daughter a copy of Sister Carrie *because a student once told me that the first time a book engrossed her was when we read* Sister Carrie *in class. The next term she got caught up in* The Grapes of Wrath, *but she thought the ending was too sad. I said, "Well, there's some hope that the Okies will get together." And she said, "Oh, I hope they do."*

Well, that's it. For young people the personal connection is very important. "Oh, I hope they do," it's as if it were happening to her own family. I have noticed that often someone who has read one of my books, a young student or someone who has come to a reading of mine, will come up and tell me about a poem they have liked, and it's almost always, "I know someone who has done this" or "I have felt this way" or "I've had this experience." They don't respond to it because it's a well-written poem; it's because there's something in the poem that touches them personally. That's always the beginning; the aesthetic thing comes later.

I was reading Sandburg my first year in this country, when I wasn't used to the language. At the same time I was reading Sandburg, I was taking my first high school English Literature course. I was reading Wordsworth and Keats and Gray and I couldn't do much with them. They were simply too difficult for me; but Sandburg, I could read, I could understand, I could respond to. I knew that Keats and Wordsworth and Shelley and the rest were supposed to be much greater poets, but that didn't mean I really liked them.

You've said that you wrote in free verse because you found "the echoes of the formal masters too strong" for your "incubating voice." Do your students have trouble with echoes?

They have echoes, but they aren't those same echoes because they largely read contemporary poetry; so there'll be echoes of maybe Mark Strand or Galway Kinnell. It's never the traditionally formal poets because my students come from two generations in which they've not been taught metric poetry. A few years ago Donald Hall was teaching a short course in writing in iambic pentameter in the Goddard MFA Program, and students flocked to it. They found it extremely difficult and they found it fascinating: they were learning *new things*. And they found it very hard because they were used to speech rhythms; they were not used to hearing stressed and unstressed syllables. It was like learning to hear poetry in that way for the first time. So everything is turned around.

I've always, for example, liked to have my students read people like Richard Wilbur, who is an absolutely marvelous poet in whatever he does, but who, among other things, is very good with forms. And also someone like Marilyn Hacker who writes not only wonderful villanelles and sestinas and sonnets, but crowns of sonnets and double villanelles. She uses these very traditional forms, but uses extremely colloquial, idiomatic, contemporary language within these forms which I think is a beautiful and interesting combination. I like my students to read these people. It doesn't necessarily mean they write like them. It is hard for them to, say, write a sonnet that doesn't sound like tenth-rate Keats.

If it's possible, I'd like you to explain this comment: "Once the tools, tricks and secrets of the trade become second nature, you lose the attention to technique which has served as a margin of safety. Suddenly you are nakedly exposed to the dangerous process of bringing a poem into existence."

I meant that period between the time you know exactly what you do because you are doing an exercise and the time when you can trust your instinct and critical judgment enough that you don't feel totally at risk. It's like a child learning to walk. The child has held onto the furniture or the hands of grownups and then she lets go and for a little while, there'll be quite a few falls until, eventually, she stops falling and can walk by herself. There is a period like that and it's very troublesome for young writers. I certainly went through that for a number of years.

I get this in workshops where people who don't have much background in writing but a great deal of enthusiasm have no sense of whether the poem works and also whether it communicates its ideas to an outside reader. Often they're very good at criticizing poems by other people but they can't do it to their own poems. I'll talk to them about a specific poem and try to help them see some of the problems and they will say, "Well, you've been very helpful and now I see what you mean, but why can't I do this myself?" There's no way except the experience of writing and writing and revising, going back, looking at your old poems. There comes a day when you can do it, when the flaws jump out at you.

It sounds as though that middle period is a time when the person hasn't really established a center for his or her work.

That's true, but it's also a matter of learning the craft. Most young writers are very awkward in their language. Even if there's a great deal of talent there, a great deal of energy, the phrasing is usually not smooth yet, not lapidary enough. It's also proportion and pace and transition, how to get from here to there, all those technical things which you have to learn by feel on your own. You develop your own voice, your own language, and that takes time.

Can having other people react to their work speed that process up?

I think it can and that's why workshops are so valuable and such a shortcut for writers. It's something I didn't have when I started to write. Students in workshops get that immediate response from a teacher who's an experienced writer and from their fellow students.

If someone couldn't go to a workshop, what would you suggest they do to teach themselves?

Read the best poets—all the good poets of their time as well as the older literature. We learn to write by imitation largely, just as we learn to speak and walk by imitation. I think most teachers—probably all poets teaching—would agree that they're merely helping along and that the reading is the primary thing. The teacher can be very valuable in helping direct students to what to read. One of the good things about the Goddard program, now at Warren Wilson College, is that each program is individually made up for a particular student, and that it requires a lot of reading. It encourages not only reading poetry and criticism and fiction, but also reading outside of literature—reading about science or architecture or psychology—other subjects that could feed into your poetry as subject matter and enrich your sense of the world. Sometimes young writers don't want to read anything outside of literature and that's a very small part . . . The world is rich. Any writer is a better writer the less insulated he or she is.

Reading widely makes you a livelier, richer person and that would feed into your writing. It's probably more important for novelists than for poets because they deal with social reality whereas poets deal largely with their inner world or how their inner world relates to the outer world, but I think it enriches the whole *context* in which you write. W. H. Auden, for example, regretted very much that he didn't know more about nature, especially botany and zoology, than he did. He felt it would have helped his poetry a great deal if he had been able to use that area of knowledge in a natural way, the way, for example, Roethke did.

Even being a good writer, but *definitely* being a *great* writer, demands a great deal of understanding and knowledge of the world. It doesn't necessarily mean a formal education, but it does involve curiosity. That's what we feel in Tolstoy and Thomas Mann and Flaubert and the great poets like Yeats or Keats. One has that sense that they were interested in a very large universe.

I'm partial to history. To me a sense of what has gone on in the past is very important to one's view of the world. Because that is my bias in writing poetry, I look at what is going on right now in my life and the life of people around me not as divorced from everything that has gone before, but in the context of the past and of what may come in the future. Now that's not everyone's bias. For some people it may be nature. Everything related to the seasonal, to the rejuvenation of nature, or perhaps it relates to landscape. There are poets whose whole world of inner experience is articulated in terms of natural images; it's as if the landscape or the weather is a metaphor always for what is going on inside them. There are many different possibilities.

I don't mean a writer can't be a wonderful writer and have a highly concentrated vision. There are writers who are obsessed by one thing and that one thing is expressed over and over and wonderfully. It's the hedgehog and the fox idea. The hedgehog is the one who burrows inside; Kafka is a typical hedgehog. He had this one idiosyncratic vision of everything, and it was such a *powerful* vision . . . perhaps if he had dissipated it, it would not have been so powerful. And then there are the foxes like Tolstoy. But I think even for the obsessive ones, knowing as much as possible is valuable and a joy.

Do you get anything from teaching?

I've enjoyed the method of tutorial teaching very much. I like working with one person at a time, being able to relate to his or her particular needs, and see the direction they're going in. I can't really help someone without understanding their poetry [and that] means trying to get into that person's mind.

I like the exchange of talking about literature. Having to do it by mail, as I've had to with my students, is laborious, but it makes you think hard about everything you say because it's down on paper and there are so many more possibilities of misunderstanding. It's taught me to think about things more clearly than I would otherwise. It's also forced me to read a lot more because I've had to keep up with the students' reading and they want to read a lot of things I haven't read. It's been stimulating for me. There is the pleasure of the intellectual-literary exchange, but also of seeing someone develop and maybe having a share in guiding their development.

Source: Nancy L. Bunge, "Liesel Mueller," in *Finding the Words: Conversations with Writers Who Teach,* Swallow Press, 1985, pp. 96–105.

Sources

Fulton, Alice, "Main Things," in *Poetry,* Vol. CLI, No. 4, January 1988, pp. 366–77.

Muratori, Fred, "Second Language," in *Library Journal,* Vol. 111, No. 15, September 15, 1986, p. 90.

Parisi, Joseph, "Second Language: Poems," in *Booklist,* Vol. 83, No. 9. January 1, 1987, p. 679.

Stitt, Peter, "The Whirlpool of Image and Narrative Flow," in *Georgia Review,* Vol. XLI, No. 1, Spring 1987, pp. 192–208.

Tanner, Lindsey, "Pulitzer for Poetry Ends In Obscurity," in *New Standard,* http://www.s-t.com/daily/05-97/05-04-97/e06ae235.htm (January 17, 2001).

Taylor, John, "Alive Together: New and Selected Poems," in *Poetry,* Vol. 171, No. 3, January 1998, p. 219.

For Further Study

Liebster, Simone Arnold, *Facing the Lion: Memoirs of a Young Girl in Nazi Europe,* Grammaton Press, 2000.
> This is the author's autobiographical account of life in the Alsace-Lorraine region of France before and during the Nazi occupation.

Posner, Gerald L., *Hitler's Children,* Random House, 1991.
> The sons and daughters of leaders of Hitler's Third Reich talk about how they feel about their childhoods.

Wyden, Peter, *The Passionate War: The Narrative History of the Spanish Civil War,* Simon and Schuster, 1983.
> Wyden weaves together interviews, memoirs, and documents into a story told to readers in a very clear and understandable way.

Cavalry Crossing a Ford

Walt Whitman

1865

"Cavalry Crossing a Ford" was first published in 1865 in *Drum Taps,* a collection of poems Whitman wrote during the Civil War, and was later incorporated into *Leaves of Grass.* The specific inspiration for this poem is not known, but Whitman did work as a nurse during the Civil War and may well have written this piece upon witnessing a cavalry troop crossing a river. Unlike the majority of poems Whitman penned during the Civil War, "Cavalry Crossing a Ford" does not use the first-person "I" to put the scene it describes into a particular context. Instead of filtering the scene through a first-person narrator, the speaker of the poem journalistically presents a series of images and entreats the reader to "behold" the scene as though he or she were the first-person observer. It is as if the speaker imagined his reader standing beside him and seeing exactly what he sees as he sees it.

Perhaps the most interesting facet of the poem concerns the perspective from which the scene is observed and presented. The panoramic quality of the images suggests that the observer (implicitly, the reader) is viewing the scene from some distance. The whole of the cavalry troop is seen at once, as though the reader were looking down from some great height. However, from this vantage the reader is ultimately unable to distinguish the particulars of the scene from the larger whole. Each individual soldier becomes merely part of the "they" that makes up the entire cavalry, and no particular individual is given special attention or distinction in the scene. The climax of the poem then comes in the

Walt Whitman

last line, when suddenly the focus is on the "guidon flags." While the reader has thus far been unable to distinguish the individuals who make up the cavalry troop, now the relatively small flags and even the particular colors they contain are described in detail. Such flags ultimately suggest political allegiance and serve to distinguish the two opposing forces of the battle. In turning attention to the flags, the poem presents a specific manner of viewing the world, one in which individual human beings are no more than their political allegiances. This mindset was no doubt prevalent during the Civil War, a time when people were compelled to choose sides, and self-preservation depended upon distinguishing one's comrades from one's enemies. That the "guidon flags" are seen to "flutter gayly" implies that the approaching cavalry troop poses no threat. The poem ends here, leaving the reader with the impression that attention to the scene is no longer necessary; the speaker has conveyed what is important.

Author Biography

The second of nine children, Whitman was born on May 31, 1819, on Long Island, New York, to Quaker parents. In 1823, the Whitmans moved to Brooklyn, where Whitman attended public school. At age eleven he left school to work as an office boy in a law office and then as a typesetter's apprentice at a number of print shops. Although his family moved back to Long Island in 1834, Whitman stayed in Brooklyn and then Manhattan to become a compositor. Unable to find work, he rejoined his family on Long Island in 1836 and taught at several schools. In addition to teaching, Whitman started his own newspaper, the *Long Islander*. He subsequently edited numerous papers for short periods over the next fourteen years, including the New York *Aurora* and the Brooklyn *Eagle*, and published poems and short stories in various periodicals.

Whitman did little in terms of employment from the 1850 to 1855. Instead, he focused on his own work, writing and printing the first edition of his collection of poems *Leaves of Grass*. Over the next few years, Whitman continued to write and briefly returned to journalism. During the American Civil War he tended wounded soldiers in army hospitals in Washington, D.C., while working as a copyist in the army paymaster's office. Following the war, Whitman worked for the Department of the Interior and then as a clerk at the Justice Department. He remained in this position until he suffered a paralytic stroke in 1873. Although he lived nearly twenty more years and published four more editions of *Leaves of Grass*, Whitman produced little significant new work following his stroke. He died in Camden, New Jersey, on March 26, 1892.

Poem Text

A line in long array where they wind betwixt green islands,
They take a serpentine course, their arms flash in the sun—hark to the musical clank,
Behold the silvery river, in it the splashing horses loitering stop to drink.
Behold the brown-faced men, each group, each person a picture, the negligent rest on the saddles,
Some emerge on the opposite bank, others are just entering the ford—while,   5
Scarlet and blue and snowy white,
The guidon flags flutter gayly in the wind.

Poem Summary

Lines 1-2

The "they" of the first line refers to the soldiers who make up the cavalry troop mentioned in the title. This abrupt beginning differs greatly from the majority of Whitman's verse, in which he uses the first-person "I" as the filter through which the poem is conveyed. Here, the "I" of the poem, the speaker, is merely implied. Instead of coloring the scene with his own perception, he relates it journalistically—objectively and with a nonjudgmental tone—presenting the image of the cavalry as it crosses a ford, a shallow place in a river. The scope of the image is so broad as to imply that the scene is being viewed from a distance and likely from some higher ground. The whole of the cavalry is presented as a vast single line twisting and turning snake-like through the landscape. The "arms" that glint sunlight in the second line refer then to the cavalry soldiers' rifles, and the "Hark," which simply means "listen," serves both as a command and an entreaty. In this manner, the speaker both asks and tells the reader to see the scene for himself or herself. It is as though he imagines the reader standing alongside him, hearing "the musical clank" of the distant soldiers' guns. While this is not a logical possibility, the speaker of the poem helps (or forces) the reader to visualize the scene by supplying images and cues. In addition, the use of assonance and consonance in these lines adds to the poem's musical quality and thus imitates the "musical clank" referred to in the poem. Indeed, "clank" is onomatopoeic, meaning that the sound of the word itself imitates the sound to which the word refers.

Lines 3-4

In these lines, the speaker continues to entreat, or command, the reader's attention. Again, the reader is asked to imagine the scene as though viewed first-hand. The first image of making up the whole picture, of course, is the landscape, the "silvery river" that the cavalry is in the process of traversing. Next are the horses that stop mid-river to drink, and finally, the "brown-faced men." Note that while the speaker says that "each person" is a "picture," implying that each is in itself worthy of our attention, no single individual is given more specific detail. In this sense, the poem seems to contradict itself. While each and every soldier is presented as being an individual, the reader is never quite able to distinguish any single person from the group. The men are still plural, part of the whole.

Line 5

Line 5 establishes again the enormity of the scene. The reader sees all at once the long line of troops stretched across the river. In ending the line with the word "while," the speaker prompts anticipation in the reader of what is to follow. The position of the subordinate conjunction "while" at the

Media Adaptations

- A 1987 video entitled *Walt Whitman,* from the *Great Works of American Literature* series, is available from Focus Media Inc. It is written by Elizabeth Ralph and directed by Jim Cronin.

- Dover Press has an audiocassette edition of *Walt Whitman's Selected Poems,* from their "Listen and Read" series, recorded in 1987.

- Mystic Fire Audio has a 1997 cassette selection of Whitman's poems available in its *Voices and Visions* series, entitled simply *Walt Whitman.*

- The audiocassette *The BBC Collection of War Poetry* uses music and sound effects to bring the best war poetry from throughout the ages to life.

- The Walt Whitman Hypertext Archive available at http://jefferson.village.virginia.edu/whitman/index.html (last accessed April 2001) has links to works by Whitman, reviews of his poetry, biographical information, etc. It is maintained by Charles B. Green (August 10, 1999).

end of the line gives it an imperative quality, a sense of importance.

Lines 6-7

Here, finally, the subordinate clause begun at the end of line 4 is brought to completion. However, line 5 postpones this sense of closure for a moment. By offering descriptive adjectives before actually defining the objects to which they refer, the line keeps the reader waiting. Whitman added this descriptive line (line 6) in 1871, some six years after the poem's original publication, and its effect on the overall reading of the poem is extremely significant. In a sense the line prolongs the reader's uncertainty about what is to follow and heightens anticipation. This is particularly important since the final image of the cavalry, the image that is most particularized in the poem, is the "guidon flags," which are carried into battle to distinguish opposing armies. In a sense, the poem then defines the cavalry and all of its members according to their political allegiance. That the banners "flutter gayly" suggests that the cavalry in question is friendly and poses no threat, and it is for this recognition that the reader has been waiting. In a sense, the reader has been observing the entire scene with this one purpose in mind—to determine whether the approaching cavalry is friend or foe. Perhaps more important, however, is the political mind-set that the poem then exemplifies. In essence, the individuals portrayed in the poem seem less important than the "flags" signifying their political allegiance. It becomes irrelevant that the men who make up the cavalry are individuals with their own values and ideas. What matters is only whether they are friend or foe.

Themes

Identity

To the speaker of the poem, the soldiers that are described here have no individual identities but are important in their function as parts of the long, serpentine line of bodies. The speaker appreciates this scene for its artistic harmony, for the way the line of soldiers fits into the overall natural setting. Symbolically, the line of soldiers resembles the river, and the men, "brown-faced," blend into the natural setting like trees. Even the flag that the men follow as a matter of honor and identity is identified with nature by the use of the adjective "snowy." Seen from a distance, these men lose their individual identities, and as a group, the men lose the defining characteristics that separate humans from nature.

There is a brief section, in the middle of the poem, where readers are told to look at the soldiers as individuals and not as parts of a group. "Behold," Whitman tells his reader, "each person a picture." A few details follow which distinguish one group from another, but no details are given to make readers envision distinct, separate individuals.

The fact that these soldiers lack individuality and appear as part of a larger unit fits in well with the goal of most military training, which is to make soldiers think in terms of how they can serve their commanders, forgetting individual needs and desires. Soldiers wear uniforms and march in formation in order to identify themselves as part of a group; in this poem, Whitman extends that way of anonymous thinking to include their faces and postures. The fact that none of these soldiers is distinct

Topics for Further Study

- Write a poem that gives an impressionistic description of something happening near where you live, viewing it from a far distance.

- Research the guidon flags of different regiments of the Union and the Confederacy in the Civil War and report on the stories behind some of them.

- Explain how the last line changes the tone of this poem. Explain how it changes the poem's meaning.

- Find memoirs of people who served in the armed forces during recent campaigns, such as the actions in the Persian Gulf or in Bosnia, and compare the ways they describe travel between battles with the way Whitman describes this army.

- Some rivers could be crossed on horseback, while others were just too wild. Find out what conditions would apply: what depth is safe to take horses across, what current they can resist, etc. Report your findings.

from the others is a testimony to their success at fitting into their military roles.

War and Peace

A reader who is drawn into the poem's picturesque description of soldiers marching off to battle might easily forget for a moment about the serious, life-and-death issues involved when war is waged. The scene presented here is one of peaceful harmony, with horses loitering and men resting, the musical clank of the men's gear reflected by the poem's musical use of alliteration (repetition of consonant sounds) and assonance (repetition of vowels). The final line, describing how the "flags flutter gaily in the wind," in some way captures the tone of carefree comfort that pervades the entire piece.

This poem is effective precisely because its view of war contradicts the brutality that readers expect to find in a war poem. By presenting warriors in their peaceful state, going about the mundane business of making their way across a river, Whitman humanizes war and reminds his readers that, aside from the excitement of battle, there are ordinary people involved in any military campaign. The contrast between the calm scene presented here and the violence usually associated with war is so extreme that the poem does not appear to be an attempt to fool readers into forgetting the horrors of fighting. Readers are actually made more aware of the danger that these soldiers may soon face by the fact that it is so completely, conspicuously, obviously absent. There is no explicit peril in this scene, but the poem's syntax—such as the abrupt break of line 5, which hints at matters that are left unexamined—serves to remind readers that the peace pictured here is only temporary in wartime life.

Nature

The fact that this is a cavalry regiment, composed of both men and horses, helps the poem emphasize the theme of nature. In one sense, the poem is a study of the interplay between nature and humankind. The military unit is a powerful symbol of humanity because it represents the extremes of human thought: the basic carnal blood thirst that drives violence, along with complex strategic logic. Unlike modern warfare, which is fought over long distances with computer-guided missiles, the soldiers of this cavalry are intimately bound to nature through their relationships with their horses and are required to adapt to the natural setting around them. In the scene presented here, it is a river, not the enemy, that they have to contend with. The fact that humans are a part of nature is emphasized by the poem's use of natural imagery: serpentine, to describe the look of the assembled column of men, and "brown-faced," which gives them a more natural tone than bare flesh and also serves to remind readers that these men have been out riding in the sun and the open air.

Order and Disorder

This poem relies upon an implied tension between what readers know about the destructive chaos of battle and the discipline of a well-trained military unit as it goes through basic maneuvers. The cavalry has various elements of rest and leisure involved in its task of crossing the river, but overall it keeps its central structure. This line of men is presented as being "in long array," using a word that usually refers to someone dressed up in formal clothes, as if their march is in itself some kind of organized presentation, a planned show, being performed for an audience. The poem supports this sense of a simple military maneuver as an orderly display by telling its readers to "behold."

Within this regimented order, though, the men and animals follow their natural tendencies toward disorder. Horses splash and loiter; men rest when they can, each following his own unique part, acting independently, depending on where he falls in the line. The implication is that someone viewing this scene up close would not be able to appreciate the cavalry's grand design, that it is only when seen from a far enough distance that the order in what they are doing becomes apparent.

Style

"Cavalry Crossing a Ford" is written in free verse, which means it adheres to no set pattern of rhyme or meter. Instead, it is organized around units composed of images and incorporates consonance and assonance in order to heighten the musicality of its verses.

Imagery refers to language used to communicate a visual picture or impression of a person, place, or thing. Images are usually defined as either fixed or free. "Fixed images," also sometimes called "concrete images," are specific and detailed enough so as to leave little to the reader's imagination. In contrast, free images are more general and depend upon the reader to provide specificity. In "Cavalry Crossing a Ford," for example, Whitman provides a series of images (both fixed and free) to present for the reader the larger picture of the cavalry troop. He writes of the "silvery river" and "the splashing horses loitering . . . to drink," as well as the image of sunlight glinting off the "brown-faced" cavalry soldiers' guns. The culmination of these "images," then, is the larger "image" of the cavalry as a whole.

Consonance refers to close repetitions of similar or identical consonant sounds where the main vowel sounds of the words are different. When such repetitions occur most frequently at the beginning of a succession of words, such consonance is called alliteration. When the repetitions come at the ends of words, they are known as slant rhymes. For example, in the lines below, the "l" sounds of "line" and "long" are alliterative. Similarly, the "nd" sounds at the ends of "wind" and "island" are slant rhymes:

> A line in long array where they wind betwixt green islands

Assonance refers to repetitions of similar or identical vowel sounds in a sequence of words. In the lines above, the long "a" sounds of "array" and "they" are examples of this. In the lines below, the repetitions of the "g" and "f" sounds exemplify consonance while the "in" sounds of "in" and "wind" are examples of assonance.

> The guidon flags flutter gayly in the wind.

Finally, "Cavalry Crossing a Ford" also incorporates what is called end-line slant rhyme, which means the last words of each line all share assonant or consonant qualities: the "n" sounds in "islands," "clank," and "drink"; the "l" sounds in "saddles" and "while"; and the "w" sounds in "while," "white," and "wind." Ultimately both assonance and consonance serve to heighten the musicality of the poem by creating a richer rhythmic texture.

Historical Context

Causes Leading to War

There were numerous causes leading to the Civil War. The most prominent was the disagreement between the Union, comprised of northern states, and the Confederacy, comprised of southern states, regarding the issue of slavery. Well before the nineteenth century, slavery was a common practice in the United States, having continued in various forms and places since Biblical times. Among the Europeans who first came to America there were "indentured servants," who were poor white Europeans brought to the new land and made to work off the cost of their passage. Sometimes this was a voluntary contractual relationship, but convicts, children, and even people abducted from the streets were forced into servitude. The indigenous people who lived on the continent before European settlers arrived were also forced into slavery, but they proved too difficult to command and too susceptible to epidemics of European diseases. Whites and Native Americans found it easy to blend into crowds of their own people whenever they escaped their captors.

The trade in African slaves existed in America as far back as 1619, when captive Africans were brought to the Jamestown colony in Virginia. By the time the United States Constitution was adopted, people were already raising questions about the morality of the practice. Seven of the original thirteen colonies had either abolished slavery or were poised to do so by 1789. The states that relied on slave labor were the southern states, where the economy was primarily based on farming. The northern states were not open enough or warm enough to sustain huge farms like the South's plantations, and so the northern economy favored industry instead. As new states were added to the Union, supporters and opponents of slavery took pains to make sure that the other side did not gain any political power.

By the 1820 census, the population in the non-slave states was significantly greater than the population in the slave states, giving the former a majority in the House of Representatives. Feeling this disadvantage, southern politicians became more aggressive in their opposition to any measures that might limit slavery. The South's economy was much stronger than the North's; for instance, their main product, cotton, increased in value a hundred times over when the cotton gin was invented in 1793. As opposition to slavery arose in the North and across the entire civilized world, southern plantation owners took any means available to make sure that there would not be any laws passed to take their slaves from them. When outrage against the inhumanity of slavery became overwhelming, slaveholders considered the option of quitting the United States—seceding—and forming their own country.

The idea that this unsolvable slavery question might lead to two countries was bought up often throughout the 1850s, particularly in 1857, when the opponents of slavery considered splitting from the slaveholders at a "Disunion Convention." By 1860, the basic economic differences had greatly expanded. There were over twice as many citizens in the free states as in the slave states, and the Union had 100,000 factories employing 1.1 million workers, whereas the Confederacy had only 20,000 factories with 100,000 workers. The Industrial Revolution that had swept across the civilized world in the nineteenth century had left the culture of the Confederacy untouched. As Kenneth C. Davis put it in his book, *Don't Know Much About the Civil War*, "Two countries, two ideologies. Despite the common ground of language, religion, race and heritage—America was primarily a white Anglo Saxon Protestant nation—the people of the day saw more differences between themselves. The simplest explanation for the war was that many in the Confederacy saw themselves being steamrolled by a northern economic machine that threatened every aspect of their way of life, hence the seemingly irrational contradiction in people proclaiming a fight for 'liberty' by defending the enslavement of someone else."

Secession began immediately upon the election of Abraham Lincoln, an opponent of slavery, in 1860. Federal officials across South Carolina quit their posts the day after the election results

Compare & Contrast

- **1865:** The United States Civil War ends when General Robert E. Lee, representing the Army of the Confederacy, surrenders to Ulysses S. Grant at Appomattox Courthouse, Virginia, on April 9. The last regiment of the Confederate army does not officially surrender until the end of the following month.

  Today: Peace treaties to end international conflicts are often supervised by an independent body, such as NATO or the United Nations.

- **1865:** The principle methods of transportation are horses, steam-powered locomotive, and the steamship.

  Today: Nearly nine million cars are sold in the United States each year, and airlines have more passengers than they can handle.

- **1865:** An American inventor is able to create ice with a compression machine that he designed.

  Today: Refrigeration and air conditioning are common and are taken for granted by most Americans.

- **1865:** After losing the Civil War, the political structure of the South is taken over by unscrupulous politicians called "carpetbaggers," opportunists who moved there with cheap luggage made of carpets in order to take advantage of the situation.

  Today: The southern states wield great power over the national political situation. On "Super Tuesday," many southern states hold primary elections for presidential candidates all at once, forcing candidates to cater to the political advantage that the South can offer them.

---

were tallied, and the state officially seceded from the Union in December. Georgia followed; then other southern states went along in the months between Lincoln's election and his inauguration in April of 1861. The month after his inauguration, the first shot of the war was fired when South Carolina militia troops fired upon Fort Sumter, a military installation maintained by the Union army.

The Civil War

The war lasted four years, from the firing on Fort Sumter to the South's surrender on April 9, 1865. The North seemed to have had the distinct advantage, with more men, more manufacturing facilities, and a navy that could keep foreign supplies from reaching southern ports. Most of the fighting was on southern soil, with the North taking a lead early—for instance, New Orleans was captured in April of 1862, costing the Confederacy its largest city and a key port for shipping goods up the Mississippi River. By the end of that year, though, the Confederacy was able to win some important victories, which gave it the momentum to invade the North at the beginning of 1863. In 1863, both sides suffered devastating losses at Gettysburg, one of the bloodiest conflicts of the war. After that, the tide shifted several times. The Union army was plagued by a lack of competent leadership, and supplies to the army of the Confederacy, as well as to the citizens of the South, fell dangerously low. The fact that the southern army was able to persevere for so long is attributed to the fact that Confederate soldiers had a sense of fighting to defend their cultural identity, rather than just fighting for an abstract principle.

In April of 1865, after a series of losses, the Confederate army finally surrendered. Over the course of the four years, more Americans died during the Civil War than have died in total in all other wars this country has fought. Five days after the surrender, President Lincoln was assassinated by John Wilkes Booth, and the business of mending a country that had been engaged in bloody battle fell to Andrew Johnson, whose policy of granting full stature to southern politicians so angered the Congress that they tried to impeach him, falling just one vote short.

Union cavalry column along the Rappahannock River, Virginia, 1862

Critical Overview

"Cavalry Crossing a Ford" is in many ways indicative of Whitman's shorter poems, especially in the vivid description of the scene. The poem differs in the manner in which the speaker situates himself on the periphery of the scene. While the majority of Whitman's work is written in the first-person, and usually the "I" of the poem is the center of the action or scene, in "Cavalry Crossing a Ford" the first-person "I" of the poem is merely implied and serves solely as a distant observer. This is particularly important in light of the fact that Whitman's biggest critical proponents argue precisely that what distinguishes his poetry is his self-referential, egocentric outlook on the world. As John Updike explained in his essay "Whitman's Egotheism," Whitman's poetic egotism is "suffused and tempered with a strenuous empathy" and serves to recognize "each man's immersion in a unique and unexchangeable ego." In other words, Whitman espouses not only his individuality but the individual nature of all persons. Yet in "Cavalry Crossing a Ford," the individual characters observed in the scene are never quite distinguished from the larger military group.

In slight contrast to this interpretation of "Cavalry Crossing a Ford," Cleanth Brooks and Robert Penn Warren, in their book *Understanding Poetry*, suggest that the original unity of the cavalry as depicted in the first line "dissolves into details." They point out that each person and each group of people is given a sense of individuality if only in that "each" is "a picture." Brooks and Warren argue that in line 5, the speaker of the poem recognizes each man's individuality. What follows is then a reassembly of the parts back into the whole. As Brooks and Warren explain, the speaker of the poem, "having fractured his general impression into these individual 'pictures' . . . then begins to reassemble the whole. Again we begin to get a sense of the column as a unit, its head emerging on the far bank, the rear entering the stream. But still the scene has not come into sharp focus. It is only when our eyes fix on the guidons fluttering 'gayly' that everything is drawn together . . . we get a feeling of how the men who, for a moment, had become individual, just men watering their horses as casually and lazily as a farmer after a day in the field, are jerked back into their places in the unit, losing their identity in the whole."

Criticism

David Kelly

Kelly is an instructor of creative writing and literature at Oakton Community College and the

College of Lake County. In this essay, he examines the reasons why Whitman used a tighter, more formal style in "Cavalry Crossing a Ford" than he used in other poems.

In Walt Whitman's poem "Cavalry Crossing a Ford," readers are presented with a rich, sublime example of how maturity can mold a writer's vision without necessarily hampering it. The poem was written after Whitman had experienced the Civil War and had been exposed to the horrible results of combat that he saw as a nurse at an army hospital in Washington. In this poem, readers do not see the immediate repulsion that he must have felt; there is no sign of war's violence, just an appreciation of the efficiency on display as dozens of humans move as one single organism, as the army has trained them to do. A reader might find the poet's control in presenting this scene to be craftsmanlike, even aloof. What is remarkable about it is the way that Whitman's style changed to reflect the gravity of life around him. Looking at his earlier work, from first editions of *Leaves of Grass*, one sees a celebration of the individual, focusing on the speaker and rambling on furiously for page after page with notions, associations, ideas, and interests. These works share the optimism that the people Whitman examined were all part of one functional body, which he identified, somewhat vaguely, as "America." As successful as these earlier, more personal, poems were, Whitman was just as successful with the camera-eye technique he used in "Cavalry Crossing a Ford." The ways in which his style differed from the earlier poems reflects the different worldview that exposure to war can cause.

The most obvious example for comparing this war poem to Whitman's earlier work would have to be "Crossing Brooklyn Ferry," which was included in the second edition of *Leaves of Grass* in 1856. Like "Cavalry Crossing a Ford," it presents masses of people involved in the task of getting across a body of water, in this case New York's East River. But that is where the similarity ends. "Crossing Brooklyn Ferry" is nearly eight pages long, composed of hundreds of lines. It does not give readers a view of the people at whom the poet is looking, but rather a view of the poet looking at the people, tracking the emotions they stir in him: "Crowds of men and women attired in the usual costumes, how curious you are to me!" the poet exclaims in the second stanza. The poem seeks to make a mystery of the mundane, to look at working people going to their jobs as some sort of nat-

> *The time that Whitman may have once spent asking himself what it means to be an American poet was spent on more serious tasks, like caring for the suffering and burying the dead. The prospect of death, as one thinker pointed out, tends to focus one's attention quite quickly.*"

ural wonder. They only seem at first to be the poet's peer group, though as the poem goes on, they appear to be different in every way. For example, a stanza from section 2 illustrates this:

> The impalpable sustenance of me from all things at all hours of the day,
> The simple, compact, well-join'd scheme, myself disintegrated, every one disintegrated yet part of the scheme
> The similitudes of the past and those of the future,
> The glories strung like beads on my smallest sights and hearings, on the walk in the street and the passages over the river,
> the current rushing so swiftly and swimming with me far away,
> The others that are to follow me, the ties between me and them,
> The certainty of others, the life, love, sight, hearing of others.

In this passage, the act of concentrating on himself drives the poet toward acute awareness of the differences between people, even as he tries to proclaim their unity. This is typical of Whitman's earlier poems. Even a poem like "I Sing the Body Electric" is made to draw attention to its central consciousness, the "I" that speaks the poem. One of Whitman's largest works is the book-length "Song of Myself," which presents a free-floating rumination about practically any subject that passes through the speaker's mind; the only real unifying factor is that it is, after all, just one mind, with broad interests and an unleashed imagination.

What Do I Read Next?

- A good anthology of poetry from the Civil War, broken down into "Confederate Poetry" and "Union Poetry," can be found at http://www.civil-war.net (October 15, 2000).

- Twentieth-century poet Robert Frost was a great admirer of Whitman, and his work certainly shows Whitman's influence. All of Frost's poetry is available in *Poetry of Robert Frost: Collected Poems, Complete and Unabridged,* published by Henry Holt in 1979.

- Emily Dickinson wrote at the same time as Whitman. Her poem "I Like to See It Lap the Miles," available in *The Collected Poems of Emily Dickinson* (1890), resembles "Cavalry Crossing a Ford" in terms of visual perspective.

- A good overview of Whitman's works, including this poem, is available in *The Viking Portable Walt Whitman* (1945), edited by Mark van Doren.

- There are many good anthologies of Whitman's works, but fans of "Cavalry Crossing a Ford" might be interested in finding a copy of *Walt Whitman's Civil War,* compiled from published and previously unpublished sources in 1961 by Walter Lowenfels.

- The book *Walt Whitman's Camden Conversations,* selected and arranged by Walter Teller in 1973, contains a number of quotations from the poet in the later years of his life, including a section with his thoughts about war.

- In 1981, Jim Perlman, Ed Folsum, and Dan Campion compiled a collection of essays, poems, and reviews about Whitman from different historical eras since his time in their book *Walt Whitman: The Measure of His Song.* Students can see how the poet's reputation has evolved over the years.

- There are numerous books dedicated to the Civil War. Students can be overwhelmed by all of the details made available by historians. One very readable book is Webb Garrison's *A Treasury of Civil War Tales* (1988), which gives a chronology of the war in anecdotal form.

The introduction to the original edition of *Leaves of Grass* explained Whitman's reasons for writing what he wrote in the way that he wrote it. The introduction is presented in prose, not in poetic verse, but in verbal style it matches the freedom that he allowed himself in poems like "Crossing Brooklyn Ferry." Amid sentences that run on for forty lines or more in places, Whitman explains that

> the expression of the American poet is to be transcendent and new. It is to be indirect and not direct or descriptive or epic. Its quality goes through these to much more. Let the age and wars of other nations be chanted and their eras and characters be illustrated and that finish their verse. Not so the great psalm of the republic. Here the theme is creative and has vista. Here comes one among the well beloved stonecutters and plans with decision and science and sees the solid and beautiful forms of the future where there are now no solid forms.

As an expression of these ideals, Whitman's style worked and has held up for a century and a half. He defined American poetry, just as he intended to, by combining a style unbound by tradition with a sharp appreciation of the American people, lingering on each person only briefly so that he would not make one seem more important than the others. In 1865, though, when he wrote "Cavalry Crossing a Ford," his point of view had shifted. He still looked at people as a group, but the imagery was no longer conveyed through an authorial "I." The speaker, whose thoughts tended to lead the earlier works from one subject to the next, is absent from this poem, giving it more focus in its use of concrete visual imagery.

Why? The most obvious answer is that the horrors of war tend to cut through any desire to look at life with a broad, philosophical perspective. The time that Whitman may have once spent asking himself what it means to be an American poet was spent on more serious tasks, like caring for the suffering and burying the dead. The prospect of death, as one thinker pointed out, tends to focus one's attention quite quickly.

The problem with accepting this easy answer is that it erases some of the importance from Whitman's earlier works. If his poetry naturally distilled down to visual objectivity when he was faced with death, and if death is inevitable, then it would seem that his later, more succinct poems are more legitimate than its free-flowing predecessors. Works like "Crossing Brooklyn Ferry" are clearly no less important or true than "Cavalry Crossing a Ford," and it would be a gross exaggeration to say that war poetry in general is more important than poetry that examines society's day-to-day operations. The idea of Whitman "maturing" during the war has to be carefully defined. Maturation put him in a different state of mind, one that was better for writing about war-ravaged America, but this is not the same as saying that the tighter, objective form of poetry is better in all cases.

Aside from the obvious change in poetic style, "Cavalry Crossing a Ford" is not really that different from "Crossing Brooklyn Ferry." It is a natural successor. In the New York City poem, the poet saw an almost infinite variety of cultures and mannerisms, so different that he could only find two elements that these people had in common: they were American, and one person was seeing them. In the war poem, there is no speaker, and the participants' national identity is established with emphasis on the uniforms they wear and the flag they march under.

Barbara Marinacci, in her book *O Wondrous Singer!* tells the story of Whitman watching columns of troops returning from a maneuver in the dead of night while he was travelling with the Union army during the 1864 Wilderness Campaign. This event was not necessarily the inspiration of "Cavalry Crossing a Ford," but his description captured the sentiments that are implied in the poem. "It was a curious thing to see those shadowy columns moving through the night," Whitman wrote later. "I stood unobserv'd in the darkness and watch'd them long. The mud was very deep. The men had their usual burdens, overcoats, knapsacks, guns and blankets. Along and along they filed by me, with often a laugh, a song, a cheerful word, but I never before realized the majesty and reality of the American people *en masse*."

His goal, then, was the same with the short war poem as it was with the longer and looser works: to pin down the nature of the American character. A reader who was only familiar with "Crossing Brooklyn Ferry" might think that "the majesty and

> *The American poet Charles Simic has said that the image '[re-enacts] the act of attention.' . . . That is, by the time we've finished reading the poem for the first time, we understand that we have been looking at a scene, or at what we might call a verbal photograph."*

reality of the American people" was only to be found in their differences from one another, in the clamor of different styles bouncing off each other and assaulting the poet's senses. It would have been easy for Whitman to be narrow-minded, to define America only as the beauty of order or the beauty of chaos. "Crossing Brooklyn Ferry" and "Cavalry Crossing a Ford" are difficult to reconcile with each other only when Whitman is not given proper credit for the scope of his vision.

Source: David Kelly, Critical Essay on "Cavalry Crossing a Ford," in *Poetry for Students,* The Gale Group, 2001.

Adrian Blevins

Blevins, a poet and essayist who has taught at Hollins University, Sweet Briar College, and in the Virginia Community College System, is the author of The Man Who Went Out for Cigarettes, *a chapbook of poems, and has published poems, stories, and essays in many magazines, journals, and anthologies. In this essay, he investigates Whitman's use of image and how it serves "Cavalry Crossing a Ford," as well as certain sound repetitions within the poem and how they and Whitman's diction or word choice work to formalize Whitman's free verse and produce "an attitude of wonder and awe."*

Walt Whitman is among the greatest and most original of American poets. He is among the most daring of poets from any age or nation, has had as much influence in our tradition as Shakespeare, and in many ways single-handedly gave birth to the modern movement in American poetry. His most significant work is "Song of Myself," but, because of its length, "Song" is rarely given the time and attention it deserves; still, students interested in Whitman should take the energies and glories offered in his shorter poems as inspiration for further reading. Much of what can be found in "Cavalry Crossing a Ford," is, for example, in "Song of Myself," which many critics believe to be one of the best poems ever written, or in "Crossing Brooklyn Ferry," which has also been considered one of the most original and haunting of all American poems. Although there is virtually no limit to the criticism available on Whitman—the reviews started coming in when the first edition of *Leaves of Grass* came out—and little limit to the approach we might take in our investigation of "Cavalry Crossing a Ford," here we'll concentrate on two poetic devices central to this poem's effectiveness and beauty, since they are both representative of Whitman's technique in general and crucial to an understanding of how all good poetry works to move and transform us. These poetic devices are (1) Whitman's use of the image and how it serves "Cavalry Crossing a Ford," and (2) certain sound repetitions within the poem and how they and Whitman's diction, or word choice, work to formalize Whitman's free verse and produce what we can call here an attitude of wonder and awe.

As many poets and other writers and critics have said in many ways and places, we cannot feel what we cannot see. This kind of statement wishes to condemn abstractions, or words expressing ideas without a direct appeal to the senses; it's the kind of statement that encourages the use of images. But what do these poets and writers mean by "image"? And how do images produce feelings? What are the images in "Calvary" actually doing? How do they work? American poet and critic Robert Bly, in "Understanding the Image As a Form of Intelligence," has this to say about the image:

> In the image the human sees his relationship to some object or a landscape. The human intelligence joins itself to something not entirely human. The image always holds to the senses, to one of them at least, smell, taste, touch, hearing, seeing of color or shape or motion. Statements such as "The good of one is the good of all" abandon the senses almost successfully. The image by contrast keeps a way open to the old marshes, and the primitive hunter. The image moistens the poem, and darkens it, with certain energies that do not flow from a source in our personal life. Without the image the poem becomes dry, or stuck in one world.

The American poet Charles Simic has said that the image "[re-enacts] the act of attention." This is a particularly useful definition to apply to Whitman's poem, since the first thing noticeable about "Calvary" is that it does indeed re-enact the speaker's observation. That is, by the time we've finished reading the poem for the first time, we understand that we have been looking at a scene, or at what we might call a verbal photograph. This verbal photograph has been made with a series of images—the poem begins with an image of a long line of men winding "betwixt green islands" and ends with an image of "guidon flags flutter[ing] gayly in the wind." Between these two lines—these are the first and seventh lines of the poem—are five more images, each one serving the poem in a number of ways.

The first line describes the line of men, as we have just seen, while the second line deepens this image by comparing the line of men to a snake with the word "serpentine." That is, the first line locates the poem in a specific time and place by telling us what the speaker is observing, and the second line makes this image of the calvary crossing the ford more complex by comparing it to a natural, earthy, and deeply symbolic or archetypal object. The second line also appeals to our sense of sound by telling us that the men crossing the water are producing a "musical clank," thus deepening our understanding of the speaker's experience on a sonic level. The third line of the poem introduces both the river, which the poet tells us is silver, and the "splashing horses" that are "loitering" because they "stop to drink." The fourth line moves away from the river and the horses and asks us to focus on the men again: "Behold the brown-faced men, each group, each person a picture, the negligent rest on the saddles." The fifth line includes an image of some men emerging "on the opposite bank" and others "just entering the ford."

A turn comes in the poem's sixth line, when the speaker shows us, with the word "while," that all his lines until this point have been preparing us for his last two images, which move away from the men, the river, and the horses to concentrate wholly on the "scarlet and blue and snowy white" flags that "flutter gayly in the wind." That is, on even a syntactical level, the poem is essentially periodic, moving gradually by way of the vehicle of one single, complex sentence to the final independent clause where the weight of the poem finally stops to rest. Thus, a kind of miracle has happened—the poet has shown us many things happening at once in a very short poem—we get to see men on both sides of the river, learn that some are "brown-faced," and some are "negligent"; we see the river itself, and the horses drinking, and yet the weight of the speaker's observation rests, in the end, on the flags. While Whitman also appeals to the senses by describing the flags in detail, this final image is also a symbol: it can be said to represent the Union Army's goal for a unified America as well as the idea of war itself. Thus, while the poem works by way of a series of linked images without making too many judgments about the pictures it presents, it nevertheless does produce, or reveal, a kind of attitude. The glorious thing about the speaker's attitude toward the calvary, and therefore the war, in this poem is that it is not specific; it is only implied. Several things about the poem's diction or word choice can now lead us to think about that attitude, tone, or stance.

Let's look again at the poem's second line. As we have just seen, the poet continues with the description he began in the poem's first line by telling us that the men "take a serpentine course" and that "their arms flash in the sun." But there's a break or pause after "sun" in that line—both the dash and the word itself, which is "hark," mark this slight stopping point. Here the poet begins a direct address that he will reinforce twice. But it's a mysterious direct address: is the speaker of the poem addressing us or is he speaking to himself? Since the poem itself does not tell us who the poet is addressing, we must assume he is addressing both his readers and himself, and just the *potential* that he could be speaking more to himself than anyone else helps to produce a feeling of self-reflection in the poem—it helps gives the scene significance, since the poet seems to be urging himself not to forget this moment: "hark," the poet says, repeating, with the word-command "Behold," this imperative twice in the poem's third and fourth lines.

Whitman's wonder about the moment can be seen, as well, in his diction or word choice. Although he's describing a profound moment—a moment of vast historical, emotional, and psychological significance—he does not choose weighted or ominous words; on the contrary, he goes to great lengths to describe the scene in glowing terms—the river is "silvery," the horses are "splashing," the flag is both "scarlet and blue" and "snowy white," and—most significant of all—the "guidon," or soldier, "flags flutter gayly in the wind." Whitman's attitude toward the calvary is, thus, an attitude of wonder: he seems almost spellbound by the sight before his eyes.

As American critic Lawrence Buell says in his introduction to the Modern Library College Edition of *Leaves of Grass,* Walt Whitman "virtually invented free verse." Much has been written on Whitman's free verse and on free verse in general since *Leaves* was first published, and although Whitman's principles of construction are too complex to cover here, it seems important to point out that "free verse" cannot or should not be used to describe formless or shapeless poetry since form is central to everything from the pineapple to the human body. One of Whitman's controlling devices is a series of linked images. Whitman also uses sound to his advantage; he's nothing if not conscious of the music he makes.

The first line of the poem establishes an interest in both alliteration and assonance, or the repetition of consonant sounds in the first case and vowel sounds in the second. The line "A *li*ne in *lo*ng *a*rray where they wind betwixt green *isla*nds" rhymes the dental *l* sounds as well the long *i* and *a* sounds, and this helps hold the poem together; it helps to formalize it in much the way complete end rhymes would in a sonnet. Whitman continues with his interest in both alliteration and assonance throughout the entire poem: he rhymes sibilants with the s sound and ends the poem in strong gutturals that he establishes early in the poem with the phrase "hark to the musical clank" and later in the poem with the words "group" and "negligent." Look at that last line again: "The guidon flags flutter gayly in the wind." Part of the pleasure we feel in this line comes from how fully it ritualizes the poet's "act of attention." The music here helps to heighten the moment the poet is observing; it raises it from the mundane and everyday; it seers first in his memory and then in ours. It might also be worth noting that there's a beautiful tension established between the more musical lines and the less musical lines in this poem: a phrase like "Behold the silvery river" can be said to knock in a kind of tense juxtaposition against a less musical line like "others are just entering the ford": the less musical lines require less attention than the more musical lines and give us a moment's pause before we move on to the next set of sound patterns.

The tension between the poem's music and the poem's subject matter also reinforces both Whitman's attitude—which is one of wonder, as we have seen—and his daring; it is uncommon to address the subject of war in these shining and harmonious terms, and yet Whitman achieves a genuine sense of feeling for the soldiers and their circumstances and his own act of observation and attention. It's the music here that helps him do that. Part of his success is his willingness to behold, as he asks himself to do, the sight before his eyes. In *Twentieth Century Pleasures,* in an essay on images, the American poet and critic Robert Hass quotes "Calvary" in full, saying this about the poem:

> [The poem] may have taken hints from the new act of photography, or from romantic genre painting, or even from Homer. It is, in any case, phenomenal—a poem that does not comment on itself, interpret itself, draw a moral from itself. It simply presents and by presenting asserts the adequacy and completeness of our experience of the physical world.

It is well known that Walt Whitman found beauty in everything—in "The carpenter singing as he measures his plank or beam, / The mason singing as he makes ready for work, or leaves off work. / The delicious singing of the mother, or of the young wife at work, or of the girl sewing or washing." Thus it should come to no surprise to us that Whitman should find a kind of wonder in watching a cavalry crossing a ford. Yet the stance or attitude is still somehow mysterious, especially to those of us who have grown up necessarily cautious about the horrors of war. This mysterious stance is the very thing that lead the American poet Randall Jarrell to say of Whitman: "they might have put this on his tombstone: WALT WHITMAN: HE HAD HIS NERVE," or to compel D. H. Lawrence, the great English novelist, to remark that "Whitman has gone further, in actual living expression, than any man, it seems to me [he] has gone forward in life-knowledge. It is he who surmounts the grand climacteric of our civilization." Given the vigor of these proclamations, students would be remiss indeed not to give Walt Whitman their own best attentions.

Source: Adrian Blevins, Critical Essay on "Cavalry Crossing a Ford," in *Poetry for Students,* The Gale Group, 2001.

Erica Smith

Smith is a writer and editor. In the following essay, she examines how "Cavalry Crossing a Ford," although a description of healthy men preparing for battle, is a tender eulogy for many of these soldiers who are about to fall in battle.

Walt Whitman's poem "Cavalry Crossing a Ford" was originally published within the volume *Drum-Taps* (1865) and was later collected within a later edition of *Leaves of Grass.* First appearing in 1855 as a self-published volume of just ninety-five pages, *Leaves of Grass* contained what came to be Whitman's most famous poem, "Song of Myself." *Leaves of Grass* swelled over the years to become Whitman's opus, absorbing all of Whitman's writing, even the volumes that were originally issued separately (as were *Drum-Taps* and, later, *Passage to India,* 1871.

Whitman wrote, cut, and rewrote *Leaves of Grass* extensively through nine editions, the last edition issued in 1891–1892. The first edition is described by critic James Woodress as "the work of [a] somewhat brash, 36-year-old Brooklyn carpenter-poet." Employing a sweeping free verse, *Leaves of Grass* was a treatise from one with an unrestrained sense of self and an epic, mystic consciousness. Within his verse, Whitman described his own style and self as "crude." Yet he persisted in finding a kind of heroism in breaking barriers: "Unscrew the locks from the doors! / Unscrew the doors themselves from their jambs!"

Although Whitman's style was inarguably his own, Whitman drew from numerous influences. The essays of Ralph Waldo Emerson were a major influence on Whitman; Whitman once remarked, "I was simmering, simmering, simmering; Emerson brought me to a boil." In addition to Emerson, the influences on Whitman's free verse seem to have been music—opera in particular—and the Bible. Like these forms, Whitman's verse was grandiose, using techniques such as symbolism, repetition of words and themes, and parallel phrases. The resulting sounds and feelings in Whitman's poetry have a natural, organic feel and are very musical if read aloud. On these influences Padraic Colum of the *New Republic* writes:

> All is urge in his poetry. His rhythms flow and break like waves. His stanzas have not the measure that belongs to the poets of a world that is established poets like Dante and Spenser, for instance but the balances that are seen in nature one living member balancing another living member, as in a branching tree.

The world's response to *Leaves of Grass* was mixed. Some, like Ralph Waldo Emerson, lauded Whitman's mysticism and individualism. In response to the first edition of *Leaves of Grass* in 1855, Emerson wrote Whitman: "I find it the most extraordinary piece of wit and wisdom that America has yet contributed. . . . I greet you at the beginning of a great career." Yet Whitman's work was not universally welcomed. Victorian sensibilities scorned the sexual themes that characterize parts of *Leaves of Grass,* particularly the "Children of Adam" poems dealing with heterosexual love and the "Calamus" poems on homosexual feelings and relationships. Yet sexuality is but one aspect of Whitman's work. More important, over the years the poet's vision was maturing; the themes of love and death were filtered through experience and wisdom. The resulting later poems have an elegiac, and sometimes haunted, feel.

The Civil War in particular had an indelible effect on Whitman. Working as a volunteer nurse in Washington and visiting Virginia battlefields during the Civil War, Whitman was often a first-hand witness to the suffering that was occurring during wartime. His anguished letters of this period, recounting details about soldiers he tended, indicate that Whitman was suffering deeply as well. Out of this experience comes *Drum-Taps,* which critic Perry D. Westbrook calls "the best collection of war poetry produced by any American writer." Of this crucial volume, "Cavalry Crossing a Ford" is a poignant touchstone.

The poem describes a line of cavalry—troops on horseback—as it travels "betwixt green islands" within a river. It is the beginning of the Civil War, and the troops are heading toward a battlefield. However, rather than being foreboding, the scene that Whitman describes here is peaceful. The troops wind their way, their weapons glinting sunlight. The cavalry's weapons and saddlery knock together; "hark to the musical clank," Whitman bids the reader.

The river itself is hushed and silvery; the "splashing horses" halt a moment to drink the water. This image of nourishment, too, is tranquil; it is not at all indicative of the battle that is to come. Whitman speaks directly to the reader, inviting one to "behold" the sight of the horses; in the next line he again implores us, "Behold the brown-faced men, each group, each person a picture, the negligent rest on the saddles." The men are tanned and handsome, presumably healthy, resting easy in their saddles as their horses drink the water.

Whitman pulls the lens back a bit, far enough to get the overall picture of the line of cavalry stopped at the islands in the river. "Some emerge on the opposite bank, others are just entering the ford." The reader gets a sense of how long the line of cavalry really is; presumably the line will keep on filing through. Whitman's view then pulls even farther back, to a flag that is waving over the troops, "scarlet and blue and snowy white." The reader is reminded of the patriotic cause for which the men are traveling and will soon fight, leaving the reader with a feeling both poignant and unsettling.

Of Whitman's poetry Colum notes, "In Whitman's epic we do not find a people. He shows us America, but it is America in vista, and it is filled not with people, but with processions." Yet the poems that surround "Cavalry Crossing a Ford" within *Leaves of Grass* come closest to giving us the feeling of the worries and experiences of individual people. The preceding poem, "The Centenarian's Story," for example, tells a very different, individualized war story. In it, a survivor of the Revolutionary War details the Battle for Brooklyn. He describes how the British troops arrived by ship just before the Declaration of Independence was read by the commanding general, likely General George Washington.

The centenarian recounts how the British troops of 20,000 men, supported amply by artillery, disembarked and prepared for war. The centenarian tells in particular of one brigade of the youngest men that went forward to engage the redcoats and were cut off and slaughtered, pounded by artillery, and attacked mercilessly by superior forces, with few surviving. The rest of the army then retreated. Whitman then imagines that he himself was an observer of the scenes leading up to this battle. He writes of seeing an army advancing for battle and then the battle slowly but steadily being joined.

"Cavalry Crossing a Ford" is given an even deeper context when considered alongside the poems that succeed it, including "An Army Corps on the March," "Come up from the Fields Father," and "Vigil Strange I Kept on the Field One Night." Here, the images of death and loss come into sharp focus. In "Come up from the Fields Father," the reader witnesses a family receiving a letter about their soldier son. The family is terrified when they read that the son has been shot in a cavalry skirmish; the daughter tries to calm her mother, noting through her sobs that the letter says he will recover soon. Yet Whitman's voice informs us that the son is already dead, and his matter-of-fact tone carries a heavy burden of grief.

"Cavalry Crossing a Ford" and its companion poems show Whitman at a crucial moment as a poet. Eulogizing the fallen soldiers and his wartorn country and soon to eulogize the fallen president who was so beloved to him, Whitman issues these verses at the height of his empathy and insight.

Source: Erica Smith, Critical Essay on "Cavalry Crossing a Ford," in *Poetry for Students,* The Gale Group, 2001.

Sources

Bly, Robert, "Understanding the Image As a Form of Intelligence," *A Field Guide to Contemporary Poetry and Poet-*

ics, edited by Friebert, Walker, and Young, Oberlin College Press, 1997, pp. 101–09.

Brooks, Cleanth, and Robert Penn Warren, *Understanding Poetry,* 4th ed., Holt, Rinehart and Winston, 1976.

Buell, Lawrence, ed., Introduction to *Leaves of Grass and Selected Prose,* by Walt Whitman, Random House, 1981, pp. xix–xliv.

Colum, Padraic, in *New Republic,* June 14, 1919, pp. 213–15.

Davis, Kenneth C., *Don't Know Much About the Civil War,* William Morrow and Co., 1996, p. 152.

Hass, Robert, *Twentieth Century Pleasures,* Ecco Press, 1984, pp. 269–308.

Jarrell, Randall, "Some Lines from Whitman," in *Leaves of Grass,* by Walt Whitman, edited by Bradley and Blodgett, W. W. Norton & Company, 1973, pp. 882–88.

Lawrence, D. H., "Whitman," in *Leaves of Grass,* by Walt Whitman, edited by Bradley and Blodgett, W. W. Norton & Company, 1973, pp. 842–50.

Marinacci, Barbara, *O Wondrous Singer! An Introduction to Walt Whitman,* Dodd, Mead & Co., 1970, p. 228.

Simic, Charles, "Images and Images," in *A Field Guide to Contemporary Poetry and Poetics,* edited by Friebert, Walker, and Young, Oberlin College Press, 1997, pp. 95–7.

Updike, John, "Whitman's Egotheism," in *Hugging the Shores: Essays and Criticism,* reprinted by Vintage Books, 1984.

Westbrook, Perry D., "'Leaves of Grass': Overview," in *Reference Guide to American Literature,* 3d ed., St. James Press, 1994.

Whitman, Walt, "Crossing Brooklyn Ferry," in *The Portable Walt Whitman,* Viking Press, 1977, p. 150.

——, Preface to *Leaves of Grass,* in *The Portable Walt Whitman,* Viking Press, 1977, p. 8.

Woodress, James, "Walt Whitman: Overview," *Reference Guide to American Literature,* 3d ed., St. James Press, 1994.

For Further Study

Morris, Roy, Jr., *A Better Angel: Walt Whitman and the Civil War,* Oxford University Press, 2000.
   Morris examines the impact of the war on Whitman's life and poetry. He weaves biographical information in with Whitman's poetry to help students understand Whitman's work.

Paludan, Phillip Shaw, *"A People's Contest": The Union and Civil War, 1861–1865,* Harper & Row, 1988.
   Paludan explores the interrelationship between two of Whitman's frequent themes, war and work, as he views war through the lens of the other great event of the nineteenth century, the Industrial Revolution.

Reynolds, David S., *Walt Whitman's America: A Cultural Biography,* Alfred A. Knopf, 1995.
   This recent biography gives a good sense of the cultural background of Whitman's time, relating his life to the social events surrounding it.

Zweig, Paul, *Walt Whitman: The Making of a Poet,* Basic Books, Inc., 1988.
   This book is mostly concerned with Whitman's earlier life and might not be of much interest to students of his Civil War poetry. Still, students desiring a broader scope will want to see his style develop into what it came to be.

The Conquerors

Phyllis McGinley
1960

Phyllis McGinley's poem "The Conquerors," which was published in her Pulitzer Prize-winning collection *Times Three* in 1960, deals with a topic that she did not often write about. Known in her time as a suburban housewife poet and a writer of light verse, McGinley most often wrote about domestic topics, things that happened in the home, in the suburbs, things that happened, as she was to say, outside her window. The topic of "The Conquerors," however, influenced by the destruction caused by World War II, is the weapons that are employed in fighting and killing and massive and epic battles or wars.

McGinley, in the book *The Writer Observed,* describes the difference between her so-called light verse and the poems with more weighty material. In the book, she states that she has arrived at a distinction between the two: "the appeal of light verse is to the intellect and the appeal of serious verse is to the emotions." And so it is with this poem, "The Conquerors," that McGinley appeals more to the intellect than to the emotions when she asks readers to look at the absurdity of war. The main thrust of the poem is even more specific: she asks that Americans in particular, with their pride soaring over the creation of their newest weapon of destruction—the atom bomb—look within themselves to re-examine their conscience. In an attempt to bring the American consciousness out of its misguided use of scientific discovery and to inspire Americans to regain a sense of morality with regard to human life, she mocks those who might

Phyllis McGinley

boast of killing masses of people with one small bomb. Her poem reminds Americans, or anyone who reads it, that there is nothing to be proud of in any kind of war. She does this in a deceivingly light tone, however, almost to the point of making her readers laugh. But this does not diminish the message. It is just McGinley's way of delivering it.

Author Biography

Phyllis McGinley was a poet who, no matter what subject matter she focused on, would seldom, if ever, hear her poetry referred to as anything other than light verse. Born on March 21, 1905, in Ontario, Oregon, and writing her first poem at the age of six and then deciding to be a poet in college after winning several writing competitions, McGinley would spend most of her professional writing career fending off criticism that tended to diminish her image of a suburban housewife poet—an image that was meant to dismiss any depth in her writing.

The fact that McGinley at first enjoyed writing poetry that focused on somewhat lightweight subjects, such as the latest fads, popular news personalities, and trivial day-to-day facets of urban living, and then collecting these poems in her first book, *On the Contrary,* gave credence to her critics' rather dismissive evaluation of her creative work. Added to this is the fact that McGinley admits that she was persuaded to continue along these lines when the *New Yorker* offered her more money if she would forget more serious topics in order to write lighter verse. McGinley is quoted in a *Newsweek* article in 1960 as having said, "Women will usually write what people want them to."

Despite the tone of her critics, McGinley's poetry won her the 1960 Nobel Prize for poetry. The book that won her the prize was *Times Three,* in which her poem "The Conquerors" is the first poem in the collection. Ironically, McGinley would eventually wear her title of Housewife Poet proudly and go on to publish a collection of essays in *Sixpence in Her Shoe,* which praised domesticity. McGinley was encouraged by her publisher to write these essays as a kind of rebuttal to writers such as Betty Friedan, who had published her book, *The Feminine Mystique,* which warned women in the 1960s that they would never find fulfillment as housewives. Sales of McGinley's book slowly climbed to the bestsellers list and then stayed there for more than twenty-six weeks.

Besides writing poetry, McGinley taught school, wrote ad copy for an advertising firm, and was the editor of poetry at *Town and Country* magazine. She also wrote books for children, a play titled *Small Wonder,* and the narration for the film *The Emperor's Nightingale.* In a *Time* magazine article titled "The Telltale Hearth," McGinley has this to say to her critics who try to undermine her poetry: "At a time when poetry has become the property of the universities and not the common people, I have a vast number of people who have become my readers. I have kept the door open." To this she adds, "If people can't understand it why write it?" In a 1954 article in the *Saturday Review,* she summed up her writing as follows: "What I have been consciously trying to do recently . . . is to narrow the gulf between 'light' and 'serious' verse. One other thing: I always try to share with my readers the immediacy of my own delight or despair of the world as I see it through my window."

McGinley was married at age thirty-one to Bill (also referred to as Charles) Hayden, an executive at the Bell Telephone Company. She was a stay-at-home mother of two girls, Julie and Patsy. She died in New York City on February 22, 1978.

Poem Text

It seems vainglorious and proud
Of Atom-man to boast aloud
  His prowess homicidal
When one remembers how for years,
With their rude stones and humble spears,   5
Our sires, at wiping out their peers,
  Were almost never idle.

Despite his under-fissioned art
The Hittite made a splendid start
  Toward smiting lesser nations;   10
While Tamerlane, it's widely known,
Without a bomb to call his own
  Destroyed whole populations.

Nor did the ancient Persian need
Uranium to kill his Mede,   15
  The Viking earl, his foeman.
The Greeks got excellent results
With swords and engined catapults.
  A chariot served the Roman.

Mere cannon garnered quite a yield   20
On Waterloo's tempestuous field.
  At Hastings and at Flodden
Stout countrymen, with just a bow
And arrow, laid their thousands low.
  And Gettysburg was sodden.   25

Though doubtless now our shrewd machines
Can blow the world to smithereens
  More tidily and so on,
Let's give our ancestors their due.
Their ways were coarse, their weapons few. 30
But ah! how wondrously they slew
  With what they had to go on.

Poem Summary

Lines 1–7

In the first line, McGinley uses the word *vainglorious*, which means conceited or to believe that one is self-important. Her use of this word sets the tone of the entire poem, as she mocks any American who might have been feeling high and mighty with regard to the U.S. victory in World War II. It is easy to infer from the first three lines of this poem that McGinley intends to knock down a few pegs anyone who might feel proud about killing fellow human beings.

By the fourth line, the reader not only can infer what McGinley's intentions are but can deduce the manner in which she will reveal her intentions—tongue-in-cheek irony. To do this, she reaches back into history and brings forward to the reader the humble beginnings of war by mentioning the rudimentary weapons of cave men. In this way, she immediately dismisses the "prowess homicidal" of modern science, stating that killing was just as effective in ancient times when people used "rude stones and humble spears." In other words, killing is killing. When someone is dead, what does it matter how they were killed? From the very beginning of the poem, McGinley questions how Americans came up with the idea that they had something to be proud of in using modern technology to kill thousands of people.

Then as a final remark, McGinley adds that although America might boast that masses of people were killed by just one atomic bomb, our ancestors could also boast that they killed, in relative numbers, just as high a percentage of their population, even if it meant that to do this, they "were almost never idle."

Lines 8–13

In the next stanza, McGinley makes it a point to put a face on the ancient people, especially the warmongers among them. In this way, she adds personality and history to an abstract idea. By delving into these historic details, she can further assault the American false pride in its role as mass murderer and conqueror. The two names that McGinley mentions are the Hittites, an aggressive ancient group of people, and Tamerlane, a ruthless conqueror.

During the second millennium B.C., the Hittites were a group of people who, at various times, ruled parts of Syria, the city of Babylon, and central and eastern Anatolia (the peninsula that modern-day Turkey occupies today). As their kingdom advanced, the Hittites displaced the former occupants by initiating brutal wars. The hub of their kingdom was rich in iron deposits, which the Hittite people mined and used for weaponry. Their iron-working technology was a major resource in ushering in the Iron Age. In a confrontation over Syria, the Hittites and the Egyptians were responsible for what has been deemed one of the greatest battles of the ancient world.

Tamerlane, also known as Timur the Lame, was a conqueror in the fourteenth century, who is remembered for his barbarity. He conquered people and land that stretched from India and Russia to the Mediterranean Sea. For thirty years, he led his band of men and was considered the last of the mighty conquerors of Central Asia. His ruthless killing gave rise to many stories of his bloody conquests. He cultivated the military arts initiated by the infamous Genghis Khan. The only weapons that were available to him were arrows and spears, but this did not deter him. He was able to cut down unarmed peasants quite easily. His surprise attacks were notorious. McGinley does not go into all these details, however, because she is a writer of light verse. This means that her way of attacking, her weapon, is not as sharp as a spear. Her weapon is rather blunt, but it nonetheless hits its mark.

Lines 14–19

From the above stanza, McGinley moves into a broader description of history. She mentions the Medes, a group of people who lived in the vicinity of Iran, northern Assyria, and Armenia. The Medes first established an empire in that area; then, in 550 B.C., the Persians conquered the Medes. Although she does not mention it, the Medes were later conquered by the Greeks, the Romans, and so many other different people that they eventually completely lost their distinctive culture. McGinley's reference to uranium is, of course, a repeated reference to the fact that the Medes were conquered without the assistance of atomic weaponry. She also mentions the Vikings, but only in passing.

She continues, bringing up the Greeks who fought with "swords and engined catapults." Well, the swords speak for themselves. They were a minor improvement over spears and bows and arrows, but it wasn't until the "engined catapult" came onto the scene that battle weaponry took on a greatly increased capacity for power. The word *catapult* comes from the Greek and means "to pierce the shield." With the mechanized catapult, the first having been built around the middle of the third century B.C., a large stone or javelin could be hurled anywhere from four hundred to eight hundred yards. Not only did this add power to the weaponry, it also allowed the two warring parties to fight at a distance from one another. This was a precursor of the atom bomb, which could be dropped from an airplane at a distance of thousands of feet. One result of this invention was that the aggressor could kill his so-called enemy without ever humanizing his target. With McGinley's mention of the catapult, readers gain the sense that she is giving them a progressive report of the development of weaponry, which they can also foresee will end with the Americans and their bomb.

With the invention of the chariot, which McGinley mentions in line 19, the Romans added speed to their war tactics. With a horse pulling a two-wheeled version of the chariot, warfare was once again revolutionized. The armies that employed them found they had greatly extended their range with the unprecedented mobility that the chariots provided. Conquerors therefore could push their troops further, expand their territories, and, of course, kill more people. First McGinley mentions the improvement in weaponry; then she insinuates the progression of power and control over other people.

Lines 20–25

In this stanza, McGinley once again opens up to a broader scope. She now mentions only the names of great historic battles. She begins with Waterloo, Napoleon's final defeat, which ended twenty-three years of war between France and the rest of Europe; then she continues to the Battle of Hastings, which occurred in 1066 and was the cause of the defeat of Harold II of England and established the Norman rule there. She also refers to the battle of Flodden (1513), a war that decided English victory over Scotland. And with the battle of Gettysburg (1863), McGinley ends her inventory of wars but not before she describes this American conflict with the word *sodden,* by which, it must be assumed, she means to convey an image of the field being soaked, not so much from rain as from blood. The battle of Gettysburg caused some of the Civil War's greatest losses—more than forty thousand men died during this battle. It is also interesting to note that, at the close of her progression of battles, McGinley ends on American soil, taking the reader back to the place where the poem started.

Lines 26–32

In the last stanza, McGinley most actively displays her mockery of war as well as her mockery of the pride of the "Atom-man" in her first stanza. To mock American pride in their development of the atomic bomb, she praises the ancestors for figuring out how to kill so many people with such primitive tools of war.

Her use of the word "machines" is fascinating, though. Since she began the poem referring to bombs, one would think that she would end with that term, but a bomb isn't really a machine. Did she use the word "machines" to find a match for "smithereens"? Or is she referring to the airplanes that were used to drop the bombs? Her choice of the phrase "more tidily" in line 28 seems to imply the airplanes. What is tidy about war and killing? The tidiness must be referring to the distance from which the airplane drops the bomb, how it allows those who drop it to get "tidily" out of its way without feeling any physical effect. She could also be referring to the fact that this distance allows a tidier psychological or emotional effect. Though the bomb causes destruction that affects thousands of people in its immediate area, which is a great expanse in itself, and though it can also cause damage to unborn generations as the radiation embeds itself into the land, the water, and the human cells, those people who drop the bomb never see the results of the destruction they have caused. From the distance that they drop it, it is even hard to imagine the destruction, unless they take the time to return to the scene, but that would probably not occur until several years later. They might see photographs. They might even visit some of the victims. But they will never see the blood. They will never hear the cries. And, therefore, they may never acknowledge their part in the destruction.

Themes

Technology and Progress

Throughout the lines of this poem, McGinley weaves a historic perspective to show the progress of technology in war weaponry. She does this, always in a tongue-in-cheek manner, to point out that there have been, over the millennia, a progression that has gone awry. She does this in two different ways. First, she demonstrates that although there has been progress in the development of more intricate, more specialized, and more complex weaponry, it always ends up that the weapons do the same thing, kill. They don't necessarily kill better, because how does one do that? Then she subtly asks if the progress is in the numbers. But then, so what if the numbers have increased. What does that mean? And is that to be considered progress?

Second, the underlying message in the poem is whether this progress is a misuse of knowledge or maybe the even greater question, Is it really progress at all? Is there something inherent in mankind that makes people need to conquer another group of people? Does invention have to focus on weaponry? Would mankind have progressed further or faster if people had not used the knowledge of metal refining to make weapons? What if atomic energy had had a focus devoid of its destructive power? Would mankind know things today that may have been lost because of the distractive nature of aggression (or so-called defense) pulling some of the greatest inventive minds into a military way of thinking rather than working on solving other, peaceful problems?

Strength and Weakness

Most apparent in this poem is the theme of conquest. Promoted throughout history (and biology, too) is the concept of the survival of the fittest. The strong shall prevail over the weak. The people with the most advanced weaponry will become the victors. Conquerors are hailed as great heroes. The vanquished are plundered to the point that they not only lose their material possessions, they lose their cultural identity. McGinley questions all these assumptions in her poem. By bringing into her poem the names of huge, ancient cultures that one by one conquered one another in their desire to control the world, to gain majesty, and to make a place for themselves in history, she makes the reader look down that road and question popular assumptions about war that might not be true. Such assumptions might include fighting for the sake of peacekeeping; fighting for the sake of democracy or some other philosophical ideal; fighting for some god, etc. In the process, she also makes Americans look at themselves in relation to historical figures. If the mass murderers of the past appear barbarous, what does that say about current world situations in which the United States claims victory with an atomic bomb? If Tamerlane was considered a brute with his spears and bows and arrows, what will historians think of the effects of radiation when used to conquer a nation?

Pride

McGinley begins her poem with the line: "It seems vainglorious and proud," emphasizing her contempt for those who would not only claim credit for murdering people but would garnish their acts with a sense of pride. The difference between aggression and defense is a fine line. It is a line that nations have dealt with all through history. When does the defense of a nation turn into an aggressive act? If an aggressor attacks, they who defend their families and loved ones deserve to be called heroes. They deserve to be proud of their courage. But war is not so cut and dry. Do conquerors know when to stop defending? They tend to become involved in retaliation, revenge, and then total obliteration. Greed and the thirst of power can also seep into the picture. Is this something to be proud of? McGinley asks.

Another aspect of McGinley's questions about pride might refer to the type of weaponry used in war, whether on the part of the aggressor or de-

Topics for Further Study

- Compare and contrast Tamerlane, the Mongol conqueror mentioned in McGinley's poem, to Hitler. Map out the areas of their conquests. Describe their tactics and their goals. What were the long-lasting effects of their assaults on other nations?

- Collect war photographs from WWII and Vietnam and give a talk on the human factors behind the military actions. Focus on the atrocities of war on one side and the benefits, if any, on the other.

- Write a rap poem (song) in the same meter and rhyming pattern as "The Conquerors." As your focus, use either the U.S. war on drugs or the war on poverty.

- Look at the economic factors behind WWII. Explain why and how WWII helped the United States out of the Great Depression.

- Write a history of the bomb from its first use to modern developments of missiles and nuclear bombs.

---

fender. Two people fighting face to face, hand to hand, in a struggle to defend what they believe is right, might be called courageous. But when a nation uses weapons of mass destruction, killing not only those who might be considered aggressors but also innocent children, mothers pregnant with the next generation, old people who have retired from the world, are these acts to be proud of?

As the number of deaths increase from cave man type hand-and-rock battles to modern techniques that are capable of wiping out whole cities in a matter of minutes, war moves into a realm of absurdity. Therefore "Atom-man" in this poem has no reason to "boast aloud" of his prowess of killing. So what if he can wipe out the world? What does that mean? Is that something to boast about or something to be ashamed of? McGinley mocks this pride by ending her poem with praise for primitive man whose "ways were coarse, their weapons few." She is, of course, not praising murder of any kind.

Rather she is exposing all murder for what it is. Killing is killing. Nothing to ever be proud of.

Style

Meter

McGinley uses an iambic meter in her poem. Iambic meter is the most common metric measure in English poetry. It consists of one unstressed syllable followed by one stressed syllable. For example, in the first line of her poem, the pattern would be broken down like this: "It seems vain-glor-i-ous and proud" with the words *it* and *vain* unstressed; and the words *seems* and the syllable *glor-* stressed; the syllable *i-* (in the middle of the word glorious) is unstressed, while the last syllable in this word *-ous* is stressed; and ending with the word *and* being unstressed and the word *proud* being stressed. This produces a somewhat singsong effect, almost like a child's nursery rhyme, but it also makes the poem very easy to read. The meter is very similar to the natural meter of conversational speech.

The poem is built on tetrameters and trimeters. This means that there are some lines that consist of four feet and some that have three feet. Feet, in poetic terms, contain two syllables each. McGinley's pattern for this poem is as follows: the first stanza is made up of two tetrameters lines, followed by one trimeter line, which in turn is followed by three tetrameter lines, followed by a final trimeter line. This pattern occurs in the first stanza and then again in the last stanza. The middle stanzas consistently follow another slightly different pattern: two tetrameter lines followed by one trimeter line, and then this is repeated. This pattern is so consistent that it draws the reader's attention to the first and last stanzas, each having an extra line. She could have done this to draw attention to the words or images portrayed in the first and last stanzas, or she might have liked the form that gives a little more weight to the beginning, where she sets up the mood of the poem, and the end, where she throws her witty punch.

Rhyme

McGinley is all about simplicity, with her rhyming scheme following suit. She uses a very regular and reliable rhyming pattern that creates a soothing rhythm. The pattern is: *aab cccb* for the first and last stanzas and *aab ccb* for all the stanzas in between. McGinley also makes a very strong point of using alternating masculine and feminine rhyming patterns. She claims, in her essay "The

Light Side of the Moon," that she employs this technique because it is "a favorite device of mine to create music and avoid monotony."

A masculine rhyme occurs on the last syllable of a word. For example, the first two lines of the poem end with the words *proud* and *aloud*. The fourth, fifth, and sixth lines end with *years, spears,* and *peers*. These are all examples of masculine rhyme. However, in the same stanza, lines three and seven end in feminine rhyme with the words *homicidal* and *never idle*. A feminine rhyme occurs when the rhyme falls on a syllable that is followed by an unaccented syllable. By ending every third line (a pattern that is thrown a little off kilter in the first and last stanza) with a feminine rhyme, McGinley not only creates a sense of music and avoids monotony, but she also creates a release, or pause, in the momentum of the poem. The line with the feminine rhyme, by definition, ends in an unstressed syllable, generating an excuse to stop and take a quick breath, much like the use of a comma in a sentence.

Style

McGinley states in a *Newsweek* article that she is "moving toward something a little different—poetry of wit, which is what the Cavalier poets used to write." This is a style that prevails in most of McGinley's works, with "The Conquerors" being no exception. The Cavalier poets were a group of English poets (Robert Herrick and Richard Lovelace were two of them) who wrote not only with wit but with simplicity. Their themes included topics such as love and loyalty, and they spoke with a very direct voice. Their poetry, like McGinley's, was considered elegant but light. "Light verse," McGinley explains, "demands brilliance of execution. The surface must be as glittering as the content; in some cases it *is* the content." In essence, what McGinley is saying is that her style is witty in the simplest and most comprehensive way that she can make it. The form of the poem is not only simple, it is also ingenious, as it adds to the poem almost as much as the content. McGinley does not believe in using an esoteric vocabulary. Her purpose is not to show off her education. The simple style that she employs reflects the way she looks at life—in a disciplined, well-planned out, witty but down-to-earth manner. Her poem "The Conquerors" is a prime example of that simplistic and Cavalier style. It is composed of simple words, rhymes, beats, and patterns. Although its topic is not simple, it is packaged in a very simple form. And it is because of its simple style that its message cannot help but reach its target. There are no complications to stop it.

Historical Context

War

McGinley alludes to no less than twelve wars in her poem. Although she mentions them almost lightly, she assumes that readers will inherently understand that she does not mean to take the topic of war in anything less than a serious tone. For she and the rest of the world, when this poem was written, were still feeling the aftershocks of one of the worst of all wars, World War II. On August 6 and 9, 1945, the cities of Hiroshima and Nagasaki were destroyed by the first atomic bombs used in warfare, which led to the end of the war and established the United States as one of the most powerful nations in the modern world. One of the aftermaths of World War II was the Cold War, which was at its height when McGinley wrote her poem. The world's two strongest powers, the USSR and the United States, aimed military weaponry at one another, and peace in the world balanced precariously on the threats these two countries thrust at one another. Each country knew that if one discharged one bomb on the other, it could ultimately mean the end of the world. In other words, war weaponry had advanced to the point where it was capable of total annihilation of human life on this planet.

During this time of the Cold War, many people began building bomb shelters in an attempt to protect themselves from an atomic bomb blast. Some families dug huge holes in their backyards and reinforced them with concrete to make an underground shelter. Then they stocked the shelter with a year's worth of food, believing that they could hide in their shelter and ride out the radiation that would infiltrate every living thing on the surface of the earth if war ensued.

This was also a time of bomb raid practices. Sirens would wail, and citizens would run for the nearest bomb shelter that was marked with a black and yellow sign. School children would duck under their desks. It was a time of simple beliefs, but also it was a time of great fear. The depths and complexities of nuclear warfare were not fully understood. The effects of radiation were just beginning to be realized.

Compare & Contrast

- **1940s:** War production during World War II brings women out of the home and into the factories. War production also brings the U.S. economy out of the Great Depression.

  1960s: The Vietnam War brings students out of the classroom to protest the draft, the war, and the deaths of thousands of their peers.

  1990s: The Gulf War causes very little reaction in the United States.

- **1940s:** The great weapon of mass destruction during World War II is the atomic bomb. Thousands of people are killed in Hiroshima and Nagasaki, and even more suffer from the effects of radiation.

  1960s: Agent Orange is used in Vietnam to defoliate the tropical jungles. Soldiers who are inadvertently sprayed with Agent Orange suffer from many physical ailments including sterility and possibly cancer.

  1990s: Biological warfare is feared during the Gulf War, and so the U.S. troops are inoculated with anthrax vaccines, which may have, ironically, contributed to what is referred to as the Gulf War Syndrome.

- **1940s:** Hitler is the main figure of World War II, the man the Allies come together to conquer.

  1960s: Ho Chi Minh is the ruler of North Vietnam, the ruler the U.S. troops attempt to defeat.

  1990s: Saddam Hussein is the aggressor in the Gulf War when he tries to take over the country of Kuwait. U.S. troops eventually defeat Hussein's armies.

- **1940s:** Literature that defines this decade includes Norman Mailer's *The Naked and the Dead,* William Saroyan's *The Human Comedy,* and Shirley Jackson's short story "The Lottery."

  1960s: Some of the most popular literature includes Harper Lee's *To Kill a Mockingbird,* the poetry of Maya Angelou and Sylvia Plath, and a children's book by Maurice Sendak called *Where the Wild Things Are.*

  1990s: Popular fiction includes many of Stephen King's books, several books by Danielle Steele and John Grisham, as well as *Sex* by Madonna, *Women Who Run with the Wolves* by Clarissa Pinkola Estes, and *Men Are from Mars, Women Are from Venus* by John Gray.

- **1940s:** American women are encouraged to leave the kitchen to fill factory positions that are vacated by men joining the armed forces.

  1960s: American women are encouraged to leave their homes, march in the streets in support of feminism, and otherwise reject the male-dominated rules of the society in which they live.

  1990s: More and more young women enter college and earn business masters degrees, then head for lucrative jobs in large corporations with realistic goals of one day becoming CEOs.

Feminism

McGinley was among a small group of women who were graduating from college in the thirties. In that sense, she was ahead of her times. But if she thought of herself as a feminist, it was a feminist with a very different definition of what women needed, what rights they should fight for. McGinley, although she held several different jobs, was a stay-at-home mom, and she not only enjoyed her domesticity, she thrived in it and glorified it in her poetry. When Betty Friedan published her book, *The Feminine Mystique,* stating that women needed to get out of the home, needed to be liberated from domesticity because they would never find fulfillment if they remained housewives, McGinley decided to fight back. She wrote a book, *Sixpence in Her Shoe,* in which she praised the housewife, stating, according to an article in a 1965 edition of *Time* that "even today's educated woman can fit happily into the framework of the home." Women at that time were just on the cusp of renewed interest in women's rights. Friedan's book might have ignited a revolution, but nonetheless McGinley's book also became a bestseller.

Anti-Communism

The 1950s, the decade in which this poem was written, was famous for its anti-communism sentiments in the United States. The Cold War, with the USSR representing the powerful communist nation, was at its height, giving America, representing the most powerful democracy, something to butt up against. And butt up against it, it did. McCarthyism was prevalent in this decade. McCarthyism is the practice of publicizing accusations of political disloyalty without sufficient evidence. It is named for Senator Joseph McCarthy, who was the leading voice in the televised hearings into alleged communist activity in the U.S. Army, the entertainment industry, and anywhere that rumors of potential allegiance to a communist philosophy might appear.

The 1950s is also the era that marked the establishment of the John Birch Society, a right-wing, anti-communist organization whose objectives were ridding the United States of all communists, repealing all social-security legislation and the graduated income tax, as well as impeaching certain government officials. Through the efforts of both Joseph McCarthy and the John Birch Society, many people lost their jobs, were persecuted as dissidents, or were made to feel paranoid about speaking against their government.

Television

Mass communications via television was born in the fifties. During this decade, more and more families were sitting around the television set at night, watching Edward R. Murrow deliver a new style of news broadcasting that was more familiar and personal than radio news and watching some of the first sitcoms, which portrayed very simplistic and yet very rigid family roles. The world that television portrayed was an ideal one: everyone belonged to the middle class; no one ever went hungry; people seldom disagreed. Television promoted the illusion that life was simple, and people out in the real world started to believe it and found themselves trying to fit the mold.

Critical Overview

In 1954, Phyllis McGinley found an image of herself on the cover of the *Saturday Review*. In 1965, she found a picture of herself on the cover of *Time* magazine. This in itself demonstrates the significance and popularity of her poetry. In 1954, the *Saturday Review* praised her collection of poetry contained in her newest publication, at that time, *The Love Letters of Phyllis McGinley*. The article inside this magazine begins with the phrase, "The news today is that Phyllis McGinley has done it again." The message in the article is that McGinley is a proliferate writer of light verse.

No matter how she is praised, or in which publication she is praised, McGinley's name is always associated with light verse. Some critics wonder why more light verse is not written. As Gerard Previn Meyer puts it in the *Saturday Review* article, "why is there not more light verse written today, verse that offers no bewildering (if sometimes fascinating) symbols dredged up from the unconscious, verse that, to the contrary, is the product of conscious art?" Not since the writing of Dorothy Parker, on the feminine side, and Ogden Nash, on the masculine, has there been a writer who is so at ease at creating light verse as McGinley is, say most of her critics.

In the article from *Time* magazine, McGinley is called "one of the most widely read and acclaimed poets in the U.S." This article praises McGinley not so much for the depth or art of her poetry but for her popular appeal. She is, according to this article, the "sturdiest exponent of the glory of housewifery, standing almost alone against a rising chorus of voices summoning women away from the hearth." In other words, in her day and time, McGinley's works were seen as the antithesis of the second wave of feminism that was just beginning to show signs of birth. This article concludes by generalizing all McGinley's poetry by stating that she has an "awesome capacity for self expression."

For criticism aimed at more specific works, there is an article in a 1960 issue of *Newsweek* that declares that because of McGinley's book, *Times Three*, in which her poem "The Conquerors" appears, her publisher must love her. But the article does not mention any specific qualities of the book, except for the fact that this book will probably make money because the Book-of-the-Month Club chose it as an alternative. W. H. Auden, however, digs deeper into the poems collected in McGinley's Pulitzer Prize-winning book. Auden compares her to Jane Austen, Colette, and Virginia Woolf, for her sensibility and imagination. He also states that her writing is very feminine, without being a "ferocious feminist." Auden then goes on to describe the difference between feminine and masculine imaginations, declaring finally that when she is "confronted with things and people who do not please her, she does not, like many male satirists, lose her temper or even show shocked surprise; she merely observes what is the case with deadly accuracy." But Auden concedes that McGinley has her fair share of masculine imagination, too, as shown in her "dexterity in rhyming." Ignoring what might today be considered sexist definitions in Auden's praise of McGinley's writing, his sentiments ring true: overall he believes that her poetry is worth reading.

Bette Richart in a 1960 article published in *Commonweal* magazine says that "certainly it is true that she is, within her tradition, an important poet, and she writes as wisely and sadly of youth and old age as anyone since Cicero, perhaps." Richart then goes on to critique light verse in general, of which she admits McGinley is one of its high practitioners, "Amusing though it is, light verse is effectively didactic, and its lessons are tolerance, self-sacrifice, and joy" in the little things of life. But Richart also states that sometimes McGinley sounds too complacent. "To glorify the commonplace is one thing . . . but to glorify the merely common is another."

A 1960 issue of the *Saturday Review* begins with great praise for McGinley's *Times Three*. It will "give Miss McGinley's expanding public an orderly cut-back inspection of the three-stage rocket which has carried an explicit poet beyond the force-field of light verse and put her into orbit." This article was written after McGinley won the Pulitzer Prize for poetry as well as during the crest of excitement about the U.S. space program, obviously. The article continues by stating that even though McGinley wrote in a field occupied by the great poetic minds of Ogden Nash and Morris Bishop, "she had her own voice to express her gaiety and wit." In direct reference to "The Fifties" chapter of *Times Three,* David McCord, the author of this magazine article, describes McGinley's satire as sharp. McCord also applauds her for "her eloquent moments, her compassion, her intuition, her ability to pare the world's wormy apple with a razor blade."

Criticism

Joyce Hart

Hart, a former college professor, is a freelance writer and copyeditor. In this essay, she examines possible reasons why McGinley's poetry is considered light verse even when the subject of her poetry is very serious, such as in the case of the poem "The Conquerors."

Although she may not have been either the first nor the last person to define her writing as light poetry, McGinley was, nonetheless, among those who agreed with this tag, although she did have some reservations. In her essay, "The Light Side of the Moon," she writes that "conscious techniques . . . are important to poetry and particularly vital to that narrow branch of the profession in which I specialize. I write what is called Light Verse (as opposed, perhaps, to Ponderous Verse)." McGinley is making three points with this statement. She is acknowledging that her poetry has been relegated by her critics to a somewhat offstage position in relation to the whole realm of poetics. Her poetry has and probably always will be referred to as "light." Next, she is making it known that even though her poetry is referred to in these terms, this does not mean that writing light verse is something that can be done without effort. In other words, poetry does not come forth from some magical place of pure inspiration, whether it is considered light verse or not. Writing poetry is deliberate work in all its forms. And finally, McGinley is saying, in her usual tongue-in-cheek manner, that even though her poetry might always be tagged with this "light" label, it does not mean that her poetry does not inspire thought.

So questions that these comments might summon up could be such as these: Why is McGinley's poetry considered light verse? Why is light verse generally considered to have little meaning? And when McGinley writes about topics as serious as war, death, and mass destruction, as in her poem "The Conquerors," how does she pull this off and still give the impression that her topic is not ponderous? How does she convey her meaning?

According to several definitions of light verse, McGinley's poem fits into the category very easily, at least in some aspects. First, her poem displays technical competence. "The Conquerors" is written in a very consciously laid out meter and includes a very carefully chosen rhyming pattern. The meter and rhyming scheme in this poem are so perfect, as a matter of fact, that they could almost be considered monotonous. The poem has a cadence that people could march to. War protesters could shout these lyrics as they paraded down Pennsylvania Avenue in front of the White House.

McGinley's choice of words in this poem demonstrates a technical grasp of vocabulary that is so competent that she can portray a powerful image in a very simple and straightforward manner. There is little if any need for most elementary school children to have to consult a dictionary to understand this poem. The historic allusions aside, the only words a fifth grade student might not know the meaning for are "vainglorious," "smiting," "garnered," and "smithereens." But these words may be somewhat unfamiliar, not because they belong to some esoteric vocabulary but because the words, themselves, are dated. They just aren't used anymore on television or in the world of an eleven-year-old child. Not only are the words in this poem easy to understand, the images that are cast through these words are right out of the movies. Once the allusions to the battles are recognized, the epic battle scenes become very familiar. They've been recreated so many times that who among McGinley's readers, or for that matter among some fifth grade class, could say that they could not imagine them?

Wit is another element that is often mentioned in reference to light verse, and McGinley definitely demonstrates her wittiness in this poem. She does this in several ways. Her rhymes are witty, for one. For example, the way she rhymes "homicidal" with "never idle" is not only a clever use of words, but it also reinforces the satire of her poem by linking these two concepts together. Satire is another element of some light verse. It is a way of highlighting human shortcomings by ridiculing them; and by linking "homicidal" with "never idle," McGinley is pretending to praise the ancestors because they were both busy and competent in their killing of one another. By setting up this image, not only is she mocking the ancestors, but she is also mocking modern warmongers as well. How can you be so proud of your homicidal prowess, she asks the omnipotent Atom-man, when long ago, long before bombs and modern weaponry were produced, people killed one another with stones? How ridiculous to be proud of some creation that does no more than a stone did. Of course, behind these words, McGinley is criticizing anyone who is proud of killing, no matter what their reasons and no matter what their weapons.

But light verse is also defined as having a trivial or playful subject. Another attribute is that light poetry has as a motive to entertain or amuse. Another is that it often involves nonsensical terms or words. "The Conquerors" has none of these elements. And yet McGinley's poem does flirt with some of these issues. Because of the meter, or rather because of the readers' association of the meter to light verse, the voice skips along the words almost happily, almost as if the poem were a limerick. An-

> *McGinley's choice of words in this poem demonstrates a technical grasp of vocabulary that is so competent that she can portray a powerful image in a very simple and straightforward manner. There is little if any need for most elementary school children to have to consult a dictionary to understand this poem."*

other factor of association is that many children are raised on this singsong tone in nursery rhymes, so the pattern feels light.

Although the subject in "The Conquerors" is serious, the tone of the poem is light enough to trick the reader into thinking that the motive is to amuse. By writing, in line 9, that "The Hittite made a splendid start," McGinley's tone sounds playful. The phrase "splendid start" conjures up memories of Mary Poppins praising her wards for having cleaned up their room or taken their medicine. This could also apply to her phrase in line 17, "excellent results," as well as in line 20, "garnered quite a yield." That Mary Poppins kind of voice also appears in the last stanza, where McGinley writes, "Let's give our ancestors their due," and "But ah! how wondrously they slew." These two lines are peppy, as if a cheerleader were sending a loud message to people in the stands watching a football game.

Since, typically, light verse was written to amuse, it was assumed that there was very little meaning above and beyond the immediate. Light verse was like a comedy or a modern sitcom. It was meant to entertain. It was narrative, a short story. It was often sung. And its topics included love, food, and social custom. Lewis Carroll's "Hunting of the Snark" and Alexander Pope's "Rape of the Lock" are often referred to as typical examples. Although this does not seem to fit McGinley's poem,

What Do I Read Next?

- *Portable Dorothy Parker,* edited by Brendan Gill and published in 1991, is an extensive collection of Parker's poetry. Parker, like McGinley, was a popular writer, known for her light verse. McGinley is often compared to Parker.

- Ogden Nash is also often compared to McGinley. His *Selected Poetry of Ogden Nash: 650 Rhymes, Verses, Lyrics and Poems* (1995) is a wide collection of his works, which are generally very humorous, a little lighter than McGinley's verses.

- In the vein of light verse, Lewis Carroll's *The Hunting of the Snark,* which was originally published in 1876, is a classic. This nonsense poem, republished in a paperback edition in 1998, involves a long sea voyage in search of the undefined snark. Critics have claimed that it had political overtones, like much of Carroll's other writings.

- McGinley wrote her book *Sixpence in Her Shoe* in 1964 after her editors suggested that she give another point of view of the modern woman in her time, contrasting her lifestyle to the budding feminist movement. The book is divided into three sections and covers such topics as higher education for women, children's literature, and keeping up with the Joneses. Although the writing might be a little outdated, her strong feelings about the joys of housewifery make for interesting reading even for modern women.

- The book that spurred the new wave of feminism, as well as McGinley's writing of her book *Sixpence in Her Shoe,* was Betty Friedan's *The Feminine Mystique* (1963). Friedan's well-researched book brought to the forefront some of the underlying elements that were making some women in the 1960s restless. Having been told for years that the woman's place was in the home, Friedan challenged this assumption, and a revolution in women's thinking began.

- Not for the faint-of-heart, Masuji Ibuse's historical novel *Black Rain* tells the horrific story of people who suffered through the atomic blast of the bomb dropped on Hiroshima. Ibuse is a powerful writer who follows the development and hardships of one Japanese family in a heart-wrenching telling of what it was like to witness the shock waves, blasts, and radiation of the bomb. This book puts readers into the middle of the destruction so that they can witness for themselves the horrific power of this historic event.

---

there is one more aspect of light verse that does define "The Conquerors" perfectly. Light verse was often irreverent but moral, its use of irony made in an attempt to bring about social change.

Although McGinley's poem is about war and mass destruction, there is no reference or mention of blood. There is no reference to pain. There is only a hint of a reference to an individual. Most of her images are big, impersonal, and somewhat vague. They are so vague at times that readers almost forget that she is talking about death and torture, and yet, at the same time, she does deliver her message. How does she do this?

McGinley writes that "light verse aims at the intellect which it wishes to amuse and divert." And then she adds that "lightness, in the meaning of shedding light, may be an adequate apology for our profession." So McGinley has turned the definition, the tag that has followed all her poetry, into something that she can better deal with. If her verse is called light, then she will make her poetry like a beam of light, a beam of intelligence. But it will not be a beam that pierces; it will be one that deflects, casts shadows; it will be a playful light, even though the subject matter is deadly.

McGinley mentions no blood or pain because that is not the picture she wants to portray. Well, it is the picture she wants because she has alluded to it, but it is a picture that has been drawn in outline only. So she will use phrases like "wiping out their peers" in line 6, instead of saying they stabbed their peers in the heart and left them, bleeding, as vultures circled overhead. She writes that the Hittites in line 9 move "toward smiting lesser nations" rather than writing that they raped and pillaged villagers, murdered children, and tortured men. And then later she writes that Tamerlane "destroyed whole populations." This statement is read with about the same emotional impact of someone stepping on a mound of ants. The picture is so broad that it is too big to have feelings about.

So McGinley's meaning is definitely directed at the intellect. First, the poem will require the intellect to figure out what her historical allusions are. She trusts that anyone who is interested will look up all the gory details if that is what they want. She has made so many allusions to so many massive battles that if readers looked up only one and followed it to its conclusion, there would be enough blood and gore in it to turn anyone's stomach. She has merely pointed the way. But she doesn't stop there. It is not her intention merely to remind readers of past wars. No, she wants to do much more than that. She wants to bring about change. She wants to see improvement. And she points this out, in an ironic way, which is also typical of light verse.

Throughout the poem, McGinley mentions many improvements in weaponry. She begins with rocks and stones, progresses through spears and bow and arrow; she jumps to chariots and cannons and ends with the atomic bomb. Now if that isn't progress, what is? But what does she do with this progression? She turns it on its head. She begins her poem with the "Atom-man" and ends her poem with "our shrewd machines," referring back to the atom bomb, but she doesn't leave it there, instead, she ends her poem by praising, once again, the ancestors with their rocks and stones. We have progressed so far, she is saying, that we have learned to split the atom. But what are we using this knowledge for? How are we improving civilization with this discovery? Just exactly what have we conquered? And, finally, she is asking, Have we really progressed at all, if all we have learned is to kill?

McGinley may be a comic at heart, but her poem has a message. She may deliver her message with a soft touch, but that does not mean that the sentiments behind her poem will not be felt. She is clever and has chosen the words of this poem very carefully. She is simple, but war is not. There have been many war protesters, many messages delivered to try to stop them. McGinley has just tried a different approach. By using a veil of nursery-rhyme meters and limerick-like rhymes, she tricks her readers into listening to a brutal message. Once again, like Mary Poppins, McGinley offers a little sugar along with her medicine.

Source: Joyce Hart, Critical Essay on "The Conquerors," in *Poetry for Students,* The Gale Group, 2001.

Newsweek

In the following review-interview, McGinley discusses her publishing success.

In her gracious living room in suburban Larchmont, N.Y., Phyllis McGinley, seated on a Louis XV sofa, a bowl of roses lighting up the coffee table in front of her, fingered a copy of her latest collection of verse, *Times Three.* "I think it's a lovely book," she said. "I mean the way it's designed. It *looks* very good. I just love my publisher."

Miss McGinley's publisher loves her, too: The collection before this one, *The Love Letters of Phyllis McGinley,* has sold an astounding (for poetry) 40,000 copies since it first appeared six years ago, and *Times Three,* covering three decades, has just been chosen as an alternate by the Book-of-the-Month Club for November.

"I think it's a very hopeful thing," said Miss McGinley, "not for me but for all poets. At least the public is being reminded what a stanza looks like on a page. And I've been building up," she said, "trying to get better. At first, back in the '30s, I was writing real light verse. I mean *really* light verse. That was when Dorothy Parker and Samuel Hoffenstein were in their heyday. But I've been moving toward something a little different—poetry of wit, which is what the Cavalier poets used to write. It wasn't until Wordsworth that there was this great dividing line between 'serious' poetry and 'light verse'."

A frequent and long-standing contributor to *The New Yorker*, she has also served on the advisory board of *The American Scholar*, and thus has a kind of official license to be considered a "serious" person. "I'm so sick of this 'Phyllis McGinley, suburban housewife and mother of two . . .'" she said. "That's all true, but it's accidental. I write about the village here, and the family, but that's only an eighth or a tenth of my work. The rest is different. There's a hell of a lot of straight social criticism."

Born 55 years ago in Oregon, raised in Colorado, and schooled in Utah, Miss McGinley came to New York and wrote "Swinburnian" poetry, then shifted into her lighter mood when a contract she

> "The usual ingredients are wit, humor, point, poise, malice, surprise, the exquisitely exact word and, if the writer has it, wisdom. Perhaps the last is the special McGinley gift. She is abidingly aware of the divine in people and things."

made with *The New Yorker* provided for higher rates per line for lighter verse. ("Women will usually write what people want them to," she said. "Women are more amenable than men.") She is married to a New York Telephone Co. executive, Charles Hayden. Her time, most recently, has been devoted to her next book, in prose, *Saint-Watching,* and the reading of history.

Miss McGinley looked across the room at a rose-marble mantel that had been bought out of Mark Twain's house on West 10th Street in New York, and suddenly spoke of her love for her art: "I've always read poetry. I read it for enjoyment, for delight, pleasure, passion, to get drunk on . . . People have been reading and enjoying poetry for thousands of years, and I just don't believe that in the past 30 or 40 years anything has changed. I don't see how it could."

Source: Newsweek, "The Lady in Larchmont," in *Newsweek,* Vol. 56, No. 13, September 26, 1960, pp. 120–21.

Louis F. Doyle

In the following essay, Doyle surveys McGinley's poetry, asserting "she is abidingly aware of the divine in people and things."

In the house of poetry there are many mansions, most of them now vacant and dark, abandoned to the spider and the bat. The traveler passing that way shouts "Is there anybody there?" but there is no answer from the illustrious ghosts of Homer and Sophocles, Dante and Virgil, Shakespeare and Dryden and Pope, who had so many luminous things to say about the universe and man and so little to say about themselves. Evidently they felt that in discussing man they had revealed everything worth revealing about themselves. They had not heard about the Ego and the Id. Consequently, their remains are now revisited only by those literary paleontologists, candidates for higher degrees, who bring with them a whole set of new tools made available by Freud and Adler and Jung. Then there are "re-evaluations" that confirm Freud and Adler and Jung.

If one says "poetry" today without further specification, he will be understood as referring to the only still-functioning branch of poetry, the lyric. Lyric poetry, as a freshman might say, is when the writer talks about himself. It is the kind of poetry about which Aristotle had nothing to say in his unfinished *Poetics.* That omission has, however, not deterred the modern critic from applying the epic and dramatic criteria of Aristotle to lyric poetry and, when they do not fit, proving once more that the Master could be wrong.

Generally speaking, the new poetry has discarded the poetic tradition in so far as that is humanly possible. From the magic casements through which his great predecessors sought truth, the modern has turned to the wells of his own subconscious in the conviction that an inventory of its contents is of supreme interest to the waiting world. In only one green plot is traditional verse still cultivated by such practitioners as Ogden Nash, Margaret Fishback, Ethel Jacobson and others. It is the field variously known as "society verse" or "smart verse" or "light verse."

The latest comer to this field is Phyllis McGinley, and it begins to look as if, Scripture-wise, the last shall be first. For it is no derogation from the brilliant talents of her competitors to say that there is a high distinction in her work that places it in a special category. Light verse is delicate and deceptive art, of course. It looks so easy at a first encounter, as if tossed off in a fine careless rapture and never touched again. All inspiration, no perspiration. The usual ingredients are wit, humor, point, poise, malice, surprise, the exquisitely exact word and, if the writer has it, wisdom. Perhaps the last is the special McGinley gift. She is abidingly aware of the divine in people and things. At least half of all true wisdom is charity, and light verse writers, as a class, are not overly stocked with charity. A wise thing said lightly wakes few echoes, whereas the banal and the obvious spoken ponderously may go booming down the corridors of time to achieve immortality.

It is not that Miss McGinley is without likes and dislikes, loves and hates, but she writes like one who has mastered both. The fool, the bore and the charlatan get short shrift at her hands, but the punishment meted out to them is somewhat like the cuffs of a mother bear, at least half love. She suffers the fool, if not gladly, at least in the spirit of a common humanity: Christ died for all. "The Old Reformer" reads

> Few friends he had that pleased his mind.
> His marriage failed when it began,
> Who worked unceasing for mankind
> But loathed his fellow man.

Who has not known the lofty soul who would die for Man but wanted nothing to do with his next door neighbor? Who could not name a half dozen specimens of "The Old Politician" who clings to the stage too long and "becomes a Public Monument through sheer longevity"? Or of "The Old Philanthropist" who gives away millions but starves his typist? There is hardly one of these four-line portraits that does not call up some present prominent public figure, all of whom shall be nameless here, needless to say.

Her gift for humanizing holy persons without flippancy or irreverence is without equal, so far as I know. Saints in the flesh can be such problems and trials to those about them that it would be hard to say which is the saintlier. St. Bridget, who conducted the first "giveaway" bankrupted her family, then borrowed from her relatives to set up a sort of one-woman Marshall plan. Miss McGinley is puzzled as to just why Simeon Stylites remained on that pillar of his—"and so was the good Lord, rather." If Simeon was seeking publicity, he got it. "The Thunderer," St. Jerome, "God's angry man . . . The great name-caller, Who cared not a dime For the laws of libel And in his spare time Translated the Bible" leaves the saint's halo at a rakish angle, but he is every inch a saint. Six of these poems on the saints first appeared in the July 10 issue of *America*.

The natural enemies of the poets of clarity are, of course, the poets of obscurity—or, should I say, the poets of the indirect approach? T. S. Eliot will live long before he is more expertly dissected than he is in "Mrs. Sweeney among the Allegories." This burlesque is replete with the quiet desperation of a sorely tried soul who waits all evening for a glimmer of sense in "The Confidential Clerk" and goes away empty. The hungry sheep looks up and is not fed, but the hungry sheep has his revenge.

"The Jaundiced Viewer" poems will not endear Miss McGinley to the purveyors of television fare but they may afford a vicarious relief to some of the inarticulate watchers of the youngest of the arts. The current avalanche of family reminiscences was, I believe, precipitated when Clarence Day wrote *Life with Father*. Since that fatal hour, we have been besieged with "I remember" books that record the most incredible collection of charming, eccentric, crotchety and dispensable characters that ever converged in one spot in literature outside of Dickens. It is Oh to be an orphan! Miss McGinley's reaction to one of these is

> The humor of family sagas is far from Shavian—
> Including the Scandinavian.

However, she disdains to advert to the familiar saga of the Idiot Husband, the Precocious Child and the Knowing Wife, which is, as all Europeans know, the authentic American family and the firm base of our national greatness. Perhaps it would have been too much like shooting a sitting duck. But her roving eye sought and found the indubitably central symbol of all small-screen art in America's most prideful product, Teeth! In "Reflections Dental"

> How pure, how beautiful, how fine
> Do teeth on television shine!
> No flutist flutes, no dancer twirls,
> But comes equipped with matching pearls.
> Gleeful announcers all are born
> With sets like rows of hybrid corn.
> Clowns, critics, clergy, commentators,
> Ventriloquists and roller skaters,
> M. C.'s who beat their palms together,
> The girl who diagrams the weather,
> The crooner crooning for his supper—
> All flash white treasures, lower and upper,
> With miles of smiles the airways teem,
> And each an orthodontist's dream.

How beautiful are our teeth upon the mountain—of luscious, denatured food!

The service the light verse writer renders in a democracy—and he cannot function elsewhere—is unique and indispensable. There are abuses and excesses that are not amenable to law and unregardful of good taste, good manners or reason so long as fame and money are in prospect. Time enough for good taste and good manners when the barbarian is firmly established, respectable enough to afford those luxuries. It is here that the well-aimed shaft of barbed laughter can sometimes penetrate the hide of the pachyderm on the make and give him pause for a moment. The silvery laughter of the Comic Muse is not always drowned out by the din and uproar of the supercolossal pitchmen.

The peculiar debt that Anglo-American civilization owes to the Celt is the corrective that the latter has administered to the absurdities of that civilization. Call the roll of them: Swift, Steele, Goldsmith, Sheridan, Wilde, Shaw. Swift, lethal as a black widow spider, probably roused more wrath than laughter. But the rest were more kindly and urbane. When Tony Lumpkin says, "I 'ates anything *low*," he speaks for a whole world of men who had looked into the glass and then gone away and forgotten what manner of men they were. The Tonies are likely to judge of a man's gentility by which finger, the forefinger or the little finger, he elevates when quaffing his liquor. If he elevates neither, he is plainly a peasant. When Wilde described a foxhunt as "the unspeakable in hot pursuit of the uneatable," he pinpointed the dead center of a whole culture. When Sheridan, looking about him on English society, selected the characters he was to M. C. in *The Rivals* and *The School for Scandal,* he was quite Celtic in his selections. And the first sound sense ever written about the true difference between the Irishman and the Englishman is Shaw's *John Bull's Other Island.*

Contrary to the popular notion, it is the unhappy Celt who is the realist and the bumbling Englishman who is content within the cocoon of his ideals and illusions. The Celt reverences God, but he is apt to play hob with household gods, popular fetishes and Pollyanna cant. When it rains in his world, it is not raining violets. That is why non-Celts are likely to find him insufferable and invite him out for a nice drink of hemlock. Incidentally, it was Peter Finley Dunne's "Mr. Dooley" who first perceived and highlighted the comic-opera aspects of the Spanish-American War when the rest of our journalists were still chanting a tribal epic about our purity of motive and prowess in war. He was also the first to turn a satirical eye on the role of the Supreme Court in politics. Those were the easy-going days before incense and anger filled the land.

Miss McGinley is in the Celtic tradition, whatever her lineage may be. The things of God she handles reverently, but the things that are Caesar's do not overly impress her. Yet there is a certain ruefulness in her humor that is reminiscent, somehow, of the old story of the two Irish farmers who waited, armed with shotguns, beside the path down which their landlord was accustomed to take his evening stroll. When midnight came and he did not, one asked the other: "What do ye make of it?" The other replied: "Well, I dinnaw. But I hope nawthin' serious has happened to the poor man." Unlike Dorothy Parker, Miss McGinley is not a killer. Mercy seasons her justice.

She can be quite serious on occasion in the workaday sense of that word, as in "Sunday Psalm." Once in an age there does come a flawless day, when all creation is as and where it should be, baptismal, pentecostal, a blessed pause in the onrush of time reminiscent of Eden, and sometimes the perfect day is, appropriately, a Sunday.

This is the day which the Lord hath made,
Shining like Eden absolved of sin,
Three parts glitter to one part shade:
Let us be glad and rejoice therein.
Tonight—tomorrow—the leaf will fade,
The waters tarnish, the dark begin.
But *this is the day the Lord hath made:*
Let us be glad and rejoice therein.

Sharply contrasted with "Sunday Psalm" is "The Day after Sunday."

Always on Monday, God's in the morning papers,
    His Name is a headline, His works are
    rumored abroad.
Having been praised by men who are movers and
    shapers.
From prominent Sunday pulpits, Newsworthy is
    God.

An unkind cut but not wholly uncalled for. During the war, when the fate of the world hung in the jittery balance, we were edified from time to time by the report that some top statesman had accorded an honorable mention to God. It was a pleasant shock. But for the most part, the place assigned to God in our press is Monday's religious page. There is a place for everything and that is the place for Him, we have determined.

The blandest heresy that has come out of the war of the sects is that reverence for God consists, not in the proper and timely use of His Name, but in utter silence on the Subject in public life. On second thought, however, the silence is not quite utter: whenever some little man wants to emphasize and underline one of his weightier statements, he reaches out for the biggest word in his limited vocabulary, and, of course, it is always the Holy Name. It would almost seem that, banished by the Pharisees, He must still consort with publicans and sinners.

It is possible to quote rather freely from *The Love Songs of Phyllis McGinley* because the book's copyright notice contains no minatory clause about "no part of this book may be used" and so on. Apparently, Miss McGinley does not consider her pearls of such great price as all that.

Source: Louis F. Doyle, "The Poems of Phyllis McGinley," in *America,* Vol. 92, No. 12, December 18, 1954, pp. 320–22.

Sources

Auden, W. H., "Foreword," in *Times Three,* Viking Press, 1960, pp. ix–xv.

Breit, Harvey, "Phyllis McGinley," in *The Writer Observed,* The World Publishing Company, 1956, pp. 211–13.

Kalb, Bernard, "The Author," in *Saturday Review,* September 18, 1954, p. 11.

"Life with a Poet: The Lady in Larchmont," in *Newsweek,* September 26, 1960, pp. 120–21.

McCord, David, "She Speaks a Language of Delight," in *Saturday Review,* December 10, 1960, p. 32.

McGinley, Phyllis, "The Light Side of the Moon," in *American Scholar,* Vol. 43, Autumn 1965, pp. 555–68.

———, *Times Three,* Viking, 1960.

Meyer, Gerard Previn, "Urbane Suburbanite," in *Saturday Review,* September 18, 1954, pp. 11–2.

Richart, Bette, "The Light Touch," in *Commonweal,* December 9, 1960, pp. 277–79.

"The Telltale Hearth," in *Time,* June 18, 1965, pp. 74–8.

For Further Study

Doyle, Louis F., "The Poems of Phyllis McGinley," in *America,* December 18, 1954, pp. 320–22.

Doyle discusses some of McGinley's poetry in terms of poetic tradition, light verse, and McGinley's gift of "humanizing holy persons," as well as her ability to present everyday things without glorifying them.

Gibson, Walker, "Gardens, Bees, A & P's," in *New York Times Book Review,* October 2, 1960.

One of McGinley's poems is cited in this article, as well as a discussion of some of her other poems, including McGinley's Pulitzer Prize-winning collection *Times Three.*

Grunwald, Beverly, "But Housework Can Be Fun," in *New York Times Book Review,* Vol. LXIX, No. 39, September 27, 1964.

Grunwald refers to McGinley's book *Sixpence in Her Shoe* that she wrote somewhat in answer to the feminist movement, but this article focuses primarily on McGinley herself, her decision to be a stay-at-home mom, and what that means to her.

Hersey, John, *Hiroshima,* Vintage, 1989.

Hersey recorded stories of victims of the atomic bomb not long after the bomb was dropped on Hiroshima, Japan, in 1945. Later, he collected these stories and published them in this book. The stories tell about the physical, psychological, and material destruction of the Japanese people.

Roleff, Tamara L., ed., *The Atom Bomb,* Turning Points in World History, Greenhaven Press, 2000.

This book provides a comprehensive history of the development of the atomic bomb, as well as a series of arguments for and against the dropping of the bomb on Japan.

Wagner, Linda Welshimer, *Phyllis McGinley,* Twayne, 1971.

A detailed account of McGinley's writings, this is the only book that is completely devoted to McGinley. Wagner has written a series of books on writers, McGinley being one of her lesser known subjects.

Darwin in 1881

Gjertrud Schnackenberg
1982

Gjertrud Schnackenberg published "Darwin in 1881" in her first collection of poems, *Portraits and Elegies,* in 1982. This book—sometimes referred to as a "chapbook" because of its short length—is divided into three sections, and "Darwin in 1881" makes up the entire second section. All three parts relate in one way or another to history, the first consisting of a series of elegies to her father, the third tracing the history of a Massachusetts farmhouse nearly two hundred years old, and the middle depicting the life of Charles Darwin one year before his death. This latter poem is layered with two primary allusions. A subtle reference compares Darwin's life to the poet's father's life, but the more obvious allusion is to Shakespeare's character Prospero from *The Tempest,* whom Schnackenberg also compares to Darwin.

To the poet, all three men—her father, Darwin, and Prospero—accomplished great things in their lives and had settled into times of quiet reflection before their deaths. In the poem, there is no description of the father's final days, but Schnackenberg relies heavily on an examination of Darwin's famous voyage to the Galápagos Islands, his controversial theory of evolution and natural selection, and his years, after the journey, at home in England. By blending in references to Prospero, who lives on an island for many years before returning to his native Milan, Italy, Schnackenberg presents a cohesive, poetic study, full of rich imagery, that points out the importance of history, science, and family in making sense of human life.

The characters here have all done remarkable things with their intellectual powers, and each has reached a point of saying farewell to his ambitious life in favor of a more solemn meditation on what the accomplishments have meant.

Author Biography

Gjertrud Schnackenberg was born on August 27, 1953, in Tacoma, Washington. Her family was of Norwegian descent and Lutheran religious faith. Walter Schnackenberg, her father, was a professor of Russian and medieval history at Pacific Lutheran University, and his early death in 1973 had a profound and lasting impact on his twenty-year-old daughter. As a youngster, Schnackenberg shared a close, warm relationship with her father, and he had a greater influence on her than anyone else in her life. They enjoyed night-fishing and other outdoor activities together, as well as quiet times of reading and study. The older Schnackenberg was a highly intellectual man, who passed on his love of history to his daughter. At nineteen, as a student at Mount Holyoke College, she began to write poetry, and her father's death the following year would become the subject of her first collection, *Portraits and Elegies,* in which "Darwin in 1881" first appeared.

Schanckenberg's talent as a poet was immediately recognized by her instructors and other members of the poetry community. She won the distinguished Glascock Award for poetry in both 1973 and 1974 and graduated summa cum laude from Mount Holyoke in 1975. Four years later, she received a Radcliffe College fellowship, and in 1983 she lived in Italy on an American Academy-Institute of Arts and Letters Rome fellowship. With the publication of her first collection in 1982, Schnackenberg earned her place among the best young writers on the American scene at the time. In spite of the many accolades, however, her work still reflected the deep feeling of loss that she felt over her father's death. *Portraits and Elegies* and her subsequent publications include direct responses to her sadness in the form of elegies to her father as well as more subtle allusions, or references, using history as the dominant subject—history, of course, being the former professor's field of teaching. In October 1987, Schnackenberg married Robert Nozick, a philosophy professor at Harvard, and the two make their home in Boston.

Poem Text

Sleepless as Prospero back in his bedroom
In Milan, with all his miracles
Reduced to sailors' tales,
He sits up in the dark. The islands loom.
His seasickness upwells,   5
Silence creeps by in memory as it crept
By him on water, while the sailors slept,
From broken eggs and vacant tortoise shells.
His voyage around the cape of middle age
Comes, with a feat of sight, to a close,   10
The same way Prospero's
Ended before he left the stage
To be led home across the blue-white sea,
When he had spoken of the clouds and globe,
Breaking his wand, and taking off his robe: 15
Knowledge increases unreality.

He quickly dresses.
Form wavers like his shadow on the stair
As he descends, in need of air
To cure his dizziness,   20
Down past the shipsunk emptiness
Of grownup children's rooms and hallways where
The family portraits blindly stare,
All haunted by each other's likenesses.

Outside, the orchard and a piece of moon   25
Are islands, he an island as he walks,
Brushing against weed stalks.
By hook and plume
The seeds gathering on his trouser legs
Are archipelagoes, like nests he sees   30
Shadowed in branching, ramifying trees,
Each with unique expressions in its eggs.
Different islands conjure
Different beings; different beings call
From different isles. And after all   35
His scrutiny of Nature
All he can see
Is how it will grow small, fade, disappear,
A coastline fading from a traveler
Aboard a survey ship. Slowly,   40
As coasts depart,
Nature had left behind a naturalist
Bound for a place where species don't exist,
Where no emergence has a counterpart.

He's heard from friends   45
About the other night, the banquet hall
Ringing with bravos—like a curtain call,
He thinks, when the performance ends,
Failing to summon from the wings
An actor who had lost his taste for verse,   50
Having beheld, in larger theaters,
Much greater banquet-vanishings
Without the quaint device and thunderclap
Required in Act 3.
He wrote, Let your indulgence set me free,   55
To the Academy, and took a nap
Beneath a London Daily tent,
Then puttered on his hothouse walk

Watching his orchids beautifully stalk
Their unreturning paths, where each descendant 60
Is the last—
Their inner staircases
Haunted by vanished insect faces
So tiny, so intolerably vast.
And, while they gave his proxy the award, 65
He dined in Downe and stayed up rather late
For backgammon with his beloved mate
Who reads his books and is, quite frankly, bored.

Now, done with beetle jaws and beaks of gulls
And bivalve hinges, now, utterly done, 70
One miracle remains, and only one.
An ocean swell of sickness rushes, pulls,
He leans against the fence
And lights a cigarette and deeply draws,
Done with fixed laws, 75
Done with experiments
Within his greenhouse heaven where
His offspring, Frank, for half the afternoon
Played, like an awkward angel, his bassoon
Into the humid air 80
So he could tell
If sound would make a Venus's-Flytrap close.
And, done for good with scientific prose,
That raging hell
Of tortured grammars writhing on their stakes, 85

He'd turned to his memoirs, chuckling to write
About his boyhood in an upright
Home: a boy preferring gartersnakes
To schoolwork, a lazy, strutting liar
Who quite provoked her aggravated look, 90
Shushed in the drawingroom behind her book,
His bossy sister itching with desire
To tattletale—yes, that was good.
But even then, much like the conjurer
Grown cranky with impatience to abjure 95
All his gigantic works and livelihood
In order to immerse
Himself in tales where he could be the man
In Once upon a time there was a man,

He'd quite by chance beheld the universe: 100
A disregarded game of chess
Between two love-dazed heirs
Who fiddle with the tiny pairs
Of statues in their hands, while numberless
Abstract unseen 105
Combinings on the silent board remain
Unplayed forever when they leave the game
To turn, themselves, into a king and queen.
Now, like the coming day,
Inhaled smoke illuminates his nerves. 110
He turns, taking the sandwalk as it curves
Back to the yard, the house, the entrance way
Where, not to waken her,

He softly shuts the door,
And leans against it for a spell before 115
He climbs the stairs, holding the banister,
Up to their room: there

Emma sleeps, moored
In illusion, blown past the storm he conjured
With his book, into a harbor 120
Where it all comes clear,
Where island beings leap from shape to shape
As to escape
Their terrifying turns to disappear.
He lies down on the quilt, 125
He lies down like a fabulous-headed
Fossil in a vanished riverbed,
In ocean-drifts, in canyon floors, in silt,
In lime, in deepening blue ice,
In cliffs obscured as clouds gather and float; 130
He lies down in his boots and overcoat,
And shuts his eyes.

Poem Summary

Lines 1–3

The opening lines of "Darwin in 1881" introduce the comparison between Darwin and Prospero, using the word "as" to indicate a likeness. In *The Tempest,* Shakespeare's last play, Prospero, the Duke of Milan, is overthrown by his brother, Antonio, and then put to sea with his young daughter to perish. As it turns out, however, Prospero and the child are shipwrecked on an island where magic and sorcery are commonplace thanks to lively spirits such as the friendly Ariel and the mischievous Caliban. Prospero acquires magical powers by donning a magician's robe and carrying a wand, and he performs many tricks over the twelve years that he and his daughter live on the island. Among Prospero's feats is his conjuring, through Ariel, a terrific storm, or tempest, bringing a ship carrying Antonio and a party of others from Milan crashing into the island. Through various magic tricks, Prospero and his spirits frighten the stranded newcomers, but the magicians eventually reveal who it is behind the sorcery. When Antonio realizes his brother and niece are still alive, he repents his act of usurping Prospero's throne and begs his brother to forgive him. Believing Antonio is sincere, Prospero makes peace with him, and all the human inhabitants of the island agree to return home where Prospero will take his rightful place as Duke of Milan. With Ariel's magical provision of friendly sea breezes, the party sails safely home on a rebuilt ship.

The references to "his bedroom" and "his miracles" in lines 1 and 2 refer to Prospero, who has given up his magical powers to live a sedate life in Italy. His miraculous adventures and accomplishments are now only a legend of "sailors' tales."

Lines 4–8

The "He" in line 4 refers to Darwin. The islands that "loom" in his mind are those he visited on his five-year expedition, beginning in 1831, as a naturalist (now more commonly called a botanist or zoologist) aboard the *H. M. S. Beagle*. Most likely, the islands are the Galápagos group where he made his greatest discoveries of the many varieties of plant and animal species. This voyage was a miserable one for Darwin, physically. He spent many seasick days in turbulent waters and reportedly contracted a tropical disease after being bitten by an insect. Whether or not that was the cause of his ailment, it is true that Darwin spent the rest of his life battling chronic stomach pains and nausea. Lines 6 and 7 contain the first direct allusion to lines from *The Tempest*. In act 1, scene 2, it is music, not "memory," that creeps by as Ferdinand describes Ariel's song: "This music crept by me upon the waters." The "broken eggs" and "vacant tortoiseshells" refer to fossils that Darwin found on his trip.

Lines 9–16

The actual cape that Darwin voyaged around was Cape Horn at the southern tip of South America. The poem, however, speaks of a time when Darwin has already rounded "the cape of middle age" and is well into his declining years. As the journey of his life comes to a close, he experiences a "feat of insight," meaning he has accomplished a true understanding of something. That something is revealed in line 16, which states that he now realizes that "Knowledge increases unreality." This statement implies that sometimes people can learn so much and be so highly intelligent that they lose touch with the real world. Before that revelation, however, Schnackenberg makes another comparison to Prospero whose own voyage "Ended before he left the stage," referring to his relinquishment of the magical powers that his robe and wand afforded him. The Duke's speech concerning "the clouds and globe" comes from act 4, scene 1, in which he states, "the great globe itself, / Yea, all which inherit it, shall dissolve / And . . . leave not a rack [wispy cloud] behind." Also, compare line 15 to Prospero's statement in Act 5, Scene 1, in which he says, "I'll break my staff, / Bury it certain fathoms in the earth."

Lines 17–24

Darwin's continuing illness often left him with insomnia as well as nausea. This second stanza depicts a sleepless night when he must go outside for

Media Adaptations

- There are many versions of Shakespeare's *The Tempest* on VCR tapes. Readings are also available on cassette, but with its superabundance of visual effects, hearing the play cannot really compare to seeing it.

some fresh air to "cure his dizziness." All his children have left home, and he likens their vacant rooms to "shipsunk emptiness." Lines 18 ("Form wavers like his shadow") and 24 ("All haunted by each other's likenesses") are references to Darwin's work with evolutionary theory and his study of why species are alike in some ways and different in others.

Lines 25–35

These lines rely on simile—a comparison of two dissimilar objects—and further allusion to Darwin's journey to various islands. On this sleepless night, he is so alone that the orchard, the moon, and even he himself seem like separate islands. The seeds that stick to his pant legs are "archipelagoes," or groups of islands, and the trees he observes are "ramifying," meaning their branches divide into new branches the way species divide and form new species in evolution. The nests he sees within the branches hold eggs "with unique expressions," just as plants and animals have developed unique looks and abilities over thousands of years. Lines 34 and 35 refer directly to Darwin's amazing discovery in the Galápagos that giant tortoises who roamed the islands were so distinct in their development that the human inhabitants could tell at a glance from which island one of the animals came.

Lines 36–44

The second half of this stanza again refers to Darwin's advancing age and an acceptance that his life is drawing to a close. Although he does not know that he will die the following year, he feels that after all the time he has spent studying nature, it is time to accept that dying is like watching nature "grow small, fade, disappear." This feeling is comparable to a traveler on a ship watching a coastline become fainter as the vessel moves farther out to sea. Upon his death, nature—the thing studied—will leave the one who studied it behind. Lines 43 and 44 imply that in the afterlife, there are no separate species and no need for something new to emerge, for there is no "counterpart."

Lines 45–54

Darwin did not become a recluse after his return from the expedition, but he did spend most of his time at home continuing his studies and developing his theory of natural selection. In spite of the controversy caused by the publication of *On the Origin of Species by Means of Natural Selection* in 1859, Darwin was highly praised by most fellow naturalists. These lines refer to an apparent award ceremony that Darwin declined to attend but that he heard a report on from friends. Schnackenberg compares Darwin to an actor playing Prospero, who refuses to return to the stage for his curtain call, regardless of the "bravos" from the audience. There is weariness in Darwin and the actor implied in this description, both tired of the spotlight and the command to perform. Lines 52–54 refer to act 3, scene 3, of *The Tempest* in which Prospero has conjured up a trick banquet for unsuspecting guests only to have the feast disappear before their eyes when they try to eat. On stage, there is the sound of thunder and the flash of lightning as Ariel appears in the form of a harpy, "claps his wings upon the table; and, with a quaint device, the banquet vanishes."

Lines 55–64

This section begins with another direct allusion to Prospero. The final two lines of *The Tempest*, spoken by the Duke of Milan in the epilogue, are "As you from crimes would pardon'd be / Let your indulgence set me free." Prospero is tired of performing magic tricks to entertain the audience, and so he asks them to release him from the obligation. In "Darwin in 1881," the tired naturalist sends a note to the "Academy" (the Royal Society for the Improving of Natural Knowledge) imparting the same sentiment—he is no longer interested in the public attention and accolades for his work. After a nap with a newspaper folded over his face, Darwin meanders by his greenhouse where he considers the evolutionary paths of orchids and how the insects that feed on them may be physically tiny but their numbers and their ability to survive are incredibly large.

Lines 65–68

The final four lines of this stanza reiterate Darwin's sedentary, domestic retirement. He prefers letting someone else accept the Academy's award for him while he spends a quiet evening at home ("Downe," in Kent, England) having dinner and playing backgammon with his wife. The wife, a reportedly very religious woman, is not impressed with her husband's theories of evolution.

Lines 69–71

These lines reflect some of the objects that Darwin had observed over the years to help him learn about the development of animal species—insect jaws, bird beaks, and the hinged shells of bivalve mollusks such as clams and oysters. The key word here is "done," mentioned twice in these lines to emphasize the end of the most spectacular part of Darwin's life. But still "One miracle remains," and it is not revealed until line 86 when it turns out to be the writing of his memoirs.

Lines 72–85

The scene here returns to Darwin's nighttime walk through his gardens while his stomach illness still swells up like seasickness. As he leans on a fence smoking a cigarette, he reminisces about one of his sons playing a bassoon in the greenhouse to see if sound can affect the movement of a plant. Darwin had ten children, seven of whom survived into adulthood. When they all lived at home in Downe, Darwin let his sons and daughters act as young research assistants, including the greenhouse scene portrayed here. Francis (Frank) Darwin would become a scientist as well, and in 1880 his father published *The Power of Movement in Plants*. These lines also use the word "done" three more times, reiterating Darwin's relinquishment of "fixed laws," "experiments," and "scientific prose," the latter of which he likens to a kind of hell where many scientific theories have been condemned by those who think them evil or sacrilegious.

Lines 86–93

These lines reveal the "miracle" that Darwin wants to accomplish before his death. He wants to write down the stories of his boyhood, a feat he has not yet attempted considering the years he has spent composing scientific theory. His mother died when he was eight years old, and he was brought up by a sister who tried to guide him in the direction of serious study in an "upright / Home." Although he attempted both medicine and theology, he did not feel inclined to become either a doctor or a minister. Instead, to the chagrin of his sister, he preferred studying snakes and bugs. This memory is a delightful one for the aging naturalist.

Lines 94–99

These lines allude again to Prospero, "the conjurer / Grown cranky with impatience" to give up his magical powers and live simply and serenely like a man in a "Once upon a time fairy tale."

Lines 100–108

These nine lines present an abstract meditation on the universe and evolutionary theory. Darwin considers the vast knowledge his years of studying nature have given him—in essence, he has "beheld the universe," and he compares it to a game of chess. This is another allusion to *The Tempest* when, in act 5, scene 1, Prospero reveals his daughter and her lover playing the game. Miranda and Ferdinand are the "two love-dazed heirs / Who fiddle with the tiny pairs" of chess pieces, in particular the king and queen. As children of royalty, they will one day "turn, themselves, into a king and queen," but what they leave behind are "numberless / Abstract unseen / Combinings on the silent board." This metaphor refers literally to the countless number of moves that can be made in a game of chess but that are never made before the game ends and figuratively to the different combinations of species that never occur in life because of the process of natural selection. Some possibilities of nature remain "Unplayed forever" in a world where form and order eventually triumph over chaos.

Lines 109–117

The words "coming day" and "illuminates" imply that Darwin has been outside nearly all night, and now dawn is breaking. This scene portrays his weariness and aging as he is described leaning against the door "for a spell before / He climbs the stairs, holding the banister" on his way back to the bedroom.

Lines 118–124

This description of Emma, Darwin's wife, sleeping uses sea imagery to show her "moored" as a ship to a dock, secure in her "illusion," or dream. Asleep, she is safe from the "storm" Darwin conjured with the publication of *On the Origin of Species by Means of Natural Selection*. This, of course, is also an allusion to Prospero who conjured a storm of his own. The "harbor" refers back to the islands Darwin visited, and lines 122–124 sum up his idea of natural selection, or the survival of the fittest. The island animals "leap from shape to shape" because only the strongest shapes survive, and they want to avoid remaining static in order not to "disappear."

Lines 125–132

"Darwin in 1881" ends with imagery of the geological phenomena that became the basis of his scientific theory. Fossils found on ocean floors and cliffs, in ice, canyons, and so forth, support the idea of evolution, and at the end of his life, Darwin himself is like a "fabulous-headed / Fossil," ready to lie down for a final time.

Themes

Family

The importance of family is at the heart of all three "layers" of "Darwin in 1881"—between Darwin and his wife and children; between Prospero and his daughter and brother; and, of course, between the poet and her father, in whose memory this poem was written. Schnackenberg portrays the main subject, Darwin, as a contemplative, somewhat frail man alternating between thoughts of his accomplishments as a scientist and his personal life as a family man with fond memories of his own childhood. He is ever mindful of the people he loves, taking note of his children's portraits as he descends the stairs in the middle of the night, dizzy and feeling ill. As he walks among the gardens and greenhouses, thinking of his long-ago voyage across the ocean to exotic islands and of the fame he incurred as a result of his studies there, his mind also returns to the life he settled into after the expedition. The greenhouse in particular reminds him of the hours his son Frank spent playing the bassoon "like an awkward angel" to see if the sound could "make a Venus's-Flytrap close." And although Darwin is "done for good with scientific prose," he joyfully considers the prospects of writing his memoirs, "chuckling" as he thinks "About his boyhood in an upright / Home," recalling his preference for gartersnakes over schoolwork. He muses over the memory of "His bossy sister itching with desire / To tattletale" and realizes that even though he has "beheld the universe," he really wants only to live a fairy tale life like a man in "Once upon a time there was a man."

Prospero is also a loving father, who brings up his daughter Miranda on an island where they are the only two humans. Perhaps Schnackenberg chose these two characters for the poem because of their very close relationship, which is similar to the one she shared with her own father. The older Schnackenberg was a studious man who loved to read, and Prospero, too, is a man who has surrounded himself with books and taught his child to

Topics for Further Study

- Read samples of both formal poetry and free verse, then write an essay explaining why you enjoy one style more than the other. Give examples of poets from each field to back up the reasons for your preference.

- Try writing a poem in the style of new formalism. Then write a brief summary of how you approached the work, explaining why it was either harder or easier than you thought it would be.

- Playwrights Jerome Lawrence and Robert Lee's 1955 drama *Inherit the Wind* is based on the Scopes Trial regarding teaching evolution in schools. Read the play and then read accounts of the actual trial. How do the two "histories" differ? How are they similar, and what aspects may have Lawrence and Lee included for dramatic effect?

- Since Darwin first suggested his theory of natural selection in the 1850s, much public debate and even violent arguments have occurred in regard to evolution versus creation. But some people claim to have no problem accepting both. Explain how evolution and creation may be compatible theories instead of opposites.

---

love them as well. For twelve years, Miranda is the only family member Prospero is with, but when his brother arrives on the island by way of a tempest and shipwreck, he eventually finds a way to forgive Antonio for the terrible acts he committed when they all lived in Milan. Even after being double-crossed and sent out to a sure death on rough seas, Prospero decides that family and forgiveness are more important than anger and revenge. Likely, this theme is prevalent in Schnackenberg's work, not only because her father was a good man but because losing him gave her an even deeper understanding of the value of being part of a family.

Resolution and Death

Individual responses to growing old and accepting the end of one's life is a common theme in many poems. In "Darwin in 1881," Schnackenberg couples the theme of death with the idea of resolution—the main characters must resolve major issues in their lives before they die. For Prospero, the decision is to give up his magical powers and return to the career he had rightfully inherited as the Duke of Milan. Although his life on the island has been filled with miraculous events and uncommon companions, he comes to understand that there is something more valuable in the world than magic and cunning and supernatural abilities. In essence, he realizes that peace of mind is the most important gift he can receive, and it will come about only by returning to a normal life as a normal man.

For Darwin, the resolution is very similar. He has not experienced the power of creating magic, but he has become a world-renowned, controversial figure whose "power" came in the form of developing a theory that changed the way humankind thought about its own origins and development. Other naturalists had considered the same theory long before Darwin, but it was his publication of *On the Origin of Species by Means of Natural Selection* that brought the concept to the public's attention and caused an uproar. In Schnackenberg's poem, Darwin is an elderly man tired of the attention—tired, even, of his own studies and scientific writings. He prefers a quiet evening at home over attending award ceremonies, and he wants to write about his boyhood instead of fossils. He may not have any magical powers to relinquish, but he does resolve to give up science in favor of domestic comforts and peace of mind. Like Prospero, Darwin wants to live out the remainder of his days as a normal man, well out of the public spotlight.

Style

New Formalism

In the 1980s, American poetry took a turn toward a more formal style of writing than the styles of the previous decades. Free verse certainly did not die out, but it did make room for the emergence of a poetic movement termed the new formalism. In this style, poets use specific form, meter, and usually rhyme, and Schnackenberg is recognized as one of the most prominent poets of the movement. "Darwin in 1881" is composed primarily in rhymed quatrains, or a series of four-line groups, following an *a-b-b-a* rhyming pattern. Consider the first four lines of the poem, with the endings "room," "miracles," "tales," and "loom." Here, lines 1 and 4 are identical rhymes, and 2 and 3 are slant, or close, rhymes. The next four lines follow a *b-c-c-b* pattern and consist of two identical rhymes: "upwells" with "tortoiseshells" and "crept" with "slept." This style is seen throughout the poem, although Schnackenberg allows herself the freedom to fluctuate between short, eight-line verses and longer ones, most divisible by four, but occasionally odd-numbered, as in the fifth stanza of this poem. After following the quatrain pattern from lines 69 through 84, suddenly line 85—the last one in the stanza—is actually the beginning of the first quatrain in the next stanza. "Stakes" is partnered with "gartersnakes," and "write" and "upright" are tucked in between. Most likely the typical stanza pattern is broken simply because the line about "tortured grammars" completes the thought begun with "raging hell," and the poet found it more sensible to opt for content over form at this point.

Because Schnackenberg writes very personal, often autobiographical poems, she may be considered a "confessional" poet, such as Sylvia Plath or Anne Sexton. What sets Schnackenberg apart, however, is that she tames her emotions and volatile subject matter with the standards of new formalism. The meter and rhyme she employs help to restrain any overly dramatic or sensationalized outbursts that free verse can sometimes allow when the topic is the poet's own grief, anger, depression, and so forth. For this reason, she has been praised for her quiet seriousness even though her poems may be about highly stressful or passionate subjects. In this case, style plays a major role in getting the poem's message across without letting emotion get in the way.

Historical Context

The same year that Charles Darwin published his controversial book *On the Origin of Species by Means of Natural Selection* (1859), another English writer, Charles Dickens, published *A Tale of Two Cities* with the opening lines, "It was the best of times, it was the worst of times." Though Dickens was referring to the era of the French Revolution, the sentiment of the statement also applies to the time in which Darwin lived *and* a hundred years after his death when Schnackenberg wrote this poem about him. During Darwin's lifetime, wars throughout the world were as common as they are today. His life spanned much of the 1800s, and during that century, Britain went to war with France in Spain and Portugal; countries in the Middle East and Far East waged battles, including Singapore, Persia, and China; India was the setting of numerous conflicts; and the young United States of America was anything but united when civil war tore the country apart. Of course, the Industrial Revolution was also underway, bringing about improvements in transportation, communication, and manufacturing, making the lives of many people much better in spite of social or political troubles. Most scientists and a part of the general public commended Darwin for making remarkable advancements in science, providing insight into biological and botanical mechanisms that would lead to a greater understanding of life itself. Another part called him blasphemous, condemning him for advocating theories that drew people away from God and a belief in the fundamental story of creation. By the 1880s, arguments still occurred between the opposing sides, but the effects of the Industrial Age were undeniable in turning more people's attention to science and technology in spite of religious beliefs.

A century later, Schnackenberg was born in the same year the Korean War ended, and she grew from adolescence to adulthood during the Vietnam War. In 1980, when she was composing the poems that would become a part of her first collection, *Portraits and Elegies*, violence was happening on the streets as much as on the battlefields. Famed Beatle John Lennon was shot dead in front of his home in New York City, and a year later, both President Ronald Reagan and Pope John Paul II were victims of assassination attempts. Darwin's theory of evolution was still being debated—as it is today—although much of the argument shifted from its authenticity to whether it should be taught in schools. Christian Fundamentalists introduced bills in a number of state legislatures to counteract the 1968 decision by the Supreme Court that any law banning the teaching of evolution was unconstitutional. Fundamentalists argued that evolution in the classroom should be balanced by the teaching of creation as well, and in the 1980s, Arkansas and Louisiana passed acts requiring such a balance in public schools. However, the acts were soon successfully challenged by opponents who said they were a violation of the separation of church and state. In the latter part of the twentieth century, many Christians accepted evolution by natural selection as compatible with religious belief. Even Pope John Paul II acknowledged this in 1981 when he told the Pontifical Academy of Sciences that the Bible should not be taken literally as a book of physics, astronomy, or biology. The Bible, he said, does not "wish to teach how the heavens were made but how one goes to heaven." (The Pope's state-

Compare & Contrast

- **1880s:** Significant advances are made in the new field of genetics. After Gregor Mendel laid the groundwork in the mid-nineteenth century for how heredity works in the genes, biologists in the 1880s discover that the material they call "germ plasm" (later, DNA) is located in the chromosomes.

  1980s: Biologists make the first successful transfer of genes from one animal to another species as genetic engineering becomes the hot topic of science. Throughout the decade, scientists prove that what has always been considered "natural" in a species can be altered and manipulated.

  Today: Pigs are the most recently cloned animals. There is much talk of using an endless supply of pig organs for human transplants, but many scientists fear the transfer of uncontrollable viruses as well.

- **1876:** The discovery of the fossil bird *Archaeopteryx,* known as the Berlin Specimen, shows the presence of teeth in the 150-million-year-old animal, supporting the Darwinian notion that birds had descended from reptiles.

  1980s: The "creation science" movement goes into full swing, putting pressure on state legislatures to require science teachers to include "abrupt appearance theory" (creationism) in their lesson plans. Although some states oblige, the courts overrule the requirements on the grounds that creationism is not legitimate science and teaching it is a violation of church and state separation.

  Today: The Kansas Board of Education is accused of banning theories of evolution and the big bang from its text books, initiating a firestorm of protests from scientists, science teachers, and much of the general public. The board, however, claims it only refused to mandate that instructors teach these theories and that students be tested in them.

---

ment was reprinted in an article on evolution on the Britannica.com web site.)

Though much of Schnackenberg's work, including "Darwin in 1881," concerns mostly individual and personal matters, it generally relates the individual to the world around him or her. Robert McPhillips, writing for the *Dictionary of Literary Biography,* claims that the poems in *Portraits and Elegies* "present a mature and unified meditation on mortality and the human capacity to impose order on and adduce meaning from life through science, history, family, and poetry." Given the world's conditions in both the poet's and her subject's times, one can find many examples when order was *not* imposed, resulting in some of the social and political troubles that occurred. But the biological and geological studies that Schnackenberg mentions in the Darwin poem reveal a definite order within the natural world. Perhaps Darwin's desire to give up his study of evolution—to abdicate his powers, like Prospero—is not as much a reaction to social turmoil and controversial science as it is a need for a more simplified life as it draws to a close.

Critical Overview

Negative criticism is not usually hard to find on any widely published writer, but Schnackenberg is an exception. From the publication of *Portraits and Elegies* in 1982 to the release of *Supernatural Love: Poems, 1978–1992,* she has been highly praised by critics and fellow poets alike. Nearly all reviewers touch on her ability to write formal poetry without falling into a trite singsong style that turns off serious, contemporary readers. Writing for the *Nation,* critic Rosetta Cohen claims that *Portraits and Elegies* shows Schnackenberg "to be a poet of enormous control, capable of working small miracles with cadence and rhyme." In the *New Repub-*

Sculptures of what were once considered prehistoric man's evolution: Pithecanthropus Erectus, the fraudulent Piltdown man, Neanderthal, Cro-Magnon

lic, critic Rosanna Warren states that the poet's "youthful work showed formal mastery verging on the ingenious." The consistent accolades are based largely on Schnackenberg's unemotional treatment of very emotional subjects. Whether she is addressing the death of her beloved father or composing a love poem, she keeps the temperament in check, depending more on stimulating a reader's intellect than on making anyone cry or scoff.

Whereas many poets have rough beginnings and must work their way into favor with publishers, readers, and fellow poets, others start out with a bang only to fizzle into oblivion with their greatest efforts sitting on the shelves of bargain basement book stores. Neither is the case with Schnackenberg. In his article for the *Dictionary of Literary Biography,* critic Robert McPhillips says of the poet that "hers was one of the most notable and enthusiastically received debuts by a young American poet in the 1980s." And, remarkably, she has not fizzled over the last two decades. Critics are just as enthusiastic over and welcoming of her recent work as they were in the beginning. If there are detractors of Schnackenberg's work out there, they must be small in number and unusually quiet.

Criticism

Pamela Steed Hill

Hill is the author of a collection of poetry, has published widely in poetry journals, and is an associate editor for a university communications department. In the following essay, she contends that the point of Schnackenberg's poem is to show the controversial naturalist in a favorable, gentle light in spite of those who would condemn him as a heretic.

When Charles Darwin wrote his autobiography in the latter part of his life, he included a section on his religious beliefs. He considered the topic at length and in the end claimed to be agnostic, basing his decision on the idea that the true origin of life cannot ever really be known by living beings. While it is true that Darwin did not adhere to the Bible as a document of literal history, he did express a respect for the ideals of morality and philanthropy described particularly in the New Testament. He went so far as to say that dedicating one's life to helping others is of far greater value than any other occupation, including his own. In spite of his humanitarian philosophy and willingness to

> *Here, Darwin's inclination is anything but blasphemous, his behavior anything but controversial.*

consider the prospect of a "personal" God, however, Darwin was harshly criticized by many and condemned outright by others for being an atheistic sinner bent on destroying Christianity worldwide.

What possible difference can a poem make in alleviating, if not reversing, the hateful, accusatory feelings that some fundamental Christians hold toward the man who made the theory of natural selection so popular? Perhaps more than one might think, if the work is read carefully with attention to the gentleness and kindness the title character seems to exude every step of the way. The reader should note, too, his apparent defenselessness, not only against the chronic illness that plagues him throughout but also against his own memories of the controversy and pain his book created among family, friends, and enemies alike. Here, Darwin is almost pitiable. Instead of provoking a reader's anger with evolution imagery, this poem tends to soften the animosity by portraying a man whose own nature—his own life—will soon "grow small, fade, disappear."

The description of Darwin suddenly sitting up in bed, sick to his stomach and feeling dizzy, must evoke heartfelt sympathy. He is utterly alone with his pain although his wife sleeps nearby, and he will spend the rest of the night alone, wandering through his gardens, reflecting on the past. And what a past it has been for the old naturalist. The years he was fortunate enough to spend at home working on his theories and raising a large family were counteracted by a tumultuous public life, sometimes rewarding him with support and admiration and sometimes blasting him with accusations of heresy. Although his personal opinions and attitude toward a supreme being were far more complex than many people gave him credit for, he now seems to weary of his own occupation and intellectual pursuit, resigned to go to "a place where species don't exist, / Where no emergence has a counterpart." Darwin appears weakened by these thoughts and takes comfort in avoiding public appearances in favor of private evenings at home with his wife. Here, Darwin's inclination is anything but blasphemous, his behavior anything but controversial.

The gentleness of Darwin's character is continued in his thoughts of the children. The scene in which "he leans against the fence" and "deeply draws" on a cigarette is very vivid in portraying both his sensitivity and his melancholy. He fondly recalls his son Frank playing a musical instrument to see if a plant in the greenhouse would respond to the sound. But this happy memory is juxtaposed against the mixed feelings he now has in regard to the science that has been an obsession for most of his life. Darwin realizes that he is "done" with everything he has experienced in his career, but he is not ready just yet to lie down and die. Instead, he wants to write his memoirs and include all those things in his life that brought him joy, from boyhood memories of a "bossy sister" and neglected schoolwork to a grown man living a fairy tale life. The image of Darwin as an old man putting onto paper these pleasant recollections is quite different from the image of him documenting results of experiments and recording his proposal for a theory of natural selection. In this poem, he appears very grandfatherly, just a kind, elderly "pop" who gets a kick out of relating those "when I was a boy" stories that grandkids love to hear. He is both loving and fragile, a combination that usually evokes a sympathetic smile, not disdain.

Schnackenberg chose the language of this poem carefully to imply a docile, almost helpless quality in her subject, all in direct opposition to the way his critics may characterize him. Just the verbs tell a story about Darwin's capabilities: he wavers, putters, leans, climbs stairs holding onto the banister, lies down, shuts a door softly, and shuts his eyes. The words supplying a blow-by-blow account of his sleepless night are also designed to make the reader sympathetic. Consider these descriptions: "He sits up in the dark"; "His seasickness upwells"; "His voyage . . . / Comes . . . to a close"; his home is full of "shipsunk emptiness"; he is "an island as he walks"; "All he can see / is how [nature] will grow small, fade, disappear"; he is a naturalist "left behind" by nature; and he likens himself to an actor who has "lost his taste for verse." It is a rather forlorn sight to picture him leaning against a fence, dizzy, trying to smoke a cigarette perhaps to calm his nerves. And it is just as pitiful to see him wander back to the house where once again he must lean against a support before making his way up the steps to his bedroom. In this year before his death, Darwin is a physically weak man, and his previous strong convictions have worn thin as well. The "scientific prose," which he once wrote so prolifically and diligently, is now a "raging hell / Of tortured grammars writhing on their stakes." In essence, he is tired of the fight—tired of the controversy and tired of defending his beliefs to people who do not really understand the ideas he has put forth for examination.

Another point that cannot be overlooked is the poet's comparison of Darwin to Shakespeare's Prospero. Obviously, there are scores of characters to choose from when a writer wants to make allusions to the playwright's works, and Schnackenberg's selection of the Duke of Milan is right in keeping with her desired portrayal of the naturalist. Both Darwin and Prospero are loving fathers, and both exhibit a willingness to put family first. Both men are intellectuals, but neither is arrogant about it, and both men make decisions toward the end of their lives that are major changes for them— Prospero gives up his magic and returns home to be a "normal" duke, and Darwin gives up his science to write his memoirs and spend quiet days with his wife. Probably the most conspicuous reason that Schnackenberg chose to allude to *The Tempest* and its main character is that Prospero is a man of extremely good will and one who is capable of weathering the worst that life has to offer while maintaining a humanitarian attitude. Even though his own brother stole his kingdom and left him to die along with his three-year-old daughter, Prospero ends up forgiving the "bad" brother, and the brother, in turn, becomes a good human being. The happy ending does not come without its price, but Prospero believes the right choice is to return home with his family, and he abides by his conscience. While the events in the lives of Darwin and Prospero may not be parallel on every count, the point of the comparison is obvious. In spite of the duke's magical abilities to stir up storms and bring conflict and unrest to the world around him, he is by no means an evil sorcerer. In spite of the viewpoint of some fundamental Christians, the same may be said of Darwin.

"Darwin in 1881" ends on an even more mournful note than the rest of the poem expresses. The allusions are no longer to a Shakespearean character but to Darwin's own past scientific pursuits. In giving up his geological and zoological studies, he becomes more a part of them than ever. It is as though his relinquishment of the fossil records has drawn him deeper into them until he

> *It is the sense of the transience of all things that is responsible for the melancholy mood that permeates the poem."*

himself becomes "a fabulous-headed / Fossil" lying down in a riverbed that will vanish over time. And once again he is alone. Although Emma still sleeps beside him in their bed, Darwin is set apart from her, not only because of the barrier his boots and overcoat present but also because he has spent the night deep in thoughts that are highly personal and difficult to convey. He knows he is an old man nearing the end of his life and is content to close his eyes for now and, soon perhaps, forever. This is hardly a portrayal of religion's "biggest bogeyman," and the poet makes that case with authority.

Source: Pamela Steed Hill, Critical Essay on "Darwin in 1881," in *Poetry for Students,* The Gale Group, 2001.

Bryan Aubrey

Aubrey holds a Ph.D. in English and has published many articles about twentieth-century literature. In this essay, he explores the significance of the many parallels in the poem between Darwin and Shakespeare's character Prospero.

Schnackenberg's "Darwin in 1881" interweaves past and present not only in the personal life of Charles Darwin but also in the evolution of the natural world that Darwin documented so exhaustively. The mood of the poem is somber, conveying the sense of a long and busy life drawing to a close. The naturalist does not look back on his life of scientific discovery with any sense of accomplishment. In spite of his vast knowledge, all he is now aware of from his many years of study is that everything in nature "will grow small, fade, disappear." The Darwin of the poem is aware only of absences, of vanishings, of things in nature that formerly were and are no more. This is of course an allusion to the extinction of species over the long course of evolution, in which the process of "natural selection" ensures that the life forms that survive are those that adapt best to their environment. Darwin also described this process as the "survival

What Do I Read Next?

- Published in 2000, Dr. Jonathan Wells's book *Icons of Evolution* gives examples of what he calls falsehoods, mythology, and hoaxes that pass for evidence of Darwinian evolution. Wells is a biologist and senior fellow of the Discovery Institute's Center for the Renewal of Science and Culture. He presents an intriguing look at how strong devotion to Darwinism has led to biology textbooks containing misinformation.

- *Charles Darwin: Interviews and Recollections,* edited by Harold Orel and published in 2000, contains over twenty excerpts from longer works by and about Darwin. The writings cover his family background, his voyage on the *Beagle* and his relationship with its captain, and his final years working at his home in Downe.

- A loving father-daughter relationship is a driving force behind much of Schnackenberg's poetry. And so it is for sportswriter Geoffrey Norman, who decided to celebrate his fiftieth birthday by climbing Grand Teton Mountain only to find out that his fifteen-year-old daughter wanted to join him. *Two for the Summit: My Daughter, the Mountains, and Me,* published in 2000, is not just an adventure story about mountain climbing but also a memoir of a good father finding an even deeper bond with his daughter.

- The so-called Scopes Monkey Trial of 1925 is reexamined in Edward J. Larson's *Summer for the Gods: The Scopes Trial and America's Continuing Debate over Science and Religion.* Published in 1997, this book provides new insight into the court battle between prosecutor William Jennings Bryant and defense lawyer Clarence Darrow when a Tennessee high school teacher, John Scopes, was arrested for teaching evolution in the classroom.

---

of the fittest." In this poem, however, Darwin links natural selection to a more general notion of death, which not only lays waste to thousands of entire species but comes inevitably to all creatures, himself included. He is acutely aware of his own impending death, "Bound for a place where species don't exist."

The poet adds a level of complexity to the poem when she equates Darwin with Prospero, the magician of Shakespeare's play, *The Tempest.* The references to Prospero pervade the poem, making it more than just a meditation on death. It also touches on issues such as the nature of knowledge, reality, dream, and illusion.

Prospero and Darwin were both men of knowledge and learning, but they represented different sides of the same coin. Darwin was a scientist. He measured, observed, and analyzed the natural world in order to determine its fixed laws of change and development. His methods were objective. Prospero, on the other hand, developed the inner rather than the outer aspects of knowledge. He became a master of the subjective world of the mind, and this gave him power over the outer world. By the power of his imagination, he could summon up events and phenomena in nature, such as the storm that produces the shipwreck that sets *The Tempest* in motion. (As a fictional character, Prospero is also, of course, the product of the imagination of his creator, Shakespeare.) Taken together, Darwin and Prospero, as was once said of the Greek philosophers Aristotle and Plato, divide the empire of the human mind.

But in the poem it seems that neither the subjective nor the objective approach to truth yields any substantial knowledge that might ward off the final reality of death and extinction. Prospero, for all his magical powers, is eventually just as bereft as Darwin. In a creative twist of her own, the poet imagines a life for Prospero beyond even the one with which Shakespeare endowed him. She pictures him, having returned from his island exile to reclaim his dukedom of Milan, as being as sleepless as Darwin. All his previous wisdom, including the magical powers that he renounced, now means nothing to him or anyone else. The seemingly miraculous acts he performed have been reduced to mere sailors' yarns, fabulous events that may never have actually occurred in real life. Like Darwin, Prospero's life's work has ended at the borders of a death that is the final outcome of everything. Prospero's famous speech in *The Tempest,* to which the poet alludes, is at one level of meaning a foreshadowing of this. In that speech Prospero announces that the world and everything in it is nothing more than an "insubstantial pageant" and will fade into nothingness. So too will all human life, the objective reality of which Prospero also calls into question: "We are such stuff / As dreams are made on; and our little life / Is rounded with a sleep."

This allusion leads Schnackenberg to her gnomic phrase, "Knowledge increases unreality," which epitomizes the theme of the poem. It suggests, first, that the more humans know, the more they are aware of how much they do not know (as Socrates is said to have remarked). Second, it means that all knowledge leads to the perception of the essential unreality of things, in the sense that everything is impermanent. Given nature's vast vanishings—the extinction of species over time—the natural world can be seen as a long, slow disappearing act (the theatrical metaphor is Prospero's and is also used by the Darwin of the poem).

It is the sense of the transience of all things that is responsible for the melancholy mood that permeates the poem. Transience is also conveyed by the pervasive sea imagery. The restless sea, always in motion, never fixed, has been used as a symbol of impermanence by poets and philosophers from ancient times to the present. In "Darwin in 1881," the sea imagery is in part prompted by *The Tempest*, which is replete with such imagery. It is also a reference to Darwin's voyage on *H. M. S. Beagle* to the Galapagos Islands, where he conducted the research that he published twenty years later in *The Origin of Species*. These sources combine to produce Schnackenberg's picture of Darwin as a lonely voyager on the inconstant sea of life, which at the last has given him no firm moorings, only a coastline fading from view and "an ocean swell of sickness."

What Schnackenberg omits in her Darwin/Prospero portrait is that Prospero does much more than give a speech about the inconstancy of things and renounce his magical powers. By cultivating the resources of his own mind, Prospero—whose name is derived from "prosper" or "prosperity"—develops the ability to shape the outer manifestations of life according to his own needs and desires. It is Prospero who creates the storm that leads his shipwrecked enemies to the island where he lives in exile. It is Prospero who conjures up various apparitions that confront the malefactors with the consequences of their own deeds. In doing so, Prospero works with providence (the benevolent guidance of God) to produce justice tempered with mercy. All things may indeed be transient, but that does not mean that humans have no control over events or that those events are purposeless. Shakespeare's *The Tempest* is as much about destiny, di-

> "Ultimately, she reveals a return to traditional poetic form that is engaged in a modern context."

vine providence, and freedom as it is about the impermanence of all things. Schnackenberg chooses to create what might be called an extra-Shakespearean, post-play Prospero who wanted to discontinue his "gigantic works," apparently for the purpose of ego-gratification, so that he could later tell stories of his exploits, "where he could be the man / In Once upon a time there was a man." This gives Prospero's actions in the play a kind of fairy-tale quality, with little implication for the real world.

Of course, the poet is entitled to interpret and recreate the figure of Prospero however she wishes, and Schnackenberg chooses not to explore the more tantalizing aspects of Shakespeare's play: the breaking down of the distinction between reality and illusion, truth and appearance. Instead, this issue is presented in a more straightforward manner. The one character in the poem who is content is Darwin's wife, Emma. But her contentment is only because she is dreaming, "moored in illusion," where everything is clear; death and extinction are cheated by "island beings," who become magical shape-shifters, adept at avoiding their own fate in real life. There is an echo here of Prospero's magical island, in which strange transformations and happenings are the rule and have beneficent consequences in the real world of the play. But in "Darwin in 1881," such events are anchored firmly in the world of illusion.

The result is that the restless Darwin of Schnackenberg's poem is, in a sense, a victim of the success of his own theory. Natural selection dealt a severe blow to Protestant Natural Theology, according to which all species were specially designed and created by God and fixed in a permanent form. Every creature was perfectly suited to the environment in which it was placed, and a beneficent God upheld the unchangeable order of creation. Darwin's theory not only demolished that static view of creation, it also called into question the Natural Theologians' belief that man, as a spiritual and moral being, had a special place in creation. For the historical Darwin, man was not unique or special; he belonged to the nature from which he emerged—a belief that is nicely conveyed in the poem as Darwin lies down "like a fabulous-headed / Fossil in a vanished riverbed."

In its belief in providential design, Natural Theology was in a sense closer to the heart of Prospero's universe in *The Tempest* than to the ruthless world revealed by the theory of natural selection. The demise of Natural Theology made it more difficult for people to believe in the traditional Christian doctrine of an afterlife in heaven for the virtuous, a thought that does not even cross the mind of the Darwin of the poem. The only heaven is for dreamers; the only eternal life creatures can hope for is to be fossilized in riverbeds or "canyon floors, in silt, / In lime, in deepening blue ice, / In cliffs." All Prospero's wizardry cannot help when the final moment comes.

Source: Bryan Aubrey, Critical Essay on "Darwin in 1881," in *Poetry for Students,* The Gale Group, 2001.

Erika Taibl

Taibl has published widely in the field of twentieth-century poetry. In the following essay, she explores Schnackenberg's poem and how it presents the relationship of historic and literary eras.

"Darwin in 1881" is a poem about the relationship of the present to the past. In the work, Gjertrud Schnackenberg explores the complexity of historical and artistic relationships as new ideas and standards replace old ones. In the poem, the reader meets the geologist Darwin a year before his death—after his theories are published, after his career has come and gone, and at a turning point in the middle-aged man's life. Schnackenberg draws parallels between Darwin's life and the life of the artist-king, Prospero, from Shakespeare's play *The Tempest*. As she strings together historic and literary times and the people that draw histories together, she explores the debt of modern poetry to the forms and traditions of a literary past.

Schnackenberg plays with form in the poem in a way that calls to mind the balance of the in-between times of history. Ultimately, she reveals a return to traditional poetic form that is engaged in a modern context. In the meeting of tradition and modernity, a hybrid form is created. The hybrid is a new self for the contemporary poet, a marriage of past and present, a joining that is carefully illustrated through the character of Darwin as he reinvents himself in the context of history and his own theories.

In the opening lines of "Darwin in 1881," Schnackenberg employs an allusion, or literary reference, to Shakespeare's play *The Tempest*. Darwin is compared to Shakespeare's Prospero, the creator king. Like Darwin in this poem, Prospero discovers in *The Tempest* that "His voyage around the cape of middle age / Comes, with a feat of insight, to a close." What is the insight? "Knowledge increases unreality." This is a cryptic revelation and only the beginning of the confusion the reader feels as the logic in the poem travels back and forth between the scientific lucidity of being "done with beetle jaws and beaks of gulls" to the less clear but more profound universe, which is compared to a "disregarded game of chess." Each stable image in the poem gives way to an uncertain wave drawing parallels between Darwin's journey in the poem and Prospero's in *The Tempest* as a cycle of self revolution that is at once quite clear and terribly confusing. The world is at once an unreal place of floating islands and the concrete place one returns to "for backgammon with your beloved mate."

As Darwin is compared to Prospero, he is also compared to Prospero's creator, Shakespeare. Darwin's geological revelations are similar to Shakespeare's literary miracles, and both, within the context of the poem, have been reduced to sailors' tales. *The Tempest* is the ultimate sailor's tale of sweeping vistas, shipwrecks, and hints of brutishness. Darwin's sailor tale took place on the *H. M. S. Beagle* as he chronicled the geological wonders of Patagonia and Tierra del Fuego. The results of this trip would be the body of Darwin's life work, *On The Origin of Species*. When the reader meets Darwin in the poem, these geological adventures are over, just as Prospero's life on the island in *The Tempest* is over. In this space of time, as era concedes to era, just before the "thunderclap / Required in Act 3," or the end of one story as another prepares in the wings, life truly takes form. Or does it? The poem suggests that at the point in life when the long-sought knowledge is at its most rich, the unreality of all of life is revealed. Should it not be the other way around? Should not the world make more sense to an individual, to an era of thinkers, after all the books have been published and theories proven? The poem, indeed, is quite wise, suggesting that the very knowledge we seek and obtain throughout our lives only increases the mystery.

The geology of the poem is the concern of the poet. This concern appears in the poem as Darwin's "form," his shadow, "wavers on the stair." The traditional verse form, for which Schnackenberg is known, wavers in the poem. Rhyme occurs throughout the lines, but without consistency. This wavering of form mirrors Darwin's mental instabilities. Darwin, the master of geological insight, wavers between strata of history. He sees "The family portraits stare, / All haunted by each other's likenesses." These faces are the figures of history imposed on his story. The poet shows the reader historic figures, real and fictional, struggling to define their own historical territory, who end up staring each other in the face. This is Schnackenberg's struggle as well: to define a new poetic voice that is poised between and haunted by traditional verse forms and modernist ideals.

In a very skilled way, Schnackenberg portrays the identity crisis of poetic form with that of Darwin's struggle in history. Darwin's scientific language and the poem's language are compared to "tortured grammar's writhing on their stakes." The struggle is Schnackenberg's, too. As a poet, Schnackenberg is considered a new formalist, the title sprung from the 1980s' movement that defied the political statements of modern open forms and challenged the contemporary reader and writer to explore the complexities of their subject matter within the *freedom* of form. Literary eras are defined by movements. Modernism is a term, as well as a movement, which is identified with concepts, sensibility, form, and style in literature and art since the First World War. Most critics agree that modernism involves a deliberate and radical break with the traditional bases of both Western culture and Western art. Modernism ultimately birthed free verse in poetry. Free verse, or open form, became a very important movement, which is still very popular today. Open forms began as Robert McPhillips suggests in his article "Reading the New Formalists," as a way to assert personal identities against a discredited version of an 'elitist' past," which suggests that open forms were a way to make a political statement, a way to express a unique and personal voice in a traditional literary society and canon. For a poet like Schnackenberg, the ideals of modernism are in themselves restrictive. In the push toward "freedom," Schnackenberg joined a group of poets issuing a challenge to return to form with the attitude of revealing something new. But neither is Schnackenberg a traditionalist. As "Darwin in 1881" shows, she is able to employ tools both of the free verse and formalist schools to emphasize the dynamics of language struggle and evolution. Critic Pheobe Pettingell in a review of *The Lamplit Answer,* the collection that contains "Darwin in 1881," writes that Schnackenberg, "recognizes a universe of ideas outside her own personal impressions and treats form as an enhancement and delight, rather than a trap." As a new formalist, Schnackenberg uses form as a way of making sense of chaos. Rosanna Warren writing in the *New Republic* said that Schnackenberg's work may be compared "to the art of tapestry. Whether woven or stitched, tapestry suggests a work whose complexity and tensile strength subordinate many disparate elements to one masterful order." This is the same tapestry thread that ties "Darwin in 1881" to Shakespeare in 1611 and the readers' eyes and ears in this year.

As Darwin's world is compared to the world of *The Tempest,* the poem is tied to an idealized world of imagination, a place of magical rejuvenation. Darwin is compared to the ruler of this imaginary land, who creates an illusion of loss to test his enemies and make them reveal their true selves. In many ways, Darwin's losses, his realizations, help him discover himself in the context of history. Darwin, the scientist, looks at the eggs of birds and knows that within them are "unique expressions," those chromosomes that will define a different future for the species, a future written on "inner staircases," codes to survive in future generations. At the same time, he knows that some, unneeded traits will fall away with time. This idea is his theory of natural selection. The falling away of traits is the loss that prompts him to be "done with beetle jaws and beak of gulls / And bivalve hinges, now, utterly done." For him, "One miracle remains, and only one." The miracle is that all his "knowledge increases unreality." The scientist sees and understands facts. Darwin built his life upon observation and hypothesis, and still, even with this knowledge, the universe becomes a "disregarded game of chess." The people, the animals, the very things that have been concrete to him, become pawns. Mystery is the only future certainty. One trait may be all that remains. But, which one? How will the world recreate itself for survival? These questions float in the poem, as do similar questions regarding poetic form.

Schnackenberg, like Darwin, is concerned with the "coastlines fading" or, in the poet's case, with the poetic lines moving away from form as they engage formlessness. Schnackenberg's worry is the poem as nature where the naturalist (the poet) has been left behind to work where "species don't exist, / where no emergence has a counterpart." She suggests that the chaos and freedom of nature cannot be articulated within freedom but must be brought to illumination within its counterpart—form. It is through death that new form takes shape. Traits, physical and poetic, fall away. New traits appear, which are counterparts. These traits define new forms. These new forms ensure future survival. The poem takes shape and reshapes itself again and again throughout literary movements and stages of history, just as the egg defines new futures with each "unique expression." Poetic forms that "fell away" with modernism are back to remind readers about what was left behind in the open forms: rhythm and a clarity of cadence. The poem struggles with these things, too, as it works to define itself in a hybrid form.

The ending of this poem is not a stable ending. Does Darwin lie down to die? The answer that history suggests is that the future holds more of him, that in death newness is revealed. That is the trust the reader must create with the poem. There will be another scientist, another great thinker that looks into family portraits and realizes a debt to the past. And that person will begin a new revolution. The same is true of the poem. New formalism will fall away and be replaced by other movements. Yet history proves that there is always a returning. With fresh eyes, the future beholds the past and recreates it. The reader cannot assume a time when the sway will cease, the revolution quiet. One of the most famous lines from *The Tempest* occurs near the end when Prospero's daughter, Miranda, declares confidence in "a brave new world." This is the world of new languages and forms, new ideas and radical concepts. Prospero tells Miranda, who represents the up-and-coming revolutionary, that the brave new world "is only new to thee." There are faces wavering in the portrait. There is history to which the present owes a debt. This marriage of past with present is the brave new world. Paul Lake, articulates what this means for poetry in his essay, "Return to Metaphor: From Deep Imagist to New Formalist," saying "Form—by which I mean the architecture of meter and rhyme and stanza—is one more piece of string for catching resemblances." The new formalists explore resemblances between past and present, the family faces of tradition and modern times. The new formalists capture this resemblance with distinct voices, and in it they find illuminations, the brave new world. Knowledge does increase unreality, and it becomes the poet's job to articulate it. What the poet creates in the resemblances, in the making sense, is fodder for "a brave new world," in which no idea is forgotten but appears again in a new form as "island beings leap from shape to shape." The poet, then, is not unlike Darwin, who goes to sleep in his coat and boots as if, in the limbo of sleep, he may be off to discover a new species.

Source: Erika Taibl, Critical Essay on "Darwin in 1881," in *Poetry for Students,* The Gale Group, 2001.

David St. John

In the following review excerpt, St. John calls Portraits and Elegies *"an exceptional first book of poems," and "Darwin in 1881" "an affectionate portrait."*

There is once again a taste for traditional forms manifesting itself in American poetry. This is good news in that it allows the reevaluation and a new appreciation, by a whole generation of younger poets, of those traditional forms and of some of our formal masters, poets like Anthony Hecht, Richard Wilbur, Donald Justice, Howard Moss, James Merrill, and W. D. Snodgrass. It is bad news because, perhaps predictably, it is helping to usher in a whole new era of decorative parlor poetry and exceedingly vapid verse. In our hunger for the least trace of formal consciousness (as teachers, poets, and reviewers), we've been too eager to leap upon the slightest trace of formal competence as the evidence of genius. As a result, we're finding too many young poets beginning to write, in my view, the same accomplished and inconsequential verse (not poetry) that finally convinced us it was time to leave the 1950s (of poetry) in the first place. While it may be true that style and content are inseparable, it is not true that technique—formal or otherwise—makes up for lack of content, or that technique itself is style. If American poetry is going to backpedal, I wish it would do it with some grace, and perhaps some substance too, though I realize I may be pushing my expectations in this regard. It should also be said that it was the popularity and fine poetry of three non-American poets, Joseph Brodsky, Seamus Heaney, and Derek Walcott, that helped initiate the present return to a concern for traditional meters and forms.

Therefore it is a special pleasure and relief to find a young poet writing in traditional forms who also has in her grasp both powerful subject matter and the intelligence to command her technique. Gjertrud Schnackenberg's *Portraits and Elegies* (David R. Godine) is an exceptional first book of poems. *Portraits and Elegies* is a book of three poems, two of which are long sequences: "Laughing with One Eye," an elegy for the poet's father, and "19 Hadley Street," a wonderful narrative poem about a house and the lives it sheltered. The book's centerpiece is an affectionate portrait of "Darwin in 1881" (a year before his death). This charming poem follows Darwin as, sleepless, he rises for a night walk; reflectively, he and the poem look back over the events of his life, of both the recent and distant past. Coming back to bed, where his wife is sleeping:

> He lies down on the quilt,
> He lies down like a fabulous-headed
> Fossil in a vanished riverbed,
> In ocean-drifts, in canyon floors, in silt,
> In lime, in deepening blue ice,
> In cliffs obscured as clouds gather and float;
> He lies down in his boots and overcoat,
> And shuts his eyes.

Source: David St. John, "Raised Voices in the Choir: A Review of 1982 Poetry Selections," in *Antioch Review,* Vol. 41, No. 2, Spring 1983, pp. 239–40.

Sources

Belz, Joel, "Witnesses for the Prosecution: *Darwin on Trial* Author Brings Together Anti-Darwin Coalition to Bring Down Evolution," in *World Magazine,* Vol. 11, No. 28, Nov. 30, 1986, p. 18.

Brittanica.com: Evolution, http://www.britanica.com/bcom/eb/article/9/0,5716,108619+7+106075,00.html (December 11, 2000).

Cohen, Rosetta, "Book Reviews: *The Lamplit Answer,*" in *Nation,* Vol. 241, Dec. 7, 1985, p. 621.

Darwin, Charles, *The Autobiography of Charles Darwin: With Original Omissions Restored; Edited with Appendix and Notes by His Granddaughter, Nora Barlow,* Norton, 1969.

Lake, Paul, "Return to Metaphor: From Deep Imagist to New Formalist," in *Southwest Review,* Vol. 74, Fall 1989, 515–29.

McPhillips, Robert, "Gjertrud Schnackenberg," in *Dictionary of Literary Biography,* Vol. 20: *American Poets Since World War II, Third Series,* Gale Research, 1992, pp. 276–80.

———, "Reading the New Formalists," in *Sewanee Review,* Vol. 97, Winter 1989, pp.73–96.

Pettingell, Phoebe, "Sound and Sense in Poetry," in *New Leader,* Vol. 83, September 1985, pp. 14–15.

Schnackenberg, Gjertrud, *Portraits and Elegies,* edited by David R. Godine, 1982.

Shakespeare, William, *The Tempest,* edited by David Bevington, Bantam Books, 1988.

Warren, Rosanna, "Book Reviews: *A Gilded Lapse of Time,*" in *New Republic,* Vol. 209, No. 11, September 13, 1993, p. 37.

———, "Visitations," in *New Republic,* September 13, 1993, pp. 37–41.

For Further Study

Feirstein, Frederick, ed., *Expansive Poetry: Essays on the New Narrative and the New Formalism,* Story Line Press, 1989.

> Published at the tail end of the decade in which the new formalism movement began, this collection of essays helps explain the reasons that some poets turned to a formal style of writing, using rhyme, meter, and a narrative voice. This is interesting reading for the serious student of poetry.

Golding, William, and Harold Bloom, eds., *William Shakespeare's "The Tempest,"* Modern Critical Interpretations, Chelsea House Publications, 2000.

> This is, of course, only one of the many publications of Shakespeare's last play. Like most, this version contains an insightful introduction to the tragicomedy and helpful interpretations throughout.

Jarman, Mark, and David Mason, eds., *Rebel Angels: 25 Poets of the New Formalism,* Story Line Press, 1996.

> As the title suggests, this anthology celebrates new formalism as a welcome and unexpected change in American poetry in the late twentieth century. Although Schnackenberg is not included, the book offers a good mix of new formalist poets, including Dana Gioia, Marilyn Hacker, and Timothy Steele.

Schnackenberg, Gjertrud, *A Gilded Lapse of Time,* Farrar Straus, 1992.

> This is Schnackenberg's third poetry collection, and it continues the theme of history through an exploration of human creation versus God's creation and the impact of myth on actual events. Written in the same style as *Portraits and Elegies,* the book will not disappoint any reader who is a Schnackenberg fan.

Daylights

Rosanna Warren
1984

"Daylights" was first published in the literary magazine *Shenandoah* and appears in Rosanna Warren's first full-length collection of poetry *Each Leaf Shines Separate,* published in 1984. It is a short poem—only twenty-eight lines in two free-verse stanzas—and, like other poems in the collection, was inspired by a famous poem. Many of the poems in the collection are also about paintings and other works of art. Using the second person "you," Warren details the response of the speaker to witnessing a New York City robbery. Full of colorful visual imagery and symbolism, the poem relates the speaker's hyper-awareness of her surroundings and her own mortality. Warren claims the poem speaks to French poet Stéphane Mallarmé's well-known poem "L'Azur," ("The Azure") and to the obsession of European romantics and symbolists with transcendental blue. Mallarmé's poem, published when he was twenty-four, isn't so much a description of the sky as it is of the sky's effects on the poet. These effects aren't feelings of beauty or love in any conventional sense but rather feelings of dread, death, and the impossibility of transcendence. The poet longs for what the blue sky promises while at the same time realizing that that promise can never be fulfilled. Warren uses blue and daylight as symbolic images of the violence and grit of urban America. She juxtaposes the symbolic promise of daylight with the harsh reality of city life. For Warren, art is always a mirror of human life and a way by which to measure it, to bring

its meaning into relief. The poem has been reprinted in *The Norton Anthology of Modern Poetry* and *The Morrow Anthology of Younger American Poets*.

Author Biography

Born on July 27, 1953, in Fairfield, Connecticut, to Robert Penn Warren and Eleanor Clark, a celebrated literary couple, Rosanna Warren was provided the kind of education that many parents can only dream of giving their children. Her father, a university professor and nationally acclaimed writer and critic, won Pulitzer Prizes for both his fiction and poetry, and her mother won the National Book Award. Warren attended the Accademia delle Belle Arti in Rome, the Skowhegan School of Painting and Sculpture, the New York Studio School, and Yale University, from which she earned her undergraduate degree in 1976. She earned her master's degree in the writing programs from Johns Hopkins University in 1980. Warren's poetry shows her training in and passion for painting and sculpture. Her intricately structured, sophisticated, and detailed poems frequently use works of art and other poems as subjects. "Daylights," for example, is inspired by Stéphane Mallarmé's poem "L'Azur." Perhaps more than any other poet writing today, her verse is directly concerned with how art can shape the way people think and experience the world.

Warren, who published *The Joey Story* in 1963 when she was only ten years old, has already had a distinguished literary career, having won a number of awards and prizes including the Nation Discovery Award in poetry, an Ingram Merrill grant for poetry, a Guggenheim fellowship, the Lavan Younger Poets Prize, the Lamont Poetry Prize, a Lila Wallace Writers' Fund award, and the Witter Bynner Prize in poetry. In addition to her chapbook of poems *Snow Day,* she has published two full-length collections, *Each Leaf Shines Separate* (1984) and *Stained Glass* (1993). A well-respected translator of classical Greek literature, she has also edited a collection of essays on the art of translation titled, appropriately enough, *The Art of Translation* (1989). A chancellor of the Academy of American Poets, Rosanna Warren is the Emma MacLachlan Metcalf Professor of the Humanities at Boston University.

Rosanna Warren

Poem Text

So the sky wounded you, jagged at the heart,
glass shard flying from liquor store window
    smashed.
They had warned you, blue
means danger. The kid runs off
zigzagging the crowd, clutching his prize of   5
    Scotch;
the liquor man yells. Those Grecian dreams
endure even New York. You think
you're safe, humdrumming along
the sidewalk's common, readable gray,
calmly digesting your hunk of daily bread,   10
with flesh enough on your bones to cast some
    shade,
but puddle flashes, car window glints,
a stranger casts you a glance from a previous life:
the sky! And there you stand
unclouded, un-named, as naked as   15
the chosen Aztec facing the last shebang—
(*his* last shebang; the globe keeps rolling along
slipslop in its tide of blood)—

So there you stand
holding your sky-stabbed heart in your hands   20
to offer—to whom?—
while the liquor man curses the daylights
out of the cop, and the crowd
clumps dully away.
And you: "What *you* lookin' at?   25
Move on!" So you

move on and grateful, by God,
in the grit gray light of day.

Poem Summary

Lines 1–7

In these lines the speaker describes an incident in which she is figuratively "wounded" by the sky after witnessing a liquor store robbery in which a window is smashed. It is important to understand that the speaker is not cut by the "glass shard" in the second line. The proximity of the image, however, evokes the extent to which she has been psychologically harmed by the sky. The "you" is a projection of the speaker. The "They" in the third line probably refers to the symbolists, a group of nineteenth-century poets including Stéphane Mallarmé, Paul Verlaine, Arthur Rimbaud, and others for whom blue symbolized the impossibility and the promise of desire. The speaker, like the boy who had just robbed the liquor store of a bottle of scotch, zigzags between the present and her thoughts on the significance of what is happening. "Those Grecian dreams" refer to the writer's own obsession with Greece and with the blue of the Aegean Sea.

Lines 8–14

These lines describe another experience of the speaker in which she is again symbolically "attacked" by the sky. While walking down the street eating ("calmly digesting your daily bread"), she observes a series of things—seemingly disconnected—which shock her into another consciousness. Her description of herself as someone "with enough flesh on . . . [her] bones to cast some shade" is an understatement, suggesting that she is not thin. Again, the sky is the symbolic image into which the speaker infuses her experience. Like "L'Azur," the Mallarmé poem that inspired this one, the sky is an interrupting force in the speaker's consciousness, reminding her of the danger in desire for transcendence. Juxtaposed with the danger of the blue sky is the "sidewalk's common, readable gray," an image of the physical world at her feet. Its description as "common, readable" suggests that it can be known and is in stark contrast to the sky, which is illegible and mysterious.

Lines 15–18

In these lines the speaker uses a simile comparing herself to "the chosen Aztec facing the last shebang." The Aztecs were the native people of

Media Adaptations

- The *Atlantic* sponsors a website at http://www.theatlantic.com/unbound/poetry/soundings/hardy.htm on which Rosanna Warren reads Thomas Hardy's poem "During Wind and Rain."

- The journal *Philosophy and Literature* carries Warren's essay "Alcaics In Exile: W. H. Auden's 'In Memory Of Sigmund Freud'" at http://muse.jhu.edu/demo/phl/20.1warren.html (last accessed April 2001), along with other interesting articles.

Central Mexico and were noted for their advanced civilization before Cortés the Conquerer came in 1519. A "shebang" is a word of unknown origin, which means situation or an affair. The meaning of the Aztec's "last shebang" is not clear, though it could allude to the conquest of the Aztec people by Cortés, or to the ritual of human sacrifice practiced by the Aztecs. Being "unclouded, un-named" and "naked" suggests the speaker's vulnerability, her innocence, and her shame. This description also suggests the speaker is in a kind of pre-linguistic consciousness, where her mind doesn't categorize the world into parts and things. Trance-like states were common for many of the symbolist poets, and it is frequently out of these states that they wrote.

Lines 19–28

This stanza begins in the same way as the first, with the offhand and conversational "so." The image of a person standing against the backdrop of an overwhelming universe—frequently symbolized by the sky—appears throughout Warren's poems, suggesting humanity's insignificance and isolation. Other poems in *Each Leaf Shines Separate* that contain this image include "Garden" and "World Trade Center." That the speaker has no one to give her "sky-stabbed heart" to underscores this sense of isolation. The symbolist image of the transcendent blue sky is echoed in the word "daylights," a slang term that also means emotional or mental stability. The speaker is figuratively paralyzed by witnessing the liquor store robbery and unnerved by what she sees around her. Readers can see her standing there wondering what to do next when the owner of the liquor store asks her what she's looking at. In the last line, the speaker "wakes up" from her trance-like state and realizes her situation. This line contains a kind of moral, as the speaker expresses gratitude, presumably for not being a part of the robbery or a victim of urban violence. It critiques the desire of looking for transcendent meaning in some other world and implicitly warns readers to keep their feet on the ground and their wits about them.

Themes

Nature

"Daylights" uses a contemporary urban setting to explore the idea of nature. By juxtaposing the gritty streets of New York with the sky, the speaker questions popular representations of nature as a benign or even a beneficent force. Here, the sky "stabs" the speaker, offering her no solace from the ugly and threatening street crime she witnesses. As lines 14–15 show, the blue sky itself makes the speaker vulnerable, "unclouding" and "un-naming" her, until she feels as if she is facing her own death. Nature for Warren, as for the symbolist poets of the nineteenth century, is not a place of refuge but rather a mirror-like entity that reflects the poet's own fears and desires. Whereas nature inspired the romantic poets, it just as often casts dread into the hearts of the symbolists, making them aware of their own aloneness in the world. Curiously, it is another human being that finally prods the speaker of "Daylights" into action after she is rendered almost catatonic by witnessing the robbery and by seeing someone from "a previous life." The speaker's gratitude, apparently for being physically unharmed, comes "in the grit gray light of day," an urban image posed in stark contrast to the blue of the "Grecian dreams" the speaker imagined earlier.

Class Conflict

In "Daylights," Warren paints a psychological profile of a person caught in the midst of urban violence. Stereotypes of the rich and the poor abound, and New York City is known for being a place where the disparity between the two is stark. Warren draws on these stereotypes to create a portrait of a person whose response to a robbery—an effect of poverty—is existential despair and gratitude that she herself is not part of the cycle of poverty

Topics for Further Study

- Make a list of the images that you would use to symbolically describe the town or city in which you live; then write a poem using those images.

- After researching the symbolist poets of the late-nineteenth century, write an essay arguing for the ways in which "Daylights" is and is not a symbolist poem.

- Write a story about a time when you encountered violence. Explain what you learned from the experience.

- Pick one other poem from Warren's collection *Each Leaf Shines Separate* and explain how it is part of another poem or work of art.

and crime. The speaker's "Grecian dreams" is the first sign that she is not of the same class as the person who committed the robbery, or even the cop, the liquor store owner, or the crowd gathered to witness the crime, all of whom she subtly characterizes as being part of the hoi polloi of seemly urban life. The despair she experiences "holding . . . [her] sky-stabbed heart in . . . [her] hands" is the despair of one caught in a world of others who cannot appreciate her own rarified way of experiencing the world. Such alienation from others is a symptom of the speaker's class consciousness, of which she herself may not be aware.

Style

Point of View

This poem uses the second person "you" as a projection of the speaker. Such use often suggests that the speaker is alienated from herself in some way, that she feels disembodied. Use of the second person has become more prominent in twentieth-century literature in general and in the last few decades of the century in particular. This use fits symbolist verse well because it is a stylized form of address when the "you" stands for the speaker.

Compare & Contrast

- **1984:** Geraldine Ferraro from New York becomes the first woman vice presidential running mate, teaming with the Democratic Party's Walter Mondale.

  2000: Joseph Lieberman becomes the first Jewish vice presidential candidate for a major party, teaming with the Democratic party's Al Gore.

- **1985:** Bernhard Goetz is charged with attempted murder for shooting teenagers on a New York City subway. Goetz claims the teenagers threatened him and attempted to rob him. New York City crime becomes front-page headlines in newspapers across the country.

  2000: Mayor Rudolph Giulliani's law and order administration is credited with the continuing drop in New York City's crime rate. However, abuses by police continue to plague the city.

- **1985:** Scientists claim that a hole in the ozone layer, first detected in 1977, is now indisputable.

  2000: The media carries first-hand reports that the polar ice cap is melting, an effect of global warming.

However, the "you" here also works to draw the reader into the speaker's experience, Warren's chief aim. The goal of the poem is not to name things in the world but to evoke an experience in readers.

Imagery and Sound

Warren employs a combination of crisp symbolic and concrete visual imagery and a variety of near-rhymes, off-rhymes, assonance, consonance, and onomatopoeia to create a verbal texture suggesting busy-ness and alarm. For example, verbs such as "humdrumming" and "zigzagging" sound like the actions they name. By using words that so accurately embody physical actions they also represent, Warren closes the distance between speaker and reader.

Historical Context

Although "Daylights" is set in New York, presumably around the time the poem was written, there is nothing specifically related to New York in it. The liquor store robbery, the inciting incident for the speaker's meditation on daylight, could happen any place. However, the appearance and reaction of the crowd and the liquor storeowner suggest a big city and the accompanying sense of anonymity people feel in them. In 1984, when "Daylights" was published, the prison population in the United States was 454,000, more than double the population in 1970. By 1999, there were more than 1.2 million people in prisons throughout the country, plus an additional half million in local jails. During the 1980s, the Reagan administration made tougher law enforcement a national priority. In 1981, Reagan declared a National Crime Victim's Week—the first of its kind—and Nancy Reagan launched her "Just Say No" anti-drug campaign. Reagan was voted into office during a time of high inflation and a soaring national crime rate, and his anti-crime initiatives were responses to these. His Economic Recovery Act of 1981 was meant to increase investment allowances, provide incentives for people to contribute to individual retirement accounts, and reduce taxes on big corporations in order to stimulate job growth and, it was hoped, reduce crime. In 1983, oil prices dropped and inflation eased. This helped Reagan and his vice president, George Bush, win a landslide election in 1984 over Walter Mondale and his running mate Geraldine Ferraro. Mondale, a moderate Democrat, emphasized the growing disparity between rich and poor during his campaign. Democrats stressed that during the 1980s the wealthiest one-fifth of Americans produced 41 percent of the national income, whereas the bottom fifth produced only 5 percent. The Republicans stressed the fact that, during the 1980s, 46 percent of the jobs created paid more than $28,000 a year and that the Consumer Price Index dropped from 13.5 percent in 1980 to 4.3 percent in 1984. In the end, Mondale proved no match for Reagan, who carried every state except for Mondale's home state of Minnesota and Washington, D.C. The Democrats, however, carried more than 90 percent of the Black vote, 65 percent of the Hispanic vote, and 53 percent of the vote among those earning less than $12,500 a year. Republicans took the majority of votes from those between the ages of eighteen and twenty-five, suggesting that the younger generation saw the Republican party as the country's best hope for improved economic opportunities.

In literature, the early 1980s saw two "schools" of poetry vie for public attention, the new formalists and the language poets. The new formalists called for the return of fixed traditional poetic forms, partly in response to the saturation of literary magazines and journals with anecdotal, first person, free verse lyrics, many of which were written by graduates of M. F. A. programs. More well-known new formalists include Molly Peacock, William Logan, Timothy Steele, and Brad Leithauser. The language poets, on the other hand, often associated with the political Left, stressed the idea that language creates rather than expresses reality. Poet and leading language poetry theorist Charles Bernstein wrote that one of the chief aims of language poetry is to expose "the optical illusion of reality in capitalist thought." Although manifestoes, essays, and poems both by and about new formalists and language poets continue to be written today, they appear mostly in academic journals and literary magazines and have little wider social appeal.

Critical Overview

No critics have written specifically on "Daylights." However, the collection in which the poem appears, *Each Leaf Shines Separate,* attracted considerable attention from reviewers. Tom Sleigh of the *New York Times Book Review* wrote that Warren's "lavish technique is disciplined by her austere moral intelligence." In their introduction to her poems in *The Norton Anthology of Modern Poetry,* anthologists Richard Ellmann and Robert O'Clair write that her poems are "highly finished, meticulously detailed, intricately composed." On the dust jacket of *Each Leaf Shines Separate,* poets Richard Eberhart and John Hollander praise Warren's work.

Eberhart writes that "Rosanna Warren's poems are like pure water falling from a hill, reflecting light and giving cool sustenance." Hollander applauds the collection's "elegant pace and timing of the way these poems unfold themselves, their precise observation, the learning and judgment at their depths and the remarkable taste that controls their surfaces."

Criticism

Chris Semansky

Semansky has published widely in the field of twentieth-century poetry and culture. In the following essay, he considers the intertextuality of "Daylights."

"Daylights" is a poem about another poem. When poems directly or indirectly reference other poems, they participate in what literary theorists call intertextuality. Simply put, intertextuality refers to the ways in which a piece of writing is involved with other pieces of writing, whether openly or covertly.

At the simplest level, "Daylights" alludes to another poem, Stéphane Mallarmé's "L'Azur," written in 1864. "L'Azur," which refers to the blue sky, is written in French and is a dramatic lyric consisting of nine quatrains. Here is the first stanza, translated:

> The everlasting Azure's tranquil irony
> Depresses, like the flowers indolently fair,
> The powerless poet who damns his superiority
> Across a sterile wilderness of aching despair.

For Mallarmé, the blue sky is a ubiquitous reminder of the poet's inability to make anything happen, to effect change, either on himself or on the world. It is a symbol of his own ennui. In the second stanza, he asks "Where can I flee?" Then he calls on the fog to "Pour your monotonous ashes down / In long-drawn rags of dust across the skies." The sky for Warren's speaker is more malicious, more active than Mallarmé's sky, which is more like a presence that taunts and harasses him. Warren begins her poem as if in the middle of another story, another thought:

> So the sky stabbed you, jagged at the heart,
> glass shard flying from liquor store window smashed.
> They had warned you, blue
> means danger....

Was the speaker daydreaming? How can the sky "wound" her? Who is the "They"? To under-

> "Poetry, like the sky, promises another world where the ideal might be achieved, but never is."

stand these questions, readers must consider not only the structure of Warren's poem but also of Mallarmé's, and the ways in which he used language. For the symbolists in general and for Mallarmé in particular, language was to be used for its effects. Symbolist poet Charles Baudelaire wrote that "everything, form, movement, number, color, perfume, in the *spiritual,* as in the *natural* world, is significative, reciprocal, converse, *correspondent.*" The symbolists saw correspondences everywhere. Between the mind and the external world, inherent and systematic analogies existed. The symbolic images they employed, often private, were meant to exploit and manifest these analogies. The sky "wounds" Warren's speaker because it suggests the promise of clarity and knowledge yet delivers, instead, the muddle of violence, danger, and surprise. She is drawing on the historical symbolism of the image of the sky, but she is also drawing on Mallarmé's use of the image in his poem. The "They" is the symbolist poets themselves.

Both poems use speakers who address themselves at various points, with Warren's speaker addressing that part of herself whose desire she is trying to tame and Mallarmé's speaker addressing his soul. Both poems evoke the sense of isolation and despair. Mallarmé's speaker has nowhere to run: "Where can I flee?" he asks. "What haggard night / Fling over, tatters, fling on this distressing scorn?" Warren's speaker comes close to being a caricature of Mallarmé's when at the beginning of the second stanza she says, "So there you stand / holding your sky-stabbed heart in your hands / to offer—to whom—?" Warren's speaker is surprised, in a state of shock, whereas Mallarmé's is world-weary and exhausted.

Both poets draw on the symbolism of the color blue. The color suggests height and depth—the blue skies above and the deep blue sea below—as well as darkness made visible. Such a range of associations is perfect for these poets, for whom the sky is a container for their own emotional and psychological projections. At one point Mallarmé writes, "The Sky is dead," mirroring his own creative and emotional torpor. Warren's blue sky, her azure, is "daylight," which in addition to daybreak also connotes clarity and mental stability, as well as the end of a successful endeavor. She plays with the associations of this word to play off Mallarmé's poem, "updating," in a sense, "L'Azur."

Both poems can also be seen as indictments of society at the end of their respective centuries. In "L'Azur," Mallarmé paints an almost Dickensian picture of his environment, as he urges pollution onto the blue sky:

> Unceasing let the dismal chimney-flues
> Exude their smoke, and let the soot's nomadic prison
> Extinguish in the horror of its blackened queues.

For Mallarmé, society is made up of people who are conformists; physical reality is itself almost unbearable. Poetry, like the sky, promises another world where the ideal might be achieved, but never is. For Warren, society is not so much a place of boredom and ennui as it is for Mallarmé, but a place of random, almost hallucinatory violence, where the poet engages with the physical world and makes a strange peace with it, realizing the folly of longing for the ideal in some transcendent symbol such as the sky. The very title of her poem underscores this idea.

Another difference between the two poems is in their form. Whereas Mallarmé's poem is a lyrical lament about the poet's internal torment, Warren's poem resembles a cautionary tale about the random violence of urban environments and the necessity to keep moving. Whereas Mallarmé evokes, Warren describes.

Most beginning readers of poetry would not know the relationship between Warren's poem and Mallarmé's, so in some ways "Daylights" is a poem which speaks differently to different kinds of readers. Readers approaching her poem for the first time and without the benefit of having read "L'Azur" or much symbolist poetry will be drawn in by Warren's crisp imagery, the drama of the robbery, and the hyperbolic manner in which the speaker details her experience, but they will no doubt be stumped by the symbolic weight she intends "the sky" to carry in line 14. However, this does not mean that the poem is the lesser one because it draws on Mallarmé's poem. Intertextuality isn't a theory used to unpack individual poems or stories but a way of thinking that acknowledges that human beings are born into a world of language. Readers and writers learn (or not) to use language based on their own experiences. Reading and writing semiotician Daniel Chandler explains intertextuality as follows:

> To communicate we must utilize existing concepts and conventions. The concept of intertextuality reminds us that each text exists in relation to others. . . . In fact, texts owe more to other texts than to their own makers. Consequently meaning is not a matter of authorial 'intention'. . . . Texts provide contexts within which other texts may be created and interpreted. The debts of a text to other texts are seldom acknowledged (other than in the scholarly apparatus of academic writing). This serves to further the mythology of authorial 'originality.' The practice of alluding to other texts and other media reminds us that we are in a mediated reality.

Chandler reminds us, then, that Warren's poem isn't necessarily a poem which describes an experience in New York City as much as it is a poem which answers another poem, the meaning of which changes the way that readers understand her own. By focusing on the relationship that poems have to one another as well as on the relationship they have to readers, readers themselves will gain a deeper and stronger appreciation for the text in front of them. They will understand that the world that they see, taste, touch, feel, and hear is only one world among many.

Source: Chris Semansky, Critical Essay on "Daylights," in *Poetry for Students,* The Gale Group, 2001.

Joyce Hart

Hart, a former college professor, is currently a freelance writer and copyeditor. In this essay, she discusses various ways of interpreting Warren's poem using an assortment of psychological models of reader response literary theory.

Some literary theorists believe that any work of creative writing possesses no fixed or final meaning. The old school of thought that purported that there was only one, so-called correct way of interpreting a piece of writing is diametrically opposed to the belief of these theorists, who are referred to as reader response theorists. Within the category of reader response theories are several different methods of obtaining that meaning, but in general the theories all contain the concept that meaning is created somewhere between the author, the reader, and the text. In other words, meaning is found somewhere between what the author implies, what the reader experiences, and what the text inspires. Using a few different approaches to reader response theory, this essay will examine Rosanna Warren's poem "Daylights" in an effort to demonstrate some of the theories as well as to try out several different possible interpretations of the poem.

> *"The reader response theory gives readers a great deal of latitude, but readers cannot simply discard parts of the poem that do not fit their interpretations. They have to find some way of understanding and interpreting the poem as a whole."*

One reader response theory uses what is called a cognitive-processing model. Under this model, readers are given a plan or model that will help them explore a work in order to eventually create their own interpretation. For example, under this model it might be suggested that the reader write down possible motives that lie behind the actions of a particular character in the piece being studied. If the motives are not easily understood, the reader might first write down a series of questions that, under a second or closer reading of the work, might later be answered. For example, to be specific to Warren's poem, the reader might ask questions such as these: Why does the speaker of this poem begin with the words "So the sky wounded you"? How could the sky wound anyone? What is it about the sky that could be piercing? Is it the brightness of the sun? Does it have anything to do with the title of the poem: "Daylights"? And why does the speaker seem to infer that the person in this poem feels safer in "readable gray" and by the end of the poem that the person in the poem feels "grateful, by God, / in the grit gray light of day?" What is it about light that appears to bother the person in the poem? Why would light bother anyone?

When using reader response theory to interpret a poem, it can be rather liberating to know that there are no concrete answers, but at the same time it can be a bit threatening. Some readers might find that it is not always easy to trust the initial thoughts that pass through their minds. Or it might just be hard to grasp them. It's also hard to forget the fact that the author of the work must have had some very specific ideas for writing the piece in the first place.

What Do I Read Next?

- Warren's poetry appears in *The Morrow Anthology of Younger American Poets,* published in 1984. This anthology showcases Warren's work as well as that of many of her contemporaries.

- In *The Roots of Romanticism,* published in 1999, editor Henry Hardy collects lectures delivered by historian of philosophy Sir Isaiah Berlin at Washington, D.C.'s National Gallery of Art in 1965. Berlin shows how romanticism would later influence twentieth-century thinkers and artists. This is an accessible and useful study of romanticism.

- Paul Horgan's study of Henriette Wyeth's art, *The Artifice of Blue Light: Henriette Wyeth,* released in 1994, argues that Wyeth's work "belongs in the first rank of contemporary American painters." Among other things, Horgan examines Wyeth's use of the color blue in her paintings.

- Warren's second collection of poems, *Stained Glass,* published in 1993, contains thirty-nine poems, most of which concern death. These poems have the intensity of visual imagery which readers have come to expect from Warren's work.

- Warren published a work of fiction, *The Joey Story,* in 1963 when she was only ten years old.

A reader response theorist might suggest that readers allow the images that the author has created to work on their thoughts, to trust the effects and power of the poem. What is important about the poem is the significance that it arouses in the reader. And to help readers grasp their thoughts while reading the work, to help them create a list of questions to ask of themselves, some theorists have suggested the following steps. First, read the work (in this case, the poem). Take notes on the parts of the poem that are bothersome, the parts of the poem that cause a reaction. For example, one reader might find it bothersome when Warren writes "glass shard flying from liquor store window smashed." Here is a person, walking "humdrumming along," when all of a sudden she hears glass cracking, sees a young kid running off "zigzagging the crowd," hears the storeowner yelling. This is a startling scene. There is uncertainty. There's been a crime. Violence has been committed, and there is a chance that more violence could follow. The person in the poem more than likely feels threatened. Some readers might find this section bothersome or unsettling. But not all readers will react to this scene. Nor will all readers react in the same way. According to reader response theory, that's the way it should be, because each reader brings different experiences to the text. However, the mere fact that something is bothersome to someone might mean that that particular part of the poem might also be one of the more interesting parts of the poem, and therefore the reader should pay more attention to it. This is the part of the poem where the reader might learn the most because this is the part that affects the reader the most.

The next suggested step is for readers to define what they don't understand about the particular piece. For instance, Warren writes in lines 6–7, "Those Grecian dreams / endure even New York." Some readers might ask, What is a Grecian dream? What things have difficulty enduring in New York? What does New York represent, especially in contrast to Greece? These questions might require a little research for some, but others might already have some ideas about Grecian culture or the lifestyle of New York. And still other readers might rely on an intuitive sense, fed by images from the rest of the poem. And that is the next step: to create hypotheses that help make the poem more understandable, forming it in a personal way so that it makes sense. In this particular situation, for instance, the reader might have images in mind that make New York seem like a difficult place to live. Everything in New York seems congested: too many people, too many cars, too many buildings. Nature is almost completely obscured in New York, whereas the Greek Isles are pictured as a place to escape modern civilization, a place to dream and reflect. Greece and its culture, in contrast to New York, may appear more romantic, more conducive to a balanced emotional life. By following these investigative steps, readers should be able to develop a more directed interpretation.

Another development in response theory is based on psychoanalytical theories of response. Under this theory, according to Richard Beach in his book *A Teacher's Introduction to Reader-Response Theories,* "the ways in which readers' subconscious fantasy themes shape the meaning of their experience" is considered. In other words, a reader "transforms experience into a conscious level that expresses, through identification with the fictional character, the reader's repressed, subconscious experience." This is a theory that is grounded in the psychological theories of Sigmund Freud. Using this aspect of a psychoanalytical theory when reading "Daylights," readers might find themselves becoming angry when they read lines 22–23: "while the liquor man curses the daylights / out of the cop." Why is the storeowner cursing the cop? The cop didn't do anything wrong. The liquor man should be cursing the thief. This anger could be a clue to readers that somewhere in their past they felt unduly charged for some disturbing consequences of which they had no part. They might never have been able to prove their innocence and have thus repressed their anger. Upon reading the poem, that anger might be released. At least, this is what Freudian psychoanalytical theorists believe.

If it is true that readers bring their experience to a text and that through that experience they interpret the text, it is only a matter of math to sum up the facts and conclude that there are multiple interpretations possible. So, taking the text of Warren's poem and examining the concepts she has given, it might be interesting to create some hypothetical interpretations.

Having been raised in an urban setting in New Jersey and having listened to Bruce Springsteen since he was twelve, some imaginary reader studies Warren's poem and concludes that this is a poem about the cold, steel and concrete environment of modern society that beats away at the soft emotions of modern man. Where does this interpretation come from? Looking at the poem, this reader sees images of a harsh urban setting with the "glass shard," the "prize of Scotch," the "puddle flashes," and the "car window glints." He also sees concrete sidewalks, dull crowds, and strangers demanding eye contact. The character in the poem feels naked in the crowd, holding her "sky-stabbed heart" in her hands while she is yelled at by someone in the crowd: "What *you* lookin' at? Move on!"

Another reader, a young woman, perhaps, having been raised in a Christian household, might read Warren's poem and see images of Christ. There is the reference to "your hunk of daily bread" that brings up the image of Christ at the Last Supper, stating that this bread is his body. There is also "the chosen Aztec facing the last shebang—." Could this not be Christ just before his crucifixion: "(*his* last shebang; the globe keeps rolling along / slipslop in its tide of blood)—"? There is Warren's reference in line 27, "grateful, by God," which suggests that there might be some religious overtones in this poem, so the Christian woman reading it is at least somewhat aided in her interpretation.

Then again, there could be a reader who recently broke off a relationship with a lover or, worse yet, may have suffered the death of a friend. For this person, with her emotions already on fire, the passion of Warren's poem might rush to the forefront. This reader might interpret the "sky wounded you, jagged at the heart" as the sentiments of a character who is suffering, a character who would prefer to remain in the shadows rather than to have her raw emotions exposed to the light. "You think you're safe, humdrumming along" might refer to the safety one feels in a crowd, lost in the unidentifiable qualities of a crowd, lost in the mass of all the unknown stories. In other words, the strangers are all unknown to one another; therefore, no emotions are exposed or need to be explained. The only reminders of emotions are the lights that come from the sky, the reflections in the puddles, the car windows—all the daylights. In this interpretation, the Aztec might take on the image of the lover who is lost, especially if that lover has died. The "stranger . . . from a previous life" could represent someone who reminds her of her lost lover, reminds her of her pain. For this reader, the "sky-stabbed heart" speaks for itself, and when she reads line 21, she might have to choke back tears because the identification is so powerful: her broken heart is in her hands and she is offering it—but "to whom?"

According to reading response theories, all the above interpretations represent hypotheses. Each is a possibility. After formulating a hypothesis, the reader should then review the text "to find information relevant to understanding" the parts he or she doesn't understand. And finally the reader should test and revise the hypothesis "against prior information" to come to a final conclusion, a cohesive interpretation, one that makes sense not only on a personal level but also makes sense in relation to the full text. So for the young man who loves Bruce Springsteen, he should look at the text to see where his interpretation might not fit. For example, how has he decided to interpret the image of the Aztec in Warren's poem? What does the title of the poem refer to? And why does the speaker of the poem say that the character is grateful to move on?

The reader with a Christian background, on the other hand, needs to figure out what the "prize of Scotch" might refer to and why the speaker of the poem says, "They had warned you, blue / means danger." And the reader who has lost a lover might have to fit into her interpretation line 15: "un-clouded, un-named, as naked as / the chosen Aztec." Do these particular lines make sense in view of these readers' personalized interpretations?

Source: Joyce Hart, Critical Essay on "Daylights," in *Poetry for Students*, The Gale Group, 2001.

Sources

Baudelaire, Charles, *Selected Letters of Charles Baudelaire: The Conquest of Solitude,* edited by Rosemary Lloyd, University of Chicago Press, 1986.

Beach, Richard, "Psychological Theories of Response," in *A Teacher's Introduction to Reader-Response Theories,* National Council of Teachers of English, 1993, pp. 71–101.

Berlin, Sir Isaiah, *The Roots of Romanticism,* edited by Henry Hardy, Princeton University Press, 1999.

Bernstein, Charles, and Bruce Andrews, eds., *The L=A=N=G=U=A=G=E Book,* Southern Illinois University Press, 1984.

Bottoms, David, and Dave Smith, *The Morrow Anthology of Younger American Poets,* Quill, 1985.

Daniel Chandler's Semiotics for Beginners, http://www.aber.ac.uk/media/Documents/S4B/sem09.html (April 25, 2001).

Ellman, Richard, and Robert O'Clair, eds., *The Norton Anthology of Modern Poetry,* 2d ed., Norton, 1988.

Horgan, Paul, *The Artifice of Blue Light: Henriette Wyeth,* Museum of New Mexico Press, 1994.

Mallarmé, Stéphane, *Collected Poems,* translated by Henry Weinfield, University of California Press, 1996.

———, *Selected Poetry and Prose,* translated by Mary Ann Caws, New Directions, 1982.

Preziosi, Donald, and Louise A. Hitchcock, *Aegean Art and Architecture,* Oxford University Press, 2000.

Sleigh, Tom, *New York Times Book Review,* July 21, 1985, p. 24.

Warren, Rosanna, *The Art of Translation: Voices from the Field,* Northeastern University Press, 1989.

———, *Each Leaf Shines Separate,* Norton, 1984.

———, *The Joey Story,* Random House, 1963.

———, *Snow Day,* Palaemon Press, 1981.

———, *Stained Glass,* Norton, 1993.

For Further Study

John Jay College of the City University of New York Staff, *Crime and Justice in New York City, 1998–1999,* McGraw Hill, 1998.

    This handbook examines the crime problem in New York City thoroughly, its causes and effects. It also looks at the components of the criminal justice system including police, courts, probation, and the death penalty.

London, Herbert, *Broken Apple: New York City in the 1980s,* Transaction Publishers, 1989.

    London examines the social and economic problems of New York City in the 1980s.

Mallarmé, Stéphané, *Collected Poems,* translated by Henry Weinfield, University California Press, 1996.

    This collection contains Mallarmé's poem "L'Azur," which influenced "Daylights".

McClatchey, J. D., ed., *Poets on Painters: Essays on the Art of Painting by Twentieth-Century Poets,* University of California Press, 1990.

    This collection presents reviews and essays by well-known poets on painters.

For the White poets who would be Indian

Wendy Rose

1980

Often, when poets create work that is inspired primarily by anger toward an individual or a group of people, the poem turns out "preachy" or too emotional. Wendy Rose's poem "For the White poets who would be Indian," first published in *Lost Copper* (1980), is based on her feelings of indignation toward non-Native American writers who claim they can understand how it *feels* to be Indian and that they can create work truly from an Indian perspective. Rose's contention is that this cannot be done. She does not call out any "White poets" in particular in this poem, but she does offer descriptive insight into the way they go about their work and the possible reasons that these poets choose to adopt another culture as their own—at least in their poetry. Because Rose is able to present her beliefs in graphic, illuminating language (as opposed to an overly emotional diatribe) and to maintain a sense of honest poetry throughout the piece, it does not fall into the ranks of dull sermonizing.

"For the White poets who would be Indian" draws upon the idea of "white shamanism," a term used by some Native American poets—including Rose—to address the issue of white writers pretending to be so entrenched in Native American ways and beliefs that they are "just as Indian" as those born into the culture. The word "shaman" refers to a very powerful and revered figure in many tribal societies, indicating one who acts as a link between the visible human world and the invisible spirit world. A shaman practices magic or sorcery to heal the sick or to control natural forces. The term "white shamanism," then, is a sarcastic comment on the hypocrisy displayed by white writers "who would be Indian," and Rose explains why in this poem.

Author Biography

Wendy Rose was born Bronwen Elizabeth Edwards on May 7, 1948, in Oakland, California. Her father was Hopi, and her mother descended from both Miwok Indian and European ancestors. The fact of her mixed blood played a large role in Rose's struggle for identity as a youth, as did her suburban upbringing in Oakland, where life exhibited much more of the European, or "white," influence than Native American, on or off a reservation.

Rose's adolescence during the 1960s was as distressed and unrestrained as the times. She dropped out of high school and into the bohemian, artistic circles of San Francisco. But even as a vulnerable teenager on her own in a large city, Rose's ongoing interests were those that would develop over the years and become a major impetus for her writing and painting—self-identity, a desire to embrace her heritage as a Hopi Indian, and fighting the exploitation of Native American culture. During this time, she began writing poetry, although many of her earliest poems would not be published for several years, her first collection, *Hopi Roadrunner Dancing,* coming in 1973. In the 1960s, she also traveled to her father's birthplace in Arizona, Hopi Indian territory, and was deeply moved by the experience, enhancing her longing to identify with her Native American heritage.

In spite of the decision to drop out as a high school student, Rose would return to school in 1966 and spend the next fourteen years earning both undergraduate and graduate degrees and completing course work toward a doctorate in anthropology. Although she was a prolific poet and painter, Rose concentrated her studies on social science and received her master's degree from the University of California, Berkeley, in 1978. Between 1966 and 1980, she also published five volumes of poetry, including *Lost Copper* in 1980, which contains "For the White poets who would be Indian."

As a part of her quest for self-identity and self-creation, Rose has experimented with her own name over the years. Many of her early works were published under the name "Chiron Khanshendel." She chose Chiron, the name of the wise centaur of Greek mythology, because of her love for horses, and Khanshendel was simply a name she devised on her own. Eventually, she settled on the abbreviated version of her birth name—Wendy in place of Bronwen—and the last name of a man with whom she had a close relationship as a young woman—Rose. Despite the fluctuation, one decision was clear: the very astute, European-sounding "Bronwen Elizabeth Edwards" would not do, and she abandoned that moniker for good.

After completing her doctorate, Rose opted to remain in academia, and she has been a teacher, researcher, and advisor, as well as head of the American Indian Studies Program at Fresno City College in California. She is also, of course, a noted anthropologist and a renowned spokesperson for Native American causes. She resides with her family in the foothills of the Sierra Nevada Mountains in California.

Poem Text

just once
just long enough
to snap up the words
fish-hooked from
to our tongues.   5
You think of us now
when you kneel
on the earth,
turn holy
in a temporary tourism   10
of our souls.

With words
you paint your faces,
chew your doeskin,
touch breast to tree   15
as if sharing a mother
were all it takes,
could bring instant and primal
knowledge.

You think of us only   20
when your voice
wants for roots,
when you have sat back
on your heels and
become   25
primitive.

You finish your poem
and go back.

Poem Summary

Line 1

It is important to single out the first line in "For the White poets who would be Indian" because it makes a significant point about the individuals addressed in the work. The line is actually a continuation of the title, which is itself a prepositional phrase that seems to open a sentence. (Notice that the main words in the title are not all capitalized as they would be normally.) The words "just once" indicate that the "White poets" for whom the poem is written would really want to "be Indian" only one time, if they were given the chance. This is the first touch of sarcasm from the poet, as she calls into question the sincerity of non-Native Americans who claim they would like to be a part of Indian culture.

Lines 2–3

These lines continue the irony, implying that white writers would be Native American "just long enough" to steal words from *real* Indians to use as their own. Rose is not accusing non-natives of literal plagiarism here but rather of a theft of style, language, and spirit—all the intangibles that are sacred to a certain culture and that outsiders cannot truly copy or lay claim to.

Lines 4–5

Here, Rose incorporates the first sense of anger and bitterness into the poem. The Indian poets' words are not just "stolen" or "taken" or even "grabbed." Instead, they are "fish-hooked from / our tongues," insinuating a violent, painful ripping away of Native American property. This metaphor is strong and well chosen in at least two ways: it connotes a feeling of personal attack on Indian writers who believe pieces of their culture have been yanked out by intruding non-Natives, and it also draws from a major activity in Indian history, culture, and economics—fishing.

Lines 6–9

In these lines, Rose refers to the deep reverence for mother earth that is a part of all Indian societies. The words imply that the white poets who try to imitate a Native American lifestyle and who pretend to hold the same values and beliefs as Indians do so only briefly when they "kneel / on the earth," presumably in a stereotypical prayer position. Again, the poet uses irony and sarcasm in saying that the non-Natives "turn holy" when they are one with the earth, as though they share the same sense of kinship with nature as is inherent in Indian culture.

Lines 10–11

These two lines present a striking contrast between the shallow superficiality of "temporary

Media Adaptations

- There do not appear to be any specific Rose recordings on tape or online, either of her reading poetry or being interviewed. However, there are many web sites that include her biography and her poems, and they can be reached by doing a general search under her name.

tourism" and the obvious depth and spirituality of "souls." Rose likens the "White poets who would be Indian" to vacationers touring places in which they have no right to enter. A tour is generally brief and whimsical, and an attempt to "vacation" in the soul of an entire race is both offensive and unfruitful.

Lines 12–15

The opening lines of the second stanza refer, metaphorically, to the lengths that white writers will go to in order to "fit in" with Indian culture. Face paint and doeskin (used primarily for gloves and boots; chewing it causes the leather to soften) are Native American symbols, and the phrase "touch breast to tree" is again mindful of the closeness between Indians and nature. The *key* phrase here, however, is "With words." It implies that white poets follow Native practices only on paper. Whereas actual members of a tribe may paint their faces for ceremonial custom or chew doeskin or *physically* touch trees, stones, the earth, and so forth, the hypocritical "wannabes" do those things only with words.

Lines 16–17

The "mother" referred to in this line is the mother earth. Rose acknowledges that human beings of all races rightfully inhabit the planet and, given that, all people share the same mother. The poet does not believe, however, that "sharing a mother" is "all it takes" to blend the races and to allow passage from one into another simply by adopting certain belief systems or appreciating the lifestyle of another culture.

Lines 18–19

These lines complete the thought started in line 15 ("touch breast to tree") by pointing out the false notion that sharing mother nature can "bring instant and primal / knowledge" to people who try to become something they cannot. The word "primal" means first or original, and it drives home the fact that a white poet can only pretend to be an Indian poet since any "knowledge" he or she may attain is necessarily second-hand. It cannot be "primal" because only *original* Indians can have original Indian knowledge. The fact that Rose placed the word "knowledge" on its own line displays the significance of its meaning in the poem. Knowledge is a powerful and sacred possession, not something that one gains "in a temporary tourism."

Lines 20–22

Line 20 ("You think of us only") is almost a verbatim repetition of line 6 ("You think of us now"), and the meaning is essentially the same—white poets think about being Indian only when the moment is "right." In this case, the moment is when the non-Natives' "voices" need "roots" or a rich heritage and cultural strength from which to gain inspiration and meaningful insight. The implication here is that the white writers lack a real cultural *core* or a sense of history within the race and that they must, therefore, borrow the roots of other people when they feel the urge for heritage and belonging.

Lines 23–24

These lines also complete the "You think of us only" phrase, but they hold a double meaning as well. On one hand, they make reference to another stereotypical Indian practice—that of sitting in a crouched position on the ground with the buttocks resting on raised heels and arms crossed over the knees. The idea is that sitting "back / on your heels" is simply another adopted (or temporarily stolen) custom that white poets use to "feel Indian," like kneeling on the earth, face painting, doeskin chewing, and touching breast to tree. But the phrase "sitting back on your heels" has also become a derogatory cliché meaning annoying complacency or the tendency to wait for something to happen and then react to it instead of taking self-initiative. In this sense, Rose takes a stab at white poets who seem to acquire their culture in passing, as though it is something that can be captured on a whim.

Lines 25–26

The fact that these two lines are made up of only one word each signifies their importance in the work. The word "become," of course, implies something that is now what it was not before. In the human sense, one who *becomes* a certain thing must not have been that way originally. What the people addressed in this poem become is "primitive." Rose again turns to irony since "primitive" (like "primal") in this case means first, earliest, or original. Try as they might, the "White poets who would be Indian" cannot actually come to be what they never were in the first place.

Lines 27–28

The last two lines of the poem are a final angry reproach of those who have been Indian "just long enough" (line 2) to feel they have written a poem from an authentic Native American perspective. Sarcastically, Rose accuses, "You finish your poem / and go back." The place the non-Natives "go back" to, of course, is their white world where they will remain until the urge to be Indian comes once again.

Themes

White Shamanism

The term "white shamanism" may be an unfamiliar one to many readers of this poem, but its significance as a theme in the work is unmistakable. First coined by Rose and fellow poets Geary Hobson and Leslie Silko, white shamanism has been misinterpreted over the years, especially by non-Native American writers who may feel a personal affront by the term. In an interview with fellow poet and author Joseph Bruchac, published in *Survival This Way,* Rose tried to explain what it really means:

> It's assumed that what we're saying is that we don't want non-Indian people to write about Indians. That's not it. Many non-Indian people have written beautifully and sensitively about Indian people.... The difference is that there are those who come out and say that they are Indian when they are not.... There are those who come out and do not claim to be genetically Indian, but who do claim that what they are writing is somehow more Indian, or more legitimately Indian, than what real Indian people are writing.... They claim to be shamans and it's impossible to be a self-declared shaman. Your community has to recognize you.

In "For the White poets who would be Indian," Rose clearly addresses those individuals who make these claims, not just any non-Indian who has ever written about Native Americans. Writing *about* a different culture or a certain race of people is not the problem. What angers Rose and others who share her position are those poets who "snap up the words / fish-hooked from" real Indians' mouths and who think they can actually "become / primitive" by simply taking on the mannerisms, behaviors, values, and customs of American Indians. The idea of white poets going so far as to consider themselves shamans is alluded to particularly in the lines "when you kneel / on the earth, / turn holy" and again in "could bring instant and primal / knowledge." The intent of these lines is to mock the belief that people from one race can ever truly understand how it feels to be from another race, much less *become* a member of it. Rose scoffs at the notion that one can gain true knowledge simply by "sharing a mother" (the earth, in this case), and she accuses the white shaman poets of thinking that that is "all it takes."

The false, hypocritical beliefs themselves are not the only cause of Indian poets' anger toward non-Natives who "practice" white shamanism; further insult is added by the fleeting, on-again off-again nature of the desire or need to be Indian. The first two lines of Rose's poem ("just once / just long enough") point sarcastically to this aspect of the problem, and the lines "in a temporary tourism / of our souls" emphasize it even more. Here, "tourism" has a negative connotation, implying a frivolous and petty jaunt so out of place in reference to human souls. The poem faults white poets who think of Indians "only / when your voices / want for roots" or only when their own words and poems seem pale and dull in comparison to those written from authentic heritage and with authentic voice. The poem ends with perhaps the greatest indignity related to white shamanism from a Native American's point of view—the tendency to shift back and forth between worlds. According to Rose's work, the white poets she addresses visit the Indian world just long enough to steal some ideas and words for their poems, and, once the work is finished, they "go back" to their own world. The insincerity this designates is at the center of the controversy over white shaman poets.

Nature

Feelings of community with nature and regarding the earth as "mother" are not unusual in American Indian culture, and it is common for ex-

Topics for Further Study

- Write an essay in response to Wendy Rose's concept of "white shamanism," keeping in mind her own explanation of it rather than the ways in which it has been misinterpreted.

- Wounded Knee, South Dakota, has been the center of attention for Indian-U.S. government relations on two major occasions. Research the events that took place there in both 1890 and 1973 and write an essay describing what happened.

- Explain how the title "For the White poets who would be Indian" makes you feel and what you would think the poem was about if the name were all you were given.

- Write a poem called "For the _____ poets who would be _____," substituting any groups of people or things into the blanks.

pressions of it to show up in the work of Indian writers. Although Rose's "For the White poets who would be Indian" is more heavily laden with the theme of white shamanism, it still speaks to the closeness and oneness this poet feels toward the natural world. Even in her angry and sarcastic remarks to non-Native American writers, she uses metaphors that draw from nature and that reveal her reverence for it in spite of the accusatory makeup of the poem. With such words and phrases as "fish-hooked," "kneel on the earth," "doeskin," "touch breast to tree," and "want for roots," Rose packs this brief piece with images that emphasize the irony in white poets' attempts to "become" Indian. The voice in the poem makes the pairing of nature imagery with hypocritical human beings obviously out of place. Even though it is the white poets who are portrayed as kneeling on the earth, chewing doeskin, and touching trees, there is an overwhelming sense of unnaturalness in their behavior. This, of course, is Rose's point—that "sharing a mother" is *not* all it takes to move from one race into another. While the nature theme may appear subtle in comparison to the complaint against white intrusion on Indian culture, it actually serves to enhance that subject. Acknowledging the role of nature in the lives of Indians is crucial in understanding the need and desire to protect it from those interested in only a tour of it.

Style

Free Verse

"For the White poets who would be Indian" is written in free verse and is a brief poem, not only in terms of its twenty-eight lines but in the relative shortness of those lines as well. Here, the form complements the simple, somewhat calm, direct address from the poet to her supposed adversaries, and, too, it reflects the poignant, down-to-earth lifestyle of most Native Americans. But simplicity does not imply artlessness. This little poem is full of staunch imagery and a compelling voice that is made stronger by its succinct, halted cadence throughout. Read the poem slowly, stopping at each line break, and notice the repetitive "drumming" effect, how the lines—including those made up of only one word—tend to sound almost dull and heavy-laden. Lines such as "our tongues," "turn holy," "of our souls," "become / primitive," and "and go back" are especially loaded with both sound and meaning, and they command the reader's voice and mind to stop and pay attention to them.

Like nearly all free verse poems, the work is not completely "free" of any poetic device. Whether near-rhyme or alliteration (like-sounding consonants and vowels) occurs by happenstance or careful planning, there are usually a few examples of them in all types of poems, and they lend "a nice ring" to the work, if nothing else. In Rose's poem, there is obvious alliteration in "now" and "kneel," "temporary tourism," "touch breast to tree," and assonance in "want for roots," and perhaps though not so obvious in "once" and "enough," "holy" and "souls," and "sat back." Though putting only one word on a line may not be considered an official poetic device, it serves to make the poem's construction more vital to the entire work. Rose intentionally stresses the words "knowledge," "become," and "primitive" because they are essential to the poem's main theme. Along the same lines, she incorporates the title of the poem into the body by presenting the words in lower case and by making the first line a continuation of the thought begun in the title. By doing so, she allows the form of the poem to intertwine specifically with its meaning.

Historical Context

Rose began writing and publishing poetry during one of the most volatile times in American history—the 1960s. Her poem "For the White poets who would be Indian" was most likely composed later in the 1970s, but regardless of the current time in which Rose was writing, the subject of most of her work is based on a history that spans hundreds of years. The plight of Native Americans since the landing of the Europeans is no secret to members of any race in the country. Their struggle has been not only to physically survive but also to retain their lands, their lifestyle, their religion, and their culture. While these battles have been going on since the first encounter between Indians and whites, Rose addresses a relatively recent problem in the relationship between the two races, among poets in particular. Probably not until the 1960s, when young Americans began to shift toward different attitudes and lifestyles, did the idea of "stealing culture" seem so threatening to those whose identities were suddenly vulnerable. American Indian society—with its sense of community, its respect for the earth, its protection of wildlife, and an overall "one with nature" perspective—was especially appealing to white youth who had tired of the urbanized, technology-driven status quo. Some only adopted the more selfless, environmentally conscious attitudes of the Native Americans, but others went too far, according to Rose, in actually claiming to "become" Indian.

Rose's own struggle for identity was fueled by her mixed-blood heritage, and it was the Hopi side to which she wanted to belong. The Hopi creation story is very indicative of what developed over the centuries into "The Hopi Way," which is based on humility and peacefulness. According to the web site "Hopi: The Real Thing," the following tells the story of the tribe's creation:

> [The tribe] the Great Spirit, Maasau'u, came to visit them and to test their wisdom. The people were divided into groups, each with their own leaders that they had chosen. Then Maasau'u placed ears of corn of different lengths in front of each leader. As each leader pushed forward to grab the biggest ear of corn the Great Spirit gave that group a name and a language. The humblest leader picked the shortest of the corn, and the name 'Hopi' was given to those people: the little ones. Hopi means to be humble and peaceful, but if the people do not live the Hopi way the name will be taken from them.

In reality, of course, the Hopi Indians experienced their share of turmoil and found it difficult, if not impossible, to remain humble and peaceful.

Compare & Contrast

- **1969:** Indians from various tribes set up an occupation of Alcatraz Island in an attempt to establish a cultural center, museum, and community for any Native American who wants to live there. The occupation lasts until 1971 when FBI agents and federal marshals forcibly remove the Indians who remained after two years of fighting with the U.S. government.

- **1973:** Members of the American Indian Movement (AIM) lead 200 Sioux Indians in a seventy-one-day takeover of Wounded Knee, South Dakota, to demand a review of at least 300 treaties with the U.S. government.

- **1989:** In Browning, Montana, the Blackfoot tribe win a dispute with the Smithsonian Institution when the museum has to return the remains of sixteen of their ancestors for burial on native soil.

- **1990:** Leaders from the United States and the Soviet Union say no to a proposal by environmentalists at the Geneva Convention to burn less oil to avert global warming. The United States accounts for 24 percent of the world's carbon dioxide emissions.

- **1992:** Columbus Day of this year marks the 500th anniversary of Christopher Columbus' first voyage to America. There are both celebrations and condemnations, as some Americans praise the explorer and others vilify him.

Not only did they have the invasion of the white man to contend with but there was also an ongoing dispute with the Navajo tribe over land ownership in northeast Arizona. Both groups laid claim to it, and in 1882 President Chester A. Arthur established the Hopi reservation along the southern end of Black Mesa, which meant the Hopi were actually surrounded by the Navajo reservation. This "settlement" was hardly appeasing, and the problems continued. An article at the web site "Hopi: The Real Thing" explains the situation:

> Because land is a part of each tribe's religion complications arose concerning the use of land by people living on land that is considered to be holy. [Today] there are eleven Hopi villages in NE Arizona on Black Mesa, a rock land table [and] current Hopi population is between 10,000 and 12,000.

Native American history is an accumulation of attempts to hold on to what is rightfully Indian—from land to lifestyle and everything in between. Given such, it is understandable that Rose and other Indian authors would address the issue in their work, incorporating both historical facts and events that are taking place around them. The 1960s and 1970s saw major political moves by Indian tribes across America. One of the most highly visible and long-lasting actions was the takeover of Alcatraz Island by members of several different tribes on November 20, 1969. A web site article entitled "Indians of North America: Alcatraz" describes this period of American Indian history:

> The nineteen-month occupation of Alcatraz Island . . . is a watershed in the American Indian protest and activist movement. . . . The Alcatraz occupation brought together hundreds of Indian people who came to live on the island and thousands more who identified with the call for self-determination, autonomy, and respect for Indian culture.

For the next decade, Native Americans would bring attention to their concerns through more than seventy uprisings and occupations, and Alcatraz is recognized as the "springboard" that gave rise to them. The article states "these occupations continued through the BIA [Bureau of Indian Affairs] headquarters takeover in 1972, Wounded Knee II in 1973, and the June 26, 1975, shootout between American Indian Movement members and Federal Bureau of Investigation agents on the Pine Ridge Reservation in South Dakota."

All these events provided much motivation for Indian poets' work. Occupations and uprisings, however, did not tell the entire story, at least as Rose and others saw it. There was a separate struggle going on, as well, and that was the fight against white shamanism. Less noticed and much less understood by the general white public, this battle is just as important to Native American writers as are the more obvious protests.

Critical Overview

Wendy Rose's most notable contribution to contemporary American poetry is her ability to present controversial subjects in an insightful manner and to make them accessible to the general reader. She has been especially acclaimed for describing the tragedies and injustices of the Native American experience and doing so in a way that retains the poetic effect while still making political or social comments. Some critics have found her words disturbing, not only for their accusatory tone but also for their sense of untamed emotion and an "if you feel it, say it" agenda. Others, however, point out that this tendency is a strength rather than a weakness.

Just as interesting as the critics' responses to Rose's work are *her* responses to the treatment of Native American writing in general. In her interview with critic and fellow poet John Bruchac in *Survival This Way,* she had this to say about reviewers:

> It's a great frustration when people won't review our work, for example, in the usual professional way, saying that they don't have "the ethnographic knowledge" to do it or something. That's a frustration to me because some of us . . . come out [of prestigious writing schools] and then find out . . . that they're culturally too obscure to be reviewed as a real writer. That's not true.

Rose has also pointed out that her books often end up in "Native American" sections of bookstores and libraries instead of in the general poetry or American literature sections. She finds this a personal affront to her work as a poet. Most store owners and librarians (and critics as well) may deny any intentional disrespect by this practice, but Rose's point is in keeping with her continuing struggle for Native American rights and acceptance.

Criticism

Pamela Steed Hill

Hill has published widely in poetry journals and is the author of a collection entitled In Praise of Motels. *In the following essay, she presents Rose's poem as a work of controlled anger, written in a voice both poetic and indignant.*

How individuals deal with feelings of injustice or anger toward an entire group of people can be as varied as the personalities of those going through the experience. Human history is full of any number of reactions to unfair treatment and intrusion on personal space—from the creation of social and political reforms to murderous revenge by a few and all out war among nations. The so-called founding and development of America by Christopher Columbus and the Europeans who followed were accepted without question for most of the 500-year history of this country. Despite the reluctant acknowledgement of how that founding impacted the lives of people who had been living on American soil for centuries, many non-Native American citizens have found ways to "justify" the usurpation of Indian lands and the deaths of those who tried to stop it. Some, however, have done a 180-degree turn in *support* of Native American causes, embracing the culture so much that they feel an actual part of it. Rather than becoming true allies of Indian tribes of the late twentieth century, these white, would-be Natives are regarded as only one more link in a long chain of invasion and injustice suffered by those who are still fighting for what is rightfully (and exclusively) theirs.

Rose is all too familiar with the struggle to find and maintain self-identity. Her poetry reflects the awkwardness and emotional stress of being caught between two worlds—the white, European heritage of her mother and the Native American world of her Hopi father. There is no doubt, however, which side she prefers, and she appears to have spent much of her life thus far in attempts to enhance and solidify her identity as an American Indian. "For the White poets who would be Indian" is a poem that may make readers think Rose is a full-blooded Native, that she has never known the bewilderment of being part of two races. Certainly, in this poem there is no indication of any sympathy for the "White poets." Instead, the voice in this work is angry, yet controlled. Rose does not fall over the edge into some mindless ranting but instills in this poem the rich imagery and provocative circumstance that create good poetry, all the while berating a race of fellow poets for their intrusion into her world.

From the outset of the poem, Rose accuses white poets of theft. The animosity is clear in the third line in which the phrase "snap up the words" conveys her belief that non-Native American writers who pretend to be Indian do so by stealing words, phrases, and topics that they think *sound* Indian. These are the poets that Rose accuses of "white shamanism," a term referring to the claim by non-Natives that they are somehow "more Indian" than actual Native Americans and that their poetry is also more Indian than that written by real Natives. One noted poet who would fall into this category, according to Rose, is Gary Snyder, whose work does often reflect and imitate Indian manner and subjects. His lifestyle, too, is patterned after that of Native Americans, and he lives "close to the earth" in the American West. Whether or not Snyder is actually guilty of white shamanism is for poets on both sides to argue, but his work is a clear example of what riles some Indian poets into angry rebuke.

Despite the indignation revealed in the opening lines of "For the White poets who would be Indian," Rose maintains a poetic sense in the image of words being "fish-hooked from / our tongues." This phrase is still angry and accusatory, but it is also creative in the use of "fish-hooked" as a strong and apt verb describing how white poets acquire the words for their Indian poems. When Rose next attacks the sincerity of these white poets, she retains a poetic voice in the fresh and unlikely metaphor of "temporary tourism / of our souls." Comparing the shallow would-be Indian poets to fleeting tourists on a holiday is an inventive way of expressing cynicism and disgust over having something as sacred as souls treated in such a frivolous manner. But sustaining the metaphorical application throughout the poem is indicative of the control Rose holds on to in spite of the very volatile subject matter.

This brief but powerful poem gains some of its strength from Wendy Rose's own striving for personal completeness—her longing to be a whole Indian. Given her lifelong struggle, the idea of becoming Indian on a whim, the way some white poets have done, must be an even harder slap in the face than usual. The web site "Voices from the Gaps: Women Writers of Color" suggests that:

> the diversity of Rose's poetry is not about distinctions, but about wholeness. Her contempt for the "whiteshaman" is out of the lack of wholeness which they represent, a wholeness which she has struggled to define in herself and her work. As she was struggling to find her identity within her mixed lineage and culture, using poetry to express herself, the "whiteshaman" simply stole from her culture. As her poetry bespeaks the position of injustice, the "whiteshaman" spoke from a privileged position.

> *The lines 'become / primitive' are cynical as Rose derides white poets for foolishly thinking they can sit like an Indian and so become one. But separating the words onto two different lines is poetically effective, serving to slow down the poem toward its end and give it a quieter impact."*

This lack of wholeness on the part of the white poets who would be Indian is implied in the second stanza of the poem especially. Rose isolates three examples of Indian practices that white poets perform only "With words." Those examples—face painting, chewing doeskin, and touching "breast to tree"—point out the incompleteness and hypocrisy of people who think *writing about* a few behaviors reminiscent of Indian culture is "all it takes" to become Native American. Rose is particularly sensitive to the notion that "primal knowledge" may be obtained instantly and easily. In her estimate, white shaman poets serve only to cheapen *real* native insight and knowledge by assuming they can gain it by *acting* Indian. Including much nature imagery and addressing Indian concerns in the work does not make a white poet an Indian poet, regardless that the two races are "sharing a mother" in the planet Earth. But the fact that Rose makes this statement by using nature imagery herself (doeskin, trees, the earth) and that she does so in interesting and unique metaphorical depiction keeps her from seeming too didactic or emotional. Her anger is mollified by creative description. Its presence is still felt, but the poetics hold it in check.

One could argue that the white poets addressed in this poem are not the only ones who "want for roots"—that Rose herself has had a perpetual struggle to claim her own roots in the Hopi Indian culture. The fact that her mother was part white seems

What Do I Read Next?

- Although published nearly forty years ago in 1963, *Book of the Hopi,* by Frank Waters and Oswald "White Bear" Fredericks, is still one of the most interesting and insightful books on this fascinating culture. It covers the complete Hopi history, including the origin of the clans, the four migrations, and common ceremonies, among many other aspects.

- In the early 1990s, editor Patricia Riley put together a provocative collection of twenty-two essays by Indian writers, called *Growing Up Native American* (1995). This book is excellent for introducing readers to Indian history, literature, culture, and Native American authors. While it does address the tragedy and hardship that many of the writers experienced, it is also full of funny stories, jokes, and recollections of mischievous pranks.

- As part Hopi, Wendy Rose has always been fascinated with learning more about her heritage, and she has had to face the challenges of the intrusion of other people on it. Frederick Dockstader's *The Kachina and the White Man: The Influence of White Culture on the Hopi Kachina Cult* was first published in 1954 when Rose was a child and presents good insight into how the pressure of white culture affected the Hopi lifestyle, with particular attention to religious changes.

- One of the most sensitive and revealing first-hand accounts of a spiritual Indian leader is *Black Elk Speaks: Being the Life Story of a Holy Man of the Oglala Sioux* (1932), with a preface by John Gneisenau Neihardt. The narratives of this visionary Native American who lived from 1863 to 1950 describe the terror, anger, and confusion that afflicted his people as they struggled to survive the invasions on their homeland. It was first published in 1932 and is just as enlightening today as it was seventy years ago.

---

to have been a thorn in the side of the daughter who wanted to be *all* Indian. In an interview with fellow poet Joseph Bruchac, in *Survival This Way: Interviews with Native American Poets,* Rose spoke candidly about her feelings on being of mixed race:

> I was in a situation where I was physically separated from one-half of my family and rejected by the half that brought me up. And in this case it was because of what there is in me that belonged to the other half. The way that a lot of us put it is you're too dark to be white and you're too white to be Indian. . . . I was in that situation where the white part of my family had absolutely no use for any other races that came into the family. . . . The Indian half is in a situation where, among the Hopi, the clan and your identity comes through the mother, and without the Hopi mother it doesn't matter if your father was full-blooded or not, you can't be Hopi.

There is a sense of resentment in Rose's statements, apparently for the white side of her family, the side that brought her up and yet rejected her as well. It is the same resentment that shows up in her poetry, although in the case of "For the White poets who would be Indian," her own partial whiteness is not mentioned. The "voices" who "want for roots" belong to the intruding Caucasian poets, and she includes herself in the Indian group in saying, "You think of us." In spite of the seeming hypocrisy here, the poetic style and control over form and expression prevent the tone from being whiny or irrational. The lines "become / primitive" are cynical as Rose derides white poets for foolishly thinking they can sit like an Indian and so become one. But separating the words onto two different lines is *poetically* effective, serving to slow down the poem toward its end and give it a quieter impact.

The final two lines of the poem bring it full-circle from the beginning. It started out with the idea that white poets want to be Indian "just once / just long enough" to steal words, create poems, and feel satisfied with their Native identity. The last lines complete that thought in saying simply, "You finish your poem / and go back." This is yet another accusation, but it is also a resignation on the part of the poet. She seems to accept that this is just the way things go and that her anger and indignation may be justified but will not likely change anything.

Wendy Rose's poetry is provocative, but it should not be mistaken for racism. Even though she singles out a particular group of people to speak against in this poem, the selection is not based on skin color alone. Rose does not convey any ill feelings toward white poets (or white *people*) in general—only those who claim to be what they are not, only those who intrude on a culture and pretend it is their own. In Rose's mind, it is the Indian who has been insulted, and poems like this would not need to be written if the attack had not been launched in the first place.

Source: Pamela Steed Hill, Critical Essay on "For the White poets who would be Indian," in *Poetry for Students*, The Gale Group, 2001.

Joyce Hart

Hart, a former college professor, is a freelance writer and copyeditor. In this essay, she projects the theme of Rose's poem "For the White poets who would be Indian" onto the larger screen of ethnopoetics, the movement in poetry that inspired the writing of the poem.

The first impression a person might have after reading Wendy Rose's "For the White poets who would be Indian," might be that Rose has a dislike (or worse) for all white poets who write about Indians. But this is not true. In an interview with Laura Coltelli (1985), Rose says that she has "no difficulty with people taking on an Indian persona and trying to imagine through their work what it would be like . . . to be a man or a woman in Indian society. Fine. As long as it's really clear that that's what it is—an act of imagination." What troubles Rose and what prompted her to write this poem are the people "who say that they have some special gift to be able to really see how Indians think, how Indians feel." It is a matter of integrity, says Rose.

Rose and fellow poet Geary Hobson have coined the phrase *white shamanism* to refer to the practice of white poets (as well as other cultural workers) who delve into Native American myths and native literary forms, taking the liberty to retranslate them according to their own literary styles (although they may have little or no knowledge of the culture or the language) and then claiming a profound understanding of the native culture to the

> "'Ethnopoetics,' says James, 'adds poetic devices such as rhyme, meter, and structure' to the older translations. If done carefully, James states, ethnopoetics could offer a more realistic representation of the native cultures and their literary forms."

point of claiming shamanistic or mystical powers. One such poet, Jerome Rothenberg (to whom Rose wrote the poem "Comment on Ethnopoetics and Literacy") is considered one of the organizers of the poetic movement called ethnopoetics. Understanding Rothenberg's philosophy as well as his reasons for organizing the ethnopoetics movement, gives the reader a better appreciation for the sentiments behind Rose's poem "For the White poets who would be Indian."

The ethnopoetics movement lasted from the late 1960s through 1980. Ethnopoetics, according to Peter O'Leary in a review of a book written by Nathaniel Tarn (another influential poet in the ethnopoetics movement), is described as follows:

> [Ethnopoetics is] a brand of American surrealism that combined poetry with anthropology by incorporating the belief that the poet, either through vocal effects that echo those of the proto-poetic shaman, or verbal and visual effects that are the latter-day remnants of those vocal effects, can retrieve or restore something of sacred reality through his or her poetry.

Meredith James, in a book review for *World Literature Today*, states that "ethnopoetics uses literary techniques to capture the vitality, complexity, humor, and artistry of traditionally oral works." Ethnopoets believe that old translations of Native American songs (poems) and myths are outdated. The old translations were done mostly by linguists, anthropologists, and missionaries who had no flare for poetics. "Ethnopoetics," says James, "adds poetic devices such as rhyme, meter, and structure" to the older translations. If done carefully, James states, ethnopoetics could offer a more realistic representation of the native cultures and their literary forms.

Unfortunately, not all translations are done carefully. And in this context, James reinforces Rose's concern for lack of integrity on the part of the poet. James adds that when the translations are not careful, "ethnopoetics creates a text that misrepresents the content and meaning of the original work, so that the stories are not so much the subject but instead the tool of ethnopoetics, telling the reader more about the translator than about the story." In order to understand this better, there is a need to look a little deeper, first, into ethnopoetics; and then into what people within the Native culture are asking for in terms of integrity. In reference to the first step, this essay will take a closer look at Rothenberg's stated definitions of and aims for ethnopoetics.

In the fall of 1970, Rothenberg published the first issue of *Alcheringa,* a journal devoted to ethnopoetics. In that issue, he printed a "Statement of Intention." Three of the intentions of the journal were: 1) to offer a place "to provide a ground for experiments in the translation of tribal/oral poetry"; 2) "to assist the free development of ethnic self-awareness among young Indians"; 3) "to combat cultural genocide in all its manifestations." The first intention was easily provided by the publication of the journal. The second, however, seems a bit pretentious in that Rothenberg appears to be stating that it is through a re-interpretation of Native poetics (namely ethnopoetics) that the "young Indians" would develop their ethnic self-awareness. According to James, as stated above, careless translation actually provides a misrepresentation of the original work. So poor ethnopoetics could lead the "young Indians" in the wrong direction from what their own ancestors had intended. Also, according to James, the so-called translator of these ancient poems becomes the focus of attention, while the story (or poem) fades somewhat into the background. Rothenberg confirms this in his "Pre-Face to a Symposium on Ethnopoetics" by emphasizing the ethnopoet's role as the shaman. The ethnopoet "performs alone . . . because his presence is considered crucial . . . [he] is needed for the validation of a certain kind of experience important to the group . . . [his madness] flows out to whole companies of shamans, to whole societies of human beings: it heals the sickness of the body but more than that: the sickness of the soul."

But it is in reference to Rothenberg's ethnopoetics third intention that Rose might very well have written her lines: "to snap up the words / fish-hooked from / our tongues." In other words, Rothenberg is a hunter who is stealing the "tribal/oral poetry," then mutilating it, and offering it back to the youths of that tribe as a gift—an act that seems quite contrary to the stated third intention. Rothenberg says that these youths are the "remnants [of hunting and gathering peoples who] exist as an endangered [and] ultimately doomed 'fourth world.'" And it is toward the goal of stopping "cultural genocide," of stopping the ultimate doomsday of this "fourth world" that Rothenberg takes on the "performance role that resembles that of the shaman." Or in Rose's words: "with words / you paint your faces / chew your doeskin, touch breast to tree / as if sharing a mother / were all it takes / could bring instant and primal / knowledge." Rose is telling Rothenberg and all *whiteshamans* that it takes more than claiming yourself to be a shaman, to become a shaman. Rose also claims that movements such as ethnopoetics can displace, marginalize and even belittle Native Americans' own stories, resulting in (contrary to Rothenberg's intentions) cultural genocide.

"You think of us only / when your voices / want for roots / when you have sat back / on your heels and / become / primitive," continues Rose's poem. And Rothenberg confirms Rose's sentiments with his statement that the poet "who had once been seer" has become an outsider in his own culture. And because the poet has become the outsider, he is constantly in search of his "primitive roots" that he believes can be found only in "something vastly older like the 'nature-related cultures'" such as the cultures of the Native Americans. Rothenberg adds that he should have learned as much from his "own origins, from which [he] had been running for most of [his] grown life." Whether it was because he lost his own roots or failed to heed them, Rothenberg believes that by reaching back to the "primitive" he will heighten his "awareness of the present [and] the future." But what does this have to do with Native Americans? Is Rothenberg trying to save their culture? Trying to rescue it from eminent extinction? Or is he searching for something else?

In her article "The Great Pretenders, Further Reflections on Whiteshamanism," Rose offers the following thoughts: "We accept as given that whites have as much prerogative to write and speak about us and our cultures as we have to write and speak about them and theirs. The question is how this is done and, to some extent, why it is done." This brings up the question of integrity. Part of the definition of integrity is discussed in Christopher Ronwaniente Jocks' article "Spirituality for Sale." First

Jocks summarizes the critiques of several Native American writers' opinions (including Wendy Rose's) concerning the adverse affects of carelessly re-translated Native American poetry and stories. There are the commercial adaptations and academic interpretations of American Indian knowledge and practice that is "often plainly inaccurate." Also, distortion often occurs when non-Native American authors try to interpret Native American concepts by using non-Native American definitions. This often occurs when non-Native American authors try to explain Native American religious concepts. An example of this is the concept of shaman, which is often associated with the Native American culture, but actually has its roots in northern European culture.

Jocks continues that there are also "numerous examples of descriptions that distort by selecting only the most pleasing (read, 'marketable') elements of Native experience to 'reveal.' Typically, practices that seem to involve 'mystical' individual experiences are promoted, while other elements considered equally or more important by Native participants are ignored: elements such as kinship obligations, hard work, suffering, and the sometimes crazy realities of everyday reservation life." Many non-Native American authors publish information for which they have not been granted permission. Much of this information is considered sacred by the Native American culture and there is a breach of ethics involved when that information is made public through "deeply offensive commercial enterprises." Jocks explains that these songs (or poems) are all parts of spiritual ceremonies and "a sacred practitioner is, by definition, a person integrated into the place and the community out of which she or he works . . . traditional American Indian ceremonial work is of a piece with traditional economic structures which, in turn, are based on reciprocal relationships within a community."

Rose's poem sums up these objections in the lines: "You think of us now / when you kneel / on the earth, / turn holy / in a temporary tourism / of our souls." Tourists come to a place from afar. They are not part of the community. What they take from that community will be designated a souvenir. What they pay for that souvenir will be in dollars. The souvenirs do not cost them anything of themselves.

Jocks elaborates next on a definition of integrity—what is required of an author who re-interprets Native American stories. He states that "knowledge cannot be traded in some imagined neutral 'marketplace of ideas,' as if it were itself a neutral, disembodied object. . . . We simply need to demand that those who put forth their interpretive opinions in public form, printed and otherwise, stand up and tell their stories fully." He believes that an author cannot learn about what goes on in a Native American community without living in it for "a long time." It takes many years to understand the "the subtleties of perception, history and communication that inform it. In fact, one really needs not just to reside, but to reside as a relative," a vital part of the community. Jocks then lists what he believes are "a few bare suggestions" on how he perceives that one can judge the integrity of an author.

First, there is reciprocation. If an author makes a living from information that he or she receives from a Native American community, there should be some kind of reciprocation made to that community. Second, authors need to "provide clear and comprehensive accounts of their relationships with the Indian communities they study." They should also be required to give to that community a full explanation of their motives. Mere curiosity or wanting to use the information to "test existing Amer-European essentialist theories" should not be considered valid reasons.

Although ethnopoetic intentions include an awareness of the challenges that face Native American communities, they do not state an intention that includes working with the community. More specifically, Rothenberg focuses on only the poetic form itself. He wants to explore and re-interpret the ancient poetry so as to hold it up against the "Amer-European" forms, and from that comparison, hopefully create a new poetry. "On the one hand," he writes, "the contemporary forms (the new means that we invent) make older forms visible: [and] on the other hand the forms that we uncover elsewhere help us in the reshaping, the resharpening, of our own tools." If this is an exchange, what is Rothenberg giving back to the community?

"Sharing of spiritual practices and knowledge can only rightly take place . . . in a discourse of mutual respect," says Jocks, "with the permission of both parties." Rose adds her thoughts by saying that this has already occurred many times before.

"Many non-Indian people have —from the stated perspective of the non-Native viewing things Native — written honestly and eloquently about any number of Indian topics. . . . We readily acknowledge the beauty of some poetry by non-Natives dealing with Indian people, values, legends, or the relationship between human beings and the American environment. [But] a non-Native poet cannot produce an Indian per-

> *"Like fishermen catching fish, white poets are in search of words, and they sink their hooks in deep to extract them. The poets Rose is addressing don't seek a holistic understanding of Native American culture and history; rather they want for the words of Indians; they want for the stories, for the traditions, for the language."*

spective on Coyote or Hawk, cannot see Coyote or Hawk in an Indian way, and cannot produce a poem expressing Indian spirituality. What can be produced is another perspective, another view, another spiritual expression. The issue, as I said, is one of integrity and intent."

From her poem, Rose summarizes all these feelings of lack of integrity, suspect intent, and non-involvement in the community when she writes: "You finish your poem and go back."

Source: Joyce Hart, Critical Essay on "For the White poets who would be Indian," in *Poetry for Students,* The Gale Group, 2001.

Judi Ketteler

Ketteler has taught literature and composition and has studied Native American literature. In this essay, she discusses the ways in which Wendy Rose's poem "For the White poets who would be Indian" is a response to her white peers, who appropriate Native American culture for the sake of their art. It looks at the cultural context for such appropriation and the ways popular culture has responded to and stereotyped Indians for centuries.

In the poem, "For the White poets who would be Indians," Wendy Rose responds to white America's appropriation of Native American culture. Specifically, she is addressing white poets who want to take part of Native American culture and make it their own for the sake of art. As a woman with both European and Indian ancestry, Rose is caught between the white world and the Indian world, between English language and Native traditions. She struggles with her own identity even as she sees that identity "borrowed" by her white peers. In fact, identity conflict is woven throughout Rose's words, as her tone floats between resentment and anger.

"For the White poets who would be Indians" was first published in 1980 in Rose's collection of poems entitled *Lost Copper*. At that time, Native American literature, as an entity, was still fairly new, having only gained critical attention and academic standing a short ten years before. Of course, that is taking into account only a narrow definition of Native American literature, which includes an oral tradition of storytelling dating back thousands of years. At the time of Christopher Columbus' arrival in 1492, there were more than 300 different Indian cultures in North America, each with its own creation stories, histories, governments, social structures, and customs. Even to speak of Native American literature is somewhat of a misnomer. In fact, it is many traditions, many histories, and many different ways of communicating those histories.

To understand the underpinnings of Rose's angry and distrustful tone, it is important to revisit American history. The seventeenth, eighteenth, and nineteenth centuries were full of shameful genocidal practices toward Indians on the part of European settlers. Policies ranged from forced removal to reservations to systematic slaughter to broken treaties and outright lies. Children were forcefully removed from home and sent to boarding schools—where they were punished if they were heard speaking their native languages. At the same time that Native Americans were encouraged to assimilate, they were cast as exotic objects, called noble savages or bloodthirsty warriors. It is a dirty history altogether, one that has shaped Native American literature throughout the centuries.

It was in the 1960s when the Native American civil rights movement came to power. Literature began to blossom, too, with the publication of N. Scott Momaday's novel *House Made of Dawn.* The 1960s were an important time for Wendy Rose as well. Born in Oakland, California, she dropped out of high school and mingled with the bohemian scene in San Francisco. In 1966, she went back to school, ultimately completing her Ph.D. in anthropology at the University of California, Berkeley.

She struggled with her identity as a mixed-blood person as well as with her identity as a scholar while at Berkeley. Rose, as quoted in the article, "The Nether World of Neither World: Hybridization in the Literature of Wendy Rose," by literary critic Karen Tongson-McCall, explains her struggles and her exclusion:

> The fact is, the only department at Berkeley that would deal with my dissertation, which involves Indian literature, is the anthropology department. Comparative literature didn't want to deal with it; the English department didn't want to deal with it, in fact the English department told me that American Indian literature was not part of American literature and therefore did not fit into their department.

That frustration is very much alive in "For the White poets who would be Indians." By the time Rose wrote this poem, however, what had changed in the academic and literary world was that to "be" Indian was suddenly in vogue. In this way, white writers are trying to appropriate, or steal and make their own, Native American beliefs and traditions. The poem opens with a violent image of theft: "just once / just long enough / to snap up the words / fish-hooked from / our tongues." Like fishermen catching fish, white poets are in search of words, and they sink their hooks in deep to extract them. The poets Rose is addressing don't seek a holistic understanding of Native American culture and history; rather they want for the words of Indians; they want for the stories, for the traditions, for the language. They don't want the identity of Indian for permanent use, just long enough to claim an artistic connection, one that makes them appear more sensitive, more in tune with the earth. And in the end, of course, they can still keep their white skin and the privilege that goes along with it. The "fish hook" Rose speaks of is a stinging image, one rooted in a bitter and misunderstood history.

Scholar Vine Deloria Jr., member of the Standing Rock Sioux Tribe, as well as theologian, attorney, and political scientist, understands this identity-snatching phenomenon some Indian scholars have labeled "white shamanism." He recounts, in a tongue-in-cheek manner, his experiences working for the government:

> During my three years as Executive Director of the National Congress of American Indians it was a rare day when some white didn't visit my office and proudly proclaim that he or she was of Indian descent. Cherokee was the most popular tribe of their choice and many placed the Cherokees anywhere from Maine to Washington State. . . . At times I became quite defensive about being a Sioux when these white people had a pedigree that was so much more respectable than mine. But eventually I came to understand their need to identify as partially Indian and did not resent them. I would confirm their wildest stories about their Indian ancestry and would add a few tales of my own hoping that they would be able to accept themselves someday and leave us alone.

Rose's poem echoes these exact sentiments. Her language is rich and forceful, calling to mind the tourist industry that has been built around Indians, presenting them in shallow and untruthful ways. "You think of us now / when you kneel / on the earth, / turn holy / in a temporary tourism / of our souls." Not only are white poets able to engage in this "tourism" of souls, white America has built an industry around it: selling cheap, unauthentic souvenirs in shops, taking advantage of limited economic resources of Indians to hire them to dress up in Plains-type headdresses when they most likely belong to a tribe nowhere near the West with a completely different culture than Plains Indians' culture. Popular culture appropriates Native American culture because there is money in it. White Americans get to "go native" by visiting an Indian reservation, buying some arrowheads, getting their picture taken with an Indian in costume, even if it resembles nothing of their traditional costume. It allows them to, as Rose says, "turn holy." And claiming Indian ancestry is just the icing on the cake.

Rose speaks of the way white poets mimic the traditional Native practices, engaging in rituals like kneeling on the earth. For these imitators, ritual is merely a commodity up for grabs, a thing with no inherent value. This is highly disrespectful and infuriating to Rose. Rose, if readers recall, has struggled with her own identity in the way she lives in two worlds. Her heart may lie with her Native American ancestry, her skin may be dark, but she writes in English for an audience of English-speakers. She is living, as the title of Karen Tongson-McCall's article suggests, in the "nether world." Rose writes about this experience herself in her introduction to *Bone Dance*, a collection of poems in which "For the White poets who would be Indian" appears. She says, "Without a Hopi mother, I am not even part of a clan. Learning all of this had a great deal to do with my writing of poetry. How can you hope to speak if you have no voice? Neither cast-offs, nor mongrels, nor assimilated sell outs, nor traditionalists, those who are like me are fulfilling in our way a certain level of existence." Therefore, not only are white poets stealing part of Rose's people's culture and identity, they are failing to understand the complexity of what they are stealing, the struggles that have shaped identities in flux, those voices from the nether world, over the past three hundred years.

"For the White poets who would be Indian" is full of images from nature, "primal" images. White poets are trying to use words to get "back to nature." "With words / you paint your faces / chew your doeskin / touch breast to tree." These writers try to adorn themselves with nature garb through their words. They practice "white shamanism" to call up spirits and write poetry about mother earth. "As if sharing a mother / were all it takes," Rose says. We can read this as an implicit critique of the way European-Americans have tended to treat the earth, as more of a dumping ground than a mother. Whereas most Native American religions posit people as the children of the earth, the caretakers of it for future generations, Christianity—and along with it, Western culture—posits people as the masters of the earth, the controllers of it. The "instant and primal knowledge" Rose refers to is that knowledge of the cycles of the earth; the "mother" she speaks of in the previous line is the earth. And while both whites and Indians share the earth, or share a mother, their relationship to that mother is completely different. For white poets to try to use words alone to reinvent a relationship to an earth-mother is preposterous from where Rose stands.

Also implicit in Rose's response to those white poets who would be Indians is the enduring image of Indians as savages, as primitive. "You think of us only / when your voices / want for roots, / when you have sat back / on your heels and / become / primitive." White American culture has repudiated the savage, casting it as the "other." At the same time, labeling Indians as savages has been the justification in the imagination of white America for the savage acts against Indians. This system of ideas is the same one used to justify slavery. If white Americans who owned slaves could cast them as the "other," as something not even human, but as property, then buying and selling them could be justified. What's different about Native Americans, however, is the romance of the West, the idea of the noble savage, the silent warrior. White poets' desire to become "primitive," then, is a shallow one, rooted only in stereotypes, mostly of Plains Indians, who represented the last American frontier.

It is perhaps the last two lines of the poem that best uncover the true posturing of the white poets. "You finish your poem / and go back." This completes the image of the "temporary tourism" of souls that Rose speaks about earlier. Because the white poets are in fact white, they can always go back. They don't live inside Indian skin from day to day or inhabit the margins of a society, desperate to find a voice. They are not silenced or cast as others because they are part of the dominant culture. *They can always go back,* and this is key for Rose. They try on a mask, take what the want, and return to the security of their whiteness—echoing the pattern of American history and Native Americans' vexed place within it.

Source: Judi Ketteler, Critical Essay on "For the White poets who would be Indian," in *Poetry for Students,* The Gale Group, 2001.

Joseph Bruchac

In the following interview excerpt, Rose clarifies her intent in "For the White poets who would be Indian."

*In his preface to your collected poems—*Lost Copper*—N. Scott Momaday said that it was a book, "not made up of poems, I think, but of songs." Would you agree with that distinction of Momaday's?*

In a subjective sense, yes. I don't think that the poems are literally songs the way that we usually understand the term. But I use them the way that many Indian people traditionally use songs. They, in a sense, mark the boundaries of my life.

So that would be one of the differences between your poetry and traditional English verse.

Yeah, I think so. My perception of them. The way that they function in my life.

Is there any other way in which they're song?

I think oftentimes that audiences feel them that way. People sometimes call them songs when they talk about them but, I don't know, I couldn't speak for what it is they are perceiving. I couldn't really put words in their mouths to try to clarify what they mean, but people call them songs and maybe they're feeling the internal parts of it the way that they have meaning for me.

In that same introduction Momaday also spoke of your language, saying, "it has made a clear reflection of American Indian oral tradition." Do you perceive a relationship between your writing and that oral tradition?

I would like to but I would have to say probably not too much. I think that there are some important differences, and I think that my particular work probably leans more toward European-derived ideas of what poetry is and of who poets are than Native American in spite of the subjective feeling that I have of the way that the poems are used in my life. There are some important differences, one of which is the sense of self-expression. The need to express the self, the need to make one's own emotions special and to explain it to other people, I don't think really exists in most Native American cultures. And I think that is an important component in my work.

Are there any other distinctions that you'd see or any other things that you would use as definitions of the American Indian interpretation as opposed to the Western interpretation of the use of song or poetry?

One way that I think perhaps they do function, and I hope it doesn't sound like I'm contradicting myself too much, is that gradually the various Native American communities are re-establishing links with people using oral tradition. And sometimes this extends even to those of us who use the printed word and who publish. So in recent years I'm finding that the poet is right there with the orators and is speaking in council. I'm finding more and more that, when there are gatherings of Indian people, there will be poets who will contribute to what's happening. This was lost for awhile because of the effect of the white man's education in that for a while Indian people were discounting the contribution that poets were making in the same way that the white man discounts the contributions of his own poets. But increasingly I think that contemporary poets in Native American communities are coming to be valued in a traditional sense even though the work itself might be different.

What are the roots of your poetry? How did you personally become a writer—and then a writer who identifies so strongly with your Native American roots?

That's a complex question. Influences as far as poetry are concerned—they're just so multiple. Perhaps the earliest one that I remember is Robinson Jeffers, who of course was not an Indian poet. But some of the first published poetry I was ever exposed to was his and that was important to me, and I think it was my first sense of being able to think in terms of putting a poet in a landscape that's familiar, because the area that he was writing about was where I grew up—the northern California and central California coast. That was an early influence. Other influences that were fairly early—I figured out that it was okay to be an Indian and a writer at the same time probably, as many of us did, through the influence of Scott Momaday. His getting a Pulitzer prize in fiction made a real dif-

> *One is the obvious thing of being biologically halfbreed, being of mixed race. I was in a situation where I was physically separated from one-half of my family and rejected by the half that brought me up . . . . you're too dark to be white and you're too white to be Indian."*

ference to us because I think so many of us had assumed that no matter what our individual goals might be, we had to somehow choose between fulfilling the goal and having any degree of integrity as Indian people. Whatever influences there are from Native American culture—I'm being fairly careful not to cite tribe here because I was born and grew up at a distance from my tribe, so I'm trying to deliberately separate myself from saying Hopi literature or Miwok literature—my community is urban Indian and is *pan* tribal. But whatever Native American traditional influences that might be in my work, I don't know if I can pick them out individually. I missed out on a great deal by not being exposed to tribal traditions as a child. In the city I was exposed on the one hand to a great many traditions and on the other hand to nothing that was really complete. I don't know. Perhaps that's an unanswerable question. I know that there was also this: in terms of identifying as an Indian writer, that was partly and perhaps mostly a function of how literature is published and distributed in this country—which is that in this particular instance if you are of a minority group and you are a writer, you are simply not allowed to do anything other than be a minority writer.

I think this would be a good place to ask you this question. In your poem "Builder Kachina," you have these lines—"a half breed goes from one-half to the other." And of course The Halfbreed Chronicles *is the name of the collection you just read that first poem from. That word "halfbreed" seems to be very important to you. What is it? What does that mean?*

Well, again, I have to answer on at least two different levels. One is the obvious thing of being biologically halfbreed, being of mixed race. I was in a situation where I was physically separated from one-half of my family and rejected by the half that brought me up. And in this case it was because of what there is in me that belonged to the other half. The way that a lot of us put it is you're too dark to be white and you're too white to be Indian. James Welch expressed it well in *The Death of Jim Loney* where Jim Loney answers someone who says to him (to paraphrase), "oh, you're so lucky that you can have the best of both worlds and choose whether or not at a given moment you will be Indian or you will be white." And he says, "it's not that we have the best of both worlds, it's that we don't really have anything of either one." I think that's really a very true statement. You don't get to pick and choose but rather you're in a position where you have no choice whatsoever. I was in that situation where the white part of my family had absolutely no use for any other races that came into the family. The white part of the family had no use for it. The Indian half is in a situation where, among the Hopi, the clan and your identity comes through the mother, and without the Hopi mother it doesn't matter if your father was fullblooded or not, you can't be Hopi. So that left me in that situation. The first years of writing, perhaps, the motivation from the very beginning was to try to come to terms with being in that impossible situation. But then maturing as a person, halfbreed takes on a different connotation and that's where *The Halfbreed Chronicles* are coming from. Now *The Halfbreed Chronicles* depict a number of people, and genetics doesn't have a great deal to do with it. For instance, the poem "Georgeline" is relating to people who are a fullblood Lakota family. There are other people who are depicted in *Halfbreed Chronicles* who would not be identified as halfbreed. People who are Japanese-American. People who are Mexican-Indian but spent their lives as sideshow freaks. People like Robert Oppenheimer. You don't think of these people in the same sense as you usually think of halfbreeds. But my point is that, in an important way, the way that I grew up is symptomatic of something much larger than Indian-white relations. History and circumstances have made halfbreeds of all of us.

Then maybe you wouldn't be offended by my bringing in something I just thought of . . . a quotation from Matthew Arnold. He described himself back in the Victorian era—"one half dead, the other powerless to be born." There seems to be, as you see it, a world dilemma not just of people of mixed Indian and white ancestry but of the modern culture that we find ourselves faced with.

Yeah, and I think that the point does come out in *The Halfbreed Chronicles* because one of the responses that I get is from people who are genetically all Caucasian, or all black, or all Indian; people who are genetically not of mixed race come up to me afterwards and say I know just what you mean by those poems. I feel like a halfbreed, too. So I know the message is getting through. We are now halfbreeds. We're Reagan's halfbreeds and Dukmejian's halfbreeds.

I find it interesting, too, that that poem, which I cited a quotation from, is called "Builder Kachina" and there is no Builder Kachina as I understand it.

No there isn't.

But you have imagined a Builder Kachina?

In a sense, yes, but based on things that my father really said to me. The poem is based on an actual conversation that I had with my biological father, which is the Hopi side of the family. And the conversation was basically my going down to the reservation and sitting down and talking to him and presenting the situation to him at a point where I was in crisis over it and saying what can I do because I can't be a member of a clan, because I can't have your clan? You're my father not my mother, I'm not entitled to any land or any rights or any privileges on the reservation. Yet, at the same time, my mother's family doesn't accept me, never has, probably never will, because of the fact that you are my father. So what do I do? His answer to me was, "Well, sometimes it's difficult, sometimes people don't point out to you what your roots are but your roots are on this land, and you just have to stand here yourself on this Hopi land and build them," and from that came the imagined person of Builder Kachina. I've invented lots of Kachinas. I hope that it's not thought of as being too sacrilegious. But I've invented Kachinas that go into outer space. I've invented Kachinas that are in the ocean and a lot that have appeared in the visual arts. This particular one appeared in poetry.

Yes, the Kachinas are something I find occurring again and again in your writing. What are the Kachinas to you? How would you define them. I know there's a definition on strictly a tribal level . . .

Well, there's no real agreement even on that definition because they aren't any one thing. They're not strictly nature spirits and they're not strictly gods. They're not strictly ancestral spirits and yet they're all of that. They are spirit beings who grow and evolve and have families and live and possibly die. Humans have to communicate with them and have to relate to them. One way that they can be thought of is if you think of the entire earth as being one being and we as small beings living on that large being like fleas on a cat. The Kachinas in a sense are aspects of that cat that are communicating with us. This is one way to look at it.

I see then in your "Builder Kachina" a sort of balance emerging out of that duality and chaos caused by the conflict between two forces which seem to be mutually exclusive. The two worlds of the European Indian. The two worlds of the two parents that you describe in your own life.

Well, of course, one thing also is that the Hopis say that the Europeans being on this continent is something that isn't all that important in the long run, that eventually the continent will be purified. The evil parts of that influence will be gone, and things will eventually return as they were and the cycle will continue. This is really only a small thing that we inflate with our own self-importance into meaning more than it does. For those of us who are in my position, I don't know whether I'm supposed to be saved with the Hopi or wiped away with the whites.

Thinking of evils, I've seen several particular evils singled out numerous times in your writings. Let me give you some examples—the California missions, the attitude of anthropology toward Indian people in general, cities and the concept of modern cities. Why do you choose those particular targets?

I don't see cities as evil first off. I don't think there should ever be more than, at most, a couple of thousand people living in one unit. I think beyond that it's impossible to be governed with any sense of integrity when you don't recognize each other and have no obligation to each other. But in any case I don't see cities as evil per se. They're evil for me. I'm not able to adapt to living in cities even though I've tried. I become intensely uncomfortable in cities and I see cities destroy people that I love. As for the other things, the California missions, of course, were not a spiritual endeavor; they were an economic endeavor. They had more to do with the conquest of a new bunch of natural resources by the Spanish crown than they did with the saving of souls. The point behind incarcerating Indian people there was to have a cheap labor force, a slave force if you will, to make blankets and to make pots and pans and various kinds of things for the Spanish settlers, for the colonist. Also to have everybody in one place so there wouldn't be any Indian people to stop settlement and there wouldn't be any Indian people out there able to act on their own. So they were incarcerated. Reduced is the actual Spanish term, the *reducciones*. It killed off some incredible number, something like during just ten years alone, in the early nineteenth century, the California Indian population was reduced by some incredibly high number like 80 percent. It was because of a combination of disease, of unnatural living conditions, and the punishment for running away. What a lot of people don't realize is there were a number of revolts against the Spanish mission by the Indians. But they don't tell you this in the museums. In fact, the museum right here in Oakland paints a ridiculous picture of the missions with the happy little natives making baskets in the shade of the adobe with the benevolent padres walking around rattling their rosaries. That just is not the way that the missions were.

And then there is the attitude of anthropology toward the Indian people. It seems linked to what we were just talking about with the missions.

In fact there's a saying that—I've heard versions of this saying from people from Africa, from Australia, from New Zealand, various American Indian people—first comes the explorer, then comes the military, then comes the missionary, then comes the anthropologist, then comes the tourist. Actually, though, as you know, in one sense it's ironic that I should be so highly critical of the field since at the moment I am teaching lower division anthropology at a junior college. However, I'm teaching it in an unorthodox way, and I hope I don't get in too much trouble for it. But, yeah, anthropologists have certainly been one of the main targets of some of my anger, probably stemming from my intimate association with them as a Ph.D. student in anthropology at Berkeley which contains both the best and the worst. I've run into some incredible racism in that department and, as faculty now, I see my Indian students running into situations that are even more bizarre than things I had experienced because it's becoming increasingly okay among the general population to become racist again or to express the racism that was always there. It's no longer cool to try to be tolerant or understanding or liberal or even to recognize that America is a plural country. There are a number of anthropologists, however, who are very, very good people and are sensitive to these issues. Unfortunately, I think they are still in a minority probably because anthropology is part of a European–derived institution run by the white male power structure. So Indian people along with many other kinds of people—women, gay people, people from fourth world nations and from third world nations—all of these people are coming into anthropology now and changing the face of it. But it's very slow because that old guard of course is still there. A lot of Indian people are going into anthropology just to become super informants and don't realize it.

In part two of Lost Copper *there are some poems that were originally published as a chapbook under the title* Academic Squaw: Reports to the World From the Ivory Tower. *I'm always interested in titles. What did you intend by it?*

Well, obviously, it was intended as ironic. The publisher inadvertently left off a postscript that was supposed to be on the title page. I think in *Lost Copper* they did put the postscript in. In the chapbook it originally appeared in, it was inadvertently left off. It explained how the term "squaw" is used in a purely ironic sense. That was really an important thing for two reasons. One is because "squaw" is an offensive term, regardless of its origin. It is now and has been for many, many years an offensive term much like "nigger" or "spic" and has been degrading not only in a racist way but in sexual ways as well. Because the image of the so-called "squaw" is a racist and a sexist image. So, on the one hand, people who are aware of that might otherwise think that I was using it without any kind of clarification, that it was just as if it were part of my vocabulary. As if I really saw myself that way. And people who don't know any better might assume the same thing not realizing there's anything special about the word. I have run into people who simply think that that is a word for Indian women. Just like they think that "papoose" is a word for Indian children and so forth.

Or "pickaninny" is a word for a black child.

Yeah. I know a man who thought that Jewish men really were called Jewboys and would call people that to their faces in total innocence because that's the only way he had ever heard Jewish men referred to. Things like this. So there is an innocence there in one sense but there's also a maliciousness.

I meant the title, of course, in a completely ironic sense and the poems were written in that context because I had just spent two years as an undergraduate at the University of California at Berkeley in anthropology and had just, in fact, by the time the book came out entered graduate school as a Ph.D. student. So the book encompasses experiences at both the graduate and undergraduate level as an anthropology major. And, as I was saying, there were some racist things that happened. There were a lot of things that happened that I had to come to terms with. There were many times when I almost dropped out. I spent the entire first year at Berkeley, in my junior year as a transfer student from a junior college, huddling in a corner in Native American Studies drinking tea and trembling. This is all coming from somebody who was raised in a relatively urban area right next to the university all her life, so I can't imagine what it must be like coming from a reservation, from someplace that's very different from Berkeley. The poems were written as a survival kit, really. And in fact one of the most pleasant things I have ever done was the day that the book came out from Brother Benet's press, I went and stuck copies of it in all my professors' mailboxes.

Why have you chosen to enter that Ivory Tower world? That world of the academic?

I'm not in the Ivory Tower. I'm a spy.

Okay, good. You say also in the poem "Handprints," "in this university I am a red ghost."

I'm a spy.

A spy. Great.

Don't blow my cover.

Oh, no. No, we'll never tell. (laughter) Let me move on to another area, Wendy. How has your art affected your writing? You now have a reputation both as an illustrator and as a writer. In fact, in some of your poems you speak directly of that world of art in rather magical terms. Sometimes you even speak as a mother speaks of her children. I'm thinking of the poem "Chasing the Paper Shaman," or the poem "Watercolors." How has your art affected your writing and how do they work together?

I can't imagine them really working apart. Nobody bothered to tell me until I was an adult that there was anything wrong with being both a visual and a verbal artist. I think that's the only reason why that isn't the case with more people, and I think that's the reason why it is the case for so many Native American people. Look at the number of Native American authors who illustrate their own work and who illustrate other people's work. There is a tremendous number. There is nothing unusual about it among Native American people at all. There's a tremendous percentage of writers who do so in contrast to the non-Indian writers, where it's very seldom the same person who does both. But the way I think of it—now I don't really know where the poems or where the art comes from, I don't know where the images come from—but however they come or wherever they come from is like communicating with a person. It's a whole person. That person shows you things and has a certain appearance but also tells you things. So as you receive images, they are either received through the ear or through the eye or through the tongue and that's just the way it feels.

Another thing that I find different about your work and also that of a number of American Indian writers (as compared to the typical writer of the traditional English mold) is your attitude toward death. Death seems to be very important in your work. Why is that so?

I don't know. I never really thought of it as being important to the work. I guess if I really think about it, yeah, I've got a lot of bones rattling around in there. I guess there's a sense of feeling—sometimes I feel like I'm dead. Like I'm a ghost. Similarly, sometimes I feel that I'm alive but there are ghosts all around me, so that's part of it. But as far as the symbols go, of things like the bones for instance, I think maybe it's argument against death. Maybe what I'm saying is that the bones are alive. They're not dead remnants but rather they're alive.

You have these images of returning to the earth and images of bones. These don't strike me as morbid images, as they would be in, say, a poem written in the eighteenth century in England.

Well, you know, the rocks are alive and all the components of a tree, for instance, live. A pine cone falls down from the tree and it's alive. It carries the life of the tree in the seeds that are in the pine cone. And I think the parts of the body must be the same way. The brain isn't all there is to human life. The consciousness that's inside the skull is not all there is.

There is a poem of yours in What Happened When the Hopi Hit New York—*"Cemetery, Stratford, Connecticut"— with these lines: "I know that what ages earth has little to do with things we build to wrinkle her skin and fade her eyes." You also say "I have balanced my bones between the petroglyph and the mobile home." These different things, balanced in some way, seem bound to lead in a different direction than just finality.*

Well, that's really what we are, isn't it? We're bones that are just covered with flesh and muscle. The part of us that is spirit is just a component that is part of that entirety. We are parts of the earth that walk around and have individual consciousness for awhile and then go back.

I could see someone looking at your poems and saying these are evidences of bitterness, of hopelessness, of a very dark perception of life.

That's what a lot of white people see in them. Indian people almost never do.

As a matter of fact, I'm playing the devil's advocate because I think there is a question we may have to address. What do you think American-Indian poems have to offer to non-Indians? Are there problems of perception like this which may make them inaccessible to the non-Indian reader?

I don't know. I want to say no, they're not inaccessible because it's a great frustration when people won't review our work, for example, in the usual professional way, saying that they don't have "the ethnographic knowledge" to do it or something. That's a frustration to me because some of us—people like Joy Harjo or any number of other people that actually have M.F.A.s from prestigious writing schools—come out and then find that they're being told that they're culturally too obscure to be reviewed as a real writer. That isn't true. I think that a person does need to stretch the imagination a little bit, perhaps, or to learn something about Native American cultures or Native American thought systems or religion, or philosophy. Just a little bit. But I don't think any more so than you need to become a Kabbalistic scholar in order to understand Jerry Rothenberg. This is a plural society and all of us have to work at it a little bit to get the full flavor of the society. I have to. Boy, do I have to work at trying to understand the Shakespearean stuff! I have students in my creative writing classes who are into Shakespeare and write tight verse and rhyme and do it very, very well. They're not doing it unsuccessfully, but I have to really work to understand where they're coming from. Just simply that what they're expressing is a dominant cultural mode in this particular country is not sufficient reason to say that that is the only way it should be. If I have to work at understanding that stuff, then I don't see why they shouldn't work a little bit to understand mine.

Hasn't it often been the other way? Literary critics have celebrated the greatness of someone like James Joyce because Finnegan's Wake *and his other books are so complicated.*

If they think the complication is individual rather than cultural, then they really love it, sure.

Good point.

But if they think it's cultural then they think that we're insulting them somehow by expecting them to understand it. That we're asking them to go out of their way. And of course, really, we're not asking any more of them than they ask of us when we pick up books in this society and read them.

What images, aside from those I've already mentioned, seem to be recurrent in your poetry?

I think I have a lot of female images. A lot of times I think that just talking about rocks or trees or spirits, where there's no real reason to put a gender on them, I automatically tend to make them female. I think that's something I've noticed more recently. Themes? I've been writing a little bit of science fiction poetry lately about colonizing other planets. But of course it's not from the colonizing viewpoint, it's from the viewpoint of the people on the planet. But that's sort of off the wall. I don't know, it's pretty hard to see the themes in your own work. I'm always amazed at what other people see in them. At first I don't believe them, and then I go back and I read it again and I realize they were right. Sometimes.

Which of your already published poems express most clearly for you what you want to say as a writer?

As a writer? Oh, boy! Of the published poems? I don't know. I guess the things that are most current in my mind or the things that I most want to say are what I've said most recently, which usually isn't published at that time. I guess what I want to say is bound up in *The Halfbreed Chronicles,* and as of now few of them have been published. One of the major focal points in *The Halfbreed Chronicles* section was published in *Ms. Magazine* in the June 1984 issue. That's kind of exciting to me to finally get a "pop" readership.

Is this the one about the woman who was . . .

The woman in the circus, about Julia Pastrana, yeah. They're publishing that one.

That's a particularly powerful poem, to me, for any number of reasons. I heard you read it about a year ago and was very moved by it.

Well, it's about a Mexican Indian woman who was born physically deformed. Her face was physically deformed to where her bone structure resembled the caricature of Neanderthal man that you sometimes see in museums. She had hair growing from all over her body including her face. So she was Neanderthal looking and hairy in visual appearance, but she was also a graceful dancer and a singer in the mid-nineteenth century. She was a very young woman. She was billed as the World's Ugliest Woman and put on exhibit, where she would sing for

the sideshow. The poem is not just about the exploitation of her being in the circus but is like a step beyond that. It's an ultimate exploitation. Her manager married her and it was, presumably, in order to control her life in the circus. She believed that he loved her, though, and really, what choice did she have emotionally? When she finally had a baby, the baby looked just like her. The baby had all the same deformities, but also had a lethal deformity of some kind and died just shortly after birth. Then she died a day or two after that. And her husband—and here's where the real *Halfbreed Chronicles* come in—her husband had her and the baby stuffed and mounted in a wood and glass case and continued to exhibit them in the circus even though she couldn't sing anymore. There was just something about the horror of that which in *The Halfbreed Chronicles* is coupled with the poem called "Truganinny" about an Aborigine woman who happened to be the last living Tasmanian native.

Truganinny went through a similar situation. She had seen her husband stuffed and mounted by the British museum people as the last Tasmanian man. She asked her aboriginal friends to please make sure that when she died that didn't happen to her. She wanted to be buried way out someplace where they couldn't find her body or just be thrown into the sea or something. And they tried but they were caught, and so she was actually stuffed and put in a museum too. Just like her husband, as the last specimen of a Tasmanian human being. The two of them together, Julia and Truganinny, represent the ultimate colonization. They're not side by side in *The Halfbreed Chronicles.* They're separated slightly by a couple of other poems. But they're intended as a pair in a sense because of the similar fate and because the circus treatment of the so-called freaks is another kind of colonization. Then too, what is it that happens to the colonized if not being made into a sideshow? So that's basically the point behind the Julia Pastrana poem and also the Truganinny poem. We are all in that situation. We are all on display that way.

There seems to be a growing consciousness on the part of American Indian women, both as writers and as people speaking up. In the postscript poem in Lost Copper *you say "Silko and Allen and Harjo and me—our teeth are hard from the rocks we eat." What do you have in common and why choose those particular women?*

This will sound sort of funny, I guess, but I could have gone on and named many, many more Indian women writers. I chose those particular ones because I felt that they were fairly well known, that a reader who has been reading very much contemporary Indian literature will immediately recognize the names. I feel that they have all made strong statements about being Indian writers, both in their creative work and peripheral statements in interviews or in articles that they have written. The actual fact of the matter is that I stopped after naming just those ones because that was the meter of the poem. (laughter) What I intend there is to go on with the list—and Hogan and north-Sun and Burns and Tapahonso and so on and so on. They're in there.

What is exciting about their work for you?

I know that when I read their work it makes chills go up and down my spine in a way that really most other people's work doesn't. It's not just Indian women's work, but work by minority American writers, by writers of color in general. It very often has that effect on me. When I read work that does have that effect on me, it is usually by such a writer. I tend to be terribly bored by the writing of white academic poets. Hopelessly bored. I really don't care how many sex fantasies they had watching a bird on a fence. If you'll pardon the phrase, I think in academia, in English departments, that the writers are just masturbating.

Of course there are also the writers who are putting on headdresses.

Yes. Yeah. There are those, but even they are not generally in the academic situation. Even they are a little too peripheral for academe.

Um. Those white poets who would be Indian as you title that one poem of yours.

Yeah. And of course that needs some clarification too because it's widely misunderstood—the whole thing about the "white shaman" controversy that Geary Hobson and Leslie Silko have addressed themselves to, that I have addressed myself to. It's widely misunderstood. It's assumed that what we're saying is that we don't want non-Indian people to write about Indians. That's not it. Many non-Indian people have written beautifully and sensitively about Indian people. Even in persona. The difference is that there are those who come out and say that they are Indian when they are not, in the case of some. There are those who come out and do not claim to be genetically Indian, but who do claim that what they write is somehow more Indian, or more legitimately Indian, than what real Indian people are writing. There are these people who claim to be what they're not. They claim to be shamans and it's impossible to be a self-declared shaman. Your community has to recognize you. And we know that the word is Siberian but we also know what is meant by it in popular usage. Yeah, it's directed toward these people and it's a matter not of subject matter but of integrity in the way in which the subject matter is approached.

You've been editor of The American Indian Quarterly, *taught Native American Literature, worked on a major bibliography of Native American writing. What do you see happening with American Indian writing today?*

Well, I think that there is a small nucleus of people who are primarily associated with the Modern Language Association who are acknowledging that it is a legitimate field of study. People like Karl Kroeber and LaVonne Ruoff and Andrew Wiget, Larry Evers. There's a whole crew there. These are people who have been interested in it all along. But through their influence and the influence of Indian writers who have become involved in that end of the writing business, the scholarship end of it, it's becoming better accepted in academe. But it's very slow as in the fact, for example, in the University where I taught (Berkeley), we were just recently told by the English Department that they would not hire people to teach anything about American Indian literature "because it's not part of American Literature." So, it's very slow. But it's gradually happening because of people like the scholars that I named . . . although it took a long time even to get to where Indian people could go speak for themselves, where Indian writers could go deal with their own work even in the Modern Language Association because the tradition for so many years was that the white scholars would sit around and talk about the work without having the writers there to deal with it themselves. That's changing.

You feel then that the current small popularity of American Indian contemporary writing is more than just a fad? That its message is large enough to go beyond this moment?

The message is large enough to go beyond the moment—whether anyone is listening or not, I'm not sure. I think that the way that a lot of us started, particularly those that are around my age in their thirties and forties, was on the basis of a fad. We were brought into it, many of us, before we were mature enough as writers, really, to do it. We were brought into anthologies and so forth, and our work was exposed to critical masses, so to speak. But I think that maybe if we work hard enough at it that we will somehow be able to make sure that it is incorporated into general American literature. And here I'm not just talking about Native American, I'm talking about Afro-American, I'm talking about Asian-American, I'm talking about Chicano and Puerto Rican, Indochinese. All of the various cultural elements have their literature that becomes modified and yet retains its cultural integrity as they come into America. Or as they leave the reservations and go into the cities that are in America. I think this is going to happen, whether anyone is out there listening or not, it's going to happen. And I know that the Indian communities respect their writers more now and that's the part that's really important to me. I would much rather be respected by the Indian community through my writing than to have my books reviewed in the *New York Times.* I really would.

Last question. What would you say to young American Indian writers now in the way of advice?

Like that old civil rights song says, don't let nobody turn you 'round. Although they probably never heard the song. (laughter)

Source: Joseph Bruchac, "The Bones Are Alive," in *Survival This Way: Interviews with American Indian Poets,* University of Arizona Press, 1987, pp. 252–69.

———, Interview with Laura Coltelli (1985), "Modern American Poetry" website at www.english.uiuc.edu/maps/poets/m_r/rose/coltelli.htm (August 8, 2000).

———, *Lost Copper,* Malki Museum Press, 1980.

Rothenberg, Jerome, "Pre-Face to a Symposium on Ethnopoetics," in *A First International Symposium on Ethnopoetics,* 1976, "Alcheringa: Ethnopoetics" at www.durationpress.com/archives/ethnopoetics/alcheringa/index.html (August 23, 2000).

———, "Statement of Intention," in *alcheringa,* Issue 1, Fall 1970, "Alcheringa: Ethnopoetics" at www.durationpress.com/archives/ethnopoetics/alcheringa/index.html (August 23, 2000).

Tongson-McCall, Karen, "The Nether World of Neither World: Hybridization in the Literature of Wendy Rose," in *American Indian Culture and Research Journal,* 1996, pp. 1–40.

Voices from the Gaps: Women Writers of Color, http://voices.cla.umn.edu/authors/WendyRose.html (July 5, 2000).

Sources

Amazon, www.amazon.com (July 11–12, 2000).

Bruchac, Joseph, "The Bones Are Alive: An Interview with Wendy Rose," in *Survival This Way: Interviews with American Indian Poets,* University of Arizona Press, 1987, pp. 249–69.

Deloria, Vine, Jr., "Indians Today, the Real and Unreal," in *Native American Literature: An Anthology,* NTC Publishing Group, 1999, pp. 7–15.

The History Channel, www.historychannel.com (July 10, 2000).

Hopi: the Real Thing, http://www.ausbcomp.com/redman/hopi.htm (July 5, 2000).

Indians of North America: Alcatraz, http://csulb.edu/~gcampus/libarts/am-indian/alcatraz/001_001_intro_text.html (July 14, 2000).

James, Meredith, Review of *Coming to Light: Contemporary Translations of the Native Literatures of North America,* in *World Literature Today,* Vol. 71, 1997, pp. 198–99.

Jocks, Christopher Ronwaniente, "Spirituality for Sale: Sacred Knowledge in the Consumer Age," in *American Indian Quarterly,* Vol. 20, 1996, pp. 415–17.

O'Leary, Peter, Review of *Scandals in the House of Birds,* in *Chicago Review,* Vol. 45, 1999.

Rose, Wendy, *Bone Dance: New and Selected Poems, 1965–1993,* University of Arizona, 1994.

———, "The Great Pretenders: Further Reflections on Whiteshamanism," in *The State of Native American Genocide, Colonization, and Resistance,* edited by M. Annette Jaimes, South End Press, 1992, pp. 403–21.

For Further Study

Brown, Dee, *Bury My Heart at Wounded Knee,* Holt, Rinehart, and Winston, 1970.

When this fully documented account of the destruction of Indians in the American West first appeared in the early 1970s, it was met with both shock and shame by the general public. It begins with the "Long Walk" of the Navajos in 1860 and ends thirty years later with the massacre of Indian men, women, and children at Wounded Knee, South Dakota. Reading this book provides insight into the basis of long-held Indian anger toward and mistrust of white society.

Coltelli, Laura, *Winged Words: American Indian Writers Speak,* University of Nebraska Press, 1990.

This book is presented in interview format and includes a photograph of each American Indian author. It includes Wendy Rose, Paula Gunn Allen, N. Scott Momaday, Leslie Marmon Silko, and others.

Rose, Wendy, *Hopi Roadrunner Dancing,* Greenfield Review Press, 1973.

This is Rose's first published collection of poems. It includes many of her early works, which she wrote during her years in San Francisco and in college, including several poems about the occupation of Alcatraz Island by Indians seeking to create a new community among tribes.

———, *What Happened when the Hopi Hit New York,* Contact II Publications, 1982.

This "middle" collection by Rose contains poems that reflect mainly on travel and that were inspired by various archaeological sites. One recognizable difference in this book is the number of humorous or light-hearted poems as opposed to Rose's typical expressions of conflict and anger.

I felt a Funeral, in my Brain

Emily Dickinson
1861

"I felt a Funeral, in my Brain" was first published in 1896. Because Emily Dickinson lived a life of great privacy and only published a handful of poems in her lifetime, the exact year of its composition is unknown; most scholars agree that it was written around 1861.

Like many of Dickinson's other poems, "I felt a Funeral, in my Brain" explores the workings of the human mind under stress and attempts to replicate the stages of a mental breakdown through the overall metaphor of a funeral. The common rituals of a funeral are used by Dickinson to mark the stages of the speaker's mental collapse until she faces a destruction that no words can articulate. As the metaphorical funeral begins and progresses, the speaker's "mind" grows "numb" until her final remark stops in mid-sentence. The poem is a staple in Dickinson's canon and reflects her ability to replicate human consciousness in a controlled poetic form. Like her poems "After great pain, a formal feeling comes—", "'Hope' is the thing with feathers—" and "I felt a Cleaving in my Mind—", "I felt a Funeral, in my Brain" uses concrete language and imagery to explore abstract issues.

The event that the funeral is used to describe, however, does not have to be interpreted as a mental breakdown. The poem allows for other readings of what constitutes the "funeral," such as an individual's being assaulted by an idea that threatens to destroy all of his or her dearly held assumptions or a mind's inability to cope with the pressures placed upon it from the outside world. The poem's ambi-

Emily Dickinson

guities allow for multiple readings, all of which, however, converge in the idea that the speaker's brain is ceremoniously "laid to rest" by the poem's conclusion.

Author Biography

Like Shakespeare, whose poetry has become an integral part of world literature but whose personal life remains very much a matter of speculation, Emily Dickinson left behind very few clues about herself besides the wealth of poetry found only after her death. She was born Emily Elizabeth Dickinson on December 10, 1830, in Amherst, Massachusetts, the second child of Edward and Emily Dickinson. Her grandfather, Samuel Fowler Dickinson (1775–1838), was a pillar of Amherst society, building the town's first brick house and cofounding Amherst College; his son Edward (Emily's father) served as the college's treasurer for thirty-seven years. Edward also served for many years in the Massachusetts legislature and spent two years in the United States Congress in the House of Representatives.

Dickinson's father was a stern, Puritanical man who sought to defend his children and church from the growing threat of radical ideas, among them New England transcendentalism, a philosophy set forth largely in the works of the essayist and poet Ralph Waldo Emerson (1803–1882). In one of her many letters, Dickinson described her father with the words, "His Heart was pure and terrible and I think no other like it exists." Indeed, Edward Dickinson felt that women (his two daughters included) ought to stay at home and leave the running of the country to their husbands and brothers. Despite these seemingly provincial views, Edward did ensure that his daughters received excellent educations; Emily attended Amherst Academy (where she studied both the liberal arts and sciences) and then Mount Holyoke Female Seminary (now called Mount Holyoke College) for a year before withdrawing in 1848, possibly because she found the coursework unchallenging.

After her withdrawal from academic life, much of Dickinson's biography becomes speculative; however, the growth of her skepticism concerning the god in whom her father so ardently believed can be attributed to her receiving a copy of Emerson's *Poems* in 1850. Emerson's radical ideas about the divinity of man and his explorations of Eastern philosophy struck a chord in Dickinson's mind, and she remained a disciple of Emerson's for the rest of her life. When, exactly, she began seriously composing verse remains a matter of some debate. It is known that, in 1862, she sent some of her poems to Thomas Wentworth Higginson, a prominent essayist whom she had never met and who showed little initial appreciation for her work (although he did gradually befriend Dickinson and help get her work in print after her death). In her lifetime, less than twenty of her poems were published and to no great acclaim. One was even mistakenly attributed to Emerson himself.

Although she was never outgoing, after the death of her father (in 1874), Dickinson withdrew from the world, never leaving the grounds of her father's house and, according to legend, dressing only in white. She did, however, continue a number of friendships through her numerous letters and continued to compose verse. Just how much verse Dickinson had been composing was discovered when, after her death from Bright's disease on May 15, 1886, her sister Lavinia discovered almost two thousand poems written on small slips of paper and sewn together in little booklets. One of these was "I felt a Funeral, in my Brain." These poems were published in a number of editions (with many textual variants) until the definitive three-volume edition of her *Poems* was released in 1955. While the "myth of Amherst," as she was sometimes called, seemed to have had an uneventful personal life, the life of her intellect was surely an adventurous and tumultuous one.

understanding about her impending devastation. Like the word *brain,* which has two meanings, the word *sense* can also refer to the speaker's physical senses, which are likewise affected by the mourners plaguing her mind.

Poem Text

I felt a Funeral, in my Brain,
And Mourners to and fro
Kept treading—treading—till it seemed
That Sense was breaking through—

And when they all were seated,   5
A Service, like a Drum—
Kept beating—beating—till I thought
My Mind was going numb—

And then I heard them lift a Box
And creak across my Soul   10
With those same Boots of Lead, again,
Then Space—began to toll,

As all the Heavens were a Bell,
And Being, but an Ear,
And I, and Silence, some strange Race   15
Wrecked, solitary, here—

And then a Plank in Reason, broke,
And I dropped down, and down—
And hit a World, at every plunge,
And Finished knowing—then—   20

Lines 5–8

As the opening lines set up the funeral as an overall metaphor for the speaker's breakdown, subsequent stanzas refer to specific parts of the funeral ritual to further convey the speaker's experience. This stanza dramatizes the speaker's growing fears and mental instability primarily through the use of sound. The mourners are all seated, representing a quiet moment, perhaps marking the end of the speaker's initial panic or mental chaos. However, the respite is short-lived, and the "Service, like a Drum" begins a fresh assault on both her physical senses and mind. The sound of the drum, like the tread of the mourners, is another attack on her sanity, an attack so fierce that she feels her mind "going numb." Numbness is a physical sensation that stands as another example of the speaker's struggle to convey her experience in understandable physical terms.

Lines 9–11

The speaker is now in what seems to be a state of shock, stunned and still like a corpse being readied for burial. However, in terms of the metaphorical funeral, her senses are still working, and again she uses the sense of hearing to describe the next stage of her breakdown. She hears the pallbearers "lift a Box," the coffin in which, perhaps, her formerly sane self is contained. These men then "creak across" her soul, which calls to mind the previous sounds of "treading—treading" and "beating—beating"; like those sounds, this creaking is unpleasant because it is the result of men with heavy "boots of lead" trampling over her. What is being trampled upon is the speaker's soul; the scope of the breakdown has expanded to include her entire conception of her own existence.

Poem Summary

Lines 1–4

"I felt a Funeral, in my Brain" is a poem in which Dickinson attempts to render into formal poetic language the experience of a mind facing its own collapse; the opening stanza presents the metaphor of a funeral that is used throughout the poem to convey the sense of this breakdown to the reader. *Brain* here refers to both the concrete physical organ and to the abstract idea of the speaker's mind; such dual meanings are used throughout the poem to convey the physical and mental effects of the breakdown. Losing one's reason is like a funeral: the final interment and burial of rational thought. The mourners can be read as symbols of the events or ideas that bring on the speaker's collapse; such events or ideas are incessant (they keep "treading—treading") and continue until the speaker begins to realize what is happening. Her "sense" (or knowledge) of what is occurring begins "breaking through" to culminate in some kind of

Lines 12–16

These lines describe the moment in the speaker's collapse when she passes from the recognizable world of rationality to a state of mind conveyable only through similes and metaphors, even more strange than those previously offered. In the real, physical world, church bells are sometimes rung as a coffin is carried to a burial plot; these same bells are ringing here but are so loud that the speaker can only describe the sound as if all space is be-

Media Adaptations

- A two-cassette set entitled *Emily Dickinson: Poems and Letters* features a recording of "I felt a Funeral, in my Brain" along with seventy-four other poems. It was released in 1989 by Recorded Books, Inc.

---

ginning to "toll." Note how the sounds of the poem have grown increasingly louder and more menacing. The tolling is so loud, in fact, that "all the heavens" seem to be one great "bell," and the speaker seems to be an "ear," open to the barrage of noise that assaults it. As the speaker now has no hope of shutting out the dreadful tolling of the bells, the speaker's soul has no hope of shutting out the madness that has possessed it. As funeral bells toll to mark the end of a human life, so the bells toll here for the figurative death of the speaker's reason and sense of self.

The speaker then finds herself "wrecked" in some "solitary" place; this place may be physically the inside of her coffin (a most solitary place, indeed) or a figurative mental place, a description of which is too difficult for her to convey. All she can say is that she is "wrecked, solitary" there. The noise that has been growing throughout the poem is still present, so much so that silence seems a part of "some strange race" that she can no longer recognize. The ambiguity of the speaker's physical and mental location in these lines suggests the difficulty of using concrete language to talk about abstract mental processes, a difficulty that will overcome her in the poem's final line.

Lines 17–20

The poem's final stanza concludes both the metaphorical funeral rites and the description of the speaker's breakdown. The mourners have come, the service has been heard, and the pallbearers have carried the casket to the cemetery. The casket being lowered into the burial plot is used to metaphorically describe the final stages of the speaker's ruin; however, while in earthy funerals a casket is rested on planks to support it prior to its being lowered into the earth, here the figurative "Plank in Reason"—the last flimsy bulwark against total insanity and devestation—snaps. As a casket is normally gently lowered into its dark earthen plot, here the speaker's mind plummets into the darkness of madness, dropping "down and down" into more indescribable depths.

Each time the speaker thinks she has reached the limits of how much she can withstand, she finds that there is still another world awaiting her further down; with each plunge she is thrown deeper into madness until she has "finished knowing." Now she can no longer trust her previously held assumptions about her own mind nor can she further describe her own mental processes in suitable terms. The poem's final word, "then," is ambiguous: either the entire poem is told from the point-of-view of one who has survived the mental "funeral" but who is now "finished knowing" anything for certain or the speaker's ability to continue her story has (like everything else) been destroyed, and she has moved to a mental place that regular, ordered language cannot describe. Either way, the poem depicts the terrors of mental collapse in language that, by its ambiguous nature, reflects the difficulties in conveying the very events that cause and comprise it.

Themes

Madness and Sanity

"I felt a Funeral, in my Brain" is a poem that, in part, presents the impending mental collapse of its speaker, a collapse that Dickinson likens to the rituals of a funeral to ultimately explore the figurative "death" of the speaker's sanity. The word *felt* in the poem's opening line suggests that the first throbbings of the collapse could be physically perceived; this merging of physical sensation and mental perception is sustained throughout the poem. By comparing the speaker's mental breakdown to a funeral, Dickinson suggests the horror and finality of such an event.

The funeral's participants and rites can be read as metaphors for the speaker's impending collapse; as the figurative funeral proceeds through its recognizable stages, the speaker's sanity becomes more endangered until it finally "dies." The mourners that the speaker feels repeatedly "treading—treading" in her brain are like the first recognizable signs (to her) that all is not well with her mind, despite the fact that her sense of what is happening to her is "breaking through" the sounds of the mourners' footsteps. The funeral service here is not a peaceful eulogy or tearful farewell but an unpleasant sound "like a drum" that plagues her mind with its "beating—beating" until she reaches the point where she cannot stand any more of it, and her mind grows numb. At this point, she has no hope of fending off her approaching breakdown. Her mind is described here in physical terms ("numb") to suggest its nearly incapacitated state. The carrying of the casket to the gravesite—the next logical step in the funeral rite—is used to convey the increased mental and even spiritual anguish of the speaker, for the pallbearers "creak across" her soul with "boots of lead" as they carry their mournful burden.

The tolling of the church bells is presented as a nearly indescribable source of pain: "all the heavens" are like one great "bell," and her entire being is like a single "ear." At this point, the speaker's trauma has become so intense that she is "wrecked, solitary, here" in a place where her ability to describe her own mind has become almost totally diminished. The lowering of the casket into the ground is compared to the final onslaught of insanity; the poem ends with the speaker being "finished knowing" anything for certain. All of her previously held assumptions about her own mind and soul have been metaphorically buried, like the remains of her sanity.

Doubt and Uncertainty

While Dickinson's poem can be read as a description of its speaker's mental collapse, this is not the only valid interpretation. Indeed, "I felt a Funeral, in my Brain" can also be read as a depiction of an individual's complete loss of religious faith. In this light, the funeral described is not one for the speaker's sanity but for those religious or spiritual assumptions previously embraced by her. While the cause of such a loss is never mentioned, the effects of it are described as devastating. Funeral rites are very often religious ones, and the "service" here can be read as an ironic metaphor: the speaker's loss of faith can only be described using religious terms. Words like "service," "soul" and "heavens" all suggest the paradox of a person attempting to describe the loss of her beliefs using language that once took its meaning from those beliefs.

The pallbearers' "creaking across" the speaker's soul with "boots of lead" suggests a system of belief being metaphorically trod upon, and the entire universe tolling like a single bell suggests that the speaker finds her recent loss of faith both inescapable

Topics for Further Study

- Research modern psychological explanations of what happens to the human mind when it is faced with clinical depression or some other mental illness. Explain how Dickinson's poem depicts these mental events in poetic terms.

- Explain how Dickinson's depiction of the human mind may have been influenced by the writings of Ralph Waldo Emerson.

- Research the ways in which groundbreaking scientific ideas were first received, such as those put forth by Galileo (whose 1632 work *Dialogue on the Great World Systems* posited the sun as the center of the solar system) or Charles Darwin (whose 1859 work *On the Origin of Species* proposed the idea of natural selection). Explain how Dickinson's poem dramatizes some of the early reactions to these radical ideas.

- Read Emerson's essay "The Poet" and then explain how Dickinson's work adheres to the ideals put forth within it.

- Research the ways that a woman's role was defined in nineteenth-century New England. Explain how Dickinson's life suited (or revolted against) the roles assigned to her by her era.

and undeniable. The poem's end thus presents a person who is "finished knowing" what she once took as an article of faith before the "plank in reason broke," that is, before her last hold on her previously held beliefs was destroyed, and she was plunged into the depths of doubt and skepticism. As Dickinson herself wrote elsewhere:

> To lose one's faith—surpass
> The loss of an Estate—
> Because Estates can be
> Replenished—faith cannot—

Style

Sound and Meter

"I felt a Funeral, in my Brain" is written in alternating lines of iambic tetrameter (four iambs per line) and iambic trimeter (three iambs per line). While this is one of Dickinson's most often used meters, its specific usefulness here lies in the ways that it reinforces in the reader's ear the steady progression of the forces that cause the speaker's mental or spiritual breakdown. In a poem such as this, where the sounds heard by the speaker are used as metaphors for her state of mind, the meter takes on added importance. In the first stanza, for example, the steady beat of the mourners' footsteps ("Kept treading—treading—till it seemed / That Sense was breaking through") is reinforced by the treading sound of the lines.

The same is true for the "Service, like a Drum" in stanza two, which "Kept beating—beating—till I thought / My Mind was going numb"; the steady rhythm of the drum hits the reader's ear and helps him or her better appreciate the sounds that eventually cause the numbness described by the speaker. Stanza three employs the meter for the same purpose when it depicts "those same Boots of Lead" that "creak across" her soul. The final stanza's description of the casket being lowered into the earth—and of the final mental blows delivered to the speaker—contains the line, "And I dropped down, and down—," another example of how Dickinson uses the unvaried meter of the poem to heighten the sense of the reader's steadily approaching and unavoidable devastation.

Historical Context

Emerson and New England Transcendentalism

Although biographers have debated the different ways in which Dickinson's reading habits affected her work, almost all concur that the single most important author that influenced her poetry was the American philosopher, poet, and essayist Ralph Waldo Emerson (1803–1882). To understand the intellectual climate of Dickinson's time, one cannot avoid an examination of this important American thinker.

Emerson was one of the founders of transcendentalism, a loose but dynamic philosophy which, in many ways, was a reaction to what its followers saw as the stifling Puritanism of America's past and, specifically, the rigid attention to reason urged by eighteenth-century enlightenment writers. Above all, transcendentalists believed in the divinity of human beings and the supremacy of the individual. Unlike enlightenment thinkers, who held that the world could only be perceived and understood through observation and rationality, transcendentalists were more like the European romantics in their focus on intuition as a means of discovering the truths of human existence. Transcendentalists also believed in the oversoul: a force present in all the universe that embodies truth, wisdom, and, above all, virtue and goodness. (Emerson's poem "Brahma" is an examination of the workings of the oversoul.)

One aim of human life was to harmonize one's individual soul with the oversoul; such a harmony would result in the fulfillment of that person's potential. Such an idea was shocking to hard-and-fast New England Calvinists, who held that God acted as a judge of man's sinful actions and doled out harsh but fitting punishments. The beauty and force of nature as an absolute good was another transcendentalist tenet, as was the value and virtue of complete self-reliance. Many of these ideas were articulated at length by Emerson in his *Essays: First Series* (1841), *Essays: Second Series* (1844), *Poems* (1846), and *Representative Men* (1850). Dickinson received a copy of Emerson's *Poems* in 1850, and the ideas behind such lines as "Beauty through my senses stole; / I yielded myself to the perfect whole" (from "Each and All") and "Beauty is its own excuse for being" (from "The Rhodora") surface throughout Dickinson's work and the work of many other New England authors who lived during Emerson's career.

Much of Emerson's work urges his readers to look to the best artists and poets for a greater understanding of both the world and themselves. For example, in his essay "Circles," he states, "All the argument and all the wisdom is not in the encyclopedia, or the treatise on metaphysics, or the Body of Divinity, but in the sonnet or the play." The great value placed here on verse as a means by which humans could better understand their worlds—a means even more powerful than the "Body of Divinity"—was a shocking one that would have certainly delighted Dickinson, whose poems often express religious frustrations and doubts.

There are even remarks in Emerson's work that echo Dickinson's decision to pursue a solitary life of the mind. In the essay "The Celebration of the Intellect," for example, Emerson commands, "Keep the intellect sacred. Go sit with the hermit in you, who knows more than you do," and in his essay "The Poet," Emerson tells potential artists, "Thou shalt leave the world, and know the muse only.

Compare & Contrast

- **1855:** Walt Whitman publishes his first edition of *Leaves of Grass,* his groundbreaking collection of free verse that revolutionizes American poetry.

  Today: Free verse is so widely used that it is no longer seen as the revolutionary style it once was. Many modern American poets such as William Carlos Williams, e. e. cummings, and Allen Ginsberg have followed Whitman's course and written much of their own work in free verse.

- **1861:** The American Civil War begins when Confederate forces attack and capture Fort Sumter in Charleston, South Carolina. The war continues until 1865, when General Robert E. Lee surrenders to Union forces.

  Today: The Civil War is perhaps the most widely studied period in American history; many contemporary artists are drawn to the Civil War as an inspiration for their work. For example, the filmmaker Ken Burns's 1997 documentary *The Civil War* has been seen by millions of television viewers, and the novelist Charles Frazier's *Cold Mountain* (1997) has been a bestseller.

- **1841:** The transcendentalist movement in America begins with the publication of Ralph Waldo Emerson's *Essays: First Series* and gains force with the publication of Emerson's *Essays: Second Series* (1844) and Henry David Thoreau's *Walden, or Life in the Woods* (1854). For a number of years, many Americans (most of them New Englanders) are drawn to the transcendentalist philosophy through these works.

  Today: While transcendentalism is no longer the vibrant philosophical force it was during the nineteenth century, millions of readers still pore over the works of Emerson and Thoreau, hoping to glean some insight from these two important American thinkers.

Thou shalt not know any longer the times, customs, graces, politics, or opinions of men, but shall take all from the muse." Finally, in his poem "Saadi," he offers the aphorism, "Men consort in camp and town / But the poet dwells alone." While the exact extent to which Dickinson responded to Emerson's individual remarks is a matter of conjecture, she did adopt something of a transcendentalist attitude in her decision (like Henry David Thoreau, who lived alone at Walden pond for awhile) to withdraw from a world founded on materialism and logic and, as she herself described in one of her poems, "dwell" in the "possibility" of discovering the truths of human existence.

Critical Overview

While some authors' reputations ebb and flow according to the times and critical caprice, the reputation of Emily Dickinson has only grown stronger since the posthumous discovery of her poems. Most critics would agree with Dickinson's recent biographer Cynthia Griffin Wolff, who (in *Benet's Reader's Encyclopedia of American Literature*) calls Dickinson "certainly America's greatest woman author and possibly its greatest poet of either gender." Generally, critics are fascinated by Dickinson's ability to present various states of mind through the use of different images that convey complex mental processes to her readers. Writing in the Introduction to *Modern Critical Views: Emily Dickinson,* Harold Bloom, one of the twentieth century's most preeminent critics, states that Dickinson presents her readers with "the most authentic cognitive difficulties" formed in "a mind so original and powerful that we scarcely have begun, even now, to catch up with her." The number of articles and books being written about Dickinson today is a testament to the truth of Bloom's remark.

"I felt a Funeral, in my Brain" has fared equally well among critics. In his important study of Dickinson's tragic poetry, *The Long Shadow,* Clark Griffith praises the poem for its embodiment of "emotional and psychological states in a hard, specific language" and concludes that the poem foreshadows "the principles and techniques of modern symbolist poetry." In his book *The Art of Emily Dickinson's Early Poetry,* David Porter states, "On the experience of psychic breakdown, perhaps no poetic expression surpasses the aptness of metaphor or the psychological authenticity of the progression of mental collapse" as Dickinson's poem. John Cody, a psychiatrist whose book *After Great Pain: The Inner Life of Emily Dickinson* offers a psychoanalytic reading of the poem, calls it "powerful" and praises Dickinson for her ability to make the reader "feel each tormenting increment of a gathering depression until vitality reaches a nadir, and reason gives way to a numb and psychotic state of reality severance." Finally, the aforementioned Cynthia Griffin Wolff, in her extensive critical biography *Emily Dickinson,* praises the way that the poem "taunts with its invitations and frustrations, and ultimately forces us to ask what we know, how we know—whether 'life' and 'death' are susceptible to understanding." These critics and many others thus praise the poem for its sharp insights into what happens to a mind facing its own destruction.

Criticism

Daniel Moran

Moran is an educator specializing in American and British literature. In this essay, he examines the ways in which Dickinson faces the difficulty of conveying complex mental processes in concrete language.

William Wordsworth's famous preface to his *Lyrical Ballads* (1798) contains his much-quoted definition of good poetry:

> Since Dickinson cannot truly replicate insanity, she instead chooses to portray it as a physical sensation; imagine trying to convey the sense of a terrible headache to one who has never had one, and then the logic behind Dickinson's choice of metaphor becomes clearer.

> Poetry is the spontaneous overflow of powerful feelings: it takes its origin from emotion recollected in tranquility: the emotion is contemplated till by a species of reaction the tranquility gradually disappears, and an emotion, similar to that which was before the subject of contemplation, is gradually produced, and does actually exist in the mind.

In other words, the poet's task is to recreate an emotion or sensation from a removed point-of-view (since someone feeling intense emotions cannot pause and then carefully compose a piece of verse) and, through the language of his or her poem, replicate that emotion or sensation in the mind of the reader. This definition suits many types of poems by many types of poets: a poet who seeks to replicate a sense of sorrow, for example, can use language that will create a sense of sorrow in the reader and thus have his work meet Wordsworth's criteria. Wordsworth's definition does, however, raise an interesting question about those poets who seek to replicate complex mental processes, for very few people (if any at all) actually think in words or phrases (much less poetic ones), and therefore any poetic replication of an individual's mind must, by its very nature, fall short of the process being described. Such poets offer their readers an imitation of the mind's working—not a poetic production and then recreation of the mind itself. This makes the subject of the poet's contemplation a difficult thing to convey, since, by its very nature, poems are ordered, grammatical, and formalized, completely unlike the human mind, which is often disordered, ungrammatical, and free-flowing.

Dickinson faced this challenge of replicating consciousness in a number of poems, among them one in which she attempts to convey the sensation of memory loss or even the loss of one's rational powers:

> I Felt a Cleaving in my Mind—
> As if my Brain had split—
> I tried to match it—Seam by Seam—
> But could not make them fit.
> The thought behind, I strove to join
> Unto the thought before—
> But Sequence raveled out of Sound
> Like Balls—upon a Floor.

Here, the inability to think is likened to a "cleaving in the mind," but even this is a questionable representation of the event, for to truly replicate something like the event being described would require language that created the same experience in the reader. If this happened, there would be no poem, only a scattering of images that did not form an artistic and aesthetic whole.

How a poet conveys the workings of any individual's mind is a tricky business, but the challenge becomes greater when the poet attempts to portray a mind on the brink of insanity or a total breakdown of rationality. Even Shakespeare faced this problem: in *Hamlet;* for example, the title character pauses during his assault on Ophelia (and on the duplicity of women in general) to state, "Go to, I'll no more on't: it hath made me mad." This moment of self-realization is certainly dramatic but psychologically suspect, for could a mind so tortured by its own destruction look outside itself and comment on its failures?

The same problem occurs in a comic vein in *Twelfth Night,* when Feste the clown is asked to read a letter from the "mad" Malvolio and does so in a loud and "mad" voice; after being asked by his mistress why he reads in such a tone, Feste remarks, "I do read but madness. And your ladyship will have it as it ought to be, you must allow *vox,*" or the letter to be read in a presumably mad voice. The problem here is the same as in *Hamlet:* if Malvolio is truly mad, how can Feste hope to convey this madness to his listeners without some sort of "*vox*" or other device? Neither Hamlet nor Feste are recollecting the insanity before them in tranquility but are instead forced by their creator to tackle a problem that he himself has a difficult time surmounting.

In literature, even the maddest of the mad often speak and think in ways that, viewed objectively, seem sane by virtue of their own self-recognition and orderly presentation. Shakespeare seems to have tackled the problem to some degree in *Othello,* when the title character—faced with the "proof" of his wife's infidelity—speaks in jumbled and fragmentary prose before falling to the ground in some sort of seizure, but even this is a physical depiction of Othello's breakdown and not a depiction in words of the experience of the breakdown itself.

Dickinson's "I felt a Funeral, in my Brain" presents the same problems to its author and reader. If Dickinson is truly interested in replicating the experience of madness (or any mental, emotional, or spiritual breakdown), her method is very strange, since the poem is written in a regular meter with a regular rhyme scheme and regular grammatical structures. Presumably the speaker is telling her story from a point in time after her mental collapse, an idea that justifies the poem's form only if the reader interprets the final line ("And Finished knowing—then—") to mean "I finished knowing anything for sure after that terrible incident" and not the equally valid interpretation in which the final "then—" marks the speaker's transition to a mental state where the representation of one's mind through language becomes impossible.

So how, then, is a reader to approach the poem? First, a reader must recognize the poem as un-Wordsworthian in its aims and design: while the sensitive reader will surely feel the horror of the

> *"If Dickinson is truly interested in replicating the experience of madness (or any mental, emotional, or spiritual breakdown), her method is very strange, since the poem is written in a regular meter with a regular rhyme scheme and regular grammatical structures."*

speaker's predicament, the reader and speaker will never truly meet in that place where the poet's subject of contemplation really does exist in the reader's mind. (This is not to dismiss Dickinson's achievement in this powerful poem, but to clarify how it should be read.) The reader must then understand that the poem is an attempt to formalize a complex and devastating mental process in familiar, recognizable images and sensations. If the poem seems a failure because it does not succeed in Wordsworthian terms, this is only because no poem depicting madness can fully replicate its subject; the best a poet can do is describe what the subject is like in a way that will make the reader appreciate it more fully than he or she did before reading about it.

Once a reader understands how to approach the poem, he or she can then examine the ways in which Dickinson uses familiar poetic devices to replicate the subject of her contemplation. The images chosen here by Dickinson all relate to a funeral: a common ritual, the devastating emotional nature of which is appropriate for a poem about the devastation of the speaker's mind. The funeral is entirely metaphoric; it is something like what the speaker felt in her brain when her mental troubles began. The metaphor of a funeral is also appropriate since a funeral is a ritual in which various stages and rites are completed before the final interment of the body; this corresponds to the various stages through which the speaker's mind passes before its final interment into the graveyard of madness. For example, the mourners that keep "treading—treading" in her brain (with their "Boots of Lead") represent the first signs of the impending catastrophe. Since Dickinson cannot truly replicate insanity, she

What Do I Read Next?

- Dickinson's "After great pain, a formal feeling comes—" (1861) describes the after-effects of profound physical, mental, emotional, and spiritual agony.

- Dickinson's "To lose one's faith—surpass," (1861), like "I felt a Funeral, in my Brain," explores the results of spiritual devastation.

- Like the speaker of "I felt a Funeral, in my Brain," the title character of William Shakespeare's *Hamlet* (1601) faces the breakdown of his rational faculties.

- Dickinson's "Much Madness Is Divinest Sense—" (1861) treats the theme of insanity in a much different way than "I felt a Funeral, in my Brain"; here, madness is likened to the spirit of non-conformity.

- The American novelist William Styron's *Darkness Visible* (1990) is a memoir of his battle with madness, specifically, clinical depression. The book is remarkable for the ways in which Styron depicts his struggle to understand the workings of his own mind.

- Robert Burton's famous psychological treatise *The Anatomy of Melancholy* (1621) examines various states of melancholy, a general term used by Burton to describe different mental illnesses. Burton's book offers a fascinating glimpse into early psychological scholarship.

- T. S. Eliot's complex poem *The Waste Land* (1922) extends the various breakdowns experienced by the speaker of Dickinson's poem to the entire twentieth century.

---

and that some of her reason was battling with the mourners who plagued her. This moment is very much like Hamlet's "It hath made me mad" in its self-reflexiveness. However, the word *sense* can also refer to the five senses, in which case the remark about her sense "breaking through" conveys the idea that her breakdown can only be portrayed in terms of an explosion of physical feeling, and physical pain is something that many readers can appreciate and imagine more easily than mental collapse. Either way, the funeral has begun and will not end until the speaker's mind is buried.

The remainder of the poem uses familiar components of the funeral ritual to convey the speaker's increased mental pressures and eventual devastation. After the mourners have arrived, the service begins. This service, however, is not a softly spoken prayer or eulogy, but rather something "like a Drum" that incessantly keeps "beating—beating" in the speaker's ears until she finds her mind is "going numb." Again, Dickinson resorts to the language of physical sensations to convey the impossible-to-replicate mental processes. This mingling of the mental and the physical is continued when Dickinson moves to the next stage of the funeral ritual: the carrying of the casket to the gravesite. The pallbearers "creak across" the speaker's soul with "Boots of Lead." Again, the impending breakdown is likened to loud noise, and this noise grows intolerable when the next part of the ritual, the tolling of the funeral bell, begins.

The bell here is so loud and threatening that it seems "As all the Heavens" are one great bell and the speaker's whole being is "but an Ear." The physical pain that must accompany such a situation is used in place of an outright description of mental pain. The bell is so loud, in fact, that silence seems a member of "some strange Race." The speaker cannot recall a time when she could not physically hear the tolling of the bell, as she cannot mentally recall what her mind was like before its "funeral" began. The casket sits ready for burial and the speaker sits on the verge of total mental destruction.

Appropriately enough, the final stanza uses the last part of the funeral ritual to dramatize the final stages of the speaker's breakdown. Caskets are often laid upon wooden planks before being lowered into the earth, but the casket in the speaker's brain proves too heavy for such supports. In terms of the physical metaphor, the speaker's mind has "broke"—its last vestiges of mental support have proven no match for the weight of the breakdown. The casket's dropping "down and down" is like the

---

instead chooses to portray it as a physical sensation. Imagine trying to convey the sense of a terrible headache to one who has never had one, and then the logic behind Dickinson's choice of metaphor becomes clearer.

At this early stage of her breakdown, the speaker seemed to feel that "sense was breaking through,"

speaker's descent into madness where she hits a "World, at every plunge." In terms of a conventional funeral, a dropping casket would eventually hit the world after falling the proverbial six feet, but this is no conventional funeral. Instead, the casket keeps "hitting bottom" only to find that there is another world beneath it. Just when the speaker thinks she has reached the limits of mental endurance, she learns that her casket can still drop another few feet. Thus, the problem of depicting the stages of derangement or mental collapse is sidestepped by Dickinson's use of physical imagery and sensation.

The poem's final line, however, presents an ambiguity (mentioned earlier) that demands examination. The speaker ends by stating that she "finished knowing—then—" a remark fraught with ambiguity. Either she "finished knowing" anything for sure and now lives as one who will never again assume anything about her own brain, or mind, to be certain or her breakdown has brought her to the point where she can no longer use conventional (or poetic) language to describe her experience. The first alternative is somewhat more comforting than the second since it implies that the speaker has had some sort of epiphany about her own mind and is now mentally strong enough to convey her experience in rational, ordered language. However, the second alternative is more in keeping with the overall problem of portraying consciousness: physical metaphors and sensations might be used to describe the onset of one's collapse, but even Dickinson herself seems to be defeated by the challenge of depicting a mind that has already dropped "down, and down." (Had she used a period instead of a dash after the last word, the problem would be solved.) As the poem stands, a reader must be satisfied with Dickinson's evocation of "powerful feelings" rather than powerful thoughts to (in Wordsworth's terms) "gradually produce" in the reader some understanding of what a funeral in the brain would be like. The impossibility of Dickinson's truly replicating the breakdown in Wordsworth's terms, however, should be regarded as somewhat of a blessing since no reader would want to read a poem capable of truly inciting a breakdown similar to the one experienced by its speaker.

Source: Daniel Moran, Critical Essay on "I felt a Funeral, in my Brain," in *Poetry for Students,* The Gale Group, 2001.

Sheldon Goldfarb

Goldfarb has a Ph.D. in English and has published two books on the Victorian author William Makepeace Thackeray. In the following essay, he

> "*The speaker is like the hero in some archetypal drama, beset by painful forces, and then somehow reaches a better state after an almost mythic confrontation.*"

seeks to illuminate the obscurity of "I felt a Funeral, in my Brain" in part by considering its narrative structure.

This is a baffling little poem, and the more it is read, the more baffling it becomes. It inspires a wide variety of responses. Some critics see it as a depiction of a real funeral. Others say that even if it originates with a real funeral about someone's physical death, the funeral image becomes symbolic and metaphorical, representing something else: some sort of agony or perhaps the process of going mad. Some critics see the poem as depicting the extinction of consciousness after death and find the poem despairing. Yet others see Dickinson as suggesting that some new way of perception can be attained after death (if the poem is about death), and they see something more positive going on. One critic (Robert Weisbuch, in *Emily Dickinson's Poetry*) says the conclusion of the poem is neither positive nor negative.

What are readers to make of all this? It does seem that Emily Dickinson has left things deliberately vague here, and perhaps that is part of her point: she is talking of the difficulty of knowing and understanding. But although there are difficulties, it does seem that the poem is telling readers that the difficulties can be worked through. At the end, the poem seems to take readers to a better place although a lot depends on the meaning of the phrase "Finished knowing" in the last line. By "Finished knowing," does the speaker mean she can no longer know anything (a rather negative conclusion) or does she mean she now knows everything she needs to know, that is, that she has finally figured things out (a much more positive suggestion)? Or does she mean she has finished with knowing because she has moved on to some better form of perception, such as feeling or intuiting or somehow connecting with the universe more successfully than through conventional forms of knowing (again a more positive view)? Has she moved from "lawyer's truth" to "the poet's truth of never knowing," as Jerome Loving puts it in *Emily Dickinson: The Poet on the Second Story?* This essay will tend toward the two positive views of the poem's ending, largely because of the last line of the first stanza and also because the structure of the poem conveys a positive sense of resolution after crisis.

Looking at the first stanza, the first point to note is that the funeral seems very much to be in the speaker's brain: the mourners "treading—treading" back and forth are, as readers learn in the third stanza, creaking across the speaker's soul; they seem to be inside her. That is, the funeral would seem to be symbolic, metaphorical, a dream-like representation of something else but not of a descent into madness, as critics like Clark Griffith and Paul J. Ferlazzo argue (in, respectively, *The Long Shadow: Emily Dickinson's Tragic Poetry* and *Emily Dickinson*). Joan Kirby (in her book *Emily Dickinson*) seems closer to the truth when she says that what is being depicted is the passing away of old thoughts, old ways of thinking, old approaches to the world. Or as Weisbuch puts it, it is the depiction of "a crucial change in . . . consciousness."

The key to understanding this crucial change may be in the last line of the first stanza, which says that as a result of the heavy tramp of the mourners, "sense was breaking through." It is as if the funeral is allowing some barrier to be destroyed so that some new sort of understanding can reach the speaker. The speaker seems to be imagining the death of something in her brain, the death of some old ways of thinking. Now, death of course is painful, even metaphorical death; so is the giving up of old ways—and the speaker does seem to be in pain, especially in stanza two, when the funeral service beats "like a Drum . . . beating—beating," until her mind seems to be going numb. But the pain in this poem seems to be a necessary price to pay for progressing to a better state; the pain is part of getting rid of old ways in order that the speaker can advance to something new.

The poem in fact reads like a miniature narrative, beginning with a crisis (the funeral and the pain), moving toward a climactic encounter, and then achieving resolution. The speaker is like the hero in some archetypal drama, beset by painful forces, and then somehow reaches a better state after an almost mythic confrontation. True, the speaker seems fairly passive in all this; it is not she, but the mourners whose tramping allows Sense to break through. Still, if the mourners are simply symbolic entities in the speaker's brain, then they are a part of her breaking through the barrier that is also part of her: it is a struggle with herself.

The immediate result of the struggle, of breaking through the barrier, is that the speaker finds herself in a surreal and terrifying landscape in which (beginning with the last line of stanza three) space begins to toll, the Heavens turn into a bell, and the speaker herself becomes simply an Ear. And she feels "wrecked" and "solitary," as if having endured an almost unendurable situation, that internal struggle represented by the funeral and the mourners.

Something gravely important has happened. What it is, is hard to tell. The poem resists being pinned down. But the tolling suggests some sort of life passage, some movement into a new stage of existence. It could be referring to life (or extinction) after death, as some critics (like John B. Pickard in *Emily Dickinson: An Introduction and Interpretation* and George Monteiro in "Traditional Ideas in Dickinson's 'I Felt a Funeral in My Brain'"), who see the funeral as a real funeral, argue. But it may be more general than that; it may simply signify any major transition.

It is interesting that in this transition there is the struggle and the terror and then a pause, as the speaker sits wrecked and solitary, having come through some wrenching experience. But the pause is brief. "A plank in Reason" breaks to begin the final stanza, again conjuring up the image of a funeral, as if the speaker is in a coffin being placed on planks before being lowered into the ground. The plank is part of reason, though, and it gives way. This seems to mean that conventional rationality is left behind, and the speaker moves into a different realm of perception, plunging down into unconscious realms where the hero in archetypal narratives goes to discover new truths. The speaker does encounter new worlds and, in the ambiguous last line, finishes knowing.

It's true that the speaker hits the new worlds, which sounds like a rather painful process. And she is dropping down at the end, which could be seen in a negative light. There is perhaps a mix of negativity and positiveness here. But the whole movement of the poem seems to be toward new discoveries. First there is sense breaking through, then there is the encounter with the tolling heavens, and finally there is the discovery of world after world. How many new worlds does the speaker hit? The poem is all about the difficult process of moving on in one's life, and as such, for all the pain it evokes, it creates a positive feeling. It is also about the difficulty of understanding, and perhaps that is why it is itself so difficult to understand.

Source: Sheldon Goldfarb, Critical Essay on "I felt a Funeral, in my Brain," in *Poetry for Students,* The Gale Group, 2001.

Paul Pineiro

Pineiro is a published poet and the supervisor of English at Montgomery High School in New Jersey. In the following essay, he considers the death of reason in "I felt a Funeral, in my Brain."

In Mark Twain's *The Adventures of Tom Sawyer,* both Tom and his pal Huck Finn get the chance to witness their own funerals and experience the heartfelt loss of those they leave behind. After creating the evidence of their feigned death, they are lucky enough to experience what most people have fantasized about at one time or another, they observe the world's response to their leaving it. They are able to see and hear the sobbing mourners crying over how much they will miss them; how unfair it was for their short lives to be ended so soon, and so on. Nevertheless, the boys are not dead, and their experience is fully external, the fantasy complete without the actual loss of life.

In "I felt a Funeral, in my Brain" Emily Dickinson also employs the perspective of a deceased narrator although in this case the experience is fully internal, and there is no rejoining the living to exploit what is learned at the ceremony. In fact, Emily Dickinson's narrator's disembodied voice is so internalized it cannot make sense of the experience in any way other than to feel it inside her brain in the form of footsteps and drum beats. It is a completely claustrophobic affair, where the narrator is at the center of the experience, yet completely detached from it. Dickinson's from-the-grave narrator is most limited in her experience because she has no context from which to build the meaning. She has only the muffled sounds of footsteps and the creaking of the box, her coffin, from which to draw any inferences about her predicament. Once the ability to build meaning becomes clearly futile, the voice collapses in on itself, dropping down and away from meaning until she "finishe[s] knowing."

The two most popular interpretations of the poem are: it is a poem about the transition from life to death; and it is a poem about the loss of reason, a slipping into a senseless void of insanity. Ar-

> "The last thing to go is the sensation of the pulsing organ itself, or better, the echo of what was once a pulsing organ dynamically absorbing existence and making sense of it."

guably, Emily Dickinson might have conceded that these are in fact not opposing views at all. Whether it is death or insanity, Dickinson sees it the same: the incapacitation of a transmitter's receiver leaves meaning ungrounded, floating senselessly in the void.

It is a curious thing to go to the trouble of granting a narrator the power to speak from the grave and then not allow her to make sense of anything. For readers trying to assert some meaning, perhaps this is the narrator's ultimate function: to dramatize that being is defined as one's ability to make sense of the world around him or her. In a later poem, "This is my letter to the World," Dickinson offers thanks to nature for having provided her with the tools necessary to assert some sense to the universe: "The simple News that Nature told— / With tender Majesty." In, "I felt a Funeral, in my Brain," her narrator is cut off from the world and "the simple News" of it, leaving her very little from which to derive an interpretation of her situation. The voice from the coffin is sealed off from the metaphors and concrete expressions of truth exhibited through nature and the world surrounding Dickinson's typically very speculative narrators.

Stanza one opens with the paradoxical notion of a concrete experience that takes place entirely at the nexus of abstract being, "I felt a Funeral, in my Brain." The choice of the word *brain* over the word *mind* is significant, for the mind is not a physical organ but a process that occurs within it. Therefore, the process of the brain, the ability to make sense of the surrounding world and even a person's existence within it, seems to be breaking down to its most base elements, its container.

Lines two and three of this first stanza move into a description of the funeral service, ignoring the limitations that it has established for itself in the first line by being only a brain. With the narrative perspective clearly entombed within itself, it has no alternative but to describe what it feels and how things seem. This perspective stands in sharp contrast to another of Dickinson's dead narrator perspectives, the voice in "I heard a Fly Buzz when I died." In the latter example, she posits the narrator on a deathbed absorbing the scenario around her, including the mourners' tears, the light from the window, and the "stumbling buzz" of the either sympathetic or opportunistic fly. In the above lines, readers do not see the world around the perspective but rather, like she, they only feel distant, muffled vibration.

> And Mourners to and fro
> Kept treading—treading—till it seemed
> That Sense was breaking through—

Things only seem to be, and the distinct characteristics of the mourners are withheld. The "sense" of which the narrator speaks is derived not from sight, sound, smell, touch, or taste but rather some experience of vibration, which the narrator reports in the next stanza:

> And when they [the mourners] all were seated,
> A Service, like a Drum—
> Kept Beating—beating—till I thought
> My mind was going numb—

Since there is no intermediary between what is going on outside the brain and the brain's interpretation of the experience, the reader may even wonder if there is any experience at all other than the waning pulse of a dying or slowly ceasing nerve center. What seems to be the narrator's final experience is simply this dying pulse of electric energy making one last reflexive connection to the mind's strongest tool of interpretation—memory, the memory of the funerals of others.

In stanza three, the narrator, in effect, repeats her earlier report regarding mourners footsteps but this time seems to be releasing the perspective of an entombed, internal self into perhaps an even more frightful, detached, abstract void.

> And then I heard them lift a Box
> And creak across my Soul
> With those same Boots of Lead, again
> Then Space—began to toll.

The narrator has shifted the perspective from its seat in the physical brain to an abstract and elusive vantage point, the soul. The blurring of the concrete and abstract continues and builds momentum. Earlier, the narrator feels the funeral through the to and fro treading of the mourners; a physical brain experiencing the sensation of physical footsteps. Now, the box (presumably a coffin or the sense of enclosure), a concrete object, creaks across her soul, an abstract concept. The image is the poem's equivalent of the Zen koan: "What is the sound of one hand clapping?" The paradox highlights the deterioration of sense and is echoed in the stanza's final line, "Then Space—began to toll." How can space, which is the absence of matter, begin to toll without anything within it to react? The dash in this stanza's last line seems to mark the place for some missing concrete element needed to catalyze meaning.

By stanza four, what was initially a report of purely physical sensation and a remaining connection to the concrete world seems to slip away toward utter detachment. The last thing to go is the sensation of the pulsing organ itself, or better, the echo of what was once a pulsing organ dynamically absorbing existence and making sense of it.

> As all the Heavens were a Bell,
> And Being, but an Ear,
> And I, and Silence, some strange Race
> Wrecked, solitary, here—

Significantly, the line reads "Heavens" as opposed to *Heaven*, suggesting that a vast, wide open emptiness of space is intended rather than a resting place or afterlife for the departed. The continuing loss of the stuff of meaning is marked by the race with "Silence" experienced by the narrative "I," who is now reduced to being but an ear. The detachment from existence is nearly complete as "Wrecked, solitary, here—" suggests those in the race become one—"solitary"—and even the faint hint or pulse of a memory of an earthly experience ends with a convergence of being and silence "here."

Finally, the narrative voice, completely cut off from concrete existence and the stuff of meaning, collapses in on itself with a swift succession of the word *and* repeated at the beginning of each line in the final stanza.

> And then a Plank in Reason, broke,
> And I dropped down, and down—
> And hit a World, at every plunge,
> And Finished knowing—then—

The "thumping of "And" that is concentrated in [this stanza]," says Cynthia Griffin Wolff, in her critical study *Emily Dickinson,* emphasizes that events in these lines occur "without pause, without yielding insight, without any logical relationship to one another, without any ordering of importance." The "and" beats create the feeling of life being "swept remorselessly along in the swift current of time, swept over the edge, perhaps to come to rest in some unfathomed end, perhaps merely to fall forever . . . [in an] undefined descent beyond understanding."

Amidst this freefall into nothingness, the narrator offers one more paradox to consider, the knowledge of (or at least the sensation of the knowledge of) "Finish[ing] knowing." Dashes surround this final moment and the final word *then* as if to mark the black-hole limbo wherein the echo of the voice continues to reside in silence. Ironically, the poem underscores its author's understanding of her own poetic process by showing the demise of it.

Source: Paul Pineiro, Critical Essay on "I felt a Funeral, in my Brain," in *Poetry for Students,* The Gale Group, 2001.

Sources

Bloom, Harold, Introduction, in *Emily Dickinson,* Modern Critical Views series, Chelsea House Publishers, 1985, pp. 1–7.

Cody, John, *After Great Pain: The Inner Life of Emily Dickinson,* Harvard University Press, 1971, p. 403.

Dickinson, Emily, *The Complete Poems of Emily Dickinson,* Little, Brown and Company, 1960.

Emerson, Ralph Waldo, *Representative Selections,* American Book Company, 1934, p. 229.

Ferlazzo, Paul J., *Emily Dickinson,* Twayne, 1976, pp. 90–1.

Frome, Keith Weller, *Hitch Your Wagon to a Star, and Other Quotations by Ralph Waldo Emerson,* Columbia University Press, 1996, pp. 83, 85.

Griffith, Clark, *The Long Shadow: Emily Dickinson's Tragic Poetry,* Princeton University Press, 1964, pp. 245–50.

Kirby, Joan, *Emily Dickinson,* St. Martin's Press, 1991, pp. 3–5.

Loving, Jerome, *Emily Dickinson: The Poet on the Second Story,* Cambridge University Press, 1986, p. 101.

Monteiro, George, "Traditional Ideas in Dickinson's 'I Felt a Funeral in My Brain,'" in *Modern Language Notes,* Vol. 75, 1960, p. 661.

Perkins, George, et al., *Benet's Reader's Encyclopedia of American Literature,* HarperCollins Publishers, 1991, pp. 261–63.

Pickard, John B., *Emily Dickinson: An Introduction and Interpretation,* Holt, Rinehart & Winston, 1967, pp. 104–05.

Porter, David, "The Early Achievement," in *Emily Dickinson,* Modern Critical Views series, Chelsea House Publishers, 1985, pp. 76–77.

Weisbuch, Robert, *Emily Dickinson's Poetry,* University of Chicago Press, 1975, pp. 105, 103.

Wolff, Cynthia Griffin, *Emily Dickinson,* Alfred A. Knopf, 1987, pp. 227–33.

For Further Study

Anderson, Charles R., *Emily Dickinson's Poetry: Stairway of Surprise,* Holt, Rinehart and Winston, 1960.
   Anderson's book examines Dickinson's poetry by examining what he sees as its four major concerns: art, nature, the self, and death. The book also features a short biographical sketch of Dickinson.

Matthiessen, F. O., *American Renaissance: Art and Expression in the Age of Emerson and Whitman,* Oxford University Press, 1968.
   While Matthissen's renowned survey of American literature only mentions Dickinson in passing, it is an invaluable study of the ways in which Emerson affected the nineteenth-century literary scene.

Robinson, John, *Emily Dickinson,* Faber and Faber, 1986.
   This short book is both a study of Dickinson's work and an examination of the intellectual climate of the New England in which she lived and wrote.

i was sitting in mcsorley's

e. e. cummings

1923

Cummings first published "i was sitting in mcsorley's" in his collection *Tulips & Chimneys*, which appeared in 1923. It has also been anthologized in *The Norton Anthology of Modern Poetry*. Different versions of the poem have been printed over time.

The poem is set in McSorley's Ale House, where cummings frequently drank. It is a New York City saloon on East Seventh between Second and Third Avenues. Known as a favorite haunt of bohemians and artists, McSorley's opened in 1854, and both Abraham Lincoln and John F. Kennedy are said to have visited the saloon. In the poem, the speaker, alternately meditative and descriptive, depicts his experience inside the saloon in typical cummings fashion, using nouns as verbs and vice versa, coining portmanteau words (words whose form and meaning are derived from a blending of two or more distinct forms), twisting syntax, and fragmenting words. The poem visually resembles prose, with its division into twelve paragraph-like sections.

Like many of the other poems in *Tulips & Chimneys*, "i was sitting in mcsorley's" embodies the opposition between the organic, natural world, and human society, what cummings refers to as "manunkind." Cummings's description of the bar is thick with sensuous and concrete images and effectively conjures the feel, smell, and sight of a saloon. The descriptions themselves also mimic the often sloppy way the brain processes perceptions and produces language when affected by alcohol.

Cummings's love for the city and his revulsion of humanity are both evident here.

Author Biography

Born October 14, 1894, in Cambridge, Massachusetts, just blocks away from Harvard Yard, Edward Estlin Cummings (known as e. e. cummings) grew up in a happy and intellectually stimulating household. His father, Edward Cummings, was a Harvard professor and, later, a Unitarian minister, who fostered a love for books and knowledge in his children. His mother, Rebecca Haswell Clarke, was descended from a long line of New England writers and intellectuals. One of them, Susanna Haswell Rowson, wrote *Charlotte Temple,* considered by many literary historians to be the first American novel.

As a child, cummings's artistic and literary interests were encouraged by his parents, and he determined early that he wanted to become a poet. After graduating from Cambridge Latin School, cummings entered Harvard, where he studied poetry and the visual arts and contributed poems to the *Harvard Advocate* and the *Harvard Monthly.* Cummings was also featured in the anthology *Eight Harvard Poets.* In 1915, he graduated with a degree in Greek and English literature and gave the commencement address. In that address, he applauded what he called "The New Art," which included cubism, futurism, impressionism, imagism, and postimpressionism.

After taking his masters degree in English from Harvard the following year, cummings, although an avowed pacifist, volunteered as a driver for the Norton-Harjes Ambulance Corps in France during World War I. Shortly after, French authorities imprisoned him for suspicion of espionage, citing letters he and his friend, William Slater Brown, had written home and cummings's outspoken criticism of France's handling of the war. Cummings describes this experience in his semi-fictional book *The Enormous Room,* often cited as a classic of American literature. This incident exemplifies cummings's disdain for bureaucracy and authority and underscores his passion for individual freedom, a concern that would help mold his writing, both thematically and stylistically, throughout his career. Cummings claimed that the goal of his writing was "unrealism," by which he meant the shattering of language's meaning-making conventions embodied in typography, grammar, and word form. He made this goal a principle of his writing and practiced that principle his entire career.

e. e. cummings

Cummings pursued his writing and painting enthusiastically after the war, returning to New York City and taking an apartment with Brown in Greenwich Village. Cummings wrote many of the poems collected in *Tulips & Chimneys* (1923), including "i was sitting in mcsorley's" during the few years after his return. In all, he published almost a dozen books, including *XLI Poems* (1925), the play *Him* (1927), and *Eimi* (1933). His poetry is gathered in *Complete Poems* (1972). He lived both in New York City and at his family's farm near Silver Lake in New Hampshire, where he spent the summers with Marion Morehouse, his common-law wife and companion for the last thirty years of his life. Cummings's awards include Guggenheim Fellowships, the Shelley Memorial Award, an Academy of American Poets' Fellowship, and a National Book Award Special Citation for *Poems 1923–1954*. On September 3, 1962, cummings died on Joy Farm in North Conway, New Hampshire.

Poem Text

I was sitting in mcsorley's.   outside it was New York and beautifully snowing.

Inside snug and evil.   the slobbering walls filthily push witless creases of screaming warmth chuck pillows are noise funnily swallows swallowing revolvingly pompous a the swallowed mottle with smooth or a but of rapidly goes gobs the and of flecks of and a chatter sobbings intersect with which distinct disks of graceful oath, upsoarings the break on ceiling-flatness

the Bar.tinking luscious jigs dint of ripe silver with warm-lyish wetflat splurging smells waltz the glush of squirting taps plus slush of foam knocked off and a faint piddle-of-drops she says I ploc spittle what the lands thaz me kid in no sir hopping sawdust you kiddo he's a palping wreaths of badly Yep cigars who jim him why gluey grins topple together eyes pout gestures stickily point made glints squinting who's a wink bum-nothing and money fuzzily mouths take big wobbly foot-

steps every goggle cent of it get out ears dribbles soft right old feller belch the chap hic summore eh chuckles skulch. . . .

and I was sitting in the din thinking drinking the ale, which never lets you grow old blinking at the low ceiling my being pleasantly was punctuated by the always retchings of a worthless lamp.

when With a minute terrif iceffort one dirty squeal of soiling light yanKing from bushy obscurity a bald greenish foetal head established It suddenly upon the huge neck around whose unwashed sonorous muscle the filth of a collar hung gently.

(spattered)by this instant of semiluminous nausea A vast wordless nondescript genie of trunk trickled firmly in to one exactly-mutilated ghost of a chair,

a;domeshaped interval of complete plasticity,shoulders, sprouted the extraordinary arms through an angle of ridiculous velocity commenting upon an unclean table.and, whose distended immense Both paws slowly loved a dinted mug

gone Darkness it was so near to me,i ask of shadow won't you have a drink?

(the eternal perpetual question)

Inside snugandevil.   i was sitting in mcsorley's
It,did not answer.

outside.(it was New York and beautifully, snowing. . . .

Poem Summary

Stanza 1

The first stanza of "i was sitting in mcsorley's" introduces the setting of the poem and one of its themes: the distinction between the inside and outside worlds. These worlds are literally the inside and outside world of the bar and the city, but they are also the inside world of reflection—focusing on self and the outside world of perception—focusing on others.

Stanza 2

The speaker describes the saloon and its "slobbering walls" as "snug and evil." This seeming contradiction highlights the simultaneous attraction and repulsion the speaker holds for the place. Cummings's trademark disregard for conventional grammar and syntax are effective here, as they help to depict a bustling, chaotic, and dirty atmosphere that is nonetheless comfortable. Adjective and adverbs such as "slobbering," filthily," "pompous," and "witless" all contribute to this description.

Stanza 3

This stanza, the longest of the poem, mixes bits of dialogue into its description of the sights and sounds of the bar. "Kiddo," "Yep," and "no sir" are all words or phrases that one might expect to hear in a bar, especially in exchanges between bartender and customer. The filmic equivalent to this stanza would be a scene from a Robert Altman film, in which simultaneous dialogues are captured. The overlapping of sight, sound, and smell give the description immediacy and highlight the many individual dramas being played out in the bar. Phrases such as "a faint piddle-of-drops" also gives cummings's description an onomatopoeic quality, as the sound of the words mimic the action depicted.

Stanza 4

Cummings frequently breaks words in unexpected places. The first word of this stanza is "steps," finishing the word "footsteps," which ends the previous stanza. Using run-on lines in this manner emphasizes the seamlessness of the speaker's perception and the relentless quality of existence itself. By stringing together his perceptions and thoughts as they happen, the speaker functions as a kind of multisensory recording device. The description in this stanza suggests an older man ("old feller") who has had too much to drink, ordering "summore."

Stanza 5

This stanza is the most conventionally coherent one in the entire poem. The speaker focuses on himself, noting that he is just "sitting in the din thinking drinking." He highlights his own pleasant feelings, regardless of the seedy surroundings, which are embodied in the image of "the always retchings of a worthless lamp." His comment that "ale . . . / never lets you grow old" alludes to the pleasant, often self-deluding effects of alcohol on one's thinking.

Stanza 6

While contemplating his experience in McSorley's, the speaker's world is interrupted by the vision of a "bald greenish foetal head," around whose huge neck "a collar hung gently." This apparition could be some combination of dog and human, which symbolizes the degenerate atmosphere of the bar and the ways in which human beings lose dignity when alcohol takes over their bodies. But more likely he is describing a man and his dog in an impressionistic manner. Phrases such as "sonorous muscle" are examples of synesthesia, a technique in which one sense is used to describe a sensation related to another sense. In this case, the speaker describes something that he sees ("muscle") with an adjective related to sound ("sonorous"). As in previous stanzas, cummings uses modifiers such as "soiling" and "unwashed" to emphasize the extreme seediness of the place and the people who frequent it. Interestingly, the speaker never implicates himself in this seediness. Rather, he positions himself as a tourist or anthropologist who doesn't see himself as a part of the world he attempts to explain.

Stanza 7

The speaker's apparitions continue when, during an "instant of semilumionous nausea," he sees a "nondescript genie of trunk" plop himself down into a "ghost of a chair." The speaker's visions suggest that he has had too much to drink and that these beings he sees are symbolic projections of his own view of humanity. But these descriptions are also cubist-like renderings of simultaneous perceptions. Whereas cubism, an early twentieth-century art form, attempted to break objects down into their geometric shapes, cummings's version of literary cubism breaks words down and coined new ones to affect the structure of experience itself. Thus, the creatures that cummings describes in this poem may be separate, a man and a dog, for example, but he is combining the words used to represent them to probe a new way of expressing the simultaneity of his perceptions.

Stanza 8

Cummings continues his linguistic inventiveness in this stanza, describing an element of time (i.e., "interval") as a physical thing, calling it "domeshaped." He references a number of perceptions in this stanza: a waitress quickly cleaning a table, a dog, and a man affectionately holding his beer. But he rearranges the words used to describe these perceptions so it appears as if they are pieces of a dream.

Stanza 9

The speaker has achieved that drunken moment of self-reflection, asking an imagined self if it wouldn't share a drink with him.

Stanza 10

Appropriately enough, this stanza shadows the previous one. The "eternal perpetual question" is

Media Adaptations

- Caedmon/HarperAudio distributes a set of audiocassettes entitled *E. E. Cummings: Nonlectures*. In these talks, cummings offers his views on art and aesthetics.

- *E. E. Cummings: The Making of a Poet* is a videocassette distributed by Films for the Humanities and Sciences. It profiles cummings's poetic development in his own words.

- Summer Stream distributes an audiocassette of cummings reading his poems as part of their Poetic Heritage Series.

- *E. E. Cummings: Twentieth-Century Poetry in English: Recordings of Poets Reading Their Own Poetry,* an audiocassette, is distributed by the Library of Congress.

- The E. E. Cummings Society's journal, *Spring,* is published annually, and includes criticism of Cummings and reviews of critical studies of the poet. *Spring*'s website, http://www.gvsu.edu/english/Cummings/Index.htm (last accessed April 2001), includes links to other useful cummings sites.

the one the speaker asks of the shadow. Cummings implicitly pokes fun at philosophical and unanswerable "eternal" questions such as, Is there a God? and What is the meaning of life?

Stanzas 11–12

These two stanzas repeat phrases and information from the beginning of the poem, giving the poem a circular shape and providing closure. That the shadow "did not answer" underscores the speaker's aloneness in the saloon, the sense of his separateness from all that surrounds him.

Themes

Language and Meaning

At the heart of "i was sitting in mcsorley's" is the question of language's capacity to sufficiently

Topics for Further Study

- Research prohibition in the United States and write an essay exploring the contradictions between the law and the reality of alcohol consumption in the country during that time.

- Using cummings's own unconventional writing style, compose a poem that focuses more on your impression of an individual than your perception of how he or she looks.

- Translate "i was sitting in mcsorley's" into conventional grammar and word form. What is changed and what is gained in the translation?

- Research a coffee house, a bar, a restaurant, or some other place in your neighborhood where artists and writers gather, then explain the appeal of that place in a short essay.

- Write a poem about a place that represents humanity at its worse.

---

name the world. Cummings's associative imagery and unconventional syntax present not a literal picture of the world within McSorley's saloon, as much as it does the speaker's emotional and subjective response to that place. That response is depicted in a rush of concrete images that are not spatially ordered or tied to narrative. The effect of this kind of description is an impressionistic rendering of the saloon, where no clearly defined shapes come into focus. The blurry nature of the picture is illustrated in the first lines of the second stanza, when cummings writes "the slobbering walls filthily push witless creases of screaming warmth chuck pillows are noise funnily swallows." Such an impressionistic representation of the physical world suggests that the role of language is not simply to name what is out there but also to question what is out there. By calling attention to language's incapacity to provide an objective depiction of the world, cummings asks readers to think about their own relationship to words and the things they represent. Language is more a prism than a window, cummings's poem suggests, and once readers acknowledge their part within that prism, they can participate in the poet's vision of the world as he sees it.

Humanity and Human Nature

Cummings has long been known as a poet who loathed the masses but loved the individual. This view of people is strikingly evident throughout the poem, as he describes McSorley's as a kind of hell and its customers as demonic and disfigured creatures. He emphasizes the "evil" nature of the saloon in his descriptions of its "slobbering walls" and its "witless creases." The people in the saloon are described in similarly unattractive terms. He writes that one of them has "a bald greenish foetal head", and he describes someone else as "a vast wordless nondescript genie of trunk." The world outside the saloon, he describes as "New York and beautifully snowing," highlighting the contrast between the world of human beings and the world of nature. The speaker confirms his own self-loathing when he describes his vision of humanity inside the bar as "this instant of semiluminous nausea." The final image readers are left with is that of a bar full of emotionally and spiritually disfigured people who choose to be inside "snugandevil" and drinking, giving vent to their baser human emotions and qualities. The innocence and purity of nature, represented by falling snow, is an ironic reminder that goodness exists but that humanity doesn't necessarily have access to it.

Style

Typography

Cummings is perhaps best known for his innovative typography and for his experiments with grammar and word form. He routinely uses capital and lowercase letters in unconventional ways, he inserts parenthesis and scatters periods and commas in a seemingly random manner; he uses nouns as verbs and vice versa, and he splits and combines words in unexpected places and ways. All of these devices slow down the poem for readers, asking them to think associatively, as the speaker thinks, and to question the ways in which reality has been described to them. In spite of all this apparent randomness, in general, each of his "stanzas" can be read as separate syntactical units.

Expressionism

Although cummings was known for his innovative typography and grammatical innovations, he

Compare & Contrast

- **1925:** Harold Ross publishes the first issue of the *New Yorker*, a weekly magazine for sophisticates that extols urban New York City.

   1985: Conde Nast chairman S. I. "Si" Newhouse Jr. buys the *New Yorker* for $168 million.

   2000: David Remnick, editor of the *New Yorker*, announces its first venture into television. "Who Wants to Be Us?" a trivia game show, will challenge contestants' knowledge of the city and the magazine.

- **1920:** On February 1, temperatures in New York City drop to 2 degrees below zero Fahrenheit, a record cold for the date for the second day in a row.

   1989: On February 1, temperatures in New York City reach 67 degrees Fahrenheit, highest for this date.

- **1925:** The United States is in its fifth year of Prohibition, which forbids the manufacturing or sale of alcohol.

   Today: The abuse of alcohol remains a major social problem; drunk driving and binge-drinking by high school and college students are major issues.

---

was essentially an expressionist. Expressionism emerged as a movement in painting in the nineteenth century and reached its peak in the 1920s. Expressionists attempted to pierce the world of illusion, the phenomenal world, to get at the truth lying beneath it. Expressionist poetry, like painting, uses symbols to express what is essentially unsayable. These symbols yoke together opposites— the individual and the collective; the outside and the inside—in an attempt to reconcile contradictions and get at the truth. Expressionists are interested in translating their subjective feelings and perceptions rather than realistically describing the empirical world. Well-known expressionist writers include Franz Kafka, Max Beckmann, and, later in the century, Beat writers such as Jack Kerouac and Allen Ginsberg.

Historical Context

After he graduated from Harvard in 1916, cummings moved to New York City, where he stayed, with time away during World War I, for most of his life. Cummings probably wrote "i was sitting in mcsorley's" around 1917, when he was living in Greenwich Village in New York City, part of that time with his friend William Slater Brown, whom he met during the war. Cummings's biographer Charles Norman notes that cummings frequented McSorley's, which he describes as follows:

> It has two rooms, each with its individual admonitory sign, "Be Good or Be Gone." The walls are crowded with photographs and lithographs in which a vanished city dwells, and dead, buxom ladies and derbied men. The room in front has the bar, but the room in back boasts a famous lady of smooth and beautiful nudeness. . . . Here writers, artists, and laborers still meet on equal terms, without distractions, to sluice down amber quarts in the abiding gloom.

Cummings was a flaneur (an idle, man-about-town) of sorts, roaming the city for hours every day, sitting in coffee shops, bars, and restaurants, soaking up the voices and sights of New York City, and using them as fodder for his paintings and poems. The early part of the century was a lively and vibrant time in Manhattan and across the country. Undergirded by a surge in industrial growth, the economy was booming, and politicians announced a New Era in world affairs. Consumerism was on the rise, as people were barraged with products they didn't even know they needed. Petroleum-based products such as rayon, acetate, and cellophane gave rise to entire new industries. Automobiles, radios, and telephones became must-have items. Americans were experiencing a sea change, or transformation, in the way that they lived. Anti-drinking activists lobbied hard for Prohibition, which took effect in 1920. The Eighteenth Amendment prohibited the manufacturing and selling of alcohol. In big cities such as New York, however, Prohibition fueled illegal activity and made drinking sexy and hip, and underground speakeasies, places where illegal alcohol was sold, sprung up across the country. Speakeasies contributed in no small part to the easing of social barriers during this time, as gangsters, businessmen, blue-collar workers, and professionals all gathered to drink. Ironically, the Prohibition movement, fueled by the fear that hordes of Europeans pouring into the country were polluting American values, helped to bring Americans of different cultures and classes together.

Across the country writers such as Theodore Dreiser, John Dos Passos, Carl Sandburg, Ernest Hemingway, and Dorothy Parker were helping to define a distinctly American brand of literary modernism and often used the new urban life as the subject of their work. In architecture, Frank Lloyd Wright was contributing to what became known as the international style, as he designed functional buildings of steel, concrete, and glass. In the visual arts Ansel Adams, Edward Hopper, and Georgia O'Keeffe were developing their own American styles. The music world was the site of experimentation as well, as jazz became popular. By the end of the decade, the good times were over, as the stock market crash, in 1929, destroyed the livelihoods and futures of millions of people and set America on a course of a recovery that would take decades.

Critical Overview

"i was sitting in mcsorley's" appeared in cummings's first collection of poetry, *Tulips & Chimneys*, published in 1923. Cummings initially put together a collection of his poems in 1919 but had no success in finding a publisher. In 1922, after Cummings had revised the contents of the collection, his friend, writer John Dos Passos, convinced Liverlight publisher Thomas Meltzer to publish the book. The book that appeared contained only sixty-six of the original 152 poems in the manuscript.

Its critical reception was mixed. Reviewing the collection for *New York World,* Robert E. Wolf writes: "It is extraordinarily good . . . it contains, in its own individual style, as beautiful poems as have been written by any present-day poet in the English language." Herbert Gorman of the *New York Times Book Review* is not as effusive, claiming that "Cummings is immensely derivative in a large part of his work," although "often he reaches a high and concentrated pitch of emotion that even his mannerisms cannot hide." *Poetry* founder Harriet Monroe writes that cummings's typography is "irritating" but that "there is a grand gusto in him, and that is rare enough to be welcomed in any age of a world too full of puling pettifoggers and picayunes." Praising the book's musicality and penchant for image-making, James Oppenheim says that cummings's poems "fill out the picture started by the prose. Open *Tulips & Chimneys* at any page, and somewhere upon that page there will be traces, oftentimes thrilling ones, of an inner musical state playing exuberantly with the materials of life."

Criticism

Chris Semansky

Semansky has published widely in the field of twentieth-century poetry and culture. In the following essay, he considers "i was sitting in mcsorley's" as an example of cummings's notion of unrealism.

"i was sitting in mcsorley's" is a painterly poem that embodies cummings's idea of what he called "unrealism." Like so many artists and writers at the beginning of the twentieth century, Cummings wanted to make his writing modern. Writing modern poetry meant to "make it new," as Ezra Pound said. This involved challenging the status quo, which at the beginning of the twentieth century was realism and its offshoots.

Realism, a literary movement rooted in the nineteenth century, uses the everyday world as its subject matter. Practitioners of literary realism considered language a tool to show readers the world as it was rather than how it should be. Realistic writing often had a reportorial feel to it. At the beginning of the twentieth century, novelists such as Virginia Woolfe, James Joyce, John Dos Passos, and others challenged this way of representing reality. In poetry, Ezra Pound, T. S. Eliot, and H. D. were similarly challenging the status quo, writing verse freed from the confines of formal diction and meter and composing a poetry in speech patterns, dense with images, whose aim was to show that the world wasn't necessarily what people thought that it was. Cummings was part of this modern movement. Claiming that the prism, not the mirror, was the symbol of all art, cummings wrote in his unpublished notebook, which can be found at the Houghton Library, that "the goal is unrealism. The method is destructive. To break up the white light of objective realism, into the secret glories which it contains."

The poem "i was sitting in mcsorley's" demonstrates the practice of cummings's unrealism in action. Ostensibly a portrait of the inside of a famous saloon in lower Manhattan, the poem doesn't show readers what the bar looks like, but rather it evokes in them a sense of the bar's complex atmosphere. Whereas realism by its very nature is selective, showing this and not that, cummings's unrealism is just the opposite, attempting to show everything at once. To accomplish this, cummings developed a method that struck at the very heart of realism's assumption about language.

When light passes through a prism it is dispersed into a number of wavelengths that the human eye experiences as colors. Cummings wants to do the same thing to language and, hence, readers' experience. He is describing the scene at McSorley's as if he were looking at it through a prism. However, instead of colors, images are dispersed. This dispersal literally destroys the linearity of cummings's sentences, the order in which he presents the images. But it creates a sense of movement and immediacy, so that readers can see and experience images and incidents simultaneously. An examination of the poem's third stanza will illustrate this method:

> the Bar.tinking luscious jigs dint of ripe silver with
>   warmlyish wetflat
> splurging smells waltz the glush of squirting taps
>   plus slush of foam
> knocked off and a faint piddle-of-drops she says I
>   ploc spittle what the
> lands thaz me kid in no sir hopping sawdust you
>   kiddo he's a palping
> wreaths of badly Yep cigars who jim him why
>   gluey grins topple to-
> gether eyes pout gestures stickily point made glints
>   squinting who's a
> wink bum-nothing and money fuzzily mouths take
>   big wobbly foot-

Using critic Rushworth Kidder's guidelines in "Cummings and Cubism: The Influence of Modern Art on Cummings' Early Poetry" for understanding cummings provides insight into cummings's method. Kidder advises readers to add punctuation and words and to rearrange words if necessary to give a cummings's poem more conventional syntactical meaning. A "translation" of the stanza into standard sentences might look as follows:

> *Ostensibly a portrait of the inside of a famous saloon in lower Manhattan, the poem doesn't show readers what the bar looks like, but rather it evokes in them a sense of the bar's complex atmosphere."*

The warm bar smelled of flat beer. You could hear the gush of squirting taps and the piddle-of-drops and see the bartender knock the slush of foam from the head of the beers. Voices could be heard above the din, saying things like "Kiddo" and "Hey you," "No sir," "Yep," "Thaz me, kid," and "Who's a bum?" You could hear the tinking of the silver mugs and see the sawdust on the floor. Tipsy people with gluey grins and smoking cigars pack the tables, winking and pointing at one another, flashing money while buying drinks, wobblying.

Cummings critic S. V. Baum, in his article "E. E. Cummings: The Technique of Immediacy," says this about cummings's technique for creating immediacy: "Because of his extreme honesty as a poet he has been compelled to describe the complex unit of experience without the presence of falsifying temporal order. Perception of the moment involves many impressions, none complete in itself; instead, they blur and overlap one into the other." To achieve this overlapping effect cummings not only fragments impressions and words, but he also creates new ones by literally reconstructing the language. "Glush" and "wetflat" are words illustrating cummings's desire to concentrate multiple sensations in the same word. Ironically, such linguistic precision makes cummings's poetry more real rather than less. Lawrence Weinstein, in his article "On the Precision of E. E. Cummings," underscores the success of this method, noting that "Cummings' precision allows him to describe objects with a particularized approach . . . he evokes exactly the object he means to describe." Weinstein cites the image of the "exactly-mutilated ghost of a chair" in McSorley's, claiming that "this description does not simply connote an old chair, but

What Do I Read Next?

- Cummings's 1922 prose work *The Enormous Room* details his experience as a prisoner of the French during World War I. Cummings was working for the American Red Cross at the time he was imprisoned for insubordination. The book is considered by many critics to be an American classic.

- Poet and critic Gerald Locklin explores the influence of cummings on contemporary poets such as Richard Kostelanetz, Edward Field, and Ronald Koertge in his 1993 essay "The Influence of Cummings on Selected Contemporary Poets."

- In addition to his biography of cummings, *Dreams in the Mirror: A Biography of E. E. Cummings* (1980), Richard S. Kennedy also wrote a critical study of cummings's work, *E. E. Cummings Revisited,* which reviews much of the more recent critical work on the poet.

- Byron Farwell's study of America's involvement in World War I, *Over There: The United States in the Great War, 1917–1918* (1999), provides an in-depth look at the United States's role in the Great War. Farwell tells the story of how the United States responded to a war it was not prepared to fight. This study helps to contextualize cummings's own formative experiences as an ambulance driver for the Allies.

---

eyes. Juxtaposition, fragmentation, and overlapping are all techniques used to heighten the sense of the subject. However, these techniques also draw attention to the medium of cummings's art and language and to the idea that words could no longer be considered the mere window onto the physical world that realists assumed they were. Cummings offers a compelling alternative to the notion that art's goal is to imitate life through an accurate depiction of the empirical world.

At the time "i was sitting in mcsorley's" was written, the United States was experiencing the aftermath of World War I. It was a time of excitement and confusion and prosperity and fear. The automobile and the telephone were changing the ways in which people thought about and experienced time and space. Movie houses were also springing up around the country, playing motion pictures and newsreels of world events, consolidating images of the past and present. The world was becoming a smaller place. By fragmenting the language he uses to describe the world, cummings presents a portrait of a fragmented world in which everything is happening at once. The demand that he places on readers to understand his poems is similar to the rapidly changing world's demand on people in their daily lives. In this sense, cummings's poems do not challenge the idea of realism as much as they help redefine realism. His "destruction" of words, word order, linearity, and sense provide readers with a hyper-real vision of things. It is a vision even truer today than it was at the beginning of the century.

Source: Chris Semansky, Critical Essay on "i was sitting in mcsorley's," in *Poetry for Students,* The Gale Group, 2001.

Erica Smith

Smith is a writer and editor. In this essay, she describes "i was sitting in mcsorley's" by e. e. cummings as a meditation on love as well as an individual's relationship with the natural world.

At first glance, e. e. cummings's poem "i was sitting in mcsorley's barely seems to be a poem at all. Arranged not in stanzas and lines like most poems, but in paragraphs like a prose passage, the poem further baffles many readers with its bizarre spelling and punctuation. Much of the poem seems to be an incomprehensible run-on sentence, the words following one another with no apparent logic. Once a reader puts aside his or her expectations of what a poem should look like, however, "i was sitting in mcsorley's" is revealed to be not only a deeply poetic piece of writing but a poem with a strong connection to the rest of cummings's work.

---

suggests precisely the particular chair in McSorley's Cummings had in mind."

Cummings also juxtaposes unlike terms in his portrait of the bar, a technique popularized by surrealists, to create his "all-in-one-effect." For example, Weinstein notes cummings's use of the description "ripe silver." "Silver," Weinstein observes, "does not ripen, but the juxtaposition of 'ripe' and 'silver' suggests precisely the comfortable, aged atmosphere of the inside of a tavern." Similarly, cummings juxtaposes snatches of dialogue with description, appealing simultaneously to readers' ears and

Throughout his long career in American poetry, cummings was know for his unorthodox style of punctuation, capitalization, and spelling. He would often leave the first letter of a line in one of his poems uncapitalized, while capitalizing a word in the middle of the line. Words would run into each other or be separated by long spaces. Lines would break in unexpected places. Cummings used these methods to bring a freshness and sense of excitement to his poems. By using such novel arrangements of his text, he also created new stresses and tensions in his poetry that would have been impossible to achieve using ordinary arrangements of words. In this way, he was following the lead of the American poet Walt Whitman, whose long lines managed to capture the exuberant rush produced by saying each line in a single deep breath.

Both poets ran words together, either to express two related ideas in a single image (such as the "wetflat" smells in line 9) or, using the technique known as juxtaposition, to force unrelated ideas together to create a fresh, new image. Cummings's unique typography also serves to make not only the individual words but the poem itself more than just words on a page. His poems become carefully arranged word pictures. In this way, he followed the lead of the founder of the imagist school, American poet Ezra Pound, who felt that each word in a poem must be like a Chinese pictogram, containing a concrete image as well as an abstract meaning.

In the case of "i was sitting in mcsorley's," cummings arranges the poem like a prose passage, with paragraphs instead of stanzas. This type of a poem is known as a prose poem. A famous example of this type of poetry is the collection of prose poems by the French poet Charles Baudelaire, *Paris Spleen*. Cummings's "i was sitting in mcsorley's" shares with *Paris Spleen* a vision of discontent, of an ugly human world into which something ugly frequently intrudes. At the same time, "i was sitting in mcsorley's" plays on two of cummings's most frequent themes: the relation between the human and the natural world, and the need and desire for love.

The first two paragraphs of the poem immediately describe the first of these themes. The poet is sitting inside McSorley's Saloon in Greenwich Village, New York City. Outside it is "beautifully snowing," (line 2) but inside it is "snug and evil" (line 3). The second paragraph is a sort of verbal collage of various impressions of the interior of the bar, mostly consisting of visual images, all thrown

> *To truly love and embrace the world, cummings seems to be saying, it's necessary to be able to embrace its ugly side, to unite with its decay, to take that risk in exchange for connection."*

together seemingly at random. Cummings's technique here serves to convey the fragmented way one would hear and see things if he or she were sitting inside the bar.

The third paragraph continues in this mode, including in its collage effect snippets of the conversations that fill the air inside McSorley's. What is most notable in this paragraph and the one before it is the palpable sense of decay that fills the inside of the bar. The imagery is full of words that sound somehow disgusting: gobs, spittle, piddle, skulch. These and the various bits of conversation related in this paragraph help to heighten the sense that it is indeed "snug and evil" inside the bar.

The noise inside the bar both brings readers closer to the other people and yet, at the same time, distances readers from them. By only allowing readers to hear little pieces of conversation, they are prevented from understanding what the people are really talking about. And by mixing up their conversations with words used to describe the way the bar looks and sounds, cummings makes it seem like the people are just a part of the bar. In fact, he never describes these people; he only gives readers parts of their conversations. This makes them seem like a part of the atmosphere in the bar and not like real people at all. At the same time, the act of eavesdropping on their conversations makes readers see the poet as something of a voyeur.

Starting with the fourth paragraph, however, there is a break in the way the poet's impressions of the bar are reported. Instead of giving readers sound impressions, he now only uses visual imagery. And at the same time, the sense of nastiness, almost of evil, is increased.

It begins with the first glimpse of the poet himself, who is sitting, drinking the ale, "which never lets you grow old" and blinking (note the sudden return to primarily visual imagery) at the ceiling, almost as if he hopes to be lifted above, or at least out of the atmosphere inside the bar. While the poet feels pleasant enough, he is constantly being reminded of where he is by the retchings of the patrons; and although he mostly just looks, his lamp remains "worthless," perhaps because it only gives light but does not illuminate.

Then into his awareness comes a stranger. This is also the first time a person is actually described in the poem. But the description is of someone monstrous: the head is "bald greenish" and "foetal"; the neck is huge and unwashed; the hands are like paws and "distended," almost as if they belong to a corpse. Yet while readers are being inundated by this sudden flood of detail, at the same time they are losing senses; while the poet first noted the head in an instant of light falling on it, soon the instant is "semiluminous," and the trunk of the other man is both "nondescript" and "wordless." This last detail is extremely important.

The poet, confronted by the approach of this strange person, seems to be filled with loathing ("nausea" is part of his sense-impressions of the man). "Darkness it was so near to me," he notes (line 32). Yet even when confronted by this apparently disgusting person, the poet does not give in to his fear but instead asks him if he would like a drink. Confronted with everything that is terrible and evil in the bar, he chooses to reach out to it, to try to connect with it.

Just as the man seems to be more than an ordinary bar patron (who has perhaps had too much to drink), so too does asking him if he would like a drink seem to be more than just a friendly invitation. The request is described as "the eternal perpetual question" and can be seen as the ultimate attempt to reach out to a world of decay and death, where one is always separated from the rest of the world, just as cummings is separated from the patrons at the bar. Thus, not only is the man (who is always described as "it") a person, he is the "Darkness" of line 32 and possibly also the world itself, or at least its evil and ugly parts. To truly love and embrace the world, cummings seems to be saying, it's necessary to be able to embrace its ugly side, to unite with its decay, to take that risk in exchange for connection.

But it does not happen in this poem. The man does not answer. McSorley's remains "snugandevil." (Note that by running the words together, cummings manages to include the word "devil" in his repeat of his first impression of McSorley's.) And outside, it remains "beautifully snowing. . . ." In contrast to the decaying human world of the bar, the outside world of natural processes (snowing) is beautiful.

Yet at the same time, the poet remains inside the bar, which is not just evil but snug. There is something comfortable about staying inside, risking the chance of human connection (which may remain forever impossible) rather than going outside into the snow, which will remain forever inaccessible to the poet.

The poem "i was sitting in mcsorley's" thus touches on two of cummings's most important themes: that love is the most important thing to have (he tries to love the man in the bar, in his own poor way, by offering him a drink) and the beauty of the outside world. At the same time, it shows the tension of trying to hold onto these beliefs in an imperfect human world. Remarkable for its brilliant collage of impressions, which manage to convey the inside of a crowded New York City bar with all its sights, sounds, smells, and tastes, "i was sitting in mcsorley's" is also a serious poem about the ache of being human.

Source: Erica Smith, Critical Essay on "i was sitting in mcsorley's," in *Poetry for Students,* The Gale Group, 2001.

Sources

Baum, S. V., "E. E. Cummings: The Technique of Immediacy," in *South Atlantic Quarterly,* Vol. 53, No. 1, January 1954, pp. 70–88.

Blackmur, R. P., "Notes on E. E. Cummings' Language," in *Hound & Horn,* Vol. IV, No. 2, 1931, pp. 163–92.

Cummings, E. E., *Collected Poems,* Harcourt Brace, 1938.

———, *The Enormous Room,* Liveright, 1922.

———, *Tulips & Chimneys,* Liveright, 1976.

———, "Unpublished Notes," Houghton Library, Harvard University.

Dendinger, Lloyd N., ed., *E. E. Cummings: The Critical Reception,* Burt Franklin, 1981.

Farwell, Byron, *Over There: The United States in the Great War, 1917–1918,* Norton & Company, 2000.

Friedman, Norman, "E. E. Cummings and His Critics," in *Criticism,* No. 6, 1964, pp. 114–33.

———, *E. E. Cummings: The Art of His Poetry,* Johns Hopkins University Press, 1960.

Gorman, Herbert, "Goliath Beats His Poetic Breast, Whilst Critics Gape," in *New York Times Book Review*, December 9, 1923, p. 5.

Kennedy, Richard S., *Dreams in the Mirror: A Biography of E. E. Cummings*, Liveright, 1980.

———, *E.E. Cummings Revisited*, Twayne Publishers, 1994.

Kidder, Rushworth, "Cummings and Cubism: The Influence of the Visual Arts on Cummings' Early Poetry," in the *Journal of Modern Literature*, No. 7, April 1979, pp. 255–91.

———, *E. E. Cummings: An Introduction to the Poetry*, Columbia University Press, 1979.

Lane, Gary, *I Am: A Study of E. E. Cummings' Poems*, University Press of Kansas, 1976.

Locklin, Gerald, "The Influence of Cummings on Selected Contemporary Poets," in *Spring*, No. 2, 1993, pp. 40–7.

Marks, Barry, *E. E. Cummings*, Twayne, 1964.

Monroe, Harriet, "Flare and Blare," in *Poetry*, January 1924, pp. 211–15.

Norman, Charles, *E. E. Cummings: The Magic-Maker*, Duell, Sloan and Pearce, 1958.

Oppenheim, James, "E. E. Cummings," in *Men Seen*, August 1924, pp. 194–200.

Rotella, Guy, ed., *Critical Essays on E. E. Cummings*, G. K. Hall, 1984.

Weinstein, Lawrence, "On the Precision of E. E. Cummings," in *Spring*, No. 3, 1994, pp.77–9.

Wolf, Robert L., "E. E. Cummings's Poetry," in *New York World*, November 18, 1923, p 9E.

For Further Study

Cohen, Milton A., *Poet and the Painter: The Aesthetics of E. E. Cummings's Early Work*, Wayne State University Press, 1987.

Cohen explores cummings's development as an artist and poet by analyzing his notes on aesthetic theory. This is an important study of cummings's influences and how his theories on writing and painting came together.

Cureton, Richard D., "Poetry, Grammar, and Epistemology: The Order of Prenominal Modifiers in the Poetry of E. E. Cummings," in *Language & Structure* Vol. 18, No. 1, 1985, pp. 64–91.

Cureton analyzes cummings's use of adjectives in his poetry, exploring the connection between cummings's adjectival order and his ideology.

McBride, Katharine Winters, ed., *A Concordance to the Complete Poems of E. E. Cummings*, Cornell University Press, 1989.

This book lists more than 13,000 words used by cumming, including combined words and neologisms (made up words) found in *Complete Poems*. This is a useful text for those doing a systematic study of cummings's poetry.

Norman, Charles, *E. E. Cummings: The Magic-Maker*, Duell, Sloan and Pearce, 1958.

This biography of cummings is thorough and well researched. Norman makes connections between cummings's emotional development and his development as an artist but does not pretend to be a psychologist.

The Idea of Order at Key West

Wallace Stevens

1934

Written in 1934, "The Idea of Order at Key West" remains one of the most difficult poems by one of America's most difficult poets. Yet, it stands as one of Stevens' most anthologized poems, and according to most critics of his work, it is one of his best. Stevens must have liked it as well, as he made it the title poem in his 1936 collection, *Ideas of Order.* As widely praised as the poem is, no authoritative reading has emerged. Indeed, there are as many different interpretations of the poem as there are readers of it.

One of the great ironies of "The Idea of Order at Key West," is that for a complex poem, its plot is rather simple. An unnamed speaker is walking along the beach of Key West and hears a woman singing a song. The song enchants the listener/speaker, and as the woman is singing, he begins to muse on the beauty of her song and its relationship to his own life, particularly his ideas on reality and imagination. Finally, after listening and thinking, the speaker experiences a kind of epiphany, a moment of insight. While few would question these basic facts of the poem, the debate takes place around what Stevens thinks of the song and what kind of epiphany he experiences.

While the poem remains too complex to be easily explicated or paraphrased here, it is accurate to say that the poem dramatizes important conflicts for Stevens: imagination and reality, presence and absence, order and chaos, nature and civilization, the mind and the body. While readers never see the female singer or actually hear what it is the woman is singing, they experience what the speaker of the poem experiences: transformation. The woman's song transforms the speaker's experience of walking along the beach, and, what's more, when he returns to town, he discovers that his perception of Key West has also been altered. Early critics cite the poem as an example of Stevens championing the creative process, but that is inaccurate, according to most recent criticism. These critics believe that the poem is about the need for poetry and the need for art. Thus, the emphasis of the poem is not so much on the song itself but what the song does to the listener. One can extend that, of course, to Stevens' hope for his own poetry—that it has the same effect on his readers as the song does on the speaker of the poem.

Author Biography

Wallace Stevens was born on October 2, 1879, in Reading, Pennsylvania, where he grew up in a typical upper-middle-class family in the American Northeast. In 1897, he enrolled at Harvard as a special student where he began writing poems seriously for the first time. He claims that, while at Harvard, he longed to be like John Keats, the famous British poet, immersed in the beauty of literature and literary pursuits. But Stevens was always pulled in multiple directions, and he was not convinced that a life devoted to literature would be an entirely masculine endeavor, nor a lucrative one.

As America was transforming into an industrial and financial powerhouse, ideas about men's roles in the world and productive professions were changing. With this in mind, upon graduation from Harvard in 1900, Stevens moved to New York to become a journalist. He believed that journalism offered the best chance for one's writing to have a direct impact on people's lives. For almost two years, he worked as a reporter for the *New York Tribune* and as an assistant editor for *World's Work*. However, Stevens and journalism were not a particularly good match, so Stevens decided to go to law school. He attended New York Law School and graduated on June 10, 1903. In 1904, he was admitted to the New York State bar and began his career as an attorney, a job he would keep his entire life.

The year 1904 was a big year for Stevens for other reasons, as well. While at home on a visit, he met Elsie Viola Moll, the woman who would become his wife five years later. Between 1904 and

Wallace Stevens

1907, Stevens worked for various law firms in New York City and dabbled in poetry. In 1908, he joined the legal staff of the American Bonding Company and wrote a small sentimental book of poems, bearing the very un-Stevens-like title of *A Book of Verses*. He not only gave the book to Elsie, it was written for her. In 1909, he wrote another book for Elsie, this time entitled *The Little June Book*. Though none of these poems reflect the kind of work Stevens would be known for, he was on his way to becoming a major poet.

In 1914, at the age of thirty-four, Stevens began publishing what scholars consider his first mature poems, but his first book, *Harmonium,* did not appear until 1923. Though *Harmonium* did not sell well, it stands as perhaps the most important first book of poems by any twentieth-century American poet. But, with the birth of his daughter Holly in 1924, Stevens stopped writing and did not publish another book until 1935, when *Ideas of Order* appeared in a limited edition by Alcestis Press and then in full release in 1935, published by Alfred A. Knopf. From this point on, Stevens was very prolific. *The Man with the Blue Guitar* hit the stands in 1937 and *Parts of a World* and the long poem "Notes toward a Supreme Fiction" appeared in 1942. Several more volumes followed: *Transport to Summer* in 1947; *The Auroras of Autumn* in

1950; *The Necessary Angel: Essays on Reality and the Imagination* in 1951; *The Collected Poems* in 1954; and *Opus Posthumous,* edited by Holly Stevens, was published in 1957, two years after Stevens died of stomach cancer.

Stevens' awards were numerous, though fairly late in coming. He was elected to the National Institute of Arts and Letters in 1945 and won the very prestigious Bollingen Prize in poetry in 1949. *The Auroras of Autumn* garnered the National Book Award for poetry in 1950, and in 1951, he received the Gold Medal of the Poetry Society of America. Stevens' *Collected Poems* won both the National Book Award and the Pulitzer Prize in 1954. Stevens died of cancer on August 2, 1955, in Hartford, Connecticut.

In 2000, a panel of scholars of poets assembled by National Public Radio voted his poem "The Snow Man" one of the ten best American poems of the century, and most scholars agree that Stevens was probably the most important and most influential American poet of the twentieth century.

Poem Text

    She sang beyond the genius of the sea.
    The water never formed to mind or voice,
    Like a body wholly body, fluttering
    Its empty sleeves; and yet its mimic motion
    Made constant cry, caused constantly a cry,   5
    That was not ours although we understood,
    Inhuman, of the veritable ocean.

    The sea was not a mask. No more was she.
    The song and water were not medleyed sound
    Even if what she sang was what she heard,   10
    Since what she sang was uttered word by word.
    It may be that in all her phrases stirred
    The grinding water and the gasping wind;
    But it was she and not the sea we heard.

    For she was the maker of the song she sang.   15
    The ever-hooded, tragic-gestured sea
    Was merely a place by which she walked to sing.
    Whose spirit is this? we said, because we knew
    It was the spirit that we sought and knew
    That we should ask this often as she sang.   20

    If it was only the dark voice of the sea
    That rose, or even colored by many waves;
    If it was only the outer voice of sky
    And cloud, of the sunken coral water-walled,
    However clear, it would have been deep air,   25
    The heaving speech of air, a summer sound
    Repeated in a summer without end
    And sound alone. But it was more than that,

    More even than her voice, and ours, among
    The meaningless plungings of water and the wind,   30
    Theatrical distances, bronze shadows heaped
    On high horizons, mountainous atmospheres
    Of sky and sea.
        It was her voice that made
    The sky acutest at its vanishing.   35
    She measured to the hour its solitude.
    She was the single artificer of the world
    In which she sang. And when she sang, the sea,
    Whatever self it had, became the self
    That was her song, for she was the maker. Then we,   40
    As we beheld her striding there alone,
    Knew that there never was a world for her
    Except the one she sang and, singing, made.

    Ramon Fernandez, tell me, if you know,
    Why, when the singing ended and we turned   45
    Toward the town, tell why the glassy lights,
    The lights in the fishing boats at anchor there,
    As the night descended, tilting in the air,
    Mastered the night and portioned out the sea,
    Fixing emblazoned zones and fiery poles,   50
    Arranging, deepening, enchanting night.

    Oh! Blessed rage for order, pale Ramon,
    The maker's rage to order words of the sea,
    Words of the fragrant portals, dimly-starred,
    And of ourselves and of our origins,   55
    In ghostlier demarcations, keener sounds.

Poem Summary

Lines 1–7

The opening stanza of the poem, along with the title, help set the stage for the action that transpires in the poem itself. Right away, Stevens distinguishes between the mind and external reality and also the singer and the sea, but as is always the case for Stevens, these divisions are never hard and fast. Readers do know a few things, though. There is a singer, who is a female. There is a speaker and also a companion, probably Ramon Fernandez of stanza six. They are all walking along the sea. Of all these agents, the agent receiving the primary attention is the female singer. The poem opens with a rather remarkable claim that she sings "beyond the genius of the sea." But Stevens describes the sea as a "wholly body" that both makes "a constant cry" and causes a constant cry. The syntax of this stanza is confusing because so many phrases may modify each other. The result of this lack of distinction is a sense of merging, a theme Stevens will develop throughout the poem. It's difficult to tell what belongs to what. What does emerge, though, is a sense that the cry takes on an inhuman significance, that it becomes an inspiring or even spiritual force that unites sea, land, speaker, and singer. The speaker of the poem may not comprehend exactly what's going on, but some sort of larger, spiritual understanding of the whole of experience is taking place.

Lines 8–14

Stevens is quick to point out in the second stanza that the sea "was not a mask," which is to say that the sea is not a static, external reality, just as the speaker is not a static, false, object. Both are in flux. They are not facades but wholly pulsing bodies. Stevens goes on to say in line ten that the cry of the sea is what the woman hears and translates into her own song. This cry, uttered by the sea, resembles the cry the young Walt Whitman experiences in "Out of the Cradle Endlessly Rocking," in that the cry of the ocean becomes the song of the poet or in this case the song of the singer. In this moment, the inhuman song of the sea fuses with the utterly human song of the woman. By uttering the song "word by word," she makes the inhuman human. What's more, the poet suggests that the woman's beautiful words actually stir the waters and the wind. However, even if this is the case, the poet reminds readers that his attention has been transferred from the sea to the woman, for it is "she and not the sea" that he hears. This is an important move for Stevens because he seems to embrace a decidedly human gesture over a gesture of nature. While this may seem a simple act, it reverses the trend of romanticism to embrace nature over people. Stevens implicit message here is that poetry remains an utterly human endeavor.

Lines 15–20

In this stanza, Stevens establishes the primacy of the individual by asserting that even though she may have gotten the idea or the source of her song from the sea, the song ultimately issues from her alone. It is her song, just as the poem is Stevens' poem. He will soften his stance on the individuality of poetic creation over the course of his career, but in his early poems, Stevens is profoundly interested in the power of the imagination. Thus, where in stanzas one and two the singer and the sea seemed a joined pair, by stanza three, the sea is merely a backdrop for her song. But even after all of this has been cleared up, a nagging question remains: "Whose spirit is this?" Is it hers? Is it the sea's? Is it the spirit of the poet observing these forces? The moment is so strong that the poet and his companion know that they must keep asking themselves, whose spirit is driving this glorious song? Stevens seems to suggest that to answer this question is to get a glimpse into the mysteries of the hazy borders between imagination and reality. In a later poem, Stevens claims that the search for reality is as important as the search for God; perhaps he is implying here that if he can discern whose spirit is animating the woman and the sea, he can begin to know not only the mysteries of human imagination and perception but also the mysteries of God as well.

Lines 21–28

Readers expecting an answer to the question posed in the previous stanza get a big disappointment in stanza four. As is the case with every question Stevens poses, there is no clear answer. The speaker wonders if the song he is hearing is "only the dark voice of the sea." And he muses if the song is nothing more than the "outer voice of sky / And cloud." In other words, he goes back over everything that has happened. This kind of reflection into the revelatory powers of nature recalls the romantic poetry of William Wordsworth, Percy Shelly, and John Keats. In poems like Shelly's "Ode to the West Wind," Keats' "To Autumn," and especially Wordsworth's "Lines Composed a Few Miles Above Tintern Abbey," the speaker enjoys a spiritual renewal through a unity with nature. Nature

Media Adaptations

- There is a video in the Voices and Visions series that situates Stevens' poetry in historical and geographical settings. Critics and other poets read and explain his work. The video, entitled *Wallace Stevens: Man Made Out of Words,* was produced by the Center for Visual History in 1988.

- You can hear Stevens read "The Idea of Order at Key West" and other poems on the cassette *Wallace Stevens Reads,* distributed by Harper Audio.

not only puts the poet in touch with the sublime, it also serves as a creative vehicle for his poem. Thus, nature serves as a kind of god in that it delivers salvation on a number of levels. Through these questions, Stevens wonders if what he is experiencing is a similar kind of conflation with the sublime. In short, he wonders if he is lucky enough to be experiencing a romantic epiphany that his poetic forefathers so passionately sought, one that seems entirely out of reach in twentieth-century America.

Lines 28–33

For the modern poet, nature cannot provide the kind of spiritual fulfillment it did for his nineteenth-century predecessors. He needs more. Readers know from the previous stanzas that what the speaker hears is not merely the sea singing through the woman's voice, nor is the woman the singular force that makes her song. Thus, when in line 28, he claims that the song is "more than that," he has come to understand that the song is more than sea, more than woman, more, even, than the trinity of woman, sea, and speaker. What, exactly, the song is remains a mystery; all he knows is that the song and the spirit driving it are beyond the totality of the external realities in his presence. This realization is a good example of ineffability in Stevens. The ineffable—the unsayable, that which is beyond language and experience—remains a constant motif for Stevens throughout his work. He may not know what the source or the design of the song is, but he knows it is greater than the "meaningless plungings of water and the wind," which means that its power is greater than natural forces. In fact, it is greater than language, greater, perhaps, than human understanding, though only possibly understood by humans who can only articulate their experiences through language.

Lines 34–38

It is language, voice, that finally brings the speaker into understanding. At first glance, these lines may appear to be a reworking of the solipsism—a theory that holds that the self can know nothing but its own modifications and that the self is the only existent thing—of an earlier poem "Tea at the Palaz of Hoon," in which Hoon imposes a kind of imperial order on the world around him. But a closer inspection reveals that what Stevens emphasizes here is not the imposition of order or the transformation of the world through perception (a rather selfish and impersonal process) but rather a celebration of the speaker's need to interpret the world around her and to articulate how she perceives this world. For Stevens, the acts of interpretation and articulation are fundamentally human acts that put people in touch with themselves and the world in which they walk and sing and dream and think. Again, Stevens wants to make a connection between the song in the poem and poetry itself. The importance of poetry lies not in the poet or even the poem but in the reader—what the reader learns about herself through an engagement with the poem.

Lines 38—43

In what remains one of the most impressive moments in modern poetry, Stevens offers a glimpse of the power of poetic engagement. In his *Adagia*, a collection of adages and aphorisms, Stevens writes, "Poetry is not the same things as the imagination taken alone. Nothing is itself taken alone. Things are because of interrelations or interactions." What Stevens means by this is that nothing is experienced alone. Really, there is no singularity. Everything stands in relation to everything else. People are all connected. This theory gets dramatized wonderfully in these six lines. The singer, the sea, and the observers all merge into one shared experience. What seemed to be autonomous, individual units in the first stanzas, becomes one shared unit by the end of this stanza. Stevens finally understands that he is not the sole maker of his reality, for his reality has been shaped by his engagement with the sea, the woman, and her song. The speaker realizes that the woman's song sharpens his perspective on the world around him and the world at large, just as a poem might do to a reader. Additionally, the song engenders in him a desire to create his own song, so that he can interact with the imagination of others the way the woman has corresponded with his. The poetic project does not exist in the private world of the singer or poet but in the public lives of other people.

Lines 44–51

To other people, the speaker turns. In an unusual poetic move for Stevens, the individual steps outside of his private meditative world and addresses another person, probably his companion on the beach, Ramon Fernandez. These lines represent a shift away from the solipsism of Hoon to a perspective shared by Ramon Fernandez and the town toward which they turn and move. Before, the song caused him to turn inward, away from nature, away from the town, but now, through the unifying power of the song (and poetry in general), the speaker turns back toward both nature and civilization with a new perspective. He re-sees the sea and his relationship to the sea. Again, he poses a question that goes unanswered. He wants to know why, after the singing ended, the lights of the boats and the town began "arranging" and "deepening" and "enchanting" the night.

While Ramon is either unable, or does not choose, to answer, the answer lies in the poem itself. He turns toward songs of humanity because the song redirected him toward human emotions, human endeavors, and human feelings. Also implied in this question is, again, the presence of something larger than the song, some spirit or force that makes human experiences more profound. Of course, a hard and fast answer will never come, but the speaker and Stevens know that the great joy and energy of being alive come from asking these very questions.

Lines 52–56

Stevens is always obsessed with words. In this final stanza, Stevens finally gets at the title of the poem by linking the desire for ordered experience with the ability to articulate experience. The "rage for order" concerns both "ourselves" and "our origins" and thus extends to the speaker, the singer, and the audience of the poem. It is important to realize that the poem is not attempting to order the readers' worlds or urging them to order the worlds of others. Rather, the song in the poem and the poem itself serve as articulations of how to begin to achieve some sort of understanding of a world that people do not understand. Or, put more philosophically, the poem dramatizes how people make the inhuman human. The "fragrant portals," then, represent openings for people, rich, rewarding passageways into places of self-location, self-awareness, and self-reflection. The song and the poem are such portals. After experiencing both, the words people utter to themselves at moments of insight and understanding will be "keener." And even though their world may contain gray areas, or "ghostlier demarcations," people might be able to access the larger spirit that is both human and inhuman, sayable and ineffable, ordered and chaotic. One of Stevens' most sensitive and passionate readers, Harold Bloom, in his book *Wallace Stevens: The Poems of Our Climate,* argues that the poem affirms a "transcendental poetic spirit yet cannot locate it." To locate that spirit would be to order the world. To leave that location up to the reader is to invite the reader into Stevens' intoxicating song.

Themes

Reality and the Imagination

Late in his career, in fact, a year before his death, Stevens was asked to define the major theme of his poetry. As quoted by Lucy Beckett in *Wallace Stevens,* Stevens wrote that there "are many poems relating to the interactions between reality and the imagination" but that these poems were marginal to the central theme of a supreme fiction. "The Idea of Order at Key West" explores both of these themes, though more explicitly it serves as a stage for the tension between human imagination and human realities. The questions the speaker asks get at the heart of this dialectic: Is the song and its power only an external reality? Or does the power of the song lie in one's ability to transform it into something personal?

In his poem, "Thirteen Ways of Looking at a Blackbird," Stevens writes, "I do not know which to prefer, 'the blackbird whistling / Or just after.'" In this poem, as in "Key West," Stevens is torn between actually hearing the songs and remembering and replying to them in his head. Finally, as Stevens suggests in the poem, one can never wholly embrace one over the other, as the imagined world is bound by the real one. The woman's song is a combination of both song and sea, and one's enjoyment of it derives out of a fusion of personal reflection and external apprehension. The poet, like the reader, must not privilege exclusively personal or public gestures but must engage both. The final stanzas of the poem offer a remedy for what Stevens calls his "reality-imagination complex"—embrace and journey into both, and you will be rewarded.

Presence and Absence

Just as Stevens is torn between the pleasures of the imagination and the pleasures of reality, so is he torn between themes of presence and absence. Not surprisingly, the two sets of themes are connected, as reality suggests a palpable presence, whereas imagination suggests an external absence. In "Key West," the female singer is both present and absent. Readers never see her. They don't even know if the poet sees her. They do not get any description of her and don't know where she is. In fact, she could be entirely illusory. However, even though she is technically absent from the poem and from the landscape in the poem, she exerts a powerful presence on the speaker and on readers through her song. Thus, while her physical body may be absent, her non-physical voice is present.

Topics for Further Study

- Do you agree with the various critical interpretations of the poem? Do you have a different reading? If so, what is the basis for your interpretation of the poem?

- Look at some other poems by Stevens, perhaps "Tea at the Palaz of Hoon," "Farewell to Florida," and "The Planet on the Table" and explain how and why the poems are similar or different? Be sure to pay attention to both formal and thematic concerns.

- Imagine the poem as a painting. What would it look like? Try to describe it as best you can. Does it remind you of any other paintings or photographs, and if so, which ones does it resemble?

- To what degree does the form of the poem mirror or compliment the theme of the poem?

- What song do you think the woman is singing? Why?

- Do you think that Stevens is the speaker of the poem? Do you think he actually experienced something similar?

- Why is a song an appropriate metaphor for a poem?

As in the quote from "Thirteen Ways of Looking at a Blackbird" mentioned above, Stevens remains attuned to the presence and absence of songs and voices. One cannot see or touch a voice, but one experiences it. Hence, a song embodies both presence and absence, as does imagination.

Just as the song suggests an interest in presence and absence, so does Stevens' search for the spirit in the poem. Both the speaker and Ramon Fernandez know that some larger, transcendent spirit is moving among them and the singer, but they can't find it, can't name it, and can't affirm it. It is present yet absent. The reality that absence can become a penetrating presence becomes a major theme for Stevens and other modern writers because it reflects larger cultural and spiritual issues of the West in the early twentieth century. The search for God, meaning, symmetry, and purpose remain present but always elusive, like the song and the spirit in Stevens' poem.

Poetry

Like most of Stevens' poems, "Key West" may be about any number of other things, but it is also about poetry. Most of Stevens' poems have to do with poetry, and, in fact, almost all of them explore the writing experience or the experience of reading and perceiving poetry. Without question, "The Idea of Order at Key West" is a sort of allegory, that is, it functions as a microcosm of a larger situation. In this case, the situation, or macrocosm, is Stevens and his work. Imagine Stevens as the female singer, her song as one of his poems, and the speaker of the poem (the listener) as the readers. In this scenario, readers become transfixed by his poetry. It moves them like nothing else and causes them to see the world in an entirely different light. If it is successful, it turns them away from the singer (Stevens) and even the song (the poem) and directs their attention toward their own reaction to reading the poem and thinking about how it affects them. In an ideal world, the poem will engender a kind of relation between Stevens, the world, his poem, and the readers. Indeed, in one of his final and best poems, "The Planet on the Table," Stevens says of his work that "his poems, although makings of his self, / Were no less makings of the sun." This means that the poem is the product of the relationship between the poet and the planet of which he, his poem, and readers are part.

Additionally, it should be noted that for Stevens, poetry is not merely, lines, symbols, rhymes, and words but a metaphor for perception and connection. For him, poetry connotes engagement; poetry is the supreme example of human interaction. Thus, poetry provides fulfillment, understanding, awareness, beauty, and relation. So, his poems about poetry are also about what poetry can do for its readers.

Style

Free and Formal Verse

"The Idea of Order at Key West" is written in both formal and free verse. It is a meditative poem, written in a relaxed iambic pentameter. This means that while most of the lines adhere to traditional for-

Compare & Contrast

- **1930s:** The United States is hard hit by the Great Depression, with unemployment reaching nearly twelve million. Upon his election in 1933, Franklin Delano Roosevelt begins instituting his New Deal initiatives that turn the economy around. By 1939, the economy finally stabilizes and begins showing signs of prosperity.

  1990s: The United States economy enjoys a period of seemingly limitless growth. In 1998, the government earns more than it spends, making a surprise budget surplus. The stock market booms thanks to low inflation, stable interest rates, and the growth of high-technology industries.

- **1930s:** The Cuban economy is unstable, and the nation undergoes a revolt headed by Fulgencio Batista y Zaldivar. Tensions between Cuba and the United States remain high for many years. President Hoover refuses to send troops to Cuba and instead sends naval ships to surround Florida.

  1990s: Nearly three-quarters of a million Cubans flee to the United States, settling mainly in southern Florida, attempting to escape the dictatorship of Fidel Castro. In 1996, the Helms-Burton Act, another embargo-strengthening measure against Cuba, passes. United States and Cuban relations remain tense as Castro insists the still faltering Cuban economy is a result of the strict U.S. embargo.

- **1930s:** Because of the depleted economy and high numbers of unemployment, a career in letters or occupations such as writing or publishing is not considered lucrative. Many people, such as Stevens, establish themselves in careers that offer more stability, such as law, medicine, or sustainable resources.

  1990s: Many people find viable and successful careers in journalism, publishing, and literature and fiction writing. Many writers, such as Stephen King, Joyce Carol Oates, Raymond Carver, and Maya Angelou enjoy both commercial and critical success and are the proud recipients of highly regarded and respected awards, such as the Pulitzer and Nobel prizes.

---

mal patterns, some do not. For instance, the basic metrical pattern of the poem is iambic, meaning that each unstressed syllable is followed by a stressed one. Because this pattern resembles English speech most precisely, it is a common metrical device. Pentameter is a form of measure or feet, denoting five stresses per line. Iambic pentameter is the most common type of poetic form, and Stevens uses it brilliantly here. The regular limping rhythm he creates mimics the regularity of the rolling waves of the ocean. But like the ocean, Stevens' poem is not perfectly symmetrical. The lines do not possess a regular rhyming pattern, and they don't always conform to the demands of traditional verse. At times, his language transgresses these expectations, just as the woman's song extends "beyond the genius of the sea." To impose an older, more traditional order on the form of the poem would be at odds with the themes of the poem itself. So Stevens tweaks traditional expectations to achieve a poetic effect in concert with his thematics.

The poem's fifty-six lines are broken into stanzas of uneven length. But the stanza breaks do correspond to the argument the poem makes, so in this sense, the poem moves along at a discernable pace. However, while the stanza breaks may suggest logic and pattern, the irregular rhymes evoke an entirely different feeling. At first, the poem offers the reader some rhymes, but as the poem progresses and builds momentum, the rhymes disappear, like waves crashing into the beach and dissolving among the sand. Thus, the poem's structure embodies one of the poem's main themes: the marriage of order and chaos. The poem as a whole reflects one of the poem's motifs: the sea transcribed into words.

Historical Context

"The Idea of Order at Key West" was published in October 1934, in a group of eight poems. While there may have been a great deal of order in Hartford, Connecticut, where Stevens lived, there was a great deal of disorder in Key West, Florida, where Stevens was visiting in February of that year. There are two main reasons for this. First, the Great Depression was in full throttle at this point in American history. This was particularly difficult for poets, as there was no great honor attached to being a Depression Poet like there was for being a War Poet just a few years earlier during World War I.

Additionally, it was hard enough to earn a living at a regular job during the depression, much less as a poet. Stevens was well aware of the effects that the Great Depression was having on his friends and his readers. By 1932, around twenty-five percent of Americans were out of work. People were losing their houses and their lives at alarming rates. Very few people had enough interest or money to buy books of poems. When Stevens was writing the poems in *Ideas of Order,* he was beginning to dabble in leftist politics and to sympathize with the sentiments of those less fortunate and more politically active than he. Though Stevens did not consider himself a political poet, he remained politically aware, and his poems, though obliquely, often serve as personal responses to public crises.

The second reason for disorder in Key West in 1934 was the presence of American battleships off the coast of Florida. In Cuba, a revolution was taking place, and Stevens seemed more attuned to the political unrest in the streets and harbors of Key West than to the flora and fauna that he typically enjoyed. In a letter to his wife, he talks of little else but the presence of warships in the port and the throngs of military men in the streets of Key West. In 1933, the Cuban economy was in bad shape, when a coup ensued, prompting the American ambassador to ask for the United States to intervene. President Roosevelt refused to send troops but did dispatch almost thirty warships to Florida to send a message to Cuba. Though Stevens seems less interested in the political disorder in Cuba than in the sense of disorder the military is causing in Key West, he does evince in his letters and journal entries a sense of uneasiness at what is happening both locally and globally. Thus, his poem about order and disorder, beauty and chaos, presence and absence, holds not only personal but public and political connotations as well.

On a larger scale, though, this was a fertile era in American arts and letters. Painting, poetry, music, fiction, sculpture, dance, and film were experiencing wild innovations. Movements like dadaism, cubism, expressionism, stream of consciousness writing, imagism, and communism had changed art and artistic expression forever. All art was becoming political in that it was challenging traditional forms and traditional ideas of beauty and expression. Stevens wants to strike a balance in his poems between the avant-garde and the conventional, and "Key West" serves as a good example of his warring desires. Formally and thematically, Stevens wrestles with his desire to write a personally fulfilling poetry yet one that speaks to and for humanity at large. Though his poem may seem more personal than political by today's standards, if one keeps in mind what was happening economically in America and politically in Cuba and in Florida, the poem acquires a heady and intriguing political and historical component.

Critical Overview

"The Idea of Order at Key West" is one of Stevens' better known poems and the most important poem in the collection *Ideas of Order.* Some critics think that this poem is one of Stevens' finest, and many cite it as among the best of his early poetry.

Early critics of the poem tended to praise what they considered a strong transforming imagination, reminiscent of the high romanticism of Keats, Wordsworth, and Shelley. One of Stevens' first major readers, Frank Kermode, in his book *Wallace Stevens,* claimed the poem "may stand as a great, perhaps belated, climax to a whole age of poetry that begins with Coleridge and Wordsworth; it celebrates the power of the mind over what they called 'a universe of death.'" Similarly, Lucy Beckett, in her book titled *Wallace Stevens,* argues that "the poem's marvelous conclusion, suggests in its triumphant but still calm cadences a glimpsed victory over poverty that could be the poet's or could be any man's." Like Kermode and Beckett, Alan Perlis, in *Wallace Stevens: A World of Transforming Shapes,* praises the ability of the singer to transform the world into her own personal song, claiming the "intellectual aspect of the heroic act, the act of localizing nature in the mind, is forcefully expressed" in "The Idea of Order at Key West." These critics tended to equate the solitary nature of the singer as she appears in stanzas two and three with

Stevens himself because their model for a strong poetic presence would choose order over disorder; however, in so doing, they miss the subtleties of the final stanzas.

More recent critics have suggested that "The Idea of Order at Key West" turns on questions of ambiguity and relation, themes that have emerged in the last ten years. These themes are also hallmarks of Stevens' work. For Joseph Carroll, in his book *Wallace Stevens' Supreme Fiction,* "The Idea of Order at Key West" is an important poem because while the poem does not locate evidence of a transcendent spirit, the "spirit that is present—first in song and in the sea and then in the glassy lights—sheds its influence all around the men who are seeking it." For him, the poem achieves spiritual presence through absence. Robert Rehder takes this reading one step further by suggesting the "poet's function in this poem is to listen rather than create." Like Carroll, he sees the poem as ultimately about a desire for connection through the poetic act. Rehder ultimately claims that the poet's rage for order is "a rage that confers a blessing."

One of the very best readers of Stevens, James Longenbach, in his book *Wallace Stevens: The Plain Sense of Things,* grounds his interpretation of the poem in its and Stevens' historical context. Drawing on Stevens' letters from Key West and his journal entries, Longenbach argues that Stevens did not see sailboats but battleships at Key West and that the rage for order described in the poem is a kind of poetic call for peace, and the poem itself is a realization of one's self in relation to others. For him, the "inexplicable magic of 'The Idea of Order at Key West' exists not in the private world of the solitary singer but in the fact that other human beings hear the song and feel its power over their minds."

Criticism

Dean Rader

Rader has published widely in the field of twentieth-century American poetry and on Wallace Stevens in particular. In the following essay, he discusses Stevens' theme of desire and the power of poetry.

Wallace Stevens is a great poet because he is a poet of many themes. His poems interrogate the borders of reality and imagination, pose questions about presence and absence, dramatize the ongoing dialogue between the body and the mind, and search

> *Perhaps what Stevens is saying is that a new music is needed, a new poetry that connects human desire with actual humans. That is, he wants to write a poetry that puts human beings back in touch with their desire through language."*

for a balance between intellect and emotion. Stevens desired both to write poems and reach a large number of people—two potentially mutually exclusive desires since few Americans read poetry. Desire is an important word for Stevens because the concept of desire may be his major theme. For Stevens, desire is the most human emotion. Everyone has desire. Everyone wants fame, love, fulfillment, closeness, happiness, good food, and a nice place to live. The list is endless. Thus, Stevens sees desire as the great universal connector. People are connected to each other through the fact that they all desire, and Stevens believes that poetry is the best art form for articulating and embodying that desire.

Since poetry and desire cannot be separated for Stevens, his poems about desire are almost always also about poetry or the power of poetry. Like Sappho, Shakespeare, Goethe, Wordsworth and many other great writers before him, Stevens tries to get at the emotional element of poetry by linking it with music and song. People tend to connect songs and music with emotions, and Stevens knows this. He also knows that poetry was originally read or sung to musical accompaniment, so he remains aware of the lyric poem's grounding in music. Stevens likes to bridge poetry and song because he sees this fusion as a kind of symbol for bridging human desire with human expression. Certainly in his first book, *Harmonium,* and in his later books, like *The Auroras of Autumn* and *The Rock,* the poems pulse with the power and urgency of desire. But, in the early 1930s, as Stevens is writing the poems that

What Do I Read Next?

- Stevens' *The Palm at the End of the Mind: Selected Poems and a Play,* reissued in 1990, is a book that contains the poems "Idea of Order at Key West" and "Thirteen Ways of Looking at a Blackbird." It also includes the play *Bowl, Cat and Broomstick* and a prose statement on the poetry of war.

- The poet most often compared to Stevens is the great American poet William Carlos Williams, who was Stevens' longtime friend. Like Stevens, Williams held an interest in art and poetic form. *The Collected Poems of William Carlos Williams* (1986) is a compilation of most of his published poetry.

- *Secretaries of the Moon: The Letters of Wallace Stevens and Jose Rodriguez Feo* (1986) collects the letters between Stevens and the talented Cuban poet with whom Stevens maintained close correspondence.

- Peter Brazeau gathers stories and other anecdotes from Stevens' friends and coworkers in *Parts of a World, Wallace Stevens Remembered: An Oral Biography* (1983).

- Another poet commonly linked to Stevens is Ezra Pound. His *Selected Poems* (1959) is a good introduction to his work.

- Stevens was very interested in painting and art theory. The Abstract Expressionist painter Robert Motherwell tries to do in art what Stevens tries to do in poetry. *Robert Motherwell* (1983), edited by H. H. Arnason and Barbaralee Diamonstein, includes both illustrations of and essays about his work.

- Another very good book on Stevens is Margaret Dickie's *Lyric Contingencies: Emily Dickinson and Wallace Stevens* (1991). In her study of the two poets, she shows how Dickinson and Stevens, both private people, write poetry that desires and intends a connection with their audience.

- Albert Gelpi's comprehensive study of modern American poetry, *A Coherent Splendor: The American Poetic Renaissance, 1910–1950,* published in 1987, offers readings of Stevens, Crane, Williams, Pound, T. S. Eliot, and other important American poets.

---

would make up *Ideas of Order,* he seems to grow somewhat skeptical of poetry's ability to embody or fully represent desire.

In "Peter Quince at the Clavier," a poem from *Harmonium,* Stevens writes that music means "desiring you," but in a different poem fourteen years later, he writes that "the waltz / Is no longer a mode of desire." Given the fact that Stevens likes to think of music as a metaphor for poetry, one might believe that Stevens feels his poetry has lost some spunk, that it cannot continue to carry the energy of human desire and emotion. However, Stevens does make a distinction between the waltz and music itself. Perhaps it is the "old music" (as he says) that cannot adequately express desire. Perhaps what Stevens is saying is that a new music is needed, a new poetry that connects human desire with actual humans. That is, he wants to write a poetry that puts human beings back in touch with their desire through language. This desire for connection seems to be a powerful theme at work in "The Idea of Order at Key West."

In his poem, "Ghosts As Cocoons," Stevens writes, "Where is sun and music and highest heaven's lust, / For which more than any words cries deeplier?" The cry is the vocalization of internal desire—the internal made external. Likewise, the new music is that which takes the internal movements of the old and transforms them into an inclusive, communal vision of the new. For Stevens, the great project of poetry is to transform private vision (the vision of the poet) into a public vision (the vision of his readers and the world around him). This is exactly what the female singer accomplishes in "The Idea of Order at Key West" and why this poem serves as a nice metaphor for his work as a whole. He wants his poetry to have the same effect on his readers that the woman's song has on the speaker of the poem.

Yet, the speaker remains separate from the shadowy singer in "The Idea of Order at Key West," and some reasons why that is might provide some insight into the transformation the speaker goes through in the poem. The gay waltz in the poem mentioned above goes unnamed. It could be any waltz, played anywhere. But "Idea of Order" is firmly located along the shores of Florida. This is important because the opening poem in *Ideas of Order* is not a welcoming but a farewell. Oddly enough, the first poem is entitled "Farewell to Florida." While few critics have noted the relationship of the two poems, there remains both explicitly and implicitly a fundamental affinity between them. The female singer in "The Idea of Order" exists as a detached, solitary figure. In the poem, she rather matter-of-factly distances herself from the person who is narrating the events. Such is the case in "Farewell to Florida," where the poet also remains distant from the female presence. But oddly enough for Stevens, opposites attract. The idea of distance makes the woman appealing. It is her detachment that seduces Stevens because it gives him perspective.

Again, desire and seduction remain key themes for Stevens because of his own desire for his poems to seduce his readers. But he knows that to do this, his poems must be attractive on an emotional level. People must be able to feel his poems. But, like most men of Stevens' era, he is uncomfortable with intimate emotions; thus his poetry is a constant struggle between the intellect and emotion. This conflict is the subject of "Farewell to Florida." The text of "Farewell to Florida" tells of a relieved Stevens who longs to return to his ordered northern (male) state of mind, but the subtext reveals something entirely different:

> From my North of cold whistled in a sepulchral
>   South,
> Her South of pine and coral and coraline sea,
> Her home, not mine, in the ever-freshened Keys,
> Her days, her oceanic nights, calling

Often Stevens associates the muse (the Greek goddesses who were in charge of inspiring poets and composers) with the tropics of Florida. Stevens is also seduced in "The Idea of Order at Key West" but not by the lushness of the woman, rather by her song. In both instances, Stevens' desire takes on a sort of rage, the likes of which readers do not find in *Harmonium*. The famous literary critic Harold Bloom, in his book *Wallace Stevens: The Poems of Our Climate,* claims that this "is so erotic a stanza that the reader needs to keep reminding himself that this Florida, as a state of mind, is a trope of pathos, a synecdoche for desire and not desire itself." True indeed, the passage is beautiful and painful. Florida and what Florida might represent to Stevens (lushness, the feminine, emotion, poetry) is an object of desire.

Because he cannot inhabit this intense landscape, he flees to the north, to the world of the snowman, the world of "the violent mind." But he is mistaken to think he can leave the muse or what Jacqueline Vaught Brogan has called his "feminine self" behind. For Stevens, Florida becomes a muse in and of itself because the South, like the muse and desire, is alive, cyclical, pungent, and ebbing. And because Stevens wants this for his poetry, the manifestation of Florida, the singing female, returns like Odysseus to the poetic ground of her making in Stevens' wonderful poem "The Idea of Order at Key West."

Not only does the singing female return, but she does so in an enhanced capacity. Of the moving first stanza, the most important lines are the first, "She sang beyond the genius of the sea" and the last two, "That was not ours although we understood, / Inhuman, of the veritable ocean." The two most important words are "beyond" and "inhuman." Indeed, taken together, the two words suggest a certain *ekstasis,* a virtual transcendence beyond the human realm. The song and singer are not "masks," nor are they anything but themselves; however, Stevens is only able to comprehend both in terms of otherness. They are not him. They are not male or northern. They are separate.

While Stevens and the singer overtly maintain a remoteness, readers should not miss the fact that Stevens does understand her. He hears what she is singing. He understands her because she is forming ideas into language. Yet Stevens also understands that he cannot translate her song into purely linguistic or human codes. What she is singing is not only beyond understanding, it also reaches beyond language: "But it was more than that, / More even than her voice, and ours, among / The meaningless plungings of water and the wind." But just as it seems like the poem is going to drift off into the ocean, Stevens brings it back to earth in the next two stanzas. What makes this an amazing poem is his ability to represent inhuman moments in human terms. Or better put, he uses language to express that which is beyond language. Like the singer's song, his poem helps transform the world. Stevens helps readers fulfill their own desires to see a richer, fuller world.

> "For all of his continuing fascination with lush tropical landscapes and fecund nature, Stevens is not even sure that the world outside of his mind even exists."

The idea that the poet is a kind of facilitator is fairly new for Stevens in the 1930s. Many people think that "The Idea of Order at Key West" marks a turning point for him, that it signals a shift from the old music of *Harmonium* to the new, more inclusive music of *Ideas of Order*. For instance, in Stevens' often quoted poem, "Tea at the Palaz of Hoon," a major poem in *Harmonium*, Hoon's chant utterly transforms the external landscape, but in "The Idea of Order at Key West," the Floridian landscape goes unchanged. It remains in disorder. The singer does not alter the external world the way Hoon does. The world goes on. Stevens realizes this and accepts it. The singer does not try to order the world. She simply sings. Neither does the listener try to order the world. He merely listens and allows the song to do the transforming. This is the new Stevens, and this the new song. The Stevens of *Harmonium* would have ended the poem after the fifth stanza, just a few more lines after the above quote, but the Stevens of 1934 adds two, somewhat puzzling stanzas, the most notable aspect of which shows Stevens turning not inward but outward:

> Ramon Fernandez, tell me if you know,
> Why, when the singing ended and we turned
> Toward the town, tell why the glassy lights,
> The lights in the fishing boats at anchor there,

The temptation is to remain, like the woman and like Hoon, in solitude, but Stevens and his companion do not turn away toward the sea (where order may be found) but toward the town, toward civilization, toward humanity. Of course the criticism can be made that a simple turn of the body is hardly an affirmative social avowal—why couldn't Stevens have simply said "I share this with all of you?"—but Stevens works subtly. His only overt social poem, "Owl's Clover," is considered by most a failure. In Stevens, gesture can be everything. While the act of singing is an act of individual will, turning that will back toward a shared experience and not inward is what delineates this poem from "Tea at the Palaz of Hoon," and other similar *Harmonium* poems. Stevens' rage in this final stanza is the rage for the "tortured words" and the "vital words" that speak concurrently for the past, present, and future. Furthermore, it is the "sibylline presence," the female singer who returns as the muse bearing the word on her voice. Through the act of poetry, Stevens is able to translate her voice and his desire into a collective voice, one that speaks and sings of the inhuman ("ghostlier demarcations") and the human ("ourselves and our origins").

Music continues to serve as an important motif for Stevens in *Ideas of Order* because music and poetry elicit a similar affectivity. Music for Stevens is essentially internal, as is poetry. Readers may hear the external notes of music, but they feel the traces the music leaves in their ears. The same goes for poetry. Music is something that is ultimately "taken in" and released over and over in the mind. The female singer in "The Idea of Order at Key West" is not just a singer but a composer both in the musical sense and in the etymological sense (from the Latin *posere,* "to place or to lie down with"). Stevens associates music with both emotion and motion, and he associates all three with poetry and with the harmonies and cacophonies of human desire. So in "The Idea of Order at Key West," Stevens actually says hello to the feminine presence that he originally said farewell to in "Farewell to Florida," and in so doing, he says hello to his feminine self. It is that self, his internal, emotive self, that allows him to link poem and song in "The Idea of Order at Key West," offering readers a vision of a world in which internal and external also begin to harmonize, fulfilling both his and others' desires.

Source: Dean Rader, Critical Essay on "The Idea of Order at Key West," in *Poetry for Students,* The Gale Group, 2001.

Greg Barnhisel

Barnhisel teaches American literature and has published articles on Ezra Pound and on the publishing industry. In this essay, he argues that "The Idea of Order at Key West" expresses Stevens' most deeply-held questions about the degree to which human perception organizes the world around the person doing the perceiving.

Along with "The Emperor of Ice-Cream," "Peter Quince at the Clavier," "Thirteen Ways of Looking at a Blackbird," and "Sunday Morning," "The Idea of Order at Key West" is one of Wallace Stevens' best-known and most anthologized poems. Like many of his works, the poem takes place largely in the head of the narrator and is a meditation on the idea of thinking, on the process of perception, on the faculty of the imagination. From his earliest days as a poet until the end of his life, Stevens' most persistent concern remained the interaction of mind and world. Is the world out there real? Does it have a material existence apart from humans perceiving it? Or is the world as it is seen, heard, and felt just a projection of human imagination? If not, is imagination somehow organizing or ordering the world for humans?

This final question is the one that drives "The Idea of Order at Key West." The poem takes place as the narrator, who is probably Stevens himself (although persona is not an essential aspect of this poem), is walking along the beach in Key West, Florida, and listening to a woman sing. Her song makes him see some kind of order in the natural world, and he begins to wonder whether her singing created that order or whether it just allowed him to see the order.

The book in which the poem in question appears takes its title from the poem. *Ideas of Order* contains many poems meditating on these issues, but Stevens' first book, *Harmonium* (1923), introduces these themes powerfully. Two of that book's poems in particular, "Anecdote of the Jar" and "Tea at the Palaz of Hoon," are prefigurations of "The Idea of Order at Key West." In "Anecdote of the Jar," the narrator speaks of placing a jar upon a hill; this jar makes "slovenly" the wilderness that "surround that hill." Continuing with his discussion of the jar's effect on the landscape, the narrator notes how the presence of the jar made the wilderness "no longer wild." Its presence organizes the apparently chaotic world around it. Throughout the poem, the narrator contrasts the disorganized fecundity of nature with the sterile organization of the manmade object. The final stanza sums up the jar's effects on the landscape:

It took dominion everywhere.
The jar was gray and bare.
It did not give of bird or bush,
Like nothing else in Tennessee.

The similarities to "The Idea of Order at Key West" are striking. In this poem, the narrator again contrasts manmade art, in this case, a simple jar, with the vast multiplicity of nature. Although he does not actually use the term in either poem, he is clearly referring to it, and in "The Idea of Order at Key West," he calls the singer an "artificer." Stevens does not mean art in the sense that someone uses the word-products of the creative process that are intended for aesthetic contemplation and enjoyment. Rather Stevens is using the term with its full etymological resonance. The word *art* derives from an Indo-European root that means "to join or fit together." From this root are derived any number of English words that indicate different types of joining or making: artifice, artisan, artifact, artful, articulate, and artificial are examples. Art is organized. It has a principle of order. In the poem, the power of human imagination, which always strives for order and organization, brings out the order in nature.

But, Stevens always asks himself, is the order inherent in nature or does the presence of an artifact that is ordered cause humans to see order that might not really be there? Another of the poems from *Harmonium* proposes an answer to that question. The first stanza of "Tea at the Palaz of Hoon," in the voice of an unnamed narrator, tells in a highly abstract tone of the narrator's "descent" through "the loneliest air". The second stanza provides us with three questions asked by the narrator: what is the ointment "sprinkled" on his beard? What songs does he hear? What sea carries him? The third stanza answers these questions: his mind provided the ointment, his ears made the "hymns," and the sea was nothing but the world of the poet himself. Concluding the poem, Stevens' narrator tells us that

I was the world in which I walked, and what I saw
Or heard or felt came not by from myself;
And there I found myself more truly and more
    strange.

In "Tea at the Palaz of Hoon," the narrator responds to the implicit questions of the "Anecdote of the Jar." The vivid sensual experiences of the second stanza are, he tells the reader, a product of "my mind" and have no basis in the real world. The sensual world is a product of the mind, the narrator says in this poem. Whether or not the world outside of the mind even exists is called into question (and this is a question that is never far from Stevens' mind).

The two *Harmonium* poems, read together, propose the preeminence of the human mind and of the faculty of the imagination. For all of his continuing fascination with lush tropical landscapes and fecund nature, Stevens is not even sure that the world outside of his mind even exists. Thirteen years later in "Key West," Stevens returns to these issues and brings together his ideas about how human imagination orders experience of the outside world with his suspicions that the human mind might actually create the outside world.

Stevens introduces the idea of creation in the very first line. "She sang beyond the genius of the sea," he tells the readers. "Genius" here must be seen not only in its customary sense, as meaning a great natural ability or intelligence. The word, which derives from a Latin word meaning a "guardian spirit," can also mean the particular spirit of a place or thing and a great natural talent for creating. Already Stevens is searching for a way to explore the difference between what is inherent in nature ("the genius of the sea" meaning the particular spirit of the sea) and what comes from human consciousness ("genius" meaning the woman's ability to create). The sea does not form "to mind or voice," Stevens specifies, meaning that no physical changes can be seen in the water, yet the sea "made constant cry," presumably in response to the song of the singer.

The next stanza continues the theme of the first stanza, further differentiating between the actual sea and the singer: Stevens wants to be certain that he is not confusing the two. In this, he is implicitly responding to the statements he makes in "Tea at the Palaz of Hoon," stating that nature is not created by the perceiver.

In the third stanza, the poem begins to respond to the questions that Stevens set out to address. The real subject of the poem is "the spirit that we sought." This "spirit" is not, Stevens takes pains to make clear in the fourth stanza, simply the voice of nature: "If it was only the dark voice of the sea . . . / If it was only the outer voice of sky / And cloud . . . / . . . it would have been deep air / . . . sound alone." But, he makes clear, "it was more than that."

When Stevens breaks the long fourth stanza in the middle, he signals the fundamental break in the poem, which is structured as a question and answer, a cause and effect. The "spirit" mentioned in the third stanza is the creative drive, the imagination, the expressive activity of the singer. "It was her voice that made / The sky acutest at its vanishing. / She measured to the hour its solitude. / She was the single artificer of the world / In which she sang." The vocabulary that Stevens chooses to describe the singer's effect—"acutest," "measured," "artificer"—is the vocabulary of organization, order, exactitude. The jar of "Anecdote of the Jar" comes to mind.

As that stanza proceeds, though, Stevens modifies his earlier rejection of the idea of human consciousness creating the world, and the reader must confront a conundrum: if the sea does exist beyond the singer, how can the singer be the "single artificer of the world / In which she sang"? When she sang, the narrator states, "the sea, / Whatever self it had, became the self / That was her song, for she was the maker." So Stevens seems to be saying that the sea does have an independent existence outside of human perception, but no one can know the nature of that existence.

And the location of the singer? Singing, creating, she is lost in her creation. "There never was a world for her / Except the one she sang and, singing, made," the poet says. But the location of the singer is not the only issue for the poet. He also wants to know what happens to the hearer and, by extension, to the audience of any human creation, or "artifice," and to the hearer's relationship to the natural world during and after the song.

Here Stevens begins speaking to his companion on the beach, Ramon Fernandez. Writing to the critic Renato Poggioli in 1954 (letter reprinted in *Letters of Wallace Stevens*), Stevens denied that the name Ramon Fernandez was intended to refer to the actual Ramon Fernandez, a French critic: "When I was trying to think of a Spanish name for "The Idea of Order," Stevens asserts, "I simply put together by chance two exceedingly common names in order to make one and I did not have in mind Ramon Fernandez." The critic Harold Bloom, among others, argues that Stevens' denials are specious, but for the purposes of this essay, that is not important. The narrator asks Fernandez, "Why, when the singing ended and we turned / Toward the town," the lights and visual sensations seemed to be ordered, organized, regular?

The last stanza begins with one of the most familiar phrases in Stevens' poetry: "Oh! Blessed rage for order." As the poem ends, Stevens seems to be saying that the human mind craves order in the universe and that the human imagination will impose order upon the chaotic natural world. In a letter that Stevens wrote, in 1935 (reprinted in *Letters of Wallace Stevens*), to his friend Ronald Lane Latimer (who edited the magazine *Alcestis,* in which Stevens published poems), Stevens explains that in "The Idea of Order at Key West"

> life has ceased to be a matter of chance. It may be that every man introduces his own order into the life around him and that the idea of order in general is

simply what Bishop Berkeley might have called a fortuitous concourse of personal orders. But still there is order.

The poem is probably Stevens' most important poem on the activities of the human mind when confronted by the sensory overload of nature. Responding to his poems of the 1920s, in which he explored the possibility of human consciousness creating the world around it, Stevens, in this poem, has arrived at the conclusion that human imagination does not create the world, but rather creates the order that is in the world and imposes that order on nature.

Source: Greg Barnhisel, Critical Essay on "The Idea of Order at Key West," in *Poetry for Students*, The Gale Group, 2001.

Wendy Perkins

Perkins is an associate professor at Prince George's Community College and has published widely in the field of twentieth-century American and British literature. In the following essay, she explores Stevens's poem as a celebration of the power of imagination.

In a letter written in November 1935, approximately one year after he wrote "The Idea of Order at Key West," Stevens comments on the role of poets:

> We are not beginning to get out of the world what it will ultimately yield through poets. If poetry introduces order, and every competent poem introduces order, and if order means peace, even though that particular peace is an illusion, is it any less an illusion than a good many other things that everyone high and low now-a-days concedes to be no longer of any account? Isn't a freshening of life a thing of consequence? It would be a great thing to change the status of the poet.

Stevens believed that it was the duty of poets to create works of art that could help readers order the chaotic experience of life. According to Stevens' premise, through the imagination of the poet, the world would become more understandable and thus the reader would experience "a freshening of life" and a sense of peace, even if that peace were only temporary or illusory. Stevens' "The Idea of Order at Key West" provides one of his best examples of this theory of the power of the poetic imagination.

William Burney, in his critical study in his book *Wallace Stevens,* notes that "the inner focus [in "The Idea of Order at Key West"] is not in the self of the poet but in the world of his poem: what Stevens later called 'my green, my fluent mundo.'" Although the poem opens with a reference to a woman singing by the sea, the focus is on that sea, which becomes a metaphor for human experience and how it can be changed through artistic expression. The poem contains a single concentrated image of meditation from beginning to end on this dominant theme. As the speaker listens to the girl's song, he contemplates the relation of poetry to reality and the power of the imagination.

> *According to Stevens' premise, through the imagination of the poet, the world would become more understandable and thus the reader would experience 'a freshening of life' and a sense of peace, even if that peace were only temporary or illusory."*

The sea suggests a state of chaos in its "constant cry," "grinding water," and "gasping wind." Later, Stevens reinforces these images with his description of "the ever-hooded, tragic-gestured sea" expressing a "dark voice." Here, the turbulence of the water symbolizes the turbulence of life. The poem illustrates the difficult task of understanding the flux of life in the following lines:

> The meaningless plungings of water and the wind,
> Theatrical distances, bronze shadows heaped
> On high horizons, mountainous atmospheres
> Of sky and sea.

The poem asserts Stevens' point that the poet's role is to help readers make sense of "the meaningless plungings" of existence. The "poet" in "The Idea of Order at Key West" is represented by a woman singing as she walks the beach at Key West. In the first stanza, Stevens illustrates the power of imagination in his juxtaposition of poetry and reality. While the sea contains its own "genius" it "never formed to mind or voice, / Like a body wholly body, fluttering / Its empty sleeves."

The poem contains a number of careful definitions and rejections where the speaker makes a clear distinction between the woman's song and the voice of the sea:

> It may be that in all her phrases stirred
> The grinding water and the gasping wind;
> But it was she and not the sea we heard.

The speaker acknowledges that "she was the maker of the song she sang." When he questions what spirit he hears through her song, he again makes a clear distinction between her voice and that of the sea:

> If it was only the dark voice of the sea
> That rose, or even colored by many waves;
> If it was only the outer voice of sky
> And cloud, of the sunken coral water-walled,
> However clear, it would have been deep air,
> The heaving speech of air, a summer sound
> Repeated in a summer without end
> And sound alone. But it was more than that,
> More even than her voice, and ours

Her song orders the turbulent sea and so makes it significant and comprehensible to the speaker who hears her:

> It was her voice that made
> The sky acutest at its vanishing.
> She measured to the hour its solitude.
> She was the single artificer of the world
> In which she sang. And when she sang, the sea,
> Whatever self it had, became the self
> That was her song, for she was the maker. Then we,
> As we beheld her striding there alone,
> Knew that there never was a world for her
> Except the one she sang and, singing, made.

Lucy Beckett, in her book on Stevens, notes, "As the poem gathers weight . . . the issues raised by the solitary figure of the girl become wider." The speaker begins to realize at this point that the girl's song is affecting not only his vision of the sea, but also his perspective on the surrounding landscape. He asks his companion,

> Why, when the singing ended and we turned
> Toward the town, tell why the glassy lights,
> The lights in the fishing boats at anchor there,
> As the night descended, tilting in the air,
> Mastered the night and portioned out the sea,
> Fixing emblazoned zones and fiery poles,
> Arranging, deepening, enchanting night.

Beckett argues that

> in the end the question is not answered at all; but the poem's marvelous conclusion, suggests in its triumphant but still calm cadences a glimpsed victory over poverty that could be the poet's or could be any man's. 'The spirit that we sought' is not defined, but it is found and found in human sense made of non-human senseless reality.

The poem itself answers the question the speaker raises. As the speaker notes the effect the girl's song has on the listeners' vision of their environment, the poem becomes a metaphor for the transforming power of the poetic voice. The song has stimulated and sensitized the listeners' imagination that organizes and clarifies their experience.

In the same letter quoted in the introduction, Stevens adds,

> There is no reason why any poet should not have the status of the philosopher, nor why his poetry should not give up to the keenest minds and the most searching spirits something of what philosophy gives up and, in addition, the peculiar things that only poetry can give.

In "The Idea of Order at Key West," Stevens has created a poem that gives "to the keenest minds and most searching spirits" his philosophy of the power of poetry. The poem offers, "Words of the fragrant portals, dimly-starred, / And of ourselves and of our origins, / In ghostlier demarcations, keener sounds." The final image is of the poet's rage to order the words of the sea, with its constantly changing ebbs, flows, and moods that symbolize the chaos of human existence. Those "fragrant portals" become doorways into a deeper experience as the poem helps readers order and therefore more fully comprehend their world.

Source: Wendy Perkins, Critical Essay on "The Idea of Order at Key West," in *Poetry for Students,* The Gale Group, 2001.

Sources

Beckett, Lucy, *Wallace Stevens,* Cambridge University Press, 1974, p. 1.

Bloom, Harold, *Wallace Stevens: The Poems of Our Climate,* Cornell University Press, 1977.

Brogan, Jacqueline Vaught, "Sexism and Stevens," in *Wallace Stevens & the Feminine,* edited by Melita Schaum, University of Alabama Press, 1993, pp. 3–22.

Burney, William, *Wallace Stevens,* Twayne, 1968.

Carroll, Joseph, *Wallace Stevens' Supreme Fiction: A New Romanticism,* Louisiana State University Press, 1987.

Fisher, Barbara, *Wallace Stevens: The Intensest Rendezvous,* University Press of Virginia, 1990, pp. 62–3.

Kermode, Frank, *Wallace Stevens,* Faber and Faber, 1960.

Longenbach, James, *Wallace Stevens: The Plain Sense of Things,* Oxford University Press, 1991.

Perlis, Alan, *Wallace Stevens: A World of Transforming Shapes,* Bucknell University Press, 1976.

Rehder, Robert, *The Poetry of Wallace Stevens,* St. Martin's Press, 1988, pp. 143–44.

Stevens, Wallace, *The Collected Poems,* Alfred A. Knopf, 1954.

——, *The Letters of Wallace Stevens,* edited by Holly Stevens, University of California Press, 1996.

——, *Opus Posthumous,* Alfred A. Knopf, 1989.

Walker, David, *The Transparent Lyric: Reading and Meaning in the Poetry of Stevens and Williams,* Princeton, 1984.

For Further Study

Bates, Milton, *Sur Plusieurs Beaux Sujects: Wallace Stevens' Commonplace Book,* Stanford University Press, 1989.

> This is a valuable collection of facsimiles and transcriptions of Stevens' poems and journal entries.

Filreis, Alan, *Wallace Stevens and the Actual World,* Princeton University Press, 1991.

> Filreis provides one of the very best books on Stevens. Like Longenbach, Filreis shows how Stevens responds in his poetry to social and political events of his time.

Fisher, Barbara M., *Wallace Stevens: The Intensest Rendezvous,* University Press of Virginia, 1990.

> This book maps the erotic and romantic progress of Stevens throughout his poetry, including an interesting reading of the female singer in "The Idea of Order at Key West."

Richardson, Joan, *Wallace Stevens: The Early Years: 1879–1923,* William Morrow, 1988.

> Richardson's work is a wonderful biography of the early phase of Stevens' life and poetic career.

——, *Wallace Stevens: The Later Years: 1923–1955,* William Morrow, 1988.

> Richardson's second volume offers an even more compelling reading than the first volume in this series.

Stevens, Holly, ed., *Letters of Wallace Stevens,* Alfred A. Knopf, 1966.

> This text edited by Stevens' daughter, is a very generous collection of his letters to various acquaintances, other writers, and publishers.

Leda and the Swan

William Butler Yeats
1928

William Butler Yeats's daring sonnet describing the details of a story from Greek mythology—the rape of Leda by the god Zeus in the form of a swan—was written at the height of the poet's career, the same year he received the Nobel Prize for literature. "Leda and the Swan" is a violent, sexually explicit poem that has all of the lyricism and complexity of Yeats's later work, with its plain diction, rhythmic vigor, and allusions to mystical ideas about the universe, the relationship of human and divine, and the cycles of history. It can be seen as a poem about the way a single event is to be understood as part of a larger scheme; the result of the god's assault on Leda is the birth of Helen of Troy, the subsequent destruction of early Greek civilization, and the beginning of the modern era. It has also been suggested that the poem, which was first written (and later revised in this present form) during the Irish Civil War of 1922–1923, is intended to draw attention to the violence that beset Yeats's homeland during that time.

"Leda and the Swan" has been considered one of the most technically masterful poems ever written in English. In the work, Yeats uses the fourteen lines of the traditional sonnet form in a radical, modernist style. He calls up a series of unforgettable, bizarre images of an immediate physical event using abstract descriptions in terse language, while at the same time offering a distanced view of that occurrence in the sweep of time. Yeats himself considered the poem one of his major accomplishments, and in addition to praising its economy of language

and skillful use of rhythm, critics have seen it as a fine example of how ideas that were central to the poet's life found expression in his poetry.

Author Biography

William Butler Yeats was born on June 13, 1865, in the Dublin suburb of Sandymount. His father was a lawyer and a well-known portrait painter, and his mother was the daughter of a shipping merchant. Yeats began writing verse in his teens shortly after entering the Metropolitan School of Art in Dublin. There he became interested in the occult, which remained a lifelong passion. In 1887, Yeats moved to London, where he became acquainted with some of the leading literary figures of his day. He also joined the Theosophical Society of Madame Blavatsky, where he furthered his interest in occult practices and magic.

In 1889, Yeats's first volume of poems, *The Wanderings of Oisin,* appeared to critical acclaim. The same year he met and fell in love with Maud Gonne, a passionate activist deeply committed to Irish nationalism. Under Gonne's influence, Yeats became increasingly involved in Ireland's political struggle for independence from Britain. Yeats was also active in societies that attempted an Irish literary revival. Together with Lady Isabella Augusta Gregory, whom he met in 1896, he founded the Irish Theatre, which was to become the Abbey Theatre, and he served as its chief playwright for many years.

In part because of the hatred and the bigotry of the Nationalist movement, Yeats became increasingly disappointed by the Irish cause, and his poetry is full of protests against it. He was further disillusioned with Irish politics when, in 1903, Maude Gonne, having turned down his own marriage proposals, married a Nationalist activist. Yeats's attitude is reflected in the works written during his middle-age years in which he writes unsparingly of Ireland as a "blind, bitter land." In 1916, Maude Gonne's husband, together with other Irish freedom fighters, was executed in the Dublin Easter Rising, prompting Yeats to write "Easter 1916," in which he eulogizes the dead heroes but offers also an honest appraisal of their activities. Maud Gonne refused yet another proposal from Yeats, and in 1917 he married Georgie Hyde-Lees, who shared his interest in mysticism and spiritualism.

By this time, Yeats was a well-known figure. He was appointed to the Irish Senate in 1922, the same year that the Irish Civil War broke out. The following year, Yeats was awarded the Nobel Prize for literature. Although he received the prize chiefly for his dramatic works, his significance today rests on his achievement as a poet. Yeats's most highly acclaimed work was actually written after he received the Nobel Prize. He finished a first version of "Leda and the Swan" (which was titled "Annunciation" originally) the same year he won the prize and had it published in 1924 in a new, radical magazine called *To-morrow.* Yeats said he was inspired to write the poem after contemplating on Ireland's place in world politics. He revised the poem six times, and it appeared in its final form in *The Tower* in 1928. That volume, together with *The Winding Stair and Other Poems* (1933) and *Last Poems and Plays* (1940) confirmed Yeats's reputations as one of the most influential twentieth-century poets writing in English. When he died on January 28, 1939, in Roquebrune, France, he was considered indisputably to be the greatest poet that Ireland had every produced.

William Butler Yeats

Poem Text

A sudden blow: the great wings beating still
Above the staggering girl, her thighs caressed
By the dark webs, her nape caught in his bill,
He holds her helpless breast upon his breast.

How can those terrified vague fingers push
The feathered glory from her loosening thighs?
And how can body, laid in that white rush,
But feel the strange heart beating where it lies?

A shudder in the loins engenders there
The broken wall, the burning roof and tower
And Agamemnon dead.
      Being so caught up,
So mastered by the brute blood of the air,
Did she put on his knowledge with his power
Before the indifferent beak could let her drop?

Poem Summary

Title

The title of the poem is important, because it is the only indication of the characters who are the subject of the poem. In the poem, Yeats assumes that the reader is familiar with the myth referred to in the title. Throughout the fourteen lines, he never uses the names of either of the characters. Zeus's name in fact appears neither in the title nor the text of the poem; the reader is expected to understand that the swan is an incarnation of the all-powerful god.

Lines 1–4

The structure of the sonnet is Petrarchan, an Italian form of the sonnet that characteristically divides its theme into an octave, in which a problem or emotion is stated, and a sestet, in which the problem or emotional tension is resolved. There is a clear separation between the first eight lines (the octave) and the final six (the sestet).

The octave is divided into two four-line stanzas, or quatrains. The first quatrain opens with a recounting of the occurrence in mid-scene. It begins abruptly, as the swan assaults Leda with "a sudden blow," which is most likely a reference to an act of sexual penetration. The use of that simple, powerful phrase (not a complete sentence) and a break before the line continues emphasizes the explosive violence of the act.

Line 1 continues with a description of the great swan hanging in the air above the girl with its wings beating. There is a pun on the word *still;* the bird's wings continue to beat and are also still as it hovers above without moving. In line 2 there is a description of Leda that indicates her physical (and perhaps psychological) state, as she staggers under her assailant. The swan has its body over Leda as she falters under him; he caresses her thighs with his webbed feet. There is an almost sensuous description in the phrase "her thighs caressed," but this is followed immediately by the grotesque image of the swan's "dark webs" in line 3 and the image of Leda's neck in his bill as he holds her helpless against him. The swan is never referred to directly as a swan, but its presence is expressed in ordinary images like "great wings" and "dark webs" that in the context of the poem seem quite extraordinary. Leda is simply "the girl" who is caught in the bird's beak like a small helpless animal. In line 4 the crushing movement of the girl pinned against the bird is reinforced by the repetition of the word *breast* as the two are joined together unwillingly as one.

Lines 5–8

The second quatrain of the octave continues with a description of the rape, but it is presented here in the form of two rhetorical questions. How, asks the speaker, can this mere mortal girl resist the power of this beast-god as he subjugates her? And how can she help but feel the beating of his heart (or his sexual organ) as he lies with her? Leda's fingers are "terrified" and "vague" because they are powerless amidst the "feathered glory" that surrounds her; and she acquiesces to the assault because she is helpless to resist; she cannot push the god's body from her "loosening thighs." She loses her identify with the continuing attack; she is no longer even "girl" but merely "body" laid in a "white rush" (referring to the bird's feathers but punning on an image of ejaculation). She feels the pulsation of the bird's "strange heart" (which, again, could refer to its penis) against her. Again in this stanza the picture of the bird is rendered in simple images using a combination of abstract and concrete descriptors that emphasize its divine and incomprehensible nature: it is a "feathered glory" with a "strange heart." The details of Leda's psychological state and physical body are presented with skillful compression and interconnectedness, with references to her "terrified" fingers and "loosening thighs."

Lines 9–11

In the final sestet the poem moves away from the description of the rape to its effect, shifting from an immediate physical description of the present to an abstract dramatization of the future. While the first part of the poem concentrated on the physicality of the act, the last stanza steps back from the present and situates it in the larger pattern of history. Also, while the first two stanzas of the poem had references to the whiteness of the swan and the blackness of its webs, the images in the final stanza are vivid with references to fire and blood.

Line 9 begins with the swan's orgasm and ejaculation, the "shudder in the loins" that, it is explained, engenders, or gives rise to, a startling series of events. The act of rape just described, the speaker says, spawns "The broken wall, the burning roof and tower / And Agamemnon dead." This compressed line and a half describe the fall of Troy (walls broken and roofs burned) and the death of Agamemnon at the conclusion of the Trojan War. That is, with the union of Leda and the swan will come the birth of Helen, and with that the series of events that culminates in the siege and fall of Troy, which signals the collapse of early Greek civilization and ushers in a new, modern age. The phrases "broken wall," "burning roof," and "tower" also have sexual connotations. The broken wall refers to the breaking of the female hymen in sexual intercourse; the burning roof refers to the vagina; the tower is a symbol of the phallus. Fire traditionally symbolizes sexual passion and represents the divine union with the human.

The break in line 11 is the only deviation from the traditional form of the sonnet, and the division stresses the completeness of thought presented in the previous eighteen words that express a vast historical process. This single event, the impregnation of the mortal woman Leda by the god Zeus signals the beginning of a new time in history. Here, in a few short lines, Yeats makes reference to his theory of history that claims that every two thousand years a new era of civilization is ushered in because of the reversal of the gyres. The mortal Leda is caught in this cosmic pattern, a helpless victim of divine forces that use her merely as a means to a larger end.

Lines 12–14

After the break in line 11 the speaker again changes tenses (this time to past) and ends the poem with another question. The use of the past tense serves to further distance the act and see it in terms of its historical significance. The speaker asks if Leda, as she was taken and ravaged so savagely by this "brute blood of the air," the god in the form of a swan, knew the consequences of what was happening to her. When she is violated by and in union with the god, does she come to some sort of divine knowledge? Does she know, as he obviously must because of his divinity, that this act portends the end of a civilization? In these lines, the description of the swan as the "brute blood of the air" identifies Zeus with a cosmic force; he is a being that is physical, animal, and divine. The poem ends in the last line with an image of the swan, after its or-

Media Adaptations

- The Nobel Internet Archive maintains a Yeats web page at http://www.nobelprizes.com/nobel/literature/1923a.html (last accessed April 2001) with links to other interesting sites.

- An audiocassette titled *The Poetry of William Butler Yeats,* which features eighty-five of Yeats's best known verses, including "Leda and the Swan," was released in 1996 by Dove Books Audio.

- The myth of Leda and the Swan has been the subject of numerous works of art, including sculptures and other decorative works from ancient times: Correggio's painting "Leda with the Swan" (1531–1532); Tintoretto's painting "Leda and the Swan" (1570–1575); Van Dongen's watercolor "Leda and the Swan" (1922); and Salvador Dali's painting "Leda atomica" (1949). Leonardo da Vinci and Michelangelo also produced paintings of the Leda myth, but both paintings have been lost—although a number of reproductions and copies of the artists' sketches survive.

gasm, as it releases its captor carelessly from its beak. He has satisfied his desire and lets her drop, indifferent to his victim's terrifying experience. The question the reader is left with is whether Leda knew that her experience would inaugurate a new cycle and whether in her terrifying union with the god she gains some type of mystical or cosmic insight.

Themes

Mythology

"Leda and the Swan" is a difficult poem to grasp fully on a casual reading because it assumes considerable background knowledge on the part of the reader of the event being described and its place in Greek mythology. The poem is also inspired by Yeats's strange and difficult theory of historical cycles. Even when one is acquainted with Yeats's sources and theories, the poem is a challenge for the student because of the complexity of the ideas to which it makes subtle reference. However, the lyrical quality and force of description in the poem can be appreciated even by those who find the ideas hard to follow. Thus the poem can be enjoyed on two levels. It is both a chilling, bizarre description of a violent act of rape and a sophisticated exploration of Yeats's ideas about the nature of cosmic history and the place of humans in it.

The ancient Greek myth that Yeats used as the source of his poem is that of Leda, the daughter of the Aetolian king Thestius. According to one version of the myth (there are at least half a dozen variations), the beautiful mortal Leda caught the eye of the god Zeus (the ruler of the Greek deities) after she had married the Spartan Tyndareus. Leda resisted the god's advances, and so he seduced her in the form of a swan. Leda gave birth, by laying eggs, to four children: the twin girls Helen and Clytemnestra and the twin boys Castor and Polydeuces. Helen, greatly famed for her beauty, later married Menelaus but then fell in love with Paris, and the couple fled together to Paris's homeland of Troy. Menelaus's attempt to win back his wife gave rise to the Trojan War. Under the command of Menelaus's brother Agamemnon (also the husband of Clytemnestra), the Greeks besieged Troy for nine years, and the city finally fell. On Agamemnon's return home to Mycenae, he was murdered by his wife and her lover. The Trojan War's lasting impact was that it marked the end of the ancient Greek mythological era and the birth of modern history.

Most accounts of the Leda myth do not describe it in terms of rape but as a seduction, yet in his poem Yeats emphasizes the unwillingness and terror of the mortal victim at the mercy of the beast-god. It is not an account of Zeus winning over Leda but of a brutal sexual assault. It is often suggested that Yeats might have based the poem on the Michelangelo painting of the Leda story (he owned a reproduction of it) or a picture of a bas-relief from an art history book, but it is likely that with the poem the poet is creating his own, idealized version of the scene.

Violence and Helplessness

Yeats wrote "Leda and the Swan" during the turbulent days of the Irish Civil War. In 1922, Britain and Ireland signed a treaty that established the Irish Free State, which gave Ireland some measure of autonomy but kept it under the firm authority of Britain. This resulted in civil war between supporters of the treaty and its opponents. Yeats, who became an Irish senator in 1922, supported the Free State, but he deplored the violence used on both sides in the war. Yeats declared that his inspiration for "Leda and the Swan" was his meditation on Ireland's place in world politics. For centuries Ireland had struggled for independence against Britain. Although there are no explicit references to Ireland or to politics in the poem, the subjugation of Leda can be seen as reflecting the brutality inflicted upon Ireland by its powerful aggressor, and the violence of the poem can be seen as an emblem of the violence of the civil war.

The focus of the poem is the violent rape, which is presented in intensely physical terms. Throughout, the helplessness of the mortal girl is contrasted with the incomprehensible and overwhelming power of the bird-god. The diction of the poem points to the swan's domination and strength ("great wings," "beating still," "feathered glory") in contrast to Leda's passivity (she is "caught," "caressed," "helpless"). The violence of the poem is also heightened by the use of the tightly controlled form of the sonnet, which describes the rape in spare but forceful terms. The act that Yeats describes brings forth a new era and civilization, and the poem thus seems to indicate that all such far-reaching transformations in history must have violent and incomprehensible beginnings. Also, with the description of the "broken wall, the burning roof and tower" that are the result of the brutal assault of Leda, Yeats seems to be suggesting that violence generates continuing violence in human history.

Annunciation

"Leda and the Swan" is one of Yeats's several "Annunciation" poems. In fact the original version of the poem, published in 1924 was called "Annunciation." In the Christian tradition, the Annunciation is the announcement by the archangel Gabriel to the Virgin Mary that she would have a child by the Holy Spirit. The Holy Spirit in the form of a dove descended upon Mary and fulfilled the angel's words. The result of this union between the divine and human was Jesus Christ, whose birth signaled the destruction of an old order and ushered in a new age and a Christian civilization. In "Leda and the Swan," Yeats describes an annunciation of a quite different type as the god Zeus, also in the form of a bird, descends upon Leda and impregnates her with Helen, who will be the cause of the destruction of Greek civilization and give rise to a new modern era. Yeats thus sees the rape of Leda by Zeus as an event parallel to the annunciation to the Virgin Mary. The children of Mary and Leda changed the world, and the moment of their conception is a pivotal moment for the universe. For Yeats, the annunciation is a moment in which the supernatural energy of a god is mingled with the human to revitalize a declining civilization.

In "Leda and the Swan," as with Yeats's other annunciation poems such as "The Magi," "Two Songs from a Play," "The Mother of God," and "The Second Coming," the violence and terror of the union of god and human is stressed. Yeats implies that any union of human and divine must be a horrifying experience. However, he thinks that there is a possibility that in that moment of merging, the mortal may attain supernatural or transcendent insight. Thus the speaker at the end of the poem asks if Leda, as she is mastered by the "brute blood of the air," gains through her experience some form of divine knowledge and divine power.

The Cycle of History

Yeats viewed history as cyclical and believed that every two thousand years a new era would be ushered in that would be the antithesis, or opposite, of the one that was being replaced. Again, although he makes no overt reference to his theory of history in the poem, Yeats uses the subject of Leda and the swan to illustrate a moment in which the cycle is begun anew. The use of tense in the poem calls attention to the timelessness of the event and so the cyclical nature of history. The rape is described in the first eight lines using present tense, but, as seen in lines 9 to 11, the act engenders consequences that are yet to be experienced in the poem—they are in the future. The poem ends using the past tense, making it clear that the events described have already taken place. The entire effect is to convey the sense that the rape is more than an assault on a particular woman at a static moment in history, but it is also a symbol for universal and recurring—although certainly violent, painful, and destructive—elements of human experiences.

In "Leda and the Swan," Yeats also seems to be pointing to his mystical theory of the universe, although he makes no overt references to it. The poem describes a moment that represents a change of era according to Yeats's historical model of gyres, which he describes in his prose work *A Vision*. In that book, Yeats conceives of history as composed of two cones rotating in opposite directions. Every moment of time moves through these spirals and so contains two opposite but interpenetrating movements, as one cone widens and the other narrows. The spiralling motions are called

Topics for Further Study

- Research the different forms of the Leda myth as they are told in ancient Greek sources. Examine how the story is represented in various paintings and sculptures from classical to modern times.

- Find examples of sonnets written in the sixteenth, seventeenth, and eighteenth centuries and compare their themes and structures to those used by Yeats in "Leda and the Swan." What are the main similarities among the poems? What are the major differences?

- In Greek mythology, Zeus took the form of a swan to seduce Leda and transformed himself into a bull to win over the princess Europa. Investigate similar accounts of such metamorphoses in myths from other traditions, including those of Africa, Asia, and the Middle East.

gyres. The times of the greatest turbulence in history are when the gyres reverse their motions, which happens every two thousand years

The rape of Leda by Zeus is an event that brings forth such a reversal. It brings forth a new era, one that is antithetical to the civilization out of which it sprang and which it replaces. Another example of an event that comes from the reversal of the gyres, according to Yeats, is the annunciation and descent of the Holy Spirit in the form of a dove to the Virgin Mary, which resulted in the birth of Christ. He held, in fact, that this event brought forth a reversal of the era that was spawned by the rape of Leda as described in "Leda and the Swan."

Style

Recurring Image

The swan is an image that is found in many of Yeats's poems. (His poetry, in fact, is full of birds of various sorts, from eagles to owls to parrots, but the swan is the most frequently recurrent bird symbol.) Although what the swan represents evolves in Yeats's poetry, it seems for him to be essentially a symbol of mystery and passion. In "Leda and the Swan," the swan is mysterious, divine, incomprehensible, violent, and brutally passionate. The use of the swan and other recurring images in Yeats's poetry also serve to draw his entire body of work into a coherent whole. By using certain images over and over again, he creates a shorthand that allows readers to recognize complex ideas that may not be explicitly mentioned in a particular poem but are the focus of other works. The swan in some of Yeats's other works, such as "The Wild Swans at Coole," "The Tower," and "Nineteen Hundred and Nineteen," represents wildness, rage, bitterness, and unsatisfied desire, and some of those thoughts will echo in this poem to a reader familiar with Yeats's poetry.

Modernist Sonnet Form

"Leda and the Swan" is a sonnet, a traditional fourteen-line poem written in iambic pentameter. The poem uses the rhyme scheme of the Shakespearean sonnet for the first two quatrains (four-line stanzas), and the rhyme scheme of the Petrarchan sonnet for the last six lines: *abab cdcd efgefg*. (The rhyme scheme of the first two quatrains of the Petrarchan sonnet is *abba abba;* the rhyme scheme of the last six lines of the Shakespearean sonnet is *efef gg*.) However, the subject matter of the work is extremely nontraditional—most sonnets are about love or public matters, not violent rape. Yeats breaks with tradition and creates a sonnet in a daring modernist style. The poem is full of such paradoxes, or oppositional elements, which is one of the sources of its richness. For example, the sonnet is one of the most precise and tightly controlled forms of poetry, but Yeats chooses this structure to describe a situation of explosive power and intensity. An act of force and violence is described within a structure of order and control. The poem is written in iambic pentameter, so it moves along in a steady, pulsating way. But Yeats uses phrases to break up the traditional meter—there is an abrupt break after the opening words, for example, and again after the description of what is engendered by the union: "And Agamemnon dead." The total effect is of a rhythm that reflects the event being explicated: a throbbing sensation is created that is broken up by dramatic moments of even greater intensity. The line break in the middle of the sestet is the only nontraditional element in terms of the sonnet's formal structure, and it is used to emphasize the sudden end of the rape and to distance the reader from the event. The rhyme used in the poem is traditional for the sonnet form, but the mixture of perfect and imperfect rhymes ("push" and "rush" in lines 5 and 7, "up" and "drop" in lines 11 and 14) add variety and interest.

Language

Because Yeats uses such a narrow, tightly ordered structure for his poem, he uses words to their maximum effect. The language and images in the poem are a mixture of concrete and abstract, which conveys a sense of the immediacy of the event as well as its greater cosmic significance. The swan is never referred to as a swan, for example, but as "feathered glory" and "brute blood of the air," which emphasizes its physical presence as well as its incomprehensible and divine nature. The use of body parts (and not their names) to refer to Leda and the swan ("thighs," "fingers," "nape," "beak," "webs," "bill") again stresses the physicality of the act. The diction in the poem is extremely simple, but the images created from them are vigorous (the "white rush," for example, calls up an otherworldly image of the swan, as it indicates its physical whiteness as well as it power).

The use of strong, simple verbs ("caught," "hold," "push," "drop") further emphasizes the sense of action. Yeats also plays on words a great deal in the poem, thus communicating several meanings in the confines of taut phrases. The images of the "broken wall, the burning roof and tower" are references to the siege of Troy but are also sexual allusions. With the phrase "the staggering girl" he draws attention to Leda's physical as well as her psychological state. Yeats manages to communicate extremely complex ideas about the ushering in of a new era through the violent union of human and divine and the cycle of history in very few words. He does this by presenting vivid images that have multiplicity of meanings and by carefully changing the tense in the poem from present to future to past to draw attention to the timelessness of the action that he has depicted in such immediate terms.

Historical Context

The history of Yeats's homeland of Ireland has been one of struggle for self-determination since the twelfth century, when Britain was formally granted overlordship of the island. In addition to the fight for independence and home rule, Ireland

Compare & Contrast

- **1922:** Ireland is partitioned, after a treaty deal with the British, into Northern Ireland and the Irish Free State. Britain maintains control of both provinces, and the Irish Civil War is fought between those who support the partition and those who oppose it.

   1949: The Republic of Ireland is proclaimed, and the country withdraws from the British Commonwealth. The British Parliament affirms the status of Northern Ireland as part of the United Kingdom. Many Irish, including those supporting the outlawed Irish Republican Army (IRA), continue to call for unification.

   1969: British troops are sent to Northern Ireland to contain continued violence that includes terrorist acts by the IRA and police retaliation. In 1971, imprisonment without trial is introduced in Northern Ireland as a measure to counter terrorism. In 1972, on what comes to be known as "Bloody Sunday," British soldiers shoot and kill thirteen protestors at a civil rights march in Londonderry. The British abolish the Northern Ireland Parliament and impose direct rule.

   1998: A historic Northern Ireland peace agreement is reached. An accord is ratified by large majorities in both Northern Ireland and the Republic of Ireland.

- **1924:** "Leda and the Swan" is condemned by members of the Irish Catholic clergy and press as filth.

   1959: An unexpurgated version of D. H. Lawrence's novel *Lady Chatterley's Lover* is published for the first time in the United States. The novel, which explores in explicit detail the sexual relationship of a man and women from different social classes, had been deemed obscene and had been suppressed from publication for more than thirty years.

   1989: The live performances and song lyrics of the rap music group 2 Live Crew's album *Nasty as They Wanna Be* provoke intense controversy. Some characterize the group's work as obscene, while others defend the band against censorship.

   1999: An exhibition of works by British artists called "Sensation," which includes a painting of the Virgin Mary decorated with elephant dung, appears at the Brooklyn Museum of Art. New York mayor Rudolph Guiliani freezes the museum's annual subsidy of more than $7 million, calling the exhibit sick.

---

has, since the seventeenth century, been beset with a bitter religious contention between Catholics and Protestants. When Yeats wrote "Leda and the Swan" in 1923, Ireland was in the midst of a bloody civil war that was the result of the Anglo-Irish conflict as well as the discord between the largely Catholic south and the Protestant north.

The failure of the British government to implement home rule led, in 1916, to the Easter Rising, during which many prominent leaders of the movement for independence were killed. The militant organization Sinn Féin, which had been founded among Irish Catholics, emerged as the dominant nationalist group during that time. They declared themselves the Irish Assembly and proclaimed an Irish republic in 1918. The group was outlawed by the British and began then to wage war underground.

The Anglo-Irish War that broke out in 1919 saw guerrilla attacks by Irish insurgents (later called the Irish Republican Army—or IRA) on British forces as well as vigorous retaliations by the British. Yeats staunchly supported the Irish cause and strongly denounced the British, in particular the tactics used by the Black and Tans, the British anti-terrorist forces. In 1920, a new Home Rule bill provided for the partition of Ireland into two separate entities. A 1922 treaty with the British finalized the partition of Northern Ireland and the Irish Free State. However, the Irish Free State and most Irish Catholics refused to recognize the finality of the partition because the close relations between Northern Ireland and Britain posed a threat to the Catholic minority in the north, and civil war broke out. Although Yeats had always supported the Irish against the British, choosing sides in the struggle of Irish against Irish was difficult for him. He elected to back the Irish Free State and was even appointed to a six-year term in the new government's Senate. The bitter civil strife ended in April 1923.

Much of Yeats's poetry written during the Anglo-Irish and Civil Wars reflects his bitterness toward those conflicts. The poem "Nineteen Hundred and Nineteen" is a harsh and relentless portrait of the destruction of civilized values and the helplessness and hopelessness left in its wake. "Meditations in Time of Civil War" (1923) is a pessimistic poem that speaks of meaningless violence, social chaos, and a fallen world.

"Leda and the Swan" makes no overt references to politics, the Anglo-Irish struggle, or the civil war, but it may be seen as representing the violence of the political events during the time. Yeats declared that he wrote the poem as he was meditating on the Irish situation, although he says, "as I wrote, bird and lady took such possession of the scene that all politics went out of it." No doubt the poem's tone of brutal violence and subjugation took its inspiration from the political events facing Ireland. The use of diction like "sudden blow," "staggering," "caught," "helpless," "terrified," "broken," "dead," and "brute blood" are certainly evocative of the savagery of war. Some critics have gone as far as to suggest that in the poem, Leda may be viewed as a symbol for Ireland, helpless and staggering underneath the brute power of her mighty British conqueror. Leda may also be seen as representative of the people and the swan as the force of law and tyrannical government.

It is also significant that the original version of the poem, called "Annunciation," was written during a time when the new Irish government was beginning to institute censorship laws that targeted works whose content was counter to Catholic morality. Yeats had been a strong supporter of the Irish novelist James Joyce whose work *Ulysses* was embroiled in a famous and lengthy censorship battle in Britain and the United States before it was published in France in 1922. In writing "Leda and the Swan," Yeats apparently hoped to arouse controversy and to flout what he thought were unjust laws targeting freedom of expression. The poem was denounced as obscene by much of the Catholic press.

Critical Overview

When Yeats first published a version of "Leda and the Swan" in 1924 in the radical monthly paper *To-morrow*, it was met with criticism from many conservatives who deplored its sexually explicit subject matter. Yeats later revised the poem (not because of the criticism but because he constantly reworked his poetry), and it appeared in his prose work *A Vision* in 1925 in a slightly amended form and as an epigraph to a lengthy discussion of his cyclical theory of history. The poem was revised four more times and appeared in its final version in the 1928 collection, *The Tower*. That volume was received enthusiastically by reviewers, and it is still regarded as one of the poet's greatest works.

Some early readers again found the sexual explicitness of "Leda and the Swan" troublesome, but for the most part it was greatly admired. Contemporary critics have been extremely generous with their praise of the poem. John Unterecker, in his *Reader's Guide to William Butler Yeats*, calls it "a nearly perfect sonnet," and Balachandra Rajan considers it "one of the most unimprovable poems ever written." Many critics have commented on the poem's intricacy of thought within the narrow confines of the sonnet, remarking at the masterful use of language and rhythm to create lyricism and complexity. A few commentators have faulted the work for its oblique references to the poet's complicated philosophical theories. Yvor Winters, for example, in his article "Leda and the Swan," says that the ideas in the poem "constitute Yeats's private fairy tale," and that they are "foolish." A few feminist writers, notably Elizabeth Butler Cullingford, have found that the poem "flirts with pornography" because of its violently sexual nature and the subjugation of Leda. Others, such as Scott C. Holstad, have suggested that in the poem Yeats plays out a rape fantasy that is the result of his unrequited love for Maud Gonne. Even critics who have found the topic of the poem troubling or distasteful, however, have conceded that "Leda and the Swan" is one of the most technically brilliant poems ever written in the English language. Yeats's choice of diction and his use of language, imagery, and rhyme, it is agreed, contribute to a powerful total effect. As Richard Ellman has written in his *The Identity of Yeats*, "He gathers his intensity and force, which have hardly been equalled in modern verse, by creating, with the aid of symbol, myth, and ritual, patterns where thoughts and feelings find unexampled voice."

Criticism

Uma Kukathas

Kukathas is a freelance editor and writer. In the following essay, she discusses Yeats's choice of a brutal rape as the subject of his poem "Leda and the Swan."

When "Leda and the Swan" was first published in 1924 (in a version somewhat different than the final form that appears in modern collections of Yeats's verse), it aroused criticism from the Catholic press in Ireland because of its sexually explicit subject matter—the violent rape of a mortal woman by a god who had taken on the form of a swan. Yeats published the poem in a radical journal and hoped to stir up controversy in order to make the point that he opposed the country's repressive attitude toward "immoral" literature.

In the early twenty-first century, "Leda and the Swan" is hardly considered an indecent work and is heavily anthologized in poetry collections as one of the finest poems written in English. While few people would argue that the poem is anything but brilliant in its technical mastery of language, some contemporary readers might still find the content of the poem troubling or objectionable because of its sexual—and perhaps sexist—nature. Is Yeats's poem sexist? Should female readers be offended by the content of the work?

The readers of "Leda and the Swan" who criticized it when it was first published did so because they thought that a sexual subject was not an appropriate topic for a work of art. More than seventy years later, sexual themes are not generally considered unsuitable for literary expression. Some feminists, however, object to the use of sexist themes in art because they perpetuate the subordination of women. The portrayal of women in television or films as being primarily objects of sexual interest, for example, is condemned as detrimental to women's status as equal members of society. The question to be explored here, then, is whether by offering a graphic image of female degradation in "Leda and the Swan" Yeats produced a sexist work and if the treatment of his female character detracts from the poem's status as great literature.

Sexism is defined in *Webster's* dictionary as "behavior, conditions, or attitudes that foster stereotypes of social roles based on sex." It is difficult to say whether in "Leda and the Swan" Yeats is presenting stereotypical portraits of Leda as female and Zeus as male. The action described is a

> "Part of the power and brilliance of Yeats's poem is that it is so unsettling, that it presents in a tightly controlled sonnet a multitude of feelings—horror, repulsion, and sexual confusion."

rape, and in that situation there is clearly an imbalance of power between the assailant and the victim. The male Zeus is clearly the strong, domineering figure and the female Leda is the weak, defenseless one. He has her "nape caught in his bill" like a small animal, and he "holds her helpless." However, simply to describe a scene in which two people of the opposite sex are shown in a particular situation is not necessarily to foster the idea that those are their natural roles. What would be more disturbing is if a woman's attitude to her assault in such a situation is characterized in terms that present an incorrect but often accepted picture of how women respond to rape. Does Yeats's characterization of Leda promote any such picture?

One often used stereotype of women is that they somehow invite rape by being seductive and alluring and that in some sense they actually want to be violated by their attackers. Clearly in Yeats's poem Leda does not invite Zeus's advances. The poem begins abruptly, and there is a clear sense that Leda is as shocked by the "sudden blow" as the reader is. She is "staggering," so she has obviously been caught off guard both physically and mentally by the massive bird. The action of the first four lines is described in terms of the swan's movements, and Leda is entirely passive. Another stereotype that is used often by rapists who claim that their sexual actions are justified is that women actually enjoy the force of rape and that in some sense their participation is consensual. As the rape begins in the first stanza, Leda appears to be a completely unsuspecting and unwilling victim of a forcible act. However, the sensual overtones of the poem also imply that the rape being described is not simply an act of violence but in some sense an erotic act.

What Do I Read Next?

- Numerous poets have used the story of Leda as a source for their poetry. The most famous of the poems about the Greek myth are Rainer Maria Rilke's "Leda" (1908), in *Selected Poems,* H. D.'s (Hilda Doolittle's) "Leda" (1921) in *Hymen,* and D. H. Lawrence's "Leda," in *Pansies* (1929).

- The 1928 volume *The Tower,* in which "Leda and the Swan" was published, is considered one of Yeats's finest collections of poetry. It includes some of his most famous works, including "Sailing to Byzantium," "Among School Children," and "The Dying Swan."

- *The Greek Myths* (1960), by Robert Graves, retells the creation myths and the legends and lives of Greek gods and heroes.

- Yeats's *Mythologies* (1962) is an anthology of Irish legends and tales of the occult that reflect the poet's deep interest in myth and preserving and celebrating Irish history and culture.

Leda's thighs are "caressed," and the swan "holds her helpless breast upon his breast" in a position that suggests intimacy or even lovemaking. As the poem progresses, there seem to be additional hints that there is in fact some consent on Leda's part.

In the second stanza, the poem moves to an examination of Leda's state of mind. It is presented in the form of two questions:

> How can those terrified vague fingers push
> The feathered glory from her loosening thighs?
> And how can body, laid in that white rush,
> But feel the strange heart beating where it lies?

The use of the interrogative to describe Leda's condition in this stanza adds a dimension of ambiguity in terms of her response to her predicament. On the one hand, she simply cannot resist: she is not being attacked by any ordinary assailant, after all, but being seized here by the all-powerful leader of the gods. How could she fight back in such a case? For this reason she appears to be stunned: her "terrified vague fingers" indicate that she is numbed by the experience. However, the use of the interrogative could point not only to the impossibility of resistance on Leda's part but to the fact that she finds the god irresistible in a sexual sense. Even though in the second stanza the poem focuses on Leda's physical and psychic state, the words used to describe her point of view hardly seem inappropriate for a woman who is being victimized.

In the midst of Leda's violation the swan is described as the "feathered glory." Leda's thighs are described not as being violently pried apart but as "loosening," perhaps in response to the rapist, again suggesting that this is a consensual act. The next two lines of the poem stress the union of woman and god. The use of the word *body* without a pronoun could imply that their two bodies are one; both together "feel" the strange heart beating. The heart is a traditional symbol of love, and the use of that word again seems hardly fitting in the context of a forcible and violent rape.

In the last stanza, there is further ambiguity with the line "A shudder in the loins." Again there is no pronoun before "loins," and it may be that the shudder is not only on the part of the swan but is felt by Leda, too. That a bestial rape would give rise to anything but horror seems unthinkable, but the ambivalence of the description again forces the possibility that there is some mutual enjoyment that results from the sexual union. At the end of the poem, after it is learned that the union between Leda and the swan-god brings about a turbulent sequence of events—the siege of Troy and, by implication, the destruction of ancient Greek civilization—another question is posed, this time about the effect of the rape on Leda: "Being so caught up, / So mastered by the brute blood of the air / Did she put on his knowledge with his power. . . ." Did Leda gain some type of insight, some knowledge about the nature of the cosmos and human history? Again, the use of the verb *caught up* can be read as being ambiguous. Leda was caught up and mastered by the god, but *caught up* can also imply being intensely involved in the act and complicit in some sense.

Although the various references do not show explicitly that Leda is a willing partner in the union with Zeus, the erotic tone of the poem and the hints at acquiescence in the act on Leda's part are unsettling. They do seem to point to the stereotype that women derive pleasure from forced sexual intercourse and, perhaps by extension, that they are somehow not entirely without blame in acts of violence against them. However, to see the poem merely as an instance of Yeats's sexism would be a mistake. Although there seem to be various clues that Yeats thinks of Leda as being erotically caught up in the event, it is obvious at the end of the poem that what has been described is a violent and contemptible abuse of a woman by a callous and indifferent aggressor.

After the speaker asks if in the union Leda "put on his knowledge with his power," it becomes clear that the god has used the mortal woman for nothing more than his sexual gratification. The swan discards her unceremoniously—he lets her drop from his "indifferent beak"—and the question is left as to whether in her horrific subjugation by a god Leda also participated somehow in the divine. Yeats uses the heightened eroticism of the act as presented throughout the poem to add to the confusion and complexity of what has taken place, and the final question gains additional force after the event has been depicted in such a manner. The rape is described in terms that are brutal, bizarre, terrifying, and erotically charged, and these various aspects contribute to the incomprehensible nature of what has taken place. Yeats's suggestions that Leda was somehow caught up in the act are used not to point to women's supposed consent to acts of violence but to add to the terrifying confusion she feels as she is not only physically raped but has her humanity violated by an indifferent god.

Although "Leda and the Swan" does seem to characterize a woman's participation in rape in ways that are found in negative and demeaning stereotypes, Yeats's intention in the poem seems not to offer a commentary on women's nature but on the terror and irresistible draw that comes with contact with the divine. The portrayal of the female rape victim thus should not be seen as sexist because what is presented ambiguously as consent on the part of Leda is used not to foster a stereotypical portrait of women but to depict the terrifying power of the god that is irresistible even in its horror and brutality. Part of the power and brilliance of Yeats's poem is that it is so unsettling, that it presents in a tightly controlled sonnet a multitude of feelings—horror, repulsion, and sexual confusion. The use of Leda's manipulation by the god and the reader's sense that she is held completely at his mercy both physically and mentally does not detract from the greatness of Yeats's poem but contributes to its intensity and adds a further dimension of complexity to this technically brilliant work of literature.

Source: Uma Kukathas, Critical Essay on "Leda and the Swan," in *Poetry for Students,* The Gale Group, 2001.

Wendy Perkins

Perkins is an associate professor of English at Prince George's Community College and has published widely in the field of twentieth-century British and American literature. In the following essay, she explores the mythological elements of Yeats's poem and how they relate to its overall themes.

In Greek mythology, Leda was the daughter of Thestios, king of Aetolia, and wife of Tyndareus, king of Sparta. The legend tells that one day Zeus, the ruler of the Greek gods, came to Leda in the form of a swan and seduced her. As a result, she bore two eggs; both would develop into two offspring each, Castor and Pollux from one egg and Helen and Clytemnestra from the other. Helen would become the breathtakingly beautiful Helen of Troy and would trigger the eventual destruction of Troy, the disintegration of early Greek civilization, and the introduction of the next cycle of Greek civilization, known as the classical age. Yeats's dramatization of this moment of annunciation in "Leda and the Swan" reveals his own spiritual and historical philosophy.

In his study of Yeats in *A History of Modern Poetry,* David Perkins notes that the poet "thought of himself as a person of religious temperament who had been deprived of religion by nineteenth-century science." In this sense, Yeats was a modernist, a term that came to be applied to a group of artists and writers who produced works in the early decades of the twentieth century. Modernists like Yeats became disillusioned with traditional beliefs in religion, political systems, and society in response to political events and the works of such scientists and thinkers as Darwin, Marx, Freud, Nietzsche, and Frazer. The devastation of World War I compounded the modernists' revolt against conventional values.

Perkins comments that in this atmosphere of cynicism, Yeats still felt a need

> to sense a spiritual depth and mystery in the universe and, beyond this, an ultimate coherence and meaning.... [He also felt] an imaginative need for concrete symbols in which the mystery could be invoked and contemplated. His religious quest was more urgently motivated by metaphysical and imaginative hungers than by moral ones.

Unable to accept the lack of faith in any established institution or doctrine, Yeats searched for

> *The poem begins with 'a sudden blow' as Zeus enters in the form of the swan with his 'great wings beating,' grasping 'the staggering' and 'helpless' girl as he begins to rape her."*

other avenues to explore in an effort to establish his own worldview. Perkins explains that Christianity was "from his point of view, impossible to believe, and his religious needs drove him to other traditions." One tradition that Yeats explores in "Leda and the Swan" is Greek mythology.

Yeats employs the myth of Leda and Zeus to illustrate his theories on the cycle of history. His book *A Vision* outlines his thoughts on historical cycles as well as his theory that the universe is made up of opposites, or antitheses, and that harmony can only be achieved through a merging of these opposites. Both of these theories figure prominently in "Leda and the Swan."

The cyclical theory of history expressed in *A Vision* centers on his idea that history moves in two-thousand-year cycles, each cycle representing a civilization that begins with a gripping mystical conception and birth. Yeats determined that the annunciation of Mary and the birth of Christ initiated the Christian era of 1–2000 A.D., and earlier the annunciation of Leda and the birth of Helen initiated the classical era of 2000–1 B.C. In his famous poem "The Second Coming," Yeats describes the end of the present two-thousand-year cycle and speculates that a new figure will emerge as a reflection of the new era as Christ represented the old. Yet his cynicism over the traumatic events of the early part of the twentieth century—World War I as well as the troubles experienced in his native Ireland—prompts a dark vision of the new Messiah in his question at the end of this poem, "what rough beast, its hour come round at last, / Slouches towards Bethlehem to be born?"

The myth that dominates the first cycle of history is illustrated in "Leda and the Swan," especially in the third stanza when the speaker notes that the result of Zeus raping Leda will be the destruction of Troy and the early Greek civilization: the act "engenders . . . / The broken wall, the burning roof and tower / And Agamemnon dead."

The poem also illustrates Yeats's theory that each era is ushered in by an act of violence, which hits the reader immediately in the first stanza. The poem begins with "a sudden blow" as Zeus enters in the form of the swan with his "great wings beating," grasping "the staggering" and "helpless" girl as he begins to rape her. B. L. Reid, in his article on Yeats for *Dictionary of Literary Biography*, notes that the speaker's point of view is that of

> an amazed and awed accidental bystander, elected voyeur and granted powers of empathy with Leda's physical experience and with some part of her mental experience. . . . [Then the poem] plunges straight ahead until the god in the swan has worked his will in this exalted rape.

Commenting on Yeats's style, Reid notes, "When Yeats boldly breaks his eleventh line he breaks, graphically, the body of Leda, the roofs of Troy, the body of Agamemnon, and the hearts of many men and women."

A merging of opposites also occurs in the poem, reflecting Yeats's view that in life a synthesis of antithetical forces must occur in order to establish permanence and a sense of harmony. Through his poetry, Yeats explores oppositions between art and reality, imagination and moral responsibility, intellect and passion. In "Leda and the Swan," Yeats asks whether a synthesis has occurred as Zeus's "brute blood" masters Leda in the final stanza: "Did she put on his knowledge with his power / Before the indifferent beak could let her drop?" Critic Charles A. Raines, in his article "Yeats' Metaphors of Permanence," concludes,

> Leda must feel the strange heart beating because a synthesis of Zeus' superhuman characteristics and Leda's human characteristics has taken place. . . . If [Zeus'] knowledge and power are obtained by Leda it must be because the supernatural has intermingled with the body, and this must be so for the result of this combination is Helen, who is considered by Yeats to have provided a source of order in the sense that she began the classical Aegean age which, for Yeats, represents permanence. Helen is considered a progenitor of permanence because she represents a synthesis of life (Leda) with the spiritual (Zeus), which produces permanence.

Perkins notes that the poem ends with the speaker's questioning whether any synthesis has taken place in the coupling of Zeus and Leda. He echoes Raines when he comments, "combining knowledge and power, the god in the form of a swan is a symbol of antitheses reconciled," but he questions whether Leda gains Zeus's knowledge:

> the antithesis Yeats poses at the end of the poem is that between the supernatural and the human. The supernatural is a whole or unified being, and the question is whether even in a fleeting moment the human is capable of such completeness.

The complex symbolic structure of "Leda and the Swan" makes it difficult to come to any absolute conclusions about the experience between Zeus and Leda. The poem does, however, provide an excellent example of Yeats's theories on the cyclical nature of history and how the opposing forces of life fit into those theories.

Source: Wendy Perkins, Critical Essay on "Leda and the Swan," in *Poetry for Students,* The Gale Group, 2001.

Sources

Cullingford, Elizabeth Butler, "Pornography and Canonicity: The Case of Yeats's 'Leda and the Swan,'" in *Law, Literature, and Feminism,* edited by Susan Sage, Heinzelman, and Zipporah Batshaw Wiseman, Duke University Press, 1994, pp. 165–88.

Ellmann, Richard, *The Identity of Yeats,* Oxford University Press, 1964.

Hargrove, Nancy D., "Aesthetic Distance in Yeats's 'Leda and the Swan,'" in *Arizona Quarterly,* Vol. 39, 1983, pp. 235–45.

Holstad, Scott C., "Yeats's 'Leda and the Swan': Psycho-Sexual Therapy in Action," in *Notes on Modern Irish Literature,* Vol. 7, No. 2, Fall 1995, pp. 45–52.

Levine, Bernard, "A Psychopoetic Analysis of Yeats's 'Leda and the Swan,'" in *Bucknell Review,* Vol. 17, No. 1, March 1969, pp. 85–111.

O'Donnell, William H., *The Poetry of William Butler Yeats: An Introduction,* Ungar, 1986, pp. 99–102.

Perkins, David, *A History of Modern Poetry: From the 1890s to the High Modernist Mode,* Harvard University Press, 1976.

Raines, Charles A., "Yeats' Metaphors of Permanence," in *Twentieth Century Literature,* Vol. 5, No. 1, 1959, p. 1220.

Rajan, Balachandra, *W. B. Yeats: A Critical Introduction,* Hutchinson University Library, 1969, pp. 132–34.

Reid, B. L., "William Butler Yeats," in *Dictionary of Literary Biography,* Volume 19: *British Poets, 1880–1914,* Gale Research, 1983, pp. 399–452.

Smith, Stan, *W. B. Yeats: A Critical Introduction,* MacMillan, 1990, pp. 113–18.

Unterecker, John, *A Reader's Guide to William Butler Yeats,* The Noonday Press, 1959, pp. 187–89.

Winters, Yvor, "'Leda and the Swan,'" in *Yeats: Poems, 1919–1935: A Casebook,* edited by Elizabeth Cullingford, Macmillan Publishers, 1984, pp. 125–27.

For Further Study

Ellmann, Maud, "Daughters of the Swan," in *m/f,* Vol. 11–12, 1986, pp. 119–62.
    This essay uses the methods of pscyhoanalysis and deconstruction to explore questions of gender and sexuality in Yeats's poems and pays special attention to "Leda and the Swan."

Ellmann, Richard, *Yeats: The Man and the Masks,* E. P. Dutton and Co., 1948.
    This is an informative introduction to Yeats and his ideas that combines biography and criticism.

Fletcher, Ian, "'Leda and the Swan' As Iconic Poem," in *Yeats Annual,* No. 1, edited by Richard J. Finneran, Humanities Press, 1982, pp. 82–113.
    This book discusses the use of the Leda myth in other works of literature and art and uses them to illuminate Yeats's treatment of the story.

Young, David, *Troubled Mirror: A Study of Yeats's "The Tower,"* University of Iowa Press, 1987, pp. 73–84.
    Young provides a detailed account of the collection in which "Leda and the Swan" first appeared, exploring how the poems interact and discussing Yeats's poetic method.

The Song of the Smoke

W. E. B. Du Bois

1907

W. E. B. Du Bois was 39 years old when "The Song of the Smoke" was published in the February 1907 issue of *Horizon,* a magazine which he himself edited. The poem is understood as "an affirmation of black pride," but Du Bois's ultimate acceptance of the need to call for black pride was the culmination of a difficult process. He was born into a community of free blacks in Great Barrington, Massachusetts, in 1868, and after his mother's death, he was given a scholarship by the primarily white town. Although he had deeply desired to go to Harvard, it was the town's stipulation that this scholarship was to be used at Fisk University, founded for the children of emancipated slaves. While Du Bois had long believed that education and a sense of purpose were all that blacks needed to gain a place as Americans after having been freed from slavery in 1865, his education at Fisk was twofold. Here he could feel what it was to engage with educated minds, with no race considerations to affect the exchange. He also was made acutely aware of "the color line" in the South, and realized it would take far more than the higher education of African Americans to overcome this barrier.

In 1895, Du Bois became the first African American to receive a Ph.D. from Harvard. His reputation as a distinguished scholar commenced with the acceptance of his dissertation, "The Suppression of the African Slave-Trade in the United States of America, 1638–1870," as the inaugural work in the Harvard Historical Studies series. Du Bois soon acknowledged, however, that his subsequent scholarly work in the new field of social science was not having the impact that he expected. Thus he turned to other forms of writing, including poetry, to present his theories and beliefs regarding "the problem of the color line," which he considered the major problem of the twentieth century. He further took responsibility for bringing this message to the public by editing the magazines *Moon, Horizon,* and the National Association for the Advancement of Colored People (NAACP) publication *Crisis,* all of which introduced the work of many new black writers, including Langston Hughes and Zora Neale Hurston.

Du Bois was one of the first African Americans to foster the idea of race-consciousness and of the African American as hero. His life's work focused on the rebuttal of the claim that the African race engendered only slaves and savages unable to make contributions to civilization and American culture. "The Song of the Smoke" clearly stands as an affirmation for African Americans, but it is also a proclamation to America as a whole of the historical and economic significance of African Americans.

W. E. B. Du Bois

Author Biography

Du Bois was born on February 23, 1868, in the western Massachusetts town of Great Barrington, to a family whose ancestry was French Huguenot on his father's side and Dutch and African on his mother's side. Du Bois' father Alfred Du Bois left his family when his son was a young boy. Du Bois lived with his mother Mary Sylvina Burghardt Du Bois until her death in 1884. Left penniless, Du Bois moved in with an aunt and worked as a timekeeper at a local mill to support himself. He graduated from high school that same year, the only black student in his class. An outstanding student, Du Bois was encouraged by his principal to attend college. With the aid of a scholarship, he enrolled at Fisk University in Nashville, Tennessee, in 1885. Du Bois graduated with a bachelor's degree in 1888 and entered Harvard University as a junior, where he graduated, cum laude, with a second Bachelor of Arts degree in 1891. Du Bois studied at the University of Berlin in Germany for two years before returning to Harvard, where he received his Ph.D. in 1895. He was the first African American to receive this degree from Harvard. From 1895 to 1897, Du Bois taught Latin, Greek, German, and English at Wilberforce University in Ohio. While Du Bois was at Wilberforce, his dissertation, "The Suppression of the African Slave-Trade to the United States of America, 1638–1870," was published in 1896 as the first installment in the Harvard Historical studies series. Also in 1896, Du Bois married Nina Gomer, a Wilberforce student. They had two children. In 1897, he moved to Atlanta University, where he taught economics and history for more than a decade. In 1903, Du Bois published his most widely acclaimed work, *The Souls of Black Folk: Essays and Sketches.*

In 1905, Du Bois expressed the desire to publish a journal that would appeal to intelligent African Americans. This coincided with his belief that the most promising blacks should be educated in colleges and universities, and they in turn would emerge to serve and lead the black race. In 1906, with the help of two Atlanta University graduates, he established a small printing shop in Memphis, Tennessee, and began the *Moon Illustrated Weekly.* A year later Du Bois established the *Horizon* in Washington, D.C. This publication was meant to be the voice of the Niagara Movement, an organization of black intellectuals founded by Du Bois in 1905. The *Horizon* did not become the official voice for the Niagara Movement, but Du Bois managed to keep the monthly publication going until 1910, at which time he merged the Niagara Movement with the newly organized National Association for the Advancement of Colored People (NAACP). He also made several other important changes in his life that same year; he resigned his faculty position at Atlanta University, became director of publications and research for the NAACP, and founded *Crisis,* a magazine he would head for almost twenty-five years. Du Bois saw this magazine as a vehicle to communicate to the world the problems faced by blacks in American society as well as those faced by other oppressed people, mainly Africans on the African continent.

Following World War I, Du Bois took an even greater interest in Africa, especially those colonies once held by the now-defeated Germans and Italians. With an agenda designed to place the problems of all blacks before the world, Du Bois helped organize the second Pan-African Congress in Paris in 1919. (A previous meeting of this body had taken place in London in 1900.) Du Bois argued for the seizure of German territories in Africa as the foundation for an international African state, and *Crisis,* which had obtained an international circulation, became the platform from which Du Bois could argue for the concept of "Africa for the Africans." The 1919 congress and subsequent meetings in 1921, 1923, and 1927 were well chronicled in the magazine.

Between 1934 and 1940 Du Bois spent much of his time teaching, conducting research, and writing. Already a prolific and well-known author, during the next five years Du Bois published two of his most important historical works, *Black Reconstruction: An Essay toward a History of the Part Which Black Folk Played in the Attempt to Reconstruct Democracy in America, 1860–1880* (1935) and *Black Folk, Then and Now: An Essay in the History and Sociology of the Negro Race* (1939). He also wrote articles for several of the leading periodicals of the time, including *Current History, Journal of Negro Education, Foreign Affairs,* and *American Scholar.* However, Du Bois still desired the forum provided by a publication of his own. He proposed a scholarly journal dedicated to research and the documentation of matters concerning race problems throughout the world. He believed this kind of research must include the study of all groups of men. He explained: "Naturally, we shall usually proceed from the point of view of black folk where we live and work to the wider world." Du Bois became editor-in-chief of such a publication in 1940 with the establishment of *Phylon* at Atlanta University. He held that position until he retired from the university in 1944.

Also in 1944 Du Bois rejoined the staff of the NAACP as director of special research, but his association with the group was terminated in 1948 as the result of political disagreements with the NAACP's executive secretary. From this point on, the influence and leadership of Du Bois began to decline steadily. By the 1950s Du Bois was shunned by most leading publishers, except those with leftist views. For years Du Bois had made no attempt to conceal his approval of Soviet Communism. After a trip to the Soviet Union in 1926, he wrote in the November issue of *Crisis:* "I may be partially deceived and half-informed. But if what I have seen with my own eyes and heard with my own ears in Russia is Bolshevism, I am Bolshevik." Du Bois's other political activities included a run for the U.S. senate on the American Labor Party ticket in 1948.

After his first wife died in 1950, Du Bois married Shirley Lola Graham in 1951. At age eighty-three he was indicted by the U.S. Justice Department as an "agent for a foreign power." Although acquitted by a federal judge, he was not allowed to leave the country until 1958. This completely disillusioned Du Bois with American democracy, and in 1961 he officially joined the Communist Party and moved to Accra, Ghana. About a year later he renounced his American citizenship and became a citizen of Ghana. Before his death, he began work on "The Encyclopedia of Africana," a project he was not able to complete. Du Bois died on August 27, 1963, in Accra, Ghana.

Poem Text

I am the Smoke King
I am black!
I am swinging in the sky,
I am wringing worlds awry;
   I am the thought of the throbbing mills,   5
   I am the soul of the soul-toil kills,
   Wraith of the ripple of trading rills;
Up I'm curling from the sod,
I am whirling home to God;
   I am the Smoke King   10
   I am black.

I am the Smoke King
I am black!
I am wreathing broken hearts,
I am sheathing love's light darts;   15
   Inspiration of iron times
   Wedding the toil of toiling climes,
   Shedding the blood of bloodless crimes
Lurid lowering 'mid the blue,

Torrid towering toward the true, 20
   I am the Smoke King
   I am black.

   I am the Smoke King
   I am black!
I am darkening with song, 25
I am hearkening to wrong!
   I will be black as blackness can—
   The blacker the mantle, the mightier the man!
   For blackness was ancient ere whiteness began.
I am daubing God in night, 30
I am swabbing Hell in white:
   I am the Smoke King
   I am black.

   I am the Smoke King
   I am black! 35
I am cursing ruddy morn,
I am hearsing hearts unborn:
   Souls unto me are as stars in a night,
   I whiten my black men—I blacken my white!
   What's the hue of a hide to a man in his might? 40
Hail! great, gritty, grimy hands—
Sweet Christ, pity toiling lands!
   I am the Smoke King
   I am black.

Poem Summary

Lines 1–2

As this poem begins, Du Bois identifies the persona of the poem as "the Smoke King." The second line proclaims that, despite this light color, the persona is "black." This was a startling proclamation for the time, as "color" had become as much of an issue in the African-American culture as outside it. Lighter skinned people "passed" as white, of course, but there was also a general acceptance of the notion in the African-American culture that lighter skin was preferable. Du Bois himself was a very light-skinned black man, and he strongly objected to this kind of distinction.

Lines 3–4

There is an immediate identification here with the characteristic of "smoke" to float upward; this will be expounded upon in lines 5–7. The poet is likely also making reference to the popular spiritual "Swing Low, Sweet Chariot," which includes the phrase "coming for to carry me home"—"home" being Heaven. The implication is that the persona has been raised up.

The use of the alliterative "wr/w" sound focuses attention on this particular image. There is, of course, the sound association with the word "ringing," which combines with the image of the persona "swinging in the sky" to create the metaphor of the Smoke King's words pealing out like a bell for all to hear. But the purpose of the words themselves is focused in "wring," which means "to twist forcibly." Hence, the Smoke King's aim is to change "the worlds," which would seem to be a reference to the two separate black and white worlds. And he wants this change to "twist" the worlds "away from the expected direction," that is, perhaps, to stop racism's effects on both black and white Americans.

Lines 5–7

The image of "smoke" takes the shape here of an idea, as well as of the smoke coming from the stacks of the factories where great numbers of blacks who had come north worked at low-paying jobs. The "thought" is the collective black memory of the extremes of labor in both the South and the North.

The use of the phrase "soul of the soul" is inextricably linked to Du Bois's own philosophy of the "two souls" of "Black Folk." Here it indicates that even after the excesses of killing labor imposed by whites through slavery and low-paying jobs there is a "soul" that lives.

"Wraith" means "a visible spirit," and probably refers to the ancestors of those who were kidnapped from Africa and brought over along trade routes to be sold into slavery in the United States. This suggests that it is vital to remember this history, the beginnings of the African American in the United States.

Lines 8–9

The Smoke King's image of "smoke," now identified with slave labor, rises from the land on which it has toiled and, as in "Swing Low, Sweet Chariot," carries itself home to God.

Lines 10–11

At this repetition of these lines the "Smoke King" becomes more than simply the light-skinned African American identifying with the darker "black" African American, but a true identification with what all African Americans have experienced as citizens of the United States.

Note that in line 2, "I am black!" is exclamatory, a proclamation. In line 11, it is stated, by use of the period, as a fact. Further note that this restatement is linked to the emotional historical content of the stanza by the use of the semicolon at the

Media Adaptations

- Du Bois, Marcus Garvey, and Booker T. Washington are the focus of a videocassette from Churchill Films called *Black Paths of Leadership,* narrated by William Marshall.

- "The Song of the Smoke" is included with poems from other African-American writers on the Audio Bookshelf recording *I, Too, Sing America,* released in 2000.

- W. E. B. Du Bois is interviewed on a Smithsonian Folkways Records 1993 cassette entitled *W. E. B. Du Bois: A Recorded Autobiography.*

- National Public Radio released a 1980 cassette with Douglas Turner Ward's renowned Negro Ensemble Company recreating Du Bois' life and times from his writings, entitled *A Sound Portrait of W. E. B. Du Bois.* It is part of their thirteen-part *A Question of Place* series.

end of line 9. Thus there is an equation between what is said prior to the semicolon and what comes in these two lines.

Lines 12–13

These lines take on the power of incantation at the beginning of this second stanza, and are now understood as well by the reader to provide a frame for the emotional memory of the history of the African American. Each stanza begins with the lines as proclamation, and each stanza concludes with their factual restatement.

Lines 14–15

The use of "wreathing" plays on a central alliterative sound used by the poet. It contrasts with "wringing" in line 4, as well as "awry." All of these words are defined as having to do with "twisting," although there is a gentler implication in "wreathing." The reference may be to these words soothing the broken hearts of African Americans at the time the poet is writing, but it also draws on the association of a wreath to honor the dead, and so honors the "broken hearts" of people kidnapped and sold into slavery, losing everything in the process.

The internal rhyme between "wreathing" and "sheathing" suggests also a gentleness, although "sheathing" might also refer to putting the "darts" into a sheath for use. In any case, these "darts" are "light" and they will be shot with "love." This likely means that the words of the Smoke King are spoken to both white and black out of love, though the words will be shot like "darts" to get the attention they deserve.

Lines 16–18

The Smoke King's words are inspired by the hard times his people have experienced; "iron" can also refer specifically to labor in northern factories. In fact, "[w]edding" is likely used to disclose that what the African American is expected to do in the North is not much different from the slave labor performed in the South. Both involve "bloodless" crimes, in that the conditions of labor under which African Americans have toiled are not intended for the purpose of individual murders or genocide of a people. Nonetheless, blood has been shed.

Lines 19–20

Alliteration and internal rhyme enhance the importance of these lines and their reference to contradictions inherent in two positions. The "blue" may refer to "high moral ground," to the Union Army whose victory brought about an end to slavery, or to being high in the sky. Hence, those whites who are at the top of the social structure in America, still do things that lower them. Contrarily, blacks who have been considered socially lower than whites, can bring themselves up toward truth, though this will require passionate ("torrid") involvement.

Lines 21–22

The matter of fact restatement of these two lines emphasizes the statement of the preceding lines 19–20. Furthermore, the lines are not "mere" restatement, but an idea closely connected to lines 14–20, as evidenced by the use of the comma at the end of line 20.

Lines 23–24

These lines become a chant that re-establishes the energy of identification with the history of the Smoke King's people.

Lines 25–26

The internal rhyme of "darkening" with "hearkening" links the purpose of these two lines, a purpose which is directly related to the poem itself through the use of the word "song." It is clear that the poet intends for this poem to inspire.

The Smoke King himself, despite his light skin, is accepting his place alongside darker blacks. Reciting his emotional history through this poem deepens his association with African Americans and allows him to understand that the wrongs that have been perpetrated on his people historically— and on each and every one of his people now—are done to him as well. This may also be a reference to the fact that a similar kind of wrong is done by blacks who line themselves up against a color line from lighter to darker.

Lines 27–29

Each line emphasizes the focus on "black." The Smoke King promises to be "black" in every possible way, historically, culturally, and politically. Thus in line 28 "black" comes to mean the race or group of the Smoke King's people, rather than a color which can be judged along a continuum from lighter to darker. Furthermore, the full acceptance of being "black," with all the historical and cultural burdens it might carry with it, is how African Americans will gain true power. The reference in line 29 is to the common knowledge that humans first appeared on this earth on the African continent. It is a reminder that even though whites believe themselves superior, the original human was black.

Lines 30–31

The Smoke King is claiming God for himself. Typically black has been associated with evil and white with good, so that Heaven is seen in visions of whiteness. The Smoke King transposes this. The reference to "swabbing Hell in white" likely refers to the fact that African Americans through kidnapping and slavery, as well as conditions of labor and culture, experienced hell on earth at the hands of whites.

Lines 32–33

The colon at the close of line 31 indicates that it is as a result of what is said in lines 25–31 that the Smoke King can make this statement.

Lines 34–35

It is because of the strengthening connection of these lines as statement at the close of each stanza—through use of comma, then semicolon, then colon—that the repetition as proclamation gains power as introduction to each succeeding stanza.

Lines 36–37

The power now established by lines 34–35 allows the Smoke King to "curse" the morning over the night. Again, this refers to an association of "black" with night, "white" with day, and by the use of the word "ruddy" refers back to the "blood" of the second stanza.

This power also manifests itself in the knowledge that to accept all of African-American history, to remember the slavery as well as the African heritage, is vital. In effect, the Smoke King sees this poem as a rehearsal for the song that African Americans as yet "unborn" will sing as they find their own hearts in the history of their people. Another interpretation of this line, however, might be that the "broken hearts" of line 14 were never truly born because they never truly lived, thus the "wreathing" of line 14 is brought into play here with "hearsing," so that the Smoke King is finally memorializing those who were cheated of African life through kidnapping and American life through slavery.

Lines 38–40

The connotation of night, with darkness and blackness, is given beauty and light through the placement in it of stars which are souls. It seems as if the Smoke King is using his association with God, begun in the first stanza, to emphasize that no soul is black or white. A further interpretation might be that shades of blackness and lightness are also irrelevant, for the color or shade of color of a person's skin has nothing to do with a human being's strength of purpose. Thus, again is sounded a call for all African Americans to identify—as black—with one another.

Lines 41–42

"Hail!" is a salute to the slaves, characterized as "hands," who labored for America. Though the slave past is "gritty" and "grimy," it is "great," and should be remembered and acknowledged as the past of African Americans. In fact, the Smoke King calls to the son of God to pity those hands which toiled on these lands.

Lines 43–44

The final chant of these two lines stands alone as an independent statement, signalled by the exclamation point at the end of line 42. This would seem to indicate that it is only through acceptance

Topics for Further Study

- In his later life, Du Bois joined the Communist Party and eventually left America to avoid harassment by the government. Read about his ideas on race relations in the 1960s and point out places in this 1907 poem that anticipate these later views.

- Find a contemporary song that you think carries the same message as this poem and point out the similarities and the differences.

- The poem makes much of the black man's ability to do physical labor, hailing "great, gritty, grimy hands." Given that this is an age of information, do you think that the capacity for manual work is still considered a positive trait? Why or why not?

- Research scientific theories about the original human beings, *homo erectus,* who first appeared on the African continent nearly 1.7 million years ago.

- Du Bois, a brilliant scholar, was the first black man to graduate from Harvard University with a Ph.D. Research the story of James Meredith, a black air force veteran whose enrollment into the University of Mississippi sparked violent protests in 1962. Report on the tension between state and federal lawmakers at that time.

of the past history of blacks as Africans and as American slaves that blacks can move forward into an identity which is independent, which in fact we now refer to as African American.

Themes

Race

This poem's historical significance is that it presents a bold, defiant image of the black man at a time when black men, especially in the South, were routinely persecuted and even murdered for such harmless activities as talking to a white woman or walking into a bar or restaurant reserved for whites. There has always been a social division between blacks and whites in America, and when that division has meant competition, the whites have always had the upper hand. "The Song of the Smoke," published more than forty years after the end of slavery, shows readers how little had changed in society since blacks had been freed. At the same time, it showed progress in the very fact that a black writer could speak so freely and intelligently about the oppression of his race, inviting the hatred of insecure whites who felt that any gain for blacks was a loss for themselves. Instead of treating blackness as something that one should be ashamed of, which would have been something of an admission that being black was the same as being inferior, the speaker of this poem embraces his blackness and proudly declares that he is "darkening" and is glad to do it because "the blacker the mantle, the mightier the man!" Insecure whites may have felt threatened by this stance, but insecure blacks received the message that not only were they not inferior but they were superior. In this way, the poem redefined assumptions that had previously been held by members of both races.

Good and Evil

It would be easy to interpret this poem as a statement that blackness represents all that is good and whiteness is a sign of evil, especially if one focuses attention on lines 30–31, where the speaker says, "I am daubing God in night, / I am swabbing Hell in white." Such a simple reading, however, does not take into account the overall mood of the poem. Though it does, in fact, make a point of asserting the good things about blackness, and does so at the expense of whiteness, the social context that Du Bois was writing in has to be considered. This poem makes more sense when understood against the perceptions of different races that were common then. It is an unfortunate coincidence that the English language uses the word "black" to refer both to the descendants of Africa and to the mysteries of evil, whereas "white" is used to represent both Caucasians and virginal purity. This trick of the language often serves, if only on a subconscious level, to encourage the stereotypical attitude that is held by some blacks and whites about the morality of the two races. "The Song of the Smoke" is not so simple that it would merely reverse the old stereotypes, as the two lines already mentioned might indicate, but it does soften these old beliefs so that neither color and neither race can be associated with absolute good or evil. In line 39, the poem states that neither race is completely made of one color or the other. In line 40, it settles the question of color and morality by asserting that skin color is irrelevant to a moral person, separating black and white from the question of good or bad. The overall assertion that black is good was necessary, given the prevailing prejudices of the early twentieth century, to move many readers toward the position that blackness is not bad.

Vitality

One of the main achievements of this poem is the way that it made its readers conscious of the power and vitality of African Americans. The old stereotype that Du Bois had to work against was one that presented blacks as "shiftless" and lazy—this idea grew out of the lack of initiative or curiosity that whites observed when the two races had any interaction with each other. The irony of this stereotype is that white society discouraged blacks from taking initiative but then frowned on their passivity. Blacks were forced to do the detestable jobs that whites would not touch, and the ones who tried to avoid this work were considered lazy. Blacks, disenfranchised from the dominant social situation, had little motivation to approach anything that they did with enthusiasm, which gave whites more reason to call them too lazy and unintelligent to participate in the social system, in a classic example of a self-fulfilling prophesy.

"The Song of the Smoke" presents a black speaker who is proud, powerful, intelligent and in control of his world. Instead of taking an apologetic attitude about black history, this poem embraces it, even with all of the hardships involved, and celebrates the obstacles that African Americans have overcome. Each stanza begins with the same two lines, proclaiming the speaker's blackness and claiming his royal status. The poem uses powerful-sounding words, including "throbbing," "toil," "towering," "cursing," "gritty," and "grimy," that all suggest action and accomplishment. For audiences who were used to thinking of black people as being passive, after generations of social institutions that were designed to break their spirits, the vitality expressed in this poem must have been shocking and perhaps a little frightening.

Order and Disorder

The image of smoke that Du Bois used to represent black pride seems somewhat inappropriate, since smoke is passive and unable to accomplish much by itself. Smoke is dark, but it does not have the destructive, frightening power that fire does. The use of this metaphor is important to the poem's meaning because it puts Du Bois's intention in sharper focus. This is not a radical poem that calls upon blacks to destroy things. Smoke billows in confusing, unexpected patterns, and it obscures vision. The words of the poem do not call for the destruction of society so much as they suggest that the rigid social rules should be less clearly defined. In some cases, the language that Du Bois uses is also confusing, with references to "toiling climes" and "hearsing hearts": phrases such as these can have two or more interpretations, but the poet obviously does not want to provide readers with any clear understanding. The poem is as inexact as its speaker wants the social order to be. It does not try to make any claims about what black people will or can do, only that, like smoke, they have a great presence and rise up toward heaven.

Style

"The Song of the Smoke" is a story-song in the tradition of ballads vocally communicated before they were ever written down. As a poetic form, the ballad preserves the notion of storytelling as well as the musicality—though the poem as ballad is rarely sung unless it is set to music, for example, as Paul Simon has done with Edwin Arlington Robinson's *"Richard Cory."*

Music is of course central to the ballad. The musicality of this poem is achieved by two distinct methods. First, the lengths of the lines in each of five blocks in a stanza are similar because the rhythm of the words creates corresponding musical patterns in blocks of 2 lines, 2 lines, 3 lines, 2 lines, and 2 lines in each of the four stanzas. The rhyme scheme of *abccdddeeab* further establishes this musical pattern or rhythm.

Secondly, "The Song of the Smoke" has a unique pattern of indention to signal the rhythm specific to each line-block. While this poem has appeared in several variations with significant alteration of the words, the most prominent difference has been in the setup of the line-blocks. The original version of the poem has the stanzas in three line-blocks each. Another version uses no indention pattern at all, setting the lines into eleven stanzas of varying line lengths. Some versions however, indent the stanzas into five line-blocks each, emphasizing the musical correspondence of rhyme scheme, rhythm pattern, and length of the lines in each block. In addition, this indention into five blocks emphasizes the repetition of the opening two lines throughout the poem by consistently setting them off at both the beginning and end of each stanza. This creates a chant or refrain that strongly reinforces the concept of this poem as a song.

The sounds of the words themselves accentuate the musicality of the poem. Alliteration manifests itself strongly in the word choices the poet makes. For example, in lines 3 and 4 of the first stanza, note the "s" of "swinging in the sky," and the "wr" and "w" of "wringing worlds awry." There is further emphasis on sound in the use of internal rhyme, exemplified in the third and fourth lines of the third stanza, "I am darkening with song, / I am hearkening to wrong!"

In addition to selection of words for their sounds, the poet pays considerable attention to the connotations of words associated with "black" (as in the word "smoke" itself, "iron," and "darkening") and with "white," as in the third and fourth stanzas, where the connotations of black and white are transposed.

Du Bois's poem presents this historical narrative of the African American in the first person "I," as if all African Americans are speaking in one voice, or as if one individual voice tells the story. The benefit of this, from Du Bois's political point of view, is that any individual African-American voice can speak this poem and experience the "author-ity" of these words. Du Bois's extensive body of work represents his mission: to place firmly in the minds of African Americans a recognition of their cultural and economic importance in order to create a sense of the rights and responsibilities of the African-American community.

Historical Context

Migration to the North

During the first decade of the twentieth century, there was a social shift in the American population. Before that time, the American economy had been primarily based upon agricultural production. The early 1900s coincided with a worldwide trend toward industrialization. Huge manufacturing plants grew up in cities. United States Steel, for example, started in 1901 with an initial investment of one billion dollars, which was twice the size of the United States government's budget for that year. In almost all industries, from building materials to petroleum to common household goods, the trend was to consolidate resources into larger, unified production facilities. Most of these were located in the northern states, which had had a history of manufacturing since the country began, with the South, because of its more temperate climate, focusing on agriculture. Workers from all over the world were drawn to the jobs that became available in cities across the northern states. Between 1900 and 1910, the population of the country grew an astonishing 21 percent, mostly from the influx of immigrants who came for jobs.

Between the end of slavery, with the Confederacy's defeat in the Civil War in 1865, and the turn of the century, two-thirds of African Americans remained in the South, where they lived under the pressures of discriminatory laws. These laws, referred to collectively as "Jim Crow" laws (after the name of a foolish black character in a 1832 minstrel show), were designed to limit where blacks could live, where they could work, where they could shop or congregate. To keep blacks from gaining the political power to change the laws, methods were devised to keep them from voting, with taxes and literacy tests administered unfairly at polling places. As the European population migrated to cities in the northern United States in search of work, so did blacks from the South. There, they still found discrimination, but they also found more opportunity than they had known previously. Colleges and newspapers gave urban blacks a sense of community that the South's violent traditions had repressed.

The Niagara Movement

In the summer of 1905, Du Bois and a coalition of twenty-nine prominent African Americans from fourteen states met at Niagara Falls, Ontario, for the purpose of drafting a manifesto calling for the end of racial discrimination in America. Their meeting was kept secret and had the main purpose of addressing the racial problem from an entirely black perspective, with no involvement from whites or support from white contributors. The manifesto that was developed at the Niagara meeting, which Du Bois helped write, called for complete self-determination for blacks and demanded equal rights, including the right to vote freely and to enjoy unhindered economic growth and open access to the political system. At the time, these simple tenants of equal protection that are taken for granted today were unheard of. The organization that came out of that meeting, called the Niagara Movement, became well known, although the con-

Compare & Contrast

- **1907:** Racial discrimination is considered legal after the Supreme Court allows for "separate but equal" accommodations for blacks and whites in the 1896 *Plessy v. Ferguson* case. Housing, transportation and medical facilities for black Americans are often not "equal," but inferior.

    Today: Federal laws strictly prohibit discrimination based on race.

- **1907:** African-American political theory is divided between the pragmatic accommodationist theories of Booker T. Washington and W. E. B. Du Bois's view that blacks should be independent and resist social injustices against them.

    Today: Despite social gains made toward equality, the same basic attitudes about African-American progress prevail among political leaders like Reverend Jesse Jackson, who works within the political system, and Reverend Louis Farrakhan, who supports self-determination for blacks.

- **1907:** An African American accused of a crime faces the likelihood of being lynched by vigilantes before standing trial, especially in the South.

    Today: In spite of gains made toward racial equality, there are still frequent accusations of unfair treatment of blacks within the criminal justice system.

- **1907:** America is a magnet for immigration: 1.29 million immigrants enter the country this year.

    Today: The country still has not received as many immigrants in a single year as it did in 1907.

- **1907:** The frustrations of racial segregation leads to race riots spontaneously breaking out in urban centers, such as Brownsville, Texas, in 1906 and Springfield, Massachusetts, in 1908.

    Today: After the turbulent and violent period of the 1960s, race riots have become rare. The most recent and notorious happens after the acquittal of policemen charged with beating black motorist Rodney King in 1992, triggering the worst violence and looting in U.S. history.

---

troversial positions it took kept people from joining it. The group went around the country, holding meetings with local black leaders in such historically significant locales as Harpers' Ferry, West Virginia, where an important rebellion against slavery was held in 1859, and Faneuil Hall in Boston where rebels met during America's colonial period to plan the Revolutionary War. Many years later, in a 1948 essay entitled "The Negro Since 1900: A Progress Report," Du Bois wrote that the Niagara Movement was "the first clear-cut demand for full citizenship rights in the twentieth century."

The movement expanded to include thirty local branches across the county and was successful in promoting the cause of racial equality in a few cases, but its existence was short-lived. Weak finances and restrictive enrollment policies that limited membership to a core of black intellectuals kept it from gaining widespread attention. A massive race riot in Springfield, Illinois, drew national attention to the problems faced by African Americans, and many white supporters became interested in supporting the cause of equality; the following year, the National Association for the Advancement of Colored People was formed. W. E. B. Du Bois shifted his affiliation from the Niagara Movement to the NAACP, and the earlier movement, having lost its most prominent member, disbanded in 1910.

The NAACP

The National Association for the Advancement of Colored People was formed in 1909 by three white supporters of civil rights: William English Walling, Mary White Ovington, and Dr. Henry Moskowitz. The three headed a conference on the problem of race in America, and from that conference came a series of meetings to establish the goals and formalize the rules of a nationwide organization. At first the group was named the National Negro Committee, changing its name the following year to the title that is familiar today. Du Bois joined the NAACP in 1910, convinced that an interracial group would be more effective to address the country's prejudices than a segregated group like the Niagara Movement. He became the Director of Publications and Research for the new group and its most prominent black member. For almost twenty-five years he was the editor of *Crisis,* the NAACP's official publication, giving it a level of serious national attention that such a publication normally would not have enjoyed.

The NAACP soon became a dominant voice in the struggle for civil rights. Throughout most of the twentieth century, the group was involved in all issues involving racial equality. Its role extended beyond discussion of the issues with the formation of the NAACP Legal Defense Fund, which was instrumental in providing representation for black defendants and for challenging racially biased laws. In the early years, the group provided resistance to hate groups such as the new Ku Klux Klan, which sought to promote white dominance through murder and intimidation. After World War II, the NAACP was more active in broader issues of equality, providing support for lawsuits that opened housing and education opportunities for all races. After the radical movements of the 1960s and 1970s, the NAACP, by then an established organization, seemed old-fashioned and even conservative. Today, the group, having hit its height of popularity in the 1950s, faces declining interest from young people who do not recognize its significance.

Critical Overview

"The Song of the Smoke" was initially published in 1907, between the time Du Bois was involved in the 1905 organization of the "radical" Niagara Movement (which demanded civil rights and other basic freedoms for black Americans), and his position as the only black founding member of the NAACP in 1909. By this time Du Bois had realized that if the African American "is regarded as an inferior creation, who can never successfully take a part in modern civilization and whose emancipation and enfranchisement were gestures against nature, then he will need something more than the sort of facts that I have set down [as a scholar]." He was, as Darwin T. Turner has noted, "a social scientist and a political leader who considered art—especially literature—to be a vehicle for enunciating and effecting social, political, and economic ideas."

Consequently, Du Bois wrote many novels and plays, as well as essays and scholarly works, and composed enough poems to fill a respectable book. He was, furthermore, as Arnold Rampersad acknowledges, the first African-American poet to "resist the concept of poetry as escape from social and political reality." As a matter of fact, his perception of the need for action against American racism was likely responsible for the belief articulated later in his life that "[a]ll art is propaganda" and that the art of black Americans had to act as propaganda "for gaining the right of black folk to love and enjoy." Turner indicates that this statement prefigured the pronouncement of the Black Aesthetic movement of the 1960s, which maintained that African Americans should "define the excellence of the artistic work according to black people's concepts of beauty."

In fact, it was Du Bois's *The Souls of Black Folk,* a book of essays published in 1903, that provided the philosophical and creative ground for "The Song of the Smoke." The essays explore the "twoness" of being both black and American, borrowing for a theoretical base the concept of "double consciousness" propounded by such leading psychologists of the time as Du Bois's former Harvard professor William James. In this book of essays Du Bois addresses the idea of the invisibility of blacks as a result of slavery and racism, suggesting also that blacks are constrained by American culture to deal with their "two souls" in, as Rampersad sees it, "a contest between memory... and amnesia" with regard to slavery and Africa. It was in this book that Du Bois established "slavery as metaphor for the black experience." Accordingly, "The Song of the Smoke," as Michael J. C. Echeruo interprets the poem, moves through "a specific cultivation of blackness that changes the contextual meaning of the word, from a generalised euphemism for the enslaved to a precise identification of a person."

But even though Rampersad declares "The Song of the Smoke" to be "the first [poem] to celebrate the beauty of human blackness," he considers that Du Bois had little real genius for the practice of art. His ultimate appraisal of Du Bois's work as a poet and novelist is that it would not have achieved critical acclaim without his other accomplishments, but that all these together "extend our understanding of the history and character of his people and, indeed, of humanism itself." Thus Du Bois accomplished, finally, what he embraced as "'the bounden duty of black America' to create, preserve, and realize 'Beauty' for America, for the aim of art and political struggle was not black power in isolation but a philosophically reconstructed universe." This poem with its proclamation that "[s]ouls unto me are as stars in a night," begins this reconstruction.

Criticism

David Kelly

Kelly is a fiction writer and playwright who teaches at two colleges in Illinois. In the following essay, he argues that W. E. B. Du Bois's poem "The Song of the Smoke" is under-appreciated by readers who ignore its artistic use of unclear language and focus on its message but not its form.

Like the works of many pioneering African-American authors, W. E. B. Du Bois's 1907 poem "The Song of the Smoke" is often recognized for its social message, but far too seldom is it given credit for its achievement as a work of art. The fact that art is often subject to individual impressions does not mean that it can be anything that any person wants to say it is: in its most basic sense, artistry can be defined by the way that the form of a piece is used to highlight its message. In the case of Du Bois, as with so many writers who raise social concerns, critics tend to spend more time looking at *what* the poem says, skipping over the details about *how* its message is conveyed. Beyond its message, there is much about the style of "The Song of the Smoke" that proves Du Bois to have been wise in his instincts as a poet, as prudent as artists with much greater reputations.

Even a beginning poetry reader can tell that the basis of this poem's structure is repetition. The phrases "I am the Smoke King" and "I am black" appear eight times each, in the very eye-catching positions at the beginning and the end of each stanza, where even lines that are not repeated would draw attention to themselves. In addition to these, the phrase "I am" (or sometimes "I'm") appears another fourteen times. Readers certainly cannot

> *The tight structure Du Bois uses serves as a constant reminder of the author's control, keeping readers aware of the fact that the ideas are results of intelligent consideration."*

come away from this poem without recognizing it as a declaration about its speaker's identity.

Judging from just these most-repeated lines alone, the identity of the speaker of this poem can be said to be made up of three main elements: blackness, kingliness, and something more vague, which can be identified as "smokiness." It is clearly part of the poem's social agenda to assert over and over again the connection between being black and being king, in order to reverse the white culture's under-appreciation of the abilities of blacks. The other main component is left a mystery, though. Readers can tell right away that smoke implies darkness, but in addition to darkness, it also has many other implications that are not nearly so easy to understand.

Du Bois's use of metaphor in "The Song of the Smoke" shows a poetic gift that is too seldom recognized. The meaning of smoke, which is given so much attention, is almost as difficult for the human mind to take hold of as actual smoke is to wrap one's fingers around. Of course, smoke means darkness, in the poem as in life, but any number of clearer images could have been used to represent darkness. It also means danger, although this seems to be only a small part of Du Bois's meaning, if it is a part of it at all. After darkness, the most salient meaning of smoke seems to be its lack of solidity, the fact that its shape is constantly changing. Many critics who think of Du Bois as a militant figure have trouble appreciating this emphasis on adaptability, especially when they are used to thinking of him in contrast to his contemporary, Booker T. Washington, whose message for the African-American community is often summarized as accommodation. It would be too easy to just forget about the idea of the smoke metaphor or to think that it does not fit in with the meaning of the poem. Many of the images

Topics for Further Study

- Many of the most important writings of Du Bois's long and distinguished career are collected in *W. E. B. Du Bois: A Reader,* edited and with an introduction by Meyer Weinburg, and originally published in 1970.

- *Autobiography of a People* (2000) is a compilation of writings by African Americans from the Colonial period to today, edited by Herb Boyd with a forward by Gordon Parks, and showing the melding of the African and American cultures into a single identity.

- James Weldon Johnson was a black author who wrote around the same time that Du Bois did. He was active with the National Association for the Advancement of Colored People (NAACP) and became its first black executive secretary in 1916. His most famous book is the novel *Autobiography of an Ex-Colored Man* (1912), which examines race relations at the time.

- The Harlem Renaissance, an artistic movement among African-American writers and scholars, is thought to have begun with Jean Toomer's 1923 book *Cane,* a collection of poems, vignettes, and stories about life in the South and the systematic destruction of the self-esteem of blacks, especially men.

- Langston Hughes was an African-American poet, playwright and short story writer of the generation after Du Bois. He looked at the tragedy of race with more humor. His poems are available in *The Collected Poems of Langston Hughes*, 1994.

- Du Bois' most influential work was his 1903 book *The Souls of Black Folk,* his semi-autobiographical musings on American life after the Reconstruction period.

here imply power and concrete hardness, with iron, molls, and toil, and there are also representations of flesh as hide or a mantle. Critics familiar with Du Bois's political views have mixed his politics with the aforementioned images of power and ended up interpreting the meaning of smoke in only one limited way.

It makes sense, though, that Du Bois would use the smoke image to contrast, not complement, the ruggedness that he ascribes to his people. The use of opposites gives his subject matter more range: it claims for the black people the multifaceted ability to be both hard-working toilers and also angelic spirits in flight. The contradictory imagery could have backfired, if Du Bois had not handled it with great care, but here it invests African Americans with a well-rounded wholeness.

The same strategy of pasting opposites together works for the poem's overall design. It is a careful, skillful mixture of a form that is strictly followed and a verbal looseness that makes "The Song of the Smoke" look, at times, as if Du Bois might have just written what came off the top of his head.

At times, the poem seems to be too tied up by the form, with every line in the last three stanzas committed to following the pattern that is established in the first one. The rhyme scheme repeats in exactly the same way time after time, the physical layout of indented lines stays the same, and, as mentioned, the same two lines repeat constantly, showing up twice in each stanza. This rigid adherence to form gives the poem a sense of tradition, of seriousness, as if the ideas being expressed are already carved in marble as universal truths. The tight structure Du Bois uses serves as a constant reminder of the author's control, keeping readers aware of the fact that the ideas are results of intelligent consideration.

The words Du Bois uses do not give this impression. They struggle against clear-cut interpretation. They seem carefully placed to match the sounds of one another, almost compulsively so, with no freedom allowed, a technique that allows little room for meaning. Not only are there solid blocks of end-rhymes (such as "mills/kills/rills" and "times/chimes/crimes"), but there are also rhymes within the third and fourth lines of each stanza. This emphasis on the sounds of words is actually what gives the poem its sense of freedom, even while seeming to make it a slave to structure. Even after going over it a dozen times, readers find themselves unable to grasp Du Bois's meaning, a marked contrast from the way that they "get" the rhythm and rhyme scheme almost immediately. Is there really any concrete way to understand a statement like "I am the soul of the soul-toil kills" or

"Sweet Christ, pity toiling lands"? Lines like these give a general impression of toiling and proud defiance, but the words do not come together in any clear way. They relate more in the way their sounds fit into a pattern than in the interaction of the meanings of the various words. There seems to be meaning, but it swirls out of grasp when a reader tries to grasp it: like smoke, it floats off into the air.

There has always been strong resistance to the idea that Du Bois may have meant the language in his poetry not to be precise in meaning. Critics who find it difficult to understand tend to look deeper and deeper, certain that there is something there, more often than not certain that it contains a hidden message about the black experience. Black American poets have often had their works examined in terms of their race, whether it is directly related to their subject matter or not. Only sometimes is this a case of crude stereotyping, of critics failing to recognize people's individuality. There is a positive side to reminding readers of the racial background of a writer of color: it tends to remind the world of black achievements and to counteract the old stereotypes about blacks' intellectual achievements. In the case of W. E. B. Du Bois, the fear of overemphasizing his race is moot, since he was so acutely aware of the place of blacks in the white-dominated American society and he worked to point out cultural inequality in just about everything that he wrote. Because of the seriousness of Du Bois's subject matter, readers tend to miss the fact that his poetry works because his use of language is simple, even light-hearted.

The dominant theme that runs through most of Du Bois's works over a career that spanned more than sixty years is a simple one: fairness. Readers tend to miss this. There are several reasons for not accepting the obvious. First, Du Bois is often characterized as an angry writer, calling for equality at a time when the field of black writers willing to express open dissatisfaction was extremely thin. Another was that he *was* angry if compared to Booker T. Washington, his intellectual opponent who favored a more timid approach to black dignity. Finally, there is the force of Du Bois's growing reputation: "fairness" seems a bit mild for a hero, and he is more often described loftily as a champion for the cause of justice. The difference in words is that one concept is somber, and the other is a simple, obvious way of life. The fairness that Du Bois championed throughout his life was not a prize; it was just, basically and obviously, the way things should be.

Readers need to look at a poem like "The Song of the Smoke" as a poem, not as a political statement. It uses words and poetic techniques to make its points, and the methods that it does use cannot be ignored. If the structure is rigid, it should be questioned; if the words do not completely make sense, readers need to ask whether there is a reason for this. It is misleading to think that these confusing aspects come from Du Bois's intellectualism or from his racial identity. They come from the requirements of art, and the poem manages to go beyond clarity in order to satisfy its own artistic requirements.

Source: David Kelly, Critical Essay on "The Song of the Smoke," in *Poetry for Students,* The Gale Group, 2001.

Erica Smith

Smith is a writer and editor. In this essay, she discusses how W. E. B. DuBois's "The Song of the Smoke" is poised within a critical moment in African-American history, reflecting the painful legacy of slavery in North America yet looking with hope toward the future.

W. E. B. Du Bois's poem "The Song of the Smoke" is a powerful statement on what it means to be an African American. Written in the early years of the twentieth century, it looks both back to the past, finding strength and sorrow in the legacy of the slave, and toward the future, hoping to find a new strength and dignity that all African Americans can unite behind.

The poem follows a song structure, including the repetition of a refrain ("I am the Smoke King / I am black"). On the one hand, this looks backward into the English folk poetry tradition, which often included song forms such as the ballad; on the other, it looks back to the rich tradition of African-American music, including the work songs sung by the slaves in the fields. The poem is filled with multiple associations and meanings like this.

Like much of Du Bois's work, this poem has a charged political content, a content that is served and exemplified by the multiple meanings that can be associated with almost every line of the poem. In his provocative and influential collection of essays, *The Souls of Black Folk* (1903), Du Bois had argued that African Americans were forever conscious of having a "twoness" of their souls—being American and, at the same time, black. The ambiguity of the poem is a literary illustration of this idea: the multiple possible meanings can be seen as reflecting the multiple ways that African Americans were forced to exist in American society. Yet,

> "The future seems destined to be the same as the present and the past for African Americans: thus, the Smoke King curses the 'ruddy morn' and, worse still, is 'hearsing hearts unborn'; for those who are born under discrimination can be said to have almost died before they were born."

almost paradoxically, the thrust of the poem is toward unity—toward fusing the often divided African-American community into a single, powerful black community.

The poem is written in the present tense, but it is almost impossible to understand its full meaning without understanding African-American history. Again, this device serves to demonstrate in a literary fashion the fact that the African-American experience is dominated by the long period in which African Americans were held as slaves in America. It also makes a subtle but potent connection between that time and the time the poem was written (1907), seemingly arguing that there is not a great deal of difference between the status of African Americans in the two times.

"The Song of the Smoke" is a poem of action and motion. Things are constantly happening in the poem; almost every important word ends in "ing." Thus, while steeped in history, the poem also conveys a sense of constant motion upwards, like the smoke "whirling home to God" in line 9. Again, this reflects Du Bois's own political views; he spent a lifetime tirelessly working for the betterment of conditions for African Americans, and he was a strong believer in African Americans lifting themselves up, without relying on white people to help them.

The poem's first two lines are repeated as a refrain throughout the poem, beginning and ending each stanza. The simple line "I am the Smoke King" contains a world of meaning. For one thing, it may refer to Du Bois's own skin color: he was a lightly-colored African-American man, a trait that was considered desirable by many African Americans at the time. Thus, his exclamation "I am black!" is a defiant cry of solidarity with all people of African descent as well as an expression of his determination not to seek preferential treatment based on his skin color. (After all, giving people different treatment because of their skin color is exactly what he spent his lifetime arguing against.) At the same time, the line "I am the Smoke King" may well represent the rise of American industry, particularly in the North. At the time the poem was written, many African Americans in the South existed in conditions of almost total economic bondage to the whites that owned the land, and discrimination prevented them from getting any jobs but the most menial. Northern industry, by providing jobs to African Americans, offered an escape from this suffocating condition. Also, industry was popularly seen as representing progress, the way to a new future, a future in which Du Bois wanted African Americans to participate. Finally, the identification of African Americans with smoke may be a reference to their rising from the ashes of slavery and the fires of the Civil War that had consumed the old slaveholding society. It may also serve as a subtle reminder that African Americans could not be expected to accept discrimination forever without fighting back: where there's smoke, after all, there's a fire as well.

Most importantly, however, the lines defiantly say that the speaker is not only black but that he is royalty—the Smoke King. This reflects a determination not only to stand up and be proud of that which the whites saw as hateful—being dark-skinned—but to take command of one's own destiny. Thus, the Smoke King is "wringing worlds awry" (line 4) by refusing to accept the role a racist society wishes to force on him.

The poem's second stanza is a bitter commentary on both the past and the present conditions of African Americans. There is the recognition that the ambitions, both public and private, of black Americans are dashed—hearts are broken, love seems impossible—but that by offering a new vision of pride in being black, the Smoke King hopes to focus and unite this suffering, healing it by breaking the pattern of racial discrimination.

Du Bois also illustrates in this stanza how much American society owes to the labor of African Americans, who "Wedd[ed] the toiling climes" (both America and Africa and the North and the South) and shed the blood of the "bloodless crimes," in this case not just slavery but the second-class status given to African Americans after the Civil War. The stanza concludes with an image of smoke hovering in the sky ("Lurid lowering 'mid the blue"). Given the popular identification of "heaven" with "sky," it can be said that Du Bois is trying to remind readers that while America might almost be a paradise for whites, it will still be flawed until racial prejudice is conquered; the next line is a reminder that African Americans will not be content to wait; they demand justice now.

The third stanza is a fantastic outburst of pride in being black, and it also clearly reminds the reader that God, who is just, is on the side of African Americans, who are unjustly persecuted. The powerful lines "I am daubing God in night / I am swabbing Hell in white" are a pointed reminder that in Christian belief it must be the innocent victims of white oppression that rise to Heaven to be with God ("daubing him with night") while their oppressors must descend to Hell. In a country that still managed to equate lightness of skin with godliness, this was a powerful statement, one that still has application to readers' own times.

The last stanza of the poem, however, is more pessimistic. The future seems destined to be the same as the present and the past for African Americans: thus, the Smoke King curses the "ruddy morn" and, worse still, is "hearsing hearts unborn"; for those who are born under discrimination can be said to have almost died before they were born. Yet at the same time, souls sparkle like stars out of the blackness of night—again demonstrating that out of blackness, that which the white people despise, incomparable beauty can shine forth. And in an arresting pairing of images, the Smoke King notes that "I whiten my black men—I blacken my white!" In this simple sentence, Du Bois cuts to the heart of the true cost of racial discrimination in America. The suffering undergone by African Americans ennobles them in a certain way: as noted in the third stanza, it lifts them up to God, who judges all men; at the same time, white people, who have discriminated against African Americans, are degraded by their own prejudice. Racial prejudice thus destroys the lives of everyone it touches, robbing African Americans of their futures, and causing white people to live in a world of hypocrisy, where the nearly sacred words of the Declaration of Independence—that all men are created equal—are reduced to a hollow mockery. Thus, the great cry that occurs in the next line (line 40), "What's the hue of a hide to a man in his might?" is not a call for brotherhood between the races, but the desperate plea for a world in which the color of a person's skin does not matter at all.

Since a religious tone has steadily been rising in the poem, it is fitting that it concludes with a prayer. (The frequent use of religious imagery in the poem may be a tacit acknowledgement of the important and influential role African-American preachers and ministers have played in the struggle against discrimination.) The prayer is, first, a call to black people to continue to better themselves through hard work ("Hail! great, gritty, grimy hands") and, second, a plea for pity from the Christian God over the "toiling lands," though whether this means the South, the North, or America as a whole is not indicated—nor does it matter much. For the most important message comes through, Du Bois's passionate plea that, united in a common history, African Americans must be united in a common pride in who they are and in a common determination to take control of their own destiny and change the future. Thus, the poem ends with its three most important words: "I am black."

Source: Erica Smith, Critical Essay on "The Song of the Smoke," in *Poetry for Students,* The Gale Group, 2001.

Sources

Du Bois, W. E. B. "The Negro Since 1900: A Progress Report," in *W. E. B. Du Bois: A Reader,* Harper & Rowe, 1970, pp. 89–98.

———, *The Souls of Black Folk,* Modern Library, 1996.

Echeruo, Michael J. C., "Edward W. Blyden, W. E. B. Du Bois, and the 'Color Complex,'" in *Journal of Modern African Studies,* Vol. 30, No. 4, 1992, pp. 669–84.

Rampersad, Arnold, "Slavery and the Literary Imagination: Du Bois's *The Souls of Black Folk,*" in *Slavery and the Literary Imagination,* edited by Deborah E. McDowell and Arnold Rampersad, Johns Hopkins University Press, 1989, pp. 104–24.

———, "W. E. B. Du Bois as a Man of Literature," in *American Literature,* Vol. 51, No. 1, March 1979, pp. 50–68.

"The Song of the Smoke," in *Exploring Poetry,* Gale Research, 1998.

Turner, Darwin T., "W. E. B. Du Bois and the Theory of a Black Aesthetic," in *The Harlem Renaissance Re-examined,* edited by Victor A. Kramer, AMS Press, 1987, pp. 9–30.

For Further Study

Banks, William M., *Black Intellectuals: Race and Responsibility in American Life,* W. W. Norton & Co., 1996.

Banks covers black intellectuals from history, like Du Bois, but he also examines the broader philosophical question of the relationship between intellectualism and the black community today.

Leamann, Nicholas, *The Promised Land: The Great Black Migration and How It Changed America,* Alfred A. Knopf, Inc., 1991.

This book, broken down by popular northern cities that blacks moved to from the South, explains how race relations in America changed between the 1940s and 1960s, making today's world different from the one Du Bois knew.

Marable, Manning, *W. E. B. Du Bois: Black Radical Democrat,* Twayne Publishers, 1986.

This biography offers a serious, yet easy-to-read, telling of Du Bois's life.

Zamir, Shamoon, *Dark Voices: W. E. B. Du Bois and American Thought, 1888–1903,* University of Chicago Press, 1995.

This book traces Du Bois's intellectual development and shows its roots in both the American and European philosophical traditions. One of the most focused and telling books ever written about Du Bois.

To His Excellency General Washington

Phillis Wheatley
1776

Phillis Wheatley's poem "To His Excellency General Washington" is as unique as the poet herself. The poem was sent to George Washington, the newly appointed Commander-in-Chief of the Armies of North America, in October of 1775, well before American Independence was declared in 1776. Washington, as busy as he was with organizing the colonies to take on the British, sent a letter back to Wheatley thanking her for the poem and inviting her to visit him if she ever came to Cambridge, Massachusetts. The two did meet in March of 1776, seven years before the war was finished and true independence was declared. Washington was roundly lauded in poems and prose *after* the successful conclusion of the Revolutionary War in 1783, but Wheatley's poem was written when the war's outcome was very uncertain, the British being the obvious favorites to win. It can be said that Wheatley was the groundbreaker in beginning the Washington legend as the "father of our country," yet she stands as a groundbreaker in even more important ways. In 1773, two years before this poem was written, Phillis Wheatley, a twenty-year-old slave, published her collection of poems entitled *Poems on Various Subjects, Religious and Moral,* the first book of poetry published by an African American, and only the second book by a woman in what would become the United States. Considering that Ms. Wheatley was bought at a slave auction in 1761, not able to read or write and incapable of speaking English, her book of poems is truly astounding. She was revered in many countries. Benjamin Franklin offered his services to her, as did many other high-

Phillis Wheatley

ranking men in America. In April of 1776, the author and political philosopher Thomas Paine published Wheatley's poem to Washington in *The Pennsylvania Magazine*. The central theme of this poem is "freedom's cause," the colonies' struggle for freedom from England, which General Washington was assigned to lead. Like many other residents of Boston, Wheatley's feelings for the British regime turned from obedient admiration to mild admonition, and finally, to support of the revolution. The poem anticipates the future for the new republic, and praises the efforts of its military leader and first president.

Author Biography

Wheatley was born in 1753 or 1754 in West Africa (present-day Senegal), kidnapped, and brought to New England in 1761. John Wheatley, a wealthy Boston merchant, bought her for his wife, Susanna, who wanted a youthful personal maid to serve her in her old age. Wheatley was frail and sickly, but her gentle, demure manner charmed Susanna. The child learned to read and write quickly and became proficient in Latin, so the Wheatleys assigned her only light housekeeping duties and encouraged her to study and write poetry. As a result, she achieved a high level of education rare for upper-class colo-

nial men, let alone women or slaves. In fact, Wheatley was treated less like a servant and more like a member of the Wheatley family. She was given a private, well-heated room and a lamp to use at night. She was free to visit with the Wheatleys' friends but forbidden to associate with other slaves.

It is believed that Wheatley began writing in 1765. Her poem "An Elegiac Poem, on the Death of That Celebrated Divine, and Eminent Servant of Jesus Christ, the Reverend and Learned George Whitefield" gained her national and international attention when it was published locally in 1770 as a broadside pamphlet and then reprinted in newspapers throughout the American colonies and in England. Wheatley continued to write elegies and honorific verses to commemorate the lives of friends and famous contemporaries as well as poems to celebrate important events.

Wheatley was freed from slavery three months before Susanna Wheatley's death in March 1774. She married John Peters on April 1, 1778. Peters was a free black man who worked as a lawyer and grocer, among other occupations, and was a writer and speaker. Peters eventually abandoned Wheatley and their three children, forcing Wheatley to work as a scullery maid in a rooming house. Two of her children died. Untrained for menial labor and physically frail, she died at the age of thirty-one on December 5, 1784. Her third child died within a few hours of Wheatley and was buried with her in an unmarked grave.

Poem Text

Celestial choir! enthron'd in realms of light,
   Columbia's scenes of glorious toils I write.
While freedom's cause her anxious breast alarms,
She flashes dreadful in refulgent arms.
See mother earth her offspring's fate bemoan,   5
And nations gaze at scenes before unknown!
See the bright beams of heaven's revolving light
Involved in sorrows and veil of night!

   The goddess comes, she moves divinely fair,
Olive and laurel bind her golden hair: 10
Wherever shines this native of the skies,
Unnumber'd charms and recent graces rise.

   Muse! bow propitious while my pen relates
How pour her armies through a thousand gates,
As when Eolus heaven's fair face deforms,   15
Enwrapp'd in tempest and a night of storms;
Astonish'd ocean feels the wild uproar,
The refluent surges beat the sounding shore;
Or thick as leaves in Autumn's golden reign,

Such, and so many, moves the warrior's train.   20
In bright array they seek the work of war,
Where high unfurl'd the ensign waves in air.
Shall I to Washington their praise recite?
Enough thou know'st them in the fields of fight.
Thee, first in peace and honours,—we demand   25
The grace and glory of thy martial band.
Fam'd for thy valour, for thy virtues more,
Hear every tongue thy guardian aid implore!

   One century scarce perform'd its destined
      round,
When Gallic powers Columbia's fury found;   30
And so may you, whoever dares disgrace
The land of freedom's heaven-defended race!
Fix'd are the eyes of the nations on the scales,
For in their hopes Columbia's arm prevails.
Anon Britannia droops the pensive head,   35
While round increase the rising hills of dead.
Ah! cruel blindness to Columbia's state!
Lament thy thirst of boundless power too late.

   Proceed, great chief, with virtue on thy side,
Thy ev'ry action let the goddess guide.   40
A crown, a mansion, and a throne that shine,
With gold unfading, WASHINGTON! be thine.

Poem Summary

Line 1
Celestial choir is the poet's muse, a device of neoclassicism. The muse is called on to inspire the poet's writing.

Line 2
"Columbia" was a term Wheatley used for America, later used by other writers.

Line 3
"Freedom's cause" is the central theme of the poem, the struggle of the colonists to be free from England, even if it meant going to war against the more powerful British.

Line 4
In this context, "dreadful" means "inspiring awe or reverence," "in refulgent arms" means "in brilliant defense." In this sense, Columbia (America) is portrayed in righteous terms for standing up against England.

Lines 5–6
The speaker of the poem points out that other countries are watching something unique occurring in the uprising. And as it turns out, the American Revolution directly inspired the French Revolution.

Lines 7–8
Heaven is affected by the struggle in a sorrowful way.

Lines 9–12
The poet describes the goddess of Freedom coming down from the heavens to become involved in the war. The ancient Greeks would use laurel to crown the victors in their games. An olive branch is a symbol of peace.

Lines 13–14
The poet calls on the muse again to be favorably disposed to inspire the poet in the retelling of the battles the American armies are going through.

Lines 15–19
The poet, through a simile, compares the American forces' battles to the power of Eolus, king of the winds.

Line 20
The "train" is the troops in file, as lining up in military formation.

Lines 21–22
The "ensign" is a flag decorated in national colors, or emblems, relating to the army displaying it. In this case, it would have been decorated with an emblem of the colonial armies sewn on it.

Lines 23–25
"Thee" is Washington, and the phrase "first in peace" is the most famous phrase in the poem, used later by Congress at Washington's funeral. There is some argument as to whether Wheatley wrote "first in peace" or "first in place," since, as commander-in-chief of the army, Washington would naturally be "first in place" over all the troops. Both versions have been published.

Lines 26–29
In 1620, a little over one hundred years before the writing of this poem, the Pilgrims first landed at Plymouth Rock.

Line 30
France was considered a strong country, skilled at warfare, with "Gallic" referring to the French.

Media Adaptations

- Phillis Wheatley, Harriet Tubman, Ida B. Wells Barnett, Sojourner Truth, and others are represented on Smithsonian Folkways' compact disc *The Negro Woman*, performed by Dorothy Washington.

- Wheatley's poem "On Liberty and Slavery" is included on an audiocassette collection from Audio Bookshelf entitled *I, Too, Sing America*, released in 2000.

- "To His Excellency George Washington" is included on an 1955 recording entitled *Anthology of Negro Poets in the USA*, edited by Arna Bontemps. It was re-released on cassette in 1992 by Smithsonian Folkways Records.

- In 1992, Smithsonian Folkways also released a cassette called *Blacks in the American Revolutionary War*, which covers individuals such as Wheatley and Crispus Atticus as well as blacks who served in the armed forces.

Lines 31–32

The speaker considers America's efforts sanctioned by heaven, and warns against those, such as England, who war against her.

Lines 33–34

The poet suggests the whole world is watching the outcome of the war, seeing which way the power may shift, hoping it may be toward the new nation.

Lines 35–38

England is described as old and tired, responsible for many deaths, inspired by a thirst for power. The colonists first tried to reason with England but had to settle for war to gain their independence.

Lines 39–42

The poet encourages Washington to continue his objective in gaining freedom for the colonists, and she argues that the goddess of Freedom is guiding his actions. If he follows the goddess and her virtue, the poet suggests that Washington will win the war and become the head of the new state.

Themes

Freedom

The date that Wheatley wrote this poem, 1776, is familiar to Americans with even the weakest sense of history as a date associated with freedom. It is mentioned every year on one of the nation's major holidays, the Fourth of July, as the date of the signing of the Declaration of Independence, which proclaimed that the colonies were no longer subject to the rule of England. In the poem, Wheatley not only asserts that America has a right to be free from British rule but goes so far as to identify America as the land of freedom. Although this poem does not make any reference to it, there is of course a good deal of irony implicit in the very fact of an African-American woman writing in 1776 to urge a white male to fight for freedom. In 1776, women were not allowed any political rights and were not even allowed to vote until the twentieth century, after decades of hard work by members of the suffrage movement. The vast majority of blacks in the colonies had even less freedom: in some Southern states, though there were as many or more blacks as whites, the blacks were slaves and subject to legal abuse for disobeying their owners. Though freedom for blacks and women was eventually won by people who stood up against the status quo and drew attention to unfairness, Phillis Wheatley was not in a position to address these concerns. Still, her poem did address an issue with which most citizens were concerned, and her praise of General Washington did serve to encourage the revolution against England. In a small, subtle way this advanced the cause of freedom for women and blacks by drawing attention to the intelligence and sensitivity of one of their rank.

Hero

In the poem, George Washington is referred to as a hero in the grandest tradition of the word, as the embodiment of all virtues that his society needs to save it from its enemies. The second stanza—the poem's longest one—lists the accomplishments of the armies under his command and then notes that it is useless to list such accomplishments for Washington, who is famed not only for his valor but for his virtue as well. A narrower sense of heroism, one that is used in everyday discourse, would claim great military might for the hero without mentioning moral righteousness. In this case, though, Wheatley claims for the hero every positive attribute possible, both physical and spiritual.

To some extent, it is unnecessary for the poem to praise Washington's military heroics because they had already been observed and accepted by all of the people of the United States. The praise that Wheatley heaps on Washington's prowess as a general in this poem is necessary for properly enumerating his accomplishments as a hero, but it represents the poem's least original thinking and may have been boring to readers and even to Washington himself, who had long since accepted his mastery of the battlefield. Wheatley goes beyond praising his accomplishments, though, and adds a dimension of righteousness to her praise of the man so that his accomplishments seem sanctioned by the will of God. The concept of a worldly hero who excels at his work is fine, but it is limited, especially when it is compared to the idea of a hero who has, as line 39 puts it, virtue by his side.

Divine Right

Students of this poem often focus on it as the work of the first woman of African descent to have her writing published in North America, but the only race that the poem itself mentions is "freedom's heaven-defended race." Just how the American people came to claim such an exalted title is not explained: instead, the poem just assumes that America is blessed, and uses that as evidence of George Washington's greatness. In assuming that the colonies' freedom from England is the will of God, Wheatley is able to heap even greater praise upon the subject of her poem, who leads the fight for America's freedom. The most successful warriors are the ones who are not held back by self-doubt, so the poem's attitude toward the righteousness of America's cause must have been the same one that Washington had to a great degree. Expressing it as the poem does, more eloquently than Washington would have been able to, conferred legitimacy on his feelings by showing the assumption of God's support to be the intelligent, poetic way to look at the war. In part, this poem's purpose was to flatter George Washington, which is clear from the fact that Wheatley sent it directly to him, but another purpose would have to have been, like all poetry, to explain the subject for readers of future generations. By claiming divine right for the colonial cause, Wheatley not only flattered

Topics for Further Study

- Write a report on the use of the word "Columbia" to refer to the United States, and how "America" came to be chosen as the country's official name.

- Throughout history, war heroes have gone from the military to political careers. Do you think that they are generally successful as politicians? Explain why or why not.

- Washington's army was at a terrible disadvantage, with fewer soldiers and resources than the British. Report on the difficulties that the army of the American Revolution faced off the battlefield and how Washington addressed these problems.

- Find another song or poem praising a great person and report on the author who wrote the piece.

the general but strongly suggested to readers that God must have supported one side of the conflict over the other.

Style

Phillis Wheatley is roundly considered to follow the neoclassical style of Alexander Pope, an early eighteenth-century poet highly regarded in Wheatley's era. She borrowed images from the neoclassical style easily, such as "realms of light," "astonish'd ocean," and "Autumn's golden reign." Wheatley also includes references to Greek mythology in her verse—the goddess of Freedom, muses and celestial choirs, Eolus, the god of wind. Her poem is written in heroic couplet, where rhyming is made within two lines, as in the last words of the second stanza's lines: "fair" and "hair," "skies" and "rise." As well as the rhyming couplets, Wheatley employed a similar number of syllables for every line—most of the lines consist of ten syllables. In the poem, the concept of freedom is abstracted,

Compare & Contrast

- **1776:** The Declaration of Independence is signed by fifty-six leaders of the American Revolution.

  Today: The Declaration of Independence is still used as an inspiration for oppressed people all over the world.

- **1776:** Wheatley lives her life in relative obscurity, unable to find a publisher for her second volume of poetry.

  Today: Wheatley is revered for breaking some of the barriers of racism. In 1998, a hand-written copy of her poem "Ocean" is bought at auction for $68,000.

- **1776:** On Christmas night, Washington leads his troops in boats across the Delaware River in a surprise attack against British troops at Trenton, New Jersey.

  Today: Washington is remembered as a superb military tactician.

- **1776:** To finance the Revolution, the Continental Congress establishes a nationwide lottery.

  Today: State lotteries become a hot trend in the 1980s and 1990s, growing into multi-state games that can reach over a hundred million dollars for a single winner.

- **1776:** This poem is the first to refer to the United States as "Columbia," after Christopher Columbus.

  Today: The word is forever linked to General Washington's name in the title of the nation's capitol: Washington, District of Columbia.

---

much in the style of neoclassicism. Yet there are also intimations toward the emotional style of the upcoming Romantic movement. Whereas neoclassicism stood for the established political and social order, Wheatley breaks with neoclassical convention in this poem by supporting the efforts of the revolutionary army. This poem is highly imaginative, also similar to the Romantic movement, as it idealizes a hard struggle that was forming all around her in the New England colonies, proclaiming the success of Washington and his troops long before it became a reality.

Historical Context

George Washington

"To His Excellency George Washington" was written to Washington when he was the commander of the American forces during the Revolutionary War, almost thirteen years before he took the position for which he is best remembered, as the country's first president. Commanding the army was a position for which Washington seemed destined, one that made the most of his strengths and minimized his personal shortcomings. He was born in 1732 to a large and moderately wealthy family in rural Virginia. As a child growing up in a British colony, he dreamed of becoming an officer in the British army but was discouraged from this dream by his mother and by an older brother who pointed out that the family lacked the connections that would be necessary for him to rise in the ranks. At the age of seventeen, he became the surveyor of Culpepper County, which gave him an opportunity to travel across the country and to earn an income allowing him to live independently from his family. A few years later, when his older brother Lawrence contracted tuberculosis, Washington traveled with him to Barbados, the only trip he ever made outside of the American colonies. Lawrence died the following year, and Washington eventually inherited the family estate, Mount Vernon, from him.

In 1753, British and French interests were in dispute over territory in the valley of the Ohio River, and Washington took the opportunity to enlist with the British. Sent to observe the French Fort

Duquesne (at a wilderness site that is now Pittsburgh), he killed a party of French soldiers that he mistook to be spies. This event set off the French and Indian War, which blossomed into a global conflict that involved Prussia, Great Britain, and Hanover against Austria, Saxony, France, Russia, Sweden, and Spain. During this war, Washington became famous throughout the colonies for his military skills. He became frustrated with the British army, though, and resigned his commission in 1759 and retired to life as a farmer and a member in the Virginia legislature.

When fighting broke out between the colonies and Britain in April of 1775, the Continental Congress convened to determine a strategy for waging war. George Washington was appointed by unanimous vote to lead the army on June 15. It was his responsibility to organize the militias of the various states into a fighting force with enough power to hold off one of the world's most powerful and sophisticated military organizations. His responsibility was not to defeat the entire British army but to convince them that it was a waste of effort to keep pouring money and troops into North America. Much of the success of the Revolution is credited to the soldiers' devotion to Washington and the near-religious awe that he inspired in them, which is reflected in the poem.

After the British quit the fighting in 1783, the colonies tried to work cooperatively as independent units, but it soon became clear that a central government had to be formed in order to oversee the situation. The Constitution was drafted in 1787, and General Washington was the clear choice to be the nation's first president. Much of the way that the government operates today is styled after traditions developed during Washington's first and second administrations. Some people feared that he would rule America until his death, and some hoped that he would, but when he willingly stepped down in 1796, it proved that the new nation would be governed by democratic vote and not become a case of a new monarchy replacing an old one.

The American Revolution

Like most armed conflicts, the Revolutionary War was the culmination of years of animosity that had built up until the moment when the two sides broke into outright hostility—with gunfire on April 19, 1775, at Lexington, Massachusetts, with the "shot heard 'round the world." The American Colonies had been settled primarily by British immigrants, but there had been other nations involved, too, primarily the Dutch and the French, who came down from the Canadian territories. From 1689 to 1763, there was a series of four wars between the English and the French regarding who would have primary control of the North American colonies. The last, the French and Indian War, led to a global conflict that left America in British hands. It also, however, left Britain with massive war-related debts, and to pay these debts, King George III of England imposed a series of increasingly harsh taxes on the colonies, seeking to draw from their untapped natural resources. Glass, tea, paint, and paper coming into the colonies were taxed at a high rate. Colonists resisted by refusing to buy goods imported from England. The British became more aggressive with their demands; the resistance of the colonists grew as well. In 1774, the British Parliament passed a resolution that came to be known as the "Intolerable Acts," punishing Massachusetts residents by shutting down their government and closing Boston Harbor. The first Continental Congress convened soon after, forming a crude form of national government. In April of 1775, the British lieutenant general Thomas Gage sent troops out into the Massachusetts countryside to collect the colonists' weapons; several scouts, including Paul Revere, rode ahead into the countryside to warn that the British were coming. The next day, at Lexington, the war began, with eight Americans dead by the end of the day.

The Revolution was fought from 1775 to 1781, when Washington's army defeated the British at Yorktown, Virginia, after a two-month-long siege. After that, open fighting between the two sides ended, although the war was not officially over until the Treaty of Paris was signed by both sides in 1783.

Critical Overview

Jay Parini, writing of Wheatley in *Columbia History of American Poetry,* explains that "from the time of her first published piece to the present day, controversy has surrounded the life and work of America's first black poet, and only its second published woman poet.... Few poets of any age have been so scornfully maligned, so passionately defended, so fervently celebrated, and so patronizingly tolerated." In *Critical Survey of Poetry, English Language Series,* John Shields points out that "one of the major subjects of her poetry is the American struggle for independence... Wheatley so energetically proclaims America's success in the political arena certainly attests her sympathies . . . that a people who find themselves unable to accept a present, unsatisfactory government, have the right to change that government, even if such a change can be accomplished through armed revolt." This poem is a description of that feeling. There has been much dissension in the criticism of Phillis Wheatley's poetry. One camp derides her for not being more vocal in her dissent against slavery. The other camp proclaims her as a true revolutionary, an African-American female slave in eighteenth-century New England, writing poetry that excels what was typically being written during her time. In *Bid the Vassal Soar,* M. A. Richmond recounts that in 1810, responding to a harsh criticism of Wheatley's poetry by none other than Thomas Jefferson, Samuel Stanhope Smith, president of the College of New Jersey, wrote: "The poems of Phillis Wheatley, a poor African slave, taught to read by the indulgent piety of her master are spoken of with infinite contempt. But I will demand of Mr. Jefferson, or of any other man who is acquainted with American planters, how many of those masters have written poems equal to those of Phillis Wheatley?" The answer was not one.

Criticism

David Kelly

Kelly is an instructor of creative writing and literature at Oakton Community College in Des Plaines, Illinois. In this essay, he recognizes the common tendency to interpret Wheatley's poem in terms of her race and her significance to blacks in America, but he urges readers to not make too much of what is not there.

To contemporary students, the story of Phillis Wheatley is often more interesting than her poems. This is especially true in the case of the historical poem "To His Excellency General Washington," which comes with a full background story, complete with a guest appearance by one of America's most famous personages. The poem's root story is fascinating and is itself an important part of the nation's heritage. It does indeed deserve to be studied today because the details about race, education, and heroism have much to tell about how the country developed to the point at which it is today. The poem is as carefully flattering as any poet laureate's work would be for any inauguration, and Washington's effort to drape modesty over his delight when corresponding with Wheatley is no different from any politician's reaction to public praise. The lack of any sign of racial identity in this particular poem—and in Wheatley's poetry in general—reflects a stance toward the country's muddled race relations that is as relevant today as it was before the country was formed; and Wheatley's quick descent after her great fame (she was dead within ten years at age thirty-one) is still a relevant warning about how quickly fame can fade away.

The circumstances around this poem have almost endless historical significance, but without the poem itself, Wheatley's story is just the interesting tale of an unusual African-American woman living in a colony that is fighting for its freedom but is about to stamp its approval on human slavery. Often, it is easier to examine any poem without taking into account the circumstances of the poet who wrote it, and many critics recommend this approach. With a poem like "To His Excellency General Washington," readers and critics have to remind themselves to look at the poem itself.

The poem's most striking feature is its use of language. The words themselves are complex, elevated, the sort of elitist words that authors have tried to avoid more and more, especially since modernism began early in the twentieth century. The audience that modern poets imagine for themselves is one of ordinary people, and they don't want to put these readers off by using words that only the most educated readers would understand. Many of the words Wheatley uses in "To His Excellency General Washington" would have been no more familiar to the average soldiers in Washington's army than they are to students today. Though most of them make themselves clear when read in context, they are not words that are readily recognizable. For example, the distinction between "refulgent" (line 4) and "refluent" (line 18) is one that could be understood by perhaps one person in a hundred.

What's more, Wheatley shows a fondness for going out of her way to shorten words by making contractions of them. In theory, she needs to do this to make them fit into her rhythm scheme, but more likely she does it to draw attention to her own nimble control of the language. Words like "enthron'd," "unnumber'd," "enwrapp'd," "fam'd," and the rest, may have fit the poem just fine if they had been put into the poem intact, but the contracted form, with its little curlicue of an apostrophe, may have made them look classy to Wheatley's audience.

To modern audiences, such verbal embellishments may be annoying, but Wheatley wrote during the Age of Enlightenment: she and her peers felt optimistic about knowledge in general and education in particular, and that optimism led to their eagerness to use any verbal trick available, almost daring readers to keep up with them. Poetry certainly was not new during the Enlightenment, but poets treated it as if human intelligence were in its infancy and waiting to be taken to new heights. The verbal excesses of writers of the eighteenth century lack the modesty that appeals to modern audiences. Eighteenth-century writers ran amok with excitement about what could be done with words and therefore showed little restraint. Critics make too little of this enthusiasm, leaving readers annoyed and baffled. Too often, they tend to mention that Phillis Wheatley was an Enlightenment poet and, having mentioned it, go on to pigeonhole her as a black writer and then to focus on the absence of black themes in her work.

Granting her the freedom to use gaudy words, modern readers can appreciate Wheatley's skill in stringing her words together. Her rhythm in this poem was flawlessly iambic, which, more than just a technical definition, is the rolling "unstressed-stressed" pattern of syllables that makes the poem so easy to read out loud, and to hear. The words might not be entirely familiar, but the rhythm is undeniable. As twenty-first-century readers know from the development of pop music over the last twenty years, rhythm is the thing that audiences connect with most. Rather than focusing on the words, readers might well appreciate "To His Excellency General Washington" for its musicality.

One other technique that Wheatley used that should be recognized as a reflection of her time is her way of calling out to the gods of antiquity. The poem is sprinkled with frequent references to the "celestial choir," the "muse," and the "goddess," in addition to such classical allusions as the one to "Autumn's golden reign." Identifying the Enlightenment's influences on her is relevant to understanding and accepting the poem because Wheatley, like all other Enlightenment writers, is clearly straining to show off all that she knows: if readers think she took these measures as a member of the social underclass, they might consider it a way of overcompensating for low self-esteem, but, in fact, it was just the way writers operated. It hardly helps modern readers appreciate the poem to tell them that Wheatley was following a fad of her time, but it is better to let them think of her as a poet of her age than to leave them to frame her as a black poet, only to find the frame empty.

> *It hardly helps modern readers appreciate the poem to tell them that Wheatley was following a fad of her time, but it is better to let them think of her as a poet of her age than leaving them to frame her as a black poet, only to find the frame empty."*

Readers who accept the poem's style but still feel uncomfortable with it may find themselves having trouble with Wheatley's excessive praise of George Washington, then the leader of the Continental Army. This is one of the clearest examples of how the passage of time has changed a poem's significance. Poetry today is more inclined to look at prominent social figures as fallen heroes. Horror became war's defining aspect in the twentieth century. After all that was written about the First and Second World Wars and the Vietnam conflict, American society has little patience for poets who try to glorify war. Students see Wheatley's images as quaint, naive relics and are as likely to believe in the nobility of "the unfurl'd ensign" and the "heaven-defined races" as they are to believe in the myth of Atlas holding the world in space on his giant shoulders.

And yet, readers still have a faint taste of the heroism that Wheatley tapped into with this poem. As ugly as political competition gets, most opponents are willing to keep quiet and support the military during times of conflict. America's most recent significant military action, the Persian Gulf War in 1991, made household names out of Generals Powell and Schwartzkopf, and there is every reason to believe that Americans, no matter how cynical, will make heroes out of the next war's generals.

The fact that George Washington went on to become president only serves to confuse the poem's message for modern readers. Presidents

What Do I Read Next?

- "To His Excellency General Washington" is included in *The Collected Poems of Phillis Wheatley* (1989), available from Oxford University Press.

- Another influential poem about a Revolutionary War hero is Henry Wadsworth Longfellow's "Paul Revere's Ride," which can be found in many poetry anthologies, as well as in *Henry Wadsworth Longfellow: Poems and Other Writings* (2000) from the Library of America.

- African-American poet Robert Hayden expresses his mixed emotions about Wheatley in his poem entitled "Letter for Phillis Wheatley," which can be found in his *Collected Poems* (1997).

- To find out more about what Washington was like, students can go to the words of the man himself. The Library of America has an authoritative collection of his letters and speeches in *Washington: Writings,* first published in 1997.

- Lerone Bennett Jr.'s book *Before the Mayflower: A History of Black America* (1993) barely mentions Wheatley, but, unlike other histories of Africans in America, it has a long section—nearly a hundred pages—on blacks in colonial America.

- Famed scholar Benjamin Quarles wrote a best-selling book in 1964 called *The Negro in the Making of America.* As the title suggests, the book has much about the role of African Americans in pre-Revolutionary times. The book was most recently updated in 1996.

- Patricia Bradley's book *Slavery, Propaganda, and the American Revolution* looks at how the founding fathers avoided addressing the issue of race while rallying colonists to stand against the British. It was published by the University of Mississippi Press in 1998.

- *George Washington: The Making of an American Symbol* by Barry Schwartz is a book devoted to examining the way the Washington legend grew.

---

have never been above criticism the way that military leaders have. Opposition is the basis of the democratic political process. Today, high praise for a politician is just as likely as not to come from the politician's supporters, who then try to make it look like the work of an innocent, ardent supporter like Wheatley. In a world of public-relations hype, Wheatley's praise of Washington sets off the modern reader's defense mechanism.

"To His Excellency General Washington" evokes greatness the old-fashioned way, with an admirer using her poetic gift and vast classical training to heap praise on a man that the world generally agreed was great. It uses figures of speech and classical symbols with which modern audiences are not comfortable, and it is direct in its praise to such a degree that readers of today's modern, ironic age hardly know what to do with it. There is a fascinating social story attached to this poem. It has to do with the fact that Wheatley was black in a world that seldom recorded the existence of black citizens, that Washington's plantation in Virginia owned two hundred slaves, that Wheatley received an exceptional education and was encouraged to develop her natural talent while most talented African Americans were taught that they were incapable of complex thought. One March afternoon in 1776, this exceptional woman and this exceptional man met and conversed for thirty minutes. The details of their meeting and its symbolic ramifications for all American history makes for a fascinating story. But it is not the story of this poem.

Source: David Kelly, Critical Essay on "To His Excellency General Washington," in *Poetry for Students,* The Gale Group, 2001.

M. A. Richmond

In the following essay, Richmond examines the interaction between George Washington and Phillis Wheatley in the aftermath of her writing "To His Excellency General Washington."

So many visitors came flocking to General Washington's headquarters at Cambridge early in 1776 that one chronicler of the proceedings there chose apologetically not to set down the long list.

"I cannot refrain, however," he interjected, "from noticing the visit of one, who, though a dark child from Africa and a bondwoman, received the most polite attention of the Commander-in-Chief. This was Phillis, a slave of Mr. Wheatley, of Boston . . . She passed half an hour with the Commander-in-Chief, from whom and his officers, she received marked attention."

Having then just attained the age of twenty-three, Phillis Wheatley was no child, but she was definitely dark, an African, and a slave, attributes sufficiently unique among Washington's visitors to prompt the chronicler's departure from his resolve not to clutter the record with an account of those who came to Cambridge. The uniqueness of the visit is underscored by the circumstances.

Washington was an uncommonly busy man at the time, having been designated by the Continental Congress only a few months earlier as Commander-in-Chief of the Armies of North America, and being occupied with the effort to fashion a reality that approximated the grandiloquence of his title. The armies were still to be created out of scattered bands of armed irregulars, and were still to face the major tests of battle against the imperial might of the British Crown.

With this burden of military duties, Washington could hardly have welcomed civilian visitors, making an exception perhaps for those who came on relevant business; that is, influential politicians, financiers, or potential suppliers and provisioners of his troops. Surely, one least likely to be welcomed at general headquarters might well have been a "dark child from Africa," who was a slave, a poet, and a woman. As a Virginia plantation owner with two hundred slaves, Washington was hardly predisposed to the polite entertainment of a slave. Nor were his intellectual interests such as to impel him to seek out the company of poets. And the male prejudices implicit in Southern chivalry would not have deemed a wartime military camp the proper haunt for a young woman, although in this instance Southern chivalry might be irrelevant because Miss Wheatley was black.

Just the same, against all the odds, the Father of His Country did grant a civil audience to the slave poet who just as fittingly may be christened the Mother of Black Literature in North America.

Events leading up to the curious encounter are shrouded with choice ambiguities. The opening shot, however, clearly was fired by Miss Wheatley with a letter and poem addressed to Washington at his Cambridge headquarters. The letter follows:

> Providence,
> October 26, 1775
>
> SIR.
>
> I have taken the freedom to address your Excellency in the enclosed poem, and entreat your acceptance, though I am not insensible of its inaccuracies. Your being appointed by the Grand Continental Congress to be Generalissimo of the Armies of North America, together with the fame of your virtues, excite sensations not easy to suppress. Your generosity, therefore, I presume, will pardon the attempt. Wishing your Excellency all possible success in the great cause you are so generously engaged in, I am, Your Excellency's mostly obedient and humble servant,
>
> Phillis Wheatley

For the next four months then there was silence, with no record that the General had received or noted the poet's offering. Finally, on February 10, 1776, writing at some length about other matters to his military secretary, Colonel Joseph Reed, Washington added almost as an afterthought:

> I recollect nothing else worth giving you the trouble of unless you can be amused by reading a letter and poem addressed to me by Mrs. or Miss Phillis Wheatley. In searching over a parcel of papers the other day, in order to destroy such as were useless, I brought it to light again. At first, with a view to doing justice to her great poetical genius, I had a great mind to publish the poem; but not knowing whether it might not be considered rather as a mark of my own vanity, than as a compliment to her, I laid it aside, till I came across it again in the manner just mentioned.

Several questions are provoked by this brief passage, chiefly: Did Washington know who his correspondent was? Were the Wheatley letter and poem saved from destruction as useless by the chance thought that they might amuse Reed?

Historians are divided in their answer to the first question. True, Phillis Wheatley had by then achieved fame as a slave poet—but it is also true that Washington's interest in poetry was so slight that she might have escaped his notice, and the reference to her "poetical genius" could rest on the one poem rather than on a knowledge of her prior work. More intriguing is his use of "Mrs. or Miss," for it was not the custom then among whites, most especially slaveowners, to dignify slaves with such titles. The chronicler who recorded the meeting between the general and the poet employed the common usage, "Phillis (no Miss or Mrs.), a slave of

Mr. Wheatley," and he *was* aware of her reputation as a poet. It would seem that the "Mrs. or Miss" is evidence not only of Washington's uncertainty about his correspondent's marital status but of a more fundamental ignorance of her identity—except for the suggestion that the secretary might be amused by the letter and poem, flavoring the entire passage with condescension and irony, which was common white sport at the expense of slaves (and, indeed, this sort of entertainment survived emancipation in white American lore). If this was the vein of the memo, there could be more mockery than courtesy in the usage of "Mrs. or Miss." However, Washington's suggestion of amusement may be attributed more charitably to modesty or the affectation of it. A general is no more likely to be a hero to his secretary than to his valet, and the Wheatley poem was so fulsome that Washington might well have been constrained to inject a deprecating note when transmitting it to Reed, especially since he was concerned with the appearance of vanity.

The controversy cannot be resolved conclusively, but its very existence says something about the black-white relationship, involving in this instance the most renowned slave and the most highly esteemed slaveowner of 1776.

However the communication to the secretary is interpreted, its tone certainly did not foreshadow what Washington was to write little, more than a fortnight later, this time directly to the poet. Dated from Cambridge, February 28, 1776, the letter reads:

> Miss Phillis, Your favor of the 26th of October did not reach my hands till the middle of December. Time enough—you will say, to have given answer ere this. Granted. But a variety of important occurrences, continually interposing to distract the mind and withdraw the attention, I hope will apologize for the delay, and plead my excuse for the seeming, but not real neglect. I thank you most sincerely for your polite notice of me in the elegant lines you enclosed; and however undeserving I may be of such encomium and panegyric, the style and manner exhibit a striking proof of your poetical talents; in honor of which, and as a tribute justly due you, I would have published the poem, had I not been apprehensive that, while I only meant to give the world this new instance of your genius, I might have incurred the imputation of vanity. This, and nothing else, determined me not to give it a place in the public prints.
>
> If you should ever come to Cambridge, or near headquarters, I shall be happy to see a person so favored by the Muses, and to whom nature has been so beneficent in her dispensations. I am with great respect, your obedient and humble servant.

The internal evidence is overwhelming that the General knew the identity of the poet. The reference to "this new instance of your genius" presupposes awareness of prior instances of it, and the open invitation to visit his headquarters also suggests acquaintance with whom his correspondent was. This time there is no ambiguity about her unmarried state, and the use of "Miss Phillis" seems like a knowing compromise: the overall tone of the letter dictating the common courtesy of "Miss" in the salutation and the first name only drawing the line of caste differentiation. One historian, whose focus is on Washington's relationship with the Negro, observed, "This . . . is probably the first time in his life that he ever accorded the civility of 'Mrs.' or 'Miss' to one of her race, or gave a Negro the unusual distinction of an invitation to pay him a social visit."

As plausible a speculation as any is that between February 10, when he wrote to Reed, and February 28, when he wrote to Phillis Wheatley, Washington was briefed by someone, possibly Reed, about his correspondent's identity, thus accounting for the striking change in attitude.

In any event, acceptance of the invitation was much more prompt than its issuance. In March, four months before independence was declared, the General and the poet met in Cambridge, neither knowing what the still infant war had in store for them. They should have been guided by the prescience that wars make generals and destroy poets.

Although the General was then forty-four and the poet only twenty-three, his former service as a secondary officer in a minor war had hardly tested his mettle as a commander of armies and a leader of men, and all the accomplishments that were to establish his place in history and legend were still before him; she, on the other hand, had completed the main body of her published literary work. The tall, physically robust soldier still had twenty-four years of life left; the slender, frail poet had less than nine.

In a sense, the poet anticipated the Washington legend, the effulgent tones of her poem seeming more in harmony with the successful conclusion of the war than with its uncertain beginning. Aside from this, an interesting claim is made for the poem: that she originated the phrase "first in peace." This seems doubtful, since in the poem's context "first in place and honours" fits better than does "first in peace and honours," although both renditions have been published.

Despite Washington's protestation that publication of the poem could be misunderstood as a token of his vanity, the poetic tribute from the black slave to the white general appeared in the April, 1776, issue of the *Pennsylvania Magazine,* then edited by Thomas Paine. Presumably Reed, residing in Philadelphia at the time, arranged for its publication. The poem follows in full, for its historical interest and as a fair example of Miss Wheatley's poetic output, both in literary form and intellectual content, at the peak of her fame.

Surely Washington may be forgiven if from a reading of this poem he could not divine that its author was either an African or a slave. The ornate style was clearly an imitation of Alexander Pope's, which was then the fashion and had, therefore, many imitators. The thought was mercantile Whig, preferred by the fashionable New England society in which the poet's owners, the Wheatleys, moved, and the suggestion of a golden throne and crown for Washington at the poem's end might easily have been no mere poetic image but an expression of political belief.

The poem poses a mystery more profound than Washington's awareness or nonawareness of the poet's identity. How did the poet comprehend her own identity? Relevant to this question is the larger background of the Wheatley-Washington exchange, a background that concerned the relationship of the Continental Army to all blacks.

On October 18, 1775, just eight days before Miss Wheatley wrote her letter to Washington, the Continental Congress adopted a resolution that barred all blacks from the Revolutionary armies. As happens so often, the Congressmen did not make policy; they merely approved a policy that the generals had already put into effect. With Washington's sanction, his council of general officers had already determined that no blacks, free or slave, were to be soldiers.

Eleven days after the Wheatley letter, on November 7, the royal governor of Virginia, Lord Dunmore, issued a proclamation that said:

> I do hereby further declare that all indented servants, Negroes, or others (appertaining to rebels) free, that are able and willing to bear arms, they joining his Majesty's troops as soon as may be.

Note that the proclamation did not refer to all slaves, only to those owned by rebels. Slaveowners loyal to the king were safe in the possession of their chattels (at least as far as Lord Dunmore was concerned, although slave rebellions and escapes, which were numerous in those unsettled times, did not await his royal dispensation). Later, the British Army did not always keep its promise of liberty, and many of its black volunteers were afterward sold into bondage elsewhere in the British colonies. But all this was later and did not affect the potential impact of Lord Dunmore's proclamation at the time of its issuance. A half-million blacks, a few free and the rest slaves, inhabited the Colonies. Their disposition could be decisive in determining the outcome of the still gathering contest. Apparently the king's governor in Virginia thought so, and his prime adversary from Virginia, General Washington, was impelled to counter this bold stroke.

Without consulting either his general officers' council or the Continental Congress, and ignoring his prior concurrence with their decisions, on December 30, 1775, Washington issued the following order from his Cambridge headquarters:

> As the General is informed, that Numbers of Free Negroes are desirous of enlisting, he gives leave to the recruiting officers to entertain them, and promises to lay the matter before the Congress, who he doubts not will approve it.

The next day Washington sent a letter to the Continental Congress with the explanation that "free Negroes who have served in this Army, are very much dissatisfied at being discarded," and that therefore he had run counter to his previous instructions from the Congress and permitted blacks to enlist. Note the date of these communications—the end of December—and then recall that in his letter to Phillis Wheatley, Washington said that hers, dated October 26, somehow did not reach his hands "till the middle of December." Was this purely coincidental, or did subordinates in his entourage consider the poet's message of insufficient importance for his attention until a change in policy on black enlistments was under consideration?

Once again, Congress voted after the fact of military action. Early in January, 1776, the Congress approved Washington's unilateral reversal of its policy, stating in its resolution:

> the free Negroes who have served faithfully in the army at Cambridge, may be re-enlisted, but no others.

More mincing than the royal governor, who promised freedom to slaves who fought for the king, the Colonial Congress promised them nothing, and even for freed blacks Congressional generosity was limited to conferring the right to bear arms only upon those who had already exercised it. Congressional apprehension at Lord Dunmore's thrust was overshadowed by solicitude for the slaveowner's property rights. After all, Washington was not the only large slaveholder among the leaders of the independence forces. Several Colonies, however, went beyond the Congress and passed laws providing freedom for slaves who fought with their armies. So it was that at least five thousand blacks fought in the armies of the American Revolution. The pressures of military necessity played a part similar, if not comparable in scope, to the part they were to play four score and seven years later, when Lincoln issued the Emancipation Proclamation.

Congressional approval of Washington's policy change came, as has been noted, in January. What effect, if any, did this have on creating the climate for Washington's gracious note to Miss Wheatley in the subsequent month? Granted, this is a question of conjecture, but it is not far-fetched. Presumably, in his position Washington was guided by considerations of state in small matters as well as large, and a modification of policy toward blacks in general would have influenced the relationship with one particular black poet.

If Phillis Wheatley was aware of the political maneuvers of Lord Dunmore and General Washington in relation to blacks and the rival armies, there is no trace of it in her communications, rhymed or prose, to the General. And if her feeling toward the Revolutionary War was in any way shaped by her condition as a black and as slave, there is no hint of it in her writing.

Who was she then? There are bone-bare facts to answer this question. Who did she think she was? Here the answer is more obscure, more complex, reflecting self-awareness, a sense of self-identity, all the influences, crude or subtle, that fashion a human mind and spirit. Traces of such influences must be sought along the path she traversed from Africa to Cambridge.

Source: M. A. Richmond, "The Poet and the General," in *Bid the Vassal Soar,* Howard University Press, 1974, pp. 3–10.

Sources

Magill, Frank N., ed., *Critical Survey of Poetry, English Language Series,* Salem Press, 1982, pp. 3051–60.

Parini, Jay, *Columbia History of American Poetry,* Columbia University Press, 1993, pp. 20–1.

Richmond, M. A., *Bid the Vassal Soar,* Howard University Press, 1974, pp. 53–4.

Shields, John, ed., *The Collected Works of Phillis Wheatley,* Oxford University Press, 1988, pp. vii–xi.

For Further Study

Foster, Frances Smith, *Written By Herself: Literary Production by African American Women, 1746–1892,* Indiana University Press, 1993.

    This book contains literature written by African-American women before the twentieth century. Many students are unaware of the amount of this type of literature.

Knollenberg, Bernhard, *Growth of the American Revolution,* The Free Press, 1975.

    This thick book covers a relatively short period of time in detail.

Neimeyer, Charles Patrick, *America Goes to War: A Social History of the Continental Army,* New York University Press, 1996.

    Neimeyer examines the soldiers who made up the Continental Army. This source has much about the role of African Americans in the Revolutionary War.

Nott, Walt, "From 'Uncultivated Barbarian' to 'Poetical Genius': The Public Presence of Phillis Wheatley," in *Melus,* Vol. 18, No. 3, Fall 1993, p. 21.

    Nott chronicles the development of Wheatley's reputation in the years after her death.

Robinson, William H., *Phillis Wheatley: A Bio-Bibliography,* G. K. Hall, 1981.

    In addition to the story of her life, this source contains a list of all of Wheatley's writings in publication.

To the Virgins, to Make Much of Time

Robert Herrick

1648

First published in 1648 in a volume of verse entitled *Hesperides,* "To the Virgins, to Make Much of Time" is perhaps one of the most famous poems to extol the notion of carpe diem. Carpe diem, or "seize the day," expresses a philosophy that recognizes the brevity of life and therefore the need to live for and in the moment. Seizing the day means eating, drinking and making merry for tomorrow we shall all die. The phrase was used by classicists such as Horace, and its spirit marks the theme of Herrick's lyric poem. Echoing Ben Jonson's poem, "Song: To Celia," the speaker of the poem underscores the ephemeral quality of life and urges those in their youth to actively celebrate life and its pleasures; however, the speaker does not urge "the virgins" simply to frolic adulterously, but to seek union in matrimony, thereby uniting the natural cycles of life and death with the rites and ceremonies of Christian worship. Although a very common theme in sixteenth- and seventeenth-century verse, and particularly in Cavalier poetry, the association of Christianity and carpe diem is not a traditional one; it is unique to Herrick and perhaps "natural" given Herrick's thirty-two year career as vicar of Dean Prior, an appointment originally bestowed by King Charles I. Written during a period of great political unrest that culminated in Britain's Civil War, the theme and the sage advice proffered by the speaker of the poem appears appropriate in this particularly transient period. The carpe diem spirit, however, has translated to modern times and is the theme of

Robert Herrick

come to power, expelled him from his vicarage. He returned to London in 1660, the year the monarchy was restored. At that time Charles II sent him back to Dean Prior, where he remained until his death in October of 1674.

Poem Text

> Gather ye Rose-buds while ye may,
> Old Time is still a flying:
> And this same flower that smiles to day,
> To morrow will be dying.
>
> The glorious Lamp of Heaven, the Sun,   5
> The higher he's a getting;
> The sooner will his Race be run,
> And neerer he's to Setting.
>
> That Age is best, which is the first,
> When Youth and Blood are warmer;   10
> But being spent, the worse, and worst
> Then be not coy, but use your time;
>
> And while ye may, goe marry:
> For having lost but once your prime,   15
> You may for ever tarry.

Henry James's *The Ambassadors* and Robert Frost's "Carpe Diem."

Author Biography

Herrick was born in the Cheapside district of London in August of 1591. He was the seventh child and fourth son of Julia Stone Herrick and Nicholas Herrick, a goldsmith who died when his son was only a year old. In 1607, Herrick became an apprentice to his uncle, also a goldsmith. He entered Cambridge University in 1613, graduating in 1620 with a master of arts degree. Herrick was ordained a minister in 1623 and four years later served as a chaplain in the Duke of Buckingham's Isle of Rhe expedition, a failed attempt to come to the aid of Protestants in predominantly Catholic France. It is believed he spent much of his time during the next several years among the social and literary circles of London, earning a reputation as a fashionable poet. He became known as one of the Sons of Ben, a group of poets greatly influenced by the work of Ben Jonson. In 1629 King Charles I appointed Herrick the vicar of Dean Prior in Devonshire. During the English Civil War, Herrick was a supporter of the monarchy, and in 1647 the Puritans, who had

Poem Summary

Lines 1–4

In the opening stanza, the poet articulates the carpe diem tenet that urges one to "Seize the Day." The gathering of roses is a metaphor for living life to the fullest. The image of roses suggests a number of things: roses symbolize sensuality and the fulfillment of earthly pleasures; as vegetation, they are tied to the cycles of nature and represent change and the transience of life. Like the "virgins," the roses are buds, fresh, youthful and brimming with life; youth, like life, however, is fleeting. Marked by brevity, life is such that one day one experiences joy, as suggested by the smiling flower, and the next day death. The poet underscores the ephemeral quality of human life. Like the rose, the virgins whom the speaker addresses, and beyond them the reader of the text, are destined to follow the same fate as the rose.

Lines 5–8

Here the poet expands on the image of fleeting time and the brevity of life. The movement of the sun in the sky underscores the passing of time as the sun has functioned quite literally as a time-

Media Adaptations

- "To the Virgins, to Make Much of Time" is one of the selections in *A Treasury of Great Poetry,* an audiocassette compilation released by Listening Library in 1986. The collection also features three other works by Herrick.

piece since ancient times (think of a sundial). Traditionally, the sun is an image of warmth, light and vitality: it is a life-giving force, nurturing growth in nature. However, the setting of the sun is a foreboding image that lends dark undertones to the poem: it is a traditional symbol of death. Like the rose, the personified sun and his progress across the sky stand as a metaphor for humankind and its ultimate fate.

Lines 9–12

In the third stanza, the speaker of the poem offers sage wisdom, which appears to have been acquired through life experience, to the naive virgins. Noting that youth, the time when one's blood is "warm" and desires and passions are readily stirred, is the "best" time of one's life, evokes the notion of carpe diem, and implies that one should celebrate this moment in life by indulging in it. However, in the final two lines of the stanza, the speaker introduces an unusually ironic and decidedly unromantic twist to the notion of pursuing love by suggesting that love is not a means by which one can escape death. Rather, the realist suggests that love must be pursued as it plays a role in life. It does not deter death, as suggested in lines eleven and twelve, but it does occupy a particular and significant place in one's life journey whose ultimate end is death.

Lines 13–16

The final stanza of the poem unites the natural cycles of life and death with the rites and ceremonies of Christian worship, thereby introducing a unique element to the carpe diem poem. Here the speaker urges the virgins, who represent all those who are young and inexperienced, to pursue love and the "natural" union of matrimony that ensues within the Christian world. By urging marriage, the speaker introduces a religious and moral element to the pursuit of pleasure and the immediate gratification of one's desires that the tenet of carpe diem suggests.

Themes

Carpe Diem

The Latin phrase "carpe diem" means "seize the day." The "carpe diem" philosophy holds that one's time on earth is shorter than one thinks and therefore must be held on to for as long as possible; those who subscribe to such a philosophy tend to value the present more than the unchangeable past or uncertain future. This attitude toward "living deep" and "sucking the marrow out of life" (as Henry David Thoreau phrased it) is a favorite theme of Herrick's and, indeed, of many seventeenth-century poets. "To the Virgins, to Make Much of Time" epitomizes the "carpe diem" philosophy by urging its readers—specifically, the young and naive "virgins" of the title—to make the most of the present before their youths have passed. The opening line, "Gather ye rose-buds while ye may," uses the symbol of the rosebuds to command the virgins to symbolically "seize" all the romantic experience they can because "Old time is still a-flying." "Still" in this context means "always," and the speaker stresses the fact that (as the saying goes) "time flies" forever. The present brings flowers that "smile" with the joy of their own beauty as well as the "glorious lamp of Heaven, the Sun," but, like everything else, these too will fade as time progresses. In a short span of time—indeed, in a span that seems as short as a single day—the flowers will "be dying" and the sun's "race" will be "run." As Feste, the clown in Shakespeare's *Twelfth Night,* sings, "Youth's a stuff will not endure."

The speaker argues that, of all the "ages" or stages through which a human life passes, the one in which the virgins find themselves now is the "best." According to him, their "youth and blood are warmer": their enthusiasm and emotions are at their highest point, and should be exploited in the search for love. Once their finite amount of youthfulness is "spent," their lives will only become "worse" until they reach old age, described here as the "worst" part of human life. However, if the virgins *do* remain "coy" and flirtatious without any

Topics for Further Study

- Write a poem that explains why youth is better than age, using examples from nature to prove your point. Give your poem a light, buoyant, youthful tone, as Herrick does.

- Compare this poem to "Virtue," by George Herbert. What is the perspective each poem takes toward death? Toward youth? Would the speaker in Herbert's poem agree with the one in Herrick's, or would he think that gathering rosebuds is pointless? Would Herrick's speaker agree with Herbert's?

- How does the tone of the poem differ in the first and last stanzas? What does this tell you about the poem's speaker?

---

that more rosebuds will bloom and the sun will rise again, Herrick's point is that physical beauty is like a *single* rosebud and a *single* day, gone forever once its time has passed. Whereas other rosebuds will bloom and other days will dawn, physical beauty is not everlasting. The virgins themselves are the ones actually "dying" here.

The poem ends with a reiteration of the importance of physical beauty for those coy virgins who have yet to marry. When they have "lost but once" their "prime," they "may forever tarry." Any individual's physical "prime" exists for a set number of days; the phrase "lost but once" implies that once this prime has passed, it is forever gone. At that point, the stubborn virgins may "forever tarry" (as they are now) because they will have lost their physical beauty and with it their desirability to men. Thus, the speaker, through his offer of an ironic possibility, attempts to frighten the virgins into considering the ephemeral nature of the beauty, which they presumably (and wrongfully) regard as fixed and eternal.

intention of committing themselves to husbands, the speaker argues that they will eventually reach a stage at which their only option is to "forever tarry" as old maids, regretful of the time they had wasted that they can never retrieve. To the speaker, adopting the "carpe diem" philosophy is the virgins' only option.

The Transient Nature of Beauty

Age is commonly regarded as a bringer of wisdom, a notion with which Herrick would most likely agree. What one gains in wisdom, however, is countered by what one loses in terms of physical attractiveness. Whereas such an emphasis on one's physical self may seem shallow to some readers, the speaker of "To the Virgins, to Make Much of Time" emphasizes the idea that physical beauty, like youth, is a commodity that lasts for a short period before fading and never returning. The virgins are advised to gather rosebuds because the rose is an immediately recognizable symbol of beauty; had the speaker urged his readers to "Gather ye orchids while ye may," his intention would be less apparent. In the same vein, the speaker describes the sun as the "glorious lamp of heaven"—a thing of divine beauty—only then to remark that "neerer he's to setting." Although a contrary reader may argue

Style

"To the Virgins, to Make Much of Time" is composed of four stanzas, each consisting of four lines of verse. Each stanza is composed of a single sentence. The poem employs end rhymes, the rhyming pattern being *abab, cdcd, efef, ghgh*.

In this poem, Herrick favors the trochaic foot, a unit of two syllables in which the first syllable is stressed and the second is unstressed. Scanning the first line of the poem, written in tetrameter form, reveals the dominance of this unit:

Ga ther / ye *rose* / buds *while* / ye *may*.

Trochaic feet are often difficult to use in a long poem as they tend to create a rocking rhythm. They are appropriate in this short poem with its short line length, where the brevity of form echoes the speaker's awareness of the brevity of life that underlies the poem's theme.

Historical Context

The English Civil War

Although a reader of his poetry may not suspect it, the world in which Herrick lived and wrote was one marked, in great part, by the chaos of war.

Compare & Contrast

- **1642:** Over four hundred years after King John signs the Magna Carta, forever limiting by law the king's power, the English Civil War begins, fought between Parliamentary forces ("Roundheads") and Royalist supporters of King Charles I ("Cavaliers").

  Today: The English monarch is a figurehead with no true legal authority; instead, the houses of Parliament are responsible for all legislation and the governing of the nation.

- **1642:** All theaters in England are closed by order of the Puritans. They will remain closed until 1660, when the monarchy is restored and Charles II is placed on the throne.

  Today: The English theater is regarded as one of the most influential and important in the world.

- **1648:** Robert Herrick's *Hesperides* is published; the collection of poems features a number of works in which the relationship between the human and natural worlds is explored.

  Today: The use of nature in British poetry is commonplace; twentieth-century poets such as D. H. Lawrence, Dylan Thomas, Ted Hughes, and Seamus Heaney have all written poems that employ natural symbols and metaphors for the human condition.

In 1637, King Charles I attempted to legally force the Scots to adopt the Anglican liturgy in place of their favored Presbyterian one. The Scots, understandably outraged, protested and eventually gathered an army that, by 1640, was bordering the northern counties of England. Refusing to back down, Charles I summoned the Long Parliament and petitioned them for money with which he could finance a war against the Scots; the Long Parliament agreed but insisted on a number of reforms in what the Puritans among them saw as a corrupted monarchy. After two years of bitter disagreements, both Charles and the Long Parliament raised armies and began the English Civil War in 1642, generally fought between the "cavaliers" (Royalists who supported Charles I) and the "roundheads" (Puritans who sought to defend the powers of Parliament).

During the years and battles that followed, one Parliamentary soldier emerged as a fierce enemy and master tactician: Oliver Cromwell. A rugged and ruthless commander, Cromwell earned the name Ironsides for his cavalry regiment and eventually defeated Charles's forces at the Battle of Naseby in 1645. This defeat—coupled with another at the hands of the Scots—led to Charles's surrender and eventual execution in 1649. After Charles's execution, Cromwell ruled England as Lord Protector until his death in 1658, although many historians argue that Cromwell became as intolerant a ruler as the king whom he had helped to overthrow. Cromwell's son, Richard, succeeded his father as Lord Protector until 1660, when General George Monck acted on behalf of many English people and brought Charles's son out of exile and onto the throne. Although tensions still existed between different religious sects and the English still argued over exactly how much power the king should have at his disposal, most agreed that the restoration of the monarchy was essential to ensure that the nation did not continue its era of unrest. Charles II reigned until his death in 1685.

Metaphysical and Cavalier Poetry

Much of the poetry that sprung from the seventeenth century can be classified as belonging to one of two genres: Metaphysical or Cavalier. The metaphysical poets (so named by the eighteenth-century writer Samuel Johnson) explored complex philosophical issues in equally complex forms; poets like John Donne, Andrew Marvell, and George Herbert sought to investigate the workings of God through involved "conceits"—extended metaphors that often run through the length of an entire work. Metaphysical poetry is, naturally, dense and challenging, offering its readers intense (and sometimes almost scientific) examinations of abstract topics. Donne's "Batter My Heart, Three Person'd God" and "A Valediction Forbidding Mourning" are two widely studied examples of metaphysical poetry.

The term cavalier refers politically to the followers of Charles I in the Civil War and to those poets who were associated with Charles's court; these poets evinced a more carefree attitude toward their subjects than their metaphysical contemporaries. Also known as the "Sons of Ben" (in homage to their idol, Ben Jonson), poets such as Thomas Carew, Sir John Suckling, and Herrick himself employed more sprightly meters and simpler forms than their metaphysical counterparts. Although cavalier poetry may strike a modern reader as less important than that produced by the metaphysicals, the cavalier poets are notable for their ability to handle complex issues in a deft and succinct manner. Herrick's "To the Virgins, to Make Much of Time," for example, explores the fleeting nature of beauty and youth, like Andrew Marvell's "To His Coy Mistress", but in a more playful way.

Critical Overview

"To the Virgins, to Make Much of Time" has been recognized as an important poem that pushes beyond the boundary of the typical Cavalry lyric extolling "Carpe diem," to reflect a unique interpretation of this notion, one that unites two seemingly contradictory belief systems, pagan and Christian. In his book *Poetry and the Fountain of Light,* H. R. Swardson, discussing another carpe diem poem by Herrick entitled "Corinna's Going A-Maying," argues that the poem does not offer mirth and the embracing of experience as a complete and utter licence to certain freedoms, as many more typical carpe diem poems do, nor does it suggest a strict and rigid Christian moral code. Rather, it mediates between the two. While avoiding a narrow understanding of Christianity, the poem draws on "the undeniable wisdom in the Christian order of life, including its action within some lawful boundary and recognizing considerations that are entirely foreign to the classical carpe diem statement." This same observation may be applied to "To the Virgins, to Make Much of Time." In the end of the poem, the advice proffered is for the virgins to marry. Thus, Herrick is able to articulate the carpe diem attitude, encouraging individuals to "seize the day" with images that suggests passion and sexual vitality, while at the same time he draws this notion into "the Christian fold," an important consideration for a clergyman living in a society deeply influenced by Christianity.

Critic George Arms, commenting in *Explicator Cyclopedia,* furthers Swardson's observations, noting that familiarity with the poem and readers' twentieth-century perspective obscure the sudden turn the poem takes in the final stanza. The image the poem develops, of virgins seeking pleasurable experiences, does not lead one to expect the pious advice to marry at the end of the poem. This unexpected advice, Arms argues, both shocks and delights the reader. Arms suggests that Herrick, in his choice of terms such as "virgin," "lamp," and "heaven," may be alluding to the parable of the wise and foolish virgins found in Matthew 25:1–13: "Then shall the kingdom of heaven be likened unto ten virgins." If this is so, the distinction between the religious advice offered at the end of the poem and the encouragement to indulge in seemingly pagan revelry is great. Pagan imagery, Karl P. Wentersdorf notes in *Studia Neophilologica,* marks Herrick's texts in a significant way. For instance, the rosebud image is linked to Dionysus, the god of wine and vegetation, who also represents fertility and life. This allusion and the classic carpe diem notion suggest a pagan or non-Christian order or belief system. Yet the poem clearly ends with an exhortation to marry. Those who disregard the Christian ethics, which locates passion within marriage, are the foolish virgins who clearly stand outside the Christian order.

Criticism

Daniel Moran

Moran is an educator specializing in British and American literature. In this essay, he explains how the speaker of "To the Virgins, to Make Much of Time" urges his "virgin" readers to marry and view the passing of time as a threat.

Although William Wordsworth is universally acknowledged as the foremost British poet of nature (with Robert Frost serving as his American counterpart), Robert Herrick certainly stands as an earlier poet who employed nature to meet his artistic ends. Worsdworth, of course, became incredibly famous in his own lifetime for poems such as "Lines Composed a Few Miles above Tintern Abbey" (1798), "I Wandered Lonely as a Cloud"

(1807) and "The World Is Too Much with Us" (1807)—all masterpieces in which the complex relationship between humans and the natural world is explored. Herrick never enjoyed such great success, but his volume *Hesperides* (1648) teems with poems that, while not at the same level of sophistication as Wordsworth's, nevertheless invite the reader to consider the ways in which the natural world offers countless metaphors and symbols through which human themes become apparent. Poems such as "To Blossoms," "To Daffodils," "Corrina's Gone a-Maying," and "Upon a Delaying Lady" stress the thematic connection between the human and natural worlds. Unlike Wordsworth, however, whose issues are as diverse as the colors of leaves in the fall, Herrick almost always returns to a central theme, epitomized by his "All Things Decay and Die":

> All things decay with time: the forest sees
> The growth and downfall of her aged trees;
> That timber tall, which threescore lusters stood
> The proud dictator of the state-like wood,
> I mean (the sovereign of all plants) the oak,
> Droops, dies, and falls without the cleaver's stroke.

Although he saw the natural world as a source of beauty, Herrick also knew that even the mightiest members of that world eventually fall prey to an enemy far more ruthless than any "cleaver": time. Even the greatest temporal power (of, for example, a "proud dictator" or "sovereign") is weak in the face of the passing years.

Read in this context, Herrick's best-known poem, "To the Virgins to Make Much of Time," stands as another example of Herrick's primary artistic concern. Although a modern reader may find the imagery and diction a trifle too quaint and the meter a bit too singsong and cute, Herrick does employ in the poem the technique of "nodding to nature" from which Wordsworth would fashion his career over a century later.

The word "Virgins" here literally refers to young, chaste women who have yet to find husbands; the poem can thus be read as a rallying cry to these delinquent maids, urging them to find suitable mates in the interest of the species as a whole. However, the word "virgin" also carries the connotation of a naive, innocent youth. Both senses are meant here, since, on the surface, the poem urges these girls to marry—but also urges them to recognize the unstoppable force of time. The virgins of the title are uninitiated both sexually and philosophically, and the speaker's aim is to persuade them to have their bodies and minds "deflowered" before they pass the point where the loss of both

> *Rosebuds die, the sun sets, blood turns cold; the innocent virgins are no longer being coddled by the speaker, who bluntly informs them that the sands in their biological, marital and emotional hourglasses are spilling faster and faster."*

literal and figurative virginity will be meaningless: an old virgin cannot bear children, nor can she make up for the time she lost in being coy.

As previously mentioned, Herrick looks to the natural world for a host of symbols that allow him to effectively make his case to his virgin readers. The poem's opening stanza presents the rosebud as a symbol of experience, specifically, the experience that involves falling in love and losing one's sexual innocence. Note that the flower is a "bud": a soon-to-blossom rose that, hopefully like the virgins themselves, will no longer hide its beauty from the world. Herrick's use of "smiles" (rather than "blooms") emphasizes the joy that will accompany the virgins' own blossoming into wives. That "same flower," however, will be dying "Tomorrow"; the speaker does not literally mean the day after its blossom, but is compressing the life of the flower to a single day to emphasize the short time nature allows all things to live (like the "proud dictator" mentioned above). Time is personified as "Old" yet "flying"—a paradoxical notion since "old" does not suggest the speed associated with "flying." In comparison to any mortal thing, however, time is, in a sense, both "old" (having existed forever) and "flying" (a person's youth passes quickly). The rhyming of "flying" (suggesting the quick passage of time) and "dying" (suggesting one's removal from time) reinforces the idea that time moves swiftly to one clear and unpleasant end.

As the first stanza presents rosebuds as symbols of marital experience, the second offers the

What Do I Read Next?

- Like "To the Virgins, to Make Much of Time," Herrick's poem "To a Gentlewoman Objecting to His Gray Hairs" (1648) explores the effects of time on physical beauty.

- Herrick's poem "To Blossoms" (1648) uses symbols found in the natural world to suggest the eventual decay and death of all living things.

- "Upon a Delaying Lady" (1648), another of Herrick's carpe diem poems, features a speaker urging his lady to "come away" with him before his love turns to "frost or snow."

- The poem "To His Coy Mistress" (1681) by Andrew Marvell, one of Herrick's contemporaries, also presents a speaker urging a young woman to adopt the "carpe diem" mentality but in a more metaphysical way than Herrick's.

- John Donne's poem "The Flea" (1633) also features a speaker trying to woo a stubborn woman; the poem is remarkable for its humorous and complex metaphysical approach to the problem.

- Christopher Marlowe's immensely popular "The Passionate Shepherd to His Love" (1599) is a poem in which a male speaker tries to entice his love to live with him forever in a pastoral setting. Unlike the speaker of "To the Virgins, to Make Much of Time," however, the shepherd's reasoning is based on a love of beauty, rather than a fear of time.

- The Irish poet William Butler Yeats's "The Wild Swans at Coole" (1916) explores the theme of fleeting youth in a melancholy tone.

---

sun as a symbol of the unstoppable progress of time. Calling the sun "the glorious lamp of heaven" emphasizes its beauty, yet, like the "flowers" of the first stanza, the beauty here is ephemeral; eventually, the sun will set and leave the world—and the coy virgins—in physical and emotional darkness. As Herrick compresses the life of a rosebud to a day, here he does the same with the span of the virgins' youth. Of course, nobody's youth lasts for only a day, but measured against a span of time as long as a human life, youth is certainly ephemeral and short-lived; it *seems* like a single day in retrospect. By speaking of the "race" that the sun runs every day, Herrick again stresses the "flying" speed of time: "And neerer he's to setting," the speaker warns, hoping that the virgins will see the symbolic importance of a common natural phenomenon. The rhyming words "sun" / "run" and "getting" / "setting" emphasize in the reader's ear this notion that time moves quickly and without any possible impediments.

The third stanza marks a change in the speaker's approach: while the first half of the poem uses symbols to make his point in a less obvious way, the second shows an increased earnestness on the speaker's part, which is conveyed in a more direct and even threatening tone. He begins by telling the virgins that they are in the "best" age of their lives, "When youth and blood are warmer." The idea of "warm-blooded youth" is a commonplace; young people are said to have "warm" blood because of the intensity of their emotions. However, such a remark also suggests that human life is a gradual frost, a dropping of bodily temperature and emotional excitement that ultimately results in death, when a person is, quite literally, physically and emotionally cold. The rhyming of "first" with the eventual "worst" stresses this inevitability. The second half of the stanza suggests that the "age" of youth will be "spent": everybody has a finite supply of youthfulness that can (and undoubtedly will) be used up. Once such a supply is depleted, all a person can expect are "worse, and worst / Times." Rosebuds die, the sun sets, blood turns cold; the innocent virgins are no longer being coddled by the speaker, who bluntly informs them that the sands in their biological, marital and emotional hourglasses are spilling faster and faster. Again the rhymes stress the point: one's "former" age is "warmer" than the one to which she is rapidly moving.

By the poem's end, the speaker has moved away from his initial use of nature as a means of persuasion to the language of direct command. The lines, "Then be not coy, but use your time / And, while ye may, go marry" gain force from their thirteen monosyllabic words leading up to "marry" and recall the idea that youth exists in a finite supply: like anything else that can spoil with time, youth must be "used" in a very practical sense. The speaker's commands can all be reduced to short phrases ("be not coy," "use your time," "go marry"), emphasizing what he sees as simple, undeniable truths. But this speaker is still not satisfied that he has made his point, so he resorts to sarcasm: "For, having lost but once your prime, / You may forever tarry." Once you have passed the window of opportunity, when your physical beauty has faded, the speaker argues, You can delay all you like—*because no one will want you.* "Marry" now or "tarry" later is drummed into the virgins' ears by way of rhyme. This may irk or offend some readers, who find the implication that physical beauty is crucial to a woman's finding a husband to be chauvinistic or even barbarous; however, many readers would agree that during one's youth, physical attraction can often lead to relationships. Beauty may be what initially brings two people together and beauty will indeed fade—but, with any luck, the marriage will not, and if the speaker feels the need to resort to language more direct than that of his opening stanzas, surely he is doing so to make what he sees as an important point.

A lesser-known poem of Herrick's, "Best to Be Merry," distills the issues of "To the Virgins, to Make Much of Time" into a very concentrated piece of verse:

> Fools are they, who never know
> How the times away do go;
> But for us, who wisely see
> Where the bounds of black death be,
> Let's live merrily, and thus
> Gratify the Genius.

The "Fools" here are like the "Virgins" in Herrick's other poem, unaware of "black death's" approach. "The times away do go," and the only possible remedy is to "Gratify the Genius" of the age: find a mate with whom one can gather rosebuds and *then* tarry—but not alone.

Source: Daniel Moran, Critical Essay on "To the Virgins, to Make Much of Time," in *Poetry for Students*, The Gale Group, 2001.

Judi Ketteler

Ketteler has taught literature and composition. In this essay, she focuses on the way Herrick uses the carpe diem theme and how this traditional literary motif is influenced by gender considerations.

One of the most well-remembered and oft-quoted lines in all of English poetry, "Gather ye Rose-buds while ye may," opens Robert Herrick's poem, "To the Virgins, to Make Much of Time." Critics have often described this work as a "carpe diem" poem. Herrick is not alone in his use of this literary motif; in fact, many seventeenth-century English poets embraced the idea of carpe diem,

> *The final lines of the poem, which instruct women to 'goe marry,' bring to bear a central question for the reader: is Herrick relegating women to marriage as the only option for happiness and fulfillment, or is he encouraging women to explore their sexuality as a means of fulfillment?"*

meaning "seize the day" in Latin. Critic Roger Rollin goes as far as to say that this is the poem "that has fixed the concept of carpe diem in the popular imagination forever." The underlying message in the poem appears to be one of uplift: waste no time; live your life to the fullest each day and embrace the moment.

In addition, "To the Virgins, to Make Much of Time," is highly readable. It rolls off the tongue, so to speak, with regular rhyme and meter, almost in a singsong way. But embedded in the poem are more serious themes—such as death and decay, the fleeting nature of youth, and sexuality—which seem to be contrary to the simplistic nature of the form. What readers have, then, is a poem whose form belies its content, and this is further complicated if readers think about Herrick's intended audience for the poem.

The seventeenth century was a tumultuous time in England, with a civil war that overthrew the monarchy and then a restoration that placed the monarchy back in power. While not overtly political in his poems, Herrick belonged to a group of poets, known as the "Cavaliers," who supported the monarchy. Sir John Suckling, Richard Lovelace, and Thomas Carew were also Cavalier poets, and all were deeply influenced by poet and playwright Ben Jonson. Herrick and the Cavaliers were known for writing lyrical love poems.

Where Herrick differs from his contemporaries, however, is in his use of Christianity—blended with traditional Pagan rituals—as an overriding theme in his love poetry, and especially in "To the Virgins, to Make Much of Time." It's no coincidence that Herrick served as a parish priest for almost twenty years. His Christian message is not overbearing in the poem, but it is significant that he advises young women to "goe marry,"—a holy sacrament, or Christian ritual. At the same time, he is sensitive to the natural rhythms and rituals of the earth. Specifically he speaks of the "glorious Lamp of Heaven, the Sun, / The higher he's a getting." Here, Herrick is hinting at Pagan tradition and mythology, which involve worshiping the sun. Time itself, which is always spelled with a capital "T" in the poem, is also part of the natural life cycle. Embracing the moment means embracing both Christian and Pagan rituals.

Herrick often brings together two disparate ideas or themes in interesting ways—a literary practice that is peppered throughout seventeenth-century poetry. "A sharpened awareness of the complex and contradictory nature of experience seems to be the feature which most generally characterizes the seventeenth-century poets," observe literary critics Alexander Witherspoon and Frank Warnke. In other words, experience is too multidimensional to present in a straightforward, one-dimensional manner; life is full of dilemmas and paradoxes; even the way people think is associative—one thing reminds them of another, or one thing depends upon another. In short, life is becoming more complicated in the seventeenth century, and literature is reflecting the modernization of the world. It makes sense that Herrick would present a poem of contrasts to capture the life/death paradox, and, as suggested earlier, the very form and content contrast with one another. What, then, is Herrick saying in "To the Virgins, to Make Much of Time" and why is it significant that he chooses to say it in the way he does?

Many seventeenth-century poets used "wit" to address the paradoxes of life. Wit, or "the ability to perceive similarities among dissimilar entities or experiences" (Witherspoon and Warnke), is one technique for presenting the contrasts of life. Herrick has his own kind of wit, not so much in that he practices literary ingenuity, weaving seemingly unconnected metaphors together to shock or surprise the reader; rather, his wit comes from his ability to use a lighthearted, conventional, lyric style—one seemingly more suited for love poems—to address the paradoxes of life, and especially, the paradox of womanhood.

Immediately, the reader feels a sense of urgency in the first stanza of the poem. The first word of the poem, "gather," is not only an action verb; it is a command to the virgins. The speaker directs the women to gather rosebuds, symbolic of beauty, love, and newness. "While ye may," is a qualifier; it suggests a limit on the gathering of rosebuds both because they may not always be available in plenty for gathering and because the reader may not always have the energy and ability needed for gathering. In the same breath, the speaker provides an explanation for this need to hurry: "Old Time is still a flying." "Time" takes on a human persona, a kind of Father Time, who is a tangible thing, and is moving forward, literally flying. "Old" and "Still" suggest time's movement is ancient and constant. Unlike the opportunity for gathering rosebuds—which will soon vanish—time knows no limits; it keeps moving forward as it always has and always will.

The first stanza closes out with another set of contrasts: "And this same flower that smiles today / To morrow will be dying." Herrick again uses the garden motif, personifying the flower. Though it stands tall and "smiles" or blooms now, death is imminent. Herrick is laying out the cycle of life, with the express purpose to show that death is part of the cycle of life. The flower almost takes on human characteristics, which connect humanity to the cycle of life and death. People are part of nature, and every minute that they live, they are one minute closer to dying.

The second stanza continues with the natural cycle motif, bringing in the sun. Like time, the sun has an ancient quality—it is dependable, and it is the way in which time is measured. "The glorious Lamp of Heaven, the Sun, / The higher he's a getting; / The sooner will his Race be run, / And neerer he's to Setting." As aforementioned, Herrick is pulling in Christian imagery, blending it with imagery from the world of nature. He connects the cycles of the sun to Christianity: the sun is not the lamp of the sky but the lamp of heaven. Herrick scholar Roger Rollin addresses the irony of this stanza: "It begins to appear that irony is a law of nature in the cosmos as in a rose garden; the nearer things are to their apogee, the closer they approach the slide down to their perigee." This is simply the way the world is ordered—and even the sun, with far more power and, readers are to believe, a kind of "wisdom," is not immune.

The third stanza further spells out the paradox of youth. "Youth and Blood" are "warmer"; innocence, then, is to be cherished. In using the word "spent" to describe the passing of time, time seems a commodity. Indeed, time is traded for experience; but once it is gone, it can never be regained. "But being spent, the worse, and worst / times, still succeed the former." Too, readers should remember that this poem is addressed to young women, who find themselves in drastically different conditions than young men of the day. The time when "Youth and Blood are warmer" is the time of beauty and innocence. In the popular imagination, a woman must maintain her beauty and her innocence and virtue to attract a man. But if time slips away, and a woman hasn't attracted a man, her beauty will fade, and her economic situation may become perilous. Unless she is of a prominent family and class, the seventeenth-century woman has limited opportunities. What does it mean, then, to "seize the day" when your options are limited by gender?

Whether Herrick wanted to debate the politics of gender is in itself a debate. His last stanza can be read in different ways: "Then be not coy, but use your time; / And while ye may, goe marry: / For having lost but once your prime, / You may for ever tarry." "Coy" in this context means a kind of reservation and modesty, or more appropriately, pretended shyness. Again, readers have the repetition of "while ye may"—first, "while ye may, gather rosebuds," and in this stanza, "while ye may, go marry." "Prime" is another way of saying beauty and attraction, and forever "tarry" is rather a euphemistic phrase for spinsterhood.

Instructing women to seize the day by marrying while they are young and beautiful lest they become bitter spinsters seems quite problematic for the twenty-first-century reader. But readers are so far historically removed from the seventeenth century and the subtleties of the final lines of "To the Virgins, to Make Much of Time." Roger Rollin has shown a way to read the nuances between the lines: "The delaying tactics that social custom prescribes for them [the virgins] are self-defeating, threatening to waste life's most precious commodities—time, youth, and love. 'Goe marry' can be taken merely as a euphemistic imperative to seek sexual liberation, but given the magisterial posture of the speaker, a literal interpretation is the most likely one: the virgins are encouraged to lose their virginity without delay but to lose it in an act of love that is socially sanctioned." Herrick was, after all, a parish priest. Whereas other seventeenth-century poets, such as John Donne and Andrew Marvell, have no problem directly addressing sexuality outside of marriage, Herrick seems to differ from them on this point.

Herrick's poem does not completely escape feminist inquiry, though. Even if the reader takes the viewpoint that "To the Virgins, to Make Much of Time" is about sexual liberation and not avoiding spinsterhood, questions still arise. The title, for example, encourages virgins to make much of *time;* why not to make much of *life?* Why not pursue dreams, liberate oneself on other fronts? Fight for economic liberation so that one may be more in control of her destiny? Is the best reason for a woman to lose her virginity because time is running out? Is a woman really fully in control of her destiny and body then?

This kind of rereading can provide interesting feminist critiques. But as readers in the twenty-first century, people have to take the poem for what it is and evaluate its message according to the tradition out of which it is written. Not only does the poem have a distinctly Christian feel, it has a Cavalier feel to it as well. Herrick was part of the upper crust of society, a supporter of the monarchy and of traditional values. While conforming to a traditional, lyrical style, he tackles serious themes in this poem, and almost by default, this poem enters into a dialog about sexuality and gender. Three hundred years later, sexuality and gender considerations are still debated in both popular culture and literature.

Source: Judi Ketteler, Critical Essay on "To the Virgins, to Make Much of Time," in *Poetry for Students,* The Gale Group, 2001.

Wendy Perkins

Perkins is an associate professor of English at Prince George's Community College in Maryland. In the following essay, she examines Herrick's unique employment of the literary motif carpe diem in "To the Virgins, to Make Much of Time."

Carpe diem, a Latin phrase from Horace's *Odes,* translates into "seize the day." The phrase has become a common literary motif, especially in lyric poetry and in sixteenth- and seventeenth-century English love poetry. The most famous poems that incorporate this motif include Edmund Spenser's *Faerie Queen,* Andrew Marvell's "To His Coy Mistress," Edward Fitzgerald's "The Rubaiyat of Omar Khayyam," and Robert Herrick's "To the Virgins, to Make Much of Time." Modern writers have also employed the motif, most notably Henry James in

> *The speaker in Herrick's poem begins on a traditional note, exhorting the listeners to 'seize the day' by giving up their virginity; yet he recommends that they accomplish this only after they have married.*

The Ambassadors and "The Beast in the Jungle," and obviously Saul Bellow in *Seize the Day*.

Typically, the speaker in a poem that uses carpe diem as its theme proposes that since death is inevitable and time is fleeting, the listener, often a reluctant virgin, should take advantage of the sensual pleasures the speaker reveals to her. H. R. Swardson in "Herrick and the Ceremony of Mirth," notes that what makes Herrick's "To the Virgins, to Make Much of Time" unique is its combination of Christian and classical traditions in its presentation of the carpe diem theme. The speaker in Herrick's poem begins on a traditional note, exhorting the listeners to "seize the day" by giving up their virginity; yet he recommends that they accomplish this only after they have married.

Most poems present a classical point of view in their expression of the carpe diem theme, reflecting the pagan spirit in nature as the speakers try to convince their listeners to give themselves up to sensual experience. For example, in Marvell's "To His Coy Mistress," the speaker's goal is to convince a young woman to join him and become like "amorous birds of prey" and "tear our pleasures with rough strife / Through the iron gates of life."

"To the Virgins, to Make Much of Time" begins in the same classical tradition. Its structure as well as its initial thematic proposal is traditional. The poem is a lyric composed of sixteen lines arranged into four stanzas. It is written in common, iambic meter with four stressed syllables in the first and third lines, three in the second and fourth.

The speaker in the first three stanzas suggests to his listeners, much like the speaker does in Marvell's poem, to "use your time" wisely by enjoying sexual love. Yet he also communicates the poignant sadness of the pursuit of pleasures as "old Time is still a-flying." Herrick uses the image of the rose in the first stanza in two traditional ways: as the symbol of beauty and of the transitory nature of life. Spenser also employs this image in *Faerie Queen* (II.xii.74–75) when the speaker suggests, "Gather therefore the Rose, whilst yet is prime."

Like the rosebuds, the virgins to whom the speaker in Herrick's poem addresses his words have not yet flowered. With this analogy, he suggests that if they give up their virginity, they will blossom into lovely roses. When he notes that the flowers "tomorrow will be dying," he reinforces his argument to his listeners that they must "make much of time" by experiencing pleasure before the opportunity passes. Whereas the inevitability of death is revealed in an almost gentle image of "old time . . . a flying" in the second line, its harsh reality emerges in the fourth when the speaker insists that the flowers will die soon after their blossoming. These images create an atmosphere of urgency. The speaker employs them to explain why he advises the virgins to gather the rosebuds "while ye may."

In the second stanza, Herrick reinforces this sense of urgency. The image of time flying in the first is echoed by the personification of the sun in the second as it runs its race in the heavens. The short life of both the flowers and the sun reflects the inevitability of death throughout nature. The sun as "the glorious lamp of heaven" is often used as it is here as a representation of life itself, its path from sunrise to sunset reflecting the stages of human life. As it sets, it seems to be dying, as did the roses, and, eventually, as will the virgins. Thus, the virgins should race against time, like the sun, to enjoy life to the fullest.

Roger B. Rollin, in his article on Herrick for *Twayne's English Authors Series Online,* notes that in the third stanza the speaker presents a two-part argument for his listeners. First, the stanza suggests, he explains, that "since human beings are subject to the law of atrophy," that they, like the roses will eventually decay and die, "youth, when growth is still taking place, has to be the optimum time of life." The "warmer blood" of youth suggests their heightened ability to feel and express passion, an ability that fades with age. Rollin notes that the second point the speaker makes here is that "the grand illusion of youth . . . is that it is forever, an illusion [he] curtly dispels with his image of adolescent heat soon giving way to the chill of age" and inevitable death. Marvell offers a similar message in "To His Coy Mistress" when his speaker slyly notes, "The grave's a fine and private place, / But none, I think, do there embrace."

Ironically, the new element that Herrick introduces in the last stanza reflects traditional Christian values. Typically in carpe diem poems, the impetus for the speaker's urging of young women to embrace their sexuality is his own pleasure as well as theirs, or it becomes an end in itself. However, in "To the Virgins, to Make Much of Time," while the speaker advises his listeners not to be coy and withdraw from sexual experience, he urges them to marry before they lose their virginity. The poem closes with a reinforcement of the speaker's main points: that since death is inevitable and time is fleeting, and since youth is the most vibrant time of life, the virgins should "seize the day." He suggests that if they do not grab this opportunity now, they may lose it forever.

Rollins suggests that the speaker proposes in the last stanza that "the delaying tactics that social custom prescribes for [the virgins] are self-defeating, threatening to waste life's most precious commodities—time, youth, and love." The charge "Go marry," Rollins notes, could be interpreted as a "euphemistic imperative to seek sexual liberation." Yet, he suggests "given the magisterial posture of the speaker" the more likely interpretation is that his purpose is to encourage the virgins "to lose their virginity without delay but to lose it in an act of love that is socially sanctioned."

Swardson argues that the poem stands out from traditional carpe diem poetry because in it, "some effort is made to assert the claims of one order of experience without denying the certain and recognized value of another order." He suggests that the "ceremonial quality" of the poem promotes "a ritual elevation, that helps give this experience a value beyond that of immediate pleasure."

In "To the Virgins, to Make Much of Time," Herrick presents a clever fusion of challenge to and support of social and religious doctrines: on the one hand, he defies custom when he encourages youth to openly embrace their sexuality; yet on the other, he upholds the belief that sexual knowledge should not be gained until one is married. Herrick's intermingling of the classical pagan call to experience fully the sensual pleasures of life with the traditional Christian attitude toward sexuality and marriage has produced a fresh and intriguing spin on the carpe diem poetic convention.

Source: Wendy Perkins, Critical Essay on "To the Virgins, to Make Much of Time," in *Poetry for Students,* The Gale Group, 2001.

Roger Rollin

In the following essay excerpt, Rollin analyzes "To the Virgins, to Make Much of Time" to determine Herrick's poetic intent.

While it is only Herrick's "Corinna's Going A-Maying" that can appropriately be compared with Marvell's "To His Coy Mistress," it is the older poet's "To the Virgins, to make much of Time" that has fixed the concept of carpe diem in the popular imagination forever. Scholarly investigation has revealed that Herrick is heavily indebted to a variety of sources—some classical, some English—in this poem, but his synthesizing is so artful that the lyric's derivativeness is hardly noticeable. Not in the least pedantic, this poem has been so popular that its opening line has become proverbial:

1. Gather ye Rose-buds while ye may,
Old Time is still a flying:
And this same flower that smiles today,
To morrow will be dying.

The admonition of the title and the image of time in flight convey some sense of urgency. However, even gathered, rosebuds are beautiful, and the personification, "Old Time," suggests a genial greybeard more than a grim reaper. The fact that this ancient is "a flying" almost makes him seem more comic than ominous. But then the ironically foreshortened image of the flower dying amid its smile manifestly darkens the mood even as it hints at the analogy between maidens and blossoms. That mood is intensified in the second stanza by an image which suggests that transiency is inherent in the cosmos as well as in sublunary nature:

2. The glorious Lamp of Heaven, the Sun,
The higher he's a getting;
The sooner will his Race be run,
And neerer he's to Setting.

The metaphoric first line of the stanza is pretentiously poetic compared to the colloquial character of stanza 1. Herrick's purpose is to inflate the eminence of the sun so that its decline, taken up in the last two lines, may seem even more swift and precipitous. It begins to appear that irony is a law of nature: in the comos as in a rose garden, the nearer things are to their apogee, the closer they approach the slide down to their perigee.

The object lesson to be drawn for the virgins from such natural phenomena is outlined in argumentative fashion in the two remaining stanzas. First, the girls are presented with a twofold proposition:

> 3. That Age is best, which is the first,
> When Youth and Blood are warmer;
> But being spent, the worse, and worst
> Times, still succeed the former.

Since human beings are subject to the law of atrophy—"*All things decay and die*"—youth, when growth is still taking place, has to be the optimum time of life. The grand illusion of youth, however, is that it is forever, an illusion the virgins' lecturer curtly dispels with his image of adolescent heat soon giving way to the chill of age. His conclusion, then, becomes almost self-evident:

> 4. Then be not coy, but use your time;
> And while ye may, goe marry:
> For having lost but once your prime,
> You may for ever tarry.

This last stanza makes it clear enough that to the speaker young women are coy by [custom or choice] rather than by nature. Their receptivity to love is under their control. The delaying tactics that social custom prescribes for them are self-defeating, threatening to waste life's most precious commodities—time, youth, and love. "Goe marry" can be taken merely as euphemistic imperative to seek sexual liberation, but given the magisterial posture of the speaker a literal interpretation is the more likely one: the virgins are encouraged to lose their virginity without delay but to lose it in an act of love that is socially sanctioned.

Source: Roger Rollin, "Cleanly-Wantonnesse and 'This Sacred Grove': Themes of Love," in *Robert Herrick*, G. K. Hall, 1999.

Sources

Arms, George, "'To the Virgins,'" in *Explicator Cyclopedia*, Vol. 2, Quadrangle Books, 1968, pp. 158–59.

Herrick, Robert, *The Poetical Works of Robert Herrick*, Oxford University Press, 1956.

Rollin, Roger, "Robert Herrick," in *Twayne's English Authors Series Online*, G. K. Hall & Co., 1999.

———, *Robert Herrick*, Twayne Publishing, 1992.

Swardson, H. R., "Herrick and the Ceremony of Mirth," in *Poetry and the Fountain of Light: Observations on the Conflict between Christian and Classical Traditions in Seventeenth-Century Poetry*, University of Missouri Press, 1962, pp. 40–63.

Wentersdorf, Karl P., "Herrick's Floral Imagery," in *Studia Neophilologica*, Vol. XXXVI, 1964, pp. 69–81.

Witherspoon, Alexander, and Frank Warnke, *Seventeenth-Century Prose and Poetry*, Harcourt Brace Jovanovich, 1982.

For Further Study

Cannon, John, and Ralph Griffiths, *The Oxford Illustrated History of the British Monarchy*, Oxford University Press, 1988.
   This comprehensive overview devotes approximately fifty pages to Charles I, the Civil War, and the Restoration.

Fowler, Alastair, *Robert Herrick*, Oxford University Press, 1980.
   This lecture delivered to the British Academy examines the overall design of *Hesperides*, Herrick's volume of verse, as well as Herrick's use of the erotic and the natural in his work.

MacLeod, Malcolm, *A Concordance to the Poems of Robert Herrick*, Oxford University Press, 1936.
   This book allows readers to locate every use of every word found in Herrick's poetry; for example, a reader could look up the word "rosebuds" and find the eight lines in Herrick's poems where the word occurs. This is a useful tool for examining the ways that Herrick uses various words and symbols throughout his work.

Press, John, *Robert Herrick*, Longman Group Ltd., 1971.
   This short study of Herrick's reputation argues that while Herrick is perhaps not one of the language's major poets, his verse still "speaks for the normal sensual man."

Scott, George Walton, *Robert Herrick*, Sidgwick & Jackson, 1974.
   This is a short biography of Herrick based on what little is known about his personal life. It also features extended analyses of Herrick's work in a very readable style.

Summers, Claude J., and Ted-Larry Pebworth, eds., *The English Civil Wars in the Literary Imagination*, University of Missouri Press, 1999.
   This collection of essays explores the ways in which different poets responded to the Puritan Revolution in their work. Though "To the Virgins, to Make Much of Time" is not specifically addressed, there is an essay on *Hesperides*, Herrick's collection of poems, as well as essays on Herrick's contemporaries.

We Live by What We See at Night

Martín Espada
1987

First published in the collection *Trumpets from the Islands of Their Eviction* in 1987, "We Live by What We See at Night" is an example of Martín Espada's longing and nostalgic voice as a Puerto Rican American distanced from his family's homeland. Using a simple tone and many images throughout, the poet imagines what it must have been like for his father as a young man, a new immigrant living in Harlem but dreaming nightly about his home. He contrasts the lush and colorful Puerto Rican landscape against the bleak New York cityscape, then shifts to the present, years later, himself now living in the same city. Although he wasn't born in Puerto Rico, Espada ends the poem expressing a sense of comfort in having "inherited" his father's nightly visions of the tropical island, memory as deeply rooted, perhaps, as race and culture. As the title might suggest, it is these dreams that sustain people and help them survive, looking forward while understanding their own past.

Author Biography

Espada was born in Brooklyn, New York, in 1957, to a Puerto Rican father and a Jewish mother. His father, a photographer whose pictures have been featured in Espada's volumes of poetry, aspired to play professional baseball. His disappointment over not having realized that goal (a difficult one for a dark-skinned Puerto Rican in the late 1940s)

I saw Puerto Rico,
I saw the mountains
looming above the projects,   20
overwhelming Brooklyn,
living by what I saw at night,
with my eyes closed.

Martín Espada

influenced the young Espada, and he later wrote about the experiences of his father in the poem "Tato Hates the New York Yankees." Espada's first book of poetry, *The Immigrant Iceboy's Bolero*, published in 1984, reflects the experiences of Spanish-speaking migrants. A tenant lawyer in Boston, Espada continues to write socially and politically informed poetry.

Poem Text

for my father

When the mountains of Puerto Rico
flickered in your sleep
with a moist green light,
when you saw green bamboo hillsides
before waking to East Harlem rooftops   5
or Texas barracks,
when you crossed the bridge
built by your grandfather
over a river glimpsed
only in interrupted dreaming,   10
the craving for that island birthplace
burrowed, deep
as thirty years' exile,
constant as your pulse.

This was the inheritance   15
of your son, born in New York:
that years before

Poem Summary

Lines 1–2

These first lines of "We Live by What We See at Night" introduce the tropical island of Puerto Rico, though readers are not sure who the poet is speaking too; who the "you" is yet (later in the poem readers learn he is referring to his father). The mountains "flicker in your sleep," suggesting this person isn't in Puerto Rico anymore, but rather, dreaming about it.

Lines 3–4

Still referring to the mountains in the first lines, here the poet describes the lush Puerto Rican landscape. Note the combination of sensory details used here: not only does the poet describe the color of the mountains, but he also uses the word "moist," allowing readers to imagine the scene using touch as well, like the feeling of a moss-covered rock under their hand. By repeating the same color twice in two lines, the poet is perhaps trying to express the overwhelming sight of green covering the entire countryside.

Lines 5–6

The poet, having described the lush green mountains of Puerto Rico in his father's dream, contrasts this with what his father saw when he woke up in New York or Texas, having been "evicted" from his homeland. Whereas the visions he saw while sleeping were natural and "green," when he wakes he sees more man-made structures like "rooftops" and "barracks," perhaps contrasting a more ideal garden-like island to cities where people have to crowd together in small apartment buildings or even bunks.

Lines 7–10

It's difficult to tell if this is a real bridge that the grandfather built, or just a figurative one. Often, the image of "crossing a bridge" is used as a metaphor to express a passage from one world to another, to express a personal growth and progression. In this case, since in the ninth and tenth lines readers learn the bridge is built over a river seen only in a dream, they might guess this is not a real bridge. Through figurative language, this image helps extend the scene into the past four generations: the poet, his father and his father's grandfather. Perhaps the poet is emphasizing the deep sense of tradition, son following father in a continuing line from the past, crossing the same bridges. Note, too, this is the second time the poet mentions dreaming, though this time it is "interrupted," suggesting his father's difficulty sleeping.

Lines 11–14

Here the poet moves from more descriptive and figurative language to a voice that tells readers explicitly how much his father must have "craved" to go back home after "thirty years exile." Again, the sense of deep tradition is emphasized through the word "burrowed," and in the simile "constant as your pulse." By using this image, perhaps the poet is reminding readers of the "bloodline," which is often used as a synonym for lineage or family record, again emphasizing the link of culture and ethnicity.

Lines 15–16

Here the poem shifts from past remembrance to the present. These lines help express how even though the poet, the son, was born in New York, he "inherited" his father's dreams of the island.

Lines 17–21

These are the first lines that introduce the speaker of the poem, the son, who insists he sees the same visions as his father. The poet transposes the mountains of Puerto Rico over the run-down city, perhaps helping create a sense of blending landscapes and cultures. Notice the verbs "looming" and "overwhelming," which seem to make the son's imagined visions predominant over the real projects in Brooklyn. It's the stories his father told of the garden-like island, perhaps, which are more important than the real city the exiled families now inhabit.

Lines 22–23

In these last lines, readers find the source of the poem's title, as well as a return to the world of dream. When the poet says he lives by what he sees at night with his eyes closed, perhaps he's suggesting that the dreams of Puerto Rico help sustain him through the harsh realities of the New York projects. Having come from a long line of exiled people, the poet learns from his father how to live on dream, hope and myth.

Themes

Inheritance

When one considers what a child inherits from a parent, the things that come to mind most often are either tangible items—money, houses, furniture, and so forth—or certain physical and personality traits—brown eyes, big feet, a hot temper, and so on. In "We Live by What We See at Night," Martín Espada addresses a different kind of inheritance, one more abstract and transcendental than the usual legacy. He has derived from his father the desire and the ability to dream of Puerto Rico, not in the typical sense of daydreaming about a beautiful tropical island but of a mental "transportation" there when he lies down to sleep.

Espada was born in New York, but his father was a native Puerto Rican. Before the poet ever had the opportunity to visit his family's homeland, he learned about its simplistic beauty and lush terrain from his father who had left the island decades before. The strong bond between the Espadas is typical of Puerto Rican family life, and not even the many years they had spent in the United States lessened the ties. It is both a sense of undying unity among family and a "craving for that island birthplace" that the father wants to pass on to his children, and this poem reflects his success in doing so.

The theme of legacy plays out not only in such direct references as "This was the inheritance / of your son" but also in the description of parallel dreams between the poet and his father. The dominant object in each is the mountainous countryside of Puerto Rico, and both men can envision it despite their actual physical surroundings of "East Harlem rooftops" and "the projects" of Brooklyn. Although much of the island's once-forested land has now been cleared for commercial purposes, still about 75 percent of the area consists of hills and mountains too steep for cultivation. This physical fact is likely a good reason that the mountainsides figure so heavily in the images that many Puerto Rican immigrants "crave" in the midst of skyscrapers and crowded streets. The father, here, has been able to convey that longing for and appreciation of the island's natural beauty to his son, although the young Espada never grew up surrounded by it.

A preference of Puerto Rico's attractive "moist green light" and the "green bamboo hillsides" over the very unattractive, poor areas of New York City is easy to understand. But an obvious partiality is not what makes inheritance so

Topics for Further Study

- Imagine a place where your ancestors lived that you would rather be in now, and write a poem describing it in detail.

- Compare the attitude of the speaker of this poem with the attitude of the speaker in Tennyson's "Ulysses." What does each poem say about experience? About family? Which speaker are you more inclined to agree with? Why?

- Do you think the beauty of Puerto Rico would be as important to the speaker if he lived in a beautiful place now? Is he saying that people should live in the past?

---

important in the Espada family. Actually, this theme stretches far beyond any one family to encompass the plight of many immigrants. People who have left their homelands to start new lives in America usually do so because they believe their lives will improve in many ways. Of course, that is not always the case, and leaving their homelands does not necessarily imply any hatred for the customs and natural surroundings of their native lands. Even though many families, including Espada's, may move to another country for economic reasons, it is very important to retain a sense of family and cultural traditions. Inheritance is valued, not just as a means of passing on whatever possessions a parent may leave to a child but as a way of holding on to the customs, beliefs, rituals, and ethics of a family's native land.

Dreams and Reality

Throughout "We Live by What We See at Night," there is an interplay of dreams and reality. The poem begins with the father dreaming about "the mountains of Puerto Rico" before he awakens to the reality of "East Harlem rooftops / or Texas barracks." The dream reference returns immediately with the father now dreaming about crossing a bridge in Puerto Rico with his grandfather, glancing at the river below. But this is a scene that he can envision "only in interrupted dreaming," implying that wakefulness and, therefore, reality, keeps interfering with his ability to satisfy "the craving for that island birthplace" when he goes to sleep. The back-and-forth scenario is not as clear in the second stanza, but now it is the son, Espada himself, who fluctuates between pleasant dreams and harsh reality. He acknowledges that he, too, envisions at night the beautiful island where his father was born and was dreaming about Puerto Rico even before he had visited there himself. Reality checks back in with a mention of the "projects" in Brooklyn, the not-so-beautiful place where the poet actually lives.

The importance of dreams in the lives of immigrants and their offspring is evident in the title of the poem itself. To say one *lives* by what the mind sees at night while asleep makes a very strong statement about what day-to-day reality must be like. Many families who left Puerto Rico for the United States after the island became an American commonwealth in 1952 found themselves crowded into the slum areas of large cities, particularly New York, where the environment was a shocking change. Many also found themselves victims of racism as well as of poverty and unemployment, so it is easy to see why pleasant dreams of their native land were such a welcome relief after a day spent trying to survive harsh conditions, both mental and physical. Espada uses this theme very effectively in "We Live by What We See at Night" by concentrating on appealing descriptions of Puerto Rico while at the same time implying more subtly the ugliness of real life in a dilapidated area of a city.

Style

"We Live by What We See at Night" is written in free verse, which means the line length varies according to the changing moods of the poem rather than being determined by a set number of metric feet or syllables, as in formal verse. In this example, Espada uses fairly short lines throughout, which help slow down the speed of the poem, perhaps matching the quiet and contemplative voice of a man recounting a fond memory. If the lines were longer, stretching across the page, the poem would seem to gain more momentum, building up a chant or prayer-like effect. Espada chose to break his lines earlier, perhaps in order to create a slower effect and isolate the images, in turn emphasizing each further.

Historical Context

So much of Martín Espada's work is a reflection of his cultural and historical perspective that nearly every poem could be discussed in terms of what it says about a political or social event, military action, or displacement of immigrants. He often makes a point about a public act by describing its personal impact on an individual, whether it is a war, a riot, or an "eviction" of a people from their native land. "We Live by What We See at Night" takes place in both Puerto Rico and New York, and it spans the time of his father's youth on the island to thirty years later when the poet is dreaming of it, just as the older man does. This puts the poem's time frame in both the 1950s and the 1980s.

Puerto Rico's history is made up of one struggle after another to survive domination by countries seeking control of this beautiful, lush island whose name is Spanish for "rich port." Spain was in control when it went to war with the United States in 1898. The Spanish-American War ended the same year it began with the signing of the Treaty of Paris granting the United States sovereign power over Puerto Rico. For decades, there was an attempt to Americanize all aspects of the island and its people, including a failed effort to make English the dominant language. American corporations took over the sugar industry, resulting in a plantation economy that meant great wealth for some and destitution for others. Throughout this time, three main political factions came into existence in Puerto Rico, all with platforms based on the island's relationship with the United States: one group favored becoming a state, a second preferred maintaining the tie but having more self-government, and the third advocated total independence. Each faction had a strong voice at one time or another over the years, but the dominant force between 1940 and 1968 was the Popular Democratic Party, which favored a new self-governing relationship with the United States. In support of this party, the American Congress passed a law in 1950 allowing Puerto Ricans to draft their own constitution and to have full local self-government. The new constitution led to the establishment of the Commonwealth of Puerto Rico in 1952, meaning it became an autonomous political entity whose association with the United States was voluntary.

Because of the booming job market in America after World War II, mass migration of Puerto Ricans began in 1947 and peaked throughout the 1950s. Between 1951 and 1959, an average of 47,000 islanders per year arrived in the United States, many settling in New York City. Such was the case with Espada's father. But, as "We Live by What We See at Night" implies, the dreams of a more prosperous and better life in America soon became nightmares for many immigrants who found themselves unwelcome in their new home. Racism, job discrimination, poverty, and a feeling of displacement all contributed to the disillusionment of immigrants, causing them to dream more of their homeland than of America.

Puerto Ricans who remained on the island during the 1950s saw an economic growth unlike any previous. As American industry moved in, many farmers and sugarcane growers became factory workers, and by 1955, income from manufacturing was greater than from agriculture. Individual income rose from $296 per year in 1950 to $1,384 per year in 1970. But the 1980s saw a downturn in both the American and Puerto Rican economies. The recession in the United States during 1980–1981 had a dramatic effect on Puerto Ricans living in both countries. Jobs with decent wages became even harder to acquire, especially for immigrants in America who were already struggling with racial and ethnic issues in the work place. In Puerto Rico, the commonwealth's gross national product declined by 6 percent in 1982–1983, and federal budget cuts resulted in the loss of a jobs program and less availability of food stamps. Tension brought on by a steadily worsening economy on the island led to increased political unrest, particularly by those groups who continued to favor a complete break from the United States. During the early 1980s, there were several terrorist attacks on American military units in Puerto Rico, but the island endured the political strife and remained a commonwealth, as it still is today.

Writing poetry and essays as a young man in the 1970s and 1980s, Espada was more familiar with the downside of Puerto Rican immigration into the United States, based partly on his father's experiences as an immigrant and on his own observations of living conditions in barrios and slums. In an essay called "Postcard from the Empire of Queen Ixolib," he relates the story of his visit to Biloxi, Mississippi, to see the place where his father had been jailed fifty years earlier. The older Espada had refused to sit in the back of a bus as he traveled across the South and was arrested because of it. When young Espada arrived there, he found the jail and bus station had been torn down and replaced by casinos. In the essay inspired by this trip, he notes the irony of a Southern effort to

Compare & Contrast

- **1950s:** "Operation Bootstrap" is set in motion in Puerto Rico, involving intensive efforts by the United States to revamp the economy, attract new industry, improve schools and hospitals, and increase manufacturing capabilities. Whereas some islanders benefit from the massive restructuring, others feel displaced and overcome by American interference.

  1980s: A Puerto Rican terrorist group calling itself the Macheteros claims responsibility for attacks on American military installations on the island. This includes a physical assault of personnel on a navy bus and the blowing up of eight air force planes at an Air National Guard site.

  Today: The question of Puerto Rico's status remains controversial. In a plebiscite called in the mid-1990s, a narrow majority of Puerto Rican voters decided to maintain the island's status as an American commonwealth.

- **1950s:** Puerto Rican poets and writers seeking to publish their work are shunned by American publishing houses, leaving many creative voices silent because of prejudice and a lack of respect for immigrants' writing abilities.

  1980s: Major New York publishers and other small presses come to recognize the commercial value in printing work by previously ignored writers, particularly Hispanics and blacks. A growing body of work by Puerto Rican writers living in New York—coined "Nuyorican" literature—is especially popular.

  Today: Hispanic authors receive more recognition than in previous decades and most university curricula include courses on Hispanic literature, as well as that of other minority groups. However, the playing field is by no means even for minorities seeking to publish their writing, and many times Hispanic writers must turn to presses such as Arte Publico Press and Bilingual Review Press for publication.

---

pave over its old mistakes while shrines to Confederate President Jefferson Davis still dot the countryside. Although the poet and essayist would likely agree that millions of immigrants to the United States have not regretted the decision to leave their homeland and have indeed lived prosperous lives in America, he would probably also point out that there is another side. That side is the one portrayed in "We Live by What We See at Night," the one that assures that family history and culture remain alive from generation to generation.

Critical Overview

"We Live by What We See at Night" was first published in Espada's second collection *Trumpets from the Islands of Their Eviction* in 1987. Many critics praise Espada for his rich and nostalgic voice while recounting an "insistent theme of migration," as Robert Creeley writes in the book's introduction. As the title of the book suggests, the poems from this collection often serve as "songs" of a dislocated Puerto Rican people, recounting the stories, hardships and longings of those islanders forced from their homeland. Concerning the book's title, Diana Vélez, in her essay included in Espada's book, points out that "Puerto Ricans are a people evicted: evicted from an island in droves in the nineteen fifties by a development program called Operation Bootstrap."

Because Espada himself was born in America, he often focuses on the life of his Puerto Rican father, who was a very influential figure in his life. The poet in turn draws from the rich source of memory, myth, and dream found in his unique culture. Linda Frost, writing for *Minnesota Review*, calls this Espada's "mythic urge—[which] collapses historical event into personal experience." "This, too," Vélez adds, "is part of the poetic function—to bring that dream material to our awareness, to help us remember or re-member ourselves to a lost wholeness via a re-reading of our dreams."

Criticism

Pamela Steed Hill

Hill is the author of a poetry collection, has published widely in journals, and is an associate editor for a university communications department. In the following essay, she explains how such a brief, apparently simple poem can have far-reaching aspects and be much more complex than it may seem.

A poem that contains a dedication line—such as, *for my wife, to John,* or, in the case here, *for my father*—often connotes sentimentality, signaling that the work is very personal, if not autobiographical. Martín Espada's "We Live by What We See at Night" is both, and on the surface it is a thoughtful poem about a son's understanding and appreciation of his father's nostalgic feelings for his native country, Puerto Rico. Espada seems to offer this work as a loving tribute to keeping family unity and ethnic tradition alive in spite of the mental and physical barriers he and his relatives encounter on a daily basis in America. At the core of it, though, is something more complex, something inevitable and disturbing, especially to those immigrants who experience mixed feelings about migration and also for those citizens of the immigrant's new country who may mistake an immigrant's doubts for ungratefulness and disrespect. In other words, the problem presented in this poem is one of duality, and it is a problem that makes some Americans say to immigrants, If you think you've got it so bad here, go home.

These are harsh words for anyone to speak, and, of course, they are even more difficult to hear if you are the one to whom they are directed. And while there is no excuse for violent responses to uncomfortable environments on anyone's part—native citizen or immigrant—it takes a real effort to sympathize with someone's situation before criticizing the newcomer's longing for home. In Espada's poem, the father has been living in the United States for at least thirty years, and his departure from Puerto Rico is called an "exile." This word is very telling of the double-edged sword that the father encountered in leaving the island, for it

> *In its back-and-forth tone the poem mirrors the duality of an immigrant's life, and it is this duality that causes so much stress and discontent. It is also what makes the word 'exile,' with its dubious meaning, so important in the poem."*

can mean two different things: on one hand, "exile" implies a forced removal from one's native land, and, on the other, it implies a self-imposed removal. So which was true of the older Espada? Did someone hold a gun to his head and tell him to get on the boat or else? Or did he feel personally compelled to leave Puerto Rico because of poor economic conditions and little hope for a successful future?

If you asked Espada, the son and poet, those questions, he would probably reply that poverty is like a gun to the head. And he would probably say that American colonialism, too, is like a pointed weapon to those who get caught in the big machine of industrialization, mass production, and other "improvements." These are points well taken, and yet there is still that other nagging side. If one is not actually physically forced to migrate to America, then there should be no complaints about the living conditions immigrants often find when they get here. If "moist green light" and "green bamboo hillsides" are what someone wants to wake up to, then East Harlem, New York, is not the place to go. So is the poem fair in its discontent with housing projects "overwhelming Brooklyn" as opposed to "the mountains"? Most likely, there is more to the disillusionment than run-down buildings and rooftops and barracks. It is more what those items represent than what they physically are.

Many immigrants see their surroundings as a "prison" in which they have been placed by inhospitable hosts in the new country. They find the same poverty they tried to leave behind with the added

What Do I Read Next?

- Born in 1928, Piri Thomas was a Puerto Rican immigrant who grew up in Spanish Harlem in New York City. After a life of racial discrimination, street fighting, drugs, and a prison sentence for shooting a police officer, Thomas wrote his now-famous account of growing up as an outsider in America, called *Down These Mean Streets*. Originally published in 1967, a thirtieth-anniversary edition came out in 1997 with a new afterward discussing the worsening conditions on the streets of Spanish Harlem.

- Martín Espada's fifth collection of poetry, *Imagine the Angels of Bread: Poems* (1996), contains a series of autobiographical poems recalling family, school, and work experiences. This is a mixture of personal and political poems in which he addresses the bread of imagination, the bread of the table, and the bread of justice.

- The Spanish-American War does not always receive as much attention in history books as other conflicts. In *Crucible of Empire: The Spanish-American War and Its Aftermath* (1993), James C. Bradford and others address the issue and show that this war was actually America's emergence as a world power.

- The classic novel *Native Son* by Richard Wright, first published in 1940, tells the story of a young black man in the Chicago of the 1930s who strikes back angrily and violently against the poverty and racism he faces on a daily basis. Some critics have claimed that American culture was changed forever after the publication of this graphic, provocative, and challenging book.

---

frustration of discrimination and sometimes violent racial attacks. The inability to secure jobs with good wages causes most to lose hope of reaching the goals of prosperity and happiness that everyone in America is supposed to attain—this, of course, in light of the millions of Americans themselves who live with hunger and poor housing conditions every day of their lives. Most people in other lands do not see that side of America and cannot even imagine it. To them, the United States is truly that land of milk and honey where everyone lives in big houses, drives big cars, and buys whatever the heart desires. Those who live here, obviously, know better, and it does not take long for reality to set in for those who arrive with a distorted image.

"We Live by What We See at Night" suggests that Espada's father must have been dreaming an American dream before he left Puerto Rico for the United States. And if it was a mistaken image that lured him from home, it was also dreams that became his solace once the truth of day-to-day life in a New York barrio became impossible to deny. As the poem indicates, the visions that the mind conjures while asleep can be both beautiful and comforting, but an agitating reminder of real life still haunts an otherwise peaceful sleep. This is implied in the words "flickered" and "interrupted." It seems the father's rest is sometimes fitful, as though there is a tug of war between the clear image of the mountains and their sudden disappearance as the picture flickers on and off in his mind. The serene view of the river is also plagued by "interrupted dreaming," as though reality keeps banging on his mind's door to get in. But the poem is not an altogether unhappy one. Nor is it completely angry and accusatory. In its back-and-forth tone the poem mirrors the duality of an immigrant's life, and it is this duality that causes so much stress and discontent. It is also what makes the word "exile," with its dubious meaning, so important in the poem.

The title of the collection in which "We Live by What We See at Night" first appeared is *Trumpets from the Islands of Their Eviction*. Even stronger than exile, eviction leaves no room for doubt about whether a removal is forced or self-imposed. As a tenant lawyer in Chelsea, Massachusetts—a poor suburb of Boston heavily populated by Hispanic immigrants—Espada certainly encountered his share of battles between immigrant renters and the landlords who served eviction notices for whatever reasons. As a poet, Espada compares this expulsion from one's house or apartment to the mass migration of Puerto Ricans to the United States after the island came under American control. And the numbers who left home were especially high during the period of "Operation Bootstrap" when many islanders got caught up in the frenzy of a new Americanized way of life in the 1950s. Whether this migration is equal to an eviction depends upon who is asked. But regardless of the debate, one thing is for certain: the feeling of displacement was very real for the new arrivals, and it was exacerbated by the animosity and mistrust that greeted them from the first day in America.

Included in this same Espada collection are many other poems depicting the emotional and physical hardships of Hispanic immigrants to the United States. Consider these lines from one called "Toque de queda: Curfew in Lawrence:" "The mobs are gone: white adolescents / who chanted USA and flung stones / at the scattering of astonished immigrants, / ruddy faces slowing the car to shout spick / and wave beer cans." This sad and violent scene is played out over and over on the streets of New York and Boston and in any other city or town where people of different colors and from different cultural backgrounds encounter one another. Given this ominous fact, it is easy to see why a native Puerto Rican may have a "craving for that island birthplace" and why it has "burrowed" itself just as deeply in the soul of the immigrant as his "thirty years' exile" has tried to dig out.

Possibly the most discouraging aspect of "We Live by What We See at Night" is the fact that it was written in the 1980s, refers to times in the 1950s, and could just as easily be written today to describe some immigrants' lives on American streets at the outset of the twenty-first century. While several anti-discrimination laws have been passed and diversity issues appear regularly in newspapers and on talk shows across the nation, day-to-day life has not changed much for some. In all fairness, many Americans will point out instances of forced reverse discrimination and their feelings of outrage over the English language taking a back seat to Spanish in some school districts. Understandably, many citizens feel threatened by a continuing influx of people from all over the world into the United States, which has added greatly to problems of overcrowding and poverty in American cities. And some say it is time to close the door. But even if new immigration laws were passed to limit or stop (a very unlikely prospect) the movement of foreign citizens into the United States, those laws would not apply to Puerto Ricans. As members of an American commonwealth, the islanders are free to come to the mainland whenever they like and to return just as easily if they choose to do so. But in spite of any speculation about future laws, an answer to long-standing problems between cultures and races is not likely to be found in legal actions anyway. And until a Puerto Rican immigrant can lie down in his bed in New York at night and dream of the life he is living in America, he will need to find comfort and peace in living with his dreams of the land he left behind.

Source: Pamela Steed Hill, Critical Essay on "We Live by What We See at Night," in *Poetry for Students,* The Gale Group, 2001.

Doreen Piano

Piano is a Ph. D. candidate in English at Bowling Green State University. In the following essay, she analyzes how cultural identity is transferred from generation to generation through the act of remembering.

Historically, the United States has been a place of new beginnings for millions of people from Europe, Africa, Asia, the Middle East, and Latin America. In fact, the "immigrant experience" is part of our cultural heritage as Americans. With its promise of economic prosperity, personal liberty, and upward mobility, the United States offers many immigrants the chance to make their lives, as well as their children's lives, better than it was in the "old country." Yet, as much as America has been described as "the land of the free and the home of the brave," expatriation, along with its attendant assimilation into an alien culture, can be a difficult experience, especially for those who still long for their homeland. In fact, the lingering memories of life before immigration and the traditions and values of the "old country" can be clung to fiercely. Therefore, for many immigrants, memories of their former homeland are an important source of cultural transference to their offspring who are first generation Americans. In his poem, "We Live by What We See at Night," Martín Espada explores the psychic landscape of the immigrant experience in the United States, revealing how cultural identity is transferred from generation to generation through the act of remembering.

Told from the son's point of view, a first-generation Puerto Rican "born in New York," the poem examines both the son's and the father's relationship to the "old world" of Puerto Rico by contrasting it to the "new world" of New York where his father now lives. The stark contrast between these two worlds is expressed in the descriptions the narrator uses. For example, the poem opens with a lengthy periodic sentence that builds up several images of Puerto Rico as a world that is tranquil, natural, and deeply familiar to the father. Thus, in the first stanza, "the mountains of Puerto Rico," the "moist green light," and "green bamboo hillsides" all reveal an intimacy with the landscape

> *The second stanza reveals the effect that the father's memories have had on the narrator. The inheritance he has been given is not economic or material gain but pride in his cultural make up."*

that only comes from having lived there and remembering what it was like. In addition, the image of "the bridge built by your grandfather over a river" illustrates how leaving the homeland also involves breaking family ties by leaving one's country of birth. To the narrator's father, Puerto Rico has become an "imagined geography," an alternative landscape that provides him with solace from the harsh world he confronts in the United States. Thus, compared to "waking to East Harlem rooftops or Texas barracks," the memories of Puerto Rico's natural beauty lull the narrator's father into a dream world that is peaceful and vibrant. In this way, Espada contrasts the rural images of Puerto Rico to the harsh image of the immigrant's current residence in a metropolitan environment to show the psychological strain that many immigrants undergo when leaving their homeland. Often what they have given up can never equal what they now have.

Espada emphasizes the idea of "imagined geographies" by referring to the memories of Puerto Rico that his father has while sleeping or dreaming. They flicker in his sleep and are glimpsed but not completely seen. For the immigrant whose life may not have turned out in the United States the way he or she had expected, the dreams of a better life are now superseded by fragmented memories of what life was like back home. These memories may have faded, but they are indelibly a part of a past that can never be forgotten. Yet these memories seem to surface only in a dream state. They create an impression of hope in what appears to be dreary circumstances by providing a space for the father to revisit his past. However, the dark side of these alluring images is that they produce a "craving for that island birthplace." They make the father restless and unsatisfied. Even after thirty years of exile, these memories are as "constant as your pulse." By holding on to these memories, the father may be unconsciously refusing to embrace his life in the United States.

Thus, in the first stanza, Espada reveals the troubled psychic landscape of the father, who dreams of returning yet knows that, either for economic or political reasons, he cannot. The desire for the homeland is emphasized by Espada's repetitious use of the subordinating conjunction *when* that opens each phrase in the first stanza. In addition, because these yearnings occur when his father is dreaming, a reader senses that actually returning to his homeland is an impossibility. Thus, the father draws on these memories of the homeland for sustenance and comfort when the day-to-day circumstances of his life are most likely difficult and harsh. Images in the poem that provide glimpses of what life is like for him in the United States are few but telling. For example, "East Harlem rooftops" suggest living in a crowded ghetto that offers little in the way of vistas or natural beauty.

However, at the same time that these memories reveal a separate reality to the one that the father lives during the day, they also promote a sense of pride in cultural heritage and family history. Despite his separation from his homeland of Puerto Rico, the father refuses to repudiate his cultural background. For many immigrants, assimilating into mainstream culture requires sacrificing their heritage, their native language, and their customs in order to be accepted as Americans. Yet the father seems to resist assimilation by relaying the memories of life in Puerto Rico to his son. In this way, the father provides the narrator with a sense of his cultural identity as a Puerto Rican despite his being "born in New York."

The second stanza reveals the effect that the father's memories have had on the narrator. The inheritance he has been given is not economic or material gain but pride in his cultural make up. Compared to the grim environment of the inner city, the memories that his father shares with him allow him to escape momentarily to an imaginary geography, as when he writes, "years before I saw Puerto Rico, I saw the mountains looming above the projects." In this way, father and son are joined by the commonality of their cultural heritage. It transcends the dire material circumstances of their lives and gives them something to "see at night." As the "we" in the title suggests, both father and son dream of the homeland that offers them an alternative reality to the one they live during the day. Interestingly enough, the poem is dedicated to Espada's father. This dedication offers the reader a hint that the poem's content may be autobiographical and may reflect on the poet's own relationship with his father. The poet Robert Creeley, in the introduction to Espada's book *Trumpets from the Islands of their Eviction,* claims that "it is the literal community and person of Frank Espada who so invests his own son's commitment. It is his father's family and relationships that preoccupy the son finally."

The power of this poem lies in its ability to reveal how cultural heritage binds father and son through the contrasting of two different environments—the natural beauty of Puerto Rico to the inner city of New York. The distinction he makes between these environments is, he suggests, like night and day. The night offers an alternative reality that daylight cannot. The verb "to see," which Espada uses repeatedly in the second stanza, engenders the dreams that his father has in the first stanza. For the son who has never been to the father's homeland, it is not difficult to imagine what life is like there as he has come to know it through his father's dream-like memories. These memories provide him with a vision of an alternate reality to the reality of the projects in Brooklyn; they are something he can *see* with his eyes closed.

Source: Doreen Piano, Critical Essay on "We Live by What We See at Night," in *Poetry for Students,* The Gale Group, 2001.

Sources

Amazon, www.amazon.com (January 5, 2001).

Campo, Rafael, Review of *Zapata's Disciple: Essays,* by Martin Espada, in *Progressive,* Vol. 63, No. 4, April 1999, p. 43.

Creeley, Robert, Foreword in *Trumpets from the Islands of Their Eviction,* Bilingual Review/Press, 1987, pp 10–11.

Espada, Martin, *Trumpets from the Islands of Their Eviction,* Bilingual Press, 1987.

———, *Zapata's Disciple: Essays,* South End Press, 1998.

Frost, Linda, Review in *Minnesota Review,* Vol. 37, Fall 1991, pp. 135–39.

The History Channel, www.historychannel.com (January 2, 2001).

"Puerto Rico," in *Worldmark Encyclopedia of the States,* 4th ed., Gale Research, 1998.

Vélez, Diana L., "Dancing to the Music of an 'Other' Voice: Martin Espada," in *Trumpets from the Islands of Their Eviction,* Bilingual Review/Press, 1987, pp. 69–89.

For Further Study

Espada, Martín, *A Mayan Astronomer in Hell's Kitchen,* W. W. Norton, 2000.

  Espada's most recent collection of poetry continues his themes of displacement and despair among various groups of people. Here, he includes a nun staging a White House vigil to protest her torture and a man on death row mourning the loss of his books.

———, ed., *El Coro: A Chorus of Latino and Latina Poetry,* University of Massachusetts Press, 1997.

  This is an excellent cross-section of contemporary Latino and Latina works. Poets range from farm workers and gang members to a medical doctor and professional chef.

Ortiz Cofer, Judith, *The Latin Deli: Prose and Poetry,* University of Georgia Press, 1993.

  Like Espada, Judith Ortiz Cofer is a first-generation Puerto Rican poet who grew up in a barrio in an American city. This is a collection of poems, essays, and short fiction that discuss Cofer's struggles with a cross-cultural childhood. Its themes are the same as those in "We Live by What We See at Night".

Ratiner, Steven, "Martin Espada: Poetry and the Burden of History," *The Christian Science Monitor Electronic Edition,* www.csmonitor.com (March 6, 1991).

  In this online interview with Espada, Ratiner calls Espada's poetry "ferocious, tender, ardently political, [and] touchingly biographical." Reading Espada's responses to the questions is helpful in understanding his poetry.

Glossary of Literary Terms

A

Abstract: Used as a noun, the term refers to a short summary or outline of a longer work. As an adjective applied to writing or literary works, abstract refers to words or phrases that name things not knowable through the five senses.

Accent: The emphasis or stress placed on a syllable in poetry. Traditional poetry commonly uses patterns of accented and unaccented syllables (known as feet) that create distinct rhythms. Much modern poetry uses less formal arrangements that create a sense of freedom and spontaneity.

Aestheticism: A literary and artistic movement of the nineteenth century. Followers of the movement believed that art should not be mixed with social, political, or moral teaching. The statement "art for art's sake" is a good summary of aestheticism. The movement had its roots in France, but it gained widespread importance in England in the last half of the nineteenth century, where it helped change the Victorian practice of including moral lessons in literature.

Affective Fallacy: An error in judging the merits or faults of a work of literature. The "error" results from stressing the importance of the work's effect upon the reader—that is, how it makes a reader "feel" emotionally, what it does as a literary work—instead of stressing its inner qualities as a created object, or what it "is."

Age of Johnson: The period in English literature between 1750 and 1798, named after the most prominent literary figure of the age, Samuel Johnson. Works written during this time are noted for their emphasis on "sensibility," or emotional quality. These works formed a transition between the rational works of the Age of Reason, or Neoclassical period, and the emphasis on individual feelings and responses of the Romantic period.

Age of Reason: See *Neoclassicism*

Age of Sensibility: See *Age of Johnson*

Agrarians: A group of Southern American writers of the 1930s and 1940s who fostered an economic and cultural program for the South based on agriculture, in opposition to the industrial society of the North. The term can refer to any group that promotes the value of farm life and agricultural society.

Alexandrine Meter: See *Meter*

Allegory: A narrative technique in which characters representing things or abstract ideas are used to convey a message or teach a lesson. Allegory is typically used to teach moral, ethical, or religious lessons but is sometimes used for satiric or political purposes.

Alliteration: A poetic device where the first consonant sounds or any vowel sounds in words or syllables are repeated.

Allusion: A reference to a familiar literary or historical person or event, used to make an idea more easily understood.

Amerind Literature: The writing and oral traditions of Native Americans. Native American literature was originally passed on by word of mouth, so it consisted largely of stories and events that were easily memorized. Amerind prose is often rhythmic like poetry because it was recited to the beat of a ceremonial drum.

Analogy: A comparison of two things made to explain something unfamiliar through its similarities to something familiar, or to prove one point based on the acceptedness of another. Similes and metaphors are types of analogies.

Anapest: See *Foot*

Angry Young Men: A group of British writers of the 1950s whose work expressed bitterness and disillusionment with society. Common to their work is an antihero who rebels against a corrupt social order and strives for personal integrity.

Anthropomorphism: The presentation of animals or objects in human shape or with human characteristics. The term is derived from the Greek word for "human form."

Antimasque: See *Masque*

Antithesis: The antithesis of something is its direct opposite. In literature, the use of antithesis as a figure of speech results in two statements that show a contrast through the balancing of two opposite ideas. Technically, it is the second portion of the statement that is defined as the "antithesis"; the first portion is the "thesis."

Apocrypha: Writings tentatively attributed to an author but not proven or universally accepted to be their works. The term was originally applied to certain books of the Bible that were not considered inspired and so were not included in the "sacred canon."

Apollonian and Dionysian: The two impulses believed to guide authors of dramatic tragedy. The Apollonian impulse is named after Apollo, the Greek god of light and beauty and the symbol of intellectual order. The Dionysian impulse is named after Dionysus, the Greek god of wine and the symbol of the unrestrained forces of nature. The Apollonian impulse is to create a rational, harmonious world, while the Dionysian is to express the irrational forces of personality.

Apostrophe: A statement, question, or request addressed to an inanimate object or concept or to a nonexistent or absent person.

Archetype: The word archetype is commonly used to describe an original pattern or model from which all other things of the same kind are made. This term was introduced to literary criticism from the psychology of Carl Jung. It expresses Jung's theory that behind every person's "unconscious," or repressed memories of the past, lies the "collective unconscious" of the human race: memories of the countless typical experiences of our ancestors. These memories are said to prompt illogical associations that trigger powerful emotions in the reader. Often, the emotional process is primitive, even primordial. Archetypes are the literary images that grow out of the "collective unconscious." They appear in literature as incidents and plots that repeat basic patterns of life. They may also appear as stereotyped characters.

Argument: The argument of a work is the author's subject matter or principal idea.

Art for Art's Sake: See *Aestheticism*

Assonance: The repetition of similar vowel sounds in poetry.

Audience: The people for whom a piece of literature is written. Authors usually write with a certain audience in mind, for example, children, members of a religious or ethnic group, or colleagues in a professional field. The term "audience" also applies to the people who gather to see or hear any performance, including plays, poetry readings, speeches, and concerts.

Automatic Writing: Writing carried out without a preconceived plan in an effort to capture every random thought. Authors who engage in automatic writing typically do not revise their work, preferring instead to preserve the revealed truth and beauty of spontaneous expression.

Avant-garde: A French term meaning "vanguard." It is used in literary criticism to describe new writing that rejects traditional approaches to literature in favor of innovations in style or content.

B

Ballad: A short poem that tells a simple story and has a repeated refrain. Ballads were originally intended to be sung. Early ballads, known as folk ballads, were passed down through generations, so their authors are often unknown. Later ballads composed by known authors are called literary ballads.

Baroque: A term used in literary criticism to describe literature that is complex or ornate in style or diction. Baroque works typically express tension, anxiety, and violent emotion. The term "Baroque Age" designates a period in Western European literature beginning in the late sixteenth century and ending about one hundred years later.

Works of this period often mirror the qualities of works more generally associated with the label "baroque" and sometimes feature elaborate conceits.

Baroque Age: See *Baroque*

Baroque Period: See *Baroque*

Beat Generation: See *Beat Movement*

Beat Movement: A period featuring a group of American poets and novelists of the 1950s and 1960s—including Jack Kerouac, Allen Ginsberg, Gregory Corso, William S. Burroughs, and Lawrence Ferlinghetti—who rejected established social and literary values. Using such techniques as stream-of-consciousness writing and jazz-influenced free verse and focusing on unusual or abnormal states of mind—generated by religious ecstasy or the use of drugs—the Beat writers aimed to create works that were unconventional in both form and subject matter.

Beat Poets: See *Beat Movement*

Beats, The: See *Beat Movement*

Belles-lettres: A French term meaning "fine letters" or "beautiful writing." It is often used as a synonym for literature, typically referring to imaginative and artistic rather than scientific or expository writing. Current usage sometimes restricts the meaning to light or humorous writing and appreciative essays about literature.

Black Aesthetic Movement: A period of artistic and literary development among African Americans in the 1960s and early 1970s. This was the first major African American artistic movement since the Harlem Renaissance and was closely paralleled by the civil rights and black power movements. The black aesthetic writers attempted to produce works of art that would be meaningful to the black masses. Key figures in black aesthetics included one of its founders, poet and playwright Amiri Baraka, formerly known as LeRoi Jones; poet and essayist Haki R. Madhubuti, formerly Don L. Lee; poet and playwright Sonia Sanchez; and dramatist Ed Bullins.

Black Arts Movement: See *Black Aesthetic Movement*

Black Comedy: See *Black Humor*

Black Humor: Writing that places grotesque elements side by side with humorous ones in an attempt to shock the reader, forcing him or her to laugh at the horrifying reality of a disordered world.

Black Mountain School: Black Mountain College and three of its instructors—Robert Creeley, Robert Duncan, and Charles Olson—were all influential in projective verse. Today poets working in projective verse are referred to as members of the Black Mountain school.

Blank Verse: Loosely, any unrhymed poetry, but more generally, unrhymed iambic pentameter verse (composed of lines of five two-syllable feet with the first syllable accented, the second unaccented). Blank verse has been used by poets since the Renaissance for its flexibility and its graceful, dignified tone.

Bloomsbury Group: A group of English writers, artists, and intellectuals who held informal artistic and philosophical discussions in Bloomsbury, a district of London, from around 1907 to the early 1930s. The Bloomsbury Group held no uniform philosophical beliefs but did commonly express an aversion to moral prudery and a desire for greater social tolerance.

Bon Mot: A French term meaning "good word." A *bon mot* is a witty remark or clever observation.

Breath Verse: See *Projective Verse*

Burlesque: Any literary work that uses exaggeration to make its subject appear ridiculous, either by treating a trivial subject with profound seriousness or by treating a dignified subject frivolously. The word "burlesque" may also be used as an adjective, as in "burlesque show," to mean "striptease act."

C

Cadence: The natural rhythm of language caused by the alternation of accented and unaccented syllables. Much modern poetry—notably free verse—deliberately manipulates cadence to create complex rhythmic effects.

Caesura: A pause in a line of poetry, usually occurring near the middle. It typically corresponds to a break in the natural rhythm or sense of the line but is sometimes shifted to create special meanings or rhythmic effects.

Canzone: A short Italian or Provençal lyric poem, commonly about love and often set to music. The *canzone* has no set form but typically contains five or six stanzas made up of seven to twenty lines of eleven syllables each. A shorter, five- to ten-line "envoy," or concluding stanza, completes the poem.

Carpe Diem: A Latin term meaning "seize the day." This is a traditional theme of poetry, especially lyrics. A *carpe diem* poem advises the reader or the person it addresses to live for today and enjoy the pleasures of the moment.

Catharsis: The release or purging of unwanted emotions—specifically fear and pity—brought about by exposure to art. The term was first used by the Greek philosopher Aristotle in his *Poetics* to refer to the desired effect of tragedy on spectators.

Celtic Renaissance: A period of Irish literary and cultural history at the end of the nineteenth century. Followers of the movement aimed to create a romantic vision of Celtic myth and legend. The most significant works of the Celtic Renaissance typically present a dreamy, unreal world, usually in reaction against the reality of contemporary problems.

Celtic Twilight: See *Celtic Renaissance*

Character: Broadly speaking, a person in a literary work. The actions of characters are what constitute the plot of a story, novel, or poem. There are numerous types of characters, ranging from simple, stereotypical figures to intricate, multifaceted ones. In the techniques of anthropomorphism and personification, animals—and even places or things—can assume aspects of character. "Characterization" is the process by which an author creates vivid, believable characters in a work of art. This may be done in a variety of ways, including (1) direct description of the character by the narrator; (2) the direct presentation of the speech, thoughts, or actions of the character; and (3) the responses of other characters to the character. The term "character" also refers to a form originated by the ancient Greek writer Theophrastus that later became popular in the seventeenth and eighteenth centuries. It is a short essay or sketch of a person who prominently displays a specific attribute or quality, such as miserliness or ambition.

Characterization: See *Character*

Classical: In its strictest definition in literary criticism, classicism refers to works of ancient Greek or Roman literature. The term may also be used to describe a literary work of recognized importance (a "classic") from any time period or literature that exhibits the traits of classicism.

Classicism: A term used in literary criticism to describe critical doctrines that have their roots in ancient Greek and Roman literature, philosophy, and art. Works associated with classicism typically exhibit restraint on the part of the author, unity of design and purpose, clarity, simplicity, logical organization, and respect for tradition.

Colloquialism: A word, phrase, or form of pronunciation that is acceptable in casual conversation but not in formal, written communication. It is considered more acceptable than slang.

Complaint: A lyric poem, popular in the Renaissance, in which the speaker expresses sorrow about his or her condition. Typically, the speaker's sadness is caused by an unresponsive lover, but some complaints cite other sources of unhappiness, such as poverty or fate.

Conceit: A clever and fanciful metaphor, usually expressed through elaborate and extended comparison, that presents a striking parallel between two seemingly dissimilar things—for example, elaborately comparing a beautiful woman to an object like a garden or the sun. The conceit was a popular device throughout the Elizabethan Age and Baroque Age and was the principal technique of the seventeenth-century English metaphysical poets. This usage of the word conceit is unrelated to the best-known definition of conceit as an arrogant attitude or behavior.

Concrete: Concrete is the opposite of abstract, and refers to a thing that actually exists or a description that allows the reader to experience an object or concept with the senses.

Concrete Poetry: Poetry in which visual elements play a large part in the poetic effect. Punctuation marks, letters, or words are arranged on a page to form a visual design: a cross, for example, or a bumblebee.

Confessional Poetry: A form of poetry in which the poet reveals very personal, intimate, sometimes shocking information about himself or herself.

Connotation: The impression that a word gives beyond its defined meaning. Connotations may be universally understood or may be significant only to a certain group.

Consonance: Consonance occurs in poetry when words appearing at the ends of two or more verses have similar final consonant sounds but have final vowel sounds that differ, as with "stuff" and "off."

Convention: Any widely accepted literary device, style, or form.

Corrido: A Mexican ballad.

Couplet: Two lines of poetry with the same rhyme and meter, often expressing a complete and self-contained thought.

Criticism: The systematic study and evaluation of literary works, usually based on a specific method or set of principles. An important part of literary studies since ancient times, the practice of criticism has given rise to numerous theories, methods, and "schools," sometimes producing conflicting, even contradictory, interpretations of literature in general as well as of individual works. Even such basic issues as what constitutes a poem or a novel have been the subject of much criticism over the centuries.

D

Dactyl: See *Foot*

Dadaism: A protest movement in art and literature founded by Tristan Tzara in 1916. Followers of the movement expressed their outrage at the destruction brought about by World War I by revolting against numerous forms of social convention. The Dadaists presented works marked by calculated madness and flamboyant nonsense. They stressed total freedom of expression, commonly through primitive displays of emotion and illogical, often senseless, poetry. The movement ended shortly after the war, when it was replaced by surrealism.

Decadent: See *Decadents*

Decadents: The followers of a nineteenth-century literary movement that had its beginnings in French aestheticism. Decadent literature displays a fascination with perverse and morbid states; a search for novelty and sensation—the "new thrill"; a preoccupation with mysticism; and a belief in the senselessness of human existence. The movement is closely associated with the doctrine Art for Art's Sake. The term "decadence" is sometimes used to denote a decline in the quality of art or literature following a period of greatness.

Deconstruction: A method of literary criticism developed by Jacques Derrida and characterized by multiple conflicting interpretations of a given work. Deconstructionists consider the impact of the language of a work and suggest that the true meaning of the work is not necessarily the meaning that the author intended.

Deduction: The process of reaching a conclusion through reasoning from general premises to a specific premise.

Denotation: The definition of a word, apart from the impressions or feelings it creates in the reader.

Diction: The selection and arrangement of words in a literary work. Either or both may vary depending on the desired effect. There are four general types of diction: "formal," used in scholarly or lofty writing; "informal," used in relaxed but educated conversation; "colloquial," used in everyday speech; and "slang," containing newly coined words and other terms not accepted in formal usage.

Didactic: A term used to describe works of literature that aim to teach some moral, religious, political, or practical lesson. Although didactic elements are often found in artistically pleasing works, the term "didactic" usually refers to literature in which the message is more important than the form. The term may also be used to criticize a work that the critic finds "overly didactic," that is, heavy-handed in its delivery of a lesson.

Dimeter: See *Meter*

Dionysian: See *Apollonian and Dionysian*

Discordia concours: A Latin phrase meaning "discord in harmony." The term was coined by the eighteenth-century English writer Samuel Johnson to describe "a combination of dissimilar images or discovery of occult resemblances in things apparently unlike." Johnson created the expression by reversing a phrase by the Latin poet Horace.

Dissonance: A combination of harsh or jarring sounds, especially in poetry. Although such combinations may be accidental, poets sometimes intentionally make them to achieve particular effects. Dissonance is also sometimes used to refer to close but not identical rhymes. When this is the case, the word functions as a synonym for consonance.

Double Entendre: A corruption of a French phrase meaning "double meaning." The term is used to indicate a word or phrase that is deliberately ambiguous, especially when one of the meanings is risque or improper.

Draft: Any preliminary version of a written work. An author may write dozens of drafts which are revised to form the final work, or he or she may write only one, with few or no revisions.

Dramatic Monologue: See *Monologue*

Dramatic Poetry: Any lyric work that employs elements of drama such as dialogue, conflict, or characterization, but excluding works that are intended for stage presentation.

Dream Allegory: See *Dream Vision*

Dream Vision: A literary convention, chiefly of the Middle Ages. In a dream vision a story is presented as a literal dream of the narrator. This device was commonly used to teach moral and religious lessons.

E

Eclogue: In classical literature, a poem featuring rural themes and structured as a dialogue among shepherds. Eclogues often took specific poetic forms, such as elegies or love poems. Some were written as the soliloquy of a shepherd. In later centuries, "eclogue" came to refer to any poem that was in the pastoral tradition or that had a dialogue or monologue structure.

Edwardian: Describes cultural conventions identified with the period of the reign of Edward VII of England (1901–1910). Writers of the Edwardian Age typically displayed a strong reaction against the propriety and conservatism of the Victorian Age. Their work often exhibits distrust of authority in religion, politics, and art and expresses strong doubts about the soundness of conventional values.

Edwardian Age: See *Edwardian*

Electra Complex: A daughter's amorous obsession with her father.

Elegy: A lyric poem that laments the death of a person or the eventual death of all people. In a conventional elegy, set in a classical world, the poet and subject are spoken of as shepherds. In modern criticism, the word elegy is often used to refer to a poem that is melancholy or mournfully contemplative.

Elizabethan Age: A period of great economic growth, religious controversy, and nationalism closely associated with the reign of Elizabeth I of England (1558–1603). The Elizabethan Age is considered a part of the general renaissance—that is, the flowering of arts and literature—that took place in Europe during the fourteenth through sixteenth centuries. The era is considered the golden age of English literature. The most important dramas in English and a great deal of lyric poetry were produced during this period, and modern English criticism began around this time.

Empathy: A sense of shared experience, including emotional and physical feelings, with someone or something other than oneself. Empathy is often used to describe the response of a reader to a literary character.

English Sonnet: See *Sonnet*

Enjambment: The running over of the sense and structure of a line of verse or a couplet into the following verse or couplet.

Enlightenment, The: An eighteenth-century philosophical movement. It began in France but had a wide impact throughout Europe and America. Thinkers of the Enlightenment valued reason and believed that both the individual and society could achieve a state of perfection. Corresponding to this essentially humanist vision was a resistance to religious authority.

Epic: A long narrative poem about the adventures of a hero of great historic or legendary importance. The setting is vast and the action is often given cosmic significance through the intervention of supernatural forces such as gods, angels, or demons. Epics are typically written in a classical style of grand simplicity with elaborate metaphors and allusions that enhance the symbolic importance of a hero's adventures.

Epic Simile: See *Homeric Simile*

Epigram: A saying that makes the speaker's point quickly and concisely.

Epilogue: A concluding statement or section of a literary work. In dramas, particularly those of the seventeenth and eighteenth centuries, the epilogue is a closing speech, often in verse, delivered by an actor at the end of a play and spoken directly to the audience.

Epiphany: A sudden revelation of truth inspired by a seemingly trivial incident.

Epitaph: An inscription on a tomb or tombstone, or a verse written on the occasion of a person's death. Epitaphs may be serious or humorous.

Epithalamion: A song or poem written to honor and commemorate a marriage ceremony.

Epithalamium: See *Epithalamion*

Epithet: A word or phrase, often disparaging or abusive, that expresses a character trait of someone or something.

Erziehungsroman: See *Bildungsroman*

Essay: A prose composition with a focused subject of discussion. The term was coined by Michel de Montaigne to describe his 1580 collection of brief, informal reflections on himself and on various topics relating to human nature. An essay can also be a long, systematic discourse.

Existentialism: A predominantly twentieth-century philosophy concerned with the nature and perception of human existence. There are two major strains of existentialist thought: atheistic and Christian. Followers of atheistic existentialism believe that the individual is alone in a godless universe and that the basic human condition is one of suffering and loneliness. Nevertheless, because there are no fixed values, individuals can create their own characters—indeed, they can shape themselves—through the exercise of free will. The atheistic strain culminates in and is popularly associated with the works of Jean-Paul Sartre. The Christian existentialists, on the other hand, believe that only in God may people find freedom from life's anguish. The two strains hold certain beliefs in common: that existence cannot be fully understood or described through empirical effort; that anguish is a universal element of life; that individuals must bear responsibility for their actions; and that there is no common standard of behavior or perception for religious and ethical matters.

Expatriates: See *Expatriatism*

Expatriatism: The practice of leaving one's country to live for an extended period in another country.

Exposition: Writing intended to explain the nature of an idea, thing, or theme. Expository writing is often combined with description, narration, or argument. In dramatic writing, the exposition is the introductory material which presents the characters, setting, and tone of the play.

Expressionism: An indistinct literary term, originally used to describe an early twentieth-century school of German painting. The term applies to almost any mode of unconventional, highly subjective writing that distorts reality in some way.

Extended Monologue: See *Monologue*

F

Feet: See *Foot*

Feminine Rhyme: See *Rhyme*

Fiction: Any story that is the product of imagination rather than a documentation of fact. Characters and events in such narratives may be based in real life but their ultimate form and configuration is a creation of the author.

Figurative Language: A technique in writing in which the author temporarily interrupts the order, construction, or meaning of the writing for a particular effect. This interruption takes the form of one or more figures of speech such as hyperbole, irony, or simile. Figurative language is the opposite of literal language, in which every word is truthful, accurate, and free of exaggeration or embellishment.

Figures of Speech: Writing that differs from customary conventions for construction, meaning, order, or significance for the purpose of a special meaning or effect. There are two major types of figures of speech: rhetorical figures, which do not make changes in the meaning of the words; and tropes, which do.

Fin de siecle: A French term meaning "end of the century." The term is used to denote the last decade of the nineteenth century, a transition period when writers and other artists abandoned old conventions and looked for new techniques and objectives.

First Person: See *Point of View*

Folk Ballad: See *Ballad*

Folklore: Traditions and myths preserved in a culture or group of people. Typically, these are passed on by word of mouth in various forms—such as legends, songs, and proverbs—or preserved in customs and ceremonies. This term was first used by W. J. Thoms in 1846.

Folktale: A story originating in oral tradition. Folktales fall into a variety of categories, including legends, ghost stories, fairy tales, fables, and anecdotes based on historical figures and events.

Foot: The smallest unit of rhythm in a line of poetry. In English-language poetry, a foot is typically one accented syllable combined with one or two unaccented syllables.

Form: The pattern or construction of a work which identifies its genre and distinguishes it from other genres.

Formalism: In literary criticism, the belief that literature should follow prescribed rules of construction, such as those that govern the sonnet form.

Fourteener Meter: See *Meter*

Free Verse: Poetry that lacks regular metrical and rhyme patterns but that tries to capture the cadences of everyday speech. The form allows a poet to exploit a variety of rhythmical effects within a single poem.

Futurism: A flamboyant literary and artistic movement that developed in France, Italy, and Russia from 1908 through the 1920s. Futurist theater and poetry abandoned traditional literary forms. In their place, followers of the movement attempted to achieve total freedom of expression through bizarre imagery and deformed or newly invented words. The Futurists were self-consciously modern artists who attempted to incorporate the appearances and sounds of modern life into their work.

G

Genre: A category of literary work. In critical theory, genre may refer to both the content of a given work—tragedy, comedy, pastoral—and to its form, such as poetry, novel, or drama.

Genteel Tradition: A term coined by critic George Santayana to describe the literary practice of certain late nineteenth-century American writers, especially New Englanders. Followers of the Genteel

Tradition emphasized conventionality in social, religious, moral, and literary standards.

Georgian Age: See *Georgian Poets*

Georgian Period: See *Georgian Poets*

Georgian Poets: A loose grouping of English poets during the years 1912–1922. The Georgians reacted against certain literary schools and practices, especially Victorian wordiness, turn-of-the-century aestheticism, and contemporary urban realism. In their place, the Georgians embraced the nineteenth-century poetic practices of William Wordsworth and the other Lake Poets.

Georgic: A poem about farming and the farmer's way of life, named from Virgil's *Georgics*.

Gilded Age: A period in American history during the 1870s characterized by political corruption and materialism. A number of important novels of social and political criticism were written during this time.

Gothic: See *Gothicism*

Gothicism: In literary criticism, works characterized by a taste for the medieval or morbidly attractive. A gothic novel prominently features elements of horror, the supernatural, gloom, and violence: clanking chains, terror, charnel houses, ghosts, medieval castles, and mysteriously slamming doors. The term "gothic novel" is also applied to novels that lack elements of the traditional Gothic setting but that create a similar atmosphere of terror or dread.

Graveyard School: A group of eighteenth-century English poets who wrote long, picturesque meditations on death. Their works were designed to cause the reader to ponder immortality.

Great Chain of Being: The belief that all things and creatures in nature are organized in a hierarchy from inanimate objects at the bottom to God at the top. This system of belief was popular in the seventeenth and eighteenth centuries.

Grotesque: In literary criticism, the subject matter of a work or a style of expression characterized by exaggeration, deformity, freakishness, and disorder. The grotesque often includes an element of comic absurdity.

H

Haiku: The shortest form of Japanese poetry, constructed in three lines of five, seven, and five syllables respectively. The message of a *haiku* poem usually centers on some aspect of spirituality and provokes an emotional response in the reader.

Half Rhyme: See *Consonance*

Harlem Renaissance: The Harlem Renaissance of the 1920s is generally considered the first significant movement of black writers and artists in the United States. During this period, new and established black writers published more fiction and poetry than ever before, the first influential black literary journals were established, and black authors and artists received their first widespread recognition and serious critical appraisal. Among the major writers associated with this period are Claude McKay, Jean Toomer, Countee Cullen, Langston Hughes, Arna Bontemps, Nella Larsen, and Zora Neale Hurston.

Hellenism: Imitation of ancient Greek thought or styles. Also, an approach to life that focuses on the growth and development of the intellect. "Hellenism" is sometimes used to refer to the belief that reason can be applied to examine all human experience.

Heptameter: See *Meter*

Hero/Heroine: The principal sympathetic character (male or female) in a literary work. Heroes and heroines typically exhibit admirable traits: idealism, courage, and integrity, for example.

Heroic Couplet: A rhyming couplet written in iambic pentameter (a verse with five iambic feet).

Heroic Line: The meter and length of a line of verse in epic or heroic poetry. This varies by language and time period.

Heroine: See *Hero/Heroine*

Hexameter: See *Meter*

Historical Criticism: The study of a work based on its impact on the world of the time period in which it was written.

Hokku: See *Haiku*

Holocaust: See *Holocaust Literature*

Holocaust Literature: Literature influenced by or written about the Holocaust of World War II. Such literature includes true stories of survival in concentration camps, escape, and life after the war, as well as fictional works and poetry.

Homeric Simile: An elaborate, detailed comparison written as a simile many lines in length.

Horatian Satire: See *Satire*

Humanism: A philosophy that places faith in the dignity of humankind and rejects the medieval perception of the individual as a weak, fallen creature. "Humanists" typically believe in the perfectibility of human nature and view reason and education as the means to that end.

Humors: Mentions of the humors refer to the ancient Greek theory that a person's health and personality were determined by the balance of four basic fluids in the body: blood, phlegm, yellow bile, and black bile. A dominance of any fluid would cause extremes in behavior. An excess of blood created a sanguine person who was joyful, aggressive, and passionate; a phlegmatic person was shy, fearful, and sluggish; too much yellow bile led to a choleric temperament characterized by impatience, anger, bitterness, and stubbornness; and excessive black bile created melancholy, a state of laziness, gluttony, and lack of motivation.

Humours: See *Humors*

Hyperbole: In literary criticism, deliberate exaggeration used to achieve an effect.

I

Iamb: See *Foot*

Idiom: A word construction or verbal expression closely associated with a given language.

Image: A concrete representation of an object or sensory experience. Typically, such a representation helps evoke the feelings associated with the object or experience itself. Images are either "literal" or "figurative." Literal images are especially concrete and involve little or no extension of the obvious meaning of the words used to express them. Figurative images do not follow the literal meaning of the words exactly. Images in literature are usually visual, but the term "image" can also refer to the representation of any sensory experience.

Imagery: The array of images in a literary work. Also, figurative language.

Imagism: An English and American poetry movement that flourished between 1908 and 1917. The Imagists used precise, clearly presented images in their works. They also used common, everyday speech and aimed for conciseness, concrete imagery, and the creation of new rhythms.

In medias res: A Latin term meaning "in the middle of things." It refers to the technique of beginning a story at its midpoint and then using various flashback devices to reveal previous action.

Induction: The process of reaching a conclusion by reasoning from specific premises to form a general premise. Also, an introductory portion of a work of literature, especially a play.

Intentional Fallacy: The belief that judgments of a literary work based solely on an author's stated or implied intentions are false and misleading. Critics who believe in the concept of the intentional fallacy typically argue that the work itself is sufficient matter for interpretation, even though they may concede that an author's statement of purpose can be useful.

Interior Monologue: A narrative technique in which characters' thoughts are revealed in a way that appears to be uncontrolled by the author. The interior monologue typically aims to reveal the inner self of a character. It portrays emotional experiences as they occur at both a conscious and unconscious level. Images are often used to represent sensations or emotions.

Internal Rhyme: Rhyme that occurs within a single line of verse.

Irish Literary Renaissance: A late nineteenth- and early twentieth-century movement in Irish literature. Members of the movement aimed to reduce the influence of British culture in Ireland and create an Irish national literature.

Irony: In literary criticism, the effect of language in which the intended meaning is the opposite of what is stated.

Italian Sonnet: See *Sonnet*

J

Jacobean Age: The period of the reign of James I of England (1603–1625). The early literature of this period reflected the worldview of the Elizabethan Age, but a darker, more cynical attitude steadily grew in the art and literature of the Jacobean Age. This was an important time for English drama and poetry.

Jargon: Language that is used or understood only by a select group of people. Jargon may refer to terminology used in a certain profession, such as computer jargon, or it may refer to any nonsensical language that is not understood by most people.

Journalism: Writing intended for publication in a newspaper or magazine, or for broadcast on a radio or television program featuring news, sports, entertainment, or other timely material.

K

Knickerbocker Group: A somewhat indistinct group of New York writers of the first half of the nineteenth century. Members of the group were linked only by location and a common theme: New York life.

***Kunstlerroman*:** See *Bildungsroman*

L

Lais: See *Lay*

Lake Poets: See *Lake School*

Lake School: These poets all lived in the Lake District of England at the turn of the nineteenth century. As a group, they followed no single "school" of thought or literary practice, although their works were uniformly disparaged by the *Edinburgh Review*.

Lay: A song or simple narrative poem. The form originated in medieval France. Early French *lais* were often based on the Celtic legends and other tales sung by Breton minstrels—thus the name of the "Breton lay." In fourteenth-century England, the term "lay" was used to describe short narratives written in imitation of the Breton lays.

Leitmotiv: See *Motif*

Literal Language: An author uses literal language when he or she writes without exaggerating or embellishing the subject matter and without any tools of figurative language.

Literary Ballad: See *Ballad*

Literature: Literature is broadly defined as any written or spoken material, but the term most often refers to creative works.

Lost Generation: A term first used by Gertrude Stein to describe the post-World War I generation of American writers: men and women haunted by a sense of betrayal and emptiness brought about by the destructiveness of the war.

Lyric Poetry: A poem expressing the subjective feelings and personal emotions of the poet. Such poetry is melodic, since it was originally accompanied by a lyre in recitals. Most Western poetry in the twentieth century may be classified as lyrical.

M

Mannerism: Exaggerated, artificial adherence to a literary manner or style. Also, a popular style of the visual arts of late sixteenth-century Europe that was marked by elongation of the human form and by intentional spatial distortion. Literary works that are self-consciously high-toned and artistic are often said to be "mannered."

Masculine Rhyme: See *Rhyme*

Measure: The foot, verse, or time sequence used in a literary work, especially a poem. Measure is often used somewhat incorrectly as a synonym for meter.

Metaphor: A figure of speech that expresses an idea through the image of another object. Metaphors suggest the essence of the first object by identifying it with certain qualities of the second object.

Metaphysical Conceit: See *Conceit*

Metaphysical Poetry: The body of poetry produced by a group of seventeenth-century English writers called the "Metaphysical Poets." The group includes John Donne and Andrew Marvell. The Metaphysical Poets made use of everyday speech, intellectual analysis, and unique imagery. They aimed to portray the ordinary conflicts and contradictions of life. Their poems often took the form of an argument, and many of them emphasize physical and religious love as well as the fleeting nature of life. Elaborate conceits are typical in metaphysical poetry.

Metaphysical Poets: See *Metaphysical Poetry*

Meter: In literary criticism, the repetition of sound patterns that creates a rhythm in poetry. The patterns are based on the number of syllables and the presence and absence of accents. The unit of rhythm in a line is called a foot. Types of meter are classified according to the number of feet in a line. These are the standard English lines: Monometer, one foot; Dimeter, two feet; Trimeter, three feet; Tetrameter, four feet; Pentameter, five feet; Hexameter, six feet (also called the Alexandrine); Heptameter, seven feet (also called the "Fourteener" when the feet are iambic).

Modernism: Modern literary practices. Also, the principles of a literary school that lasted from roughly the beginning of the twentieth century until the end of World War II. Modernism is defined by its rejection of the literary conventions of the nineteenth century and by its opposition to conventional morality, taste, traditions, and economic values.

Monologue: A composition, written or oral, by a single individual. More specifically, a speech given by a single individual in a drama or other public entertainment. It has no set length, although it is usually several or more lines long.

Monometer: See *Meter*

Mood: The prevailing emotions of a work or of the author in his or her creation of the work. The mood of a work is not always what might be expected based on its subject matter.

Motif: A theme, character type, image, metaphor, or other verbal element that recurs throughout a single work of literature or occurs in a number of different works over a period of time.

Motiv: See *Motif*

Muckrakers: An early twentieth-century group of American writers. Typically, their works exposed the wrongdoings of big business and government in the United States.

Muses: Nine Greek mythological goddesses, the daughters of Zeus and Mnemosyne (Memory). Each muse patronized a specific area of the liberal arts and sciences. Calliope presided over epic poetry, Clio over history, Erato over love poetry, Euterpe over music or lyric poetry, Melpomene over tragedy, Polyhymnia over hymns to the gods, Terpsichore over dance, Thalia over comedy, and Urania over astronomy. Poets and writers traditionally made appeals to the Muses for inspiration in their work.

Myth: An anonymous tale emerging from the traditional beliefs of a culture or social unit. Myths use supernatural explanations for natural phenomena. They may also explain cosmic issues like creation and death. Collections of myths, known as mythologies, are common to all cultures and nations, but the best-known myths belong to the Norse, Roman, and Greek mythologies.

N

Narration: The telling of a series of events, real or invented. A narration may be either a simple narrative, in which the events are recounted chronologically, or a narrative with a plot, in which the account is given in a style reflecting the author's artistic concept of the story. Narration is sometimes used as a synonym for "storyline."

Narrative: A verse or prose accounting of an event or sequence of events, real or invented. The term is also used as an adjective in the sense "method of narration." For example, in literary criticism, the expression "narrative technique" usually refers to the way the author structures and presents his or her story.

Narrative Poetry: A nondramatic poem in which the author tells a story. Such poems may be of any length or level of complexity.

Narrator: The teller of a story. The narrator may be the author or a character in the story through whom the author speaks.

Naturalism: A literary movement of the late nineteenth and early twentieth centuries. The movement's major theorist, French novelist Emile Zola, envisioned a type of fiction that would examine human life with the objectivity of scientific inquiry. The Naturalists typically viewed human beings as either the products of "biological determinism," ruled by hereditary instincts and engaged in an endless struggle for survival, or as the products of "socioeconomic determinism," ruled by social and economic forces beyond their control. In their works, the Naturalists generally ignored the highest levels of society and focused on degradation: poverty, alcoholism, prostitution, insanity, and disease.

Negritude: A literary movement based on the concept of a shared cultural bond on the part of black Africans, wherever they may be in the world. It traces its origins to the former French colonies of Africa and the Caribbean. Negritude poets, novelists, and essayists generally stress four points in their writings: One, black alienation from traditional African culture can lead to feelings of inferiority. Two, European colonialism and Western education should be resisted. Three, black Africans should seek to affirm and define their own identity. Four, African culture can and should be reclaimed. Many Negritude writers also claim that blacks can make unique contributions to the world, based on a heightened appreciation of nature, rhythm, and human emotions—aspects of life they say are not so highly valued in the materialistic and rationalistic West.

Negro Renaissance: See *Harlem Renaissance*

Neoclassical Period: See *Neoclassicism*

Neoclassicism: In literary criticism, this term refers to the revival of the attitudes and styles of expression of classical literature. It is generally used to describe a period in European history beginning in the late seventeenth century and lasting until about 1800. In its purest form, Neoclassicism marked a return to order, proportion, restraint, logic, accuracy, and decorum. In England, where Neoclassicism perhaps was most popular, it reflected the influence of seventeenth-century French writers, especially dramatists. Neoclassical writers typically reacted against the intensity and enthusiasm of the Renaissance period. They wrote works that appealed to the intellect, using elevated language and classical literary forms such as satire and the ode. Neoclassical works were often governed by the classical goal of instruction.

Neoclassicists: See *Neoclassicism*

New Criticism: A movement in literary criticism, dating from the late 1920s, that stressed close textual analysis in the interpretation of works of literature. The New Critics saw little merit in historical and biographical analysis. Rather, they aimed to examine the text alone, free from the question of how external events—biographical or otherwise—may have helped shape it.

New Journalism: A type of writing in which the journalist presents factual information in a form usually used in fiction. New journalism emphasizes description, narration, and character development to bring readers closer to the human element of the story, and is often used in personality profiles and in-depth feature articles. It is not compatible with "straight" or "hard" newswriting, which is generally composed in a brief, fact-based style.

New Journalists: See *New Journalism*

New Negro Movement: See *Harlem Renaissance*

Noble Savage: The idea that primitive man is noble and good but becomes evil and corrupted as he becomes civilized. The concept of the noble savage originated in the Renaissance period but is more closely identified with such later writers as Jean-Jacques Rousseau and Aphra Behn.

O

Objective Correlative: An outward set of objects, a situation, or a chain of events corresponding to an inward experience and evoking this experience in the reader. The term frequently appears in modern criticism in discussions of authors' intended effects on the emotional responses of readers.

Objectivity: A quality in writing characterized by the absence of the author's opinion or feeling about the subject matter. Objectivity is an important factor in criticism.

Occasional Verse: Poetry written on the occasion of a significant historical or personal event. *Vers de societe* is sometimes called occasional verse although it is of a less serious nature.

Octave: A poem or stanza composed of eight lines. The term octave most often represents the first eight lines of a Petrarchan sonnet.

Ode: Name given to an extended lyric poem characterized by exalted emotion and dignified style. An ode usually concerns a single, serious theme. Most odes, but not all, are addressed to an object or individual. Odes are distinguished from other lyric poetic forms by their complex rhythmic and stanzaic patterns.

Oedipus Complex: A son's amorous obsession with his mother. The phrase is derived from the story of the ancient Theban hero Oedipus, who unknowingly killed his father and married his mother.

Omniscience: See *Point of View*

Onomatopoeia: The use of words whose sounds express or suggest their meaning. In its simplest sense, onomatopoeia may be represented by words that mimic the sounds they denote such as "hiss" or "meow." At a more subtle level, the pattern and rhythm of sounds and rhymes of a line or poem may be onomatopoeic.

Oral Tradition: See *Oral Transmission*

Oral Transmission: A process by which songs, ballads, folklore, and other material are transmitted by word of mouth. The tradition of oral transmission predates the written record systems of literate society. Oral transmission preserves material sometimes over generations, although often with variations. Memory plays a large part in the recitation and preservation of orally transmitted material.

***Ottava Rima*:** An eight-line stanza of poetry composed in iambic pentameter (a five-foot line in which each foot consists of an unaccented syllable followed by an accented syllable), following the *abababcc* rhyme scheme.

Oxymoron: A phrase combining two contradictory terms. Oxymorons may be intentional or unintentional.

P

Pantheism: The idea that all things are both a manifestation or revelation of God and a part of God at the same time. Pantheism was a common attitude in the early societies of Egypt, India, and Greece—the term derives from the Greek *pan* meaning "all" and *theos* meaning "deity." It later became a significant part of the Christian faith.

Parable: A story intended to teach a moral lesson or answer an ethical question.

Paradox: A statement that appears illogical or contradictory at first, but may actually point to an underlying truth.

Parallelism: A method of comparison of two ideas in which each is developed in the same grammatical structure.

Parnassianism: A mid nineteenth-century movement in French literature. Followers of the movement stressed adherence to well-defined artistic forms as a reaction against the often chaotic expression of the artist's ego that dominated the work of the Romantics. The Parnassians also rejected the moral, ethical, and social themes exhibited in the works of French Romantics such as Victor Hugo. The aesthetic doctrines of the Parnassians strongly influenced the later symbolist and decadent movements.

Parody: In literary criticism, this term refers to an imitation of a serious literary work or the signature style of a particular author in a ridiculous manner. A typical parody adopts the style of the original and applies it to an inappropriate subject for humorous effect. Parody is a form of satire and could be considered the literary equivalent of a caricature or cartoon.

Pastoral: A term derived from the Latin word "pastor," meaning shepherd. A pastoral is a literary composition on a rural theme. The conventions of the pastoral were originated by the third-century Greek poet Theocritus, who wrote about the experiences, love affairs, and pastimes of Sicilian shepherds. In a pastoral, characters and language of a courtly nature are often placed in a simple setting. The term pastoral is also used to classify dramas, elegies, and lyrics that exhibit the use of country settings and shepherd characters.

Pathetic Fallacy: A term coined by English critic John Ruskin to identify writing that falsely endows nonhuman things with human intentions and feelings, such as "angry clouds" and "sad trees."

Pen Name: See *Pseudonym*

Pentameter: See *Meter*

Persona: A Latin term meaning "mask." *Personae* are the characters in a fictional work of literature. The *persona* generally functions as a mask through which the author tells a story in a voice other than his or her own. A *persona* is usually either a character in a story who acts as a narrator or an "implied author," a voice created by the author to act as the narrator for himself or herself.

Personae: See *Persona*

Personal Point of View: See *Point of View*

Personification: A figure of speech that gives human qualities to abstract ideas, animals, and inanimate objects.

Petrarchan Sonnet: See *Sonnet*

Phenomenology: A method of literary criticism based on the belief that things have no existence outside of human consciousness or awareness. Proponents of this theory believe that art is a process that takes place in the mind of the observer as he or she contemplates an object rather than a quality of the object itself.

Plagiarism: Claiming another person's written material as one's own. Plagiarism can take the form of direct, word-for-word copying or the theft of the substance or idea of the work.

Platonic Criticism: A form of criticism that stresses an artistic work's usefulness as an agent of social engineering rather than any quality or value of the work itself.

Platonism: The embracing of the doctrines of the philosopher Plato, popular among the poets of the Renaissance and the Romantic period. Platonism is more flexible than Aristotelian Criticism and places more emphasis on the supernatural and unknown aspects of life.

Plot: In literary criticism, this term refers to the pattern of events in a narrative or drama. In its simplest sense, the plot guides the author in composing the work and helps the reader follow the work. Typically, plots exhibit causality and unity and have a beginning, a middle, and an end. Sometimes, however, a plot may consist of a series of disconnected events, in which case it is known as an "episodic plot."

Poem: In its broadest sense, a composition utilizing rhyme, meter, concrete detail, and expressive language to create a literary experience with emotional and aesthetic appeal.

Poet: An author who writes poetry or verse. The term is also used to refer to an artist or writer who has an exceptional gift for expression, imagination, and energy in the making of art in any form.

Poete maudit: A term derived from Paul Verlaine's *Les poetes maudits* (*The Accursed Poets*), a collection of essays on the French symbolist writers Stephane Mallarme, Arthur Rimbaud, and Tristan Corbiere. In the sense intended by Verlaine, the poet is "accursed" for choosing to explore extremes of human experience outside of middle-class society.

Poetic Fallacy: See *Pathetic Fallacy*

Poetic Justice: An outcome in a literary work, not necessarily a poem, in which the good are rewarded and the evil are punished, especially in ways that particularly fit their virtues or crimes.

Poetic License: Distortions of fact and literary convention made by a writer—not always a poet—for the sake of the effect gained. Poetic license is closely related to the concept of "artistic freedom."

Poetics: This term has two closely related meanings. It denotes (1) an aesthetic theory in literary criticism about the essence of poetry or (2) rules prescribing the proper methods, content, style, or diction of poetry. The term poetics may also refer to theories about literature in general, not just poetry.

Poetry: In its broadest sense, writing that aims to present ideas and evoke an emotional experience in the reader through the use of meter, imagery, connotative and concrete words, and a carefully constructed structure based on rhythmic patterns. Poetry typically relies on words and expressions that have several layers of meaning. It also makes use of the effects of regular rhythm on the ear and may make a strong appeal to the senses through the use of imagery.

Point of View: The narrative perspective from which a literary work is presented to the reader. There are four traditional points of view. The "third person omniscient" gives the reader a "godlike" perspective, unrestricted by time or place, from which to see actions and look into the minds of characters. This allows the author to comment openly on characters and events in the work. The "third-person" point of view presents the events of the story from outside of any single character's perception, much like the omniscient point of view, but the reader must understand the action as it takes place and without any special insight into characters' minds or motivations. The "first person" or "personal" point of view relates events as they are perceived by a single character. The main character "tells" the story and may offer opinions about the action and characters which differ from those of the author. Much less common than omniscient, third person, and first person is the "second-person" point of view, wherein the author tells the story as if it is happening to the reader.

Polemic: A work in which the author takes a stand on a controversial subject, such as abortion or religion. Such works are often extremely argumentative or provocative.

Pornography: Writing intended to provoke feelings of lust in the reader. Such works are often condemned by critics and teachers, but those which can be shown to have literary value are viewed less harshly.

Post-Aesthetic Movement: An artistic response made by African Americans to the black aesthetic movement of the 1960s and early 1970s. Writers since that time have adopted a somewhat different tone in their work, with less emphasis placed on the disparity between black and white in the United States. In the words of post-aesthetic authors such as Toni Morrison, John Edgar Wideman, and Kristin Hunter, African Americans are portrayed as

looking inward for answers to their own questions, rather than always looking to the outside world.

Postmodernism: Writing from the 1960s forward characterized by experimentation and continuing to apply some of the fundamentals of modernism, which included existentialism and alienation. Postmodernists have gone a step further in the rejection of tradition begun with the modernists by also rejecting traditional forms, preferring the antinovel over the novel and the antihero over the hero.

Pre-Raphaelites: A circle of writers and artists in mid nineteenth-century England. Valuing the pre-Renaissance artistic qualities of religious symbolism, lavish pictorialism, and natural sensuousness, the Pre-Raphaelites cultivated a sense of mystery and melancholy that influenced later writers associated with the Symbolist and Decadent movements.

Primitivism: The belief that primitive peoples were nobler and less flawed than civilized peoples because they had not been subjected to the corrupt influence of society.

Projective Verse: A form of free verse in which the poet's breathing pattern determines the lines of the poem. Poets who advocate projective verse are against all formal structures in writing, including meter and form.

Prologue: An introductory section of a literary work. It often contains information establishing the situation of the characters or presents information about the setting, time period, or action. In drama, the prologue is spoken by a chorus or by one of the principal characters.

Prose: A literary medium that attempts to mirror the language of everyday speech. It is distinguished from poetry by its use of unmetered, unrhymed language consisting of logically related sentences. Prose is usually grouped into paragraphs that form a cohesive whole such as an essay or a novel.

Prosopopoeia: See *Personification*

Protagonist: The central character of a story who serves as a focus for its themes and incidents and as the principal rationale for its development. The protagonist is sometimes referred to in discussions of modern literature as the hero or antihero.

Proverb: A brief, sage saying that expresses a truth about life in a striking manner.

Pseudonym: A name assumed by a writer, most often intended to prevent his or her identification as the author of a work. Two or more authors may work together under one pseudonym, or an author may use a different name for each genre he or she publishes in. Some publishing companies maintain "house pseudonyms," under which any number of authors may write installations in a series. Some authors also choose a pseudonym over their real names the way an actor may use a stage name.

Pun: A play on words that have similar sounds but different meanings.

Pure Poetry: poetry written without instructional intent or moral purpose that aims only to please a reader by its imagery or musical flow. The term pure poetry is used as the antonym of the term "didacticism."

Q

Quatrain: A four-line stanza of a poem or an entire poem consisting of four lines.

R

Realism: A nineteenth-century European literary movement that sought to portray familiar characters, situations, and settings in a realistic manner. This was done primarily by using an objective narrative point of view and through the buildup of accurate detail. The standard for success of any realistic work depends on how faithfully it transfers common experience into fictional forms. The realistic method may be altered or extended, as in stream of consciousness writing, to record highly subjective experience.

Refrain: A phrase repeated at intervals throughout a poem. A refrain may appear at the end of each stanza or at less regular intervals. It may be altered slightly at each appearance.

Renaissance: The period in European history that marked the end of the Middle Ages. It began in Italy in the late fourteenth century. In broad terms, it is usually seen as spanning the fourteenth, fifteenth, and sixteenth centuries, although it did not reach Great Britain, for example, until the 1480s or so. The Renaissance saw an awakening in almost every sphere of human activity, especially science, philosophy, and the arts. The period is best defined by the emergence of a general philosophy that emphasized the importance of the intellect, the individual, and world affairs. It contrasts strongly with the medieval worldview, characterized by the dominant concerns of faith, the social collective, and spiritual salvation.

Repartee: Conversation featuring snappy retorts and witticisms.

Restoration: See *Restoration Age*

Restoration Age: A period in English literature beginning with the crowning of Charles II in 1660 and running to about 1700. The era, which was characterized by a reaction against Puritanism, was the first great age of the comedy of manners. The finest literature of the era is typically witty and urbane, and often lewd.

Rhetoric: In literary criticism, this term denotes the art of ethical persuasion. In its strictest sense, rhetoric adheres to various principles developed since classical times for arranging facts and ideas in a clear, persuasive, appealing manner. The term is also used to refer to effective prose in general and theories of or methods for composing effective prose.

Rhetorical Question: A question intended to provoke thought, but not an expressed answer, in the reader. It is most commonly used in oratory and other persuasive genres.

Rhyme: When used as a noun in literary criticism, this term generally refers to a poem in which words sound identical or very similar and appear in parallel positions in two or more lines. Rhymes are classified into different types according to where they fall in a line or stanza or according to the degree of similarity they exhibit in their spellings and sounds. Some major types of rhyme are "masculine" rhyme, "feminine" rhyme, and "triple" rhyme. In a masculine rhyme, the rhyming sound falls in a single accented syllable, as with "heat" and "eat." Feminine rhyme is a rhyme of two syllables, one stressed and one unstressed, as with "merry" and "tarry." Triple rhyme matches the sound of the accented syllable and the two unaccented syllables that follow: "narrative" and "declarative."

Rhyme Royal: A stanza of seven lines composed in iambic pentameter and rhymed *ababbcc*. The name is said to be a tribute to King James I of Scotland, who made much use of the form in his poetry.

Rhyme Scheme: See *Rhyme*

Rhythm: A regular pattern of sound, time intervals, or events occurring in writing, most often and most discernably in poetry. Regular, reliable rhythm is known to be soothing to humans, while interrupted, unpredictable, or rapidly changing rhythm is disturbing. These effects are known to authors, who use them to produce a desired reaction in the reader.

Rococo: A style of European architecture that flourished in the eighteenth century, especially in

France. The most notable features of *rococo* are its extensive use of ornamentation and its themes of lightness, gaiety, and intimacy. In literary criticism, the term is often used disparagingly to refer to a decadent or overly ornamental style.

Romance:

Romantic Age: See *Romanticism*

Romanticism: This term has two widely accepted meanings. In historical criticism, it refers to a European intellectual and artistic movement of the late eighteenth and early nineteenth centuries that sought greater freedom of personal expression than that allowed by the strict rules of literary form and logic of the eighteenth-century Neoclassicists. The Romantics preferred emotional and imaginative expression to rational analysis. They considered the individual to be at the center of all experience and so placed him or her at the center of their art. The Romantics believed that the creative imagination reveals nobler truths—unique feelings and attitudes—than those that could be discovered by logic or by scientific examination. Both the natural world and the state of childhood were important sources for revelations of "eternal truths." "Romanticism" is also used as a general term to refer to a type of sensibility found in all periods of literary history and usually considered to be in opposition to the principles of classicism. In this sense, Romanticism signifies any work or philosophy in which the exotic or dreamlike figure strongly, or that is devoted to individualistic expression, self-analysis, or a pursuit of a higher realm of knowledge than can be discovered by human reason.

Romantics: See *Romanticism*

Russian Symbolism: A Russian poetic movement, derived from French symbolism, that flourished between 1894 and 1910. While some Russian Symbolists continued in the French tradition, stressing aestheticism and the importance of suggestion above didactic intent, others saw their craft as a form of mystical worship, and themselves as mediators between the supernatural and the mundane.

S

Satire: A work that uses ridicule, humor, and wit to criticize and provoke change in human nature and institutions. There are two major types of satire: "formal" or "direct" satire speaks directly to the reader or to a character in the work; "indirect" satire relies upon the ridiculous behavior of its characters to make its point. Formal satire is further divided into two manners: the "Horatian," which ridicules gently, and the "Juvenalian," which derides its subjects harshly and bitterly.

Scansion: The analysis or "scanning" of a poem to determine its meter and often its rhyme scheme. The most common system of scansion uses accents (slanted lines drawn above syllables) to show stressed syllables, breves (curved lines drawn above syllables) to show unstressed syllables, and vertical lines to separate each foot.

Second Person: See *Point of View*

Semiotics: The study of how literary forms and conventions affect the meaning of language.

Sestet: Any six-line poem or stanza.

Setting: The time, place, and culture in which the action of a narrative takes place. The elements of setting may include geographic location, characters' physical and mental environments, prevailing cultural attitudes, or the historical time in which the action takes place.

Shakespearean Sonnet: See *Sonnet*

Signifying Monkey: A popular trickster figure in black folklore, with hundreds of tales about this character documented since the nineteenth century.

Simile: A comparison, usually using "like" or "as," of two essentially dissimilar things, as in "coffee as cold as ice" or "He sounded like a broken record."

Slang: A type of informal verbal communication that is generally unacceptable for formal writing. Slang words and phrases are often colorful exaggerations used to emphasize the speaker's point; they may also be shortened versions of an often-used word or phrase.

Slant Rhyme: See *Consonance*

Slave Narrative: Autobiographical accounts of American slave life as told by escaped slaves. These works first appeared during the abolition movement of the 1830s through the 1850s.

Social Realism: See *Socialist Realism*

Socialist Realism: The Socialist Realism school of literary theory was proposed by Maxim Gorky and established as a dogma by the first Soviet Congress of Writers. It demanded adherence to a communist worldview in works of literature. Its doctrines required an objective viewpoint comprehensible to the working classes and themes of social struggle featuring strong proletarian heroes.

Soliloquy: A monologue in a drama used to give the audience information and to develop the speaker's character. It is typically a projection of the speaker's innermost thoughts. Usually delivered while the speaker is alone on stage, a soliloquy is intended to present an illusion of unspoken reflection.

Sonnet: A fourteen-line poem, usually composed in iambic pentameter, employing one of several rhyme schemes. There are three major types of sonnets, upon which all other variations of the form are based: the "Petrarchan" or "Italian" sonnet, the "Shakespearean" or "English" sonnet, and the "Spenserian" sonnet. A Petrarchan sonnet consists of an octave rhymed *abbaabba* and a "sestet" rhymed either *cdecde, cdccdc,* or *cdedce.* The octave poses a question or problem, relates a narrative, or puts forth a proposition; the sestet presents a solution to the problem, comments upon the narrative, or applies the proposition put forth in the octave. The Shakespearean sonnet is divided into three quatrains and a couplet rhymed *abab cdcd efef gg.* The couplet provides an epigrammatic comment on the narrative or problem put forth in the quatrains. The Spenserian sonnet uses three quatrains and a couplet like the Shakespearean, but links their three rhyme schemes in this way: *abab bcbc cdcd ee.* The Spenserian sonnet develops its theme in two parts like the Petrarchan, its final six lines resolving a problem, analyzing a narrative, or applying a proposition put forth in its first eight lines.

Spenserian Sonnet: See *Sonnet*

Spenserian Stanza: A nine-line stanza having eight verses in iambic pentameter, its ninth verse in iambic hexameter, and the rhyme scheme *ababbcbcc.*

Spondee: In poetry meter, a foot consisting of two long or stressed syllables occurring together. This form is quite rare in English verse, and is usually composed of two monosyllabic words.

Sprung Rhythm: Versification using a specific number of accented syllables per line but disregarding the number of unaccented syllables that fall in each line, producing an irregular rhythm in the poem.

Stanza: A subdivision of a poem consisting of lines grouped together, often in recurring patterns of rhyme, line length, and meter. Stanzas may also serve as units of thought in a poem much like paragraphs in prose.

Stereotype: A stereotype was originally the name for a duplication made during the printing process; this led to its modern definition as a person or thing that is (or is assumed to be) the same as all others of its type.

Stream of Consciousness: A narrative technique for rendering the inward experience of a character. This technique is designed to give the impression of an ever-changing series of thoughts, emotions, images, and memories in the spontaneous and seemingly illogical order that they occur in life.

Structuralism: A twentieth-century movement in literary criticism that examines how literary texts arrive at their meanings, rather than the meanings themselves. There are two major types of structuralist analysis: one examines the way patterns of linguistic structures unify a specific text and emphasize certain elements of that text, and the other interprets the way literary forms and conventions affect the meaning of language itself.

Structure: The form taken by a piece of literature. The structure may be made obvious for ease of understanding, as in nonfiction works, or may be obscured for artistic purposes, as in some poetry or seemingly "unstructured" prose.

Sturm und Drang: A German term meaning "storm and stress." It refers to a German literary movement of the 1770s and 1780s that reacted against the order and rationalism of the enlightenment, focusing instead on the intense experience of extraordinary individuals.

Style: A writer's distinctive manner of arranging words to suit his or her ideas and purpose in writing. The unique imprint of the author's personality upon his or her writing, style is the product of an author's way of arranging ideas and his or her use of diction, different sentence structures, rhythm, figures of speech, rhetorical principles, and other elements of composition.

Subject: The person, event, or theme at the center of a work of literature. A work may have one or more subjects of each type, with shorter works tending to have fewer and longer works tending to have more.

Subjectivity: Writing that expresses the author's personal feelings about his subject, and which may or may not include factual information about the subject.

Surrealism: A term introduced to criticism by Guillaume Apollinaire and later adopted by Andre Breton. It refers to a French literary and artistic movement founded in the 1920s. The Surrealists sought to express unconscious thoughts and feelings in their works. The best-known technique used for achieving this aim was automatic writing—transcriptions of spontaneous outpourings from the unconscious. The Surrealists proposed to unify the contrary levels of conscious and unconscious, dream and reality, objectivity and subjectivity into a new level of "super-realism."

Suspense: A literary device in which the author maintains the audience's attention through the buildup of events, the outcome of which will soon be revealed.

Syllogism: A method of presenting a logical argument. In its most basic form, the syllogism consists of a major premise, a minor premise, and a conclusion.

Symbol: Something that suggests or stands for something else without losing its original identity. In literature, symbols combine their literal meaning with the suggestion of an abstract concept. Literary symbols are of two types: those that carry complex associations of meaning no matter what their contexts, and those that derive their suggestive meaning from their functions in specific literary works.

Symbolism: This term has two widely accepted meanings. In historical criticism, it denotes an early modernist literary movement initiated in France during the nineteenth century that reacted against the prevailing standards of realism. Writers in this movement aimed to evoke, indirectly and symbolically, an order of being beyond the material world of the five senses. Poetic expression of personal emotion figured strongly in the movement, typically by means of a private set of symbols uniquely identifiable with the individual poet. The principal aim of the Symbolists was to express in words the highly complex feelings that grew out of everyday contact with the world. In a broader sense, the term "symbolism" refers to the use of one object to represent another.

Symbolist: See *Symbolism*

Symbolist Movement: See *Symbolism*

Sympathetic Fallacy: See *Affective Fallacy*

T

Tanka: A form of Japanese poetry similar to *haiku*. A *tanka* is five lines long, with the lines containing five, seven, five, seven, and seven syllables respectively.

Terza Rima: A three-line stanza form in poetry in which the rhymes are made on the last word of each line in the following manner: the first and third lines of the first stanza, then the second line of the first stanza and the first and third lines of the second stanza, and so on with the middle line of any stanza rhyming with the first and third lines of the following stanza.

Tetrameter: See *Meter*

Textual Criticism: A branch of literary criticism that seeks to establish the authoritative text of a literary work. Textual critics typically compare all known manuscripts or printings of a single work in order to assess the meanings of differences and revisions. This procedure allows them to arrive at a definitive version that (supposedly) corresponds to the author's original intention.

Theme: The main point of a work of literature. The term is used interchangeably with thesis.

Thesis: A thesis is both an essay and the point argued in the essay. Thesis novels and thesis plays share the quality of containing a thesis which is supported through the action of the story.

Third Person: See *Point of View*

Tone: The author's attitude toward his or her audience may be deduced from the tone of the work. A formal tone may create distance or convey politeness, while an informal tone may encourage a friendly, intimate, or intrusive feeling in the reader. The author's attitude toward his or her subject matter may also be deduced from the tone of the words he or she uses in discussing it.

Tragedy: A drama in prose or poetry about a noble, courageous hero of excellent character who, because of some tragic character flaw or *hamartia*, brings ruin upon him- or herself. Tragedy treats its subjects in a dignified and serious manner, using poetic language to help evoke pity and fear and bring about catharsis, a purging of these emotions. The tragic form was practiced extensively by the ancient Greeks. In the Middle Ages, when classical works were virtually unknown, tragedy came to denote any works about the fall of persons from exalted to low conditions due to any reason: fate, vice, weakness, etc. According to the classical definition of tragedy, such works present the "pathetic"—that which evokes pity—rather than the tragic. The classical form of tragedy was revived in the sixteenth century; it flourished especially on the Elizabethan stage. In modern times, dramatists have attempted to adapt the form to the needs of modern society by drawing their heroes from the ranks of ordinary men and women and defining the nobility of these heroes in terms of spirit rather than exalted social standing.

Tragic Flaw: In a tragedy, the quality within the hero or heroine which leads to his or her downfall.

Transcendentalism: An American philosophical and religious movement, based in New England from around 1835 until the Civil War. Transcendentalism was a form of American romanticism that had its roots abroad in the works of Thomas Carlyle, Samuel Coleridge, and Johann Wolfgang von Goethe. The Transcendentalists stressed the importance of intuition and subjective experience in communication with God. They rejected religious dogma and texts in favor of mysticism and scientific naturalism. They pursued truths that lie beyond the "colorless" realms perceived by reason and the senses and were active social reformers in public education, women's rights, and the abolition of slavery.

Trickster: A character or figure common in Native American and African literature who uses his ingenuity to defeat enemies and escape difficult situations. Tricksters are most often animals, such as the spider, hare, or coyote, although they may take the form of humans as well.

Trimeter: See *Meter*

Triple Rhyme: See *Rhyme*

Trochee: See *Foot*

U

Understatement: See *Irony*

Unities: Strict rules of dramatic structure, formulated by Italian and French critics of the Renaissance and based loosely on the principles of drama discussed by Aristotle in his *Poetics*. Foremost among these rules were the three unities of action, time, and place that compelled a dramatist to: (1) construct a single plot with a beginning, middle, and end that details the causal relationships of action and character; (2) restrict the action to the events of a single day; and (3) limit the scene to a single place or city. The unities were observed faithfully by continental European writers until the Romantic Age, but they were never regularly observed in English drama. Modern dramatists are typically more concerned with a unity of impression or emotional effect than with any of the classical unities.

Urban Realism: A branch of realist writing that attempts to accurately reflect the often harsh facts of modern urban existence.

Utopia: A fictional perfect place, such as "paradise" or "heaven."

Utopian: See *Utopia*

Utopianism: See *Utopia*

V

Verisimilitude: Literally, the appearance of truth. In literary criticism, the term refers to aspects of a work of literature that seem true to the reader.

Vers de societe: See *Occasional Verse*

Vers libre: See *Free Verse*

Verse: A line of metered language, a line of a poem, or any work written in verse.

Versification: The writing of verse. Versification may also refer to the meter, rhyme, and other mechanical components of a poem.

Victorian: Refers broadly to the reign of Queen Victoria of England (1837–1901) and to anything with qualities typical of that era. For example, the qualities of smug narrowmindedness, bourgeois materialism, faith in social progress, and priggish morality are often considered Victorian. This stereotype is contradicted by such dramatic intellectual developments as the theories of Charles Darwin, Karl Marx, and Sigmund Freud (which stirred strong debates in England) and the critical attitudes of serious Victorian writers like Charles Dickens and George Eliot. In literature, the Victorian Period was the great age of the English novel, and the latter part of the era saw the rise of movements such as decadence and symbolism.

Victorian Age: See *Victorian*

Victorian Period: See *Victorian*

W

Weltanschauung: A German term referring to a person's worldview or philosophy.

Weltschmerz: A German term meaning "world pain." It describes a sense of anguish about the nature of existence, usually associated with a melancholy, pessimistic attitude.

Z

Zarzuela: A type of Spanish operetta.

Zeitgeist: A German term meaning "spirit of the time." It refers to the moral and intellectual trends of a given era.

Cumulative Author/Title Index

A

Acosta, Teresa Palomo
   My Mother Pieced Quilts: V12
An African Elegy (Duncan): V13
Ah, Are You Digging on My Grave?
   (Hardy): V4
Alabama Centennial (Madgett):V10
American Poetry (Simpson): V7
An Arundel Tomb (Larkin): V12
Anasazi (Snyder): V9
Angelou, Maya
   Harlem Hopscotch: V2
   On the Pulse of Morning: V3
Angle of Geese (Momaday): V2
Annabel Lee (Poe): V9
Anonymous
   Barbara Allan: V7
   Go Down, Moses: V11
   Lord Randal: V6
   The Seafarer: V8
   Sir Patrick Spens: V4
   Swing Low Sweet Chariot: V1
Anorexic (Boland): V12
Any Human to Another (Cullen): V3
A Pièd (McElroy): V3
Arnold, Matthew
   Dover Beach: V2
Ars Poetica (MacLeish): V5
As I Walked Out One Evening
   (Auden): V4
Ashbery, John
   Paradoxes and Oxymorons: V11
At the Bomb Testing Site (Stafford): V8
Atwood, Margaret
   Siren Song: V7
Auden, W. H.
   As I Walked Out One Evening: V4
   Funeral Blues: V10
   Musée des Beaux Arts: V1
   The Unknown Citizen: V3
Auto Wreck (Shapiro): V3
Autumn Begins in Martins Ferry,
   Ohio (Wright): V8

B

Ballad of Orange and Grape
   (Rukeyser):V10
Baraka, Amiri
   In Memory of Radio: V9
Barbara Allan (Anonymous): V7
Barbie Doll (Piercy): V9
Ballad of Birmingham (Randall): V5
Barrett, Elizabeth
   Sonnet 43: V2
The Base Stealer (Francis): V12
The Bean Eaters (Brooks): V2
Because I Could Not Stop for Death
   (Dickinson): V2
Bedtime Story (MacBeth): V8
The Bells (Poe): V3
Beowulf (Wilbur): V11
Beware: Do Not Read This Poem
   (Reed): V6
Beware of Ruins (Hope): V8
Birch Canoe (Revard): V5
Birches (Frost): V13
Birney, Earle
   Vancouver Lights: V8
A Birthday (Rossetti):V10
Bishop, Elizabeth
   Brazil, January 1, 1502: V6
   Filling Station: V12
Black Zodiac (Wright):V10
Blake, William
   The Lamb: V12
   The Tyger: V2
A Blessing (Wright): V7
Blood Oranges (Mueller): V13
Blumenthal, Michael
   Inventors: V7
Bly, Robert
   Come with Me: V6
Boland, Eavan
   Anorexic: V12
Bradstreet, Anne
   To My Dear and Loving
      Husband: V6
Brazil, January 1, 1502 (Bishop):
   V6
Bright Star! Would I Were Steadfast
   as Thou Art (Keats): V9
Brooke, Rupert
   The Soldier: V7
Brooks, Gwendolyn
   The Bean Eaters: V2
   The Sonnet-Ballad: V1
   Strong Men, Riding Horses: V4
   We Real Cool: V6
Browning, Elizabeth Barrett
   Sonnet 43: V2
Browning, Robert
   My Last Duchess: V1
Burns, Robert
   A Red, Red Rose: V8
The Bustle in a House
   (Dickinson):V10
Butcher Shop (Simic): V7
Byron, Lord
   The Destruction of Sennacherib: V1

C

Cargoes (Masefield): V5
Carroll, Lewis
   Jabberwocky: V11
Casey at the Bat (Thayer): V5
Cavalry Crossing a Ford (Whitman): V13
The Charge of the Light Brigade (Tennyson): V1
Chicago (Sandburg): V3
Chocolates (Simpson): V11
Clifton, Lucille
   Miss Rosie: V1
Coleridge, Samuel Taylor
   Kubla Khan: V5
   The Rime of the Ancient Mariner: V4
Come with Me (Bly): V6
The Constellation Orion (Kooser): V8
Concord Hymn (Emerson): V4
The Conquerors (McGinley): V13
Cool Tombs (Sandburg): V6
The Courage That My Mother Had (Millay): V3
Crane, Stephen
   War Is Kind: V9
The Creation (Johnson): V1
The Cremation of Sam McGee (Service): V10
Cullen, Countee
   Any Human to Another: V3
cummings, e. e.
   l(a: V1
   i was sitting in mcsorley's: V13
   maggie and milly and molly and may: V12
   old age sticks: V3
The Czar's Last Christmas Letter. A Barn in the Urals (Dubie): V12

D

Darwin in 1881 (Schnackenberg): V13
Dawe, Bruce
   Drifters: V10
Daylights (Warren): V13
Dear Reader (Tate): V10
The Death of the Ball Turret Gunner (Jarrell): V2
The Death of the Hired Man (Frost): V4
The Destruction of Sennacherib (Byron): V1
Dickey, James
   The Heaven of Animals: V6
   The Hospital Window: V11
Dickinson, Emily
   Because I Could Not Stop for Death: V2
   The Bustle in a House: V10
   "Hope" Is the Thing with Feathers: V3
   I felt a Funeral, in my Brain: V13
   I Heard a Fly Buzz—When I Died—: V5
   My Life Closed Twice Before Its Close: V8
   A Narrow Fellow in the Grass: V11
   The Soul Selects Her Own Society: V1
   There's a Certain Slant of Light: V6
   This Is My Letter to the World: V4
Digging (Heaney): V5
Do Not Go Gentle into that Good Night (Thomas): V1
Donne, John
   Holy Sonnet 10: V2
   A Valediction: Forbidding Mourning: V11
Dove, Rita
   This Life: V1
Dover Beach (Arnold): V2
Drifters (Dawe): V10
A Drink of Water (Heaney): V8
Drought Year (Wright): V8
Dubie, Norman
   The Czar's Last Christmas Letter. A Barn in the Urals: V12
Du Bois, W. E. B.
   The Song of the Smoke: V13
Duncan, Robert
   An African Elegy: V13
Dugan, Alan
   How We Heard the Name: V10
Dulce et Decorum Est (Owen): V10

E

The Eagle (Tennyson): V11
Easter 1916 (Yeats): V5
Eating Poetry (Strand): V9
Elegy Written in a Country Churchyard (Gray): V9
Eliot, T. S.
   Journey of the Magi: V7
   The Love Song of J. Alfred Prufrock: V1
Emerson, Ralph Waldo
   Concord Hymn: V4
Espada, Martín
   We Live by What We See at Night: V13
Ethics (Pastan): V8
The Exhibit (Mueller): V9

F

Facing It (Komunyakaa): V5
Falling Upon Earth (Bashō): V2
A Far Cry from Africa (Walcott): V6
A Farewell to English (Hartnett): V10
Fenton, James
   The Milkfish Gatherers: V11
Fern Hill (Thomas): V3
Fifteen (Stafford): V2
Filling Station (Bishop): V12
Fire and Ice (Frost): V7
For An Assyrian Frieze (Viereck): V9
For Jean Vincent D'abbadie, Baron St.-Castin (Nowlan): V12
For the Union Dead (Lowell): V7
For the White poets who would be Indian (Rose): V13
The Force That Through the Green Fuse Drives the Flower (Thomas): V8
Four Mountain Wolves (Silko): V9
Francis, Robert
   The Base Stealer: V12
Frost, Robert
   Birches: V13
   The Death of the Hired Man: V4
   Fire and Ice: V7
   Mending Wall: V5
   Nothing Gold Can Stay: V3
   Out, Out—: V10
   The Road Not Taken: V2
   Stopping by Woods on a Snowy Evening: V1
   The Wood-Pile: V6
Funeral Blues (Auden): V10

G

Ginsberg, Allen
   A Supermarket in California: V5
Glück, Louise
   The Gold Lily: V5
Go Down, Moses (Anonymous): V11
The Gold Lily (Glück): V5
A Grafted Tongue (Montague): V12
Graham, Jorie
   The Hiding Place: V10
Gray, Thomas
   Elegy Written in a Country Churchyard: V9
Gunn, Thom
   The Missing: V9

H

H.D.
   Helen: V6
Hall, Donald
   Names of Horses: V8
Hardy, Thomas
   Ah, Are You Digging on My Grave?: V4
   The Man He Killed: V3
Harlem (Hughes): V1
Harlem Hopscotch (Angelou): V2
Hartnett, Michael
   A Farewell to English: V10
Having a Coke with You (O'Hara): V12

Hawk Roosting (Hughes): V4
Hayden, Robert
   Those Winter Sundays: V1
Heaney, Seamus
   A Drink of Water: V8
   Digging: V5
   Midnight: V2
Hecht, Anthony
   "More Light! More Light!": V6
The Heaven of Animals (Dickey): V6
Helen (H.D.): V6
Herrick, Robert
   To the Virgins, to Make Much of Time: V13
The Hiding Place (Graham):V10
High Windows (Larkin): V3
The Highwayman (Noyes): V4
Holmes, Oliver Wendell
   Old Ironsides: V9
Holy Sonnet 10 (Donne): V2
Hope, A. D.
   Beware of Ruins: V8
Hope Is a Tattered Flag (Sandburg): V12
"Hope" Is the Thing with Feathers (Dickinson): V3
The Hospital Window (Dickey): V11
Housman, A. E.
   To an Athlete Dying Young: V7
   When I Was One-and-Twenty: V4
How We Heard the Name (Dugan):V10
Hughes, Langston
   Harlem: V1
   Mother to Son: V3
   Theme for English B: V6
   The Negro Speaks of Rivers:V10
Hughes, Ted
   Hawk Roosting: V4
Hunger in New York City (Ortiz): V4
Hurt Hawks (Jeffers): V3

I

I felt a Funeral, in my Brain (Dickinson): V13
I Hear America Singing (Whitman): V3
I Heard a Fly Buzz—When I Died— (Dickinson): V5
i was sitting in mcsorley's (cummings): V13
The Idea of Order at Key West (Stevens): V13
In a Station of the Metro (Pound): V2
In Flanders Fields (McCrae): V5
In the Land of Shinar (Levertov): V7
In Memory of Radio (Baraka): V9
Inventors (Blumentha): V7
An Irish Airman Foresees His Death (Yeats): V1
Island of the Three Marias (Ríos): V11

J

Jabberwocky (Carroll): V11
Jarrell, Randall
   The Death of the Ball Turret Gunner: V2
Jeffers, Robinson
   Hurt Hawks: V3
   Shine Perishing Republic: V4
Johnson, James Weldon
   The Creation: V1
Journey of the Magi (Eliot): V7

K

Keats, John
   Bright Star! Would I Were Steadfast as Thou Art: V9
   Ode on a Grecian Urn: V1
   Ode to a Nightingale: V3
   When I Have Fears that I May Cease to Be: V2
Kenyon, Jane
   "Trouble with Math in a One-Room Country School": V9
King James Bible
   Psalm 8: V9
   Psalm 23: V4
Kinnell, Galway
   Saint Francis and the Sow: V9
Kooser, Ted
   The Constellation Orion: V8
Komunyakaa, Yusef
   Facing It: V5
Kubla Khan (Coleridge): V5
Kunitz, Stanley
   The War Against the Trees: V11

L

l(a (cummings): V1
The Lamb (Blake): V12
Lament for the Dorsets (Purdy): V5
Landscape with Tractor (Taylor):V10
Larkin, Philip
   An Arundel Tomb: V12
   High Windows: V3
   Toads: V4
Lawrence, D. H.
   Piano: V6
Layton, Irving
   A Tall Man Executes a Jig: V12
Leda and the Swan (Yeats): V13
Lee, Li-Young
   The Weight of Sweetness: V11
Levertov, Denise
   In the Land of Shinar: V7
Leviathan (Merwin): V5
Levine, Philip
   Starlight: V8
Longfellow, Henry Wadsworth
   A Psalm of Life: V7
   Paul Revere's Ride: V2

Lord Randal (Anonymous): V6
Lost Sister (Song): V5
The Love Song of J. Alfred Prufrock (Eliot): V1
Lowell, Robert
   For the Union Dead: V7
   The Quaker Graveyard in Nantucket: V6

M

MacBeth, George
   Bedtime Story: V8
MacLeish, Archibald
   Ars Poetica: V5
Madgett, Naomi Long
   *Alabama Centennial:*V10
maggie and milly and molly and may (cummings): V12
The Man He Killed (Hardy): V3
A Martian Sends a Postcard Home (Raine): V7
Marvell, Andrew
   To His Coy Mistress: V5
Masefield, John
   Cargoes: V5
Matsuo Bashō
   Falling Upon Earth: V2
   The Moon Glows the Same: V7
McCrae, John
   In Flanders Fields: V5
McElroy, Colleen
   A Pièd: V3
McGinley, Phyllis
   The Conquerors: V13
   Reactionary Essay on Applied Science: V9
McKay, Claude
   The Tropics in New York: V4
Meeting the British (Muldoon): V7
Mending Wall (Frost): V5
Merriam, Eve
   Onomatopoeia: V6
Merwin, W. S.
   Leviathan: V5
Midnight (Heaney): V2
The Milkfish Gatherers (Fenton): V11
Millay, Edna St. Vincent
   The Courage That My Mother Had: V3
Milton, John
   [On His Blindness] Sonnet 16: V3
Mirror (Plath): V1
Miss Rosie (Clifton): V1
The Missing (Gunn): V9
Momaday, N. Scott
   Angle of Geese: V2
   To a Child Running With Outstretched Arms in Canyon de Chelly: V11
Montague, John
   A Grafted Tongue: V12
The Moon Glows the Same (Bashō): V7

"More Light! More Light!" (Hecht): V6
Mother to Son (Hughes): V3
Muldoon, Paul
   Meeting the British: V7
Mueller, Lisel
   Blood Oranges: V13
   The Exhibit: V9
Musée des Beaux Arts (Auden): V1
Music Lessons (Oliver): V8
My Last Duchess (Browning): V1
My Life Closed Twice Before Its Close (Dickinson): V8
My Mother Pieced Quilts (Acosta): V12
My Papa's Waltz (Roethke): V3

N

Names of Horses (Hall): V8
A Narrow Fellow in the Grass (Dickinson): V11
The Negro Speaks of Rivers (Hughes): V10
Nemerov, Howard
   The Phoenix: V10
Neruda, Pablo
   Tonight I Can Write: V11
Not Waving but Drowning (Smith): V3
Nothing Gold Can Stay (Frost): V3
Nowlan, Alden
   For Jean Vincent D'abbadie, Baron St.-Castin: V12
Noyes, Alfred
   The Highwayman: V4

O

O Captain! My Captain! (Whitman): V2
Ode on a Grecian Urn (Keats): V1
Ode to a Nightingale (Keats): V3
Ode to the West Wind (Shelley): V2
O'Hara, Frank
   Having a Coke with You: V12
   Why I Am Not a Painter: V8
old age sticks (cummings): V3
Old Ironsides (Holmes): V9
Oliver, Mary
   Music Lessons: V8
[On His Blindness] Sonnet 16 (Milton): V3
Ondaatje, Michael
   To a Sad Daughter: V8
On Freedom's Ground (Wilbur): V12
Onomatopoeia (Merriam): V6
On the Pulse of Morning (Angelou): V3
Ortiz, Simon
   Hunger in New York City: V4
Out, Out— (Frost): V10
Overture to a Dance of Locomotives (Williams): V11
Owen, Wilfred
   Dulce et Decorum Est: V10
Oysters (Sexton): V4

P

Paradoxes and Oxymorons (Ashbery): V11
Pastan, Linda
   Ethics: V8
Paul Revere's Ride (Longfellow): V2
The Phoenix (Nemerov): V10
Piano (Lawrence): V6
Piercy, Marge
   Barbie Doll: V9
Plath, Sylvia
   Mirror: V1
A Psalm of Life (Longfellow): V7
Poe, Edgar Allan
   Annabel Lee: V9
   The Bells: V3
   The Raven: V1
Pope, Alexander
   The Rape of the Lock: V12
Pound, Ezra
   In a Station of the Metro: V2
   The River-Merchant's Wife: A Letter: V8
Psalm 8 (King James Bible): V9
Psalm 23 (King James Bible): V4
Purdy, Al
   Lament for the Dorsets: V5
   Wilderness Gothic: V12

Q

The Quaker Graveyard in Nantucket (Lowell): V6
Queen-Ann's-Lace (Williams): V6

R

Raine, Craig
   A Martian Sends a Postcard Home: V7
Randall, Dudley
   Ballad of Birmingham: V5
The Rape of the Lock (Pope): V12
The Raven (Poe): V1
Reactionary Essay on Applied Science (McGinley): V9
A Red, Red Rose (Burns): V8
The Red Wheelbarrow (Williams): V1
Reed, Ishmael
   Beware: Do Not Read This Poem: V6
Revard, Carter
   Birch Canoe: V5
Richard Cory (Robinson): V4
The Rime of the Ancient Mariner (Coleridge): V4
Ríos, Alberto
   Island of the Three Marias: V11
The River-Merchant's Wife: A Letter (Pound): V8
The Road Not Taken (Frost): V2
Robinson, E. A.
   Richard Cory: V4
Roethke, Theodore
   My Papa's Waltz: V3
Rose, Wendy
   For the White poets who would be Indian: V13
Rossetti, Christina
   A Birthday: V10
Rukeyser, Muriel
   Ballad of Orange and Grape: V10

S

Sailing to Byzantium (Yeats): V2
Saint Francis and the Sow (Kinnell): V9
Sandburg, Carl
   Chicago: V3
   Cool Tombs: V6
   Hope Is a Tattered Flag: V12
Schnackenberg, Gjertrud
   Darwin in 1881: V13
The Seafarer (Anonymous): V8
The Second Coming (Yeats): V7
Service, Robert W.
   The Cremation of Sam McGee: V10
Sexton, Anne
   Oysters: V4
Shakespeare, William
   Sonnet 18: V2
   Sonnet 19: V9
   Sonnet 29: V8
   Sonnet 30: V4
   Sonnet 55: V5
   Sonnet 116: V3
   Sonnet 130: V1
Shapiro, Karl
   Auto Wreck: V3
Shelley, Percy Bysshe
   Ode to the West Wind: V2
Shine, Perishing Republic (Jeffers): V4
Silko, Leslie Marmon
   Four Mountain Wolves: V9
Simic, Charles
   Butcher Shop: V7
Simpson, Louis
   American Poetry: V7
   Chocolates: V11
Sir Patrick Spens (Anonymous): V4
Siren Song (Atwood): V7
Small Town with One Road (Soto): V7
Smith, Stevie
   Not Waving but Drowning: V3
Snyder, Gary
   Anasazi: V9
The Soldier (Brooke): V7
Song, Cathy
   Lost Sister: V5

Sonnet 16 [On His Blindness] (Milton): V3
Sonnet 18 (Shakespeare): V2
Sonnet 19 (Shakespeare): V9
Sonnet 30 (Shakespeare): V4
Sonnet 29 (Shakespeare): V8
Sonnet 43 (Browning): V2
Sonnet 55 (Shakespeare): V5
Sonnet 116 (Shakespeare): V3
Sonnet 130 (Shakespeare): V1
The Song of the Smoke (Du Bois): V13
The Sonnet-Ballad (Brooks): V1
Soto, Gary
   Small Town with One Road: V7
The Soul Selects Her Own Society (Dickinson): V1
Stafford, William
   At the Bomb Testing Site: V8
   Fifteen: V2
Starlight (Levine): V8
Stevens, Wallace
   The Idea of Order at Key West: V13
Stopping by Woods on a Snowy Evening (Frost): V1
Strand, Mark
   Eating Poetry: V9
Strong Men, Riding Horses (Brooks): V4
A Supermarket in California (Ginsberg): V5
Swing Low Sweet Chariot (Anonymous): V1

T

A Tall Man Executes a Jig (Layton): V12
Tate, James
   Dear Reader: V10
Taylor, Henry
   Landscape with Tractor: V10
Tears, Idle Tears (Tennyson): V4
Tennyson, Alfred, Lord
   The Charge of the Light Brigade; V1
   The Eagle: V11
   Tears, Idle Tears: V4
   Ulysses: V2
Thayer, Ernest Lawrence
   Casey at the Bat: V5
Theme for English B (Hughes): V6

There's a Certain Slant of Light (Dickinson): V6
This Life (Dove): V1
Thomas, Dylan
   Do Not Go Gentle into that Good Night: V1
   Fern Hill: V3
   The Force That Through the Green Fuse Drives the Flower: V8
Those Winter Sundays (Hayden): V1
Tintern Abbey (Wordsworth): V2
To an Athlete Dying Young (Housman): V7
To a Child Running With Outstretched Arms in Canyon de Chelly (Momaday): V11
To a Sad Daughter (Ondaatje): V8
To His Coy Mistress (Marvell): V5
To His Excellency General Washington (Wheatley): V13
To My Dear and Loving Husband (Bradstreet): V6
To the Virgins, to Make Much of Time (Herrick): V13
Toads (Larkin): V4
Tonight I Can Write (Neruda): V11
The Tropics in New York (McKay): V4
The Tyger (Blake): V2

U

Ulysses (Tennyson): V2
The Unknown Citizen (Auden): V3

V

A Valediction: Forbidding Mourning (Donne): V11
Vancouver Lights (Birney): V8
Viereck, Peter
   For An Assyrian Frieze: V9

W

Walcott, Derek
   A Far Cry from Africa: V6
The War Against the Trees (Kunitz): V11
War Is Kind (Crane): V9

Warren, Rosanna
   Daylights: V13
We Live by What We See at Night (Espada): V13
We Real Cool (Brooks): V6
The Weight of Sweetness (Lee): V11
Wheatley, Phillis
   To His Excellency General Washington: V13
When I Have Fears That I May Cease to Be (Keats): V2
When I Was One-and-Twenty (Housman): V4
Whitman, Walt
   Cavalry Crossing a Ford: V13
   I Hear America Singing: V3
   O Captain! My Captain!: V2
Why I Am Not a Painter (O'Hara): V8
Wilbur, Richard
   Beowulf: V11
   On Freedom's Ground: V12
Wilderness Gothic (Purdy): V12
Williams, William Carlos
   Overture to a Dance of Locomotives: V11
   Queen-Ann's-Lace: V6
   The Red Wheelbarrow: V1
The Wood-Pile (Frost): V6
Wordsworth, William
   Lines Composed a Few Miles above Tintern Abbey: V2
Wright, Charles
   Black Zodiac: V10
Wright, James
   A Blessing: V7
   Autumn Begins in Martins Ferry, Ohio: V8
Wright, Judith
   Drought Year: V8

Y

Yeats, William Butler
   Easter 1916: V5
   An Irish Airman Foresees His Death: V1
   Leda and the Swan: V13
   Sailing to Byzantium: V2
   The Second Coming: V7

Cumulative Nationality/Ethnicity Index

Acoma Pueblo
Ortiz, Simon
   Hunger in New York City: V4

African American
Angelou, Maya
   Harlem Hopscotch: V2
   On the Pulse of Morning: V3
Baraka, Amiri
   In Memory of Radio: V9
Brooks, Gwendolyn
   The Bean Eaters: V2
   The Sonnet-Ballad: V1
   Strong Men, Riding Horses: V4
   We Real Cool: V6
Clifton, Lucille
   Miss Rosie: V1
Cullen, Countee
   Any Human to Another: V3
Dove, Rita
   This Life: V1
Hayden, Robert
   Those Winter Sundays: V1
Hughes, Langston
   Harlem: V1
   Mother to Son: V3
   The Negro Speaks of Rivers: V10
   Theme for English B: V6
Johnson, James Weldon
   The Creation: V1
Komunyakaa, Yusef
   Facing It: V5
Madgett, Naomi Long
   Alabama Centennial: V10
McElroy, Colleen
   A Pièd: V3

Randall, Dudley
   Ballad of Birmingham: V5
Reed, Ishmael
   Beware: Do Not Read This Poem: V6

American
Acosta, Teresa Palomo
   My Mother Pieced Quilts: V12
Angelou, Maya
   Harlem Hopscotch: V2
   On the Pulse of Morning: V3
Ashbery, John
   Paradoxes and Oxymorons: V11
Auden, W. H.
   As I Walked Out One Evening: V4
   Musée des Beaux Arts: V1
   The Unknown Citizen: V3
Bishop, Elizabeth
   Brazil, January 1, 1502: V6
   Filling Station: V12
Blumenthal, Michael
   Inventors: V7
Bly, Robert
   Come with Me: V6
Bradstreet, Anne
   To My Dear and Loving Husband: V6
Brooks, Gwendolyn
   The Bean Eaters: V2
   The Sonnet-Ballad: V1
   Strong Men, Riding Horses: V4
   We Real Cool: V6
Clifton, Lucille
   Miss Rosie: V1

Crane, Stephen
   War Is Kind: V9
Cullen, Countee
   Any Human to Another: V3
cummings, e. e.
   l(a: V1
   i was sitting in mcsorley's: V13
   maggie and milly and molly and may: V12
   old age sticks: V3
Dickey, James
   The Heaven of Animals: V6
   The Hospital Window: V11
Dickinson, Emily
   Because I Could Not Stop for Death: V2
   The Bustle in a House: V10
   "Hope" Is the Thing with Feathers: V3
   I felt a Funeral, in my Brain: V13
   I Heard a Fly Buzz—When I Died—: V5
   My Life Closed Twice Before Its Close: V8
   A Narrow Fellow in the Grass: V11
   The Soul Selects Her Own Society: V1
   There's a Certain Slant of Light: V6
   This Is My Letter to the World: V4
Dove, Rita
   This Life: V1
Dubie, Norman
   The Czar's Last Christmas Letter. A Barn in the Urals: V12
Du Bois, W. E. B.
   The Song of the Smoke: V13

Dugan, Alan
   How We Heard the Name: V10
Duncan, Robert
   An African Elegy: V13
Eliot, T. S.
   Journey of the Magi: V7
   The Love Song of J. Alfred Prufrock: V1
Emerson, Ralph Waldo
   Concord Hymn: V4
Espada, Martín
   We Live by What We See at Night: V13
Francis, Robert
   The Base Stealer: V12
Frost, Robert
   Birches: V13
   The Death of the Hired Man: V4
   Fire and Ice: V7
   Mending Wall: V5
   Nothing Gold Can Stay: V3
   Out, Out—: V10
   The Road Not Taken: V2
   Stopping by Woods on a Snowy Evening: V1
   The Wood-Pile: V6
Ginsberg, Allen
   A Supermarket in California: V5
Glück, Louise
   The Gold Lily: V5
Graham, Jorie
   The Hiding Place: V10
Gunn, Thom
   The Missing: V9
H.D.
   Helen: V6
Hall, Donald
   Names of Horses: V8
Hayden, Robert
   Those Winter Sundays: V1
Hecht, Anthony
   "More Light! More Light!": V6
Holmes, Oliver Wendell
   Old Ironsides: V9
Hughes, Langston
   Harlem: V1
   Mother to Son: V3
   The Negro Speaks of Rivers: V10
   Theme for English B: V6
Jarrell, Randall
   The Death of the Ball Turret Gunner: V2
Jeffers, Robinson
   Hurt Hawks: V3
   Shine, Perishing Republic: V4
Johnson, James Weldon
   The Creation: V1
Kenyon, Jane
   "Trouble with Math in a One-Room Country School": V9
Kinnell, Galway
   Saint Francis and the Sow: V9

Komunyakaa, Yusef
   Facing It: V5
Kooser, Ted
   The Constellation Orion: V8
Kunitz, Stanley
   The War Against the Trees: V11
Levertov, Denise
   In the Land of Shinar: V7
Levine, Philip
   Starlight: V8
Longfellow, Henry Wadsworth
   A Psalm of Life: V7
   Paul Revere's Ride: V2
Lowell, Robert
   For the Union Dead: V7
   The Quaker Graveyard in Nantucket: V6
MacLeish, Archibald
   Ars Poetica: V5
Madgett, Naomi Long
   Alabama Centennial: V10
McElroy, Colleen
   A Pièd: V3
McGinley, Phyllis
   The Conquerors: V13
   Reactionary Essay on Applied Science: V9
McKay, Claude
   The Tropics in New York: V4
Merriam, Eve
   Onomatopoeia: V6
Merwin, W. S.
   Leviathan: V5
Millay, Edna St. Vincent
   The Courage that My Mother Had: V3
Momaday, N. Scott
   Angle of Geese: V2
   To a Child Running With Outstretched Arms in Canyon de Chelly: V11
Montague, John
   A Grafted Tongue: V12
Mueller, Lisel
   The Exhibit: V9
Nemerov, Howard
   The Phoenix: V10
O'Hara, Frank
   Having a Coke with You: V12
   Why I Am Not a Painter: V8
Oliver, Mary
   Music Lessons: V8
Ortiz, Simon
   Hunger in New York City: V4
Pastan, Linda
   Ethics: V8
Piercy, Marge
   Barbie Doll: V9
Plath, Sylvia
   Mirror: V1
Poe, Edgar Allan
   Annabel Lee: V9
   The Bells: V3
   The Raven: V1

Pound, Ezra
   In a Station of the Metro: V2
   The River-Merchant's Wife: A Letter: V8
Randall, Dudley
   Ballad of Birmingham: V5
Reed, Ishmael
   Beware: Do Not Read This Poem: V6
Revard, Carter
   Birch Canoe: V5
Ríos, Alberto
   Island of the Three Marias: V11
Robinson, E. A.
   Richard Cory: V4
Roethke, Theodore
   My Papa's Waltz: V3
Rose, Wendy
   For the White poets who would be Indian: V13
Rukeyser, Muriel
   Ballad of Orange and Grape: V10
Sandburg, Carl
   Chicago: V3
   Cool Tombs: V6
   Hope Is a Tattered Flag: V12
Schnackenberg, Gjertrud
   Darwin in 1881: V13
Sexton, Anne
   Oysters: V4
Shapiro, Karl
   Auto Wreck: V3
Silko, Leslie Marmon
   Four Mountain Wolves: V9
Simic, Charles
   Butcher Shop: V7
Simpson, Louis
   American Poetry: V7
   Chocolates: V11
Snyder, Gary
   Anasazi: V9
Song, Cathy
   Lost Sister: V5
Soto, Gary
   Small Town with One Road: V7
Stafford, William
   At the Bomb Testing Site: V8
   Fifteen: V2
Stevens, Wallace
   The Idea of Order at Key West: V13
Tate, James
   Dear Reader: V10
Taylor, Henry
   Landscape with Tractor: V10
Thayer, Ernest Lawrence
   Casey at the Bat: V5
Viereck, Peter
   For An Assyrian Frieze: V9
Warren, Rosanna
   Daylights: V13
Wheatley, Phillis
   To His Excellency General Washington: V13

Whitman, Walt
   Cavalry Crossing a Ford: V13
   I Hear America Singing: V3
   O Captain! My Captain!: V2
Wilbur, Richard
   Beowulf: V11
   On Freedom's Ground: V12
Williams, William Carlos
   Overture to a Dance of Locomotives: V11
   Queen-Ann's-Lace: V6
   The Red Wheelbarrow: V1
Wright, Charles
   Black Zodiac: V10
Wright, James
   A Blessing: V7
   Autumn Begins in Martins Ferry, Ohio: V8

Australian

Dawe, Bruce
   Drifters: V10
Hope, A. D.
   Beware of Ruins: V8
Wright, Judith
   Drought Year: V8

Canadian

Atwood, Margaret
   Siren Song: V7
Birney, Earle
   Vancouver Lights: V8
Layton, Irving
   A Tall Man Executes a Jig: V12
McCrae, John
   In Flanders Fields: V5
Nowlan, Alden
   For Jean Vincent D'abbadie, Baron St.-Castin: V12
Purdy, Al
   Lament for the Dorsets: V5
   Wilderness Gothic: V12
Strand, Mark
   Eating Poetry: V9

Canadian, Sri Lankan

Ondaatje, Michael
   To a Sad Daughter: V8

Cherokee

Momaday, N. Scott
   Angle of Geese: V2
   To a Child Running With Outstretched Arms in Canyon de Chelly: V11

Chilean

Neruda, Pablo
   Tonight I Can Write: V11

English

Alleyn, Ellen
   A Birthday: V10
Arnold, Matthew
   Dover Beach: V2
Auden, W. H.
   As I Walked Out One Evening: V4
   Funeral Blues: V10
   Musée des Beaux Arts: V1
   The Unknown Citizen: V3
Blake, William
   The Lamb: V12
   The Tyger: V2
Bradstreet, Anne
   To My Dear and Loving Husband: V6
Brooke, Rupert
   The Soldier: V7
Browning, Elizabeth Barrett
   Sonnet 43: V2
Browning, Robert
   My Last Duchess: V1
Byron, Lord
   The Destruction of Sennacherib: V1
Carroll, Lewis
   Jabberwocky: V11
Coleridge, Samuel Taylor
   Kubla Khan: V5
   The Rime of the Ancient Mariner: V4
Donne, John
   Holy Sonnet 10: V2
   A Valediction: Forbidding Mourning: V11
Eliot, T. S.
   Journey of the Magi: V7
   The Love Song of J. Alfred Prufrock: V1
Fenton, James
   The Milkfish Gatherers: V11
Gray, Thomas
   Elegy Written in a Country Churchyard: V9
Gunn, Thom
   The Missing: V9
Hardy, Thomas
   Ah, Are You Digging on My Grave?: V4
   The Man He Killed: V3
Herrick, Robert
   To the Virgins, to Make Much of Time: V13
Housman, A. E.
   To an Athlete Dying Young: V7
   When I Was One-and-Twenty: V4
Hughes, Ted
   Hawk Roosting: V4
Keats, John
   Bright Star! Would I Were Steadfast as Thou Art: V9
   Ode on a Grecian Urn: V1
   Ode to a Nightingale: V3
   When I Have Fears that I May Cease to Be: V2
Larkin, Philip
   An Arundel Tomb: V12
   High Windows: V3
   Toads: V4
Lawrence, D. H.
   Piano: V6
Marvell, Andrew
   To His Coy Mistress: V5
Masefield, John
   Cargoes: V5
Milton, John
   [On His Blindness] Sonnet 16: V3
Noyes, Alfred
   The Highwayman: V4
Owen, Wilfred
   Dulce et Decorum Est: V10
Pope, Alexander
   The Rape of the Lock: V12
Raine, Craig
   A Martian Sends a Postcard Home: V7
Service, Robert W.
   The Cremation of Sam McGee: V10
Shakespeare, William
   Sonnet 18: V2
   Sonnet 19: V9
   Sonnet 30: V4
   Sonnet 29: V8
   Sonnet 55: V5
   Sonnet 116: V3
   Sonnet 130: V1
Shelley, Percy Bysshe
   Ode to the West Wind: V2
Smith, Stevie
   Not Waving but Drowning: V3
Tennyson, Alfred, Lord
   The Charge of the Light Brigade: V1
   The Eagle: V11
   Tears, Idle Tears: V4
   Ulysses: V2
Williams, William Carlos
   Queen-Ann's-Lace: V6
   The Red Wheelbarrow: V1
Wordsworth, William
   Lines Composed a Few Miles above Tintern Abbey: V2
Yeats, W. B.
   Easter 1916: V5
   An Irish Airman Forsees His Death: V1
   Leda and the Swan: V13
   Sailing to Byzantium: V2
   The Second Coming: V7

German

Blumenthal, Michael
   Inventors: V7
Mueller, Lisel
   Blood Oranges: V13

The Exhibit: V9
Roethke, Theodore
   My Papa's Waltz: V3

Ghanaian
Du Bois, W. E. B.
   The Song of the Smoke: V13

Indonesian
Lee, Li-Young
   The Weight of Sweetness: V11

Irish
Boland, Eavan
   Anorexic: V12
Hartnett, Michael
   A Farewell to English: V10
Heaney, Seamus
   Digging: V5
   A Drink of Water: V8
   Midnight: V2
Muldoon, Paul
   Meeting the British: V7
Yeats, William Butler
   Easter 1916: V5
   An Irish Airman Foresees His Death: V1
   Leda and the Swan: V13
   Sailing to Byzantium: V2
   The Second Coming: V7

Italian
Rossetti, Christina
   A Birthday: V10

Jamaican
McKay, Claude
   The Tropics in New York: V4

Japanese
Bashō, Matsuo
   Falling Upon Earth: V2
   The Moon Glows the Same: V7

Jewish
Blumenthal, Michael
   Inventors: V7
Espada, Martín
   We Live by What We See at Night: V13
Piercy, Marge
   Barbie Doll: V9
Shapiro, Karl
   Auto Wreck: V3

Kiowa
Momaday, N. Scott
   Angle of Geese: V2
   To a Child Running With Outstretched Arms in Canyon de Chelly: V11

Mexican
Soto, Gary
   Small Town with One Road: V7

Native American
Momaday, N. Scott
   Angle of Geese: V2
   To a Child Running With Outstretched Arms in Canyon de Chelly: V11
Ortiz, Simon
   Hunger in New York City: V4
Revard, Carter
   Birch Canoe: V5
Rose, Wendy
   For the White poets who would be Indian: V13
Silko, Leslie Marmon
   Four Mountain Wolves: V9

Osage
Revard, Carter
   Birch Canoe: V5

Russian
Levertov, Denise
   In the Land of Shinar: V7
Merriam, Eve
   Onomatopoeia: V6
Shapiro, Karl
   Auto Wreck: V3

Scottish
Burns, Robert
   A Red, Red Rose: V8
Byron, Lord
   The Destruction of Sennacherib: V1
MacBeth, George
   Bedtime Story: V8

Senegalese
Wheatley, Phillis
   To His Excellency General Washington: V13

Spanish
Williams, William Carlos
   The Red Wheelbarrow: V1

Swedish
Sandburg, Carl
   Chicago: V3

Welsh
Levertov, Denise
   In the Land of Shinar: V7
Thomas, Dylan
   Do Not Go Gentle into that Good Night: V1
   Fern Hill: V3
   The Force That Through the Green Fuse Drives the Flower: V8

West Indian
Walcott, Derek
   A Far Cry from Africa: V6

Subject/Theme Index

***Boldface** denotes dicussion in *Themes* section.

A

Abstinence
   To the Virgins, to Make Much of Time: 225–228, 230
Adulthood
   Birches: 24
   Blood Oranges: 41, 43–44
Adventure and Exploration
   Darwin in 1881: 84–87
Africa
   An African Elegy: 2, 4, 6–8, 10–11
Alienation
   Birches: 20–21
Alliteration
   Cavalry Crossing a Ford: 52–53
   The Song of the Smoke: 197–198, 202
Ambiguity
   Birches: 25–26
American Civil War
   Cavalry Crossing a Ford: 54–55
American Northeast
   Birches: 18–19, 27–28, 30
   Daylights: 100, 103–104, 108–109
   i was sitting in mcsorley's: 150–152, 154–156
   To His Excellency General Washington: 211, 216–218
   We Live by What We See at Night: 239–244, 246–247
American Northwest
   To His Excellency General Washington: 211–224

American South
   Cavalry Crossing a Ford: 54–56
   The Idea of Order at Key West: 169–170, 173
American West
   For the White poets who would be Indian: 128–130
Anger
   For the White poets who would be Indian: 111, 113–115, 118–120, 124–125
   We Live by What We See at Night: 245–246
Annunciation
   Leda and the Swan: 184
Asia
   The Conquerors: 67, 71–72
Authoritarianism
   Blood Oranges: 33, 35–40

B

Beauty
   i was sitting in mcsorley's: 151–152, 154–156
   The Idea of Order at Key West: 162, 165, 168–169
   To the Virgins, to Make Much of Time: 227–228, 230–235
   We Live by What We See at Night: 241–243
Bloomsbury Group
   An African Elegy: 2, 4, 6

C

Carpe Diem
   To the Virgins, to Make Much of Time: 225–228, 230, 233

Childhood
   Blood Oranges: 35, 37, 41–43
Christianity
   To the Virgins, to Make Much of Time: 225, 227, 230, 234–235
City Life
   Daylights: 100, 103
Class Conflict
   Daylights: 103
Classicism
   Leda and the Swan: 191–192
   To His Excellency General Washington: 219–220
   To the Virgins, to Make Much of Time: 236–237
Communism
   The Conquerors: 73
Conquest
   Birches: 17
Courage
   Darwin in 1881: 98
   To His Excellency General Washington: 214, 219
Crime and Criminals
   Daylights: 100, 102–104
   For the White poets who would be Indian: 113–117
   The Song of the Smoke: 197–199, 201, 203
Cruelty
   Blood Oranges: 33, 35–36, 39
   Leda and the Swan: 180, 182, 184–191
Cubism
   i was sitting in mcsorley's: 153
The Cycle of History
   Leda and the Swan: 185

Cynicism
- Birches: 30–31

D

Death
- An African Elegy: 2, 4–8, 10–11
- Blood Oranges: 35–41
- The Conquerors: 67–68, 74, 76
- Darwin in 1881: 82, 84–86, 88–91, 94–96
- I felt a Funeral, in my Brain: 135, 137–140, 142–148
- To the Virgins, to Make Much of Time: 225–229, 236–237

Description
- Birches: 15–16
- Darwin in 1881: 82, 86–87
- Daylights: 100, 102
- I felt a Funeral, in my Brain: 138–140
- i was sitting in mcsorley's: 150, 152, 154, 157–158
- Leda and the Swan: 182–184, 186

Dictatorship
- Blood Oranges: 35, 38–40

Divine Right
- To His Excellency General Washington: 215

Doubt and Uncertainty
- I felt a Funeral, in my Brain: 139

Dreams and Reality
- We Live by What We See at Night: 242

Dreams and Visions
- Birches: 29–30
- We Live by What We See at Night: 239–243, 245, 248–249

E

Emotions
- An African Elegy: 4–5, 7, 9
- Birches: 17, 24
- The Conquerors: 65, 69
- Darwin in 1881: 89, 91
- Daylights: 102, 106, 108–109
- For the White poets who would be Indian: 111, 118–119, 126, 132
- I felt a Funeral, in my Brain: 142–143
- i was sitting in mcsorley's: 154, 156
- The Idea of Order at Key West: 167, 171–174
- Leda and the Swan: 182
- The Song of the Smoke: 197–199
- To His Excellency General Washington: 216
- To the Virgins, to Make Much of Time: 227, 231–232

- We Live by What We See at Night: 247

Eternity
- i was sitting in mcsorley's: 152–153
- To the Virgins, to Make Much of Time: 227–228, 230

Europe
- Blood Oranges: 33–44
- The Conquerors: 67–68
- Darwin in 1881: 82, 84, 86, 88–90
- Leda and the Swan: 180, 183–184, 186–188, 191–192
- To His Excellency General Washington: 212–215, 217

Evil
- Darwin in 1881: 86
- i was sitting in mcsorley's: 159–160

Exile
- We Live by What We See at Night: 245–247

Expressionism
- i was sitting in mcsorley's: 155

F

Family
- Darwin in 1881: 87

Farm and Rural Life
- Birches: 17–19, 27, 29–30

Fate and Chance
- Blood Oranges: 45–46, 48
- For the White poets who would be Indian: 128–133
- To the Virgins, to Make Much of Time: 236–237

Fear and Terror
- Leda and the Swan: 189–191

Feminism
- The Conquerors: 72–73

Folklore
- Leda and the Swan: 188

Forgiveness
- Darwin in 1881: 84, 88

Freedom
- To His Excellency General Washington: 212–215

G

Ghost
- For the White poets who would be Indian: 128, 131–132
- i was sitting in mcsorley's: 152–153
- The Song of the Smoke: 197, 199, 201

God
- The Conquerors: 79–80
- Leda and the Swan: 180, 182–185, 189–191

- The Song of the Smoke: 197, 199–200, 208–209
- To His Excellency General Washington: 215

Good and Evil
- The Song of the Smoke: 200

Grief and Sorrow
- An African Elegy: 4–7
- I felt a Funeral, in my Brain: 137–140, 142–148

H

Hatred
- The Conquerors: 68–69
- To His Excellency General Washington: 214, 217–218

Heaven
- Birches: 23–26

Hero
- To His Excellency General Washington: 214

Heroism
- Blood Oranges: 35–36, 38, 42–43
- I felt a Funeral, in my Brain: 145–146
- To His Excellency General Washington: 214–215, 218–219

History
- Blood Oranges: 40, 42, 44, 45, 48
- The Conquerors: 67–69
- Darwin in 1881: 82, 90, 96–98
- For the White poets who would be Indian: 113–114, 116–117
- Leda and the Swan: 180, 182–186, 188
- The Song of the Smoke: 197–203, 205
- We Live by What We See at Night: 243–245

Homosexuality
- An African Elegy: 1–2, 4, 7–8

Honor
- For the White poets who would be Indian: 121–123

Humanity and Human Nature
- i was sitting in mcsorley's: 154

Humor
- The Conquerors: 78–80

I

Identity
- Cavalry Crossing a Ford: 52

Ignorance
- Blood Oranges: 33, 37, 40

Imagery and Symbolism
- An African Elegy: 2, 4–11
- Birches: 15, 17, 19, 22–26, 30–31
- Blood Oranges: 36, 38–40, 44, 46–48

Cavalry Crossing a Ford: 52–53
Darwin in 1881: 82, 87, 95
Daylights: 100, 102–106
For the White poets who would be Indian: 113, 115–116, 118–119
I felt a Funeral, in my Brain: 135, 137–140, 142–146
i was sitting in mcsorley's: 152–154, 159–160
The Idea of Order at Key West: 177–178
The Song of the Smoke: 197, 201, 204–206
To the Virgins, to Make Much of Time: 226–227, 229–232, 234
Imagination
   Birches: 13, 16–17, 20–24
   The Idea of Order at Key West: 162, 165–168, 170, 175–177, 178

The Imagination vs. the Real World
   Birches: 17
Immigrants and Immigration
   We Live by What We See at Night: 239, 242–248
Inheritance
   We Live by What We See at Night: 241
Insanity
   I felt a Funeral, in my Brain: 138–139, 142–143, 145
Irony
   Blood Oranges: 33, 35
   For the White poets who would be Indian: 113–115, 129–130

K

Killers and Killing
   Blood Oranges: 33, 35, 39–40
   The Conquerors: 67–72, 74–77
Kindness
   Darwin in 1881: 92
Knowledge
   The Conquerors: 69
   Darwin in 1881: 85–87, 96–98
   For the White poets who would be Indian: 114–116, 118

L

Landscape
   An African Elegy: 2, 4–11
   Cavalry Crossing a Ford: 49, 51–53, 55–56, 60–61
   Darwin in 1881: 84, 86–88, 90
   The Idea of Order at Key West: 162–167, 169, 171, 173–178
   We Live by What We See at Night: 239–242, 244, 248–249

Language and Meaning
   i was sitting in mcsorley's: 153
Law and Order
   Daylights: 104
   For the White poets who would be Indian: 117
   The Song of the Smoke: 202–204
Limitations and Opportunities
   Birches: 15–21
Literary Criticism
   An African Elegy: 9
   To the Virgins, to Make Much of Time: 234
Literary Eras
   Darwin in 1881: 97
Loneliness
   Birches: 27
Love and Passion
   An African Elegy: 11
   Birches: 13, 16–19, 23–24
   Darwin in 1881: 87–89, 91
   Daylights: 109–110
   i was sitting in mcsorley's: 159–160
   Leda and the Swan: 183–184, 186, 188
   To the Virgins, to Make Much of Time: 227–228, 230, 234–237
Loyalty
   Cavalry Crossing a Ford: 50, 52
   The Conquerors: 71, 73

M

Madness and Sanity
   I felt a Funeral, in my Brain: 138
Memory and Reminiscence
   We Live by What We See at Night: 247–249
Mental Instability
   I felt a Funeral, in my Brain: 137
Middle East
   The Conquerors: 67–68
Miracle
   Darwin in 1881: 84, 86, 88, 90
Modernism
   Darwin in 1881: 97–98
   Leda and the Swan: 191
Monarchy
   An African Elegy: 2, 4–6
   Darwin in 1881: 84, 87
   The Song of the Smoke: 197–199, 203, 207–209
   To the Virgins, to Make Much of Time: 225, 229–230
Money and Economics
   Darwin in 1881: 89
   We Live by What We See at Night: 241–244
Mood
   Darwin in 1881: 93, 95
Morals and Morality
   The Song of the Smoke: 198, 200–201

Murder
   Blood Oranges: 33, 36, 38, 40
   The Conquerors: 67, 69–70
   The Song of the Smoke: 198, 200, 203–204
Music
   Cavalry Crossing a Ford: 51–54, 60–62
   The Conquerors: 79–80
   For the White poets who would be Indian: 126, 132, 134
   I felt a Funeral, in my Brain: 137, 139–140
   i was sitting in mcsorley's: 155–156
   The Idea of Order at Key West: 162–178
   The Song of the Smoke: 194–195, 199, 201–202
Mystery and Intrigue
   Blood Oranges: 36, 39–41
Mythology
   Leda and the Swan: 183
Myths and Legends
   An African Elegy: 5, 7–8
   Leda and the Swan: 180, 182–186, 188–193

N

Narration
   Birches: 21
   I felt a Funeral, in my Brain: 146–148
   The Idea of Order at Key West: 175–176
   We Live by What We See at Night: 248–249
Naturalism
   Darwin in 1881: 85–86, 88, 92–93
Nature
   An African Elegy: 5–7
   Birches: 17–18, 20, 24–27, 30
   Blood Oranges: 35
   Cavalry Crossing a Ford: 52–53, 56
   Darwin in 1881: 85–87, 93–96
   Daylights: 103
   For the White poets who would be Indian: 113–116, 125
   i was sitting in mcsorley's: 154
   The Idea of Order at Key West: 162, 165–166, 170, 174–177
   Leda and the Swan: 182, 184–186, 188–191
   To the Virgins, to Make Much of Time: 230–232
The Need for Limits
   Birches: 17
1980s
   Daylights: 104–105
North America
   Cavalry Crossing a Ford: 54–55

The Conquerors: 69, 71–73
The Idea of Order at Key West: 169–170
The Song of the Smoke: 197, 202
To His Excellency General Washington: 211, 215, 217
We Live by What We See at Night: 239–249

Nuclear War
The Conquerors: 65, 67–69, 71–72

O

Order and Disorder
Cavalry Crossing a Ford: 53
The Song of the Smoke: 201

P

Painting
i was sitting in mcsorley's: 155–156

Pastoralism and Nature Poems
Birches: 17

Perception
The Idea of Order at Key West: 162, 163, 165–169

Permanence
Leda and the Swan: 192

Persecution
An African Elegy: 2, 4–6
The Conquerors: 69, 73
Leda and the Swan: 183–184, 189–191

Personal Identity
For the White poets who would be Indian: 124–125
To His Excellency General Washington: 218

Philosophical Ideas
Birches: 28–30
For the White poets who would be Indian: 131
I felt a Funeral, in my Brain: 140–141
To the Virgins, to Make Much of Time: 225, 227–230

Plants
Birches: 13, 15–17, 19–25

Pleasure
To the Virgins, to Make Much of Time: 236–237

Plot
I felt a Funeral, in my Brain: 137–138

Poetry
An African Elegy: 1–2, 4–12
Birches: 13, 15–31
Blood Oranges: 33–48
Cavalry Crossing a Ford: 49–54, 56–63
The Conquerors: 65–79
Darwin in 1881: 82, 85, 87–99
Daylights: 100–110
For the White poets who would be Indian: 111–126, 128, 131–133
I felt a Funeral, in my Brain: 135–148
i was sitting in mcsorley's: 150, 152–160
The Idea of Order at Key West: 162–178
Leda and the Swan: 180–186, 188–193
The Song of the Smoke: 194–195, 197–202, 204–209
To His Excellency General Washington: 211–224
To the Virgins, to Make Much of Time: 225–237
We Live by What We See at Night: 239–249

Politicians
Cavalry Crossing a Ford: 54–55
Daylights: 104
To His Excellency General Washington: 211–213, 216–218, 221, 223

Politics
An African Elegy: 7–8
Blood Oranges: 33, 35–40
Cavalry Crossing a Ford: 50, 52–55
The Conquerors: 69, 73
Daylights: 102–105
The Idea of Order at Key West: 169–170
Leda and the Swan: 184, 187–188
The Song of the Smoke: 199, 202–205, 207–208
To His Excellency General Washington: 212–214, 216–218, 221, 223–224
To the Virgins, to Make Much of Time: 225, 229–230
We Live by What We See at Night: 242–244

Presence and Absence
The Idea of Order at Key West: 167

Pride
The Conquerors: 65–70

Psychology and the Human Mind
An African Elegy: 1, 4, 6–8
Daylights: 107–109
I felt a Funeral, in my Brain: 140–143
We Live by What We See at Night: 248

Purity
Blood Oranges: 37

R

Race
For the White poets who would be Indian: 111, 113–131, 134
The Song of the Smoke: 194–195, 197–205, 207–209
To His Excellency General Washington: 220–224
We Live by What We See at Night: 239, 241, 243–244

Race and Racism
An African Elegy: 6

Racism and Prejudice
The Song of the Smoke: 194–195, 197, 199–204, 208–209

Realism
i was sitting in mcsorley's: 156–158

Reality and the Imagination
The Idea of Order at Key West: 167

Religion and Religious Thought
Birches: 26
The Conquerors: 80
Darwin in 1881: 86, 89, 91, 93, 95
For the White poets who would be Indian: 116–117, 123
I felt a Funeral, in my Brain: 139–140
Leda and the Swan: 184–185, 187, 190–192
The Song of the Smoke: 209
To His Excellency General Washington: 217
To the Virgins, to Make Much of Time: 227, 229–230

Resolution and Death
Darwin in 1881: 88

Revolution and Revolt
Blood Oranges: 38

Roman Catholicism
Leda and the Swan: 187–188

S

Saints
The Conquerors: 79

Science and Technology
The Conquerors: 65, 67–69
Darwin in 1881: 82, 85–90, 92–93, 96–97

Self-Realization
To His Excellency General Washington: 219

Sensuality
Blood Oranges: 38

Setting
Cavalry Crossing a Ford: 52–53

Sex and Sexuality
An African Elegy: 6, 8–9
Leda and the Swan: 180, 182–184, 186–191

To the Virgins, to Make Much of Time: 226, 230–231, 233, 235–237
Sexism
   Leda and the Swan: 189, 191
Sexual Abuse
   Leda and the Swan: 180, 182–186, 188–191
Slavery
   Cavalry Crossing a Ford: 54
   The Song of the Smoke: 194–195, 197–200, 202–204, 207–209
   To His Excellency General Washington: 211, 214, 218, 220–224
Solitude
   Birches: 17–18, 26–27
   I felt a Funeral, in my Brain: 138–140, 148
Sonnet
   Leda and the Swan: 180, 182–184, 186, 188
Soul
   I felt a Funeral, in my Brain: 137–140
Spiritual Leaders
   For the White poets who would be Indian: 111, 114–115, 121–123
Spirituality
   I felt a Funeral, in my Brain: 139
Sports and the Sporting Life
   An African Elegy: 10–11
Storms and Weather Conditions
   Birches: 13, 15–17, 19–24
   Blood Oranges: 35–36, 39, 41
   Cavalry Crossing a Ford: 52–54, 60–61
   Darwin in 1881: 84–85, 87–88

Strength and Weakness
   The Conquerors: 69
Structure
   Leda and the Swan: 182, 186
   The Song of the Smoke: 205–207

T

Technology and Progress
   The Conquerors: 69
Time and Change
   Darwin in 1881: 82, 85–87, 89–91, 93, 95
   i was sitting in mcsorley's: 159–160
Tone
   Birches: 28
   Cavalry Crossing a Ford: 51–53
   The Conquerors: 66–67, 71, 75
Transcendentalism
   I felt a Funeral, in my Brain: 140–141
The Transient Nature of Beauty
   To the Virgins, to Make Much of Time: 228

U

Ugliness
   i was sitting in mcsorley's: 159–160
   We Live by What We See at Night: 239–245, 247–249
Understanding
   I felt a Funeral, in my Brain: 137, 140, 142
   The Idea of Order at Key West: 165–168

V

Violence and Helplessness
   Leda and the Swan: 184
Vitality
   The Song of the Smoke: 201

W

War and Peace
   Cavalry Crossing a Ford: 52
War, the Military, and Soldier Life
   Blood Oranges: 33, 35–40
   Cavalry Crossing a Ford: 49–63
   The Conquerors: 65–77
   Darwin in 1881: 89
   The Idea of Order at Key West: 169–170
   Leda and the Swan: 180, 183–184, 187–188
   To His Excellency General Washington: 211–224
   To the Virgins, to Make Much of Time: 225, 228–230
   We Live by What We See at Night: 240, 242–244
Wealth
   Darwin in 1881: 82, 84–88, 90, 93–96, 98
White Shamanism
   For the White poets who would be Indian: 114
Wildlife
   An African Elegy: 2, 4–6, 10
   Darwin in 1881: 85–87, 90
   Leda and the Swan: 180, 182–191
Wisdom
   To the Virgins, to Make Much of Time: 225, 227–228, 230
World War II
   Blood Oranges: 33, 35–44
   The Conquerors: 65, 67, 71–72

Cumulative Index of First Lines

A

A brackish reach of shoal off Madaket,— (The Quaker Graveyard in Nantucket) V6:158
"A cold coming we had of it (Journey of the Magi) V7:110
A line in long array where they wind betwixt green islands, (Cavalry Crossing a Ford) V13:50
A narrow Fellow in the grass (A Narrow Fellow in the Grass) V11:127
A poem should be palpable and mute (Ars Poetica) V5:2
A wind is ruffling the tawny pelt (A Far Cry from Africa) V6:60
About me the night moonless wimples the mountains (Vancouver Lights) V8:245
About suffering they were never wrong (Musée des Beaux Arts) V1:148
Across Roblin Lake, two shores away, (Wilderness Gothic) V12:241
After you finish your work (Ballad of Orange and Grape) V10:17
"Ah, are you digging on my grave (Ah, Are You Digging on My Grave?) V4:2
All Greece hates (Helen) V6:92
All night long the hockey pictures (To a Sad Daughter) V8:230
All winter your brute shoulders strained against collars, padding (Names of Horses) V8:141
Anasazi (Anasazi) V9:2
And God stepped out on space (The Creation) V1:19
Animal bones and some mossy tent rings (Lament for the Dorsets) V5:190
As I perceive (The Gold Lily) V5:127
As I walked out one evening (As I Walked Out One Evening) V4:15
At noon in the desert a panting lizard (At the Bomb Testing Site) V8:2
Ay, tear her tattered ensign down! (Old Ironsides) V9:172
As virtuous men pass mildly away (A Valediction: Forbidding Mourning) V11:201

B

Back then, before we came (On Freedom's Ground) V12:186
Bananas ripe and green, and ginger-root (The Tropics in New York) V4:255
Because I could not stop for Death— (Because I Could Not Stop for Death) V2:27
Before the indifferent beak could let her drop? (Leda and the Swan) V13:182
Bent double, like old beggars under slacks, (Dulce et Decorum Est) V10:109
Between my finger and my thumb (Digging) V5:70
Beware of ruins: they have a treacherous charm (Beware of Ruins) V8:43
Bright star! would I were steadfast as thou art— (Bright Star! Would I Were Steadfast as Thou Art) V9:44
By the rude bridge that arched the flood (Concord Hymn) V4:30

C

Celestial choir! enthron'd in realms of light, (To His Excellency General Washington V13:212
Come with me into those things that have felt his despair for so long— (Come with Me) V6:31
Composed in the Tower, before his execution ("More Light! More Light!") V6:119

D

Darkened by time, the masters, like our memories, mix (Black Zodiac) V10:46
Death, be not proud, though some have called thee (Holy Sonnet 10) V2:103

Devouring Time, blunt thou the lion's paws (Sonnet 19) V9:210
Do not go gentle into that good night (Do Not Go Gentle into that Good Night) V1:51
Do not weep, maiden, for war is kind (War Is Kind) V9:252
(Dumb, (A Grafted Tongue) V12:92

E

Each day the shadow swings (In the Land of Shinar) V7:83

F

Falling upon earth (Falling Upon Earth) V2:64
Five years have past; five summers, with the length (Tintern Abbey) V2:249
Flesh is heretic. (Anorexic) V12:2
From my mother's sleep I fell into the State (The Death of the Ball Turret Gunner) V2:41

G

Gather ye Rose-buds while ye may, (To the Virgins, to Make Much of Time) V13:226
Go down, Moses (Go Down, Moses) V11:42
Gray mist wolf (Four Mountain Wolves) V9:131

H

"Had he and I but met (The Man He Killed) V3:167
Had we but world enough, and time (To His Coy Mistress) V5:276
Half a league, half a league (The Charge of the Light Brigade) V1:2
Having a Coke with You (Having a Coke with You) V12:105
He clasps the crag with crooked hands (The Eagle) V11:30
He was found by the Bureau of Statistics to be (The Unknown Citizen) V3:302
Hear the sledges with the bells— (The Bells) V3:46
Her body is not so white as (Queen-Ann's-Lace) V6:179
Her eyes were coins of porter and her West (A Farewell to English) V10:126
Here they are. The soft eyes open (The Heaven of Animals) V6:75
Hog Butcher for the World (Chicago) V3:61
Hope is a tattered flag and a dream out of time. (Hope is a Tattered Flag) V12:120
"Hope" is the thing with feathers— (Hope Is the Thing with Feathers) V3:123
How do I love thee? Let me count the ways (Sonnet 43) V2:236
How shall we adorn (Angle of Geese) V2:2
How would it be if you took yourself off (Landscape with Tractor) V10:182
Hunger crawls into you (Hunger in New York City) V4:79

I

I am not a painter, I am a poet (Why I Am Not a Painter) V8:258
I am the Smoke King (The Song of the Smoke) V13:196
I am silver and exact. I have no preconceptions (Mirror) V1:116
I am trying to pry open your casket (Dear Reader) V10:85
I cannot love the Brothers Wright (Reactionary Essay on Applied Science) V9:199
I felt a Funeral, in my Brain, (I felt a Funeral in my Brain) V13:137
I have just come down from my father (The Hospital Window) V11:58
I have met them at close of day (Easter 1916) V5:91
I hear America singing, the varied carols I hear (I Hear America Singing) V3:152
I heard a Fly buzz—when I died— (I Heard a Fly Buzz—When I Died—) V5:140
I know that I shall meet my fate (An Irish Airman Foresees His Death) V1:76
I sit in the top of the wood, my eyes closed (Hawk Roosting) V4:55
I'm delighted to see you (The Constellation Orion) V8:53
I've known rivers; (The Negro Speaks of Rivers) V10:197
I was sitting in mcsorley's. outside it was New York and beautifully snowing. (i was sitting in mcsorley's) V13:151
If ever two were one, then surely we (To My Dear and Loving Husband) V6:228
If I should die, think only this of me (The Soldier) V7:218
"Imagine being the first to say: *surveillance*," (Inventors) V7:97
In 1936, a child (Blood Oranges) V13:34
In China (Lost Sister) V5:216
In ethics class so many years ago (Ethics) V8:88
In Flanders fields the poppies blow (In Flanders Fields) V5:155
In the groves of Africa from their natural wonder (An African Elegy) V13:3
In the Shreve High football stadium (Autumn Begins in Martins Ferry, Ohio) V8:17
In Xanadu did Kubla Khan (Kubla Khan) V5:172
Ink runs from the corners of my mouth (Eating Poetry) V9:60
It is an ancient Mariner (The Rime of the Ancient Mariner) V4:127
It little profits that an idle king (Ulysses) V2:278
It looked extremely rocky for the Mudville nine that day (Casey at the Bat) V5:57
It seems vainglorious and proud (The Conquerors) V13:67
It was in and about the Martinmas time (Barbara Allan) V7:10
It was many and many a year ago (Annabel Lee) V9:14
Its quick soft silver bell beating, beating (Auto Wreck) V3:31

J

Januaries, Nature greets our eyes (Brazil, January 1, 1502) V6:15
Just off the highway to Rochester, Minnesota (A Blessing) V7:24

just once (For the White poets who would be Indian) V13:112

L

l(a (l(a) V1:85
Let me not to the marriage of true minds (Sonnet 116) V3:288
Listen, my children, and you shall hear (Paul Revere's Ride) V2:178
Little Lamb, who made thee? (The Lamb) V12:134
Long long ago when the world was a wild place (Bedtime Story) V8:32

M

maggie and milly and molly and may (maggie & milly & molly & may) V12:149
Mary sat musing on the lamp-flame at the table (The Death of the Hired Man) V4:42
Men with picked voices chant the names (Overture to a Dance of Locomotives) V11:143
"Mother dear, may I go downtown (Ballad of Birmingham) V5:17
My black face fades (Facing It) V5:109
My father stands in the warm evening (Starlight) V8:213
My heart aches, and a drowsy numbness pains (Ode to a Nightingale) V3:228
My heart is like a singing bird (A Birthday) V10:33
My life closed twice before its close— (My Life Closed Twice Before Its Close) V8:127
My mistress' eyes are nothing like the sun (Sonnet 130) V1:247
My uncle in East Germany (The Exhibit) V9:107

N

Nature's first green is gold (Nothing Gold Can Stay) V3:203
No easy thing to bear, the weight of sweetness (The Weight of Sweetness) V11:230
Nobody heard him, the dead man (Not Waving but Drowning) V3:216
Not marble nor the gilded monuments (Sonnet 55) V5:246
Now as I was young and easy under the apple boughs (Fern Hill) V3:92
Now as I watch the progress of the plague (The Missing) V9:158

O

O Captain! my Captain, our fearful trip is done (O Captain! My Captain!) V2:146
O Lord our Lord, how excellent is thy name in all the earth! who hast set thy glory above the heavens (Psalm 8) V9:182
O my Luve's like a red, red rose (A Red, Red Rose) V8:152
"O where ha' you been, Lord Randal, my son? (Lord Randal) V6:105
O wild West Wind, thou breath of Autumn's being (Ode to the West Wind) V2:163
Oh, but it is dirty! (Filling Station) V12:57
old age sticks (old age sticks) V3:246

Once upon a midnight dreary, while I pondered, weak and weary (The Raven) V1:200
Once some people were visiting Chekhov (Chocolates) V11:17
One foot down, then hop! It's hot (Harlem Hopscotch) V2:93
one shoe on the roadway presents (A Piéd) V3:16
Out walking in the frozen swamp one gray day (The Wood-Pile) V6:251
Oysters we ate (Oysters) V4:91

P

Poised between going on and back, pulled (The Base Stealer) V12:30

Q

Quinquireme of Nineveh from distant Ophir (Cargoes) V5:44

R

Red men embraced my body's whiteness (Birch Canoe) V5:31

S

Shall I compare thee to a Summer's day? (Sonnet 18) V2:222
She came every morning to draw water (A Drink of Water) V8:66
She sang beyond the genius of the sea. (The Idea of Order at Key West) V13:164
Side by side, their faces blurred, (An Arundel Tomb) V12:17
Since the professional wars— (Midnight) V2:130
S'io credesse che mia risposta fosse (The Love Song of J. Alfred Prufrock) V1:97
Sleepless as Prospero back in his bedroom (Darwin in 1881) V13:83
so much depends (The Red Wheelbarrow) V1:219
So the man spread his blanket on the field (A Tall Man Executes a Jig) V12:228
So the sky wounded you, jagged at the heart, (Daylights) V13:101
Softly, in the dark, a woman is singing to me (Piano) V6:145
Some say the world will end in fire (Fire and Ice) V7:57
Something there is that doesn't love a wall (Mending Wall) V5:231
Sometimes walking late at night (Butcher Shop) V7:43
Sometimes, a lion with a prophet's beard (For An Assyrian Frieze) V9:120
Sometimes, in the middle of the lesson (Music Lessons) V8:117
South of the bridge on Seventeenth (Fifteen) V2:78
Stop all the clocks, cut off the telephone, (Funeral Blues) V10:139
Strong Men, riding horses. In the West (Strong Men, Riding Horses) V4:209
Sundays too my father got up early (Those Winter Sundays) V1:300
Swing low sweet chariot (Swing Low Sweet Chariot) V1:283

T

Take heart, monsieur, four-fifths of this province (For Jean Vincent D'abbadie, Baron St.-Castin) V12:78

Tears, idle tears, I know not what they mean (Tears, Idle Tears) V4:220

Tell me not, in mournful numbers (A Psalm of Life) V7:165

That is no country for old men. The young (Sailing to Byzantium) V2:207

That time of drought the embered air (Drought Year) V8:78

That's my last Duchess painted on the wall (My Last Duchess) V1:165

The apparition of these faces in the crowd (In a Station of the Metro) V2:116

The Assyrian came down like the wolf on the fold (The Destruction of Sennacherib) V1:38

The broken pillar of the wing jags from the clotted shoulder (Hurt Hawks) V3:138

The bud (Saint Francis and the Sow) V9:222

The Bustle in a House (The Bustle in a House) V10:62

The buzz saw snarled and rattled in the yard (Out, Out—) V10:212

The courage that my mother had (The Courage that My Mother Had) V3:79

The Curfew tolls the knell of parting day (Elegy Written in a Country Churchyard) V9:73

The force that through the green fuse drives the flower (The Force That Through the Green Fuse Drives the Flower) V8:101

The green lamp flares on the table (This Life) V1:293

The ills I sorrow at (Any Human to Another) V3:2

The instructor said (Theme for English B) V6:194

The king sits in Dumferling toune (Sir Patrick Spens) V4:177

The land was overmuch like scenery (Beowulf) V11:2

The last time I saw it was 1968. (The Hiding Place) V10:152

The Lord is my shepherd; I shall not want (Psalm 23) V4:103

The man who sold his lawn to standard oil (The War Against the Trees) V11:215

The moon glows the same (The Moon Glows the Same) V7:152

The old South Boston Aquarium stands (For the Union Dead) V7:67

The others bent their heads and started in ("Trouble with Math in a One-Room Country School") V9:238

The pale nuns of St. Joseph are here (Island of Three Marias) V11:79

The Phoenix comes of flame and dust (The Phoenix) V10:226

The river brought down (How We Heard the Name) V10:167

The rusty spigot (Onomatopoeia) V6:133

The sea is calm tonight (Dover Beach) V2:52

The sea sounds insincere (The Milkfish Gatherers) V11:111

The Soul selects her own Society— (The Soul Selects Her Own Society) V1:259

The time you won your town the race (To an Athlete Dying Young) V7:230

The whiskey on your breath (My Papa's Waltz) V3:191

The wind was a torrent of darkness among the gusty trees (The Highwayman) V4:66

There are strange things done in the midnight sun (The Cremation of Sam McGee) V10:75

There is the one song everyone (Siren Song) V7:196

There's a Certain Slant of Light (There's a Certain Slant of Light) V6:211

They eat beans mostly, this old yellow pair (The Bean Eaters) V2:16

they were just meant as covers (My Mother Pieced Quilts) V12:169

They said, "Wait." Well, I waited. (Alabama Centennial) V10:2

This girlchild was: born as usual (Barbie Doll) V9:33

This is my letter to the World (This Is My Letter to the World) V4:233

This is the black sea-brute bulling through wave-wrack (Leviathan) V5:203

This poem is concerned with language on a very plain level (Paradoxes and Oxymorons) V11:162

This tale is true, and mine. It tells (The Seafarer) V8:177

Thou still unravish'd bride of quietness (Ode on a Grecian Urn) V1:179

Tonight I can write the saddest lines (Tonight I Can Write) V11:187

tonite, *thriller* was (Beware: Do Not Read This Poem) V6:3

Turning and turning in the widening gyre (The Second Coming) V7:179

'Twas brillig, and the slithy toves (Jabberwocky) V11:91

Two roads diverged in a yellow wood (The Road Not Taken) V2:195

Tyger! Tyger! burning bright (The Tyger) V2:263

W

We could be here. This is the valley (Small Town with One Road) V7:207

We met the British in the dead of winter (Meeting the British) V7:138

We real cool. We (We Real Cool) V6:242

Well, son, I'll tell you (Mother to Son) V3:178

What dire offense from amorous causes springs, (The Rape of the Lock) V12:202

What happens to a dream deferred? (Harlem) V1:63

What thoughts I have of you tonight, Walt Whitman, for I walked down the sidestreets under the trees with a headache self-conscious looking at the full moon (A Supermarket in California) V5:261

Whatever it is, it must have (American Poetry) V7:2

When Abraham Lincoln was shoveled into the tombs, he forgot the copperheads, and the assassin ... in the dust, in the cool tombs (Cool Tombs) V6:45

When I consider how my light is spent ([On His Blindness] Sonnet 16) V3:262

When I have fears that I may cease to be (When I Have Fears that I May Cease to Be) V2:295

When I see a couple of kids (High Windows) V3:108

When I see birches bend to left and right (Birches) V13:14

When I was one-and-twenty (When I Was One-and-Twenty) V4:268

When I watch you (Miss Rosie) V1:133

When to the sessions of sweet silent thought (Sonnet 30) V4:192

When, in disgrace with Fortune and men's eyes (Sonnet 29) V8:198

When the mountains of Puerto Rico (We Live by What We See at Night) V13:240

Whenever Richard Cory went down town (Richard Cory) V4:116

While my hair was still cut straight across my forehead (The River-Merchant's Wife: A Letter) V8:164

While this America settles in the mould of its vulgarity, heavily thickening to empire (Shine, Perishing Republic) V4:161

Who has ever stopped to think of the divinity of Lamont Cranston? (In Memory of Radio) V9:144

Whose woods these are I think I know (Stopping by Woods on a Snowy Evening) V1:272

Why should I let the toad *work* (Toads) V4:244

Y

You are small and intense (To a Child Running With Outstretched Arms in Canyon de Chelly) V11:173

You were never told, Mother, how old Illya was drunk (The Czar's Last Christmas Letter) V12:44

Cumulative Index of Last Lines

A

a man then suddenly stops running (Island of Three Marias) V11:80

a space in the lives of their friends (Beware: Do Not Read This Poem) V6:3

A sudden blow: the great wings beating still (Leda and the Swan) V13:181

A terrible beauty is born (Easter 1916) V5:91

About my big, new, automatically defrosting refrigerator with the built-in electric eye (Reactionary Essay on Applied Science) V9:199

Across the expedient and wicked stones (Auto Wreck) V3:31

Ah, dear father, graybeard, lonely old courage-teacher, what America did you have when Charon quit poling his ferry and you got out on a smoking bank and stood watching the boat disappear on the black waters of Lethe? (A Supermarket in California) V5:261

All losses are restored and sorrows end (Sonnet 30) V4:192

Amen. Amen (The Creation) V1:20

Anasazi (Anasazi) V9:3

and all beyond saving by children (Ethics) V8:88

And all we need of hell (My Life Closed Twice Before Its Close) V8:127

and changed, back to the class ("Trouble with Math in a One-Room Country School") V9:238

And Death shall be no more: Death, thou shalt die (Holy Sonnet 10) V2:103

And drunk the milk of Paradise (Kubla Khan) V5:172

And Finished knowing—then— (I Felt a Funeral in My Brain) V13:137

And gallop terribly against each other's bodies (Autumn Begins in Martins Ferry, Ohio) V8:17

and go back. (For the White poets who would be Indian) V13:112

And his own Word (The Phoenix) V10:226

And I am Nicholas. (The Czar's Last Christmas Letter) V12:45

And life for me ain't been no crystal stair (Mother to Son) V3:179

And like a thunderbolt he falls (The Eagle) V11:30

And makes me end where I begun (A Valediction: Forbidding Mourning) V11:202

And 'midst the stars inscribe Belinda's name. (The Rape of the Lock) V12:209

And miles to go before I sleep (Stopping by Woods on a Snowy Evening) V1:272

And not waving but drowning (Not Waving but Drowning) V3:216

And oh, 'tis true, 'tis true (When I Was One-and-Twenty) V4:268

And reach for your scalping knife. (For Jean Vincent D'abbadie, Baron St.-Castin) V12:78

and retreating, always retreating, behind it (Brazil, January 1, 1502) V6:16

And settled upon his eyes in a black soot ("More Light! More Light!") V6:120

And shuts his eyes. (Darwin in 1881) V13: 84

And so live ever—or else swoon to death (Bright Star! Would I Were Steadfast as Thou Art) V9:44

and strange and loud was the dingoes' cry (Drought Year) V8:78

and sweat and fat and greed. (Anorexic) V12:3

And that has made all the difference (The Road Not Taken) V2:195

And the deep river ran on (As I Walked Out One Evening) V4:16

And the midnight message of Paul Revere (Paul Revere's Ride) V2:180

And the mome raths outgrabe (Jabberwocky) V11:91

And the Salvation Army singing God loves us. . . . (Hope is a Tattered Flag) V12:120

and these the last verses that I write for her (Tonight I Can Write) V11:187

And those roads in South Dakota that feel around in the darkness . . . (Come with Me) V6:31
and to know she will stay in the field till you die? (Landscape with Tractor) V10:183
and two blankets embroidered with smallpox (Meeting the British) V7:138
And would suffice (Fire and Ice) V7:57
And Zero at the Bone— (A Narrow Fellow in the Grass) V11:127
As any She belied with false compare (Sonnet 130) V1:248
As far as Cho-fu-Sa (The River-Merchant's Wife: A Letter) V8:165
As the contagion of those molten eyes (For An Assyrian Frieze) V9:120
As they lean over the beans in their rented back room that is full of beads and receipts and dolls and clothes, tobacco crumbs, vases and fringes (The Bean Eaters) V2:16
aspired to become lighter than air (Blood Oranges) V13:34
at home in the fish's fallen heaven (Birch Canoe) V5:31

B

Back to the play of constant give and change (The Missing) V9:158
Before it was quite unsheathed from reality (Hurt Hawks) V3:138
Bless me (Hunger in New York City) V4:79
But be (Ars Poetica) V5:3
but it works every time (Siren Song) V7:196
But there is no joy in Mudville—mighty Casey has "Struck Out." (Casey at the Bat) V5:58
But, baby, where are you?" (Ballad of Birmingham) V5:17
But we hold our course, and the wind is with us. (On Freedom's Ground) V12:187

C

chickens (The Red Wheelbarrow) V1:219
clear water dashes (Onomatopoeia) V6:133
Comin' for to carry me home (Swing Low Sweet Chariot) V1:284

D

Dare frame thy fearful symmetry? (The Tyger) V2:263
"Dead," was all he answered (The Death of the Hired Man) V4:44
Delicate, delicate, delicate, delicate—now! (The Base Stealer) V12:30
Die soon (We Real Cool) V6:242
Down in the flood of remembrance, I weep like a child for the past (Piano) V6:145
dry wells that fill so easily now (The Exhibit) V9:107

E

Eternal, unchanging creator of earth. Amen (The Seafarer) V8:178

F

fall upon us, the dwellers in shadow (In the Land of Shinar) V7:84
Fallen cold and dead (O Captain! My Captain!) V2:147
Firewood, iron-ware, and cheap tin trays (Cargoes) V5:44
Fled is that music:—Do I wake or sleep? (Ode to a Nightingale) V3:229
For I'm sick at the heart, and I fain wad lie down." (Lord Randal) V6:105
For nothing now can ever come to any good. (Funeral Blues) V10:139

H

Had anything been wrong, we should certainly have heard (The Unknown Citizen) V3:303
Had somewhere to get to and sailed calmly on (Mus,e des Beaux Arts) V1:148
half eaten by the moon. (Dear Reader) V10:85
Happen on a red tongue (Small Town with One Road) V7:207
Has no more need of, and I have (The Courage that My Mother Had) V3:80
Hath melted like snow in the glance of the Lord! (The Destruction of Sennacherib) V1:39
He rose the morrow morn (The Rime of the Ancient Mariner) V4:132
He says again, "Good fences make good neighbors." (Mending Wall) V5:232
Has set me softly down beside you. The Poem is you (Paradoxes and Oxymorons) V11:162
How at my sheet goes the same crooked worm (The Force That Through the Green Fuse Drives the Flower) V8:101
How can I turn from Africa and live? (A Far Cry from Africa) V6:61
How sad then is even the marvelous! (An Africian Elegy) V13:4

I

I am black. (The Song of the Smoke) V13:197
I am going to keep things like this (Hawk Roosting) V4:55
I am not brave at all (Strong Men, Riding Horses) V4:209
I could not see to see— (I Heard a Fly Buzz—When I Died—) V5:140
I have just come down from my father (The Hospital Window) V11:58
I cremated Sam McGee (The Cremation of Sam McGee) V10:76
I never writ, nor no man ever loved (Sonnet 116) V3:288
I romp with joy in the bookish dark (Eating Poetry) V9:61
I see Mike's painting, called SARDINES (Why I Am Not a Painter) V8:259
I shall but love thee better after death (Sonnet 43) V2:236
I should be glad of another death (Journey of the Magi) V7:110
I stand up (Miss Rosie) V1:133
I stood there, fifteen (Fifteen) V2:78
I turned aside and bowed my head and wept (The Tropics in New York) V4:255
I'll dig with it (Digging) V5:71
If Winter comes, can Spring be far behind? (Ode to the West Wind) V2:163

In a convulsive misery (The Milkfish Gatherers) V11:112
In balance with this life, this death (An Irish Airman Foresees His Death) V1:76
In Flanders fields (In Flanders Fields) V5:155
In ghostlier demarcations, keener sounds. (The Idea of Order at Key West) V13:164
In hearts at peace, under an English heaven (The Soldier) V7:218
In her tomb by the side of the sea (Annabel Lee) V9:14
in the grit gray light of day. (Daylights) V13:102
In the rear-view mirrors of the passing cars (The War Against the Trees) V11:216
iness (l(a) V1:85
Into blossom (A Blessing) V7:24
Is Come, my love is come to me. (A Birthday) V10:34
is still warm (Lament for the Dorsets) V5:191
It asked a crumb—of Me (Hope Is the Thing with Feathers) V3:123
it's always ourselves we find in the sea (maggie & milly & molly & may) V12:150
It was your resting place." (Ah, Are You Digging on My Grave?) V4:2

J

Judge tenderly—of Me (This Is My Letter to the World) V4:233
Just imagine it (Inventors) V7:97

L

Laughing the stormy, husky, brawling laughter of Youth, half-naked, sweating, proud to be Hog Butcher, Tool Maker, Stacker of Wheat, Player with Railroads and Freight Handler to the Nation (Chicago) V3:61
Learn to labor and to wait (A Psalm of Life) V7:165
Leashed in my throat (Midnight) V2:131
Let my people go (Go Down, Moses) V11:43
Like Stone— (The Soul Selects Her Own Society) V1:259
Little Lamb, God bless thee. (The Lamb) V12:135

M

'Make a wish, Tom, make a wish.' (Drifters) V10: 98
make it seem to change (The Moon Glows the Same) V7:152
midnight-oiled in the metric laws? (A Farewell to English) V10:126
More dear, both for themselves and for thy sake! (Tintern Abbey) V2:250
My love shall in my verse ever live young (Sonnet 19) V9:211
My soul has grown deep like the rivers. (The Negro Speaks of Rivers) V10:198

N

never to waken in that world again (Starlight) V8:213
No, she's brushing a boy's hair (Facing It) V5:110
no—tell them *no*— (The Hiding Place) V10:153
Noble six hundred! (The Charge of the Light Brigade) V1:3
Nothing gold can stay (Nothing Gold Can Stay) V3:203
Nothing, and is nowhere, and is endless (High Windows) V3:108
Now! (Alabama Centennial) V10:2
nursing the tough skin of figs (This Life) V1:293

O

O Death in Life, the days that are no more! (Tears, Idle Tears) V4:220
O Lord our Lord, how excellent is thy name in all the earth! (Psalm 8) V9:182
O Roger, Mackerel, Riley, Ned, Nellie, Chester, Lady Ghost (Names of Horses) V8:142
of gentleness (To a Sad Daughter) V8:231
of love's austere and lonely offices? (Those Winter Sundays) V1:300
of peaches (The Weight of Sweetness) V11:230
Of the camellia (Falling Upon Earth) V2:64
Of the Creator. And he waits for the world to begin (Leviathan) V5:204
Of what is past, or passing, or to come (Sailing to Byzantium) V2:207
Old Ryan, not yours (The Constellation Orion) V8:53
On the dark distant flurry (Angle of Geese) V2:2
On the look of Death— (There's a Certain Slant of Light) V6:212
On your head like a crown (Any Human to Another) V3:2
One could do worse that be a swinger of birches. (Birches) V13:15
Or does it explode? (Harlem) V1:63
Or help to half-a-crown." (The Man He Killed) V3:167
or nothing (Queen-Ann's-Lace) V6:179
ORANGE forever. (Ballad of Orange and Grape) V10:18
outside. (it was New York and beautifully, snowing . . . (i was sitting in mcsorley's) V13:152
owing old (old age sticks) V3:246

P

Perhaps he will fall. (Wilderness Gothic) V12:242
Petals on a wet, black bough (In a Station of the Metro) V2:116
Plaiting a dark red love-knot into her long black hair (The Highwayman) V4:68
Pro patria mori. (Dulce et Decorum Est) V10:110

R

Rage, rage against the dying of the light (Do Not Go Gentle into that Good Night) V1:51
Remember the Giver fading off the lip (A Drink of Water) V8:66
Rises toward her day after day, like a terrible fish (Mirror) V1:116

S

Shall be lifted—nevermore! (The Raven) V1:202
Singing of him what they could understand (Beowulf) V11:3
Singing with open mouths their strong melodious songs (I Hear America Singing) V3:152
slides by on grease (For the Union Dead) V7:67
Slouches towards Bethlehem to be born? (The Second Coming) V7:179
So long lives this, and this gives life to thee (Sonnet 18) V2:222
Somebody loves us all. (Filling Station) V12:57

Stand still, yet we will make him run (To His Coy Mistress) V5:277
startled into eternity (Four Mountain Wolves) V9:132
Still clinging to your shirt (My Papa's Waltz) V3:192
Stood up, coiled above his head, transforming all. (A Tall Man Executes a Jig) V12:229
Surely goodness and mercy shall follow me all the days of my life: and I will dwell in the house of the Lord for ever (Psalm 23) V4:103
syllables of an old order. (A Grafted Tongue) V12:93

T

Take any streetful of people buying clothes and groceries, cheering a hero or throwing confetti and blowing tin horns ... tell me if the lovers are losers ... tell me if any get more than the lovers ... in the dust ... in the cool tombs (Cool Tombs) V6:46
That then I scorn to change my state with Kings (Sonnet 29) V8:198
That when we live no more, we may live ever (To My Dear and Loving Husband) V6:228
That's the word. (Black Zodiac) V10:47
The bosom of his Father and his God (Elegy Written in a Country Churchyard) V9:74
The dance is sure (Overture to a Dance of Locomotives) V11:143
The garland briefer than a girl's (To an Athlete Dying Young) V7:230
The guidon flags flutter gayly in the wind. (Cavalry Crossing a Ford) V13:50
The hands gripped hard on the desert (At the Bomb Testing Site) V8:3
the knife at the throat, the death in the metronome (Music Lessons) V8:117
The lightning and the gale! (Old Ironsides) V9:172
the long, perfect loveliness of sow (Saint Francis and the Sow) V9:222
The Lord survives the rainbow of His will (The Quaker Graveyard in Nantucket) V6:159
The man I was when I was part of it (Beware of Ruins) V8:43
the quilts sing on (My Mother Pieced Quilts) V12:169
The red rose and the brier (Barbara Allan) V7:11
The shaft we raise to them and thee (Concord Hymn) V4:30
The spirit of this place (To a Child Running With Outstretched Arms in Canyon de Chelly) V11:173
the unremitting space of your rebellion (Lost Sister) V5:217
The woman won (Oysters) V4:91
There is the trap that catches noblest spiritts, that caught—they say—God, when he walked on earth (Shine, Perishing Republic) V4:162
there was light (Vancouver Lights) V8:246
They also serve who only stand and wait." ([On His Blindness] Sonnet 16) V3:262
They rise, they walk again (The Heaven of Animals) V6:76
They think I lost. I think I won (Harlem Hopscotch) V2:93
This is my page for English B (Theme for English B) V6:194
This Love (In Memory of Radio) V9:145
Tho' it were ten thousand mile! (A Red, Red Rose) V8:152
Though I sang in my chains like the sea (Fern Hill) V3:92
Till human voices wake us, and we drown (The Love Song of J. Alfred Prufrock) V1:99
Till Love and Fame to nothingness do sink (When I Have Fears that I May Cease to Be) V2:295
To every woman a happy ending (Barbie Doll) V9:33
to its owner or what horror has befallen the other shoe (A Piéd) V3:16
To strive, to seek, to find, and not to yield (Ulysses) V2:279
To the moaning and the groaning of the bells (The Bells) V3:47

U

Until Eternity. (The Bustle in a House) V10:62
unusual conservation (Chocolates) V11:17
Uttering cries that are almost human (American Poetry) V7:2

W

War is kind (War Is Kind) V9:253
Went home and put a bullet through his head (Richard Cory) V4:117
Were not the one dead, turned to their affairs. (Out, Out—) V10:213
Were toward Eternity— (Because I Could Not Stop for Death) V2:27
What will survive of us is love. (An Arundel Tomb) V12:18
When I died they washed me out of the turret with a hose (The Death of the Ball Turret Gunner) V2:41
When you have both (Toads) V4:244
Where deep in the night I hear a voice (Butcher Shop) V7:43
Where ignorant armies clash by night (Dover Beach) V2:52
Which Claus of Innsbruck cast in bronze for me! (My Last Duchess) V1:166
which is not going to go wasted on me which is why I'm telling you about it (Having a Coke with You) V12:106
white ash amid funereal cypresses (Helen) V6:92
Wi' the Scots lords at his feit (Sir Patrick Spens) V4:177
Will hear of as a god." (How we Heard the Name) V10:167
Wind, like the dodo's (Bedtime Story) V8:33
With gold unfading, WASHINGTON! be thine. (To His Excellency General Washington) V13:213
with my eyes closed. (We Live by What We See at Night) V13:240
With the slow smokeless burning of decay (The Wood-Pile) V6:252
With what they had to go on. (The Conquerors) V13:67

Y

Ye know on earth, and all ye need to know (Ode on a Grecian Urn) V1:180
You live in this, and dwell in lovers' eyes (Sonnet 55) V5:246
You may for ever tarry. (To the Virgins, to Make Much of Time) V13:226
you who raised me? (The Gold Lily) V5:127